STRATEGIC MANAGEMENT AND ORGANISATIONAL DYNAMICS

STRATEGIC MANAGEMENT AND ORGANISATIONAL DYNAMICS

Ralph D Stacey

Professor of Management
University of Hertfordshire Business School

Pitman Publishing
128 Long Acre, London, WC2E 9AN

A Division of Pearson Professional Limited

© R D Stacey 1993

First published in Great Britain 1993

British Library Cataloguing-in-Publication Data
A catalogue record for this book is available from the
British Library.

ISBN 0 273 60098 2

10 9 8 7 6 5 4

Printed in England by Clays Ltd, St Ives plc

Contents

Contents in detail

List of key concepts

List of illustrations

Chapter 9

Chapter 10

Chapter 11

List of figures

List of exhibits

Preface

Not another textbook on strategic management! Since I am adding to the pile, I owe it to the reader immediately to explain why.

At least ninety per cent of the contents of all the textbooks on strategic management that I know of are devoted to that part of the management task which is relatively easy – the part that has to do with running the organisational 'machine' in as surprise-free a way as possible. Thus, most textbooks focus heavily on techniques and procedures for long-term planning, on the need for visions and missions, on the importance and the means of securing strongly shared cultures, on the equation of success with consensus, consistency, uniformity and order. This relative emphasis in content terms has the effect of reinforcing a conventional wisdom that today dominates the approach of Western managers to strategic management, namely the belief that the purpose of strategic management is to reduce the level of surprise, to increase the level of predictability, and thereby improve the ability of those at the top to control the long-term destiny of their organisation. These beliefs are promoted and reinforced through the persistent failure of most textbooks to question the most fundamental belief upon which that conventional wisdom is built: namely, the belief that organisations succeed when they operate in states of stability and harmony to adapt intentionally to their environments.

Reflection on why an organisation needs managers at all, however, reveals how exceedingly odd this conventional wisdom is. Organisations need managers primarily to handle the surprises that all organisations must inevitably encounter as they move through time. Managers, from the first supervisory level right up to the chairman of the board, justify their existence when they apply their intuition and judgement to those situations in which the techniques, procedures, rules, structures and so on turn out to be inadequate in some way – a machine may break down, operators may suddenly quarrel, bank loans may be recalled, new market opportunities may appear and so on. If we could rely on the absence of such events, that is if the techniques and prescriptions of the conventional wisdom could be relied on to work, then of course there would be very little need for managers – it would suffice if one or two managers were available to maintain the systems. We need armies of managers because organisational life is inevitably full of ambiguities, uncertainties and surprises and no matter how perfect the techniques and how hard we try this is still so.

The real management task, then, is that of handling the exceptions, rapidly and under pressure, as and when they unexpectedly occur. In other words, the real management task is that of coping with and even using unpredictability, clashing counter-cultures, disensus, contention, conflict, and inconsistency. In short, the task that justifies the existence of all managers has to do with instability, irregularity, difference and disorder – matters that most textbooks devote less than ten per cent of their content to.

Furthermore, there is evidence available that the conventional wisdom – all explanations and prescriptions that encourage managers to focus on uniformity, stability and regularity – leads to failure rather than success in rapidly changing and highly competitive conditions. The evidence suggests that organisations succeed in highly uncertain environments when they sustain states of instability, contradiction, contention and creative tension in order to provoke new perspectives and continual learning. In this manner successful organisations create and discover their own environments and their innovative strategies emerge without prior, organisation-wide intention. In such circumstances no-one can be in control of future direction.

Yet another textbook on strategic management is therefore justified, I suggest, by the need for a critical treatment of today's dominant conventional wisdom; a treatment that juxtaposes the conventional perspective of success as a state of stability with its direct opposite, success flowing from instability. This textbook therefore turns convention on its head and devotes less than ten per cent of its contents to order, stability and lack of surprise, and the remaining ninety per cent to the tasks of coping with and using instability and difference.

The concern with real life instability pursued in this book is reflected in the emphasis on the study of the dynamics of organisations: that is, the patterns of change that organisations display as they move through time and the properties of the systems driving those patterns.

To study the dynamics, it is necessary to understand that an organisation is a feedback system. A dynamic study of organisations is a study of the properties and consequences of their feedback system nature. Most textbooks today, however, focus heavily on the static analysis of competitive positions and largely ignore the dynamics. This follows from the fact that they provide almost no explicit examination of the feedback systems nature of organisations. This lack is now made particularly serious by the discoveries that mathematicians and natural scientists have made about the dynamics of feedback systems – the properties of chaos and self-organisation. These discoveries have important implications for how it is possible to manage an organisation strategically.

Yet another textbook on strategic management is therefore required to fill the need for a focus on organisational dynamics and thus the feedback system properties of organisations. An understanding of the dynamics leads to greater insight into those processes of strategic management that may lead to success.

The particular concern this book has with the dynamics of feedback systems has methodological consequences. The key point about such systems is that the links between cause and effect may be lost in the detailed behaviour of the system and it therefore follows that a reductionist approach to understanding such systems will prove to be seriously misleading. That is to say, we will develop a defective understanding of the whole organisation if we follow a procedure of splitting it into discrete levels and other parts, then identify cause-and-effect links to understand each part, and finally put it all together again in the expectation of now understanding the whole. Instead, when feedback systems operate in states where cause-and-effect links disappear, we have to try to comprehend the system's functioning in terms of overall patterns in its behaviour across many levels. We have to sacrifice precision and logical rigour to gain more useful qualitative images and insights into how the system evolves.

There is, therefore, in what follows no sequential approach to behaviour at the individual level, building into behaviour at a group and then an organisational level. Instead, the argument is structured into examinations of different kinds of feedback process. One way a feedback system can operate is through negative feedback processes, which, in certain conditions, generate stability. So, early on in the book, we look at theories and models of negative feedback systems and what they might mean for overall patterns of behaviour across levels in an organisation. Then the focus shifts to positive feedback, where once again a number of different models are presented to enhance understanding of the patterns of development that positive feedback systems generate across levels in an organisation. Finally, the same procedure is applied to systems that flip between positive and negative feedback. The remainder of the book then uses this distinction between different kinds of feedback to identify implications of major importance for the process of strategic management in practice.

In using a number of different theories and models to shed light on the pattern of development that different types of feedback produce, there has been little concern with presenting those theories in any kind of chronological order. The rationale for what is presented and when it is presented is that of maximising the appreciation of feedback patterns, rather than providing a chronological development of ideas on strategic management.

Furthermore, because the book is structured around the implications of different types of feedback, it will sometimes happen that a particular topic is dealt with in a number of places. For example, politics and group behaviour may be interpreted by some writers in a manner that implies negative feedback, while others may deal with these matters in a way that uses positive feedback concepts. Although the topic is the same, the feedback implications are different and thus that topic is repeated, but from a different angle.

Another methodological point relates to the balance between prescription and description. Some textbooks adopt a heavily prescriptive approach; that is, they specify general sets of prescriptions that managers should apply in a wide range of strategic situations if they are to be successful. Others, however, may tilt the balance toward the description of what managers can be observed to do, leaving it to the reader to draw direct conclusions about best practice. This book falls more into the latter category. It is primarily concerned with trying to explain what managers do, why they do it, and what the consequences are in different kinds of decision and control situations. The reason for this is that it is impossible to develop general sets of prescriptions at the cutting edge of strategic management. If it were possible to develop such general prescriptions we would be back to the no-surprise situation discussed at the beginning of this Preface. Instead, managers have to develop unique responses to each unique strategic situation they face. As far as general prescriptions are concerned, therefore, Chapter 2 presents the prescriptions of the conventional wisdom, but argues that they are inadequate, while at the end of Chapter 11 some rather loose prescriptions for encouraging learning organisations are presented. Elsewhere it is up to readers to extract their own conclusions and prescriptions from the explaining and understanding that develops.

Some readers may want a fuller appreciation of the structure of the argument we are going to pursue, rather than waiting for it to unfold through the book. Such a preview can be acquired by reading Chapter 1, then the introductory sections of Chapters 7 and 10, and finally Chapter 12.

The book is aimed at students in the final year of undergraduate business degrees and at practising managers taking post-experience courses, for example Diploma in Management Studies and Master of Business Administration. It is intended to serve as a textbook for courses on business strategy, business policy, strategic management, change management, managerial decision-making, and organisational behaviour.

Let me make some other points about the presentation of the material in the book. Most chapters identify key concepts, highlighted by placing them in boxes. The rationale behind selecting an idea for inclusion in the list of key concepts is that of underlining the fundamental tools for understanding organisational dynamics. This is why the idea of 'cause and effect' appears as a key concept, while that of 'competitive advantage' does not. There is no intention of saying that one is more important than the other, simply that, in developing an understanding of the dynamics of organising, one is more fundamental than the other. In addition to the key points, the text also highlights case examples and other illustrative material in boxes. At the end of the book there is a set of case studies for use in discussing the concepts developed in the book. The cases are given at the end rather than attached to particular chapters because they are about strategic management as a whole, not some neat compartment of it – the point about systems and reductionism again. The cases can be used to think about a number of aspects that cover more than one chapter. A Lecturer's Guide containing teaching notes on the cases, as well as comments on the chapters and how that might be used in teaching, is also available from the publishers.

I wish to thank the International Institute for Management Development, Lausanne, Switzerland for permission to reproduce a number of the case studies and also the following authors of case studies: Francis Bidault, Kimberly Bechler, John Pringle, David Hover, Vijay Jolly, Manfred Kets de Vries, Christine Czyzewska, Brenda Zimmerman and Bengt Johanisson. I am also grateful to Martyn Pitt of Bath University for his very helpful comments. Finally I thank students and colleagues at the University of Hertfordshire Business School, as well as consulting colleagues and clients, for the assistance they perhaps unknowingly provide in the way I come to see things.

RDS
London
September 1992

1

The nature of strategy

1.1 Introduction

Strategy is a serious, exciting and often bizarre game that managers play every day. It is a game that groups of managers play with other groups in their own and other organisations and with individuals both inside and outside their organisation. The smallest players in the game are individual managers, single-person households and one-person businesses. The largest players are powerful teams of top managers in global corporations and government organisations. Some of the internal players are called departments, others business units, and yet others project teams. Some of the external players are called customers, others suppliers, and yet others competitors, regulators, or financiers.

Honda versus General Motors

A well-known example of the strategy game runs like this. In the late 1950s, Honda's managers made a move into the United States motor cycle market. They tried to get support for this move from MITI, the Japanese trade ministry, but were denied it. They went ahead anyway with their intention of selling large motor cycles in the US but they found that potential customers were not interested. So, the Honda executives displayed their entrepreneurial flare by selling their small 50cc Super Cub range of motor cycles instead and that worked (Pascale, 1984).

Managers at General Motors paid no attention to this move. Why should they? They produced automobiles, not motor cycles, and they were the most powerful of the players in the US market with their 50 per cent share. The arrival of a tiny motor cycle importer on the West Coast was hardly worth noticing.

But competition comes from unexpected quarters in the strategy game and Honda turned out to be one of the tiny changes that would escalate into a transformation of the market. In the 1960s Honda built up its automobile manufacturing capability in Japan, again without the support of MITI, and by the 1970s was exporting cars to the US. By 1978 it had a 2.4 per cent market share and a decade later it had its own US manufacturing capability and a market share of over 7 per cent. Other Japanese manufacturers were developing much the same posture and imports of cars into the

US rose from almost nothing in the late 1950s to around 30 per cent of the market by the late 1980s. The General Motors' market share fell from 50 per cent to 33 per cent and with its market share, its profits and share price tumbled too – its performance deteriorated markedly. Today, in 1992, General Motors is still deteriorating – it recently announced a huge decline in profits and is currently undergoing a major contraction and restructuring.

These changing positions and postures over more than thirty years were clearly the consequences of the strategies that the managers in the different companies were pursuing, that is of the patterns in their actions. For example, during the 1970s General Motors continued to supply all segments of the market, responding to higher fuel costs and foreign imports of small cars by reducing the size of its vehicles across the whole product range. General Motors' managers called the strategy *downsizing* (Quinn, 1985). Honda on the other hand, after initial difficulties with quality, concentrated on differentiating its products by quality in a relatively narrow range of products (Quinn, 1990). We could label that a strategy of *focused differentiation*. In the late 1970s, 80 per cent of General Motors vehicles were recalled for quality defects while only 20 per cent of Japanese vehicles were. However we label them, one strategy or pattern in actions was clearly leading to success while another was not. It is also clear that both strategies came about through the decision-making processes employed by managers in each organisation. The key to success has to do with the processes of strategic decision-making and action.

Variations on this particular Far Eastern version of the game have, as we all know, been played in a number of other industries in the USA and in Europe too. And this version of the game, in which those from the Far East almost always win, is still being widely played. The game, however, is not confined to such dramatic moves and large players. Managers in a small family business selling fertiliser in East Anglia in the UK have to play the game too, against ICI and Norsk Hydro, if they wish to survive. The same applies to not-for-profit organisations such as Oxfam, hospitals, educational institutions and other bodies in the state sector, where they have to play against each other for the funds that keep them alive.

Why a game?

It is important right at the outset to think of strategy as a game that people play, because when it is discussed more seriously there is a strong tendency to slip into talking about it as a response that 'the organisation' makes to 'an environment'. When we do that, we depersonalise the game and unwittingly slip into understanding it in mechanical terms, where one 'thing' moves in predetermined ways in relation to another 'thing'. The inevitable result is a lack of insight into the real complexities of strategic management because in reality organisations and their environments are not things, one adapting to the other, but groupings of people interacting one with another. When we think about strategy as a game, therefore, we focus on how success or failure flows from the circular process of moves a player makes that provoke responses from other players, in turn feeding back into counter-responses from the first, and so on from day to day. That is to say, we focus on the feedback process and the dynamics it generates, and this leads to a sharper insight into the nature of strategy.

When managers think in terms of one thing adapting to another, they play the strategy game in unimaginative, predictable ways that are unlikely to lead to winning positions. If, however, they understand the dynamic patterns of interaction between suppliers, competitors and customers, they are much more likely to design successful moves. Our task as students of strategic management is to try to determine which patterns of moves lead to success and which do not, and this means that we too must pay attention to the dynamics.

The **first key question** we will be addressing throughout this book, therefore, is **what can we say about the dynamics of organisations** and the impact this has on how managers make strategies? Let me clarify this point on dynamics and in so doing define the key features of the strategy game.

1.2 Defining the key features of the strategy game

Some of the most essential features of the dynamic strategy game – the underlying nature of moves like those made by the managers at Honda and at General Motors over many years – can be illustrated in the manner shown in *Figure 1.1*.

The figure depicts a continuing loop over time connecting the actions of people in an organisation to the responses of people outside it, and the reactions to those responses.

Starting at the left-hand side of *Figure 1.1*, we see that people in the environment of Organisation A do something that people in Organisation A discover. People in Organisation A choose how to respond and then act upon that choice. The actions of people in Organisation A also have consequences for people in the environment, for example customers, competitors, suppliers and regulators. Thus, in the above example, Honda discovered that there might be an opportunity in the United States, chose to set up an operation in that country and sold small, high-quality cars. The consequence was a decline in General Motors' market share.

Returning to *Figure 1.1* we can see how it depicts people who are the environment discovering the consequences of Organisation A's actions, choosing how to respond and then acting. For example, General Motors responded to Honda's action by reducing the size of all of its cars but paid little attention to improved quality.

Returning once more to *Figure 1.1* we can see how the actions of people in the environment then have further consequences for people in Organisation A. The latter in turn discover, choose and act. People both within and outside any organisation are therefore continuously moving around feedback loops, that is processes through which they interact to make the decisions and take the actions that control and develop their organisations.

This brings us to the **second key question** that we will be exploring throughout this book: **what do we know about the operation of the feedback systems** that drive an organisation and about the patterns of behaviour those feedback systems produce?

Studying the dynamics

We can look back in time from the present, t_0 in *Figure 1.1* and, if we are able to perceive a pattern in past actions, we call this pattern the strategy of the organisation.

Figure 1.1 The Strategy Concept

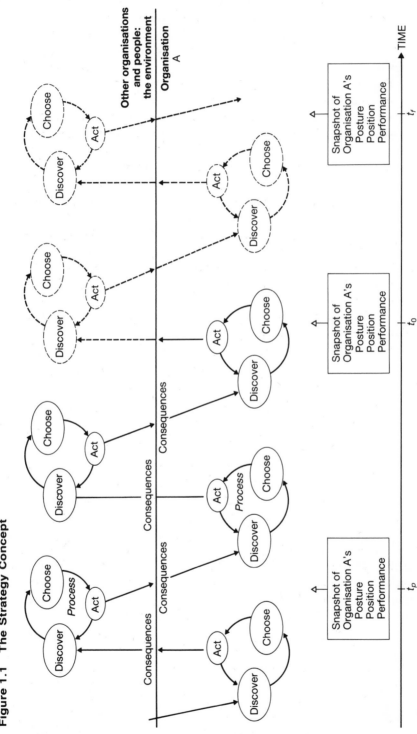

If we are able to look forward to time t_f we might perceive a pattern, or strategy, in future actions. Strategy is a perceived pattern in actions past or yet to come. We cannot touch a strategy or feel it – it is an interpretation we make of what has happened or what we expect to happen next. A strategy is simply a category into which we put certain patterns of action: for example Honda's actions to establish differentiation through superior quality or General Motor's actions to downsize its product line. Strategy is a label applied to patterns in action.

The patterns in action are generated by the circular loop between discovery, choice and action, that is the management process: strategic management is a feedback loop connecting discovery, choice and action. For example, General Motors discovered the likely increase in fuel costs and foreign competition through its analysis of the market. It chose to respond by formulating a plan to downsize its product range and acted by implementing that plan. At the same time Honda was discovering the importance of quality from customer feedback, choosing to focus on quality and acting to improve that quality.

When we seek to understand strategy in terms of patterns over time and strategic management in terms of the feedback processes generating those patterns, we are conducting a study of the dynamics of organisations. In a dynamic study we are concerned with the ebb and flow over time in the game managers in an organisation are playing, and with how they constitute an interactive system. We are concerned with how the players are provoking responses from each other and whether their moves are regular and predictable or not. Dynamics is concerned with the stability or instability of a system and the conditions that produce that stability or instability.

Static analysis

Figure 1.1 also depicts a snapshot at some past point in time, t_p, showing the posture of the organisation and the position it occupied in relation to the actors in its environment at that past time point.

The posture of an organisation refers to matters such as:

- the composition of its activities in terms of product lines and markets operated in;
- the technologies on which those activities are based;
- the manner in which the organisation is structured and controlled;
- the predominant shared behaviours or culture of the people in the organisation.

In other words, the posture of an organisation is a picture of what it looks like, its shape and its capabilities. The *posture* of an organisation is what you see when you stand at the organisational boundary and *look inwards*.

We could describe the position of the organisation in terms of aspects such as:

- market shares in particular segments;
- customer image;
- competence in relation to competitors;
- relative importance to suppliers

Position, then, is a picture of how an organisation relates to the people that are its environment. The *position* is what you see when you stand at the organisational boundary and *look outwards*.

The posture and the position of the organisation are the result of the strategy, the pattern in actions, it has pursued. That posture and position determine its performance at the time and performance refers to:

- financial dimensions such as cost levels, return on capital, profit growth; and
- operational dimensions such as quality and service levels.

When we seek to understand the position, posture and performance of an organisation at a particular point in time, we are concerned with static analysis. Static analysis is about a situation and its determinants at a point in time. So we might understand the General Motors situation in the late 1980s by analysing the structure of the US automobile market and the competitive capability of the firms operating in it. We would describe General Motors' position in terms of its 33 per cent market share, its image for poor quality, and its decline relative to Honda. Its posture could be analysed as that of an operator with a wide product range, hierarchical structures, bureaucratic processes and conservative cultures. Its performance would be measured in terms of profitability and product quality.

Comparative statics

We can also take a snapshot at the present time, t_0 in *Figure 1.1*. This will show the current organisational posture, position and resulting performance. The change in posture, position and performance from t_p to t_0 is the result of the strategy that has been pursued.

When we seek to understand strategy in terms of comparisons between one point in time and another, we are concerned with comparative static analysis. For example, in a comparative static analysis we would compare the 50 per cent General Motors' market share in the late 1970s with its 33 per cent share in the late 1980s and look for the causes of this decline.

The future – uncertainty and ambiguity

We study the dynamics of organisational life, and we analyse the past performance and decision-making processes of large numbers of organisations, because we hope to identify the fundamental laws governing successful organisational development. If we can do this we will be able to prescribe what to do to create and manage organisations that will succeed in the future.

The task of strategic management is that of somehow producing a posture and position for a particular organisation that will yield acceptable performance at some long-term future point, t_f in *Figure 1.1*. To do this it is necessary to determine the pattern in actions (the strategy) that will lead to the required posture and position. And to do that it is necessary to establish the particular feedback processes, the form of strategic management, that will lead to the required patterns. *Figure 1.1* shows the processes of strategic management to be undertaken in the future as dotted feedback loops.

As soon as we approach the task of identifying successful future strategies and strategic management processes, we are confronted by the problems of uncertainty and ambiguity. The strategy game is a turbulent one in which everything keeps changing – people's attitudes, their requirements for goods and services, their tastes and fashions change all the time as do technologies, government policies and many more factors. Therefore, managers have to make decisions and take actions now that will have uncertain consequences – the world in which managerial actions bear fruit will be different to the one in which they were initiated. At the time of taking a decision managers will not be sure of the meaning of many of the changes they are trying to cope with – these changes will be ambiguous.

For example, at any particular point in time, the managers at General Motors could quite legitimately have attached different meanings to the success that Honda was achieving in the US automobile market. Some of General Motors' managers could have concluded that Honda was being successful because Honda cars were small and therefore low fuel consumers. Other General Motors managers, however, could quite sensibly have argued that Honda's success was due to their lower price. Yet others could have insisted that Honda's success was due to higher quality. The situation would have been ambiguous and the conclusions drawn would have depended upon the shared way in which groups of managers were making sense of their world. That is to say, the explanation most managers accept at any one time depends upon what they together believe is important about their business. During the 1970s the prevailing belief amongst General Motors' managers was that customers were looking for small, fuel-efficient cars. The particular meanings that the most powerful group of General Motors' managers identified and believed in determined what they subsequently did.

The point we have to pay attention to throughout our study of strategic management, therefore, is that of the effect of uncertainty and ambiguity on the behaviour of people as they go about the tasks of deciding and acting strategically. People decide and act in one way when they operate close to certainty but, when they find themselves far from certainty, they have to decide and act in different ways.

The **third key question** that will arise again and again in the following chapters is that of just **what uncertainty and ambiguity mean** for the processes of strategic management.

This discussion about uncertainty and ambiguity also raises the **fourth key question** that will concern us much in what follows, namely the central importance to an understanding of strategic management of **the nature and role of shared ways of understanding the world**. Another word for a shared way of understanding the world is a paradigm and the same meaning is conveyed by the terms 'the conventional wisdom' or the 'company recipe'. A *paradigm* is a set of deeply held, unquestioned beliefs about what makes particular organisations successful, how they should be managed, and what is important about the needs they serve. How managers act in a strategic sense has a great deal to do with the paradigm they share. The views managers and writers of textbooks have on the nature of successful strategic management processes also depends upon their paradigm.

The management process and intention

Most people believe that any order they observe in a human system, such as a society or an organisation, has been put there by a designing mind. They believe that organisations follow the strategies they do because this is what their leaders have decided; the practice of paying large bonuses to chief executives when their organisations improve performance and then firing them as soon as their organisations falter is the practical expression of this belief. Quite consistent with this belief in the designing mind is the belief that the circular process of discovery, choice and action that is strategic management is a deliberate and intentional one. It is most frequently believed to be a process of:

● setting a goal in which the organisation's capability is matched to the requirements of its environment;
● analysing the environment and the capability of the organisation;
● deriving from the analysis those options that will achieve the goal;
● selecting the best option and then implementing it.

This is a model of the strategy process that deals in an analytical, rational way with the questions:

● How did we get here?
● Where do we want to go now?
● How shall we get there?

The important point to bear in mind is that this interpretation of what managers do or should do reflects a particular paradigm: a belief in the importance of intention, stability and regularity for the success of a system. There are, however, other interpretations. The process of discovery, choice and action could be interpreted as a process in which managers:

● discover in an intuitive rather than an analytical way;
● make unconscious, automatic choices rather than consciously intentional ones;
● carry those choices out in a reflexive, automatic way rather than a deliberate one.

They might not ask the questions in the rational model at all. They might:

● discover changes by chance;
● make choices on the basis of emotion and power; and
● carry those choices out in a tentative, trial-and-error way.

In this alternative interpretation, managers are not necessarily going around the loop in a deliberate way and what happens may not be intentional – it may simply emerge and may even be contrary to intention. This second interpretation of how managers might discover, choose and act also flows from a paradigm; this time based on the belief that human systems are so complex that no individual or small group of individuals can understand them fully enough to intend what happens to them. Order may nevertheless emerge despite a lack of intention.

This leads to the **fifth key question** that we will return to frequently as we proceed through the chapters that follow: **to what extent is successful strategy the result of organisational intention** and to what extent does it emerge from the complex interactions between people in organisations?

If we are to develop a deep understanding of strategy and strategic management we have to avoid jumping to immediate conclusions about the nature of the successful process. The nature of the successful process is what we have to explore carefully, not what we have to start off assuming. We need to try to expose the paradigms that lead to different views on the nature of successful strategic management processes. It is for this reason that I have used the words 'discovery', 'choice' and 'action'. They are intentionally vague and general enough to be open to many different interpretations. The posture, position and level of performance that discovery, choice and action lead to could all be intentional, or they could all just emerge. Our task in studying strategy is to identify the conditions that must be satisfied for it to be possible to make intentional strategies and the conditions within which there is no choice but to encourage emergent strategy. That task is far from easy as we shall see in the next section.

1.3   Difficulties in studying strategic management

Strategy is a deadly serious game because the livelihood, and indeed the lives, of all of us depend upon how and with what results it is played. Strategy is also a challenging and exciting game because it is so uncertain and fast moving, with extreme outcomes ranging from great success to catastrophic failure. Furthermore, it is in many ways an amusingly bizarre, Alice-in-Wonderland kind of game because it is so often extremely difficult to work out what the players are doing and why they are doing it. Simply asking them what they are doing, and why, is frequently of little use because they often act in skilled automatic ways that they find difficult, or even embarrassing, to explain. It is this sometimes bizarre aspect that makes the game so interesting to reflect upon and so difficult to draw conclusions about.

Saying one thing and doing another

For example, ask a sample of managers what they do and they will usually tell you something along these lines: organising and planning the work of others to achieve the organisation's goals. Managers still say this with great frequency despite the research evidence (Mintzberg, 1975a; Stewart, 1983) showing that they dash around under great pressure, spending a few minutes on each task, with very little visible sign of organising and planning.

Or, ask the members of a board of directors of a large company what the role of that board is. They will almost certainly say that the role is one of formulating the strategy of their company and overseeing its implementation. If you sit and watch them at work in the boardroom, however, you will observe that they usually spend 90 per cent of their time together reviewing past results against budget, legitimising decisions already taken, and attending to administrative matters, in that order of importance. This leaves less than 10 per cent of the time for what all board members say is their principal function.

As they play the strategy game, managers frequently say they are doing one thing when they are really doing another. It is often rather difficult to explain why they are doing this and even harder to change what they are doing. This clearly makes the study of strategic management a tricky business – all may not be as it seems.

This tendency to say one thing while doing another is particularly noticeable when people become anxious, and few things arouse anxiety and conflict as much as the uncertain and the ambiguous. Any realistic study of strategic management will therefore have to take account of how people discover, choose and act when they become anxious and conflict with each other.

The **sixth key question** that we will keep returning to in later chapters is therefore to do with the **behaviour of people in groups** and the impact this has on the way they choose and act strategically. The importance of the behavioural aspect is reinforced when you consider the frequency with which myths grow up in organisations.

Myths

To make the study of strategic management even more difficult, myths often grow up around how things happened. Sometimes the managers themselves come to believe the myths, but sometimes they do 'remember' how it 'actually' happened if they are asked the right questions.

Take the entry of Honda into the USA. It is usually described in terms of carefully laid plans by top Honda executives to do with global domination; or in terms of strong strategic intent, or vision, to build core competences in engines and a global presence in the automobile market (Hamel & Prahalad, 1989). We also often hear that Japanese companies win because they are backed by their government. These, however, appear to be myths.

Interviews with the Honda executives involved in the US market entry reveal a different story (Pascale, 1984). A small group of Honda executives was despatched to San Francisco on a trial basis. No market research had been carried out and there was no long-term plan; the executives concerned simply thought that there might be a market for large motor cycles in the United States. After many months of failing to sell those large motor cycles, the executives were on the verge of withdrawal, when by chance they noticed that people were interested in the small 50cc Super Cub that they were using for their own personal transport to save on scarce foreign currency. So they abandoned the idea of selling large motor cycles for a time and concentrated on selling Super Cubs instead – they had enough determination and initiative to use chance when it arrived. Also, we saw above that the Japanese government refused to back Honda; they did it on their own.

Few managers, however, describe the realisation of their strategies in such opportunistic terms, preferring to give more rational, even if mythical accounts. Again these tendencies create problems for the serious study of strategic management and therefore for deriving prescriptions on how to do it successfully. When you ask managers how they manage strategically you have to be careful about the myths. They may in reality not be using the visible formal organisation where they implement plans; they may be acting instead through the shadowy informal organisation that consists of a network of personal contacts where decisions are made on intuitive and political grounds.

It is all too easy to focus on the formal organisation and the myths about its use, and so miss what managers are actually doing when they manage strategically.

This **question of the role of the informal organisation is the seventh key one** that we will visit many times in the chapters that follow.

Winners and losers

The Alice-in-Wonderland quality of the strategy game is particularly evident when it comes to judging which organisations are winning and which are losing: we keep changing our minds about who is a success and who is a failure. During the mid-1980s UK commentators hailed the business folk heroes of the Thatcher era; for example, Ralph Halpern of Burtons, George Davies of Next, and Alan Sugar who built up the Amstrad consumer electronics empire. Some five years later, Burtons and Next together with their principal architects are seen as 'has-beens'. Alan Sugar and Amstrad come in for periodic criticism.

In the USA, Ford Motor Company is praised for its business skill during some periods and written off in others. General Electric is held up as a model for all to follow in some periods and then knocked down as an overweight conglomerate during others. In the early 1980s IBM was regarded as an excellent company, then it was widely judged to be 'dead', and by the late 1980s it was once again being acclaimed as an example to the rest of the business world. Clearly, we judge success to be a state of steady performance – a state of stability – but that state seems to be an extremely elusive one.

This raises **key question number eight** that we will pose a number of times in later chapters: **is success to be found in states of stability**, consistency, and consensus, or does it have more to do with instability, contradiction, and conflict?

This leads to the **ninth key question** that will occupy our attention as we move through the book, namely that to do with **paradox**. We will see that organisational success is not a matter of *either* stability *or* instability, but one of *both* stability *and* instability. In other words real organisations have to deal with the simultaneous presence of completely opposed forces, that is a paradox. This does not apply to questions of stability and instability alone but to many other aspects of organisational life. For example, organisations have to achieve both low prices and high quality; and people want both to be individuals and to lose themselves in a group.

1.4   Outline of the book

To summarise, the strategies of any organisation are the *perceived patterns*, over a long time period, in the sequences of actions undertaken by people in that organisation. They are categories into which we can sort typical patterns in action; they are labels we can apply to experience.

These patterns in action flow from the circular feedback *processes* of discovery, choice and action employed by people in organisations. The strategic management processes may be deliberate ones that produce intentional outcomes. On the other hand, those processes may not be deliberate and so produce unintended, emergent outcomes. The processes may be the visible ones of the formal organisation, or the much less visible ones of the informal organisation, and it is quite possible that managers may be using the latter without being all that aware of it.

Strategic actions have widespread, long-term consequences that establish the *posture* (that is, the internal shape and capability) of an organisation and its *position* (that is, its relationship to customers, competitors, suppliers, regulators, and financiers). The organisation's posture and position determine its *performance*. Today's posture, position and performance feed back into the process of strategic management to determine the next unfolding of patterns in action.

The strategy is the pattern in actions. The source of the strategy is the circular feedback process of strategic management employed. The result of the strategy is the posture and position of the organisation. Together posture and position determine performance and they provide the platform from which further patterns in action are developed.

The definitions say nothing about the presence or absence of stability, regularity or predictability in the patterns in action, positions, postures and performance levels. The definitions say nothing about the sources and nature of uncertainty and ambiguity, or about their impact on people and processes. Nor do the definitions say anything about the presence or absence of organisational intention. All these matters, and the connection between them and success, are what we need to explore through the study of strategic management. We have to avoid making assumptions about these matters before we embark on the study.

Key concerns

We have identified six important aspects of strategy, all made to start with the letter P (after Mintzberg, 1987b) because that is a fashionable thing to do in management books! These six Ps establish a broad but rather empty framework that is to be filled in with meaning as we study strategic management in the chapters that follow. The key questions we will need to keep posing to fill in the meaning have to do with:

1 The dynamics or patterns of change in organisational development, their stability and predictability or otherwise.
2 The circular feedback process of discovery, choice and action that generates the dynamics.
3 The effect of uncertainty and ambiguity on that circular feedback process.
4 The central part played by shared beliefs and shared ways of making sense of the world in determining management actions.
5 The role of shared intention in driving organisational strategy as opposed to the possibility of emergent strategies.
6 The impact of group behavioural dynamics on the choices and actions of managers.
7 The role of formal and informal systems in the successful management of an organisation.
8 The relationship between success and stability.
9 The presence of paradox and how managers cope with it.

We have also identified three different approaches to understanding all of this. One is the dynamic route that focuses on patterns and circular processes over time. The other two are forms of static analysis that focus on the determinants of postures, positions and performance at particular points in time. As we examine the different views of writers in the chapters that follow we will seek to identify the form of analysis they use and the manner in which they take account of the dynamics.

The whole point of studying strategic management is to find out what managers need to do to develop an organisational posture and position that will yield successful performance at some point in the future. In other words, we study strategic management quite simply because we are looking for the recipe for success, that is for general prescriptions we can apply to many different strategic situations. The trouble is that in matters as complex as strategic management there may be no reliable general recipes for success that managers can use in a wide variety of strategic situations. To the extent that strategic situations are unique and exceptional, managers will have to develop a unique way to handle each strategic situation as they face it. In such circumstances, general sets of prescriptions will be misleading and far more useful will be explanations of how things work, patterns of the kinds of general things that tend to happen, that can be used in a loose way to design custom-made responses to unique situations as they crop up. This book will argue that the approach of understanding systems and seeing patterns is far more useful than trying to set out lists of generic prescriptions. The matter of general prescriptions is dealt with in Chapter 2 and some prescriptions are presented at the end of Chapter 11, but the rest of the book is concerned with explanation and descriptive material that aids in explanation. Armed with insight and understanding of the dynamics managers may cope far better with the ambiguous and uncertain than they will if all they have is sets of general prescriptions that cannot by definition apply to unique situations. This is not, however, today's conventional wisdom.

Chapter 2, therefore, provides a summary of the conventional wisdom on strategic management; it sets out the general prescriptions for success that command most attention in the management literature and among practising managers. The conventional wisdom prescribes:

- general attributes to do with structure and behaviour that managers must install in their organisations in order to make them excellent;
- techniques to formulate, evaluate, select and implement plans to achieve performance objectives;
- systems to control performance against those plans;
- particular styles of management that are appropriate to particular environments.

This 'wisdom' is 'conventional' in the sense that the majority of managers profess to be at least aiming to behave according to it. It is also 'conventional' in the sense that most popular books on management reinforce it. This should not be taken to mean that the 'conventional wisdom' is some monolithic, uniform body of explanation and prescription. On the contrary, it consists of a number of approaches that may well conflict with each other and certainly appear to be very different. For example, one set of prescriptions is concerned with establishing very general qualitative 'visions' of the future to be achieved by trial-and-error action made consistent by the culture that all strongly share. Opposed to this view is another set of prescriptions to do with quantitative objectives and analytical techniques to determine optimal ways of achieving those objectives.

However, despite the marked differences, all the conventional approaches share a set of basic assumptions in common that are rarely questioned. Chapter 3, therefore, tries to make sense of the conventional wisdom by examining the unquestioned assumptions that underlie the prescriptions presented in Chapter 2. The chapter shows how these assumptions constitute a paradigm, a way of looking at the world, that I will label *the stable equilibrium organisation*. We have then a conventional wisdom that the majority of managers easily accept even though it consists of rather different and often conflicting prescriptions. But that wisdom is accepted without reflecting much on the fact that these conflicting prescriptions flow from exactly the same way of looking at the world, that is from the paradigm of the stable equilibrium organisation. This paradigm leads to a primarily static analysis in which strategic management is largely understood as an intentional process of deciding and acting within a formal organisation, or a carefully ordered informal one.

Chapter 4 turns to the criticisms that have been levelled at the conventional wisdom and demonstrates that they amount to an attack on the assumptions that the conventional wisdom makes about organisational dynamics. In other words, the attack is upon the dominant stable equilibrium organisation paradigm itself, that is the assumption that organisations succeed when they manage to achieve stability and regularity, when they get close to a state of stable equilibrium in which they are adapted to their environments. It will be argued that this way of looking at the problems of strategic management gives a rather shallow understanding of what managers actually do, or can do.

Chapter 5 explores the roots of the paradigm of the stable equilibrium organisation. Those roots lie in particular theories about feedback systems, namely cybernetics (or the engineer's approach to control), general systems theory, models of planned organisation development, and studies of overt political activity in organisations. So in Chapter 5 we will be exploring a number of explanations of the operation of negative feedback, that which is required to produce the stable equilibrium on which the conventional wisdom is built.

In Chapter 6 we will explore the important aspects of real life management that are ignored when we focus primarily on negative feedback and consequent stable equilibrium. That is, we will be exploring a number of models of management based on amplifying, or positive, feedback and the complex behaviour that positive feedback leads to. These models and explanations do not occupy a central position in the literature and have so far failed to command the attention of most practising managers, but they nevertheless give important insights into real-life strategic management. These are largely models that explain organisational behaviour in terms of amplifying feedback that often produces unintended results – vicious circles, covert political activity, organisational defence routines, and bizarre group behaviour.

By the time we reach Chapter 7 it will be clear that organisations are simply webs of what are called *nonlinear feedback loops*. When these loops are dominated by negative feedback then an organisation may be stable. On the other hand, when the loops operate in a positive mode an organisation is explosively unstable. By the time we reach Chapter 7 it will also be clear that innovative organisations must avoid the exclusive use of one or other of these forms of feedback and must instead employ both at the same time. Chapter 7 is concerned with new scientific explanations of what happens to such systems when they operate simultaneously in positive and negative feedback modes: their long-term futures become inherently unpredictable, that is completely unknowable. In such circumstances any form of long-term planning and any form of driving an organisation according to a specific vision becomes impossible. Instead strategies can only emerge from the interaction between people. This chapter and its presentation of chaos and self-organisation theory is a pivotal one – the conclusions it reaches justify the discussion in the rest of the book.

Chapter 8 examines what these conclusions about inherent unpredictability and emergent strategy mean for the kinds of change managers have to deal with and how they make decisions when faced with a spectrum stretching from predictable closed change to open-ended change where outcomes are unknowable. It will become clear why the decision-making processes prescribed by the conventional wisdom can be applied only when managers are dealing with the predictable; they have no choice but to use more complex, messier processes if they are to cope at all with the ambiguous and uncertain open-ended. What we will be doing in this chapter is looking at how we might understand decision-making when we accept that innovative organisations are driven not by either negative or positive feedback, but simultaneously by both in a way that generates inherent irregularity.

Chapter 9 explains what open-ended change and the decision-making processes required to deal with it mean for managers' ability to control an organisation. We will be exploring the forms of control that it is possible to practise in different change situations. What we will be doing in this chapter, therefore, is looking at how we might understand the control of an organisation once we recognise that innovative organisations are driven by both negative and positive feedback at the same time in such a way that their behaviour is inherently unstable. The conclusion we will reach is that the simultaneous presence of both positive and negative feedback and the chaos it generates creates a paradox: the need to practise two directly opposing forms of control at the same time; in fact the need simultaneously to practise two contradictory forms of management. I will call these *ordinary* and *extraordinary management* for reasons that will become clear as we proceed. We will discover that the conventional wisdom's prescriptions help us a great deal to practise ordinary management, but become redundant when we face the tasks of extraordinary management. In the latter case management with, and of, chaos becomes important.

Chapter 10 is concerned with how managers practise ordinary management. Ordinary management is concerned with the control and development of an organisation within a framework of beliefs that is accepted and agreed upon by people in that organisation. Such management may be concerned with the day-to-day running of the activities of the organisation, or with matters that are strategic in the sense that they have to do with the long-term continuation of the existing activities of the organisation. Managers carry out the tasks of ordinary management through the formal organisation and this is perfectly adequate in conditions of predictable change. By the time we get to this stage we will be able to see that, because today's conventional wisdom is based firmly on the paradigm of the stable equilibrium organisation, it can provide explanations and prescriptions for ordinary management only – the taking up of roles in a hierarchy and a bureaucracy, or in a band of firm believers led by a charismatic leader. The development of formal hierarchies and reporting structures and the use of Management Information and Control Systems will also be examined.

Chapter 11 will explain what managers do when they practise extraordinary management. It will become clear in this chapter how the new scientific theories of chaos and self-organisation point to explanations of organising and managing that have received rather little attention over the past thirty years. We will see how ordinary management is not enough when an organisation has to innovate and cope with the ambiguous, the uncertain, and the unpredictable. Then managers have also to practise extraordinary management in which they continually challenge and destroy the existing ordinary management frameworks in order to create new ones. To do this they have to switch to operating through the informal organisation. Chapter 11 explores the nature of the informal organisation, sometimes called the network organisation, and the role it plays as the cutting-edge tool for strategic management. For the great majority of organisations, success paradoxically requires both ordinary and extraordinary management at the same time. We will be exploring how managers cope with this paradox in Chapter 11.

It is usual to draw a distinction between the short-term day-to-day management of an organisation and the long-term strategic management of that organisation. The distinction between the two forms of management lies in the time span of organisational intention; that is, the time period into the future over which the consequences of managerial action will occur and therefore the time period managers have to take account of and think in terms of. Chapters 9, 10 and 11 will argue that it is more useful to draw a distinction between management that is conducted within a given set of beliefs and management that is about changing that set of beliefs, because these two different forms of management involve such different, in fact directly contradictory, processes. Ordinary management is about stable processes, of either the rational or the ideological kind, that secure the continuity of existing organisational activity, while extraordinary management is an unstable, political process that destroys existing beliefs and leads to innovation and new strategic direction. Strategic management can be ordinary when it is about building on existing strengths to do more of what the organisation is already good at, and extraordinary when it is about doing the new. It is clearly the latter that is the cutting edge of strategy. The distinction between ordinary and extraordinary management is based not on the time span of intention but on the extent to which people in the organisation share a common paradigm.

Chapter 12 concludes by summarising the argument of the book and pointing to some consequences of the tensions and paradoxes inherent in management. The main consequence is anxiety and this may explain why some managers cling to formal, rational explanations of management even where they cannot work – the appearance of rationality may act as a defence against anxiety.

2

How to make successful strategies

The conventional wisdom

2.1 Introduction

This chapter sets out the most widely prescribed routes to organisational success, the ones that constitute today's conventional wisdom. The term 'conventional wisdom' is used here to encompass all those explanations of, and prescriptions for, the successful practise of strategic management that the majority of managers and consultants subscribe to. The conventional wisdom is what you hear most often when you ask managers and consultants what happens and what ought to happen when they practise strategic management. The conventional wisdom is what is to be found in the best-selling books on management and in most of the textbooks. This conventional wisdom is, however, not a monolithic body of knowledge, but rather a collection of explanations that differ from each other and indeed often contradict each other, as we shall see in this chapter.

In this chapter we will largely explore what the conventional wisdom has to say about the routes to success, mentioning only some of the practical difficulties encountered in trying to apply that advice and some of the more obvious criticisms of it. The deeper conceptual limitations of the conventional wisdom will be examined in the next chapter.

First, we consider the 'one best way' prescriptions. These are usually derived from studies of excellent organisations that identify the key features those organisations have in common and then conclude that these key features are the sources of excellence. The 'excellence' prescription can be summarised as follows:

1 An organisation is successful because it possesses a small number of key attributes, primarily leadership and cultural factors, that can be identified by studying how managers in successful organisations behave. These attributes can be imitated by and installed into other organisations which will then also succeed. The key attributes

postulated to be necessary for success relate to behaviour: success follows when groups of people work together in harmony to adapt to their environment; when they strongly share the same values and the same vision of the future. The prescription is, therefore, to install the key attributes: that is, establish a centrally intended vision for the future, promote internal harmony by encouraging a shared culture, empower people, and continually adapt to the external environment through trial-and-error action. (The next section of this chapter will explore this prescription.)

The excellence approach received a great deal of attention during the 1980s because of a reaction against the widespread view that success can be secured simply by the rational formulation and implementation of quantitative long-term plans. The reaction took the form of emphasising the importance for organisational success of factors that are the opposite of the rational: for example, vision, emotion, charismatic leadership, belief, ideology and culture.

However, although this visionary and ideological approach to strategy has had a powerful impact on the way managers talk and think, the rational formulation and implementation of long-term plans has continued to be the most widely presented route to success. The next set of prescriptions we will consider, therefore, is concerned, first of all, with formulating and selecting strategic plans according to given rational criteria. This approach in effect rejects the idea that there is 'one best way' and presents instead a procedure for identifying a specific acceptable way for each individual organisation, determined by its own particular circumstances. The next four conclusions about success (to be explored in the section after the next) are concerned with evaluating and selecting long-term plans:

2 Organisations succeed when their managers set appropriate long-term goals, formulate the right plans to achieve those goals, and then implement their plans. The prescription is for top managers to set the objectives and formulate the plans, or at least approve the plans prepared by subordinates that provide the framework for others to act.

3 Appropriate goals and the right long-term plans are those that produce performance that is acceptable to the most powerful groups of stakeholders in an organisation. The prescription that flows from this conclusion is that managers should apply certain well-known analytical techniques to the specific situation of their organisation to determine in advance whether particular patterns in action are likely to yield acceptable performance.

4 Appropriate goals and the right long-term plans are those that produce performance that is acceptable and patterns in action that are feasible. The prescription here is that managers should identify, through advance analysis, whether they will have the resources and skills to carry out their proposed strategy.

5 Appropriate goals and the right long-term plans are those that produce performance that is acceptable, patterns in actions that are feasible, and what is called 'fit' or suitability. Fit or suitability is a requirement for patterns in action and their consequent positions and postures to be consistent with each other, as well as with long-term goals and with the demands of the environment. This is really saying that organisations are successful when they intentionally achieve internal harmony and external adaptation to their environment. The prescription is for managers to use analytic techniques to identify consistent relationships between the elements of their strategy, their objectives, the capability of their organisation, and the demands of their environment. Managers should analyse their organisation's strengths, weaknesses and opportunities. They should then use the analysis to guide actions that build on their strengths, secure opportunities consistent with those strengths, and avoid threats and activities where they are weak. In short, to be successful, managers should generally stick to what they do best.

Rational approaches to organisational success have focused mainly on selecting the right strategy in advance of action. It has, however, been increasingly recognised that the implementation of a selected strategy cannot be taken for granted. This has led to further conclusions and prescriptions (to be explored in a later section of this chapter):

6 Even when managers do follow the prescriptions for selecting long-term strategies, many still fail because of problems with implementing their plans. The prescriptions that follow from this conclusion are that managers should analyse the organisation's culture and power structure to identify what the obstacles to implementation will be and then prepare plans to overcome these obstacles in advance of action. Such plans might involve, for example: installing a new management reporting structure; training and developing people; installing new information, control and reward systems; or changing the whole culture of an organisation.

7 Furthermore, managers should monitor the performance of their organisation against their long-term plans and take corrective action to stay on course. In other words, managers should attend as much to the question of control as they do to that of selecting the right plan in the first place.

Finally we will consider some conclusions and prescriptions about the process of strategic management and the overall strategic stance that should be adopted if organisations are successfully to select and implement long-term plans (to be explored in a later section of this chapter):

8 The style of strategic management has to do with the role that managers at different levels – corporate, business unit and functional – play in the strategic management of the whole enterprise so as to cope with the inevitable tensions between short- and long-term objectives, between the parts and the whole of the organisation, and many more tensions. The conventional wisdom holds that an organisation's style has to be appropriate to its nature and to the environment it operates in. Some of the prescriptions that flow from this are as follows. Where an organisation consists of a number of overlapping businesses and has to operate in a highly turbulent environment, then it will succeed if the corporate level adopts a top-down long-term planning style and the other levels implement what the top has decided. On the other hand, where the organisation consists of a number of largely independent, mature businesses operating in stable environments, then it is appropriate for the corporate level to adopt a short-term financial control style of managing the whole organisation and leave the development of strategies to managers in the different business units. There will then be no corporate long-term plans, only business unit ones. Yet other configurations of organisational characteristics and environmental factors lead to other appropriate styles; for example, a style in which top management controls the process of planning but leaves the formulation of the content to managers lower down.

We turn now to an examination of the first set of prescriptions, those to do with the installation of excellence.

2.2 Installing the attributes of excellence

In the early 1980s Peters and Waterman (1982) published a study of forty-three major American corporations. The sample included such household names as Disney, Boeing, IBM, Mars, McDonalds, Dupont, Levi-Strauss, Procter and Gamble, 3M, Caterpillar, Hewlett Packard, Kodak, Wang, and Atari. All forty-three companies were selected because they were judged to be excellent according to six financial yardsticks and because they had been innovative and adaptable over reasonably long time periods. The study reached the conclusion that the cause of the excellence displayed by these companies lay in eight prominent attributes they shared in common. The conclusion drawn was that, if other companies imitated these eight attributes, they too would become excellent. The eight attributes are listed below; they are particular characteristics of pattern in actions, position, posture and process.

The attributes of excellence

1 Stick to the knitting. This attribute relates to the pattern in sequences of strategic actions undertaken by excellent companies. They build on their strengths or core competences and they never diversify far away from these. Because successful companies stick to what they know and avoid that which they do not, senior managers can have a clear understanding of their business. It is this knowledge and experience that provides the basis of their management intuition and credibility. For example, McDonalds sticks to fast foods and avoids diversifying into hotels.

2 Close to the customer. This attribute relates to the position an excellent company adopts in relation to its environment. Excellent companies actively listen to their customers and place great emphasis on delivering quality, reliability and high levels of service. They set very high standards in these regards and ensure their achievement through reward systems that include emotional rewards, for example reward ceremonies. The excellent companies succeed because by listening to their customers they become better adapted to their environments than their competitors.

3 Productivity through people. The posture that excellent companies adopt towards their people is one of major importance. They express concern for the feelings of their people and try to foster attitudes in which people perceive themselves as belonging to an extended family.

4 Autonomy and entrepreneurship. Excellent companies adopt a posture and process that encourage local initiative and practical risk-taking; they empower people to make decisions about their own jobs. The cultural values are such that people are not penalised for the failures that must sometimes flow from taking risks. Eccentrics are tolerated, provided that they are doers.

5 Hands on, value driven. In their decision-making processes, excellent companies place particular emphasis on cultural values and beliefs. The leaders of the company articulate and preach a set of beliefs to which they convert others. It is this strongly shared common culture that is the principal cause of the harmony to be found in excellent companies. The role of the leaders is also to create a strong sense of direction by expressing a vision of the future state the organisation is to occupy. The vision and the core values are not open to question, other than at the fringes. Leaders are inspirational and involved in the activities of the organisation, not superior or aloof monitors of previously planned actions.

6 Bias for action. This also refers to the management processes employed by excellent companies. Excellent companies rely heavily on informal communication and employ small, temporary task forces with voluntary membership inspired by visionary product champions to progress many different projects. On this view, organisations make strategic choices in a political manner because the choice depends upon how much support the champion can build for his or her idea.

Excellent companies are interested in tangible results, not lengthy reports; they do not wait for the results of analyses, but rather try ideas out, rapidly one after the other. Their posture and the processes of management they use emphasise fast trial-and-error action through which they learn about their environment.

Note, however, that learning here is of a rather simple kind in which managers are learning about the consequences of their actions. Their learning prompts a change of action, but not a change in beliefs. The previous attribute (all people strongly sharing the same visions and values) means that people will not question basic beliefs and attitudes. This must exclude the more complex forms of learning that takes place when people question the deepest beliefs and assumptions that their views and actions are based upon, and in so doing change them.

7 Simple form, lean staff. Excellent companies adopt a structural posture that involves small corporate headquarters with the rest decentralised into small autonomous units. Authority is pushed down the line. Complicated matrix forms of organisation are avoided. People are encouraged to see organisational sub-units as flexible and permeable. Rigid job descriptions are discouraged.

8 Simultaneous loose–tight properties. Excellent companies adopt a control posture in which there are two elements. These elements sound contradictory, but the manner in which they are used means that they are not contradictory in practice. On the one hand, excellent companies encourage simple fluid structures with high levels of autonomy and positive attitudes to risk taking where people are empowered to take their own decisions. On the other hand, excellent companies apply tight short-term financial controls to the performance of all their units and they fiercely guard the core values. But they find it possible to combine individual initiative and enterprise (the loose) with central organisational intention and control (the tight) in a consistent and harmonious way because of the belief system that all strongly share.

Harmony and consistency is thus preserved, so solving the apparent contradiction between the tight and the loose.

The conclusion drawn is that if managers install these eight attributes into their organisations then people will be motivated to carry out the trial-and-error actions required to reach the vision shared by all. The top sets the vision and the values and then relies on people in the organisation to find the route to that vision. Peters and Waterman explain that rapid change and high levels of uncertainty make it impossible to forecast enough of what is going to happen to make it possible to prepare stable plans well in advance of acting, that is to tell people well in advance what they are expected to do. It follows that managers have to discover the route to the future position they wish to occupy through trial-and-error action. The drive to undertake large volumes of trial-and-error action comes from what people believe, hence the heavy emphasis of the eight attributes on ideology, culture and vision.

Peters and Waterman argued that managers were being misled by a belief that they ought to be rational and were consequently spending too much time on research and analysis that diminished the urge to act – the result was paralysis by analysis. The argument about rationality and the extent to which managers need to use rational criteria to make decisions or to adopt some other approach still continues. Unfortunately, the debate is greatly confused by the fact that rationality has a number of meanings and debaters do not always make it clear which of these meanings they are using. *Key Concept 2.1* sets out the different senses in which the word rationality will be used throughout the rest of this book. Peters and Waterman condemn the excessive use of rationality in its technical and reasoned senses in strategic management and focus instead on 'reality-testing' forms of rationality.

■ **Key concept 2.1**
RATIONALITY

The word 'rational' can be used in a number of different ways and its use can cause confusion in discussions about management processes. It is important to distinguish one meaning from another. There are three common meanings of the word 'rational':

1 *Sensible, reasonable in the circumstances, sane, not foolish, absurd or extreme. Rationality here is behaving and deciding in a manner connected to reality and judged likely to bring about desired, intended consequences. Irrationality consists of fantasy-driven behaviour, while rationality involves testing for reality where that reality may well be of an emotional, ideological or cultural kind. I will use the term reality-testing for this kind of rationality and keep the word 'rational' for its next meaning.*

2 *Rejecting that which cannot be tested by reason applied to objective facts. Rationality here is behaving and deciding only on the basis of propositions that can be consciously reasoned about, rather than on the basis of customs, norms, emotions and beliefs. Irrationality here consists not only of fantasy, but also of behaviour driven by emotions and beliefs even if they are connected to an emotional and ideological reality. I will use the word rational in this sense throughout the book.*

3 *A method of deciding that involves setting clear objectives, gathering the facts, generating options, and choosing one that maximises or* satisfices *(i.e, approximately satisfies) the objective. Irrationality here is any behaviour whatsoever that is not preceded by fixing objectives and weighing up options based on observable facts. I will refer to this as* technical rationality.

It is quite possible, indeed highly likely, that reality-testing will lead to the conclusion that technical rationality should be avoided. That is, it may be quite 'rational' in sense 1 to avoid being rational in sense 3. So, in a totally unpredictable environment, under strict time pressures, it would not be logical or sensible to try to make decisions in a painstaking manner that could never anyhow succeed in meeting all the criteria of rationality in its sense 3 meaning. (These criteria will be discussed in Chapter 8 in the section on models of decision making far from certainty.)

It could also be rational in terms of meaning 1 (reality-testing) to avoid meaning 2. You may achieve a better response from others if you base your behaviour on emotion and belief in certain circumstances. To do so would therefore be rational in sense 1 but not in sense 2.

The meaning of discovery, choice and action: vision and ideology

We can see now how the excellence approach to organisational success fills in the meaning of the discovering, choosing and acting loop that was discussed in Chapter 1. Choice is embodied in the vision and the values that all share – people make choices through a political process in which champions build support for their projects, but those projects all flow from the ideology that everyone in the organisation believes in. Any project not consistent with the ideology would not even

Figure 2.1   How the excellence approach defines discovery, choice and action

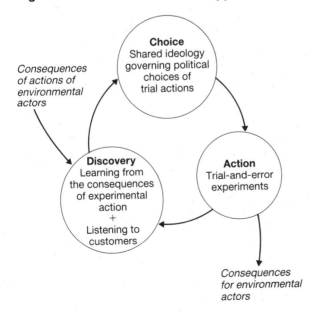

be perceived by most and, even if it was perceived, it would not attract sufficient support to be implemented. Central to the choice process is the role of charismatic leaders and the exciting and emotional response they arouse in their followers. This is not a cold, rational mode of choosing what to do, but an exciting, emotional one.

The focus is on action and, when they act, people take trial actions that they build on if the action succeeds and discontinue if it fails. In this way they discover, or learn from, the consequences of their trial actions and that discovery leads to the next trial action until the vision is realised. Discovering also means listening actively to customers. These definitions are depicted in *Figure 2.1*.

At this point it should be noted how the vision/ideology interpretation of the strategic management process is one that is clearly based on organisational intention (see *Key Concept 2.2*). In other words, successful organisations, it is held, follow sequences of actions that their leaders intend. As we shall see in Chapter 3 this amounts to an assumption about organisational dynamics and as we shall see in later chapters it is possible to make other assumptions that will lead us to question the central role of organisational intention.

■ **Key concept 2.2**
ORGANISATIONAL INTENTION

In its fullest sense, organisational intention means that: everyone in an organisation, or at least key groups of managers, are deliberately sharing an intention to achieve some relatively distant future state relating to posture, position and performance; and they are deliberately sharing an intention to achieve that future state through a particular strategy, that is pattern in actions. Organisational intention here has to do with conscious, purposeful, deliberate design of both the future state and the actions leading to that state. It has to do with a concept of predetermined direction shared by the key decision makers if not by all involved.

Few would seriously suggest that an organisation could be controlled and developed over the long term in a fully intentional manner. However, it is the conventional wisdom that it is possible to get close enough to the conditions for intentionality, to make long-term planning an effective approach. This seems to be a natural assumption to make when the only alternative is thought to be haphazard action or short-term reaction. But there is another possible alternative – that of emergence. The practically useful juxtaposition is that of intentionality *and* emergence. *It is perfectly possible for future states and patterns of action to emerge from the continuing interactions between people and groups operating in a complex system. This need not be haphazard.*

In his book, Managing on the Edge, *Richard Pascale (1990) describes how Ford transformed itself in the 1980s from a huge loss maker to a profitable and acclaimed excellent company. It is a story of a number of independent initiatives on quality, design, employee participation, executive development, studies on Japanese competitors, management workshops and many more, that somehow came together in a mutually reinforcing way. All of this happened in conditions of conflict and tension and there was no central plan or vision. The outcome emerged from many individual intentions and actions. Pascale describes what happened as the 'coincident unfolding of events' where it is impossible to envision that coincidence without the benefit of hindsight. The idea of no organisational intention and patterns in action emerging from the detail of actions and interactions is therefore not at all far-fetched.*

There is then a spectrum of possibilities. At one end of the spectrum all the conditions for full intentionality are satisfied (see Chapter 9): managers can then establish in advance what the long-term outcome will be and they can identify in advance the pattern of actions necessary to get them there. The mode of strategic management is that of long-term planning. At the other end of the spectrum none of the conditions are satisfied; managers then have no idea of what the long-term outcome will be and they can only detect the pattern in what they have done with the benefit of hindsight. In this case the strategy will emerge from the detail of what they do and the mode of strategic management here is a complex form of learning (see Chapter 11). Between these two extremes there is the possibility of intending the final outcome but discovering how to achieve it. The mode of strategic management here is visionary and ideological.

The Peters and Waterman study and the principles it identified have had a very powerful effect on companies throughout the world. During the 1980s many companies cut out layers of management to make their organisations lean and simple. They embarked on major programmes to change the cultures of their organisations and to empower people; they devoted time to forming visions and preparing mission statements; and terms such as vision, values and culture came to occupy a prominent place in the vocabulary of most business people.

The enduring contribution made by the Peters and Waterman study is the attention it focused on the important role that values, culture and beliefs play in organisational success. We will be returning to these matters on a number of occasions in later chapters, particularly in Chapters 10 and 11.

The Peters and Waterman study also directed attention to the informal aspects of an organisation and the role that organisational politics plays in the process of strategic management by emphasising the role of leaders, product champions, project teams, and task forces. These are much the same kinds of processes that have been observed in studies of political activity in organisations and we will be looking at these in more detail in Chapters 5, 6, 8 and 11. Informal organisational processes and the implications of empowering people will be discussed in Chapter 11.

The model of the strategic management process presented by Peters and Waterman in their eight-attribute analysis, with its emphasis on trial-and-error action, is close to a model developed by Quinn (1980) called logical incrementalism and we will be examining this in more detail in Chapter 8 in the section on models of decision-making far from certainty.

Despite the importance of the Peters and Waterman study, however, it has not identified *the* definitive route to success. The eight-attribute plan proved to be a disappointment because, within five years, two-thirds of the companies in the sample had slipped from the pinnacle, some to return later, others to remain in the doldrums. A number of other studies followed (for example, Goldsmith & Clutterbuck, 1984), but none so far can be judged to have found the one best way for all companies.

We now turn to prescriptions for selecting and implementing plans. The excellence approach prescribes shared beliefs that motivate people to use their own initiative and judgement to undertake the actions required to realise a centrally determined vision.

The technically rational approach, on the other hand, prescribes the application of analytical techniques to select particular sequences of actions to achieve goals well in advance of acting; people on this view are first told, or agree on what to do and they then get on and do it.

2.3   Formulating and selecting strategic plans according to technically rational criteria

The first prescription of the technically rational approach to strategic management is that managers should formulate a long-term plan.

To do this, managers must first identify and agree upon the performance levels, both financial and operational, that they are going to achieve by some point in the long-term future; that is, they must set the quantitative and qualitative objectives that they are going to strive for. Those objectives must satisfy the rational criteria of acceptability, feasibility and suitability that we will discuss below.

The second step in formulating a long-term plan is the specification of the future organisational posture and position that will produce the performance objectives. You will recall from Chapter 1 that the performance of an organisation at any one time is the consequence of its posture and the position it occupies in its environment at that time. However, before much can be said about an appropriate future position and posture for an organisation, it is necessary to find out something about the future environment in which that position and posture is to be taken; some postures and positions are possible and successful in some environments but not in others. The requirement for success, according to the conventional wisdom, is that an organisation must be adapted to its environment. It follows that we cannot plan a position and posture to do this until we know something about what that environment will be.

Finding out about a future environment is a process of analysing the past and the present and then using that analysis as the basis for forecasting. Once managers know something about the nature of their future environment they can then deduce what alternative positions and postures might deliver their performance objectives. For each of these alternatives they will also need to identify the patterns in actions, the plans, that will produce the position and the posture. The range of future positions and postures realistically open to an organisation at some future point, and the appropriate range of actions required to get to those future positions and postures, constitute the organisation's strategic options. The rational criteria of acceptability, feasibility and suitability, to be discussed in the next section, must then be applied to evaluate each option and select that option which best satisfies the criteria. This becomes the organisation's strategy. An example of this kind of prescription is given in *Illustration 2.1*.

The meaning of discovery, choice and action: technical rationality

We can now see how the technically rational approach fills the discovery, choice and action loop with meaning. Discovery is a process of systematically gathering the

Figure 2.2 How the technically rational approach defines discovery, choice and action

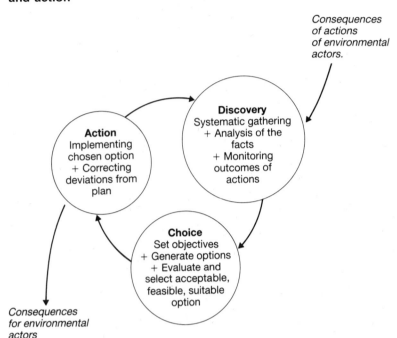

objective facts and analysing them. This forms the basis of choice and choice is the selecting of performance objectives, the generating of options to achieve them, and the evaluation and selection of an acceptable option as the long-term plan. Action is the implementation of the plan. Since the outcomes of actions will deviate from planned intentions, discovery is also a process of monitoring that feeds deviations back into the choice process, which in turn leads to corrective action to move the organisation back on to plan.

As managers move around this loop they will discover changes that require them to alter their objectives and their plans. Although we have described the process as a step-by-step one running from objectives to options to plans and then to action, it is clearly a circular process and the description could start at any stage.

■ **Illustration 2.1**
ANSOFF'S STRATEGIC SUCCESS HYPOTHESIS

Ansoff (1990) presents a strategic success hypothesis stating that a firm's performance will be optimal when:

- the aggressiveness of the sequence of actions undertaken by the firm matches the level of turbulence in its environment;
- the responsiveness of the firm's capability matches the aggressiveness of its actions;
- the elements of the firm's capability are supportive of one another.

Ansoff defines levels of turbulence in terms of rising levels of unpredictability and complexity and he distinguishes five levels: repetitive, expanding, changing, discontinuous, and surprising.

Strategic aggressiveness is defined in terms of the size of the break with past strategies and the speed with which they are implemented. He identifies five levels of aggressiveness: stable, reactive, anticipatory, entrepreneurial, and creative.

He then distinguishes five levels of capability responsiveness: custodial which is precedent-driven and suppresses change; production-oriented which is efficiency-driven and adapts to change; marketing orientation which is market-driven and seeks familiar change; strategic which is environment-driven and seeks new change; flexible which seeks to create the environment and seeks novel change.

Strategic logic means, for example, that flexible capability and creative action is required in surprising environments. Ansoff maintains that all these levels can be identified in advance of acting by strategic diagnosis.

Having said something about the nature of planning we turn now to the different kinds of planning that are prescribed for organisations. Since most organisations of any size consist of a collection of different activities organised into units, a distinction is drawn between corporate plans and business unit plans (Hofer & Schendel 1978; Porter, 1987).

The corporate plan

This is concerned with the pattern of actions that is to apply to the organisation as a whole. It is what is supposed to make the whole add up to more than the sum of its parts, a phenomenon known as *synergy*. The justification for grouping a number of related activities together, rather than having them operate as separate organisations, lies in the value that the corporate level adds. And it adds value by reaping synergies and by coordinating and making the parts consistent.

Corporate strategy is concerned with what activities or businesses the organisation should be involved in and how the corporate level should manage that set of businesses. In other words corporate strategy is about a portfolio of businesses and what should be done with them. The key question for corporate strategy is: what collection of activities do we need to put together, and how should we manage this collection, to achieve corporate objectives in the end set by shareholders?

Business unit plans

A business unit plan sets out how that business unit is going to build a posture and position that is superior to that of its rivals so enabling it to achieve the performance objectives set by the corporate level. In other words, business unit strategy is about the means of securing and sustaining competitive advantage. The key question for business unit strategy is: how do we secure competitive advantage so as to achieve the objectives set by the corporation?

Finally, since business units are generally organised on a functional basis – finance, sales, production and research departments, for example – the business unit strategy will have to be translated into functional or operational strategies.

Functional and operational plans

These set out the actions that a function is to take to contribute to the whole strategy of the business unit, just as the business unit strategy contributes to the corporate one. The key question for functional plans is: what actions must we take to contribute our share to the business unit plan?

What we have, then, is a hierarchy of long-term objectives and plans, the corporate creating the framework for the business unit, and the business unit creating the framework for the functional. Furthermore, this collection of long-term plans provides the framework for formulating shorter-term plans and budgets against which the organisation can be controlled in the short term (see *Key Concept 2.3*).

■ **Key concept 2.3**
PLANS AND PLANNING

The words 'plans' and 'planning' are often used loosely by managers. For example, managers may say that they have a long-term plan simply because they have set out some long-term financial targets or because they have identified one or two specific actions that they intend to undertake, for example make an acquisition. Managers also sometimes claim that they are planning, when what they are doing is following a technically rational decision-making process. As students of strategic management, we need to be more precise in using the words plan and planning.

Managers can only be said to be planning the future of their organisation when, as a group, they share a common intention to achieve a particular future posture, position and level of performance for the business (you may wish to refer back to Chapter 1, Figure 1.1); that is, when they select aims and objectives for the business well in advance of acting. In addition to choosing a future state, managers must also share a common intention to pursue a sequence of actions to achieve that chosen future state, if their behaviour is to qualify as planned. Before managers can intentionally choose an intended state and an intended sequence of future actions, however, they have to identify the future environment in which they are to achieve their aims – their intentions must be anchored to a specific future reality. In other words, managers cannot possibly plan unless they can also make reasonably reliable forecasts of the future time period they are planning for. The future must not only be knowable, it must be sufficiently well known in advance of required performance.

In addition, to qualify as controlling and developing the business's long-term future in the planning mode, managers must set milestones along the path to the intended future state, couched in terms of results. This will enable the outcomes of actions to be checked and deviations from plan corrected. Action is both implementation of the planned sequence of actions and corrections to keep results on course. Only then is control being exercised in a planned manner. The ability to control by plan depends upon the possibility of establishing organisational intention.

The key question to address now is how managers at whatever level are supposed to select the plans that will lead them to success. The prescribed way of selecting successful plans is to use analytical criteria to evaluate the options.

Evaluation criteria are intended to enable managers to conclude whether or not a particular sequence of actions will lead to a particular position and posture and whether that position and posture will in turn produce some target measure of performance. The criteria are there to enable managers to form judgements about the outcomes of their proposed actions before they take those actions; that is, judgements as to whether a choice of strategy is likely to turn out to be a good one before they do anything at all to implement it. The purpose is to prevent surprises and ensure that an organisation behaves over long time periods in a manner intended by its members and leaders. There are three very widely proposed sets of criteria for doing this.

Acceptability or desirability

(To be discussed in detail in the next section.) According to this criterion strategies will turn out to be successful only if their consequences are acceptable to the organisation's most powerful stakeholders. These consequences must be acceptable not only in the obvious terms of financial performance but also in terms of meeting other stakeholder expectations, including the impact on their power positions and their cultural beliefs. The stakeholders of an organisation are its owners, managers, employees, customers, suppliers, trade bodies, trades unions, government authorities and community pressure groups. If a pattern of actions is not acceptable to powerful groups from any of the stakeholder categories then the strategy may well fail.

Feasibility

(To be discussed in detail in the section after the next.) This criterion states that a strategy will be a success if it is feasible in the sense that the financial and other resources, the technology and the skills are all available to carry out the strategy. A strategy is feasible when there are no insurmountable obstacles to its implementation. Many strategies have failed and will fail because they require investments of resources, or applications of skill and technology, beyond the capability of the organisation trying to carry them out.

Suitability, appropriateness or fit

(To be discussed in a later section below.) This means that strategies will be successful when they relate to the key features identified by strategic analysis; that is, when the patterns in actions, positions, postures and performance fit with the objectives and the environment of the organisation. The strategy is suitable when it takes advantage of strengths and opportunities, as well as dealing with weaknesses and threats. This then associates success with a strategic logic, or rationale, matching patterns of action to market situations, competitive capability and the culture of the organisation. We can summarise all this by saying that an organisation fully satisfies the suitability criteria when it is in a stable equilibrium state completely adapted to its environment.

We turn now to the first of the three widely accepted criteria for selecting some future sequence of actions that will make an organisation successful.

ACCEPTABILITY

There are at least three senses in which strategies have to be acceptable if we are to conclude that they will be successful. First, performance in financial terms must be acceptable to owners and creditors. Second, the consequences of the strategies for the most powerful groupings within the organisation must be acceptable to those groupings in terms of their expectations and the impact on their power positions and cultural beliefs. Third, the consequences of the strategies for powerful groups external to the organisation must be acceptable to those groupings. Consider what each of these senses entails.

1   Acceptable financial performance

If they are to be successful then managers must determine in advance of acting whether their long-term plans are likely to turn out to be financially acceptable. They determine this by forecasting the financial consequences of each strategic option open to them: cash flows, capital expenditures and other costs, sales volumes, price levels, profit levels, assets and liabilities including borrowing and other funding requirements. Next, they use the forecasts to calculate prospective rates of return on sales and capital.

A rate of return is calculated by expressing some measure of profit as a percentage of some measure of the sales that yield that profit or the assets used in generating it. So, if the business earns a profit of £1m from sales of £5m and in order to make these sales it had to use assets of £10m, then the rate of return on sales is 20 per cent and on capital employed it is 10 per cent.

However, complexities arise because it is possible to define profits and assets in many different ways. Managers may be interested in profits before tax or after tax, before allowing for the depreciation of assets or after depreciation, before interest paid on loans or after interest. They may be interested in total assets employed or in net assets employed, that is after deducting amounts owed to the organisation. They may be interested in fixed assets (land, buildings, plant and machinery) or variable assets such as inventories and debtors. There are therefore many different rates of return on sales and capital and the one used depends upon the purpose of use and also on accounting conventions.

No matter what particular rate of return is selected, there will be many difficulties of measurement to be overcome. For example, it may be difficult to measure just how much of an asset has been used up in a particular period of use – the problem of measuring depreciation. Or it is often difficult to know how to allocate the costs of the corporate level of management to the business units.

Once managers have identified what the relevant performance measures are and dealt with the difficulties of measurement, they then have the information they can use to determine the likely financial acceptability of their plans. Financial acceptability rests on a balance between rewards and risks and we will now discuss how the information on performance can be used to measure rewards and associated risks for those who provide the organisation's funds.

Acceptable financial performance is a relative concept and is defined in terms of the next best opportunity open to the owners of the organisation for using or investing their funds. In the case of state and not-for-profit organisations those alternatives are established through political choices and those choices depend upon the relative power of people interested in the choice.

In 1991, the UK government decided to permit British Rail to build a Channel Tunnel rail link that will pass through east London rather than south London. The reason for choosing an eastern rather than a southern route was most probably because the pressure groups of people living in the east are far less powerful than the pressure groups of the much more affluent inhabitants of the southern parts of the city. Furthermore, the decision to invest government funds in this project constitutes a choice not to use those funds to build, say, a refuge for the homeless. Again that choice reflects the relative power positions of industry that wants the rail link and the homeless who need somewhere to live.

Although the alternative uses of funds in state and not-for-profit bodies are inevitably the result of political decisions, those concerned to apply a more technically rational approach prescribe the use of analytical techniques to identify and compare the costs and benefits of alternative political choices. The argument is that, even if at the end of the day the choice is made on the basis of relative power, those making the choice should at least be aware of what the costs will be of the benefits provided by each option open to them.

Cost/benefit analysis

Cost/benefit analysis (Rowe, Mason, Dickel & Snyder, 1989; Mirsham, 1980) attempts to place money values on all the costs and benefits of a particular strategic action option. The difficulty lies in the fact that state bodies and not-for-profit organisations are particularly concerned with intangible, non-traded costs and benefits.

So, for example, an investment in a new road has clear monetary costs relating to its construction, but there are much less clearly measurable costs in terms of the destruction of the countryside, the noise imposed on nearby households and so on. Many of the road's benefits are also not traded, for example the reduction in time wasted in traffic jams. It is therefore difficult to measure and even more difficult to value a great many of the costs and benefits that the particular types of organisations we are talking about get involved in.

The analysis therefore involves many subjective judgements upon which there is likely to be disagreement that cannot be resolved by rational argument in either its technical or reasoned senses (see *Key Concept 2.1*). In the end the decision has to be made by political processes of persuasion and conversion, or even force. The analysis is there to aid this process by making the factors that need to be taken into account explicit and by creating the appearance of technical and reasoned rationality. This appearance of rationality can be instrumental in persuading people to accept a particular choice and it legitimises the decision, in effect giving it a seal of 'scientific' approval even though such rationality was not actually used to make the choice.

The rest of this section considers organisations in the business sector, where the ability to measure and value costs and benefits is far greater. But bear in mind that, even there, that ability to measure is far from perfect.

Performance benchmarks

For the majority of organisations in the business sector, alternative investment opportunities for owners are established, not by a political system but by the capital markets. Over the long term it is the operators on the capital markets who will judge whether the performance of a business is acceptable or not and they will do so in terms of the financial return on their investment. The exception to this is family-owned private companies, where alternative investment opportunities are also determined by the capital markets, but where the shareholders have the freedom to choose some definition of acceptability other than financial return. However, non-family-owned business organisations will only continue to receive financial backing if capital market operators judge that the rate of return on the assets employed bears some reasonable relationship to long-term interest rates, taking account of likely rates of inflation and different levels of risk. Companies that persistently fail to achieve rates of return on assets and rates of growth in profit levels that are acceptable in these terms, and that are comparable with similar kinds of businesses, will be prime candidates for takeovers. *Illustration 2.2* sets out how benchmark performance measures of this kind can be calculated.

■ **Illustration 2.2**
BENCHMARK PERFORMANCE MEASURES

Investors look for income, capital appreciation, or some combination of the two. Acceptable financial performance for a business organisation means some combination of dividend yield and profit growth (the justification for capital appreciation) that is comparable to alternative investment opportunities involving the same level of risk.

Suppose that we were seeking to establish benchmark performance standards for pharmaceutical company A in the UK. If shareholders are to find the shares of this company attractive then it must achieve a performance record at least equal to the industry average. If it consistently underperforms its share price will fall, opening it up to the threat of takeover. The publications of stockbrokers, or a report such as Business Ratios (published by ICC Information Group Limited), provide information on profit growth rates in a wide range of different companies and different business sectors. These reports may show that sales in the pharmaceutical sector have been growing at 8 per cent per annum on average and profit levels at 12 per cent on average. Stockbroker reports may indicate that these growth rates are expected to continue. (Since the rate of return on capital for pharmaceutical companies is regulated by the government, it is profit growth rates that will be the main indicators of performance, but if we were dealing with the electronics industry, we would also be interested in the rate of return on capital.) The top executives of company A would use this comparative information to form a judgement on the sales and profit growth rates their company should be targeting to achieve in order to satisfy shareholders. Achieving more than the sector average will mean a rapidly rising share price and thus protection from takeover threats. So top executives in company A may decide to set targets of 10 per cent per annum growth in sales and 15 per cent per annum growth in profits. These targets would then be communicated to the responsible line managers, who would be judged on how closely they were achieved.

Gap analysis

Benchmark performance measures may be used to perform what is called gap analysis (Argenti, 1980). To carry out a gap analysis, the performance of a company is first projected on the basis that it continues to follow existing policies. The resulting levels of profitability, rates of return and rates of profit growth are then compared with the benchmarks and the gap between them calculated. That gap measures the contribution that will be required from the development of new strategies. It is these new strategies that must fill the gap between what is acceptable and what is likely from continuing to run the business as before. Whether a set of strategies fills the gap or not becomes a criterion for successful strategy selection. *Illustration 2.3* gives an example of how gap analysis is used.

■ Illustration 2.3
USE OF GAP ANALYSIS

Suppose the corporate level of the pharmaceutical company A referred to in *Illustration 2.1* sets growth rate objectives for one of its divisions. It requires the division to achieve annual growth rates of 10 per cent in sales and 15 per cent in pre-tax profits for the next five years. The division carefully examines its product portfolio and concludes that two of its major product lines – call them X and Z – will be coming off patent towards the end of the five-year period, opening up the way for inevitable competition and loss of market share. The remaining product lines, C and D, are old ones unlikely to grow at all. The divisional managers then examine the new product development portfolio and conclude that there is no way in which new products coming on stream, E and F, could compensate for the lack of growth in revenues and profits from the existing product portfolio. It is now possible to quantify the negative gap between the corporately set objective for the division and the outcome likely to be generated by existing and new product portfolios by the end of the five-year period.

Divisional management conclude that in order to plug the gap they will have to adopt a strategy of acquiring products and/or companies. A divisional long-term plan is put together, setting out the objectives, the financial projections and the general strategy of acquisition. Here analysis of the gap between what is required and what is likely prompts plans to close the gap.

To use gap analysis it is necessary of course to project the profit consequences of continuing to pursue existing policies and the consequences of alternative proposals to fill the gap. This projection and comparison of different courses of action for a firm as a whole is greatly facilitated by the use of computerised corporate financial models. Most companies of any size nowadays have models to forecast future sales volumes and prices. These may be complex and sophisticated regression models or they may be simple rules of thumb. Most companies also have forecasting procedures to form the basis of production scheduling and inventory control. A corporate or financial model combines partial models of this kind with the relationships in the profit and loss account and the balance sheet to constitute a financial model of the corporation as a whole.

Financial models and scenarios

Such corporate models can then be used to simulate the future of the corporation on the basis of different scenarios (Cooke & Slack, 1984; Shim & McGlade, 1984; Beck, 1982; Rowe, Mason, Dickel & Snyder, 1989). The use of scenarios involves specifying a number of different possible future environments for a company. Key variables specified by each of these scenarios, for example the rate of growth in the volume of market demand, are then plugged into the corporate model. The performance of the company is thereby simulated for each of the possible scenarios. This is done to assist managers to decide in advance whether a particular set of strategies is likely to result in acceptable performance or not. Simulating the performance of the company in different scenarios for the future allows different calculations of the performance gap.

The use of scenarios, simulation and corporate models is illustrated in *Illustration 2.4*.

Investment appraisal techniques

So far, we have been concerned with evaluating the impact of possible strategies on the financial performance of a corporation as a whole. In addition, each of the specific elements of any strategy, that is each of the investment projects required to put it in place, also have to meet criteria of acceptability. There are a number of techniques of investment appraisal available to test whether individual projects meet the requirements of acceptable return; they are now outlined.

Payback period

This is simply the period of time it takes to pay back the original investment. Thus, if the proposal is to build a new factory to produce concrete building blocks at a cost of £10m, and we estimate that it will take four years for the profits flowing from that factory to add up to £10m, then the payback period is 4. A corporation would set payback targets and require that investment proposals should meet them if they are to be acceptable. So, the target may be a payback of five years or less in which case our concrete block factory proposal passes the hurdle.

Average rate of return

Here we would estimate what the profit level in the first full year of operation would be and then calculate the rate of return that this represents on the original investment.

Thus if the concrete block plant yields a profit of £1.5m in its first year of full operation and it costs £10m, then the rate of return is 15 per cent. A corporation using this method would set a target rate of return, say 12.5 per cent, and reject all investment proposals that fell below this.

Discounted cash flow analysis

The drawback of the payback and the average rate of return methods is that they do not take account of the fact that money in the hand today is worth more than a promise of money tomorrow – if you have money today you can invest it and earn interest on it. Discounted cash flow methods meet this objection by discounting all the cash flows back to the present.

To discount the cash flows, it is necessary to estimate the cash flow for each year in the life of the investment. So, in the case of the concrete block plant, we might decide to calculate cash flows for the next 25 years. The cash flow for the first year would be −£10m because we are spending money on building the plant and getting nothing in return.

Next year we believe that we will make sales of say £12m as we start to attract customers for the plant, but commissioning problems and low capacity usage mean that costs are expected to run at £15m, producing another negative cash flow: −£3m. The year after that we believe that we will double sales and keep costs at the same level producing a positive cash flow of £9m. Estimates of this kind need to be made for the next 25 years.

Then we use estimates of interest rates to discount each year's cash flow back to the present. For example, suppose today's interest rate is 10 per cent and we invest £7.44m at that rate, then in two years' time it will be worth £9m. So the present value of £9m in two years' time at a discount rate of 10 per cent is £7.44m. When we have performed this calculation for each year's cash flow, we can add them up and if the net result is positive, then the investment is worthwhile in the sense that it will earn more than an investment at today's interest rate. In fact we will want to set a higher discount rate to take account of the fact that investing in a block plant is a great deal riskier than investing in the bank. The discount rate we set might be, say, 18 per cent when interest rates are 10 per cent. If the net cash flow is still positive at this rate, then we can conclude that it is as good an investment as putting the money in the bank. The discount rate that yields a zero net present value is also clearly the rate of return that the investment will earn.

A corporation using this method of investment appraisal would set a target rate of return and require that investment proposals should meet it. Suppose it sets an 18 per cent discounted cash flow (dcf) rate of return and finds that a proposal yields only 13 per cent, then it would reject it as unacceptable to its shareholders because they could earn more in a risk-adjusted sense by keeping their money in a bank.

The difficulty of forecasting cash flows and interest rates for many years ahead is recognised by those who use that approach. Most therefore make calculations for a number of different scenarios of the environment in which an investment project may operate. A number of different market environments, cost and regulatory regimes are postulated, and the calculations made for each of them. In other words, the future performance of the investment is simulated.

Practical difficulties arise as the number of different scenarios increases. The number of scenarios required in practice to cover the most likely eventualities usually turns out to be so large that managers lose track of what they all mean. The experts preparing the scenarios and simulations end up making literally hundreds of small assumptions about prices, volumes, costs and many other matters. These are so numerous that the line managers who have to take the decision cannot be aware of what they all are. The result can be confusion as to the reasons why an investment is being undertaken. There is also, in common with cost/benefit analysis, the difficulty of incorporating important intangible, difficult-to-measure and value elements. So in practice you find that managers include rather arbitrary values to represent the benefits of synergy between the investment they are considering and some other activity. In practice the use of what appear to be highly rational techniques may all too often simply be a rational 'cover-up' for decisions being taken on other bases.

Risk and sensitivity analysis

The use of scenarios and simulations at both total corporate and specific investment project levels allows sensitivity analyses to be performed. The purpose of these analyses is to identify those variables to which performance is particularly sensitive. So a particular company, or a particular investment project, may not be all that sensitive to changes in the exchange rate, but it may be highly sensitive to changes in regulations on pollution control. Sensitivity analysis allows managers to gain some idea of how serious a change in some variable, such as the interest rate, will be for the future performance of an investment or of the corporation as a whole. The manner in which this provides a tool for analysing risk is shown in *Illustration 2.4*.

■ **Illustration 2.4**
SENSITIVITY ANALYSIS

Suppose a steel production company, the local electricity supply company and a construction company form a consortium to build and operate a small gas turbine power station. The power station is estimated to cost £100 million and in order to provide acceptable financial returns the investors are looking for net profits of £12 million per annum.

The key factors affecting profit levels are the price of gas, the capacity utilisation of the generating plant, and the price of electricity. In order to test the sensitivity of the return on the investment to these three factors we can construct a number of scenarios.

For example we might assume that plant capacity utilisation will be around 60 per cent and the gas price will remain at a level of 100. We can then calculate the profit levels that will be achieved in these circumstances at different prices of electricity:

at 3.5 pence per unit a profit of £15m is achieved;
at 3.0 pence per unit a profit of £12m is achieved;
at 2.5 pence per unit a profit of £8m is achieved;
at 2.0 pence per unit a loss of £2m is made.

We could then take one of these price levels, say 3 pence per unit, and calculate the effects of higher and lower capacity utilisation and gas price levels. Suppose these showed that profit is even more sensitive to changes in gas prices and capacity utilisation. We might then conclude that we will only undertake the investment if we can secure long-term demand contracts for the electricity and long-term supply contracts for the gas. The main risk, to which profit is highly sensitive, will then be electricity prices. We would then have to consider whether the major generators could afford to allow prices to fall as low as 2 pence per unit. We might decide that they are unlikely to do this and that therefore the risk of price fluctuation is a reasonable one to take; or we might judge that the generators will artificially suppress prices for a time to discourage those who wish to make investments like ours. We might then judge that the proposed investment is too risky.

Financial ratios

There are a number of indicators of the level of financial risk that are used to make judgements about the acceptability or otherwise of performance in financial terms. These indicators take the form of financial ratios and the following are among the most important.

Gearing ratios

A gearing ratio is a measure of how heavily or otherwise an organisation depends on borrowed funds. An organisation can finance its operations using money contributed by its shareholders or it can borrow the money it needs. On that borrowed money it must pay interest whether it earns a profit or not, while on shareholders' funds it pays a dividend only if it earns a profit. Depending on borrowed funds therefore creates risk and it is necessary to make judgements about the level of risk and manage that risk.

A gearing ratio is the ratio of some measure of borrowing to some measure of shareholders' funds. So, if an organisation has borrowings of £50m and shareholders' funds of £100m, then the gearing ratio is 50 per cent. Whether this is too high or too low, and therefore whether it is particularly risky or not, is a matter of judgement. That judgement will be heavily influenced by what is regarded by operators in the capital markets as the norm for companies of a particular type. ICC ratios (already referred to above in *Illustration 2.2*) publish information on gearing ratios and managers can compare the gearing ratio that their plans would produce with that of other companies. If the gearing ratio is judged by investors and lenders to be too high, share prices will fall and lenders will refuse to extend further loans.

Another measure of exposure to borrowing is provided by the ratio of profits to interest paid, a measure known as interest cover. If profits cover interest 20 times, this would probably be judged to be low risk. But, if profits cover interest payments only twice, this would probably be judged to be high risk.

Liquidity ratios

Liquidity ratios provide a measure of how quickly an organisation could realise its assets. Obviously, the faster it can turn its assets into cash the more easily it will be able to deal with any financial crisis that occurs. The most liquid asset is of course cash and therefore the cash ratio is a prime measure of liquidity. This is calculated as the percentage of total assets that are in the form of bank deposits, or capital market instruments such as bonds. Another liquidity ratio would be current assets as a percentage of total assets. Current assets are cash plus inventories plus debtors minus creditors, all reasonably realisable in a short time period.

Inventory turnover

This is a measure of how many times a year the inventories of a business are realised. So, if it takes a year to sell all that is held in inventory, then the inventory turnover is 1. If it takes only a month to sell the whole inventory and replace it, then the turnover is obviously 12. The faster inventories are turned over, that is the more rapidly they can be sold, the safer the business.

So much for determining whether plans will produce financial performance acceptable to shareholders and creditors in terms of both risk and reward levels. Even if plans pass this test, however, they must still pass others – they must meet the expectations of those with power in the organisation.

2   Acceptable consequences for internal power groups

In addition to financial risk and reward, long-term plans have other consequences for people within an organisation. If carried out, strategic plans may well change the way people work, who they work with, what relative power they have, how they are judged by others and so on. Long-term plans could produce consequences that people believe to be morally repugnant or against their customs and beliefs in some other way. If this is the case, those plans are unlikely to succeed because people will do their best to prevent the plan being implemented. Managers must therefore submit their long-term plans to another acceptability test: they must analyse the impact of their plans on the expectations, relative power positions, and cultural beliefs of key individuals and groups within the organisation.

Illustration 2.5 gives an example of how managers rejected what they had calculated to be the most acceptable option in financial terms, because it conflicted with the expectations of some key individuals.

■ Illustration 2.5
CASTINGS PLC

Some 15 months ago Castings PLC acquired a company in Colchester which produces castings using three processes:

- sand/Shaw where wooden patterns are used to make ceramic moulds for the casting;
- lost wax where metal moulds are filled with wax and the ferrous casting subsequently made from the wax shape;
- lost was used to manufacture aluminium castings.

The customers for the Colchester factory's products, large companies in the aerospace and general engineering industries, demand high-precision castings at low prices. Demand for product from the lost wax process has been growing rapidly as customers turn to the higher quality and lower cost that this process gives compared to sand/Shaw or machining. Although sand/Shaw is therefore on the wane, it is still cheaper for short runs.

When it acquired the Colchester factory, Castings PLC already had another ferrous casting business using lost wax. This is located at Peterborough and it makes higher-volume less-complicated castings than the new acquisition. Another Castings PLC business uses lost wax to cast aluminium and it is located at Leicester. These are both very profitable businesses.

Over the first year the newly acquired company with sales of under £2m incurred a £0.5m loss. Losses over the first three months of this financial year have been stemmed, but not reversed. Now the landlord has given notice that the premises occupied by the acquisition must be vacated in 9 months' time.

The board of Castings PLC therefore considered the options open to it. The Finance Director prepared a schedule showing the sales, costs, profits and rates of return of a number of options as follows:

1 Relocating the Colchester factory to a nearby site would yield an average return on capital (ROC) for the next five years of minus 4.8 per cent.
2 Relocating the sand/Shaw business at Colchester to a nearby site, moving the lost wax ferrous business to Peterborough and the aluminium to Leicester would yield a five-year average ROC of 9.1 per cent.
3 Moving everything to Peterborough would yield a five-year average ROC of 20.9 per cent.
4 Closing Colchester down would yield a five-year average ROC of minus 0.1 per cent.

Despite the high rate of return to be gained from concentrating the whole business at Peterborough the board chose option 2. They did this because they knew that the managers of the successful Peterborough business did not want to have to deal with the problem of a declining sand/Shaw business. They would be distracted from their own profitable business. Furthermore, key personnel at Colchester would probably not move and therefore would be lost to the company. Customers too might be disaffected by the change in location. Perhaps most important of all, although it was hardly discussed at the board meeting, was the impact closure would have on operators on the stock market. The closure of Colchester would have to be made public, amounting to an admission of failure on the part of Castings PLC board members who had promoted the acquisition in the first place.

The option chosen therefore met a number of people's non-financial expectations, even though it was not the best financial option according to the prescribed way of making that calculation.

Organisational culture

In order to determine whether a plan is likely to be acceptable in cultural terms it is necessary to analyse the core beliefs that people in an organisation share. Analysis of the culture will reveal whether options being considered fall within that culture or whether they require major cultural change. One would not necessarily reject options that require major cultural change, but then plans to bring this about would have to be formulated – a matter we will discuss in Section 2.4.

The nature of an organisation's culture can be analysed by studying the stories people in the organisation tell. For example, there may be well-known stories about the organisation's founder or other memorable leaders that are always told to new joiners. They may tell the story about the company founder who used to stand at the door each morning to see who was arriving late. The story is a way of emphasising one of the rules that all accept about not being late. In another organisation the leader may wear casual clothing and sit in an open plan office. The leader's clothes are a cultural symbol of a core belief in informal relationships. The culture is revealed by the myths, the heroes, the rituals and symbols that are used. The culture is reflected in leadership and management styles.

When analysing the culture the strategist will identify what the core beliefs are and how strongly people believe in them. Some approaches to classifying cultures will be discussed in the section on implementing strategic plans later on in this chapter.

■ Key concept 2.4
THE CULTURE OF AN ORGANISATION

The culture of any group of people is that set of beliefs, customs, practices and ways of thinking that they have come to share with each other through being and working together. It is a set of assumptions people simply accept without question as they interact with each other. At the visible level the culture of a group of people takes the form of ritual behaviour, symbols, myths, stories, sounds, and artifacts.

Power structure

It will also be necessary to analyse the power structure of an organisation to determine whether plans are likely to be acceptable (see *Key Concept 2.5*).

■ Key concept 2.5
POWER

Power flows from relationships, built up over time, between individuals and groups that determine how one affects or responds to another in making organisational choices. Power enables one person or group to force or persuade another to do something that the other does not want to do, or could not otherwise do, or would not otherwise have thought of doing. The sources of power lie in:

- *Sanctions. Power increases with the ability of one person or group to reward or punish another in terms of prestige, status, money or career progression.*
- *Interdependence. One individual or group is relatively more powerful than another if*

> *it: controls more resources; has greater access to information; performs critical activities upon which the others depend for their performance; has greater access to communication channels or the more powerful; has control over communication agendas or the decision-making situations.*
>
> ● Contribution. *Relative power increases with the personal skills and expertise of particular individuals and their ability to interpret ambiguous situations and so reduce uncertainty for others.*
>
> *The source of power has much to do with the form it takes. Power can take the form of authority when it is exercised and consented to because of hierarchical position and because of the rules and regulations of the organisation. Or power can take the form of influence where it is based on interdependence between people and the contributions they make to common endeavours. Or power can take the form of force.*

Having analysed the source and form of power, the strategist has to identify its location and that means identifying the dominant coalitions in the organisation. This may be difficult because the power structure does not necessarily accord with the formal hierarchy – it will be necessary to identify which individuals and groups exercise much influence even though they have less authority. It will be necessary to look for potential alliances between coalitions. *Illustration 2.6* gives some examples of how the power structure affects the acceptability of strategies.

■ **Illustration 2.6**
POWER AND THE ACCEPTABILITY OF STRATEGIES

Some strategies will require large injections of funds that can only be obtained by the issue of new shares. This may weaken the control of particularly powerful shareholders, making the strategies unacceptable to them despite acceptable financial performance. Where the ownership of a company is concentrated in the hands of one or two individuals, then acceptability to those individuals in personal power or other terms may count for much more than acceptable performance. So the owner may tolerate below-average performance for years because it is found unacceptable to replace relatives in key positions.

It is not just acceptability to owners that counts. Some strategies may be unacceptable to a powerful subsidiary of one division of a corporation because it will undermine that division's power position in the corporation. Suppose a relatively small division proposes to expand its activities from its domestic base to foreign countries. If this is unacceptable to a larger more powerful division already operating in foreign markets, the strategy could well fail for this reason alone. The battles between these two divisions could lead to failure as attention is diverted from the markets. Or, to take another example, for reasons that have little to do with performance, a powerful chairman may have certain preferences. For example, this chairman may favour the expansion of a house-building subsidiary because his son runs it. Because that subsidiary will require substantial investment, the chairman may be against diversification. Attempts to pursue diversification strategies are then unlikely to succeed.

3   Acceptable consequences for external power groups

Power groups outside an organisation also determine the acceptability of that organisation's strategies. A community pressure group may find the noise level of a proposed factory expansion unacceptable. Even if the factory itself turns out to be a financially acceptable investment, the total consequences for the image of the corporation could render the strategy unsuccessful. Another example is provided by the electricity and gas industries in the UK. To succeed, strategies of companies in these sectors have to be acceptable to the industry regulators and consumer pressure groups. A further example is where the strategies of one organisation could have damaging consequences for the distributors of that organisation's products or for the suppliers to that organisation. Such damage could provoke those distributors and suppliers to retaliate in highly detrimental ways, as shown in *Illustration 2.7*.

■ Illustration 2.7
KITCHEN QUEEN

In the 1970s a small company distributing fitted kitchens was set up in Manchester – Kitchen Queen. This company grew rapidly for a number of years because of its policy of advertising and displaying quality fitted kitchens, supporting the product with design and installation services and meeting reliable delivery time criteria. After some years of rapid growth, it was floated on the stock market and then pursued a policy of diversification. It purchased Di Lussio, a firm producing DIY flat-pack fitted kitchens of a high quality. By this move Kitchen Queen diversified into production and the profitability of Di Lussio relied on its distributors, competitors to the original Kitchen Queen business. The distributors were thus an important power group outside Kitchen Queen and the strategy of the latter would have to be in some sense acceptable to those distributors.

   The acquisition worked and before long the production activity of the Kitchen Queen Group was generating most of the profit. Then a number of further diversifications were undertaken, including the purchase of a mail order company. The decision was then made to distribute all of Di Lussio's product through the mail order acquisition. When the distributors got wind of this they cancelled all their orders and dumped all their stocks of Di Lussio product onto the market at very low prices. This was one of the major causes of Kitchen Queen's bankruptcy not long afterwards.

Source: Kitchen Queen Case Study, Case Clearing House, Cranfield.

The reactions of competitors to strategies is also of major importance. Some strategies pursued by one company could provoke more than normal competitive responses from competitors. Those competitors may regard the strategies of the first company as unfair competition and this could lead to price wars, hostile mergers, lobbying of the national political institutions, all of which could cause a strategy to fail. For example, North American and European countries have passed laws against imports from Japanese competitors or insisted on voluntary restraints.

FEASIBILITY

Analysis may show that strategies are likely to be acceptable in terms of financial performance, and to major power groupings both within and outside the organisation, but yet fail because they are not feasible. To be feasible there must be no insurmountable obstacle to implementing a strategy. Such obstacles could be presented by:

- inadequate resources
- resources of insufficient quality
- inappropriate technology
- timing in relation to other events
- competitor strength.

Feasibility and financial resources

One of the immediately obvious resources that must be available if a strategy is to be carried out is the money to finance the strategy over its whole life. If a company gets half-way through a strategy, which is on target to yield acceptable performance, but nevertheless runs out of the funds to continue, then clearly the strategy will fail. The prescription is therefore to carry out a flow-of-funds analysis of the strategy options, before embarking on any of them, to ascertain the probability of running into cash flow problems.

A flow-of-funds analysis identifies the timing and size of the capital expenditures and other costs required for each project that makes up the strategy, and the timing and size of the revenues that those projects will generate. These revenue and expenditure flows then need to be related to projected cash inflows and outflows for the corporation as a whole. The intention would be to identify any potential crisis point in the net flows of cash into the business, well in advance of it occurring.

Normally, an investment project first produces negative cash flows and profit levels – costs are incurred before any revenues can be earned. Later, the cash flows and the profit levels turn positive if the project is a success. The point of change from the negative to the positive is known as *break-even*. A flow of funds analysis makes it possible to calculate this break-even point, where a project, a set of projects constituting a strategy, or a corporation as a whole makes neither a loss nor a profit. An example of break-even analysis is provided in *Illustration 2.8*.

What managers should do, therefore, to establish the feasibility of their strategy is to calculate the flows of funds and the break-even points for different strategic options in different scenarios. This will help them to identify the financing requirements for their strategy, the timing of those requirements, and the key conditions required for the move out of any initial negative cash flow situation.

The flow-of-funds analysis indicates how much money a strategic option will require if it is to be implemented. It may well be that this money cannot be generated by the existing business of a company and it will therefore have to raise more funds from its shareholders, or borrow, if it wishes to proceed. However, there is a limit to the amount of new capital that can be raised from shareholders and there are limits to borrowing. At some point further increases in borrowing will raise the level of risk:

■ **Illustration 2.8**
BREAK-EVEN ANALYSIS

In break-even analysis, we identify a few crucial factors upon which success is likely
to depend. For example, success may depend heavily on achieving certain volumes
of production. These volumes can only be sustained if certain market shares are
achieved. So for strategy option A we calculate that we can achieve break-even, that
is neither loss nor profit, at a market share of 10 per cent. But for strategy B we
discover that we would have to achieve 20 per cent to break even. Given our
knowledge of competitor power, we may decide that strategy A is therefore more
feasible.

---

the gearing ratio will rise above that regarded as prudent and the stock market will
therefore mark the company's shares down; the number of times profit covers
interest payments will fall and lenders will be less and less willing to extend further
loans.

At some point, then, a strategic option will be feasible only if it generates positive
cash flows in some areas to provide the cash requirements of other areas. The
prescription is that a strategy must establish a balanced collection, or portfolio, of
activities such that the positive profit and cash flow generated by one activity offset
the negative flows of others. A balanced portfolio also reduces risk – while the
markets for one activity may experience unexpected declines, those for another
activity may do unexpectedly well.

The technique available to conduct this test of balance and hence feasibility is called
portfolio analysis. The building blocks of portfolio analysis are the concepts of the
product life cycle and the experience curve. We will first consider these and then see
how they can be combined to provide a portfolio analysis.

The product life cycle

This idea is based on the observation that most products follow the typical
evolutionary pattern illustrated in *Figure 2.3*:

- An *embryonic* stage in which the product is developed. Here market growth
  potential may be great but it will be very uncertain; there will be few competitors,
  little in the way of entry barriers to the market, and perhaps the technology will
  be new too.
- A *growth* stage in which rapid market growth materialises, attracting other
  competitors. Competitors develop customer loyalty, so making it harder for more
  new competitors to enter.
- A *shake-out* stage in which some of the competitors who entered find that they
  cannot compete and therefore leave.
- A *mature* stage in which growth in the demand for the product slows and a small
  number of competitors come to dominate the market.

Figure 2.3   The product life cycle

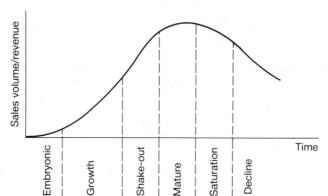

- A *saturation* stage in which demand for the product stabilises and competitors have difficulty in filling their capacity.
- A *decline* stage in which demand begins to switch to substitute products.

These stages in the evolution of a product indicate different general types of strategies – different generic strategies. Which of these generic strategies is appropriate is said to be dependent upon the stage of evolution of the product's market and the competitive strength of the company producing it. So a company with a strong capability should invest heavily in the embryonic stage and establish a position before others arrive. During the growth phase it should continue investing, push for rapid growth, and so defend its strong position against new arrivals. By the time the mature phase is reached, this company should have established market leadership and, as the product gets to saturation level, the aging stage, the dominant company should defend its position but withdraw cash from the business. In a declining market it will be able to continue harvesting cash, while weaker competitors withdraw.

Throughout, strong competitors are supposed to follow strategies of cost leadership. The weaker competitors will have to pursue very different strategies, however. In the embryonic stage they will have to identify a niche in the market for the product and occupy that; for example, they may make a luxury, high fashion version of the product and target a particular age or social group. Through the evolution of the market they will have to pursue strategies of making their product different – differentiation – rather than trying to make it cheaper as the dominant competitors can. In the later stages of product evolution, the weaker competitors will find that they have to withdraw (Porter, 1980).

Figure 2.4 illustrates the points made above about the relationship between product stage and strategic option. We now turn to the second block upon which product portfolio techniques are based – the experience curve.

The experience curve

The idea of the experience curve is based on the observation that the higher the volume of a particular product that a company produces, the more efficient it becomes

Figure 2.4   Generic strategies and the stage of industry development
Source: M. Porter (1985), *Competitive Advantage: Creating and Sustaining Superior Performance*, New York: The Free Press

Stage of 'industry' development

	Growth	Maturity	Decline
Leader	Keeping ahead of the field	Cost leadership Raise barriers Deter competitors	Redefine scope Divest peripherals Encourage departures
Follower	Imitation at lower cost Joint ventures	Differentiation Focus	Differentiation New opportunities

Strategic position of organisation

at producing it. The cost per unit therefore declines as volume increases, at first rapidly and then more slowly as the learning opportunities for that particular product are exhausted. As a company moves down the learning curve it is in a position to reduce the price it charges customers for the product because its costs are falling. The price curve therefore follows the learning/cost curve as shown in *Figure 2.5*.

From these curves it can be seen that although unit profits are typically high at low volumes, total profits are of course low. As volumes increase, unit profits fall but this is offset by the higher volumes and so total profits increase.

These price and cost curves can be linked to the idea of a product life cycle and the different strategies that strong and weak competitors should pursue. In the early stages of product evolution, a strong competitor will achieve higher volumes than a weak one and so move further down the learning curve. This will enable the strong

Figure 2.5   The experience curve

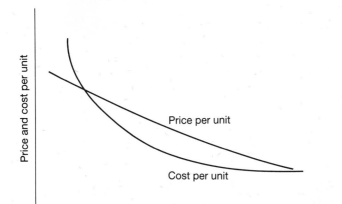

competitor to reduce prices faster, stimulating demand and so increasing volumes even more to move even faster down the learning curve. Soon, the weaker competitor, or the latecomer, will have no chance of catching up.

Furthermore, there will be typical patterns in the cash flows and profit levels of companies as a product evolves. At first, all the companies developing a particular product have negative cash flows as they invest and probably incur losses. Later in the growth stage most may still experience negative cash flows as they continue to invest to stay ahead, but the profit levels of the strong competitors will turn positive. Then in the mature stage, investment in the product declines and cash flows run positive for the strong, while profitability becomes less attractive than it was. The weak may be forced to withdraw at this stage. These typical patterns lead to the idea of a product portfolio.

The product portfolio

The earliest and simplest form of product portfolio analysis is the Boston Consulting Group (BCG) growth share matrix (Henderson, 1970). To analyse their organisation in this way, managers review their whole business, dividing it up into all its different products, or market segments, or business units. They then calculate the market share they hold for each product, or market segment, or business unit, and then divide it by the share of their nearest rival. This is then the relative market share of that product, segment or business and it is plotted along the horizontal axis of the diagram given in *Figure 2.6*. If the relative share is much greater than 1, then the firm is dominant in that market. If the relative share is well below 1, then the firm is very weak in terms of competitive capability. The relative market share provides a measure of the firm's competitive capability with regard to that product, segment or business unit, because a high market share indicates that the firm is well down the experience curve compared to rivals.

Next managers must calculate the rate of growth of the product demand or market segment, represented on the vertical axis of *Figure 2.6*. The rate of growth is held to

Figure 2.6   The BCG product portfolio matrix

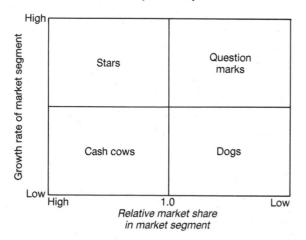

be a good measure of the attractiveness of the market – the stage in its evolution that it has reached. Rapid rates of growth indicate the entrepreneurial and growth stages of evolution. For each product, market, or business, market share and market growth will therefore be represented by a point plotted on the diagram shown in *Figure 2.6*.

Each quadrant of the diagram has a label:

- *Question marks* are products, market segments or business units that are growing rapidly, and the company has a relatively low share. The product life cycle and the experience curve analysis tell us that question marks will require heavy investment, are unlikely to yield profit for some time, and may face strong competitors. They are called question marks because the firm will have to decide how feasible it is to pursue these.
- *Stars* are products, markets or businesses that are growing rapidly, and the firm has a high relative share. Product life cycle and experience curve analysis tell us that these products will require heavy investment (negative cash flow) but may produce high levels of profit. The strategy indicated is one of concentrating effort and money on the stars.
- *Cash cows* are products in mature slow-growth markets in which the firm has a relatively high market share. The prescription is to cut down on investment in these products and harvest the cash. Cash flow will be strongly positive for cows and profit levels rather low.
- *Dogs* are products in slowly growing markets in which the firm has a low share. Both cash flow and profit could be negative. It is in a weak position and should therefore withdraw.

When managers set out all their products, markets or businesses, and the strategic options they are considering, on such a diagram, they can then see how feasible each strategic option will be in financial terms. The feasible options will be those that have some balance between the different quadrants. If a firm has enough cash cows, it will be able to use the money milked from those businesses to support the stars and perhaps try to develop some of the question marks. It can sell dogs and use the money so raised for the same purposes. An unbalanced portfolio – too many stars and not enough cows for example – will mean either that the company has to borrow heavily or it will generate big cash surpluses without knowing what to invest them in.

Criticisms of the BCG matrix

There have been many criticisms of this product portfolio approach (Slatter, 1980). First, it is obviously far too simple to equate competitive capability with high market share, large volumes and low cost. This places too great an emphasis on cost; it assumes that dominant firms can achieve their position only through low costs when we know that they may well do so by differentiating themselves through the quality they provide. It is also too simple to equate the attractiveness of a market with the growth rate and hence the stage of the product cycle. Even declining markets can provide attractive opportunities for some. Hanson PLC has consistently followed a strategy of acquiring businesses that would be classified as cash cows or sometimes even dogs, and yet it has consistently improved its performance.

To overcome the criticism, others have developed more complex product matrices.

For example, General Electric developed what it calls the business screen and Shell developed a similar directional policy matrix shown in *Figure 2.7.*

This differs from the BCG matrix in that it does not use simple quantified measures but the judgements of managers as to whether the market is attractive in a number of ways and as to whether they have a strong or a weak position in that market according to a number of criteria. More factors are thus taken into account, but the idea remains that of building a balanced portfolio of businesses to make strategies feasible. The idea is also still that there are generic strategies appropriate for different market conditions and different competitive capabilities.

Even the most complex matrix is still subject to serious drawbacks however. It is all too easy to slip into thinking that the market segments identified for the purpose of the analysis will remain unchanged. For example, in the 1970s General Foods conducted a portfolio analysis and concluded that its coffee business was a cash cow. That business was then starved of funds which were diverted to businesses classified as stars. However, competitors began to segment the coffee market in different ways. They developed coffee products suitable for different kinds of coffee – capucino, filter coffee, specially ground coffee for espresso, decafeinated coffee and so on. Because they had differentiated coffee in this way they were able to charge higher prices and attract business away from more traditional coffee suppliers. General Foods became aware of what was happening just in time to prevent the disappearance of its coffee business. Changing the way a market is segmented may thus be more important than applying standardised strategies determined by portfolio analysis.

Furthermore, portfolio analysis makes the assumption that the different products or businesses plotted on the matrix are independent of each other. However, some

Figure 2.7   A directional policy matrix

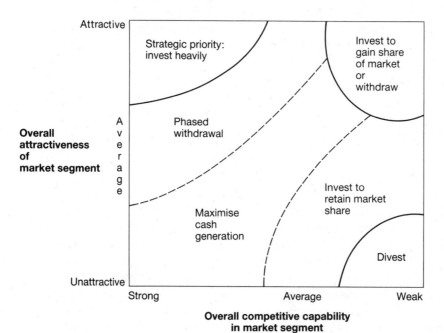

product that qualifies as a dog may be a crucial component or provide a crucial skill for another product that qualifies as a star. If the standard strategic advice is followed and the dog disposed of, this could damage the competitive position of the star (see *Illustration 2.9*).

Finally, there are those who say that it is the role of the investor to spread risk and balance portfolios by holding a mix of shares in different companies. They claim that it is the role of a company to take risks in a particular business and look to lenders and shareholders for the funds they need.

Some other aspects of feasibility

In addition to financial resources, the availability of the right quality of skilled people will also be a major determinant of the feasibility of strategic options. This makes it necessary for managers to audit the human resources inside their organisation, those available outside, and the availability of training resources to improve the skills of people.

Timing constraints are also important in determining feasibility for obvious reasons. An organisation may have the capability to carry out a strategy and it may have all the skills and resources to do so, but the opportunity the strategy is required to address may be available for only a short time in the near future. This timing constraint may make it impossible for the organisation to mobilise its resources fast enough.

The techniques we have just discussed to identify financial feasibility also clearly have other messages about feasibility too. For example, it will not be feasible to enter a market already dominated by a low-cost producer, unless the focus is to be on a small niche and the strategy is one of differentiation. Product portfolios, life cycles and experience curves indicate relative market power and in doing so say something about feasibility from a market perspective as well as a financial one.

We turn now to the third criterion for the evaluation and selection of successful strategies.

■ **Illustration 2.9**
CIBA-GEIGY

Ciba-Geigy is a diversified multinational company based in Switzerland and engaged in the production of fine chemicals, dyestuffs and pharmaceuticals. In 1980 its sales amounted to nearly 12 billion Swiss francs, of which about 3 billion were generated by its Pharmaceuticals Division.

That Division was organised into product groups based on therapeutic areas: cardiovascular, central nervous system, rheuma and pain, infectious diseases, and other therapeutic areas. The last-named product group included dermatological products. In each product group there were product managers for each of the specific lines that the product group consisted of – there were twenty such managers in the Division. In 1981 the Pharmaceuticals Division prepared strategic plans using the company's newly installed portfolio planning system based on the concept of Strategic Business Units (SBUs). One of the main difficulties of this technique lies in how the

SBUs are to be defined in practice. In the case of the Pharmaceuticals Division, the product groups were defined as the SBUs. But was this right?

While most managers thought that it was sensible to regard each Division as an SBU, some were doubtful about regarding product areas within the Division as SBUs because they were so interdependent. Medical representatives handled products from a number of product groups, the production facilities and R&D were shared, as were most of the administration costs. To think of the product groups as businesses that could be handled separately might therefore lead to the wrong conclusions. On top of that, each group included specific products that differed from each other in important respects: age, technical maturity and expected growth potential. So if an SBU was defined as a distinctive product grouping, different from others, then perhaps the individual products should be the SBUs.

Source: Buzzel, 1983.

SUITABILITY OR FIT: ADAPTING TO THE ENVIRONMENT

Having established that their strategies are acceptable and feasible, the next hurdle managers must cross to achieve success is that of demonstrating that those strategies have a *strategic logic*. Strategic logic means that a proposed sequence of actions is consistently related to the objectives of the organisation on the one hand and matches the organisation's capability (including its structure, control systems and culture) to its environment on the other. The idea is that all the pieces of the strategic puzzle should fit together in a predetermined manner – the pieces should be *congruent*. When this happens we can say that the strategies fit, that they are suitable. The prescription is to use analytical techniques to determine the strategic logic of a sequence of actions, how all the pieces do or do not fit together (Hofer & Schendel, 1978). The analytic techniques available to do this are briefly summarised in this section.

SWOT analysis

This is a list of an organisation's strengths and weakness as indicated by an analysis of its resources and capabilities, plus a list of the threats and opportunities that an analysis of its environment identifies. Strategic logic obviously requires that the future pattern of actions to be taken should match strengths with opportunities, ward off threats, and seek to overcome weaknesses.

Life cycle analysis

We have already discussed product life cycles in an earlier section of this chapter as criteria against which to measure the feasibility of strategies. Later in this chapter in the section on implementing strategies we will discuss the life cycles that have been identified for organisational cultures, and in Chapter 10 the life cycles of organisational structures will be explored. Strategic logic demands that a selected sequence of actions for the future should be appropriate to the life cycle in product, structural and cultural terms. So products or markets may be at the mature stage of their life cycle and consistent, matching strategies would probably then have to do with maintaining market share through cost leadership strategies. Or an organisation may have passed through structural stages from the simple structure with a fluid culture to a divisionalised machine bureaucracy with a rather rigid culture. Matching strategies would then consist of many small incremental steps rather than one revolutionary change.

Portfolio analysis

This technique has also been discussed in an earlier section of this chapter as a criterion for feasibility, but it too is concerned with consistency and fit. Strategies that demonstrate strategic logic are those that take the organisation to a more balanced portfolio of activities. According to portfolio analyses, strategic logic requires a company to divest itself of businesses that have low market shares in stagnant markets, to withdraw cash from businesses with high market shares in mature markets, and invest the proceeds in businesses with high market share potential in growth markets.

PIMS

Here statistical relationships have been derived, relating typical performance in a particular market segment back to the causes of that performance. When managers identify the consequences of some strategy option they are considering, say the market share it leads to, they can plug that information into the statistical relationships and calculate the performance it would lead to. In this way the suitability, or strategic logic, of strategy options can be tested (Buzzell & Gale, 1987).

Synergy

This is the extra benefit that comes from linking two or more separate activities together. For example, if a corporation can link a business selling financial services to one selling real estate, then it may be possible to reduce costs because only one rather than two retail outlets will be required. Even more important, one business will generate customers for the other – customers arriving to buy a house might also be sold an insurance policy. The prescription then is that the results of potential interconnections between activities should be analysed to identify synergies. Strategic logic requires building in synergies as much as possible.

Industry structure and value chain analysis

These analytical techniques identify key aspects determining the relative market power of an organisation and its ability to sustain excess profits. Strategic logic entails taking actions that are consistent with and match the nature of the organisation's market power. Industry structure determines what the predominant form of competitive advantage is. Some market structures mean that sustainable competitive advantage can only be secured through cost leadership strategies. Other structures mean that competitive advantage flows from differentiation. Strategic logic means matching actions to those required to secure competitive advantage. Value chain analysis identifies the points in the chain of activity from raw material to consumer that are crucial to competitive advantage. Since these market structure and value chain techniques have attracted widespread attention, they will now be discussed in somewhat greater detail.

Porter's industry structure and generic strategy analysis

Michael Porter (1980 & 1985) has put the classical economic theories of market form into a framework for analysing the nature of competitive advantage in a market and the power of a company in that market.

Defining the market

The first step in analysing industry structure is to define the market (or, as he calls it, the industry). A market is an interaction between a grouping of customers who have similar requirements of a particular good or service on the one hand, and a strategic group of competitors competing to meet those requirements on the other hand. The boundary around a market is defined in terms of similarities in what is demanded and in terms of the closeness of the competition.

For example, when analysing the construction industry managers would be ill advised to regard construction as one market. This is because the 'construction' market contains some very different groupings of customers and competitors. It would be more accurate to talk about a market for private houses because there we can find a reasonably clear group of customers – families who share a similar need for a home – and a relatively constant strategic group of large housebuilders who account for most of the houses built. It might even be necessary to break this market down further, for example into a small-house market for first-time buyers, a market for medium-size homes and a market for luxury homes. In addition, there is a quite separate market for large structures: roads, office blocks and hospitals for example. Here again we find customers looking for much the same thing: organisations with the ability to manage large and complex construction programmes that take long periods of time to complete. We also find that there is a relatively constant group of about 20 or so companies in the UK that compete to fulfil this need. Then there is a market for small structures and repair work. In this market customers are not looking for a management service but for those who will do the work directly. The competitor group is a shifting population of small companies. Each of these markets is very different from the other and therefore different strategies may be appropriate in those different markets. There are no hard and fast rules about drawing the boundaries around a market, but how that boundary is drawn will have a major effect on the analysis.

We have also seen in the General Foods example, discussed in an earlier section in relation to product portfolio analysis, that the boundaries around a market can change quite rapidly. In that example, one homogeneous coffee market split into a number of rather different ones. Managers will therefore have to keep questioning the definitions of the market that they are using to conduct their strategic analysis.

Analysing the five competitive forces

Having defined the market, the next step in the analysis is to identify the structure of that market. We can do this by analysing the five competitive forces that shape the prices firms can charge, the costs they have to bear, and the investment they must undertake to compete. In other words, the competitive forces determine the relative market power of competitors, the kind of competition they engage in, the factors that give some of them a competitive advantage, and the relative attractiveness of that market compared to others. These competitive forces are depicted in *Figure 2.8* and then summarised below.

1 *The threat of new entrants* New entrants would obviously add production capacity and seek to fill that capacity with volumes competed away from existing firms. This would lead to lower prices and hence lower profits. Those already in the market will therefore seek to use or build barriers against the entry of others and if they succeed in this they will be able to hold prices above the minimum level necessary to keep firms in the business. Entry barriers make excess profits possible and so make the market more attractive to firms. Those companies that can shelter behind the barriers come to occupy a powerful market position and the nature of their competitive advantage is tied up with the nature of the entry barrier. One of the most common entry barriers is the need to invest large sums in the production facilities necessary to produce the product.

For example, it is difficult for new firms to enter the automobile market because of

Figure 2.8 Porter's five market forces

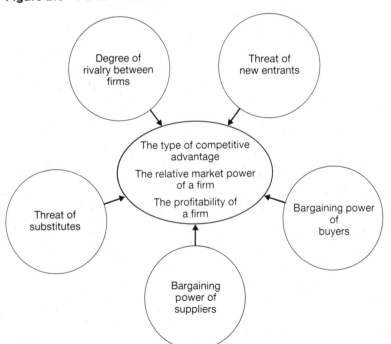

the need for large factories. This is not true of the construction markets, but in some of them we still find entry barriers. For example, in the market for large structures it is rare to see new entrants because it takes time to acquire the skills of managing large construction projects. On the other hand, in the market for small structures, the skills are easier to acquire and we therefore find firms coming and going. Some other barriers to entry are provided by brand images, patent laws, and government trade protection policies.

Where the entry barrier is provided by the need to invest large amounts in facilities, we will usually find that a firm's market power, its competitive advantage, lies in its ability to achieve low costs. Where, however, the barriers are provided by brand images or other differentiators such as quality, then we will find that a firm's competitive advantage lies in its ability to differentiate itself from its rivals. Where the entry barriers are low, the threat of new entrants will force firms to compete on cost or try to build a market niche and focus on that.

2 *The threat of substitute goods or services*   Another threat that will force competitors to keep their prices low will be that of some substitute for their product or service.

3 *The bargaining power of buyers*   Customers have bargaining power if there are few of them. They also have bargaining power if they are buying a product or service to incorporate into something they themselves are producing, and what they buy represents a high proportion of their costs or a critical element of their quality. The importance of what they are buying will make them more demanding customers. A buyer is also powerful when that buyer purchases a significant proportion of a firm's output. Powerful buyers mean that a firm has to keep its prices low.

4 *The bargaining power of suppliers*   Suppliers are powerful in relation to a particular firm when they are few in number, if they are supplying a product or service that is not crucial in cost or quality terms to the business of the particular buying firm, or if they are not supplying a major part of their own output to that particular buying firm. Powerful suppliers will mean that a firm's costs will be higher than they otherwise would have been, making profits lower and the market less attractive.

5 *The rivalry among existing competitors*   If rivalry is intense, marketing costs are higher or prices lower than they would otherwise have been. Once again the market is less attractive.

Once the competitive forces have been identified, a judgement has to be made on which are the relatively most important because they could be working in different directions. Thus, a firm may face weak buyers but powerful suppliers, or there may be little in the way of entry threats but rivalry amongst those already in the market may be intense. Analysing the forces and making judgements on their relative importance should lead managers to see how they can deal with and influence the forces.

Identifying competitive advantage

The analysis indicates what the source of competitive advantage is. For example, the private housing market in the South East of England has weak buyers because there are many families purchasing homes and there is very little threat from substitutes – people mostly live in houses rather than tents or caravans. It is the suppliers of land to build the houses on who are in a powerful position because land is so scarce in the South East of England. Once a house-building company has built up a land bank, that company is in a powerful position because its land bank represents an entry barrier to others. The source of competitive advantage lies primarily in the ability to acquire land. In a less densely populated area, however, the ability to acquire land will not be the source of competitive advantage. Instead it may be the ability to arrange finance for buyers or the ability to build houses at low cost.

When we analyse the structure of a market, we are identifying the position a firm should occupy and the posture it should adopt to generate acceptable performance. The purpose of identifying a market's structure, and the sources of competitive advantage it causes, is to draw conclusions about the strategies that will match or fit the environment. When managers select strategies that are adapted to the environment in this way, then, according to the technically rational, analytical approach, they will be successful.

Porter expresses this relationship between the form of competitive advantage and the matching strategy in the manner shown in *Figure 2.9*. Porter identifies two types of competitive advantage: firms compete either on the basis of lower cost than their rivals, or on the basis of differentiation where they provide some unique and superior value to the buyer allowing them to charge higher prices. Firms can use these competitive advantages in either a broad or a narrow way – their competitive scope. Advantage and scope together create four kinds of strategy.

Where the industry structure is such that low cost is the source of competitive advantage then a firm will succeed only if it takes a broad approach and goes for cost leadership or if it targets narrowly and adopts a strategy of cost focus. For example, producers of standardised silicon chips have to vie for the position of lowest-cost producer – high-cost producers are soon squeezed out. But there is also a market for small numbers of customised chips to be incorporated into large complex pieces of equipment such as body scanners in hospitals. Some chip manufacturers target this

Figure 2.9   Porter's generic strategies

Source: M. Porter (1985), *Competitive Advantage: Creating and Sustaining Superior Performance*, New York: The Free Press

	Competitive advantage	
	Lower cost	Differentiation
Broad target	1. Cost leadership	2. Differentiation
Narrow target	3A. Cost focus	3B. Differentiation focus

(Competitive score)

small segment and produce at lower cost than the big chip manufacturers because they have more flexible production methods.

Where, however, the industry structure is such that differentiation is the source of competitive advantage, then a firm will succeed only if it takes a broad approach and differentiates its whole range of products from those of its rivals, or if it targets and adopts a strategy of differentiation focus. For example, in the 1970s General Motors supplied cars across the spectrum of demand; it had a car for every price bracket and differentiated itself from rivals in each price bracket through the styling of its cars. Jaguar on the other hand focused on the luxury car segment and sought to create a distinctive image compared to say BMW. Porter's prescriptions for success are:

- Select the strategy that matches the particular market structure your firm faces.
- Make a clear choice between one strategy and another: cost leadership, or differentiation, or focus and avoid the ambivalence of being 'stuck in the middle' with a strategy that is partly cost leadership and partly differentiation.

Having identified the market structure and the matching generic strategy, managers must next identify where costs should be cut and how products and service should be differentiated. To do this they must conduct a value chain analysis.

Porter's value chain analysis

The value chain traces the path a product or service follows right from the raw material stage through production and distribution to the final customer. As it travels along this chain, value is added at each point, accumulating into the combination of values that the customer is looking for. The total value chain therefore consists of a number of firms as illustrated in *Figure 2.10*.

The first stage of the analysis is to identify which links in the chain are the crucial ones for achieving low cost or differentiation. It is these links that will control the whole chain and therefore provide the most attractive opportunities. The kinds of strategy a firm will be able to follow will depend upon the links of the value chain it covers – strategy will have to fit the location in the total value chain.

For example, take the value chain in the market for biscuits: farmers grow the wheat, millers make the flour, biscuit manufacturers produce the biscuits, and supermarkets sell them. The key source of competitive advantage is probably differentiation – taste, variety, attractive packaging are the value that the customer is looking for. The key link in providing these values is the small number of powerful supermarket chains. Each supermarket chain competes with the others on the basis of differentiation and many of the brands of biscuits are sold under a supermarket's own label. They have sufficient power to require the biscuit manufacturers to produce biscuits specified by the supermarket and packaged as the supermarket's product. Biscuit manufacturers will find that they have to compete on the basis of low cost.

By understanding the value chain, managers may be able to change it to the benefit of their company. For example, an ice cream manufacturer, also subject to the power of the supermarkets, may decide to acquire its own retail outlets and promote its own image as Haagen Däzs ice cream has done.

The notion of a value chain is also relevant to each firm in the total value chain. Every company takes in inputs and uses some process to add value to those inputs,

Figure 2.10 The industry value chain

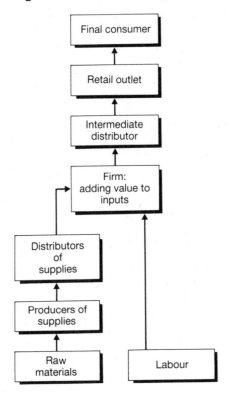

so producing outputs that it passes to the next link in the total value chain. A way of analysing the value chain within a firm is shown in *Figure 2.11*.

The value chain consists of primary activities and support activities that together ultimately produce the firm's profit margin. The primary activities consist of:

- *Inbound logistics*: the activities of receiving, storing, handling and distributing the inputs required to produce the product or service, as well as controlling inventories.
- *Operations*: the process of transforming the inputs in some way so that they take on greater value for the ultimate consumer. This would cover making components, testing them, assembling them into a product, and packaging that product.
- *Outbound logistics*: storing the firm's final product and distributing it to the next link in the total value chain.
- *Marketing and sales*: making customers aware of the product and ensuring that it is available.
- *Service*: all the activities that enhance or maintain the value of the product such as installation, advice, repairs, spares and so on.

Each of these primary activities have a need for support activities:

- *Procurement*: the administrative activity of ordering the inputs to the primary activities.

Figure 2.11   The firm's value chain

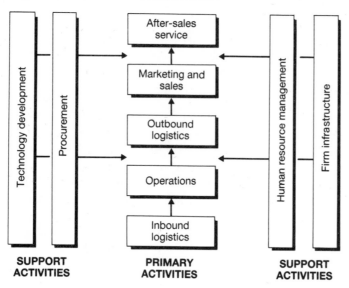

- *Technology development*: the activity of researching and developing the processes through which inputs are transformed into outputs.
- *Human resource management*: the activity of recruiting, training, motivating and rewarding the people necessary for the primary activities.
- *Management systems*: the activity of planning, financing and controlling the primary activities.

Having specified their firm's value chain, managers are then in a position to identify which of the primary activities and which of the support activities are the most crucial to providing the competitive advantage either of low cost or of differentiation. To fit or match the situation, a strategy will have to focus particularly on those links. For example, the primary activities of inbound logistics and the support activity of procurement are crucial to keeping the costs of supermarkets competitive. For this reason, supermarkets do not decentralise responsibility for these activities to their store managers. While some specific links will be of particular importance, the value chain must also be managed as a whole system, not simply a collection of separate parts. Reconfiguring the chain, relocating or eliminating activities in the chain, may lead to improved competitive position.

So far in this section, we have been looking in some detail at how managers can use analytical techniques to determine whether the strategic options they are examining satisfy the criterion of suitability or fit. They can use market structure and value chain analysis, for example, to ascertain whether a proposed cost reduction strategy matches the structure of their market and their position in the value chain, or whether some form of differentiation would provide a better match. The suitability criterion is basically saying that whether a strategy is successful or not depends upon, is contingent upon, its capability and its environment. The theoretical justification for this postulated relationship between success and the matching of an organisation to its environment lies in what is called contingency theory. It will be helpful, therefore, briefly to review contingency theory.

Contingency theory

The development of contingency theory (see *Key Concept 2.6*) was a reaction against the idea that there is 'one best way' in management. At the time it was developed that 'one best way' was scientific management, Management By Objectives (MBO) and related sets of prescriptions. Contingency theory substitutes the 'it all depends' approach for the 'one best way'. The approach derives from empirical research (Burns & Stalker, 1961; Woodward, 1965; Lawrence & Lorsch, 1967) which showed that success was not correlated with a simple single set of factors. Instead, the effectiveness of a particular organisational structure, culture, or sequence of actions is contingent upon, depends upon, a number of factors. The most important of these contingency factors are usually held to be:

- the environment, particularly the market
- the size of the organisation
- the technology it employs
- the history of the organisation
- the expectations of employees and customers.

The theory states that success will be secured when the organisation secures a good match between its situation and its strategies and structures. For example, mechanistic bureaucracies are said to be appropriate for stable environments, but flexible, organic structures are required for turbulent environments. Child (1984) summarises the theory as follows:

> Contingency theory regards the design of an effective organisation as necessarily having to be adapted to cope with the 'contingencies' which derive from the circumstances of environment, technology, scale, resources and other factors in the situation in which the organisation is operating.

■ **Key concept 2.6**
CONTINGENCY

Contingency is a theory about the nature of cause and effect. It makes statements like these. If an organisation is operating in an environment that is very complex and changing rapidly, then it requires organic forms of organisation to succeed. If, however, it operates in simple, slow-moving environments, then it requires mechanistic structures to succeed. If an organisation is small, then it requires a simple structure. If an organisation is large, then it requires a divisionalised structure.

Contingency theory postulates a complex web of interconnections between the features of organisations and their environments in which the causal connections are linear in the sense that they run in one direction. It is a particular environment that causes a particular kind of successful strategy and that causes a particular kind of successful structure. The theory does not contemplate circular causation in which the

> structures of organisations cause them to follow certain strategies which then create certain kinds of environment to which they respond.
>
> Contingency theory is based on the assumption that approximately the same cause will have approximately the same effect. It does not envisage escalation in which a tiny difference between two causes leads to two completely different outcomes. It does not, for example, allow for the possibility that two organisations operating in the same environment may develop in totally different directions simply because one gained a slightly bigger market share than the other in a particular product line at a particular point in time.
>
> By making particular assumptions about the nature of cause and effect, contingency theory is making particular assumptions about the dynamic of organisations. Success is assumed to be a state of equilibrium and, because they are close to equilibrium, the future time paths of successful organisations are predictable. These are all assumptions that are open to question, as we shall see in Chapter 3.

The contingency concept, and its consequent prescription of consistency and congruence, runs in terms of a large number of different combinations of strategies, structures, cultures and so on, each suited to a particular environment and a particular set of objectives at a particular time. Organisations then adopt whichever of these satisfies the consistency criteria. We have to specify the circumstances rather precisely before we can identify the appropriate combination of strategy, structure and so on. On the other hand, the configuration approach, to which we now turn, tries to identify a relatively small number of typical combinations of strategies, structures and so on, into which we can classify most organisations.

Configuration

The concept of configuration (see *Key Concept 2.7*) is a development of the ideas of contingency and congruence. Whereas contingency theory adopts an 'it all depends' approach, configuration is concerned with 'getting it all together' (Mintzberg, 1989).

■ Key concept 2.7
CONFIGURATION

A configuration is some typical constellation of structural, cultural, strategy pattern, control system features and other organisational factors appropriate to a particular environment. In other words, a particular configuration is one of a limited number of categories, based on many interrelated and mutually supportive features, into which we can classify organisations. A configuration therefore describes a typical or archetypal organisational system.

According to the configuration approach, examples of which are given in *Illustration 2.9*, success flows from selecting and designing an organisation and its strategies from a fairly limited number of archetypes. Empirical studies have been undertaken (reviewed in Miller, 1986) to demonstrate the following propositions:

1 There are only a limited number of possible constellations of strategies, structures, cultures and other organisational attributes that are feasible in any environment (Hannan & Freeman, 1977; Aldrich, 1979; McKelvey, 1980). Companies following these survive because they are more adapted to the environment, while other less well adapted organisations do not survive. The environment in effect selects out various common constellations of organisational attributes. Success flows from convergence upon a viable configuration. And it is postulated that this convergence will occur in short bursts, after which the successful organisation will display stability. We will return to this point in Chapter 4 in the section on revolutionary change.

2 Organisations are driven toward a few common configurations in order to achieve internal harmony and consistency between structures, cultures, strategies and contexts. Instead of an infinite number of combinations of elements, organisations tend to pursue one of a relatively small number of central themes that marshal all the elements into a coherent pattern where attributes are complementary and self-reinforcing. So a machine bureaucracy organisation with its highly specialised, routine operating tasks and highly formalised procedures can only function in stable environments in which its inflexibility is not overly limiting; but consistently stable environments enable operating procedures to be formalised, giving the advantage to machine bureaucracies. Machine bureaucracies in stable markets tend to pursue cost leadership strategies; but stable markets encourage growth to a scale that can reap cost benefits. Here the idea of configuration is stressing circular causation, whereas contingency stresses linear causation.

3 Organisations tend to change the elements of their configuration in a manner that either extends a given configuration (incrementally builds on existing strengths), or

Figure 2.12   The 7S framework

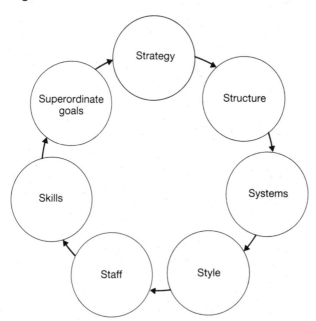

moves very quickly to a new configuration (strategic revolution) which will then be preserved for a long time. Piecemeal moves to a new configuration will often destroy the complementarities among elements in the configuration and will thus be avoided. Only when a configuration change is absolutely necessary or extremely advantageous will organisations move rapidly to a new configuration. The rest of the time organisations will build on their existing configuration.

A particularly well-known use of the concept of configuration is the 7S framework (Waterman, Peters & Phillips, 1980) shown in *Figure 2.12*. This framework indicates how the success or otherwise of an organisation follows from a configuration of seven attributes that are all interconnected, all part of one system. It is no use getting just one or two elements right; since they are all interdependent, they must all fit together and be consistent with each other.

■ Illustration 2.10
EXAMPLES OF CONFIGURATION

Miller (1986) describes four configurations:

- Small firms operating in niche markets with simple structures in fragmented industries.
- Large machine bureaucracies operating in stable concentrated industries with high entry barriers pursuing cost leadership strategies.
- Organic adhocracies where the strategy is differentiation through innovation in embryonic or growth industries.
- Large companies pursuing diversification strategies in mature industries with divisionalised conglomerate structures.

According to a configuration view therefore, the suitability criterion for selecting a sequence of actions is a set of closely interwoven attributes. Elements make sense in terms of the whole. Success flows from selecting patterns of action, positions, postures and performance that all fit together as a puzzle does to produce stability, consistency and regularity, harmony and fit. The criteria for successful choice are provided by a relatively small number of rather standard patterns, not a large number of separate criteria.

We turn now to the matter of implementing the strategic plan selected and the use of that plan to control an organisation.

2.4   Strategy implementation and strategic control

The main emphasis of technically rational approaches to strategic management has always been on the formulation, evaluation and selection of appropriate strategies.

It is always recognised, however, that none of this analysis is of much use unless the strategies so developed are implemented. It is also often pointed out that in practice managers spend most of their time on implementation rather than formulation and that the failure of strategy is most frequently due, not to poor formulation, but to the difficulties of implementation. Despite the recognition of its importance, however, the question of implementation continues to receive relatively little research attention and some hold that the consequent lack of practical and theoretically sound models to guide managers' actions during implementation is a major cause of implementation failure (Alexander, 1991).

When the question is dealt with, successful implementation is held to follow from the installation of a number of key organisational elements. To implement their formulated strategies managers must:

1 Design a hierarchical reporting structure that is appropriate to the strategy they have formulated.
2 Install and operate the management information and control system that will enable them to keep the organisation on its planned path.
3 Install and operate reward systems for people that will provide the monetary incentives for them to carry out the strategy.
4 Change the culture or belief system of people in the organisation to provide the non-monetary motivation for them to carry out the strategy.
5 Develop appropriate social and political behaviour that will not block the implementation of strategy.

We will now consider further each of these elements of implementation.

Installing structures to implement strategy

The structure of an organisation is the formal way of identifying:

● who is to take responsibility for what;
● who is to exercise authority over whom; and
● who is to be answerable to whom.

The structure is a hierarchy of managers and is the source of authority, as well as the legitimacy of decisions and actions. It is normally held that the appropriate structure follows from the strategy that an organisation is pursuing and that organisational structures display typical patterns of development or life cycles (Chandler, 1962).

Chandler identified four stages in the structure life cycle:

1 Embryonic organisations have very simple structures in which people report rather informally to someone that they accept as their leader. They tend to do whatever needs to be done with relatively little separation of functions. When they embark on a growth strategy, however, they will find it necessary to change the structure to one based on more formal specialisation of functions and identification of authority and responsibility. If this is not done, managers will find it impossible to implement their strategy of growth and the organisation will probably fail.
2 As they pursue their growth strategy, managers will find that they have to carry out strategies of cost reduction to stay ahead and they will be more and more

confronted with the problem of integrating specialised functions. The structure will therefore have to be made even more formal with clearer definition of lines of authority and communication. It will also be necessary to systematise and improve the techniques of marketing, manufacturing and materials procurement.

3 Then, as managers pursue strategies of diversification into new products and markets, they find it necessary to set up marketing and manufacturing organisations in different geographic areas: they install additional structures.

4 As they continue their strategy of diversification, the number of additional structures multiplies and they have to restructure to ensure a better 'fit' with the diversification strategies they are pursuing. They might secure this fit by forming a larger functionally departmentalised structure, with departments at the centre shared by many geographic areas; or by setting up largely independent subsidiaries as divisionalised or holding company structures. Another label for such organisations is Mintzberg's (1991) 'machine bureaucracy.'

Implementation, then, means installing a structure appropriate to the strategy being pursued and this typically results in a life cycle for hierarchical structures. We will be returning to a more detailed discussion of organisational structure in Chapter 10.

Systems installation and control

The information and control systems of an organisation are basically procedures, rules and regulations governing:

- what information about the performance of an organisation should flow to whom and when;
- who is required to respond to that information and how they are authorised to respond, in particular what authority they have to deploy the resources of their organisation.

To implement the strategies they have formulated, managers will have to ensure that their information and control systems:

- are adequate enough for the flows of information that implementation requires;
- provide appropriate control mechanisms to enable managers to monitor the outcomes of the strategy implementation and do something if those outcomes are not in accordance with the strategy.

Management control is defined as the process of ensuring that all resources – physical, human and technological – are allocated so as to realise the strategy. It is a process in which a person or a group of people intentionally affects what others do. Control ensures proper behaviour in an organisation and the need for it arises because individuals within the organisation are not always willing to act in the best interests of the organisation (Wilson, 1991). The process of control involves setting standards or targets for performance, or expected outcomes of a sequence of actions, then comparing actual performance or outcomes against standards, targets or expectations, and finally taking corrective action to remove any deviations from standard, target or expectation. Control takes a *feedforward* form when corrective action is taken on the basis of predictions with the aim of avoiding deviations from expectations. It takes on a *feedback* form where the predictions cannot be accurate enough. In the feedback form, monitoring detects a deviation that has already occurred and then takes action to correct it. Most business control systems are a mixture of feedforward and feedback control.

The principal form taken by the control system in most organisations is that of the annual plan or budget. Strategy implementation is held to depend upon an effective budgeting system. The budget converts strategy into a set of short-term action plans and sets out the financial consequences of those action plans for the year ahead. Control is then a process of regularly comparing what happens to what the budget said would happen. Budgets allocate the resource of the organisation with which different business units and functions are charged to carry out the strategy. Budgets establish the legitimate authority for using the resources of the organisation. The budget will normally be prepared in great detail, showing what people in each business unit and function are required to bring in as revenue, what they are permitted to spend and on what, and therefore what surplus they are required to earn, or deficit they will be allowed to incur.

The budget, however, is a short-term instrument, only the first step in the implementation of the strategy. Some have therefore sought to identify the differences between short-term control and strategic control. For example, Hurst (1982) points out that strategic control requires more data from more sources, particularly external sources, and the data must be oriented to a longer-term future. Strategic control is therefore inevitably less precise and less formal than budgetary control. It is concerned more with the accuracy of the premises on which decisions are based and much less with quantitative deviations from standards. Strategic control has to be more flexible and use variable rather than rigidly regular time periods for reporting. The relationships between corrective action and outcome are therefore weaker in strategic control. The conclusion drawn is that although planning and control in a strategic sense is very difficult, a system to compare expectations and outcomes is even more necessary than it is for the short term.

Goold and Quinn's (1990) research shows that very few companies have a strategic control process that is anything like as formal and comprehensive as their budgetary control system. Even where managers do set strategic milestones that would allow them to check on their progress as the strategy was implemented, those milestones take the form of events rather than results. So the milestone might be the completion of a new factory; managers might set this for a period two years hence and then after two years check if the factory is indeed complete. If it is, they may conclude that they are keeping to their strategy. However, since this is an event rather than a result, they will not know if the financial results their strategy was supposed to achieve are in fact being achieved. The reasons for the lack of a proper results-based monitoring and control system was identified as the length of time lags between action and outcome and the risks and uncertainties that long-term plans were subject to. Despite the difficulties, however, Goold and Quinn recommend trying harder to use formal strategic control systems based on milestones for comparison.

Clearly, the technically rational planning approach to strategic management has difficulty with the matters of implementation and strategic control, difficulties that have so far not been satisfactorily resolved. We will be returning to the question of strategic control in the next section of this chapter and again in Chapter 9, but before that we consider the third aspect of strategy implementation.

Installing and operating human resource systems

Effective strategy implementation should occur when the people required to take action to this end are motivated to do so. One of the most powerful motivators is the organisation's reward system (Galbraith and Kazanjian, 1986). Appropriate rewards stimulate people to make the effort to take actions directly relevant to the organisation's strategy. The way in which people's jobs are graded and the pay scales attached to these grades will affect how people feel about their jobs and the effort they will make. Differentials need to be perceived to be fair if they are not to affect performance adversely. Bonuses, profit-related pay, piecework and productivity schemes are all ways of tying monetary rewards to the actions that strategy implementation requires.

Non-monetary rewards are also of great importance in motivating people. These rewards include promotion, career development, job enrichment, job rotation, training and development. They all help individuals to be more useful to the organisation while developing greater self-fulfilment. Simpler forms of reward are also of great importance, for example praise, recognition and thanks.

Training and development is an important implementation tool, not only because it motivates people, but also because it provides the skills required for strategy implementation (Hussey, 1991). The objectives of training and development programmes should be aligned with those of the organisation's strategy and those objectives should consist of measurable changes in corporate performance. Lorenz (1986) describes how ICL put 2000 managers through a development programme designed to improve ICL's competitiveness against the Japanese. Such programmes allow managers at all levels to develop a comprehensive understanding of what their organisation's strategy actually means.

Culture-change programmes

Just as the reporting structure of an organisation should fit the particular strategy it wishes to pursue, so should its culture, the attitudes and beliefs that people within an organisation share. Handy (1981) classifies organisational cultures into four categories:

1 The *power* culture is typically found in small entrepreneurial companies controlled by powerful figures. People in this culture share a belief in individuality and in taking risks. They believe that management should be an informal process with few rules and procedures.
2 The *role* culture is associated with bureaucracies where people's functions are defined in a formal way and they specialise. People here share a belief in the importance of security and predictability. They equate successful management with rules and regulations.
3 The *task* culture is found where people focus on their job, or on a project. People share a belief in the importance of teamwork, expertise and in being adaptable.

4 The *person* culture occurs where people believe that the organisation exists so that they can serve their own personal interest, for example barristers and architects, and many other professionals.

Just as structures need to fit a particular strategy and just as they tend to follow a life cycle from the simple to the functional to the divisional, so too do cultures. The power culture is appropriate to the early stages of a firm's life when its structure is simple. Later it will have to change to the role culture as it grows and installs a functional structure. Then it will have to develop a task culture to fit in with a divisionalised structure.

Implementation may well therefore require that an organisation change its culture and the conventional wisdom prescribes that such change should be planned. The reasons why people might resist a change in culture need to be identified and plans formulated to overcome the resistance. Participation, communication and training are all seen as ways of overcoming resistance. The process of overcoming resistance involves a stage called unfreezing when the existing culture is questioned and is followed by a period of reformulation where people consider what new beliefs they need to develop and share with each other. Finally there is the re-freezing stage where the new culture is fixed in place. We will be returning in Chapter 5 to these matters of planned change in belief systems – the discipline of Organisation Development.

Developing appropriate political behaviour

It is inevitable that people in an organisation will conflict and, when they do, they engage in political behaviour (Pfeffer, 1981). As an organisation differentiates into functions and units, those functions and units develop their own objectives, some of which will be different to those of the organisation as a whole. But differentiation brings with it interdependence so that no single function or unit can achieve its objectives on its own. They will have both to compete with each other for scarce resources and to cooperate with each other to reach their objective. Interdependence, heterogeneous goals and scarce resources taken together produce conflict. If the conflict is important and power is distributed enough, then people will use political behaviour, that is persuasion and negotiation, to resolve their conflict. If power is highly centralised then most will simply do as they are told – they will not have enough power to engage in political behaviour.

The kinds of political strategies people employ to come out best from conflict are the selective use of objective criteria, the use of outside experts to support their case, forming alliances and coalitions, sponsoring those with similar ideas, empire building, intentionally doing nothing, suppressing information, making decisions first and using analysis afterwards to justify them, and many more.

The above view of politics as a manipulative process of dubious ethical validity leads to a conventional belief that steps should be taken to reduce the incidence of political behaviour. Such steps are those that reduce the level of conflict and the most powerful of these is to preach and convert people to a common ideology. Creating excess resources should also reduce levels of conflict.

In the conventional approach, political activity is seen as a way of managing that is likely to be necessary, but will be a difficult and dangerous task, something to avoid if only it were possible.

We now turn to a matter closely connected with strategy implementation and strategic control – strategic management styles.

2.5   Installing strategic management styles

So far we have discussed the criteria managers should use to select appropriate strategies, as well as the steps they should take to implement and control the consequences of those strategies. The question now is: what part should the various levels of management play in the formulation and implementation of strategies and in strategic control? In other words, the question is to do with how managers at various levels add value to the strategy process. It is the manner in which various levels of management contribute to the strategy process that determines what we might call the management style of the organisation. In this section we will consider three well-known ways of categorising the strategic style of an organisation.

Mintzberg's types of strategy

Mintzberg and Waters (1985) distinguish the following eight styles of strategic management:

- *Planned.* Top managers articulate precise intentions and embody these in formal plans that set out what the levels of managers below them are to do. Top management then exert control by monitoring outcomes against plan.
- *Entrepreneurial.* The organisation here is under the personal control of the leader and strategies flow from the unarticulated vision of a single leader.
- *Ideological.* Strategies are the intended patterns in action expressed in collective beliefs. Here top managers articulate inspirational and relatively immutable beliefs that govern the actions of those lower down and so become the strategy. The ideology embodies the organisation's intention and control is through indoctrination and socialisation.
- *Umbrella.* Here the leaders define the overall targets and set the boundaries within which managers lower down actually formulate the content of the strategy. Control is exerted by monitoring achievement against target and behaviour against the boundaries.
- *Process.* The leaders control the process of strategy, for example the reporting structure, the planning timetable and the appointment of managers, and then leave the content to those lower down. Control is exerted through keeping people to timetables and through allocating resources, that is through exercising a final veto.
- *Unconnected.* Here there is either no central intention or groups of people produce strategies in direct contradiction to central intention. The organisation's strategy therefore flows from a collection of unconnected strategies formed by groups within the organisation.
- *Consensus.* People in the organisation converge on a common theme through

agreement with each other, without any central managers directing them. Here strategies emerge without prior organisational intention.

- *Imposed*. This occurs where the environment dictates what has to be done.

Mintzberg and Waters (1985) relate these strategic management styles to the kind of environment that managers face. For mature diversified corporations, planned strategic management styles are appropriate for stable environments, but umbrella or process styles will be more suitable in turbulent ones. This corresponds with the distinction usually drawn between top-down and bottom-up planning. For different kinds of organisation in turbulent environments we will tend to find entrepreneurial, unconnected or consensus strategic management styles.

Mintzbeg (1991) also distinguished between five types of organisation:

- The *simple structure* in which the entrepreneurial style of management is usually found.
- The *machine bureaucracy* which works according to rules and regulations established by the centre of the organisation. This is appropriate for stable environments and the planned style of strategic management fits with it.
- The *professional bureaucracy* which is bureaucratic but not centralised, such as schools, universities and hospitals. The strategic management style here will normally be of the unconnected type.
- *Divisionalised structures* where the choice of style would lie between planned, process or umbrella.
- The *adhocracy*, which are highly organic organisations with little in the way of formal structures, rules and procedures. They consist of teams of specialists, for example management consultants. The strategic management style here might be entrepreneurial, consensus or ideological.

Miles and Snow's categories

Miles and Snow (1978) provide another way of categorising strategic management style. They distinguish between the following:

- *Defenders*. Managers in these organisations concentrate on a relatively well-defined market area. They concentrate on increasing their expertise and improving their position in this market, rather than searching for alternative strategies.
- *Prospectors*. Managers here are always searching for new opportunities and they often create change and uncertainty.
- *Analysers*. Managers in this kind of organisation operate in both stable and unstable areas; in the former they use formalised structures while in the latter they adopt a more organic approach.
- *Reactors*. Here managers perceive change and uncertainty but are unable to respond effectively. They lack a consistent strategy and act when the environment forces them to.

Goold and Campbell's strategies and styles

Goold and Campbell (1987) define strategic management styles in terms of the manner in which the corporate level of an organisation resolves a number of tensions.

They distinguish between five key tensions:

- *Multiple perspectives versus clear responsibility.* This is the dilemma created when people are given clearly defined jobs in a system that restricts them to those jobs. The result is greater efficiency at the defined job, but it leads to narrow thinking and therefore reduced ability to deal with change. If the organisation moves in the direction of multiple perspectives, however, it suffers a reduction in efficiency.
- *Detailed planning reviews versus entrepreneurial decision making.* This presents an organisation with a similar dilemma. It can secure greater control and higher levels of efficiency if it plans carefully and regularly reviews actions against plan. But this narrows the focus of people and their motivation to act so that many new opportunities will be lost.
- *Strong leadership versus business autonomy.* The dilemma here is that between strong central control with the synergies it brings and local autonomy with the flexibility to deal with unexpected change.
- *Long-term objectives versus short-term objectives.* The tension here occurs because short-term profitability and cash flow is high when a company does not invest in expensive new facilities and research and development, but this failure to invest will reduce long-term profitability.
- *Flexible strategies versus tight controls.* This dilemma is created by the need to set out precisely what people are to do in order to have a firm basis for monitoring their performance. When this is done, however, it removes the flexibility individuals have to handle unexpected changes.

Goold and Campbell argue that successful organisations resolve these tensions in a manner that matches a number of factors internal to the organisation with a number of factors external to it. The internal factors are matters such as the nature of the business portfolio, the extent to which businesses overlap each other, and the skills and personalities of people in the businesses. The external factors include the level of uncertainty the environment presents and the intensity of the competition. A strategic management style is a choice that resolves the tensions to secure equilibrium. The three most important choices of styles they identify are:

The financial control style

One choice is to operate in market segments that are highly stable so that most of the tensions described above are avoided. The organisation can then adopt an uncompromisingly simple, flat, decentralised organisational structure. It can focus firmly on short-term objectives and practise tight short-term control using quantitative management information and control systems. Unforeseen change, the strategic and the long term are all dealt with by the entrepreneurial initiative of the managers closest to the action and/or by an entrepreneurial approach to acquisitions at the corporate level.

The strategic planning style

Here companies adopt complex, centralist structures and practise top-down long-term planning. They place great weight on the achievement of long-term objectives and are tolerant of non-achievement in the short term. They make these choices because they are pursuing interconnections and synergies; they are trying to develop competitive advantage and achieve balance in the portfolio of businesses under their control. This style choice will be appropriate where changes in customer requirements and competitor groupings are turbulent and competition intense. This choice is also appropriate where there are significant interconnections between business units in terms of shared customers or shared operational processes and technology.

The strategic control style

These companies strike a balance between short- and long-term objectives, sacrificing short-term profit where there is a reasonable prospect of this leading to greater long-term profit. They usually choose simple, flat, decentralised organisational structures to allow effective short-term control, but try to promote collaboration to enable some interconnections and synergies to be taken advantage of. They adopt the more facilitating forms of management, relying more on the processes of persuasion and negotiation than on instruction. Planning is then of the bottom-up type. This style choice is far less clear than the other two, but it does offer advantages of flexibility. It is likely to be appropriate where the company consists of businesses that are not significantly interconnected in customer or operational and technology terms, and operates in markets characterised by rapid change arising in contained situations.

If you choose a strategy that focuses on synergy and that requires integrated operational responses and common approaches to customers, then a successful choice is the strategic planning style, with all it means in terms of structures, roles and cultures. If you choose to sacrifice some synergy and operate in rather more independent market segments, which do not have common customer bases and do not require integrated operational responses, then strategic control is the successful choice. This choice also leads to particular structural, cultural, role and systems requirements to fit or match.

2.6   Does the conventional wisdom work?

We have now briefly examined the core prescriptions that form today's conventional wisdom on strategic management. We have also reviewed the explanations of the nature of management and organisation from which these prescriptions are derived. Recall that we have defined the 'conventional wisdom' as those explanations and prescriptions that the best-selling management books focus on, that occupy the bulk of the discussion in most textbooks on the subject, that are recognised and articulated by most managers. Note that the conventional wisdom consists of a number of different and sometimes conflicting explanations of strategic management: the technically rational views on how to design strategic plans, the visionary/ideological views on how to innovate, and the idea of configurations of limited numbers of archetypes of organisational success. In the next chapter we will consider what all these diverse explanations have in common. But first we must ask how well this conventional wisdom works. If we have succeeded in identifying a reliable set of prescriptions for strategic success, then we would expect to find at least a small sample of companies that have mastered those prescriptions. We would expect to find samples of excellent companies that remain successful for long periods of time.

In fact, it seems that no sooner does anyone identify a sample of excellent companies than most of them slip from grace. As we have seen, in the early 1980s, Peters and Waterman (1982) identified 43 excellent companies in the USA but within five years two thirds could no longer be included in the sample. Goldsmith and Clutterbuck (1984) carried out a similar analysis of 25 UK companies and much the same fate befell their sample. The rankings of the Fortune 500 companies and the *Financial Times* top 100 companies change dramatically over five-year periods.

It is therefore extremely difficult to find a sample of companies that have consistently mastered the task of successful strategic management for a reasonably long period of time. The usual reason given for this difficulty is that the environment is too turbulent to allow continuing success, or that companies fall from the category of excellence because they are incompetently managed.

It has also proved very difficult to establish any connection between the existence of formal planning in an organisation and superior performance (Greenley, 1986). That may be because few companies actually use long-term plans as control instruments. A recent survey of large companies in the UK (Goold and Quinn, 1990) shows that only 15 per cent of those that do have formal planning systems use them as templates against which to monitor actions. Even those 15 per cent monitor their plans against events such as building a factory rather than by results such as making a profit. It seems that most managers do not use the espoused recipes for success as they are intended to be used; and we cannot establish much of a link between the use of the recipe and success.

Apparently only 20 per cent of Japanese companies practise formal long-term planning (Argenti, 1984). In many other respects these successful global rivals of Western companies seem to do things very differently. Hamel and Prahalad (1989) identify the relative success of the Japanese with a superior model of strategy in which they do not attempt to adapt to environments but create core competences and build market share. Hampden-Turner (1990) describes how Japanese managers are more comfortable with dilemmas and paradoxes than Western managers are. Nonaka (1988) describes how Japanese managers intentionally develop the instability of counter-cultures, while the Western approach is to attempt to secure even more conformity.

Today's strategic management prescriptions do not provide reliable answers to the question of how to create and sustain effective and long-lived organisations. Royal Dutch Shell conducted a survey in 1983 and found that the average life-time of the largest industrial corporations was less than forty years (De Geus, 1988). Corporations do not live as long as individual people! Some people are not concerned about this short life-span, holding that the continuous failure of old organisations and creation of new ones is how innovation occurs. This might be an acceptable argument if we knew how to create successful new organisations – the high failure rate of new companies indicates only too forcefully that we do not. Furthermore, securing innovation through allowing the old organisations to die and bringing on the new ones means continually re-experiencing the same problems of turning small companies into large ones. That way we continue to learn old lessons instead of learning how to develop new forms of large organisation. Our failure reliably to create and sustain organisations is therefore an indictment of the conventional wisdom.

The argument, then, is that today's dominant prescriptions for strategic management – the planning, envisioning, controlling and ideology sharing described in this chapter – are not leading the corporations of Europe and North America to success. Managers in the Far East see the world through different lenses (Pascale, 1990; Hampden-Turner, 1990) and for decades now they have been winning the strategy game. This is certainly not a new conclusion: arguments along these lines have been presented many times over the past few years (for example, Hayes & Abernathy, 1980; and Hamel & Prahalad, 1989).

The usual response

This recognition of relative failure normally provokes an intensified effort to improve a selected number of the existing prescriptions. Larger numbers of organisations are researched and the approaches to planning, envisioning, strategically controlling and consensus building are further refined.

For example, the study of large UK companies already referred to identified that only 15 per cent of those who formulated long-term plans subsequently monitored and reviewed action against them (Goold and Quinn, 1990). The conclusion drawn by the researchers was that managers were behaving in an ineffective way. Despite the admitted difficulties of doing so, managers were advised to devote more effort to setting strategic milestones and reviewing their actions against those milestones. The implicit assumptions the researchers were making are these:

- Companies will be successful if they formulate consistent long-term plans and then sustain stability by acting in accordance with those plans.
- Such stability can be secured only by reviewing and monitoring action outcomes against milestones.
- Levels of uncertainty are not such as to make all of this completely impossible.

But the managers in the sample of companies knew all about setting milestones and monitoring outcomes. They were doing exactly this when they used budgets for short-term control systems. Why did the majority in the sample not carry the procedure over to the long-term control of their organisation? They all knew about the importance of the long term. Perhaps they did not carry short-term reviewing procedures over to the long term because it did not make much practical sense to do so. Perhaps the level of uncertainty was too high. Repeating advice that has been heeded only superficially for decades now is surely not a useful response to a serious difficulty. But this is exactly what the conventional wisdom predisposes us to do.

Is a different response required?

When confronted by the evident failure of strategic management prescriptions to produce consistent organisational success, the conventional wisdom leads us to ascribe this to some combination of environmental turbulence and management incompetence. We then do more research, try to refine the prescriptions further, and exhort managers to try harder. But there is another possibility and this is that there is something fundamentally wrong with the conventional wisdom. The next chapter explores this possibility by examining the basis upon which the conventional wisdom is built.

2.7 Summary

This chapter has briefly described the main prescriptions for successful strategic management that are to be found in the textbooks and that are subscribed to by practising managers. These prescriptions constitute the conventional wisdom, that which managers say they do. The conventional wisdom is not monolithic, but consists of different and sometimes conflicting explanations. The chapter has classified these prescriptions according to:

- The 'one best way' which prescribes the installation of a number of attributes of success to create an organisation that is flexible enough to deal with high levels of uncertainty. This has been referred to as the 'excellence' approach or as the 'visionary/ideological' model of strategic management. Proponents of this approach condemn reliance on technical rationality.
- A specific best way for each set of circumstances. Here the prescription, based on contingency theory, is to formulate and select long-term plans according to technically rational criteria, then implement those plans, and monitor performance against them. This has been labelled the technically 'rational planning' approach.
- A configuration approach that tries to identify a limited number of constellations of factors that taken together produce a successful organisation.

In practice, managers claim they are using some combination of these approaches. At the end, however, we have to admit that we have found no reliable answers in our quest for the route to successful organisations. The reason usually given for the failure to sustain organisational success is the incompetence of managers or their ignorance of all the changes they have to deal with. It is the purpose of the next chapter to question this conclusion by digging deeper into the nature of the conventional wisdom.

Further reading

Highly recommended reading is Peters & Waterman (1982). Although this book has not identified the one best way, it is important because of its exposition of the role of culture and belief in organisational success. To obtain further information on analytical techniques and models for evaluating strategies turn to Hofer & Schendel (1978) as well as Rowe, Mason, Dickel & Snyder (1989). Also Johnson & Scholes (1988) or Bowman & Asch (1987).

3

Making sense of the conventional wisdom

Today's dominant management paradigm

3.1 Introduction

In the last chapter we explored the strategic management prescriptions that constitute today's received or conventional wisdom; that is, the routes to successful organisations that most textbooks set out and that most managers subscribe to. We identified a rational approach, a visionary/ideological approach, and an approach based on the idea of configuration. These three approaches differ dramatically in the prescriptions for success that they present. In this chapter we will be concerned with the view of the world of organisations that these different approaches are based upon and we will see that despite their differences they share fundamentally the same view of the organisational world. We also saw in the last chapter, that it is not at all clear that the prescriptions of the conventional wisdom work as they are intended to. In this chapter, therefore, we will begin to explore why the prescriptions may not be working and we will begin to see that this failure has something to do with the fundamental view of the world that all the conventional approaches share.

Sensible prescriptions are always based on something and that something could range from a simple hunch to an elaborate explanation or a well-researched theory. In the case of the strategic management prescriptions we have been considering in Chapter 2, the basis is a number of research studies, descriptions and theories on the nature of management, leadership, control, and the functioning of organisations.

Therefore, if we want to understand why managers are having difficulty in achieving success through the conventional prescriptions, we must explore the fundamental nature of those explanations of managing and organising that underlie the prescriptions. And just as our prescriptions are derived from the way we explain what is going on, so our explanations are derived in turn from our paradigm or way of perceiving the world. It follows that, if we are to get at the fundamental nature of strategic management explanations, we must first understand what a paradigm is and how paradigms underlie all human efforts to understand any world from the universe to the functioning of a human organisation, or the behaviour of an individual person.

Once we have reviewed the role that paradigms play in the way we make sense of the world, we will try to identify the paradigm, that is the unquestioned assumptions made, in the approaches to strategic management discussed in Chapter 2. As soon as we do this it will become evident that it is quite possible to make dramatically different assumptions and so produce completely different explanations and prescriptions for successful strategic management. The next chapter will explore why we might need to make dramatically different assumptions about the way organisations function and the chapters after that will examine what those different assumptions might be and what they might mean for the successful practice of strategic management.

3.2 How paradigms govern what we see and do

What every one of us sees, understands and does in any situation depends upon the perspective from which we view that situation. Such a perspective is called a paradigm, a very general way that each of us uses to make sense of the particular world we are operating in. The term is explained in *Key Concept 3.1*. How teachers, researchers and consultants understand the strategy game and therefore advise on it, how managers understand it and therefore play it, all depend in the end upon their paradigm.

■ **Key concept 3.1**
PARADIGM

A paradigm is the set of preconceptions we bring from our past to each new situation we have to deal with. The paradigm is, as it were, the lens through which we look at the world and it therefore determines what we perceive. A paradigm is a set of beliefs or assumptions we make about the world, normally beneath the level of awareness and therefore mostly never questioned. As we live and work with other people we come to share a particular way of focusing on the world and that shared paradigm determines what explanations we develop and agree upon amongst ourselves. The origins of all our explanations of everything, therefore, lie in the process of socialisation, in the shared cultures formed by people in groups. The paradigm flows from shared past experience and is reflected in our skilled behaviour, that is the rapid actions we take automatically to perform complex tasks without thinking about how, and often why, we are performing them.

I can perhaps make clearer what I mean by the importance of paradigms by asking you to look at *Figure 3.1*, which you have no doubt seen before, and construct a story around what you see. If you focus on the white space, seeing the black as

Figure 3.1 Perception

unimportant background, you will see a container. Your story will have something to do with a cup, or a vase, and what it might be used for. If you focus on the black spaces, seeing the white as unimportant background, you will see two people facing each other. Your story will have to do with who they are, why they are looking at each other, and what they might do next.

How you focus (the equivalent of your paradigm) determines what you see, and what you see determines what you do, in this case the story you tell. And as you tell your story, the telling itself provokes new thoughts to be added to that story.

In the terminology introduced in Chapter 1, how and what you *discover* (your paradigms and the perceptions they lead you to) directly affects what you *choose* to do since you cannot choose what you have not perceived, and that choice in turn determines your *actions*. And it is through your actions that you make further discoveries, leading to other choices and actions in a continuing feedback loop. Even when you do something as simple as look at *Figure 3.1* and construct a story around it, you are in effect following a feedback loop in which one discovery or action leads to others, just as was the case in the strategic management process illustrated in *Figure 1.1* of Chapter 1. Furthermore, it is your paradigm, how you focus, that determines how you go around the feedback loop. How you go around the loop determines the patterns of change in the behaviour you generate, that is the dynamics of your behaviour. The paradigms that the managers of an organisation share will therefore determine how they practise strategic management and what strategies they pursue.

To see this, consider what happens if, as in *Figure 3.1*, you focus on the white space of stability, consistency, harmony and adaptation. You will then tell a tale of strategic management that has to do with objectives and visions, plans and shared ideologies. Instability and contradiction will be unimportant background. The story you choose to tell will drive much of what you actually do and so you will establish planning systems to deal with your strategic problems, or you will try to set out visions for the future. This will encourage you to follow stable patterns of behaviour that inevitably build on your existing strengths and repeat successful behaviour from the past. In an age where survival depends upon innovation, exclusive reliance on this form of behaviour might be questionable.

If, however, you focus on the direct opposite, on the black space of instability, contradiction, conflict and creative interaction, then you will tell a tale of strategic management that has to do with challenging and provoking political interactions, personalities, group dynamics and learning. If your story is one of politics and learning you may try to create conditions in which people will develop new perspectives. This will mean unstable patterns of behaviour, conflict and tension, but such behaviour might produce innovation.

Our paradigm, then, ultimately determines what we do in every sphere of life – it comes before any visions we may form and it is prior to any rational analysis. For example, the development of every science is conditioned by the paradigm that a particular community of scientists shares (Kuhn, 1970). In the same way, the paradigm shared by scholars, students and practitioners of strategic management also determines the explanations and prescriptions they put forward on organisational success. It will help us to understand the nature of strategic management, therefore, if we examine Thomas Kuhn's explanation of how paradigms relate to the development of a science.

Kuhn on scientific revolutions

In the framework that Thomas Kuhn uses to explain the development of the natural sciences, he draws a distinction between what he calls normal science and extraordinary science.

Normal science is what most scientists spend most of their lives doing. It is conducted within a paradigm that the great majority of those in a particular discipline share. That paradigm is a set of shared mental models that are largely tacit, that is below the level of consciousness and therefore hardly every questioned. The paradigm consists of the beliefs that a community of scientists share about:

- what their world of study consists of;
- what the core generalisations on the functioning of that world are;
- what the key problems confronting them are;
- what is acceptable as solutions to the problems;
- what methods are to be employed to study the field and carry out experiments;
- what examples are regarded as typical of the phenomena being dealt with.

The paradigm is therefore far more general than a set of rules or procedures; rather, it constitutes a whole way of thinking that conditions how normal science is carried out.

Normal science

Normal science does not try to invent or discover something completely new; it is not a search for novelty or surprise, but rather the methodical activity of solving puzzles posed by the paradigm, using criteria and rules of procedure that are set by the paradigm. Puzzles have known solutions; it is the method of solving them that is unknown and the challenge is to achieve the anticipated in a new way. The method for doing this is rational argument backed up by evidence and it is the paradigm that sets the ground rules for this rational argument – people can only have a rational argument when they share a paradigm. Examples of normal science and its dependence on a paradigm are given in *Illustration 3.1*.

Every paradigm, however, is a simplification of reality and therefore the conduct of normal science will eventually uncover anomalies that undermine the paradigm. In other words, scientific experiments will inevitably produce discrepancies that cannot be explained within the beliefs of the paradigm and the rules and procedures for conducting experiments that are derived from it. *Illustration 3.1* also gives examples of how normal science produces anomalies.

Thus, normal science is about avoiding surprises and certainly does not set out to undermine and change the paradigm. However, the more diligent the conduct of normal science, the more rapid the build-up of the anomalies that will lead some to question the paradigm.

In a field where the paradigm is being questioned, most of the scientists in that field will at first resist the threats to the paradigm because belief in the paradigm is vital to the continuing conduct of normal science. What is vital to normal science then becomes the enemy of further scientific development.

Extraordinary science

Eventually, however, as more and more anomalies come to light, they generate a crisis in which there is no widely shared paradigm in the field of study. Instead there is a battle between competing paradigms seeking to substitute for the now discredited one. Only when a new paradigm is once again shared can normal science be resumed. This crisis period of paradigm destruction and new paradigm creation is a scientific revolution and this is how all major scientific advances occur.

■ **Illustration 3.1**
RELATIVITY AND X-RAYS

During the 19th century scientists believed that light was a wave that moved through a substance called ether and scientists therefore deduced that light was governed by Newton's laws of physical mechanics. So, theories of light were simply extensions of Newtonian theory. If ether did exist, however, it should have been possible to detect the drift of planets through the ether, that is the way in which the ether slowed their movement; in the course of normal science, expensive equipment was built to detect this drift. No such drift was detected but, despite this, scientists continued to conduct their normal scientific experiments on the assumption that ether existed.

Then in the last two decades of the 19th century Maxwell developed his electromagnetic theory. He continued to believe that light and electricity were displacements of the ether governed by Newton's laws – his normal scientific work continued to be governed by the ether paradigm. However, the theory he had developed did not include ether drag and it proved impossible to incorporate it. Many attempts were made to detect ether drag in electricity, but they failed. Thus the anomalies that could not be explained within the ether paradigm built up and eventually created a crisis for Newtonian theory's assumptions of absolute time and space. It was this crisis that led Einstein to develop his relativity theories and they resulted in a change in paradigm, a switch in perception from Newton's absolute classical mechanics to a relativist view of the world.

Another example is provided by the accidental discovery of X-rays. While conducting a normal experiment with cathode rays, Roentgen noticed that a barium platino-cyanide screen at some distance from his shielded apparatus glowed during the experiment. Further investigation indicated that the cause of the glow was X-rays, which could of course pass through the shielding around Roentgen's apparatus. This discovery was greeted with shock by other scientists and some said it was a hoax. At that time, the design of laboratory equipment and procedures, as well as the rules for interpreting results, were all based on the assumption that a phenomenon such as X-rays did not exist. Consequently, if the existence of X-rays was to be accepted, equipment and procedures would have to be changed and experiments repeated because previous results could have been due to, or at least affected by, X-rays of which the experimenters were ignorant.

It is important to understand the process through which one paradigm comes to substitute for another – it is a process that is very different from what most people understand by the term 'scientific'.

Normal science is conducted through logical argument against rational criteria backed up with evidence. In case of conflict it will be possible for the arguments of one scientist to prevail over those of another on purely rational grounds. This is possible because they share the paradigm and this means that they in effect agree to follow the same rules of argument and accept the same items of evidence. But when it comes to changing the paradigm, this rational process can no longer apply because that which provides the commonly shared rules is no longer shared.

Two scientists arguing about a paradigm have no prior set of concepts or higher intellectual authority to whom they may appeal to settle the argument. Kuhn (1970, p. 199) puts it as follows:

> Debates over [paradigm] choice cannot be cast in a form that resembles logical or mathematical proof. In the latter, premises and rules of inference are stipulated from the start. If there is disagreement about conclusions, the parties to the ensuing debate can retrace their steps one by one, checking each against prior stipulation. At the end of that process one must concede that he has made a mistake, violated a previously accepted rule. After that concession he has no recourse and his opponent's proof is then compelling. Only if the two discover instead that they differ about the meaning or application of stipulated rules, that their prior agreement provides no sufficient basis for proof, does the debate continue in the form it inevitably does during scientific revolutions. That debate is about premises, and its recourse is to persuasion as a prelude to the possibility of proof.

So, when trying to establish a new paradigm, strictly logical, rational ways of resolving any conflict break down. They break down because rationality and logic require the prior existence of some shared set of rules that people agree to abide by and not question. As soon as they do question the paradigm they remove the basis of rationality. A new paradigm can eventually come to be shared only through a political process of persuasion and conversion:

- Some individual or small group of individuals perceives a new paradigm through some process of intuition prompted by the build-up of anomalies under the preceding paradigm.
- That new paradigm champion then uses political processes to persuade the group of scientific colleagues to share it.

Note how the processes used in revolutionary or extraordinary science are completely different to those used in normal science and in many ways are diametrically opposed to them. Yet the conduct of science involves both normal and revolutionary science and indeed the latter is prompted by, and leads to, improvements in the former. Without revolutionary paradigm-destroying science there would be no real advance in scientific knowledge, that is there would be no innovation. Note how extraordinary science is the enemy of normal science, and how normal science necessarily seeks to block the extraordinary, and yet how progress requires this paradox, this contradiction.

Kuhn's views, and his research into the history of science to back them up, are of great importance because they make untenable the traditional view that science is a purely rational activity based on observable facts. From the traditional perspective, science is the activity of progressively uncovering the immutable laws of nature through a process of formulating hypotheses about phenomena in a particular area and testing them by experiment. If the testing of the hypothesis predictions against observed fact fails to falsify the hypothesis, then that hypothesis is accepted until such time as it might be falsified and replaced by a better one.

Science, on this view, was held to be free of any distortions due to human perceptions, beliefs, values or cultures. What Kuhn so convincingly demonstrates is that this is not so. At any one time, the laws of science reflect the perceptions, the paradigm of the scientific community, and a paradigm is a culturally conditioned, shared way of understanding the world that arises through social processes and is changed by political activity.

Simply accepting the laws of any science at face value is therefore unwise. What we need to do instead is understand the paradigm, the set of unquestioned assumptions, that underlie those scientific laws. This applies to managing and organising too and it is to this task that we now turn.

3.3 The unquestioned assumptions underlying the conventional wisdom on strategic management

In Chapter 2, we saw that today's conventional wisdom on strategic management is built on one or all of these propositions:

- Organisations will succeed if they install the key behavioural attributes shown by research into successful organisations to be the causes of excellence.

- Organisations will succeed if they formulate and select long-term plans using given analytical criteria, then implement those plans and monitor development against them.
- Organisations will succeed if they select the appropriate configuration, that is a complex combination of structure, strategy, environmental and other factors that all fit together.

To see what unquestioned assumptions these propositions make, take the first of the analytical criteria for selecting long-term plans, namely the one that requires strategies to yield acceptable financial performance.

1 Rational strategy selection criteria: financial acceptability

In Chapter 2 we saw that financial performance is measured in a number of ways: flows of cash; levels of profit; rates of growth in profit; profit as a rate of return on assets employed; relationships between liquid and illiquid forms of assets; relationships between shareholder and borrowed forms of funds. In order to determine whether any of these measures is acceptable or not, we have to find some benchmark against which to compare them. The most important financial benchmarks are derived from the operation of the capital markets and from comparisons with other companies operating in similar markets. There are a number of techniques available for using performance measures and benchmarks to analyse performance: for example, gap analysis and discounted cash flow investment appraisal. The argument is that measures of performance and the benchmarks with which to compare them can be applied to evaluating past performance and to selecting future sequences of actions that will lead to success. What unquestioned assumptions is this argument based on?

Evaluating past financial performance

The evaluation of past financial performance to reach judgements about its acceptability or otherwise is important, first, as a trigger to corrective action. Managers spend substantial parts of their working day reviewing past performance in order to identify where action needs to be taken to keep to acceptable levels. Secondly, evaluating the past in this way is important because it is one step in learning from past experience. By measuring, analysing and explaining past performance, managers identify lessons about both success and failure that will be relevant to what they do next. Thirdly, such evaluations play an important part in determining the monetary and promotion rewards of managers.

However, if managers are to use measures of performance and benchmarks to fulfil these functions, then they have to collect information within some conceptual framework and store it within that framework. This means that current financial information will have been collected and stored in ways that were fixed by past modes of thinking and it will be difficult to retrieve the information in a form suitable for another mode of thinking.

For example, a parcels express delivery company may collect information on the deliveries it makes according to how long it takes to make the deliveries: the categories for collecting and storing information on sales may, then, be 'next day delivery' and 'later than next day delivery'. When reviewing past experience a key question may emerge in relation to the weight of the parcels delivered. It may be discovered that profitability is related more to weight than to speed of delivery because costs increase more with weight than with delivery speed. However, current information will not have been collected with that question in mind and it may be very difficult to retrieve it from the delivery data, even with flexible software and very powerful computers. Indeed it may not be possible at all, simply because managers may not have recorded information on weight. At the time they set up their information system, they might not have thought that weight was an important variable to measure.

What this example makes clear is that in order to ensure that information will always be retrievable in the form required at future dates, it is necessary to know in advance all the questions that will require answers in the future. You would have to be able to forecast, even if all you wanted to do was to be sure of always having adequate data to review the past.

Another example of this kind of difficulty relates to the use of discounted cash flow analysis (see the section on financial performance and acceptability in Chapter 2). Many large companies nowadays prepare this analysis before they proceed with a large investment project but, once that investment is generating cash, the actual cash flows are measured in terms of the normal accounting framework. The data is collected, communicated and reviewed on a business-by-business basis according to the formal organisational structure, rather than on a project-by-project basis. Managers therefore find it very difficult to see if any investment is actually yielding the cash flows shown in the discounted cash flow analysis used to make the decision in the first place. The performance of the project is not monitored against the performance that was promised. To do this would require a special exercise and this faces the difficulties of identifying which parts of a total integrated business cash flow can be accurately identified with a particular project. This could only be done if the development of the business without the project could be forecast and compared with the development of the business with the project; the difference would then be the actual cost or benefit of the investment project for comparison with the original discounted cash flow analysis.

Evaluating future financial performance

When we try to use measures of performance, benchmarks, and associated analytical techniques to select acceptable strategies for the future, we face much the same problem of forecasting. Using financial measures in a future-oriented way requires forecasts of what will happen to an organisation's cash flows and profit levels over long periods into the future. While everyone recognises the great difficulty of doing this, most continue to believe that it is possible to forecast accurately enough to justify using the criterion of financial acceptability. Under what conditions will this belief be justified?

It is possible to predict the performance outcome of a sequence of actions if, and only if, there are clear-cut connections between causes and effects. Only when this is true can we say that, in principle at least, if we pursue action A in circumstance B then it will lead to performance C. We may still have great difficulty in forecasting because we may not be sure whether circumstance B will actually occur or not and we may not accurately know the quantitative relationship between A and C. But we will be able to make some kind of forecast with some probability of success. However, if a sequence of actions is being generated by a system in which the relationships between cause and effect are lost in the minute detail of what happens, then it becomes impossible in principle even to predict, let alone to forecast, specific outcomes. We will not be able to predict if the outcome depends upon chance and in Chapter 7 we shall see that it might well do so. *Key Concept 3.2* explains the relationship between a prediction and a forecast.

■ Key concept 3.2
PREDICTING AND FORECASTING

A prediction is a conditional statement of the following type: if the UK economy grows at 5 per cent next year and the rate of inflation falls to 4 per cent then the profits of the corporate sector will grow by 25 per cent. In order to be able to make such a statement with any degree of confidence we must construct a model of the corporate sector of the UK which contains relationships between economic growth, inflation and profit levels. In other words, there have to be laws governing this system and those laws must be such that if growth is approximately 5 per cent and inflation is approximately 4 per cent then profits will be approximately 25 per cent.

In principle, if we are to be able to predict we must have laws that establish clear-cut connections between causes and effects and these connections must not require perfectly exact measurements, since perfect measurement is impossible to achieve. In other words, the laws must not be such that outcomes depend upon chance amplifications of tiny differences in causes.

The conditions for reliable forecasts are more onerous than this. All the conditions for predictability must be present but in addition we must be able to say that economic growth will be 5 per cent and inflation will be 4 per cent so that profits will be 25 per cent. In a forecast we are trying to say what will actually happen – the statement is no longer conditional. We then need models for the economy, as well as models for the corporate sector, to enable us to stipulate most likely outcomes for growth and inflation, from which we can derive most likely outcomes for profit.

It follows that when we put forward financial acceptability as one of the criteria for selecting future strategies we are making the unquestioned assumption that it is possible to forecast the future of an organisation to a reasonably useful degree. In other words, we are assuming that it is possible and sensible to make, at the very least, some assumptions about what the future of our organisation will look like. And to make this assumption about forecasting, we have to be assuming that we can, in principle, predict the future of an organisation even though it may be very difficult to do so in practice. Furthermore, to make this assumption about the possibility of prediction in principle, we also have to be assuming that there are clear-cut links between cause and effect (see *Key Concept 3.3* on the nature of causality). Since we are making a specific assumption about the links between cause and effect, we are therefore also making assumptions about the nature of the system that is generating the behaviour we are talking about. We have to be assuming that the system is one that tends to some form of equilibrium, either stable or unstable (see *Key Concept 3.4* for a description of equilibrium). In other words we are making particular assumptions about the system dynamics of an organisation (see *Key Concept 3.5* for a definition of dynamics).

The unquestioned assumptions

To summarise then, the prescription to select a strategy well in advance of acting that satisfies the criterion of acceptable financial performance makes the following unquestioned assumptions:

- Organisations are systems that are driven by laws producing predictable long-term futures. Although it is difficult to identify what those laws are, and it is also difficult to use them to make accurate forecasts, it is nevertheless possible to do so in principle. Progress therefore lies in gathering data and researching the laws and the techniques of forecasting.
- Those laws establish clear-cut links between a cause and an effect, between an action and its outcome.
- Organisations are successful when they are close to a state of stable equilibrium.
- The dynamics of successful organisations are therefore those of stability, regularity and predictability where any tensions or contradictions have been resolved.

In other words, in order to believe that we can use the techniques on financial acceptability in a future-oriented manner, or even with very high levels of reliability in a past-oriented manner, we have to be making some rather specific assumptions about the dynamics of organisations. And as we will see in later chapters, it may be quite realistic to make completely the opposite assumptions, in which case we will build diametrically opposed explanations of the successful strategic management process. In the meantime, let us look at the other criteria that the conventional wisdom puts forward for selecting strategies.

■ Key concept 3.3
THE NATURE OF CAUSALITY

The dominant way of thinking about the relationship between cause and effect in Western culture is what we might call linear *and* unidirectional. *We observe some variable Y whose behaviour we wish to explain. We immediately regard it as dependent and look for other 'independent' variables, X_1, X_2, ..., that are causing it. We usually reason that more of a cause will lead to proportionally more of the effect.*

In Chapter 2 we looked at ways of explaining organisational success. The usual way is to say that success is caused by a particular culture, a particular management style, a particular control system. The more we apply that culture, style, or control system the more successful we will be. We say that the demand for our product depends upon the behaviour of our customers. Opposition parties always say that the government of the day has caused the recession and the inflation. More of the government's policies will, they say, lead to more recession and more inflation. All of this is what is meant by straightforward unidirectional, linear connections between cause and effect.

Scientists, both social and natural, are increasingly realising that this view of the relationship between cause and effect is far too simple and leads to inadequate understanding of a system's behaviour. Greater insight comes from thinking in terms of the mutual or circular causality we find in feedback loops. The demand for a product does not depend simply on customer behaviour; it also depends upon what the producing firm does in terms of price and quality: the firm affects the customer who then affects the firm. Management style may cause success but success affects the style managers adopt. The government's policies may cause recession and inflation, but recession and inflation may also cause the policies they adopt.

When we think of organisms and organisations as systems then we become aware of more complex forms of causality to do with interconnection and interdependence, *where everything affects everything else.*

In addition to the circular causality and interdependence of feedback systems, there is also nonlinearity. This means that one variable can have a more than proportional effect upon another. Nonlinear feedback systems then involve very complex connections between cause and effect, a matter we will discuss in some detail in Chapter 7. It may become unclear what cause and effect mean. The links between them may become distant in time and space and those links may even disappear for all practical purposes. If in these circumstances we proceed as if simple linear links exist even if we do not know what they are, then we are likely to undertake actions that yield unintended and surprising results.

Most managers today think in terms of linear, unidirectional causality; and mainstream strategic management prescriptions are based on this kind of thinking too.

■ Key concept 3.4
EQUILIBRIUM

Equilibrium is a possible state of behaviour for a system. It takes a stable form when the behaviour of a system regularly repeats its past and when it is very difficult to change that behaviour to some other state. It requires significant change to shift a system from a state of stable equilibrium. For example, in economic theory markets are assumed always to tend to a state of stable equilibrium. If there is an increase in demand, then prices will rise to encourage an increase in supply to match the demand. If demand then stays constant, so will price and supply. Any chance movement of the price away from its equilibrium level will set in train changes in demand and supply that will rapidly pull price back to its equilibrium level. It will take a noticeable change in demand or supply to alter this behaviour.

Equilibrium can take an unstable form. Here the system will produce behaviour that diverges rapidly from its past state, but in a perfectly regular way. For example, a population may grow at a constant compound rate of growth, say doubling every five years. This is perfectly regular behaviour but it is explosively unstable because it cannot be sustained – sooner or later, the population will run into food constraints and collapse.

Dynamic equilibrium is a state in which a system continuously adapts to alterations in a continually changing environment.

The key point about all forms of equilibrium behaviour is that they are regular, orderly and predictable. Most theories of management and organisation have been developed within an equilibrium framework. Of course, to be regular, orderly and predictable, the links between cause and effect have to be clear cut. In equilibrium there are clear-cut links between cause and effect and consequently behaviour is predictable.

However, scientists are now explaining the functioning of nature in terms of behaviour that is far from equilibrium, a matter we will come to in Chapter 7. We can therefore no longer accept without question explanations that are based on unquestioned assumptions of equilibrium behaviour. Later chapters will explain far-from-equilibrium behaviour and what it might mean for explanations of strategic management.

■ Key concept 3.5
DYNAMICS

Dynamics is the study of how a system changes over time: classical dynamics establishes laws of motion through time for physical bodies; thermodynamics establishes laws of heat dissipation over time; population dynamics establishes the patterns of change in populations over time; economic dynamics attempts to establish and explain patterns of economic development over time; psychodynamics tries to explain the human behaviour patterns over time that are generated by contradiction and tension, for example by the need to be part of a group and yet be a free individual, by the feeling of love and hate for the same person, and so on. Dynamics is concerned with the effects of tension on a system, with the manner in which contradictions cause tension and so create the energy that drives behaviour.

Dynamics, as we saw in Chapter 1, may be contrasted with statics, the study of states of rest of phenomena, of patterns and positions at a point in time, of snapshots at a point in time.

Dynamics can also be contrasted with comparative statics, the study of change by comparing two snapshots taken at different points in time.

Dynamics is concerned with the path from one state to another, to the next and so on, generated by feedback processes. Amongst the more important questions raised by dynamics are those relating to whether the system being studied is moving from one stable equilibrium state to another, whether the movement is stable and orderly, and whether the movement is predictable. The dynamics is generated by the manner in which a particular system feeds back the information on the outcome of one action to at least partly cause the next one. Dynamics therefore involves the circular causality that flows from feedback systems, matters to be dealt with in Chapters 6 and 7.

Organisational and managerial dynamics will be concerned with how organisations and managerial actions change over time and with the feedback processes that lead to such changes. The study of dynamics is a difficult matter and therefore most of the literature on managing and organising can probably be classified as statics or comparative statics.

2 Rational strategy selection criteria: political acceptability

Consider next the unquestioned assumptions we make when we say that we can use the criterion of political acceptability to select long-term plans. To do so we must be able to predict how political acceptability will change in the future. In order to be reasonably confident that a proposed strategy will be acceptable to the most powerful groupings relevant to that strategy at a particular future time, we would have to be able to predict the steps in a highly dynamic political game. We would have to be able to predict how the preferences of powerful organisational actors are going to change as they interact with each other over the future. If that political game is such that small unnoticeable consequences could set off massive counter-responses, then it will be impossible to decide in advance whether a strategy is going to turn out to be politically acceptable or not. The usefulness of this as a criterion for the prior selection of strategy therefore depends upon the possibility of prediction. The discussion above indicated how the possibility of prediction depends upon the nature of the links between cause and effect and hence on the nature of the organisational dynamic. The criterion of political acceptability can be applied only to equilibrium systems.

3 Rational strategy selection criteria: feasibility

The possibility of using feasibility criteria as prescribed rests on the same assumptions as do the prescriptions on political and financial acceptability. We can select strategies, in advance of acting, on the basis of feasibility, only if we are able to predict the specific future consequences of those strategies. Once again the prescription to analyse feasibility as a strategy selection criterion is built on assumptions about the nature of cause and effect and therefore of the organisational dynamic – it can apply only to equilibrium systems.

4 Rational strategy selection criteria: suitability or fit

Strategies are judged to be suitable if they bring about consistent relationships that produce stability and regularity over time, harmony within the organisation, and continuing adaptation of the organisation to its environment. From this definition it is quite easy to see what unquestioned assumptions are being made about successful organisational dynamics: success is seen to flow from the achievement of continuing stable equilibrium adaptation to the environment. Another way of expressing this requirement for fit is the notion of contingency (see *Key Concept 2.6* in Chapter 2).

Contingency

You will recall that contingency theories make particular assumptions about the nature of cause and effect and therefore about the dynamics of organisations. Success is assumed to be a state of equilibrium in which future time paths are predictable.

Contingency, the idea that an organisation must fit its environment if it is to succeed, implicitly makes the following assumptions:

1 The choice of structures and strategies is not an essentially political one. Thus, it

is assumed that, if all the contingency factors are the same, two organisations will not make different structure and strategy choices. In fact we find that they do because of different compromises and bargains between people within and outside the organisation. It is quite possible that two organisations making completely different choices will both be successful. *Illustration 3.2* gives an example of this. While contingency theory allows a choice, it seems to imply at least a very limited range of choice within a given set of circumstances if the organisation is to succeed. The choice seems to be between making the right decision in those circumstances or the wrong one. In practice the range of choices seems to be much wider than this.

2 The environment an organisation reacts to is a given set of facts. In fact we find that the environment may be an interpretation made by managers in the organisation. Managers in two different organisations could interpret the same environment differently and so act differently and yet both could succeed.

3 Cause and effect are linked in a straightforward manner (see *Key Concept 3.3*). In fact, an organisation is a system that is part of an even larger environmental system consisting of other organisations and, because they all interact with each other, causation is circular. What managers in one organisation do affects other organisations and so the managers in these other organisations react, leading to a response from managers in the first and so on. This circular causation means that managers are taking part in creating their own environment and this kind of creativity leads to considerable ambiguity when we come to the concept of adapting to the environment. If managers create and invent their own environments, then what is causing what and who is adapting to whom? The contingency idea of organisations adapting to their environment seems too simple from this point of view.

■ Illustration 3.2
LITTON INDUSTRIES AND TEXAS INSTRUMENTS

Both Litton Industries and Texas Instruments were small entrepreneurial companies in the 1950s. By 1983 Litton Industries had a sales level of $4.7 billion generated by operations in the electronics industry. Texas Instruments had a sales level of $4.6 billion also generated by operations in the electronics industry. These two companies did not operate in exactly the same segments of the industry. Texas produced silicon chips and sold consumer electronics, while Litton did neither of these. Litton concentrated relatively more than Texas on control systems and defence equipment. But they were corporations of the same size operating in broadly the same markets, markets sharing the same general characteristics in terms of degrees of uncertainty and type of competitive advantage. Contingency theory would therefore lead one to expect two approximately similar companies in terms of strategies pursued, organisational structures and control systems. In fact these two companies were very different from each other in 1983.

Litton Industries had loose structures, developed its strategies in a rather informal way, and pursued opportunistic strategies of acquisition, focusing on niche markets. It had an aggressive entrepreneurial culture. Texas on the other hand had rather rigid structures, pursued cost leadership and market domination strategies, and had tight formal control systems. Strategy processes were based on formal planning and analysis.

In the period since 1983 these two companies have pursued very different paths. Miller (1990) describes how Litton has followed a strategy of acquisition that made it an unstable, unwieldy conglomerate of unrelated companies. It spent the late 1980s cutting back to core businesses. Miller also describes how Texas pursued a strategy of paying more and more attention to detail and getting further and further away from what customers wanted. In the late 1980s Texas replaced its authoritarian leaders and encouraged broader participation in decision-making. It reduced its reliance on the silicon chip market and concentrated on more lucrative segments. It introduced systems to secure flexibility and keep closer to its customers.

Contingency factors would suggest that Litton and Texas should look similar and develop along similar time paths. In fact they only looked similar at the start of their lives and have pursued very different time paths ever since. This suggests that the idea of contingency has little dynamic content. A dynamic explanation should indicate how two systems in much the same environment can develop in totally different ways.

Source: Quinn (1985b)

Porter and clear choices of generic strategy

Another concept central to the idea of securing adaptive fit with the environment is that of Porter's industry structure analysis. You will recall from the discussion of this form of analysis in Chapter 2 that it is one of the most popular analytical methods for identifying whether a strategy is likely to fit the environment. The technique is to identify the characteristics of the five competitive forces that are said to determine the competitive structure of a market – threat of entry, threat of substitutes, buyer power, supplier power, and competitor rivalry. The balance of these forces determines the relative power of the players in the market and the nature of that power. So one constellation of forces determines that the lowest-cost producer wields the greatest power, and another combination of forces means that it is the differentiated player, for example the highest-quality firm, that will exercise the greatest power. This is clearly a contingency theory and makes all the assumptions that such theories do.

The industry structure analysis is based on the assumption that there are clear-cut links between cause and effect and that markets tend to a state of stable equilibrium determined by the five forces. To be useful in actually selecting strategies for the future it would also be necessary to forecast the future structure of a market. The Porter analysis makes exactly the same assumptions as the other criteria required for selecting sound strategies. In addition the Porter analysis makes another assumption clear. The advice is that firms must make a clear choice between low cost, widespread differentiation, or focus strategies. Porter explicitly advises against 'getting stuck in the middle'. What this amounts to is an assumption that success comes when managers solve or resolve contradictions or paradoxes. Since higher quality costs more money to deliver, it is the opposite of low cost; they are contradictory forces that cannot be present at the same time, paradoxes between which managers must choose if they want to succeed. The assumption amounts to one that success follows from reducing or relieving the tensions that contradiction and paradox bring.

Some have criticised this assumption about paradox. Hendry (1990) has pointed out that there is no economic reason why a firm should not be a below-average-cost producer and yet achieve above-average quality that allows the charging of above-average prices. In fact, Japanese firms do not accept this approach to solving paradox, but sustain the paradox. Instead of choosing between low cost and high quality they demanded both and, when they turned their minds to finding out how to secure both, they came up with flexible manufacturing methods and Just-In-Time delivery and inventory control systems. Instead of simply accepting that quality costs more they sought ways of reducing costs while they spent more on quality. They found that they could reduce costs if they developed better relationships with suppliers such that supplies would be delivered more rapidly when they were required. Thus they cut down on inventory holding costs and the result was the concept of JIT. They also found that they could provide people with the variety of features they wanted on a product and still keep the costs low if they developed more automated ways of re-tooling and of controlling production – the concept of flexible production.

The Porter approach to dealing with paradox is widespread in today's Western conventional wisdom on strategic management. You will recall the Goold and Campbell analysis of styles of strategic management in the section on installing strategic management styles in the last chapter. Their analysis identified five important tensions that organisations are under, for example the tension between long-term and short-term objectives. They defined the style of strategic management in terms of the manner in which managers resolve or relieve the tension. They described managers as making 'either/or' choices: either they choose long-term objectives or they choose short-term objectives. This analysis of styles is also couched in terms of equilibrium and in terms of adaptation to a particular environment. It too is a contingency theory.

Another much-discussed example of how Western managers deal with paradox is provided by the prescription for loose/tight controls (see the section on installing the attributes of excellence in Chapter 2). The orderly conduct of the day-to-day activities of an organisation requires tight controls – setting quantitative targets and monitoring performance against them. Innovation, however, requires that people feel empowered to conduct many experiments that fall outside the normal activities of the organisation and, for this purpose, controls need to be loose. The conventional advice is not to sustain this paradox but to resolve it by persuading all to share the same belief system. Although people are free and empowered, they are nevertheless controlled by beliefs that they may not question in any fundamental way. The loose control is loose largely in appearance.

Those making these prescriptions also advise that hierarchies and bureaucracies be replaced by new flat, flexible organisational structures. Here too there is no thought of operating in two different modes at the same time – the bureaucratic and the flexible – but a resolution of the paradox by removing the bureaucracy (Peters, 1988).

The conventional assumptions about the nature of, and responses to, paradox have had a major impact on the kinds of prescriptions that make up the conventional wisdom. It will assist in later discussions therefore if we clarify what a paradox is and how we normally deal with it.

3.4 Paradox and how we normally deal with it

There are a number of different definitions of a paradox. First, it may mean an apparent contradiction, a state in which two apparently conflicting elements appear to be operating at the same time. Paradox in this sense can be removed or resolved: by choosing one element above the other all the time; or by choosing one element at one time and another element at another time; or by reframing the problem to remove the apparent contradiction. This is the way in which the conventional wisdom that we have been surveying defines and deals with paradoxes and the tensions they cause. But there is another definition of paradox.

A paradoxical state may be one in which two diametrically opposing forces are simultaneously present, neither of which can ever be removed. The choice is not therefore between one or the other, both must be accommodated, and this can be done only by continually rearranging them (Quinn & Campbell, 1988).

To see what paradox means return to *Figure 3.1*. You can look at that figure in a manner which involves switching your focus: one second you see the container and the next you see the people. Alternatively you could sustain both perceptions at the same time. This is somewhat harder to do, but if you succeed then you will tell a more complex tale of containers and people. Instead of your story being about *either* containers *or* people, it will be a more sophisticated tale about *both* containers *and* people. If you can sustain contradictory notions you will be capable of working with sophisticated both/and perceptions as opposed to simple either/or ones (Weick, 1969/79).

When it comes to a world that is much more complex than *Figure 3.1*, the world of organisational strategy, it becomes much more difficult to switch focus from one paradigm to another and even more difficult to see your world in two different ways at once. But if you succeed in this, then you will develop a much more complex understanding and practice of strategy: one that is not the simple either/or choice between stability and instability that the dominant paradigm leads to; one that is instead a sophisticated both/and choice combining stability and instability in appropriate and creative ways.

This is a matter of major importance for Western managers. Western culture, Western scientific traditions and forms of education have strongly encouraged the either/or way of thinking. The major competitors in the Far East, however, are far more accustomed to both/and thinking, to paradoxes and dilemmas (Pascale, 1990; Hampden-Turner, 1990). If Western managers are to compete they will have to learn to see the world of organisations in this more sophisticated both/and way.

■ **Key concept 3.6**
PARADOX

As it is used in this book, the word paradox means the presence together at the same time of self-contradictory, essentially conflicting forces, none of which can be removed. The word is not used in the sense of a dilemma, that being a situation where a choice must be made between two equally undesirable possibilities. Dilemmas are solved by making an either/or choices. Paradoxes are resolved or orchestrated by making both/and choices. A state of contention is thus the consequence of a paradox in a human system. Contention is positively expressed as dialogue around the paradoxical forces and negatively expressed as unresolvable conflict. Paradoxes are mutually exclusive and simultaneously present, for example the requirement that control systems should be loose–tight. Neither side can win and the result is creative tension. Creative people wrestle with the irreconcilable until they discover a new frame of reference and only then is the creative tension released. Pascale (1990, p. 110) puts it thus:

> Paradox has had a pervasive role in creative activities of all types. One pioneering investigation into the essence of creativity studied the milestone contributions of fifty eight famous scientists and artists, including Einstein, Picasso, and Mozart. They shared a common pattern: *all* breakthroughs occurred 'when two or more opposites were conceived simultaneously, existing side by side – as equally valid, operative and true.' The research report continues: 'In apparent defiance of logic or physical possibility, the creative person consciously embraced antithetical elements and developed these into integrated entities and creations.' (Rothenburg, 1979)

A paradox forces people to think outside the current paradigm, to transcend the contradiction and see things in a new way (Rothenburg, 1979).

Organisations are paradoxical

Any human organisation is quite clearly paradoxical for the following reasons.

In even the simplest human system we find it necessary for efficiency reasons to divide up the tasks that need to be done. We develop specialisations. But as soon as we do that we create the problem of integrating the divided tasks back into a whole again; we create the problem of control. There is no choice between *either* task division *or* task integration. We have to choose *both* task division *and* task integration if we are to succeed. Paradoxes require both/and choices; either/or choices are not possible.

Each individual in an organisation has a paradoxical desire for freedom and the excitement that goes with chance and uncertainty, while at the same time fearing the unknown and wanting order and discipline. This is the paradoxical human need to fuse into a group and yet remain an individual. There are many other examples of such paradoxes. Businesses have to produce at the lowest cost, but they have to increase costs to provide quality. Organisations have to control what their employees do, but they have to give them freedom if they want to retain them and if they want them to deal with rapidly changing circumstances. All of these examples require both/and rather than either/or choices.

Today's conventional wisdom emphasises either/or choices. It prescribes either stability and success, or instability and failure. It usually does not recognise paradox as fundamental and, when it does, it prescribes some kind of harmonious, equilibrium balance between the paradoxical forces. In this way the paradox is in effect removed; its existence is a nuisance that is not fundamental to success. We normally deal with paradox by seeking to remove it, to find the solution so as to reach equilibrium.

The way we perceive paradox says much about the way we understand organisational dynamics. The idea that paradoxes must be resolved, and the tension they cause must be released if we are to be successful, is part of the paradigm that equates success with the dynamics of stability, regularity and predictability. The notion that paradoxes can never be resolved, only endlessly rearranged, leads to a view of organisational dynamics couched in terms of continuing tension-generating behaviour patterns that are irregular, unstable and unpredictable.

3.5 The paradigm of the stable equilibrium organisation

As soon as we ask the question 'What are the criteria for choosing successful strategies?', we make an assumption that we do not usually make explicit because it seems so obvious. The assumption is that someone, or some small group of people, in the organisation intend the strategy and its outcome. It is being assumed that it is possible for a person, or a small powerful group, to intend the strategy of the organisation; that successful strategies do not simply emerge but have to be chosen (see *Key Concept 2.2* on organisational intention).

This assumption about organisational intention implies a particular view on the nature of organisational control. If someone is choosing the strategy, someone must be in control of the organisation. That someone is the top executive who should know where the organisation is headed and how it is going to get there. Such notions constitute a mental model in which it is unquestioningly assumed that someone can, and must, be *in control* of the organisation if it is to succeed, that its behaviour cannot be controlled without this. We are then excluding the possibility that there may be mechanisms that lead to controlled group behaviour despite the fact that no one is in control of the group.

As soon as we believe that someone at the top is in control, that that someone knows and intends the future direction of the organisation, it is an easy step to assume that there are frameworks of one kind or another that the top can install to cause the organisation to change in ways that those in control want.

These assumptions all flow from those about the nature of success. Success is seen as a state in which the organisation is adapted to its environments; successful organisations adapt more rapidly and more completely to their environments than their rivals do. Competition performs the task of natural selection. The force driving successful change, the dynamics, is therefore the need to achieve continuing dynamic equilibrium with the environment of a stable kind. Such stable equilibrium states are characterised by regular patterns of behaviour, by consistency in the manner in which the parts of the system are related to each other, by harmony.

The assumptions being made about the dynamics of organisations and the environments they operate in mean that there are straightforward relationships between cause and effect: small changes are not blown up out of all proportion and therefore the future time path of the system is, in principle, predictable, although in practice it may be difficult to forecast it. Because of this predictability, successful organisations make their adaptations before the change occurs or, when unforeseen, through gradual adaptation to them.

We can summarise all of this by calling it the paradigm of the stable equilibrium organisation (see *Key Concept 3.7*).

■ **Key concept 3.7**
THE STABLE EQUILIBRIUM ORGANISATION

While a system operates in a state of equilibrium it continues to follow exactly the same pattern of behaviour, until some external disturbance promotes a change. That pattern may be a very simple one of sticking to a constant value or it may be one of some kind of regular cycle. So the behaviour of a system in equilibrium may be one of change but that change will be regular and thus perfectly predictable.

A stable equilibrium organisation, therefore, is one where internal behaviour is harmonious, all the elements of the organisation and its strategies are consistent, and the organisation remains fully adapted to its environment. The stable equilibrium organisation follows a predictable course into the future, with no surprises. New developments are dictated by changes in the environment. This idea constitutes a management paradigm in which successful organisations are seen as those moving closer to a state of stable equilibrium, disturbed only by environmental changes that it was not possible to predict. Instability comes from outside and can be reduced by gathering and analysing more data and making more effective forecasts. This represents a particular view of dynamics.

Most of this chapter has been concerned with demonstrating how the prescriptions of the rational planning model of strategic management fall within a clear paradigm. This paradigm applies just as much, however, to the visionary/ideological model of strategic management and to notions of configuration. For example, a manager can have a vision of a future state and then undertake trial actions to realise it, only if there are clear-cut connections between a cause and an effect, an action and an outcome. This can only be true of systems operating close to equilibrium. Also, the visionary/ideological model lays great stress on shared cultures or belief systems; that is, it prescribes internal harmony and consistency, another clear sign of stable equilibrium thinking. Although the visionary/ideological model recognises greater levels of uncertainty and greater complexity in human behaviour than the planning model does, it still does so within the same overall paradigm. The same point applies to approaches based on the idea of configuration; there, too, success is equated with the harmonious fitting together of a puzzle, to ideas of adaptation and fit. Configuration is all about success following when structures, strategies, systems and other aspects of an organisation all fit together and match the environment; the conceptual foundations here have to do with consistency, adaptation, harmony and predictability, and these are all clearly aspects of the stable equilibrium paradigm.

We have then a conventional wisdom consisting of different, conflicting sets of prescriptions but, when we examine the conceptual foundations upon which all of them are built, we find that they are all built on the same foundation. They all assume success to be a state of stable equilibrium; they all assume that there are, in principle, straightforward links between cause and effect even though those links may be difficult to identify. If we find that successful organisations have to operate in states where cause-and-effect links disappear, then the conventional wisdom will have to be seen as a limited special case applicable in very restricted circumstances only. We would not then be surprised that this conventional wisdom provides inadequate guidance for strategic management.

3.6   Summary

In this chapter we have identified the assumptions that underlie today's dominant explanations of, and prescriptions for, successful strategic management. In doing so, we have been attending to the key questions identified in Chapter 1. All the strategic management prescriptions explored in Chapter 2 deal with the key questions in the following way:

- Organisational success is assumed to follow when an organisation strives for and gets close to a state of stable equilibrium. In this state the dynamics, or patterns of behaviour over time are characterised by predictability, regularity, consistency and harmony.
- In the circular feedback process that generates this stable dynamic, discovery is defined as a process of formally scanning the environment or of listening to the customers, that is gathering the observable facts. Choice is then either a matter of analysing the facts to generate the options available for achieving the objectives and then choosing the best option, or a matter of selecting trial-and-error experiments that are consistent with a shared ideology and are aimed at realising a vision or selecting a configuration. Action is then either the implementation of the selected option to achieve the objective, or carrying out the trials to reach the vision.
- The ambiguity and uncertainty that inevitably accompanies the strategic is to be dealt with by gathering more facts and carrying out more analysis on the one hand, or it is to be dealt with by abandoning long-term plans and using political processes to identify issues, and trial and error to discover how to realise a vision. Uncertainty and ambiguity makes strategic management more difficult on this view, but both models of strategic management still assume that success flows from organisational intention.
- In the analytical planning approach to strategy, little attention is paid to the way in which managers make sense of the world and the manner in which their shared beliefs affect what they do. This is because in this approach success is assumed to flow from analysing observable facts, and matters of culture and ideology are seen as facts to be analysed in preparing acceptable strategies and as obstacles to be overcome in implementing those strategies. In the visionary/ideological approach to success, a single shared ideology is assumed to drive successful action.
- In all of today's dominant approaches to successful strategy, it is organisational intention that drives the strategy. In other words, the strategy that an organisation follows is assumed to result from the shared intention on the part of the top management team, at least, to achieve a range of objectives or visions.

- In the technically rational planning approach the behaviour of people in groups is not seen to be an important determinant of successful strategy. Such behaviour is a fact to be analysed and an obstacle to be removed. In the visionary/ideological approach more attention is paid to the matter of group dynamics, but it is assumed that success follows when people interact in groups in a stable harmonious manner.
- In the rational planning approach, the formal organisation is the instrument managers use to formulate and implement strategies, while the informal organisation is a fact to analyse and an obstacle to remove. The visionary/ideological approach lays great stress on the role of the informal organisation in the making of strategies, but it assumes that the informal organisation is effective when it produces harmony and rapidly resolves conflict.
- In both approaches, where organisational paradoxes are recognised, it is assumed that success follows when the paradox is resolved in some way, when the tension it creates is relieved.

The way in which these questions are dealt with is a consequence of the paradigm that most subscribe to about organisational success, namely that of the stable equilibrium organisation. The key unquestioned assumptions here are that organisations are systems in which there are clear-cut connections between cause and effect and as a result it is possible in principle to predict long-term outcomes.

In the next chapter we turn to the anomalies that should lead us to question the whole stable equilibrium paradigm and therefore all of today's dominant explanations and prescriptions for successful strategic management.

Further reading

It is well worth reading Kuhn (1970), the classic work on paradigms and scientific revolutions. Hampden-Turner (1990) provides an interesting account of how organisations deal with paradoxes and Quinn & Campbell (1988) explore the theoretical issues. Hurst (1986) provides the practitioner's viewpoint on the inadequacy of the conventional wisdom. Stacey (1991) gives a more detailed account of the assumptions underlying the conventional wisdom.

4

Why today's dominant management paradigm must be questioned

Simplistic assumptions about organisational dynamics

4.1   Introduction

In the last chapter we saw how every science is conducted within a common paradigm, a shared set of unquestioned assumptions that governs what tasks scientists carry out and how they do them. We identified that the study and practice of strategic management is also conducted within a paradigm, mostly within a dominant one that we may call the paradigm of the stable equilibrium organisation. We saw that the unquestioned assumptions of this paradigm have to do with the dynamics of organisations; clear-cut links between cause and effect are assumed to generate behaviour that is predictable in principle and that keeps an organisation in a state of dynamic equilibrium in which it is adapted to its environment. It follows that the behaviour patterns of successful organisations are assumed to be patterns of order, regularity and consensus around a stable belief system.

In the last chapter we also saw that, as scientists carry out their tasks, they uncover anomalies that eventually lead them to question the paradigm and replace it. This process of uncovering anomalies that undermine the dominant paradigm has also been occurring in the field of strategic management.

This chapter will examine those anomalies and show how they are providing the basis for a new paradigm, that of the far-from-equilibrium organisation. This new paradigm is different because of the way it sees the dynamics of organisations. Instead of regularity and consistency it sees irregularity, contradiction and creative tension as the essence of the successful organisation. Success on this view focuses on changing the belief systems that govern how organisations operate. When an organisation faces a rapidly changing environment it faces the paradox of needing consistency and stability in order to conduct its existing business in an efficient day-to-day manner, and also needing to shatter that consistency and stability in order to generate creative new moves. In this chapter we will be reviewing studies showing that successful strategic management is a creative, innovative process that requires exposure to and management of contradiction.

We will also be reviewing studies that question the idea of success as a state in which the organisation fits or is adapted to its environment. Instead, success is seen to flow from innovatively using resources to create the environment.

A framework that relates success to far-from-equilibrium conditions of contention, that relates success to creative interaction with the environment, soon leads to the idea that innovative strategies cannot be selected in advance by any criteria, that innovative strategies cannot flow from prior, central, organisation-wide intention. This framework leads to an understanding of innovative strategies as emerging from a complex organisational learning process in real time.

4.2 Successful organisations create as well as adapt to their environment: Hamel and Prahalad's analysis

Hamel and Prahalad (1989) have studied a number of global companies in America, Europe and Japan. They suggest that what distinguishes the noticeably successful (Honda, Komatsu and Canon, for example) from the noticeably less so (General Motors, Caterpillar and Xerox, for example) is the different mental models of strategy guiding their respective actions. This research questions one of the basic tenets of the conventional wisdom, namely the notion that successful organisations are those that fit, or adapt to, their environments.

Hamel and Prahalad found that the less-successful companies follow the conventional prescriptions and so seek to maintain strategic fit. This leads them to trim their ambitions to those that can be met with available resources. Such companies are concerned mainly with product-market units rather than core competences, they preserve consistency through requiring conformity in behaviour, and they focus on achieving financial objectives. These companies attempt to achieve their financial objectives by using generic strategies, selected according to criteria of strategic fit, in order to secure sustainable competitive advantage. Hamel and Prahalad report that this approach leads to repetition and imitation.

On the other hand, Hamel and Prahalad found that successful companies focus on leveraging resources, that is using what they have in new and innovative ways to reach seemingly unattainable goals. The main concern of these companies is to use their resources in challenging and stretching ways to build up a number of core competences. Consistency is maintained by all sharing a central strategic intent and the route to this successful state is accelerated organisational learning, recognising that no competitive advantages are inherently sustainable. Here, managers are not simply matching their resources to the requirements of the environment, leaving to others those requirements their resources are incapable of delivering. Instead, managers creatively use the resources they have, they create requirements of the environment which they can then meet, they push to achieve stretching goals, and so they continually renew and transform their organisation.

While these authors question one central assumption of the stable equilibrium model of organisational success, they preserve the other central assumptions. In particular, they continue to see organisational success as flowing from clear, prior organisation-wide intention. They stress what they call strategic intent, a challenging shared vision of a future leadership position for the company. This strategic intent is stable over time. It is clear as to outcome but flexible as to the means of achieving the outcome. It is an obsession with winning and winning on a global scale cannot be secured either through long-term plans or through some undirected process of intrapreneurship or autonomous small task forces. Instead success is secured by discovering how to achieve a broad, stretching, challenging intention to build core competences.

This study questions the idea of adapting to the environment, proposing instead creative interaction. But in other respects – intention, harmony and consistency – it falls within the stable equilibrium paradigm. We turn now to other studies that move further away from this paradigm.

4.3 Success flows from contradiction as well as consistency: the analyses of Miller and Pascale

As our discussion in Chapter 2 moved from 'one best way' criteria for successfully choosing strategies, through criteria based on contingency approaches, to those based on the idea of configuration, we have always made the unquestioned assumption that success requires harmony, consistency, stability and regularity. At its most sophisticated these assumptions have led us to view success as the consequence of establishing a suitable configuration. Closer examination, however, points to all manner of anomalies, neatly summarised by one of the leading developers of the configuration idea, Mintzberg (1989, p. 97):

> Many organizations seem to fit naturally into one of these categories, more or less. We all know the small aggressive entrepreneurial firm, the perfectly machine-like Swiss hotel, the diversified conglomerate, the professional collegial university, the freewheeling intrapreneurial Silicon Valley innovator. But some organizations do not fit, ... and even many that seem to, on closer examination reveal curious anomalies. It is difficult to imagine a more machine-like organization than McDonald's; why then does it seem to be rather innovative, at least in its own context? And why is it that whenever I mention to an executive group about a 3M or a Hewlett Packard as innovative in form, someone from the audience leaps up to tell me about their tight control systems. Innovative adhocracies are not supposed to rely on tight controls.

It is the consideration of anomalies such as these, and research into how organisations seemingly belonging to clear configurations develop, that lead one to the idea that success may have a great deal to do not simply with harmony and consistency but also with contradiction and instability.

Mintzberg (1989), Miller (1990) and Pascale (1990) all make the point, backed by empirical research, that the harmony, consistency and fit achieved by a firm that reaches a viable configuration is at one and the same time its strength and its downfall. The tendency is for companies in this position to concentrate on doing better that which they already do well. Their strategies become ones of repetition and excess. Or, in another sense, they become over-adapted to their environment and, when that environment changes, they have great difficulty in changing.

Miller's analysis of the causes of failure

Miller (1990, p. 3) puts it like this. He has researched a number of companies to look for the reasons for failure and finds these in the Icarus paradox.

> The fabled Icarus of Greek mythology is said to have flown so high, so close to the sun, that his artificial wax wings melted and he plunged into the Aegean sea. The power of Icarus's wings gave rise to the abandon that doomed him. The paradox, of course, is that his greatest asset led to his demise. And that same paradox applies to many outstanding companies today: their victories and their strengths often seduce them into excesses that cause their downfall. Success leads to specialization and exaggeration, to confidence and complacency, to dogma and ritual.

Miller detects four trajectories, patterns in action, through which organisations extend and amplify the strategies, policies, attitudes and events that led to their success in the first place:

- The focusing trajectory that takes Craftsmen organisations (those with strong engineering and tight operational controls as their major sources of competitive advantage) and turns them into Tinkerers (insular firms whose technocratic culture alienates customers with perfect but irrelevant offerings). By focusing on their quality or cost leadership strategies, their engineering and operational strengths, these companies come to ignore their customers. Periods in the history of Digital, Disney, Caterpillar and Texas Instruments illustrate this path.
- The venturing trajectory converts entrepreneurial Builders (high-growth companies managed by imaginative leaders and creative planning staffs) into Imperialists (companies overtaxing their resources by expanding too rapidly into businesses they know little about). Examples here are provided by ITT, Litton Industries, Gulf and Western, Dome Petroleum.
- The inventing trajectories along which Pioneers (companies with excellent R&D departments, flexible think tank operations, and state of the art products) move to become Escapists (run by cults of scientists who squander resources in the pursuit of grandiose futuristic inventions). Examples here are Federal Express, Wang, Apple, Rolls Royce and Polaroid.
- The decoupling trajectory which transforms Salesmen (companies with developed marketing skills, broad markets and prominent brand names) into Drifters (companies whose sales fetish obscures design issues and who become aimless and bureaucratic producing me-too offerings). Examples here are Proctor and Gamble, General Motors and IBM.

Miller makes the point that outstanding organisations are characterised by consistency and harmony – the parts fit together and they constitute typical configurations called builders, craftsmen, pioneers and salesmen. Organisations keep extending the central theme of their configuration. They keep building upon, reinforcing and modifying what has made them successful. They do this because of the mental models with which they design their actions and because of the decision-making processes they use. The result is a momentum for the organisation that suppresses variations and pushes it down typical trajectories that lead to disaster. Momentum is the result of amplifying existing strengths and it leads to a vicious circle of excess. What Miller describes is an example of an amplifying feedback process, that is a self-reinforcing pattern of circular behaviour that can become either virtuous or vicious. These are important ideas that we will develop later in Chapter 7.

Pascale's analysis of the causes of success

Pascale (1990) reaches very similar conclusions to those of Miller and he takes the analysis further in a number of ways. He stresses the need to change today's predominant management paradigm. The existing paradigm with its emphasis on order and stability, Management by Objectives, planning and incremental changes simply focuses on doing better what companies already do well. The existing paradigm blocks alternatives. Pascale calls for a new paradigm that recognises the non-equilibrium nature of innovative organisations and the connection between tension and destruction on the one hand and creativity on the other.

According to Pascale, successful organisations are characterised by a paradox. On the one hand they have to achieve *fit*. By fit, Pascale means a state of coherence, centralisation, tight central control, synergy and fit between the 7Ss (see the section on configuration in Chapter 2) of the organisation. But successful organisations also require *split*. By split, Pascale means breaking apart, decentralising, differentiating, variety and rivalry. They require split because without it they cannot develop new perspectives and innovative actions. Developing new perspectives means shattering old paradigms and changing old structures – creativity requires destruction. The need for an organisation simultaneously to display fit and split creates tension. But this is creative tension that provokes inquiry and questioning. It is this tension that leads to the learning organisation with its continual dialogue between contradicting points of view. Pascale stresses the importance of dialogue as opposed to argument.

■ **Key concept 4.1**
DIALECTICS AND DIALOGUE

The word dialectic describes the process through which paradoxes are arranged, or orchestrated, to yield a transcending new configuration. It is a process characterised by constructive tension. For example, in an organisation it is necessary to concentrate power in order to operate efficiently. It is simultaneously necessary to distribute power in order to cope with high levels of uncertainty in a rapidly changing environment. Making an either/or choice will not do – it will sacrifice either efficiency or flexibility and we need both. An effective organisation may continually cope with the paradox through shifting patterns of power concentrated for some purposes at some times and dispersed for other purposes at other times. This would be a dialectic process. Note that this

> *resolution through a shifting pattern is not a solution; it throws up its own problems of continuing contention that need to be resolved, so that there is never a solution.*
>
> *Dialogue is where two parties exchange views about paradoxical situations, each having the intention of modifying their position in the light of the views and evidence presented by the other. Each participant is open to being influenced by the other. Argument is simply stating positions without any intention of moving. Dialogue is thus the required process for dialectics.*
>
> *Note the connection between the concepts of paradox, contention, creative tension, dialectics and dialogue.*

Tension leads to what Pascale calls *contend* (see *Illustration 4.1*), the positive use of tension and conflict to create and generate new perspectives. Through this clash of opposites the organisation *transcends* to a new constellation of fit and split. This view of organisational development is a dialectical one (see *Key Concept 4.1*) in which opposites produce, through learning, a new synthesis consisting of more complex forms of strategy and structure. Organisations use fit and split at the same time to produce sudden jumps to new positions and postures. Pascale stresses the need to orchestrate rather than balance, to preserve the tension rather than move to stable equilibrium. The choices facing an organisation are and/both, not either/or. It is necessary to avoid the extremes of split and fit because they lead to excess and failure. Instead organisations have to use both ends of the fit/split spectrum at once.

Another point made by Pascale is that organisations fail because they are not good at perceiving weak signals from the environment. The concern here is that many of the most important changes start off in a small, almost unnoticeable way. Those small changes can escalate to have major consequences for the organisation. So it becomes a matter of importance to pay attention to small changes and the weak signals they send, before the organisation is engulfed by major consequences (see Chapter 7).

■ **Illustration 4.1**
THE VECTORS OF CONTENTION

Pascale (1990) puts forward seven contentions (based on the 7S framework) that lead to the disequilibrium and creative tension that prompts inquiry. Inquiry and dialogue lead to the new. The seven contentions are:

- planned versus opportunistic strategy
- elitist versus pluralist structures
- mandatory versus discretionary systems
- managerial versus transformational style
- individuality versus collegiality in the treatment of staff
- hard minds versus soft hearts in terms of shared values
- maximise (making more efficient, earning more profit from doing the same thing better) versus 'meta-mise' (transforming the problem or opportunity into the creatively new).

A far-from-equilibrium paradigm

The views being put forward by Miller and Pascale contrast starkly with the discussion in Chapter 2 on the criteria for selecting strategies. The latter emphasise stability and harmony, while the former point to the importance of instability, contradiction and rivalry. The reader should also contrast the Miller and Pascale views with the way in which recognised organisational tensions are treated by other writers. For example in Chapter 2 in the section on installing strategic management styles, we saw that Goold and Campbell's styles of strategic management are also based on organisational tensions that are very similar to the ones enumerated by Pascale. But Goold and Campbell's successful organisations are ones that find an equilibrium balance between the tensions. On the Pascale view this leads to failure not success. Also note the difference between Pascale and the Hamel and Prahalad (1989) model discussed earlier: the latter relate success to intention, harmony and consistency, while the former relates success to contention and conflict that leads to emergent strategy.

The Miller and Pascale studies are built on assumptions that are dramatically and fundamentally different to those we identified in Chapter 3 to be the basis of today's conventional wisdom. The conventional wisdom is based on an unquestioned assumption that the criteria for success has to do with consistency, regularity and stability – the paradigm of the stable equilibrium organisation. What the studies in this section are suggesting is that we need to revise this view. They point to the conclusions that: continuing movement towards equilibrium is failure; success requires the maintenance of a position away from equilibrium; contradiction between stability and instability, between tight and flexible controls, between centralised and decentralised structures, are all essential to success. Success seems to have something to do with the ability of an organisation to sustain and manage contradiction and tension. And this ability seems to be closely tied to creativity, a point made some time ago by the economist Schumpeter (1934). He pointed out that progress was a process in which companies continually destroyed existing forms of competitive advantage to make way for new ones.

■ **Key concept 4.2**
THE FAR-FROM-EQUILIBRIUM ORGANISATION

While a system operates in a state far-from-equilibrium it never follows exactly the same pattern of behaviour. It follows complex patterns that are not regular and predictable. Instead, behaviour patterns exhibit features of stability and instability, but not in a predictable manner. A far-from-equilibrium organisation is thus characterised by contradiction and contention, not harmony and consistency. Because of this it generates new perspectives and new forms of behaviour. Such systems have the potential for innovation not possessed by equilibrium systems. They may experience sudden revolutionary changes of direction; they may suddenly move through a crisis to new forms of order.

What the Pascale and Miller studies represent is a new management paradigm, a different view on the nature of organisational dynamics. We are presented with a picture of patterns of change that are circular, that amplify small changes, that generate vicious and virtuous circles (see Chapter 7). This is in sharp contrast with patterns of change that are orderly, predictable movements towards stable equilibrium. This new view of the nature of organisational dynamics is also very much in evidence in the latest framework developed by Michael Porter. In Chapter 2 we discussed his industry structure and value chain analyses. In his latest book he has cast these ideas in a more dynamic framework that we now go on to discuss.

4.4 Success flows from being part of a self-reinforcing system as well as organisational intention: Porter's analysis of the competitive advantage of nations

Porter (1990) puts forward an explanation of how nations develop competitive advantage. Since competitive advantage is embedded in organisations and is the consequence of the strategies they pursue, his explanation is also an explanation of strategic change in a single organisation. This approach sees a particular company as part of a complex system consisting of other competing, supplying, supporting, customer and governmental organisations. The pattern of change any one company in this system displays depends upon a self-reinforcing interplay between what all of them are doing. Clusters of supporting and competing companies emerge in particular areas as a result of spreading benefits between them – a form of feedback between them that amplifies advantages and disadvantages and sets off virtuous and vicious circles of development. In this process, partly affected by chance, the cause and effect of individual determinants becomes blurred.

When we discussed Porter's industry structure and value chain analysis in Chapter 2, we painted a picture of managers in an organisation who analyse a given environment and then choose a particular strategy that they then implement. If they choose the right strategy, that is if they formulate the right organisational intention and then actually carry it out, they will succeed. This is a picture of orderly, intentional adaptation to the environment. In the later analysis being discussed here, however, each firm is part of a complex system and therefore what happens to any individual firm will be a consequence, not of the shared intention of its top managers, but of the evolution of the whole system of which that firm and its top managers is a part. This way of looking at the strategic development of a firm is consistent with the approach that Miller and Pascale adopt and like their analysis it represent a decisive break with the conventional wisdom. It is for this reason that we discuss it here.

The analysis is conducted in terms of what Porter calls the 'national diamond' reproduced as *Figure 4.1*. A nation, and therefore any individual firm within it,

Figure 4.1   Porter's model for analysing the competitive advantage of nations
Source: M. Porter (1990), *The Competitive Advantage of Nations*, London: Macmillan Press

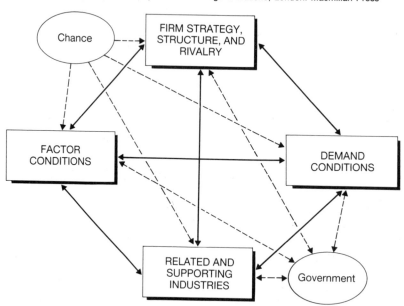

achieves success in a particular industry when it develops a favourable configuration between the following:

- *Factor conditions* such as skilled labour, the transport and education infrastructure, knowledge resources.
- *Demand conditions* such as the size of markets and the sophistication of buyers.
- *Related and supporting industries.* The point here is that one firm has competitive advantage when it is part of a whole value chain that is competitive. So Italian shoe manufacturers have advantages because they are part of a cluster of industries containing support in the form of leather suppliers and designers. This support industry is made possible by the existence of related firms such as handbag manufacturers.
- *Firm strategy, structure and rivalry.* The way firms are managed and formulate their strategies affects their competitive advantage. The more intense the rivalry between firms the more effective and efficient they will have to be to survive and therefore the more internationally competitive they will be.

In addition to these four determinants, the development of firms in a cluster depends on chance and on the government. Chance inventions or other events outside the control of companies or their governments create discontinuities that can reshape an industry. Government policies are part of the system too because they can add to or detract from competitive advantage (see *Illustration 4.2*).

These determinants create a system within which the nation's firms are born and develop. They gain advantage when the cluster they are part of is more favourable than competing clusters. This is a self-reinforcing system because the effect of one determinant depends upon the state of the others. Favourable demand conditions only lead to success if the state of rivalry is such that firms respond.

■ **Illustration 4.2**
SILICON VALLEY AND THE ITALIAN SHOE INDUSTRY

Research centres of excellence in microelectronics and information technology at Stanford and Berkeley, together with the availability of skilled labour, played an important part in the development of Silicon Valley in California. The availability of advanced technology made this an attractive location for electronics manufacturers in the early stages of that industry's development. These businesses in turn attracted component suppliers and other support companies. What we can observe is a feedback process through which a particular constellation of industries is built up.

A similar process can be observed around Cambridge in the UK. Once again a research centre of excellence has played an important part in the initial attraction of electronics and information technology firms. Feedback connections attracted others to establish a whole new industrial area. Similar developments are to be observed between Reading and Bristol, for similar reasons.

But the specific composition of the industries, which have grown up around San Francisco, around Cambridge and between Reading and Bristol, are quite different. For example, neither of the two UK areas contain silicon chip manufacturers. These differences may be due to government policies, to some other factor, or even to small chance differences between locations and the way people responded.

Similar patterns of geographic development in fashion clothing and shoes can be observed in Northern Italy around Milan. The process is the same. Some initial advantage attracts a small cluster of companies. Through feedback, support industries are attracted and so the pattern develops.

We can detect and recognise these patterns of geographic economic development, but their specific form seems to be unpredictable, depending to a significant extent on chance. Failed attempt after attempt by governments artificially to establish such geographic concentrations through planned industrial policies attests to this unpredictability.

This framework, like the studies by Miller and Pascale, presents a fundamentally different perspective on the dynamics of organisational development to that which has conditioned most of our thinking about the sources of success. Porter is stressing the importance of the notion of an organisation as a complex system within an even larger complex system. He shows how that system develops in an amplifying feedback fashion, where small changes are escalated and generate virtuous and vicious circles (see Chapter 7). He brings in the part played by chance.

Before pursuing where these implications about the dynamics lead us, consider now how an organisation changes over time. In choosing strategies for the future, will success flow from gradual evolution or does it require revolution?

4.5 Successful organisations display revolutionary as well as incremental changes: the analyses of Greiner and of Miller & Friesen

The debate here centres on whether organisations typically act strategically in a gradual incremental manner, converging in an evolutionary way on some state adapted to the environment, or whether strategic actions occur as sharp frame-breaking revolutions.

Incremental strategic change

In the conventional wisdom, a successful organisation sustains dynamic equilibrium with its environment. If the environment changes suddenly and dramatically then a successful organisation in that environment will have to change in a revolutionary way. However organisational environments seem to be changing all the time, so we would expect to find that successful organisations develop by continually taking small steps to stay adapted. We would not expect successful companies to drift away from equilibrium and then have to make dramatic, revolutionary changes to get back in step – that would represent some kind of failure to plan rationally.

Based on his study of ten large corporations, Quinn (1980) identified a pattern of strategic change which he called logical incrementalism. Here managers have an intended destination for their organisation, but they discover how to reach it by taking logically connected decisions step by step. They do not make major changes

Figure 4.2 Incremental change
Source: G. Johnson (1987), *Strategic Change and the Management Process*, Oxford: Blackwell

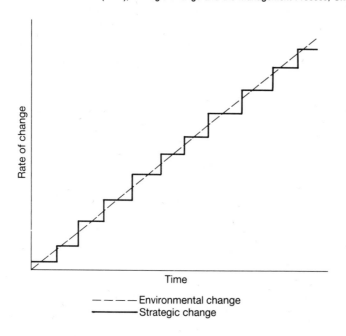

Time

– – – – Environmental change
———— Strategic change

but build incrementally in a consistent manner on what they already have. They sense the changes in their environment and gradually adapt to those changes so maintaining a continuing dynamic equilibrium with their environment. This pattern can be illustrated as in *Figure 4.2*.

Revolutionary, frame-breaking strategic change

Other studies however, particularly those by Mintzberg (1989), Miller & Friesen (1980), Greiner (1972), Johnson (1987) and Tushman & Romanelli (1985), have identified a different pattern of change. Here managers resist changes that conflict with their predominant way of understanding their organisation and its environment, until some crisis makes it impossible to continue doing so. We therefore get patterns of strategic change in which the organisation is driven down the same path by its own momentum, becoming more and more out of line with its environment. This gives rise to strategic drift. When that drift has taken the organisation too far from its environment, it then makes sudden revolutionary adjustments. These inevitably involve breaking the old frames they were working within and establishing new ones. This idea of momentum, drift and revolutionary change is illustrated in *Figure 4.3*.

Greiner's development model

Greiner (1972) presents a model of the typical pattern of development experienced by all companies. He holds that all companies must pass through a number of stages if they are to sustain acceptable levels of performance. He describes five phases of growth that are punctuated by crises. In order to make the necessary move from one phase of growth to another, an organisation must pass through a crisis. These phases and their related crises are as follows:

- *Growth through creativity.* In the early stages of its life, when it has simple structures and is small, a company grows through the creative activity of small close-knit

Figure 4.3 Strategic drift and revolutionary change
Source: G. Johnson (1987), *Strategic Change and the Management Process*, Oxford: Blackwell

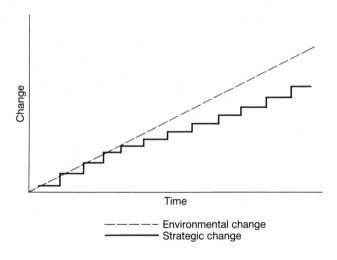

teams. At some point however they face the crisis of leadership. As the company increases in size it can no longer be managed in highly personal, informal ways.

- *Growth through direction.* If the leadership crisis is successfully resolved through 'professionalising' the management, specialising its functions and setting up more formal systems, the company proceeds to grow in a centrally directed way. This leads to the crisis of autonomy. As the organisation gets bigger and bigger, employees feel restricted by the hierarchy and the top finds it more and more difficult to maintain detailed control.
- *Growth through delegation.* If the autonomy crisis is successfully resolved through changing formal structures and decentralising, then growth proceeds through delegation. This brings with it a crisis of control. The top feels it is losing control and parochial attitudes develop in the divisions of the company.
- *Growth through coordination.* If the control crisis is successfully resolved through installing systems to bring about greater coordination and cooperation then the growth of the company proceeds. As it grows larger and more complex it is brought to the crisis of red tape. Increasingly bureaucratic controls create sharp divisions between head office staffs and operating divisions.
- *Growth through collaboration.* Here the crisis of red tape is resolved through strong interpersonal collaboration and control through cultural sharing rather than formal

Figure 4.4 Greiner's model of strategic change

Source: L. E. Greiner (1972), 'Evolution and revolution as organizations grow', *Harvard Business Review*, July–August

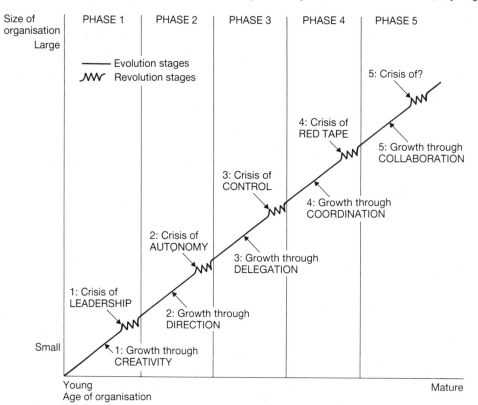

controls. Greiner thinks that this growth stage may lead to a crisis of psychological saturation in which all become exhausted by teamwork. He thinks there may be a sixth growth phase involving a dual organisation: a 'habit' structure for daily work routines and a 'reflective' structure for stimulating new perspectives and personal enrichment.

We have then two different views about the time path of successful change in an organisation. There is the incremental view on the one hand and the revolutionary, crisis-punctuated view on the other. Just as the difference between views on the criteria for successful strategy reflect different interpretations of the dynamics of organisational development, so too do these differences of view about time paths. The incremental approach assumes the dynamics of the stable equilibrium organisation proceeding intentionally towards known goals. The revolutionary view is consistent with the far-from-equilibrium dynamics implicit in Porter's analysis and made quite explicit in the Pascale analysis. And this far-from-equilibrium dynamics is entirely consistent with the idea that strategies may emerge from complex organisational interactions rather than be intended in a prior, central manner by the organisation.

4.7 Summary

In this and the previous chapter we have been concerned with how a particular paradigm leads us to adopt a particular view of the source of organisational success.

The stable equilibrium frame of reference discussed in the last chapter leads us to look for certain limited configurations of characteristics, identifiable in advance of change occurring. It leads us to look for criteria for selecting successful strategies in advance of acting.

Actual practice, however, throws up a number of anomalies when compared to the expectations generated by this stable equilibrium mental model. These anomalies lead us to question the underlying assumptions and consider the kind of model used by Pascale and by Porter to explain why organisations succeed. We can call this a far-from-equilibrium mental model where the assumptions are that successful organisations are complex systems, in turn part of even larger complex systems that exhibit continuing instability taking the form of contradictions and tensions, as well as chance developments. Such instability provokes continuing enquiry and learning from which strategies can emerge without anyone specifically intending them. What emerges can be a paradigm-shattering form of revolutionary strategy.

Key conclusions

The arguments presented in this chapter and the previous one together lead to important conclusions:

1 The most widely accepted view of the cause of organisational success today is based on a particular set of assumptions about the nature of organisational dynamics.

These assumptions are that success is achieved when an organisation gets close to a position of stable equilibrium. Here it produces regular patterns of behaviour over time; it displays internal harmony and external adaptation to its environment. On this view organisations can reach success by selecting strategies that are acceptable, feasible and suitable. Successful organisations stick to one of a limited number of configurations. Because of the assumptions on the dynamic it is assumed to be possible to predict the long-term outcomes of strategies to some extent, even if that extent is only a qualitative vision. Successful strategies can therefore be selected in advance and systems put in place to deliver success. Leaders choose future strategies and are in control of the organisation and intend its future direction.

But recent studies are increasingly raising question marks over this widely accepted view. These studies lead to the following conclusions, ones that produce a totally different view of the sources of success to that summarised in conclusion 1 above. The difference is so great that we may talk about a new paradigm for strategic management. The differences centre around what we are assuming about the dynamic.

2 According to Porter, companies are successful, in the sense that they are globally competitive, when they are part of an interrelated and interactive cluster consisting of demanding customers, strong rivals, innovative suppliers and support industries, as well as a highly skilled workforce and a developed knowledge base. The point is that a successful firm is a part of a feedback system in which it and other members of its cluster are playing an important part in creating their own environment through their interaction with each other. They are not simply adapting, they are creating. (This is also one of the key points of the Hamel and Prahalad study.) Porter also makes it clear that the outcomes produced by this complex feedback system, of which a firm is a part, also depends to some extent on chance or luck. What Porter is talking about in this analysis is a self-reinforcing feedback system that amplifies advantages and disadvantages to generate virtuous and vicious circles, with outcomes that depend partly on creative management action and partly on chance. Success here is being related to a particular view of the dynamics of businesses as systems, a view far outside mainstream understandings of strategic management.

3 Companies show strong tendencies to develop typical configurations of attributes characterised by consistency and harmony – they are stable equilibria. The connection between such configurations and success is a complex one. At first a particular configuration may be the source of success, but firms show a strong tendency, according to Mintzberg, Miller and Pascale, to continue developing the configuration to excess and ultimate failure. Success therefore is strongly related to the maintenance of contradiction: developing configuration but then breaking it.

Another version of the essential contradiction of organisations is the fit/split paradox. Organisations are pulled by forces that are disintegrating on the one hand and integrating on the other. Both of these forces have to be present at the same time, but they need to be orchestrated or arranged. What these findings are suggesting is that a successful business system is one that resists the strong pull to stability and integration on the one hand and the equally strong pull to instability and disintegration on the other. This again represents a particular view of the dynamics of successful businesses that is not yet part of mainstream strategic management thinking.

4 Success also seems to be related to the ability of an organisation to pick up and act upon weak signals from its environment. Both Porter (1990) and Ansoff (1990) make this point. The implication then is that small barely noticeable changes can escalate to have significant consequences.

5 Looking at the pattern of development over time of successful companies, we find that they make incremental adjustments much of the time, but occasionally they experience crises that provoke revolutions or sudden jumps to new configurations. The idea here is that creativity is closely related to destruction, that instability is required to shatter existing paradigms so making way for the new. This is an essentially dialectical view of how organisations develop: confronted by two opposites, they temporarily arrange the conflict in a particular way, but the opposites remain, generating tension that will eventually force a rearrangement of the conflicting forces.

6 Researchers keep identifying rather similar configurations, or categories, of companies. Very few companies ever fit these categories exactly. What we keep seeing is qualitative patterns that we recognise, patterns whose chief characteristic is their irregularity. This too says something about the dynamic as we shall see in Chapter 7.

It seems then that some of the latest work on strategic management is pointing away from equating success with a movement to stable equilibrium. It seems to be pointing to success as having to do with being away from equilibrium and in a state of contradiction and instability. It seems to be doing so in the context of feedback systems that show self-reinforcing and amplifying behaviour, generating virtuous and vicious circles. It seems to be behaviour characterised by qualitative patterns that are irregular. And development over time for this far-from-equilibrium, amplifying feedback system occurs through paradigm-shattering crises and revolution that produce newly negotiated paradigms and configurations. Since these views are all so closely related to how we understand the dynamics of organising and managing, the next two chapters will explore these dynamics in greater detail. First, in Chapter 5 we look at the dynamics that the conventional wisdom focuses on and then in Chapter 6 we consider the dynamics that it largely ignores. In Chapter 7 we will come to important new discoveries about the complex dynamics of feedback systems, discoveries that explain the key conclusions reached above.

Further reading

For further insight into the dynamic explanations of success read Pascale (1990), Miller (1990) and Porter (1990).

5

Exploring today's dominant assumptions about organisational dynamics

Stable equilibrium systems

5.1 Introduction

In Chapter 1 we identified the discovery, choice and action feedback loop as a suitable general framework for reviewing explanations of strategic management. In Chapter 2 we saw how two rather different attempts to explain the successful strategic management process – the visionary/ideological and the rational planning models – attach meaning to that loop. Then in Chapter 3 we saw how, despite their differences, both of these meanings are based on the same unquestioned assumption about how the discovery, choice and action feedback loop works. That unquestioned assumption is that, when it is operating successfully, the loop functions in such a way as to produce a state of stable equilibrium. In this chapter we are going to examine how the feedback loop produces stability.

It is of great importance to explore this question of how feedback loops produce stability rather carefully because, as we saw in Chapter 4, there is research that has identified serious anomalies that cannot be explained by the stable equilibrium perspective. That research points to a view of successful organisational dynamics that is the direct opposite of stable equilibrium. This difference of view is absolutely fundamental to how we explain and prescribe organisational success and, in order to make an intelligent judgement as to which of these views to rely on, we need to understand organisational dynamics in some depth.

Four theoretical approaches to the dynamics of stable equilibrium are to be discussed in this chapter: cybernetics, general systems theory and an important application of general systems theory known as Organisation Development (OD), and, finally, an explanation of political activity in organisations. The ideas in these theoretical approaches form the bedrock of the dominant paradigm that most managers today explicitly adhere to. All of these approaches are based on the assumption that successful organisations employ negative feedback only. The mechanism that systems use to sustain stable equilibrium is called negative feedback.

5.2   Negative feedback and equilibrium

The concept of negative feedback is set out in *Key Concept 5.1*. To fix ideas on exactly what negative feedback means, consider, first, two commonly quoted examples: a domestic central heating system and the Watt steam engine governor.

A domestic heating system consists of an appliance and a regulator. The regulator contains a device that senses room temperature connected to a device that turns the heating appliance on and off. A desired temperature is set in the regulator. When the room temperature falls below this desired level, the control sensor detects the discrepancy between actual and desired states. The regulator responds to a negative discrepancy with a positive action – it turns the heat on. When the temperature rises above the desired level the opposite happens. By responding to the deviation of actual from desired levels in an opposite or negative way, the control system dampens any movement away from desired levels. The controls keep the room temperature close to a stable level over time utilising negative feedback. *Figure 5.1* illustrates this negative feedback loop.

■ **Key concept 5.1**
NEGATIVE FEEDBACK

Negative feedback simply means that the outcome of a previous action is compared to some desired outcome and the discrepancy between the two is fed back as information that guides the next action in such a way that the discrepancy is reduced until it disappears. Thus, when anything at all disturbs a system from its state of equilibrium, it will return to that equilibrium if it is governed by some form of negative feedback control. Negative feedback is the process required to produce the dynamics of stability.

The same principle applies to the steam engine governor. As the boiler of the engine is stoked, steam pressure rises causing the engine to speed up. If this speed exceeds a preset desired level, the governor responds by opening a valve to release the steam and so pull the engine speed back to the desired level. As soon as the speed falls below the desired level the valve closes, steam pressure rises, and the engine speed increases to the desired level. Here too the operation of the control system is such that fluctuations around the desired level are damped and predictable. Stable equilibrium behaviour is thus preserved through the use of negative feedback. *Figure 5.1* also illustrates this example.

Figure 5.1   Negative feedback

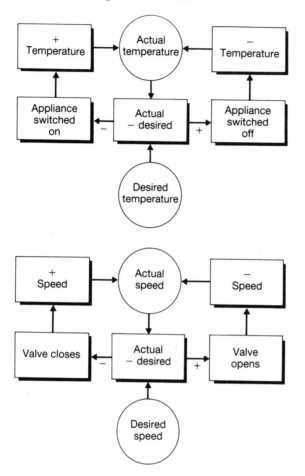

Negative or damping feedback is the mechanism that is widely used in nature and in engineering for automatic control or regulation. It is also used for this purpose in organisations.

Damping feedback loops and organisational control

The decision-making processes and control systems of an organisation are quite clearly feedback loops and we almost always think about them as negative, damping feedback.

For example, managers fix targets for profits and then prepare annual plans or budgets setting out the time paths for product volumes, prices and costs required to yield those profit targets. The plans also establish the actions that are to be taken to secure projected volumes, prices and cost levels. As the business moves through time, outcomes are measured and compared with the plan projections to yield variances or deviations. Frequent monitoring of those variances prompts corrective action to bring performance indicators back onto their planned paths. When profits

Figure 5.2   Negative feedback in business control systems

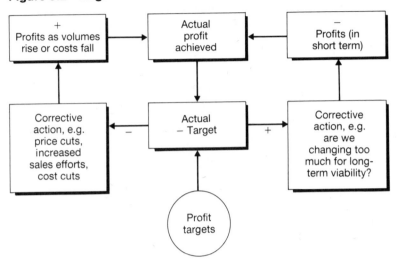

fall below desired levels we take corrective action to increase them – negative feedback. When profits exceed target, then the target may be raised, or more usefully, managers may enquire into why this is happening. It may be that they are exploiting a short-term monopoly advantage. In this case, short-term profit may be high, but competitors will be attracted and customers may be alienated. From a long-term perspective it may therefore be wise to lower prices and pull profits back onto target. Time lags and unforeseen environmental changes will mean that the adjustments are never perfect. But when the control system is operating effectively the actual outcome should fluctuate, in a tightly constrained manner, around the planned levels. The feedback loop is illustrated in *Figure 5.2*.

The scheduling, budgetary and planning control systems of a business utilise negative feedback to operate in a damping manner in exactly the same way as central heating controls or steam engine governors. The outcome is supposed to be the same – the organisation should be kept on its stable, predetermined equilibrium path.

This idea of the dynamics of successful organisations is the most widely accepted one today. It is based on a number of assumptions which we need to surface if we are to judge how useful the approach is. We can surface these assumptions by briefly considering four important developments in the theory of managing and organising: the cybernetic and general systems models of organisations, the discipline of Organisational Development (OD), and theories of political activity in organisations.

5.3   Negative feedback, control and cybernetic theory

Cybernetics is an application of the engineer's idea of control to human activity. During the Second World War, the superiority of the German air force led British scientists to consider how they might improve the accuracy of anti-aircraft defences. One of these scientists, Norbert Wiener, saw a way of treating the evasive action of enemy aircraft as a time series that could be manipulated mathematically to improve the gunner's predictions of the enemy plane's future position:

> When we desire a motion to follow a given pattern, the difference between the pattern and the actually performed motion is used as a new input to cause the part regulated to move in such a way as to bring the motion closer to that given pattern. (Wiener, 1948, p. 6.)

This thought prompted Wiener and his colleagues to see the importance of feedback loops in most human actions – a loop in which the gap between desired and actual performance of an act just past is fed back as a determinant of the next action (see *Figure 5.3*).

If you are trying to hit an object by throwing a ball at it and you miss because you aimed too far to the right, you then use the information from this miss to alter the point at which you aim the next shot: you aim further to the left, trying to offset the last error. In this sense the feedback is negative – it prompts you to move in the opposite direction. You keep doing this until you hit the object. Wiener and his colleagues saw how this negative feedback was essential to controlled behaviour and how breaking the feedback link led to pathological behaviour. Those who do not correct their behaviour in the light of what they have learned about the consequences of such behaviour are in some sense ill.

The systems scientists also realised that when such negative feedback becomes too fast, or too sensitive, the result could be uncontrolled cycles of over- and under-achievement of the desired state. So for example, you may be taking a shower and find the water too hot. This leads you to raise the flow of cold water. If you do not take sufficient account of the lag between your action and the subsequent drop in

Figure 5.3 Negative feedback in cybernetics

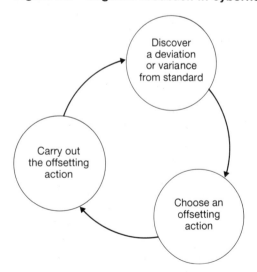

temperature you may increase the cold water flow again. This may make the water too cold so you raise the flow of hot water which then makes it too hot again. Unless you get the time lag between your action and its consequence right, you may increase the hot water flow until it becomes too hot again. So, if your negative feedback control system is operating too rapidly, the temperature of the water will fluctuate in an unstable manner instead of settling down to a desired level. Negative feedback systems can be highly unstable.

Those studying such systems therefore became very concerned to establish the conditions for stability and instability in negative feedback control systems. As a result of this kind of work governments came to accept that their attempts to remove cycles in the level of activity in the economy were usually counterproductive. Just as the economy was recovering from a slump, impatient governments tended to cut taxes and increase expenditure so fuelling an excessive boom accompanied by rapid inflation. Just as that boom was collapsing on its own, fearful governments increased taxes and cut expenditure so pushing the economy into a deeper slump than it would otherwise have experienced. To secure stability through negative feedback you must be able to predict not only the outcome of an action but also the time lag between an action and its outcome. The design of a control system that works at the right speed and the right level of sensitivity relies upon such predictions. Given the ability to predict, it is then possible to specify in a precise mathematical way exactly what conditions will produce stability for any negative feedback system.

Having outlined what cybernetics is all about we can now turn to how it has been applied to the control of organisations. Two writers have been of major importance in developing cybernetic theory, particularly as it applies to organisations: Roy Ashby (1945, 1952, 1956) and Stafford Beer (1959/67, 1966). In this chapter we are trying to identify what those who focus on negative feedback systems have to say about the forces driving such systems and the patterns of behaviour they display. On these matters Ashby and Stafford Beer have made the key points set out in the paragraphs below.

Goal-seeking adaptation to the environment

Cybernetics postulates that two main forces drive an organisation over time. The first force is the drive to achieve some purpose: organisations are goal-seeking systems and the goal drives their actions. The second force arises because organisations are connected through feedback links to their environments: they are subsystems of an even larger environmental suprasystem. Reaching the goal requires being adapted to those environments.

Thus, in the cybernetics tradition, organisations are driven by attraction to a predetermined desired state which is equilibrium adaptation to the environment. The state a given organisation comes to occupy is determined by the nature of its environment.

For example, on this view, a company operating in say the electronics industry may be driven by the goal of achieving a 20 per cent return on its capital. In order to achieve this it must deliver what its customers want. If customers have stable requirements for standardised low-cost silicon chips to be used as components in their own products, then our company has to adapt to this environment by employing mass production methods to produce standardised products at lower costs than its rivals. It will have to support these production methods with particular forms of organisational structure, control systems and cultures: functional structures, bureaucratic control systems, and conservative, strongly shared cultures. Our company will look much the same as its rivals in the same market because the overall shape of each is determined by the same environment.

If, however, the electronics market is a turbulent one with rapidly changing technology and many niche markets where customers look for customised chips, then we will get very different kinds of organisation, according to cybernetics theory. Our company will then have to adapt by emphasising R&D and continually developing new products to differentiate itself from its rivals. It will support these production methods with particular forms of structure, control systems and culture: decentralised structures of separate profit centres, greater emphasis on informal controls, and change-loving cultures.

Cybernetics, the reader will by now have recognised, is a contingency theory (see *Key Concept 3.2* in Chapter 3).

But how do organisations come to be adapted to their environments and achieve their goals?

Regulators

According to cybernetics, organisations deploy regulators that utilise negative feedback in order to reach their goals and the desired states of adaptation to their environments. The central problem is how to keep an organisation at, or near to, some desired state and the answer to the problem lies in the design of the regulator, that is the design of the control system. Cybernetics is the science of control, and management is the profession of control. At the heart of that science and that profession lies the design of regulators. You can see how this kind of thinking accords with one of the dominant paradigm's major concerns – that to do with being in control.

There are two types of regulator: the error-controlled regulator and the anticipatory regulator. In Ashby's scheme, disturbances from its environment (D in *Figure 5.4*) impact on the organisation (T in the figure) leading to an outcome (E in the figure). The problem is where to put the regulator (R in *Figure 5.4*).

Anticipatory regulation

If we place the regulator so that it senses the disturbance before that disturbance hits the organisation, then we can take anticipatory action and offset the undesirable impact of the disturbance on the outcome (the top part (A) of *Figure 5.4*).

An immediately recognisable example of this kind of regulator is of course a planning system. Such a regulator takes the form of a sensing device using market research questionnaires or analyses of market statistics. On the basis of these, realistically achievable desired states are established. These desired states are forecasts of sales volumes, prices and costs at some future point; that is, the

Figure 5.4   Regulation in control systems
Source: W. R. Ashby (1956), *Introduction to Cybernetics*, New York: Wiley

A

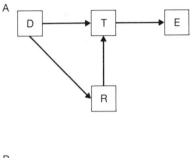

B

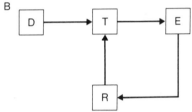

positions and postures required to achieve the performance target or goal. Action plans to realise these forecasts are also prepared; that is, patterns in future actions are identified. As the company moves through time it continually senses the environment, picks up disturbances before they occur, and prepares planned actions to deal with them before they hit the organisation. This is the ideal control without making mistakes: preventing deviations from plan occurring in the first place. It was referred to as feedforward control in the section on implementing strategic plans in Chapter 2.

Error-controlled regulation

If it is not possible to establish such an anticipatory regulator, or if such a regulator cannot work perfectly, then we have to place a regulator so that it can sense the outcome once that outcome has occurred. This is the classic error-controlled regulator (the lower part (B) of *Figure 5.4*).

An immediately recognisable example of this type of regulator is the monitoring, reviewing and corrective action system of an organisation. It is what a company's board of directors does each month when it meets to review what has happened to the business over the past month, monitors how the performance measures are moving, and decides what to do to correct deviations from plan that have already occurred.

It is clearly preferable to anticipate disturbances as far as possible because there are time lags: first in detecting what is happening; then in deciding what should be done; then in doing it; and then in the outcome materialising from the action. These time lags mean that relying entirely on the error-control system will not produce the intended performance. Since it takes time to correct a deviation, and since time lags can cause instability in performance, we should aim to prevent deviation in the first place. But anticipating disturbances relies on the ability to forecast them and this can never be perfect. Therefore an organisation will have to rely on both anticipatory and error-control regulators. This is exactly what the managers of a business do when they prepare budgets and plans and then monitor and review the environment and the company's performance each month. Note, however, that even error-controlled regulators depend on some form of predictability. When a deviation between a desired and an actual outcome appears, you take action in one period. When the next period comes around and the deviation has still not been removed, do you take further action? You would only do so if the last period's action has already had its effect and that effect was insufficient. You would not do so if the effects were still working their way through. This means that when you take a corrective action you have to be able to predict the timing of its effects if error-controlled control is to be reliable.

Reliance on statistics

An essential requirement for the most effective application of this whole approach to control is the availability of quantitative forecasts of future changes in the organisation and its environment, as well as forecasts of the consequences of proposed actions to deal with these changes. The tools we have for such quantitative forecasts are those derived from statistical theory. Statistical forecasting methods are based on the assumption that the disturbances hitting the organisation from its environment take the form of groupings of large numbers of closely similar events that can be described by a probability distribution. It is implicitly assumed that uniquely uncertain events will be relatively unimportant.

This distinction can be clarified by two examples. An example of a unique event is the Iraqi invasion of Kuwait in August 1990. It is of course unique because it only occurs once. We cannot describe it in terms of an observed probability distribution – either it occurs or it does not. Because of its uniqueness we cannot apply standard statistical techniques to forecast its occurrence. An example of a grouping of events that can be described by a probability distribution is the number of television sets a company sells each month, or the number of faulty television sets customers return to the company each month. By looking at the records for a number of months we will be able to say that the most likely level of demand is say 1000 units and usually some 10 are returned each month. These different possibilities are illustrated in *Figure 5.5*. If the business is primarily affected by events that can be described by probability distributions we will be able to use tried-and-tested statistical techniques to forecast them. Statistical techniques require data generated by many repetitions. If most of the events hitting our business are unique we will not be able to rely on these techniques. If we cannot use these techniques, then practising anticipatory and error-controlled control in the way proposed by cybernetics will not be possible.

The law of requisite variety

However, cybernetics sees the main cause of the difficulty in designing regulators not in terms of the uniqueness of events, but in terms of their variety, or complexity.

Figure 5.5 Distribution of events

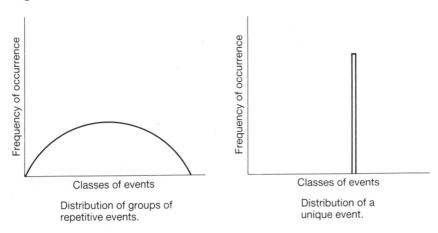

Distribution of groups of repetitive events.

Distribution of a unique event.

Variety is the number of discernibly different states the environment can present to the organisation and the number of discernibly different responses the organisation can make to the environment. It is the function of the regulator to reduce variety so retaining stability within a system, despite high variety outside it. That is, the huge variety of disturbances presented by the environment must be neutralised by a huge number of responses such that the outcome can match the one desirable state selected in advance that will fit the environment. In order to be able to do this, the regulator must be designed to have as much variety as the environment; the number of potential responses must match the number of potential disturbances so that they can cancel each other out and produce a single desired outcome. This is Ashby's Law of Requisite Variety: the complexity and speed of the firm's response must match the complexity and speed of change of the environment. *Key Concept 5.2* gives examples of the forms which requisite variety might take.

■ Key concept 5.2
THE LAW OF REQUISITE VARIETY

According to cybernetics, an organisation must achieve the goal of continuing adaptation to its environment if it is to survive and succeed. In order to so adapt, it has to employ a control system or regulator. It will successfully adapt when the complexity and speed of the responses enabled by its regulator match the complexity and speed of the changes occurring in its environment; that is, when it controls its business according to the law of Requisite Variety.

Suppose an organisation faces a stable environment in which changes follow regular predictable patterns. Then it will succeed when it uses an anticipatory regulator of the comprehensive planning kind. Here it forecasts the changes that will occur and prepares a single comprehensive plan to deal with all the future changes it faces over a given time period: it decides in advance on the sequence of actions it is to follow for a particular time period, then it implements that sequence of actions.

In this case we have a simple rather than a complex environment. We also have an environment in which there is little variety: it is regular and we are able to predict the single pattern it will follow in the future. Because the environment is simple and low in variety we can design a regulator that is simple and low in variety; we can establish one single set of intended actions, the comprehensive plan, which we can then follow.

Now suppose that the environment is more complex and displays greater variety. This inevitably means that we have greater difficulty in forecasting what will happen. Using the simple regulator – one plan for the future – is likely to lead to failure because we will not be responding to a great many of the unforeseeable events that are occurring. To succeed, the regulator must be given greater variety. This can be done by preparing a number of different forecast scenarios (see Chapter 2, the section on financial acceptability) and putting together contingency plans for each scenario. As it becomes clearer which scenario is unfolding we can pull the requisite contingency plan from the file and implement it.

In effect we make the whole planning procedure more flexible and keep changing our long-term plans every few months in order to match them to unforeseen changes as those unforeseen changes emerge. So, we may have one plan for an environment in which oil prices are low, exchange rates favourable, rates of growth in demand high, own product prices high, and competitor moves sluggish. We can then develop a different plan for the reverse of all of these environmental conditions, or for only some of them.

Notice how we respond to a higher level of complexity and variety by increasing the complexity and variety of the regulator, in this case the planning system, the range of plans available, and the frequency with which they are changed.

At some point the changes in the environment may become so rapid and unpredictable that we have to give up on even contingency planning; too many contingencies may arise to make it practicable to have a plan ready for all of them. The regulator will therefore no longer take the form of a planning system. Instead it may take the form of a loose, changing set of project teams or, what Peters and Waterman called skunkworks (Peters & Waterman, 1982). (We discussed this in Chapter 2 under the heading of the excellence approach.) Here each team is working on some project to deal with some possible change in the environment. Each team conducts trials to test out possible market responses. One team will be experimenting with one kind of product that might suit say a rapid-growth low-oil-price environment and another may be experimenting with a product that suits a slow-growth high-oil-price environment. The regulator takes the form of trial-and-error testing of responses that the changing environment might require. The organisation is thus developing a large number of potential responses to a large number of potential environmental changes. Those experiments that succeed are continued with and those that fail are abandoned. The more experiments conducted, the greater and faster the action, the more likely the organisation is to deal with what the environment throws at it.

Here then we have a regulator that has even more variety and complexity built into it so as to match the much higher level of complexity and variety in the environment. The visionary/ideological model of strategic management depends crucially upon the validity of this idea and as we shall see in Chapter 7, in the section on what chaos means for organisations, its validity is questionable.

Cybernetics and causality

The law of requisite variety makes it unnecessary, according to the cybernetics tradition, to understand the internal feedback structures of the organisation and the environment. Let me explain.

Cyberneticists recognised that feedback means circular causality – event A causes event B which then causes event A (see *Key Concept 3.3* on the nature of causality). They argued that we can determine the direction this circular causality takes for any pair of events simply by observing which precedes which in a large number of cases. But when we are dealing with large numbers of interconnected pairs it all becomes too difficult. These internal structures are so complex that we cannot hope to understand them – they constitute a 'black box'. Note how an unquestioned assumption is being made here. Those arguing this position are assuming that there is always a specific cause for each specific outcome, the problem being that it is all too complex for us to understand. We will see later in Chapter 7 that there is another way to tackle this difficulty: it may be impossible to reduce our understanding to specific cause-and-effect links because the links themselves are lost in the detail of what happens; the alternative is then to think in terms of patterns in the behaviour of systems as a whole.

The cyberneticists, however, argued that causal connections exist but we do not need to understand them because we can observe a particular type of disturbance impacting on a system and we can observe the outcome of that disturbance, that is how the system responds. If the regulator has requisite variety, that is a large enough variety of responses to counteract the variety of disturbances, then it will normally respond to a particular type of disturbance in the same way. From large numbers of observations of such regularities we can establish statistical connections between particular types of disturbance and particular organisational responses.

The importance of this notion of causal connection is that it allows us to use statistical techniques to control in a negative feedback way, despite system complexity so great that we cannot hope to understand it, at least according to the cyberneticists. What matters to them is pragmatic factors such as what we observe and what we do. We do not need to devote much energy to understanding and explaining, they claim, because observing and doing is what matters in a complex world. These writers were not concerned about the dynamic patterns of behaviour that organisations generated or with the complexities of the internal workings of the organisation. No importance is attached to perceptions, to pictures of, or feelings for, the patterns of behaviour generated by systems as a whole.

Note how the law of requisite variety and the view taken of complex causality amount to an assumption that the laws of large numbers, or probability, apply. Large numbers of random disturbances from the environment are to be offset by equally large numbers of responses from the organisation. But since we cannot know the complex causal relationship between these, according to cybernetic theory, we will have to rely on a process of cancelling out. Because causality is so complex we cannot determine exactly the right response for each disturbance, so some responses will be too weak and others too strong, but taken together the deviations from what is required should cancel out over large numbers.

Now, this is only possible if the disturbances and responses are not unique; that is, they do not take the form of a disturbance requiring one and only one response at a particular point in time if it is to be handled effectively in goal-seeking terms. If amplifying feedback could cause a tiny disturbance to escalate, then it would require an immediate response of exactly the right offsetting nature to stop this happening. If such escalation was not immediately stopped it could swamp the behaviour of the whole system – the cancelling out of inappropriate responses to disturbances would not occur. Without this cancelling out, the law of requisite variety would not be enough to secure control.

This assumption about uniqueness and large numbers is therefore of great significance to the view we have of control, a matter which we will be returning to in Chapters 7 and 9. There we will discover that successful organisations are characterised by amplifying feedback with the result that the law of requisite variety is not a useful way of thinking about control. We have already seen that the law of requisite variety underlies the visionary/ideological approach to strategic management. Its inapplicability therefore undermines the usefulness of that way of thinking about strategic management.

Cybernetics, then, is an approach that seeks to control an organisation by using feedback without understanding the feedback structure of the organisation itself. It sees effective regulators as those that cause the system to be largely self-regulating, automatically handling the disturbances which the environment bombards it with. It sees effective regulators as those that maintain continual equilibrium with the environment. The result is stable behaviour, predictable in terms of probabilities of specific events and times.

These aspects of the cybernetic tradition have had an important impact on the prescriptions for designing management control and information systems. The assumptions upon which cybernetics is based are shared by rational, scientific schools of management thought. These assumptions are still the dominant ones in the mental models employed by managers today and they underlie the planning and visionary/ideological approaches to strategic management. But as we shall see in later chapters, what cybernetics omits makes the whole approach of only limited use. In cybernetics:

- Behaviour patterns themselves are thought not to be interesting enough to warrant special comment.
- Circular causation is recognised but then sidestepped by saying it is too complex to understand.
- No particular importance is attached to nonlinearity: that is, the possibility that one even may lead to a more-than-proportional response in terms of the next event is not seen to have any special implications.
- Positive, self-reinforcing or amplifying feedback is largely ignored.

The key points on organisational dynamics made by the cybernetics tradition are summarised in *Figure 5.6*. Whenever managers use planning, monitoring, reviewing and corrective action forms of control, they are making the same assumptions about the world as those made by cyberneticists. Whenever management consultants install such systems they too make the same assumptions. Whenever managers engage in trial-and-error actions in the belief that this will take them to an envisioned end-point in a turbulent environment, that is whenever they implement the advice of Peters and

Figure 5.6 Cybernetics: main points on organisational dynamics

- Organisations are goal-seeking feedback systems adapting to their environments by utilising negative feedback.
- Change is caused by the environment to which the organisation is linked by feedback loops. Instability comes from the environment.
- Feedback links mean circular causality. This makes the relationships so complex that we cannot understand their causal structures. But we can observe statistical links between disturbances and organisational responses.

- Predictability of specific events and their timings is therefore possible in a probabilistic sense. Disturbances coming from the environment are not primarily unique.
- Effective control requires anticipation and a control system that contains as much variety as the environment.
- Nonlinearity and positive feedback are of no particular importance.
- Effective organisations are self-regulating, an automatic mechanical feature flowing from the way the control system is structured.
- Success is a state of stability, harmony and consistency.

Waterman (1982), then they are assuming that the Law of Requisite Variety is valid. The problem is that managers and consultants are normally not all that aware of what they are assuming. They hardly ever ask whether their assumptions make sense or not.

5.4 Adaptation and general systems theory

Around the same time as the development of cybernetics, there also appeared the closely related ideas of general systems theory. In a number of papers and books between 1945 and 1968 the German biologist Von Bertalanfy put forward the idea that organisms, as well as human organisations and societies, are open systems. They are systems because they consist of a number of component subsystems that are interrelated and interdependent on each other. They are open because they are connected by feedback links to their environments, or suprasystems of which they are a part (see *Illustration 5.1*).

Each subsystem within a system and each system within its environment has a boundary separating it from other subsystems and other systems. For example, the sales department in an organisation is a subsystem separated by a boundary from the production and accounting departments. One organisation such as IBM is a system separated by a boundary from the other organisations and individuals that form its environment.

Within each system or subsystem, people occupy roles, they conduct sets of activities, and they engage in interrelationships with others both within their part of the system and in other parts or other systems.

Each subsystem within a system and each system within an environment is open in the sense that it imports materials, labour, money and information from other subsystems or systems and in turn exports outputs, money and information to other subsystems and systems.

Open systems explanations of managing and organising therefore focus attention on:

- behaviour of people within a subsystem or system;
- nature of the boundary around a subsystem or system;
- nature of the relationships across the boundaries between subsystems and systems;
- requirements of managing the boundary.

The open system concept provides a tool for understanding the relationship between:

- the technical and the social aspects of an organisation;
- the parts and the whole organisation (for example, the individual and the group, the individual and the organisation);
- the whole organisation and the environment.

Negative feedback

Changing one component in an open system will clearly have knock-on effects in many other components because of the prevalence of interconnection. Changes in the environment will have an impact on changes in the subsystems of an organisation. What happens in one system will affect what happens in another system and that in turn will affect the first.

You can see the importance of the insight provided by open systems theory if you consider how the technical subsystem of an organisation is interconnected with its social subsystem (Trist & Branforth, 1951).

Scientific, technically rational management tends to concentrate on the technical subsystem. This system consists of the primary tasks that the organisation is there to carry out: for example, the techniques, technology and sets of tasks required to produce coal in the case of a coal mining business. The prescription for success made by the scientific management school is to make the task subsystem as efficient as possible. So, if you introduce the latest technology for mining coal together with rules and regulations about quality and efficiency to govern the work of coal miners, then you should succeed according to scientific management. Success here depends primarily on the technical subsystem.

The behavioural school of management, on the other hand, focuses primarily on the psycho-social subsystem. Its prescriptions for success stress the establishment of a social system in which people are motivated and participate in making decisions about the nature of the tasks and the technology. To succeed you must consult those who perform the organisation's primary tasks, involve them in decision making, and introduce reward structures that will motivate them to operate efficiently. Success here depends primarily on the social subsystem.

The insight that comes from open systems theory is that the technical and social systems are so interconnected that it makes no sense to regard one as dominant and the other as subordinate. Both subsystems have to be handled together in a manner that takes account of their interdependence.

The importance of this interconnection was demonstrated many years ago in a study of the coal mining industry in the UK by Trist and Branforth (1951). In the late 1940s, the British coal industry introduced the more efficient long-wall method of mining coal. This technology however, required changes in the set of tasks performed by coal miners. These changes broke up the cooperative teams in which miners were accustomed to working, teams that reflected their social arrangements in the coal mining villages in which they lived. Because of the consequent resistance to working in the new way, the technology failed to yield its technical potential.

The message is that, if changes are to succeed, then they have to be based on a realistic understanding of the interconnection, or feedback, between the social and the technical subsystems. And that interconnection is not simply taken account of by introducing participation or reward schemes for individuals. Instead, general systems theory prescribes a match between the two subsystems, one that establishes stable equilibrium.

Like cybernetics therefore, the general systems strand of thinking sees an organisation as a feedback system. It also sees that feedback system as one that maintains equilibrium with its environment, and between its parts, by utilising the mechanisms of negative feedback.

Paradox and conflict

In general systems theory, open systems are thought of as having maintenance subsystems to sustain orderly relationships between the parts of the system (Lawrence and Lorsch, 1967). In an organisation this would be the management information and control systems and the cultures that keep people working harmoniously together. However, it is recognised that these maintenance systems are conservative by nature. They are intended to hold the system together; to prevent it from changing too rapidly; to keep it efficiently carrying out its main tasks. The inevitable consequence of this maintenance form of control is that the overall system and its subsystems become out of balance as time goes by and things change. They become out of balance with each other and with the environment.

Note how close this idea is to that which Miller talks about in describing trajectories that take organisations to excess. Also note the similarity to Pascale's idea of organisations moving to a state of 'fit'. (Both are discussed in the section on success flowing from contradiction in Chapter 4.)

But organisations also have adaptive mechanisms that promote change so as to keep them in dynamic equilibrium with the environment. These two subsystems, the maintenance and the adaptive, inevitably conflict but successful organisations sustain a stable balance between them, according to general systems theory.

Note that general systems theory recognises fundamental conflict inherent in the structure of the system, the paradox of stability and instability, but assumes that successful systems deal with this by sustaining equilibrium. Recall that Pascale proposes that success occurs when the conflict is sustained and the paradoxical forces rearranged in a dialectical process.

■ **Illustration 5.1**

THE ORGANISATION AS AN OPEN SYSTEM

Kast and Rosenzweig (1970) conceived of the organisation in terms of suprasystems and subsystems:

- *Environmental suprasystem*. This can be divided into general societal and specific task systems. The general environment system covers the culture of the society of which the organisation is a part, its general level of technology, its politics, and so on. The task systems include customers, suppliers, competitors and so on. The more complex and unstable the environmental system, the more complex and differentiated the internal structuring of the organisation will have to be to cope.
- *Goals and values subsystems*. These flow from relationships between five levels: individuals within the organisation; groups of people within the organisation; the organisation as a whole; the task environments; and society at large.
- *Technical subsystem*. This relates to the knowledge required to perform tasks. It includes the technology of production specific to the organisation, the degrees of specialisation and automation required and applied, and the extent to which tasks are routine and non-routine.
- *Psychological subsystem*. This is created by individuals and groups in interaction. Individual behaviour and motivation, status and roles, group dynamics and political interactions are all part of this subsystem. It is clearly influenced by all the other subsystems and suprasystems.
- *Structural subsystem*. This covers the ways in which tasks are divided up and then integrated again. Organisational charts and job definitions, as well as formal communication flows, are the more visible manifestations of this subsystem. It also includes the informal organisation with its networks of personal contacts and casual information flows.
- *Managerial subsystem*. This spans the entire organisation and it relates the organisation to its environment, developing goals and plans, designing structures, and establishing control processes. Its primary role is an integrating one.

Differentiation and integration

Lawrence and Lorsch (1967) used the conceptual approach of open systems to research the functioning of a number of large organisations. They concluded that as organisations increase in size they differentiate into parts, and the more they differentiate, the more difficult becomes the consequent task of integration.

So as the environment becomes more complex and as they grow in size, companies differentiate into functions – finance, operations, sales and so on. But each part or function then faces the problem of relating to the other parts, if the firm is to operate effectively. Integrating what people in the production department do with what those in the sales or finance departments do then becomes more and more of a problem.

As organisations deal with their external environment they become differentiated into separate units, each dealing with a part of the environment. Think of large multinational companies, such as ICI or IBM, with perhaps hundreds of different subsidiary companies across the world. They have reached advanced stages of differentiation and face well-known and very difficult-to-solve problems of integrating all their activities.

The authors found a relationship between variables external to the organisation and the states of differentiation and integration within that organisation. They found that organisations become more differentiated as their environments become more diverse.

Citibank operates in a large number of countries, a complex environment, through a great many national subsidiaries. This is a differentiated organisation. Since the environment demands more interdependence and cooperation, the organisation responds with greater integration. So, Citibank superimposes upon its national subsidiaries a central activity to serve its multinational clients wishing to deal with one central point, not hundreds of subsidiaries (Buzzell, 1984).

As environments become more diverse and organisations more differentiated, the tasks of integration become greater leading to a proliferation of complex integrating devices. Citibank finds that conflicts grow up between the national subsidiaries and the central body dealing with multinational clients. It has to set up rules and systems to try to resolve the conflicts.

Lawrence and Lorsch also found that the more unpredictable the environment becomes the more decentralised the organisation becomes, pushing the locus of decision making down the hierarchy. We encountered this kind of reasoning in Chapter 2 when discussing contingency theory. The general systems approach is also a contingency theory. (See *Key Concept 2.2* in Chapter 2).

Note how general systems theorists clearly recognise fundamental paradoxes of organising: the need simultaneously to divide tasks up and to integrate them; the need for maintenance control systems for stability but the inevitable drift from the demands of the environment as such maintenance control is applied. Note how they interpret organisations dealing with these paradoxes. They, in effect, see them as solving them, the solutions being dictated by the need to adapt to the environment. Recall again how Pascale suggests a different perspective, one we will be coming back to in Chapter 7.

General systems theory has made an important contribution to our understanding of the nature of managing and organising in a number of ways. It focuses our attention on:

- interdependence, interaction and interconnection between parts of an organisation and between organisations;
- the importance of the boundaries between parts of an organisation and between one organisation and others;
- the roles of people within and across the boundaries and the nature of leadership as management of the boundary.

These ideas have been important in developing our understanding of group dynamics within an organisation, a matter to be discussed in Chapters 6 and 11, and in the discipline of Organisation Development which we now go on to discuss.

Figure 5.7 General systems theory: main points on organisational dynamics

- An organisation is an open system: a set of interconnected parts (individuals, informal groups, formal groups such as departments and business units) in turn interacting with other organisations and individuals outside it.
- Interconnection means that a system imports energy and information from outside itself, transforms that energy and information in some way, and then exports the transformed result back to other systems outside of itself.
- An organisation imports across a boundary separating it from other systems, transforms the imports within its boundary, and exports back across the boundary. The boundary separates a system from its environment but also links it to its environment.
- Relationships across the boundary are always changing, the environment is always changing. The boundary therefore exercises a regulatory function: on the one hand it protects the system from fluctuations in the environment and on the other it relays messages and prompts changes within the boundary so that the system adapts to its environment.
- It is the role of leadership to manage the boundary, to regulate so that the system is protected and changes adaptively.
- Successful management keeps an organisation adapted to its changing environment through a process of negative feedback producing stable equilibrium.
- Adaptation to the environment determines the stable equilibrium balance between differentiation and integration, between maintenance control systems and change, required for success. Organisational paradoxes are thus solved in a unique way determined by the environment.
- Success is therefore a state of stability, consistency and harmony.

5.5 Planned organisational development and culture change

One of the most prominent applications of general systems theory is to be found in the discipline of Organisation Development. The central concern of those practising this discipline is the planning and management of changes in the beliefs, values, cultures, social interactions and behaviour of people in an organisation in order to improve its effectiveness.

Organisation Development (OD) recognises that it is not sufficient to analyse the environment and then set out the planned actions logically required to achieve the organisation's goals in that environment. What actually happens in an organisation does not depend on such rational considerations alone; it depends just as much on the behavioural factors: belief systems, social interactions, cultures, group behaviour and individual psychology. It is not enough to focus on technical or primary task subsystems; it is also necessary to operate on the psycho-social subsystem. Action plans will simply not be implemented if they run counter to the belief system, or if they adversely affect social structures, or if they do not motivate people. For this reason it is necessary to plan changes in beliefs and cultures to support the required actions, according to OD.

OD is therefore a long-term programme of intervention in the social, psychological, cultural and belief systems of an organisation. These interventions are based on certain principles and practices which are assumed to lead to greater organisational effectiveness.

These principles and practices are to do with identifying those beliefs, values and cultures conducive to achieving the organisation's goals – the desired culture – and then designing a systematic and deliberate change programme to move from the current to the desired culture.

One of the pioneers of this line of thinking was Kurt Lewin (1947, 1951) and we can explore the main assumptions on organisational dynamics made by OD practitioners if we look briefly at some of the key points he made. His models of the change process in organisations have had an important impact on subsequent thinking. The discipline and practices of OD, with its culture-change programmes, has been heavily influenced by Lewin's thought and is now widely accepted by practising managers.

Lewin (1947) saw social planning as a means of improving the functioning of organisations. He saw such social planning processes in terms of circular feedback in which goals were clarified, paths identified, and actions kept to the path, through the operation of negative feedback.

Lewin thought of the organisational change process in the following terms:

● At the beginning of any social change we can think of the organisation as being in a state of stable equilibrium: a state of harmony in which all share the same culture.

Figure 5.8 Negative feedback and organisation development

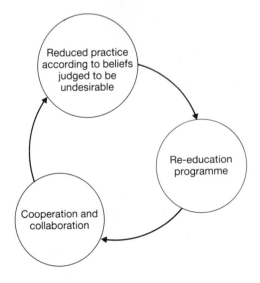

Figure 5.9 Lewin's concept of a force field

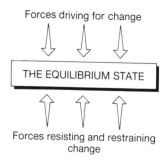

Forces driving for change

THE EQUILIBRIUM STATE

Forces resisting and restraining
change

- Stable equilibrium means that the forces driving for change and the forces resisting change just balance each other. In other words, driving and restraining forces create what he called a *balanced force field*, illustrated in *Figure 5.9*.
- Then some trigger such as falling profitability, or an announcement of reorganisation, or the setting-up of some programme of planned culture change, upsets the balance between the driving and resisting forces. In other words, some environmental change causes some internal change that unbalances the force field. Consequently, the existing management recipe on what the business is all about and how it should be run is challenged. This is the first stage of organisational change and Lewin called it *unfreezing*.
- When the balance between driving and restraining forces is upset, it causes confusion in which people search for new recipes. This is the second stage of organisational change, called *reformulation*. It comes to an end once a new management recipe has been identified, one that is believed to match the changed environment.
- The third stage is *re-freezing* in which people are converted and persuaded to accept the new recipe. The organisation thus returns once more to the harmony and stability characterised by all sharing the same culture. If the organisation is to survive, this new recipe must be one that is more appropriate to the changed environment.

This is clearly a feedback loop, one that will keep the organisation adapted to its environment, if it functions effectively. To function effectively, the feedback loop must be negative in its operation so as to keep the organisation moving to a desired state established by the environment. The dynamics of successful change are quite clearly to do with the drive to equilibrium and they are characterised by regularity and stability.

Now, the organisational change process could just occur as the environment changed or it could be planned, and OD is based on the belief that such change should be planned along the following lines.

1 The analysis

The first step in planned social change is that of analysing the force field existing at any one time in a specific organisation to identify what the driving forces are and what the resisting forces are.

For example, consider the problems faced by any one of the electricity utilities in the UK in 1989 as they began to prepare to operate as privately owned corporations rather than state bodies. The forces driving change were the new government policies on the ownership of the electricity industry, the European Community Directives on tighter control of pollution, and perhaps the appointment of a new chief executive from the commercial sector to oversee the change. The driving forces were creating a need for a whole new culture, one that focused on profit rather than engineering considerations. The resisting forces were created by the engineering culture of the utility, by the existing beliefs and patterns of work.

Suppose that OD consultants are hired to help with the change process. What would those consultants do? They would first form a clearer picture of the nature of the drivers of and resistances to change. They would do this by holding many discussions with managers and employees. These discussions would surface the main concerns. The consultants would start to form hypotheses about the main resistances to change and then check these by distributing and analysing questionnaires to large samples of managers and employees. The analysis would reveal much about the attitudes, the satisfactions and dissatisfaction of people throughout the organisation, the strengths and weaknesses of the organisation.

2 Developing the plan

The second step in planned social change is to prepare a plan for change that strengthens the favourable driving forces and weakens the blocking resisting forces.

The OD approach to developing such a plan is one that employs process consulting. This means that the consultant does not operate as an expert selling advice to the organisation in response to a need that the organisation has already defined. Nor does the consultant act as the company doctor who diagnoses what is wrong, recommends what to do and then leaves. The process consultant (Schein, 1987, 1988) helps the client to perceive and understand what is going on in the environment and within the organisation and then assists the client to develop appropriate responses. The emphasis is on clients helping themselves.

Indeed the OD approach heavily emphasises what it regards as the most effective way for clients to help themselves, namely through widespread participation. The OD process for developing plans for change is one based on an ideology of planned participation and democracy. It focuses very much on the importance of leadership in this process, but leadership of a facilitating, encouraging kind rather than authoritarian, directing kinds.

Typically therefore, OD consultants follow a sequence of activities such as the following:

- A top client group is established consisting of the most senior and politically powerful executives. Sometimes the client is simply the most powerful executive. The analysis of the driving and restraining forces described above is presented to this client and the hypotheses on them discussed. Together the client and the OD consultants identify what changes need to be brought about. So for example, top management and OD consultants in the electricity utilities mentioned above might identify the prime need to change the culture from an engineering to a profit-centred one, to remove the old bureaucracy and cut staff levels. They might agree on a programme of regular meetings at a number of different levels in the hierarchy to set financial and staff reduction targets and then review their part of the business against those targets and take corrective action.

- The top executives might start the process off by going away for a weekend to put together a mission statement setting out what new key values are to drive the business. They might set some broad overall financial targets.
- The next step would then be to 'roll down' the mission statement throughout the organisation. The next most senior level of managers would be formed into a group and a programme of meetings arranged for it. At the first few meetings that group would examine the mission statement prepared by the top team for the whole organisation. They would translate that into a mission for their level.
- Then teams of managers would be established for different business units or for different functions such as sales and production. These teams would then take the mission statements and translate them into mission statements for their own business units and functions.
- As the programmes of meetings continued, members would spend time identifying how to turn the missions into more precise objectives and what plans to prepare to achieve those objectives.

In this way, an orderly hierarchy of management teams pursue a programme of clarifying objectives and roles and preparing plans for change, all in accordance with a broad framework established at the top of the organisation.

3 Implementing the plan

The final step in planned social change is to implement the culture-change plan.

In a sense, implementation is proceeding alongside the development of objectives and plans because managers at many levels in the hierarchy are behaving in a way they did not do before. They are attending planning and reviewing meetings and working collaboratively on developing plans. The process of rolling down the mission statements and the objectives may itself be implementation in so far as the participation motivates people to accept changes in behaviour.

The planned changes in behaviour to more collaborative forms may be specifically reinforced by team-building exercises and training in group skills. So managers may be sent on presentation and assertiveness courses, or they may be sent away in groups for long weekends where they take part in team-building exercises. This may involve playing business games, or taking part in physical activities such as rock climbing, or finding the way through some wilderness. Such exercises are believed to build team spirit and establish bonds between people who have shared hardships or pleasurable activities together.

The top executive team will also probably engage in such team-building activities. These could include exercises in which the executives use questionnaires to identify the personality types to which they belong (Belbin, 1981; Kiersey & Bates, 1978). They then explore how these different personality types interact with other types and what impact this has on their working together as a group.

All of these OD interventions are of course a form of social engineering which could have sinister overtones, were it not for the insistence of OD that culture-change programmes will work only if they are collaborative. The culture-change programme must be one that leads the people involved to see for themselves why they should change their culture to a new desired state.

OD is therefore about a comprehensive approach to planning changes in behaviour in organisations. This kind of thinking leads to the rejection of piecemeal culture change as the effective way to alter belief systems. Simply affecting one of the driving or resisting forces is thought unlikely to move the whole system. The whole system must move if the organisation is to change enough. These thoughts lead to the current popularity of the large-scale culture-change programmes adopted by many companies.

Note how OD is built firmly on the idea that negative feedback, planning and

Figure 5.10 Organisation development: main points on organisational dynamics

- Organisations are normally in a state of stable equilibrium in terms of cultures and belief systems. The forces driving change and those resisting it balance each other.
- When it becomes necessary, analytical methods can be used to identify some new desirable state for the culture and the belief system. Analysis can also determine which driving and resisting forces to focus on in order to realise the desired change. Someone can know what an appropriate culture is. Specific actions lead to specific changes in beliefs and social structures and small chance events can be prevented from escalating into major changes in beliefs and social interactions – it is possible to prevent chain reactions and bandwagon effects (see Chapter 6, the section on positive feedback and nonlinearity in organisations).
- There are collaborative group techniques available to persuade and convert people to the new required belief system. Once rational people of goodwill see why they should change, for the common good, what they believe and how they interact socially, then they will. In other words, OD consultants implicitly assume that it is possible to ignore or overcome deeply buried unconscious group processes which lead people to behave 'irrationally'. (See Chapter 6, the section on Bion's models, which discusses sensitivity training and the Tavistock method. This approach which focuses on unconscious group processes is usually criticised by OD consultants and is very rarely used by them.)

- It is thus possible to install new belief systems and it is possible for someone in the organisation to be in control of the process.
- Once the change process is over, the organisation returns to its normal stable state.
- Successful change is planned, regular, hierarchical. It is secured through harmonious collaboration, the application of negative feedback.

reviewing leads to success. Note how the dynamics are described in terms of strong tendencies towards states of stability and harmony.

5.6   Orderly overt political activity

We saw in Chapter 2, in the section on implementing strategic plans, how conflict inevitably flows from the development of an organisation: as it differentiates into different functions and different business units, the members of these functions and units identify more closely with each other than with the organisation as a whole. They consequently develop conflicting objectives. Power and politics are resorted to as a means of dealing with such conflict in organisations. When it is judged to be operating beneficially, this kind of overt political activity is usually seen as a form of negative feedback control as shown in *Figure 5.11*.

Some studies of political activities in organisations have identified broad phases that managers follow as they deal with high levels of uncertainty and internal conflict. These conclusions are based on detailed studies over time of individual companies (Pettigrew, 1985) and cross-sectional studies of a sample of highly innovative and much less innovative companies in the USA (Kanter, 1985).

Galvanizing events

The cycle of political activity is triggered by some crisis (Pettigrew, 1973, 1986), a galvanizing event: departure from tradition, shifts in leadership, upset to existing perceptions, non-routine ways of doing things (Kanter, 1985). The consequence is some ideological shift, the development of different perceptions and points of view (Srivasta & Barrett, 1986). This increases uncertainty, leading to divergent goals, conflict, and unwillingness and inability to commit to any course of action.

For example at the beginning of the 1980s in the UK, three firms (Metal Box, Nacanco and Francis Packaging) were supplying paint cans to paint manufacturers, amongst whom ICI and Crown Paints were dominant. In the early 1980s, ICI decided to switch the packaging of its emulsion products from tin to plastic containers to

Figure 5.11   Negative feedback and politics

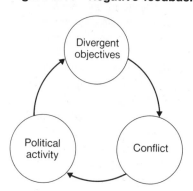

increase customer satisfaction. The tin can manufacturers did not respond quickly to this new requirement, so two plastic packaging companies (Mardon Illingworth and Superfos) entered the market and took away a substantial part of the tin can market. In 1985, Francis Packaging was acquired by the conglomerate Suter PLC, who removed the managing director and installed a new chief executive. These galvanizing events generated great uncertainty and the remaining managers had to develop new perspectives on what their business was all about and how they should change it. They had to deal with the often suppressed conflict which ensued.

Support building

The change in perspectives and the conflict have to be worked through before action can occur (Pettigrew, 1986). Particular individuals with vision are prime movers in bringing this about and they do so by developing special interests, making demands and generating support. Individuals or organisational sub-units identify uncertain changes that will affect them in some way and they make demands for particular choices in their own interests. To further these demands they obtain support from other individuals and units (Pettigrew, 1973); or, from the observations of other writers, individuals and groups acquire information on what is going on, they define the problems emerging from the questioning of old ways, and build coalitions to gain attention for the problem and their solution to it (Kanter, 1985; Quinn, 1980; Pfeffer, 1981; Bacharach & Lawler, 1980). All this support-building and coalition-forming is focused not just on the problems and opportunities generated by change, but also on individual careers and sub-unit positions and aspirations.

This could be detected at Francis Packaging. Coalitions formed around closing some of the plants to respond to the decline in demand and this inevitably affected the career prospects of some of the managers. Others formed coalitions around the issue of updating some of the plant to improve the quality of the remaining business. The new chief executive had to build political support for proposals to develop the business.

Building support is an exercise in building power. Power is the ability of one individual or group to get others to do something against their will. Power involves overcoming resistance (Pettigrew, 1973; Pfeffer, 1981). Power is usually distinguished from authority. The latter derives from the structures, rules and procedures of the organisation and the former not. Power in this sense is seen by some as illegitimate in organisational terms (Mayes & Allen, 1977). Most writers define power as both authority and influence. They see the utilisation of power as an inevitable and necessary process for making organisational choices in conditions of uncertainty and ambiguity. They see it as inevitable because it arises from the very structure of the organisation itself. The division of tasks, the design of separate functions and business units, immediately leads to differing sub-unit goals, in turn generating conflict which can only be resolved by the application of power (Pettigrew, 1973; Pfeffer, 1981).

Yet others take an even more favourable view of power as the ability of one individual or group to enable others to do what they could not otherwise have done (Srivasta & Barrett, 1986). Here the focus is on cooperation, consensus seeking and organisational transformation. Power seen as influence is also the ability to enable others to do what they would not otherwise have done because they lacked the information or the perception (Kanter, 1985). Here the emphasis is on cooperative discussion to develop ideas. Further, power can take an unobtrusive form in which the decision situation or the cultural norms around decision making are manipulated to prevent different perceptions, and thus conflict, from emerging (Pettigrew, 1986).

Power, then, is a relationship between individuals and groups that determines how one affects or responds to the other in making an organisational choice. The relationships existing now are strongly affected by those which existed and were built up in the past (Pettigrew, 1973; Pfeffer, 1981). The choices that an organisation makes are determined by relative power built up over a number of periods. Once the power source of the actors involved has been identified and their relative power positions determined, the choice itself is predictable. (The sources of power were discussed in Chapter 2 in the section on implementing strategic plans.)

Choice

Once power has been deployed to build enough support, the political cycle moves to its third phase – choice (Pettigrew, 1973; Pfeffer, 1981). Some writers describe this as mobilisation and completion, or the acquiring of legitimacy from higher authorities (Kanter, 1985). The outcome is the overcoming of conflict, the avoidance of conflict, cooperation, innovation, and new strategic direction. For some, this choice is part of an incremental process (Quinn, 1980). For others it can be a revolution (Mintzberg, 1978).

At Francis Packaging, the power of the Suter board and the individual power of the Francis chief executive resolved important conflicts to do with the closure of some plants, rationalisation and selective investment.

Planned implementation or trial-and-error action

Having made the strategic choice, implementation may be realised by following an agreed plan setting out the action steps required to achieve the chosen goal; or, where the environment is characterised by great uncertainty, that goal may be reached by trial-and-error action. Here the success of each trial step is judged against criteria for success. Such criteria usually relate to the core values of the business and to some logical connection with its existing activities. Francis Packaging decided to invest in some new facilities to produce tin products for segments it had not operated in before. Some of them turned out to be reasonably successful. It also started negotiations with Metal Box to buy those Metal Box subsidiaries that competed with it. This particular trial-and-error action ended up with Metal Box buying the business of Francis Packaging instead. Not long afterwards, Metal Box sold its packaging interests to a French company.

It is held that certain conditions can be established in which the kind of political behaviour required to secure innovation will occur. This will happen when (Kanter 1985; Srivasta & Barrett, 1986):

● People are free and empowered: the required conditions are the wide dispersal of power, local autonomy, and decentralised resources.

- People participate and collaborate with each other, and there is a willingness to share: team building and the fostering of strongly shared cultures is thus essential.
- There is a culture of commitment and pride in the organisation and its accomplishments: it must also be a culture which values and loves change.
- The cultures, structures, systems and relationships between people are integrative rather than segmentalist.
- There is open communication and networks which operate both informally and are built into the structures.
- Job assignments are ambiguous and non-routine: job definitions are loose and job territories intersecting.
- Leadership is persuasive and visionary, but also sets tough standards.
- There is an orientation to action.

It is postulated that when these conditions are established, people will participate in the kind of discovering, choosing and action that produces innovation. The negative feedback nature of these models of organisational politics is illustrated in *Figure 5.12*.

Figure 5.12 Overt political activity: main points on organisational dynamics

- The messiness, the difficulties, the tendency to regress from cooperative activity observed in practice, are all recognised descriptively, but do not form essential parts of the explanation of political activity.
- Although disorder and chance may be mentioned in passing, in most explanations of political activity they are in a shadowy background, not at the centre of the stage. Any disorder starts the process off, but is not used to explain how it unfolds. The impact of group dynamics, and the possibility of dysfunctional group dynamics and neurotic forms of leadership, are not part of the explanation. The interactive impact of personality differences on what choices are made is not incorporated. Thus the dysfunctional politicking, which in practice always accompanies functional political learning, is separated out as 'raw politics' (Kanter, 1985) and its impact on what happens is not built into the explanation in an essential way. Chance influences on political outcomes are not incorporated into the explanations.
- Current models of political decision-making present an orderly sequential process that occurs to overcome an initial disorderly state of ambiguity and conflict. The outcome is predictable once the sources of power have been identified and measured, once the relative power positions have been determined. Deterministic laws on power relativity yield predetermined outcomes.
- The normal state of the successful organisation is one of commitment, consensus and cooperation.
- Innovative outcomes will occur if power is widely enough dispersed, and people participate and show continuing commitment and consensus under persuasive, visionary leadership which stresses action. Disorder at an individual level does not contribute to the outcome in any essential way other than to start the whole process off.

5.7 Summary

This chapter has briefly outlined the theoretical foundations of what are today's dominant ideas on controlling and developing organisations. They are dominant in the sense that managers are more exposed to these ideas than to any others, and managers themselves most widely proclaim these ideas as the basis of their actions. Cybernetics and general systems theories are the foundations of today's management information and control systems, the hardware of control. They are also the foundation of OD, the planned change of behaviour, or the software of control. Both the hardware and the software are based on the following particular set of selective and rather narrow assumptions about the dynamics of organising:

- Organisations are goal-seeking systems kept on the path to the goal by negative feedback.
- What they are depends upon their environments and they change because their environments change.
- Understanding and explaining the cause-and-effect links in the feedback system which is an organisation is very difficult if not impossible. But this does not matter because we can identify statistical regularities between events in the environment and consequences within organisations.
- Statistical connections enable us to forecast and plan in advance of doing. Even if we cannot understand cause and effect, the link is still there.
- Unique changes are not the norm.
- Nonlinearity and positive feedback are of no special importance to success.
- Success is a regular state of stability and harmony.
- Individual and group unconscious behaviours are not of any particular importance in determining the patterns that an organisation follows over time.
- The systems that lead to success, of both the behavioural and the bureaucratic type, can be installed in advance of action.
- Success requires that someone should intend and be in control of the direction of the organisation.
- Consensus is the norm and the role of political activity is to resolve conflict as rapidly as possible.

If these assumptions are violated in real life then the approaches most managers now espouse on controlling and changing their organisations will be flawed. In the two following chapters, we will be examining and questioning all of the above assumptions. It will be argued that by reversing all of them we will reach a more useful understanding of the dynamics of successful organisations. We will be questioning the need to assume that groups of people must be pursuing a known objective, that they must have a purpose before they can form a group or an organisation. We will be questioning whether such a purpose is necessary before there can be control. We will want to question whether successful organisations adapt to their environments and whether they pursue the logical step-by-step thinking and acting implied by negative feedback forms of control. We will be asking whether it is really necessary to identify the links between specific cause and specific effect to understand how a system works. We will be asking whether there is not some other form of understanding instead.

Further reading

More detail on Organisation Development can be obtained by reading any of the standard texts on organisational behaviour, for example Robbins (1986). Models of political activity can be read about in greater detail in Mintzberg (1983), Pettigrew (1973) or Pfeffer (1981). For an overall view of the role of feedback in human societies, Richardson (1991) provides a very useful overview.

6

What stable equilibrium systems ignore about real life

Amplifying feedback and complexity

6.1 Introduction

In the last chapter we saw how today's conventional wisdom on strategic management is built upon a particular assumption about the dynamics of the successful organisation. The assumption is that successful organisations are dominated by negative feedback processes that generate regular, predictable patterns of behaviour over time – success equals stable equilibrium.

In this chapter we will see how this assumption leads us to ignore the widespread presence of positive, amplifying feedback in all human systems and how, when we ignore this fact, we find it difficult to explain and deal with the messy irregular dynamics we observe in real-life management.

First, we look at the nature of feedback systems, because it is feedback systems and their properties that generate the dynamics. Then we go on to examine a number of studies that identify positive feedback processes in organisations. After that we explore the implications of explanatory models developed by Weick (1969/79), Jay Forrester (1961), Argyris (Argyris and Schon, 1978; Argyris, 1990), Greiner and Schein (1988), and Bion (1961). These explanations all take account of the dynamic consequences of nonlinearity and positive feedback for a system's behaviour. These explanations are not usually accorded much attention in discussions on strategic management, but they are nevertheless of great importance: through the insights they provide, we may begin to understand the surprising, contradictory, counter-intuitive events and outcomes so often to be observed in the development of organisations. Armed with this understanding, we will be able to provide more realistic explanations and prescriptions for the process of strategic management.

6.2 The nature of feedback systems, nonlinearity and positive feedback

A feedback loop is established as soon as two people interact with each other. Take the following sequence of events as an example. As you walk down a street you may look at an attractive stranger. The stranger may return your admiring glance with an equally appreciative one, prompting you to smile. The stranger may smile too and greet you. So encouraged, you may then stop and find some excuse to start a conversation. That conversation may lead to dinner and that dinner could escalate into many shared meals. The circle of interaction between you and the former stranger could continue for years.

What is happening here is that one action on your part leads to an action on the other's part, which feeds back into a further action on your part. And in this case the feedback is a self-reinforcing amplification of a small chance encounter into a life-long relationship.

Feedback loops are set up whenever one action (event, piece of information) determines some other action (event, piece of information) which then in turn affects the first action (event, piece of information). When an environment causes a decision that in turn affects the environment, then we have feedback. So, when competitors cut their prices, managers in a company have to make a decision as to whether to cut their prices too. If they do, this could prompt the competitors to cut their prices even further and so the pattern of feedback may take the escalating, amplifying form of a price war.

When the output of a machine (or any other system) is monitored back as an information input to regulate or otherwise affect the behaviour of that machine (or system), then we have feedback. When we see managers detecting a negative profit variance, that is profits coming in below target, and then taking positive action to close the gap, we are witnessing feedback at work. This time the feedback is limiting and regulating rather than amplifying and self-reinforcing.

Feedback, a circle of interdependence or mutual causality, is ubiquitous in human systems and in nature's systems too.

Feedback between two individuals

At its most basic, any organisation consists of interactions between individual people (Weick, 1969/79). Interactions between people are always, as we saw above, feedback loops. We can represent such interactions in the diagrammatic form shown in *Figure 6.1*, which depicts the following sequence of events:

1 Manager X acts, and draws an accusation of sexual harassment made by employee Z against supervisor Y to the attention of supervisor Y.
2 Supervisor Y listens, so discovering what accusation X is making.
3 Supervisor Y considers what to do and makes a choice to deny the accusation.
4 Supervisor Y acts and denies the accusation.
5 Manager X listens to the denial, so discovering the consequences of the action of making the accusation in the first place.

Figure 6.1 Feedback interaction between two people

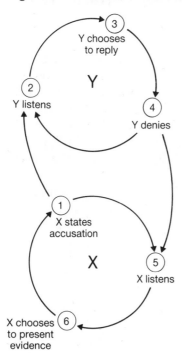

6 Manager X considers what to do next and chooses to continue with the confrontation by presenting evidence to Y.

7 Manager X acts, setting out the alleged time and place of the incident and asking where Y was at the time and what Y was doing.

And so both X and Y continue to move around a feedback loop in which each acts, discovers the consequences of their action in terms of the other's actions, chooses what to do in the light of the discovery, and then acts once again.

Feedback between three individuals

To illustrate how the web of feedback loops builds up, consider what happens when employee Z is summoned by the manager to a meeting with the supervisor Y. We now need to look at the feedback interactions between three people, each of whom is discovering, choosing and acting. This is illustrated in *Figure 6.2*.

Now when manager X makes a statement – suppose X repeats the accusation – it is heard (discovered) by both Y and Z. Each then considers the available choices for responding. Suppose Y repeats the denial and Z chooses to remain silent. Now X discovers the consequences of acting, namely the denial of Y and the silence of Z, and chooses to take the matter no further. X announces that the matter is closed and asks Y and Z to leave the office. Both Y and Z now discover the consequences of their behaviour. Suppose Z chooses to respond to this discovery and then takes violent action against Y. Now both Y and X discover the consequences of their behaviour. Y chooses to retreat and does so, while X chooses to intervene and tries to restrain Z.

Figure 6.2   Feedback interaction between three people/groups/organisations

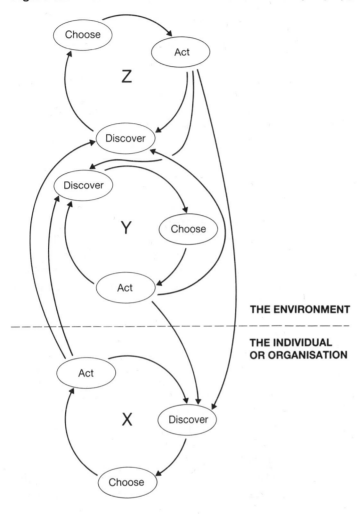

Feedback and the environment

What *Figure 6.2* also depicts is the nature of an environment. Manager X operates in an environment that consists, on this occasion, of two people, Y and Z. We can think of manager X as a feedback loop or system that is part of a web of feedback loops constituting an environment. Note how the environment of manager X is not some 'given' to which X adapts, but a sequence of perceptions and behaviours which X plays a major part, with others, in creating.

Feedback and groups

We can easily use *Figure 6.2* to describe sequences of interactions between three groups of people in an organisation. For example X can stand for the Marketing and Sales Department, Y for the Production Department, and Z for the R&D Department.

If we are looking at what happens from the point of view of Marketing and Sales we would see the other departments as its environment. An example of the feedback patterns that might emerge is as follows.

Marketing and Sales might write a memo on a new product idea to R&D. R&D receive it and discuss what it means (discovery). They then choose a response and conduct a prototype experiment (action). The Production Department is consulted, considers the production options, and experiments with some of those. The Marketing and Sales Department receives the prototype, chooses some trial customers, and tries them for a response. Marketing and Sales then write a report which they send to R&D and Production.

Feedback and organisations

Alternatively, we could use *Figure 6.2* to follow the evolving pattern of interaction between a whole Organisation X and the Organisations Y and Z that constitute its environment. So Organisation X may decide to boost volumes by severely cutting prices. Organisations Y and Z may respond by even bigger cuts and improvements in product quality as well. This compels X to cut prices even further and so the pattern of feedback takes on the form of a price war.

Positive and negative feedback

As we saw in the last chapter, feedback may take a negative or damping form, for example when managers use budgets to control the development of their business. When they practise budgetary control, managers react to profit variances by taking action to remove them so that feedback operates in a limiting way to maintain stability – negative feedback.

However, feedback systems can also operate in a positive manner. If you return to the two examples of negative feedback at the beginning of Chapter 5 you can see quite clearly how positive feedback operates. Central heating and steam engine regulators that operate in a positive feedback manner would take temperature or engine speed further and further away from the desired level. A tiny increase in temperature above the desired level would turn on the heat, so increasing the deviation from the desired level. That deviation would result in continued application of heat so that the room temperature rose even further. Eventually, the inhabitants would die of heat exhaustion. In the case of the steam engine, a small increase in engine speed would partially close the valve, raising steam pressure and thus engine speed. The valve would consequently be closed even further, so increasing the steam pressure and engine speed even more until the engine blew up.

Amplifying feedback here generates a vicious circle that escalates small changes. We would describe the behaviour of the system as 'runaway' or 'explosive'. The operation of the control system is such that fluctuations are amplified, leading to predictable equilibrium behaviour of a highly unstable kind.

No sane engineer designs engine or heating control systems that act in an amplifying manner and set off on predictably unstable paths to explosion. And no sane manager designs business control systems that could lead to increasingly divergent behaviour such that the organisation simply disintegrates. We therefore almost always think of business control systems in terms of negative or damping feedback. As we proceed through this and later chapters, we will be questioning this notion.

Feedback and nonlinearity

In addition to their positive and negative properties, feedback systems may be either linear or nonlinear. All the feedback systems we will be talking about in this chapter are nonlinear and that nonlinearity has very important consequences for the patterns of behaviour generated by the feedback loops.

Nonlinearity occurs when some condition or some action has a varying effect on an outcome, depending on the level of the condition or the intensity of the action. So the availability of a stock of goods in an inventory affects the shipment rate, but the effect varies. When the stock is close to a desired level, there will be virtually no impact of stock levels on shipment rates. The firm ships according to its order inflow rate. When inventory is very low, stock availability has a powerful constraining effect on shipments.

Another example is where extra labour is hired. At first, extra labour may lead to proportionally extra output but, given fixed equipment, a point will be reached where extra labour adds proportionally less and less to output. Eventually adding extra labour causes output to decline as large numbers interfere with efficient operation. These effects cannot be captured in simple linear relationships where a cause always exerts the same degree of effect on an outcome.

Feedback loops in organisations are nonlinear because of basic economic laws and basic human behaviour. As a firm sells more output its profit levels first rise because it is able to spread fixed cost, but eventually further increases in output lead to falling profit levels as prices have to be cut to sell more. At first demand for a new product rises slowly as a few people try it out. Then the demand may rise very rapidly as more people see that their neighbours have it; the desire for it spreads through the consumer population. But then the demand growth slows as demand reaches saturation levels. Organisational life does not proceed in proportional terms or straight lines; it proceeds non-proportionally, following curves. In this sense organisational life is a consequence of nonlinear feedback.

The important point about nonlinear systems is that they can operate in both negative and positive feedback modes.

Nonlinearity, positive and negative feedback

For example, the behaviour of a population of, say, insects is clearly driven by a feedback system. The size of the population feeds back through the birth and death rates to determine tomorrow's population size. You can see that this feedback system is nonlinear when you consider the two sets of forces driving population changes. The first set of forces is that which generates growth: factors such as better nutrition lead to rising fertility and birth rates as well as declining mortality rates. We can represent this by means of a feedback loop in which population now (P_t) is some multiple (c) of population in the last period (P_{t-1}):

$$P_t = cP_{t-1}$$

This is a positive feedback loop determining that the insect population will grow for evermore. What we are describing is simply the phenomenon of compound growth such as that applied to interest-bearing bank deposits.

But this is not the only set of forces governing the population level. As the population rises, food becomes scarcer and conflict and stress rise as overcrowding increases. In other words, there will also be a negative feedback loop governing population levels at the same time as the positive one. To represent the negative loop we can use the following formula that shows population now (P_t) falling as population of the previous period gets larger:

$$P_t = 1 - P_{t-1}$$

Since both of these sets of forces are acting upon the population level at the same time, we can express the relationship as follows:

$$P_t = cP_{t-1} (1 - P_{t-1})$$

This is the famous logistic difference equation that has been widely used in analyses of populations of all kinds and many other phenomena besides. We can represent it in diagram form as the positive and negative feedback loops shown in *Figure 6.3*.

The reason for going to all the trouble of setting out these equations and loops is the very interesting properties they display, properties we will explore in much greater detail in Chapter 7.

At low levels of the population, the positive growth feedback loop dominates and the population grows. At higher levels, the negative loop dominates and the population declines. Here we have a system with positive and negative loops and loop domination changes because of the nonlinearity in the relationship. A system governed by nonlinear feedback structures, where positive and negative feedback are both present, may move in a regular way to a stable equilibrium when the negative loop dominates. Then it may suddenly flip and operate in a self-reinforcing, explosive direction. After some time it might flip back again. These alterations in behaviour will be due simply to the structure of the system and have nothing to do with changes in the environment. This is a very important difference from the models discussed in Chapter 5 that concentrate simply on linear damping loops. As this section will

Figure 6.3   Positive and negative feedback in population growth

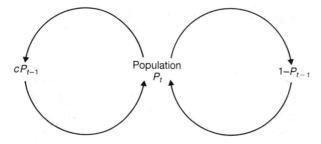

show, adding nonlinearity and positive loops leads to the capture of far more of the complexity of real-life organisational behaviour than the models surveyed in Chapter 5 can encompass.

So a human system may be unstable simply because it has a nonlinear, amplifying feedback structure, reasons that have nothing to do with the environment or the competence of individual agents within the system. It will then be rather foolish to look for the cause of failure in some person, some external event, or some scapegoat. It will make little more sense to heap praise on a person or identify the causing event when things go very well.

Feedback, paradigms and perspectives

There is another important point that we need to make about human nonlinear feedback systems. *Figure 6.2* illustrated how the behaviour of each individual in an organisation is a feedback loop connecting discovery to choice, choice to action, and action back to discovery again. You will recall how the process of making sense of *Figure 3.1* (the container and the people example in Chapter 3) could also be described as one of discovering, choosing and then acting. The point made in that discussion was this: it is the way we frame our understanding of the world that determines what we perceive or discover. And what we perceive determines what we choose to do. And what we choose to do determines what we actually do. And what we do affects our perceptions and so determines the nature of the further discoveries we make. Feedback loops in human behaviour, then, are heavily conditioned by paradigms and the perceptions those paradigms lead to. When we relate human feedback loops to the impact of paradigms and perceptions we see how environments are social constructions of reality, that is how an environment is a perception that people have woven together through their social intercourse.

Note that the feedback concept is one of a circle and because it is a circle it may be impossible to say what causes what, or what precedes or follows what. We may be acting out part of a sequence of actions before we discover fully what the consequences of those actions will be. If we are considering the feedback loops in the behaviour of groups of people, then in relation to the same issues some groups may be acting before or while other groups are discovering the consequences of those actions. In complex situations it may well be impossible to say whether actions precede or follow choices and discoveries.

Feedback, dynamics, change, control and success

By now enough has been said to make it clear that any group of people, any organisation, is a system consisting of a web of nonlinear feedback loops operating as part of a larger system or environment that is also simply a web of nonlinear feedback loops (see *Key Concept 6.1*).

Why is it so important to base a discussion of strategic management so firmly on what is so simple and obvious a notion?

The reason, as will be made much clearer in later chapters, is that strategic management is, above all, about dealing with change, and the patterns of change a system displays over time depend entirely on the nature of the feedback interaction of that system. It is the nature of the feedback that determines the dynamics of the system and therefore the nature of the change it has to cope with. When we talk about positive feedback and nonlinear systems, therefore, we are talking about systems in which the potential for under- and over-reaction, the potential for the escalation of tiny changes, are inbuilt characteristics of how the system behaves. What processes of strategic management are possible and effective will depend upon the dynamic and the consequent nature of change. Effective strategic management will take cognisance of the dynamics and the dynamics are a feature of feedback.

It is quite clear how negative feedback controls a system to produce stability. You can also, however, see the connections between feedback, dynamics and control if you consider a price war. The pattern of change, the dynamic, is an escalating vicious circle. It is a sequence of changes that have a predictable outcome – the bankruptcy of the players. That dynamic, or pattern of change, is a consequence of the fact that feedback in this case is positive or amplifying. Feedback has set up a self-reinforcing circle that is having increasingly disastrous consequences. The system is moving along a dynamic path that we may label as explosive equilibrium and it is rapidly heading out of control. This perfectly predictable equilibrium state of explosion and loss of control clearly does not lead to success. So far, it seems that negative feedback produces stability and control, while positive feedback generates instability and a loss of control.

However, to return to the example of positive feedback given above involving feedback loops between Sales & Marketing, Production and R&D departments as they developed a new product: one change led to further amplifying changes, positive feedback, and yet there was control. There was control because there were constraints – each department was significantly constrained by the power of the others. Control then takes on a self-organising form in the sense that the relative power of each department is exercising a controlling influence without anyone directing it. Amplifying feedback within constraints, unstable dynamics within boundaries, can lead to controlled behaviour.

■ Key concept 6.1
FEEDBACK SYSTEMS

A system is an organised body of things, a set of relationships connecting the parts of a complex whole together. Whenever humans group they constitute a system in which they are bound together by their interrelated actions and information exchanges.

Perhaps the central feature of human systems is their feedback nature. Feedback is a circle of interaction, a loop connecting one action or piece of information to another that is in turn connected to the first. The patterns of behaviour in such a loop are linked, each influencing the other and in turn responding to the behaviour of the other. The concept of a system in which the connections are feedback loops therefore involves mutual interdependence and circular causality (see Key Concept 3.3).

In a feedback loop, variable A causally influences variable B, which then causally influences A, in turn feeding back to affect B again, and so on. This feedback connection can be positive in which case the behaviour of A reinforces the behaviour of B, which reinforces the behaviour of A. Feedback here is amplifying and leads to either virtuous or vicious circles of behaviour. Unstable equilibrium is an example of positive feedback.

Alternatively, feedback may be negative in which case the behaviour of A dampens the behaviour of B, which dampens the behaviour of A, and so on. Negative feedback is also self-reinforcing but in a damping way, diminishing and counteracting tendencies to move away from some given position. Negative feedback systems move strongly to stable equilibrium.

Feedback systems may be linear, where one response is proportional to the one which caused it, so keeping the system moving at a regular speed as it were. Or the system may be nonlinear where one response is more (or less) proportional to the one which caused it, so that each response is an increasingly exaggerated one, causing the speed of the system to accelerate or decelerate as it were.

Feedback with its circular causality makes it very difficult to define what is the cause and what is the effect, particularly where the system is nonlinear. An effect may easily be distant from its cause in both time and space and the links between cause and effect may even be lost in the complex detail of what happens.

6.3   Positive feedback and nonlinearity in organisations

We have already come across amplifying feedback processes at work within an organisation, and between one organisation and the other organisations and individuals that constitute its environment. In Chapter 4 we saw how Porter explains the emergence of national competitive advantage as a self-reinforcing amplifying process. In that chapter both Miller and Pascale talked about organisations getting caught up in self-reinforcing spirals in which they build on existing strengths to the point of excess and disaster. Consider further important examples of positive feedback in organisations.

Vicious circles

The vicious (or virtuous) circle is a widely used concept and this too is nothing other than a positive feedback loop. An early model of vicious circles in organisations is provided by Gouldner (1964). He studied a gypsum plant in the USA and developed a model to explain what he observed. This is illustrated in *Figure 6.4*.

Senior managers at the gypsum plant were concerned to manage efficiently and believed that this required reduced tension between managers and workers. Such tension could be reduced, they thought, if power relations became less visible and all behaved according to impersonal rules. The intention was to emphasise the 'rationality' of the rules and conceal the fact that power was being exercised. No reasonable person could object to rules designed to improve efficiency and those who had to enforce them could deny the personal exercise of power and simply say they were doing their job. Conflicts around the distribution of power would then be removed.

Figure 6.4 Gouldner's model of intended and unintended consequences

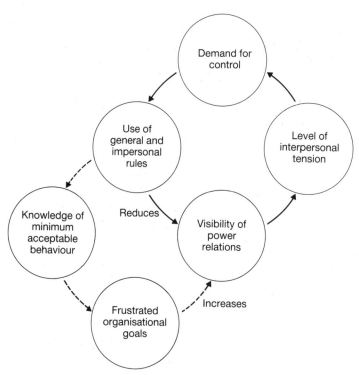

Thus, the demand by senior managers for greater control led to the use of general and impersonal rules intended to decrease the visibility of the power of senior management and hence interpersonal tension. In this way managers hoped to establish a damping, negative feedback loop producing intended consequences of reduced tension.

These actions, however, set up another loop that produced unintended consequences. The rules created norms about minimum performance in terms of time of attendance and output levels. People stuck to the minimum norms, frustrating senior management expectations of increased performance. That led to a call for closer supervision and closer control which had the effect of increasing the visibility of power and thus increasing the level of tension. More impersonal rules were then required. An unintended positive loop was generating unintended consequences. And that loop came to dominate what was going on, causing a vicious spiralling circle of tighter controls and more tension.

Self-fulfilling prophecies

Merton (1952) developed a model of organisations in terms of self-fulfilling prophecies, another example of positive feedback at work. Many managers argue that most people are not all that competent and cannot be left to make decisions for themselves in relation to their work. They argue that efficiency requires rules. But constant compliance with rules causes individuals eventually to lose the capacity to make decisions for themselves. The constant reliance on rules leads to the rules becoming ends in themselves instead of means to ends. As a consequence of being compelled to obey rules they did not originate, employees lose the capacity for independent thought. The result is trained incapacity. Rule-bound organisations encourage unimaginative people to join them and the imaginative leave. The prophecy that people are incompetent is fulfilled by the means taken to deal with its originally supposed existence.

This is shown in *Figure 6.5*. Managers demand greater control in order to secure reliability in service terms. Employees fulfil the stipulated reliability criteria by sticking to the rules. The result is employees who stick to the rules and supply customers strictly in accordance with them. If this leads to trouble with customers, employees can show how they have kept to the rules. This is the intended feedback loop – negative and damping. But such rigid behaviour and the organisational defences it involves lead to more and more difficulties with clients. Growing customer dissatisfaction leads to top managers calling for greater reliability and more rules. So another positive loop is set up, a vicious circle with unintended consequences.

Bandwagon effects and chain reactions

A bandwagon effect is the tendency of a movement to gain supporters simply because of its growing popularity; or it is the well-observed economic phenomenon of

Figure 6.5　Merton's model of intended and unintended consequences

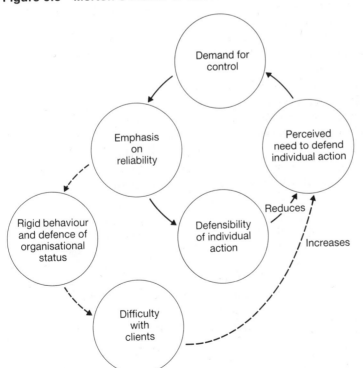

'keeping up with the Jones's' – the demand for a product increases simply because more and more people see that other people have it. This phenomenon of products spreading through consuming populations is another example of a positive feedback loop, this time creating a virtuous circle for the producer of the product. A small gain in market share by one product can, through this spreading and copying effect, be escalated into market domination. So although Sony's Betamax is the technically superior video recorder, Matsushita's VHS recorder obtained a small market lead in the early days of market development. This led to more stores stocking titles in the VHS format. That led to a further increase in VHS recorder market share and therefore more stockists turned to VHS films, and so on.

A similar phenomenon is the chain reaction. Here a positive feedback process

---

■ Illustration 6.1
CHANGING THE COCA-COLA FORMULA

In April 1985, the Chairman of Coca-Cola announced that the original formula for the world-famous soft drink was to be changed to a new sweeter variety to be called 'New Coke'. This announcement followed the two years of research and planning, costing some $4m, that had gone into the development of a new strategy to counter the market share gains being made by Pepsi Cola. Market research had shown that the New Coke would boost Coca-Cola's market share and add some $200m in sales. Taste tests had demonstrated that people preferred the New Coke taste.

New Coke was launched on 23 April 1985 at a press conference attended by 200 newspaper, magazine and TV reporters. They were unconvinced by the New Coke and their stories were generally negative.

The word about the change in Coca-Cola spread quickly. Within 24 hours, 81 per cent of the US population knew about it and early results were encouraging despite the negative media response. About 150 million people tried New Coke and most commented favourably. But the protests were also mushrooming. In the first four hours, the company received 650 calls. By mid May calls ran at 5000 per day, and there was a mass of angry letters – around 40 000 letters were received that spring and summer. The company had to hire new staff to handle the complaints.

People talked about Coke as an American symbol and they felt betrayed. Some threatened to switch to tea or water. Before May, 53 per cent of sample surveys said they liked the New Coke. In July that fell to 30 per cent. Anger spread across the country, fuelled by the media. The Chairman's father threatened to disown him for tampering with a national symbol.

On 11 July 1985 the company acknowledged that it had made a mistake, top executives apologised to the public and announced the restoration of the old Coca-Cola. TV programmes were interrupted to convey the news.

No satisfactory linear cause and effect explanation has been found for this sequence of events. What this demonstrates is how some small change, added sweetness to a soft drink, can escalate into a major consequence through the operation of positive feedback taking the form of herd instinct, bandwagon effects.

Source: Hartley, (1991)

escalates a small change into major consequences. Police firing a shot into a demonstrating crowd may touch off a chain reaction which leads to a massive riot or even the overthrow of a government. *Illustration 6.1* gives an example from business.

There is convincing evidence that almost any human system one can think of is characterised by nonlinear relationships and by the powerful effects of positive amplifying feedback, as well as by negative feedback loops. Models that ignore this nonlinearity and the presence of positive feedback must inevitably give a very one-sided, and therefore suspect, understanding of the dynamics of organising. Such deficient understanding must lead to questionable prescriptions for success. It will be argued in later chapters that today's dominant received wisdom on how to practise strategic management is characterised by just this problem of a deficient understanding of positive nonlinear feedback.

The rest of this chapter is devoted to considering what the literature has to say about this matter. Bear in mind that the rest of this chapter covers material that has remained largely outside the mainstream received wisdom on strategic management. It is interesting to note how resolutely the mainstream views on strategic management ignore the widespread prevalence of positive feedback, despite the fact that we are all aware of its manifestations as bandwagon effects and vicious circles, and despite the fact that these phenomena have been written about for at least forty years now. The conventional approach to strategic management says, in effect, that the escalation, the virtuous and vicious circles should not be happening. The prescription is to use rational approaches to remove such phenomena. The reality is that positive feedback is an inescapable feature, an irremovable structural property of human systems. Instead of building models that suppose we can remove feedback phenomena, we need to be building models of how to use and cope with those phenomena.

6.4 Karl Weick's models: managers create their environment

Karl Weick approaches the understanding of organisations from a psychological and sociological point of view. He analyses the problems of managing and organising at the level of interactions between individuals. He sees those interactions in terms of positive and negative feedback loops. As with the models discussed in Chapter 5, he is talking about a system, that is a set of interactions and interrelationships between people in groups. In common with the systems models of organisations already discussed in Chapter 5, Weick explains the operation of the system in terms of feedback interactions. However, his model differs significantly from those discussed in Chapter 5 in two important respects:

- the incorporation of both negative and positive loops in the feedback behaviour; and
- the implicit recognition of nonlinear relationships that cause systems autonomously to change from dominant positive to dominant negative feedback modes.

Figure 6.6 Weick's model: events at a meeting

Source: K. Weick (1979), *The Social Psychology of Organizing*, Reading, MA: Addison-Wesley

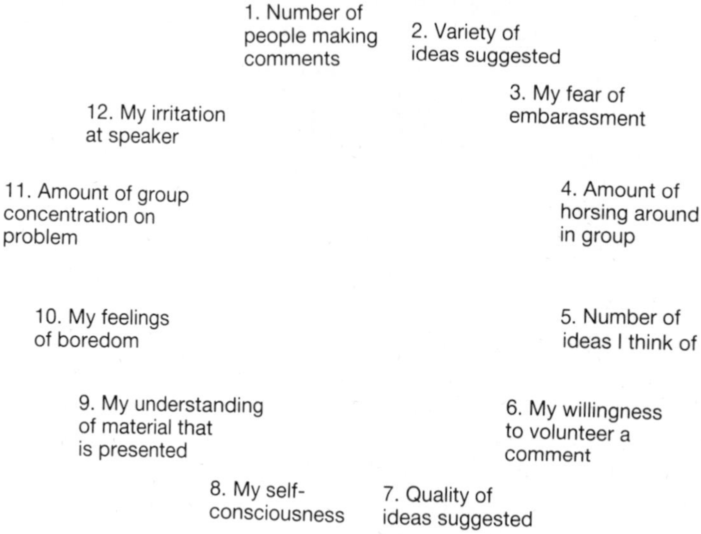

1. Number of people making comments

2. Variety of ideas suggested

12. My irritation at speaker

3. My fear of embarassment

11. Amount of group concentration on problem

4. Amount of horsing around in group

10. My feelings of boredom

5. Number of ideas I think of

9. My understanding of material that is presented

6. My willingness to volunteer a comment

8. My self-consciousness

7. Quality of ideas suggested

Weick (1969/79) invites his readers to see the feedback nature of organisations for themselves by working on the diagram shown in *Figure 6.6*.

This figure depicts a number of variables that affect what happens at a meeting between two or more people in an organisation. The reader is invited to connect the phrases in the diagram with causal arrows showing the effect of one variable on the others, indicating with a plus sign when one variable causes another to increase and with a minus sign when one variable causes another to decrease. The result will be a set of interconnected positive and negative feedback loops. What happens at this meeting will depend upon whether positive or negative loops dominate, and that domination could change during the course of the meeting. The system will be stable or unstable depending upon the dominant form of feedback (see *Illustration 6.2*).

So right at the most basic level of an organisation, that is at the level of interactions between individuals, the unfolding of events will depend upon the nature of the feedback structure that defines these interrelationships.

■ **Illustration 6.2**

FEEDBACK INTERACTIONS AT A MEETING

Suppose we are at a meeting which I am chairing. Suppose that, as my willingness to proffer comments declines, the rest of the group engages in more horseplay (negative link between the boxes 6 and 4 in *Figure 6.4*). Then suppose that, as the level of horseplay increases, it diminishes my understanding of the material being presented at the meeting (negative link between boxes 4 and 9 in *Figure 6.4*). As my understanding falls, my fear of embarrassment rises (negative link). And as my fear of embarrassment rises, my willingness to volunteer comments declines (negative link).

The decrease in my comments leads to even more horseplay and so we continue around the amplifying, vicious circle that makes us more and more ineffective as a group. Because we have four negative links, an even number, the feedback loop as a whole is positive. With that kind of structure our meeting is unstable and we will not get much done.

But there could be other links in the loop. Suppose my level of boredom rises as the amount of horsing around increases (positive link). The more bored I become the less self-conscious I become (negative link). This fall in self-consciousness increases my willingness to comment (negative link). That willingness to comment cuts down on the horseplay (negative link). We have here a limiting or self-regulating loop whereby the increase in horseplay sets off automatic responses that tend to hold it in check. This loop has one positive and three negative links. It is therefore a negative feedback loop. It exerts a damping effect, pushing the system towards an equilibrium.

At some point the level of horseplay may become so great that the second loop (the negative one) dominates the first (the positive one) and the meeting will move from a vicious spiral of ineffectiveness onto a path towards more effective communication. Note that the behaviour of the system moves of its own accord, because of its nonlinear feedback structure, from an unstable to a stable state.

Because relationships between people in a group inevitably take this complicated, changing feedback form, decision making cannot be as coherent a process as rational models of any kind would lead us to believe. This becomes even clearer when we take account of the impact of the unconscious on group behaviour. We could add boxes to *Figure 6.6* to represent the unconscious responses people make to each other and to some situations. For example, when they are confronted by great uncertainty, a group of individuals may regress to infantile defence mechanisms that impair their ability to learn, work and make decisions. This possibility will be discussed in the final section of this chapter.

Tight and loose coupling

Weick points to added levels of complexity in interrelationships and decision making as we move from single groups to the collections of groups that constitute an organisation. Organisations are typically not tightly coupled sets of groups alone. Organisations are more typically sets of groups that are tightly coupled for some purposes, but constitute a loosely coupled system for other purposes.

Groups or systems are *tightly coupled* when there are clear-cut direct connections between them; when they are so closely coordinated that a decision or action in one has immediately apparent implications for decisions or actions in another. So we get tight coupling in an efficient assembly production process, where one group assembling the components on a television set work in a highly coordinated way with another group putting the components into a plastic casing. Any failure in the first assembly operation has an immediate impact on the later operation and vice versa. Tight coupling is highly efficient while all moves according to plan. But unforeseen changes in one area have rapid and major implications for what happens in other areas. A small failure in one small part could bring the whole system down. Tight coupling is characterised by (Perrow 1984):

- no delays in processing;
- no variation in sequences of events;
- only one method of achieving the goal;
- no slack in the flow of activity from one part of the system to another;
- any buffers built in at the design stage;
- possible substitution of supplies or equipment built in at the design stage.

Loose coupling, on the other hand, means that there is a buffer between one group and another. There is the possibility of delays and changes in the sequences of events. Parts of the system can continue to function while failures in other parts of the system are attended to. Alternative methods can be employed and additional resources called upon. Buffers and redundancies are available to deal with the unforeseeable.

Clearly, loosely coupled systems are less efficient, but they are also far safer. The more unpredictable the situation, the more helpful it will be to have a loosely coupled system. So in the assembly operation above we could turn the system into a loosely coupled one by introducing the possibility of building up unplanned inventories at each stage. If the group putting the assemblies into plastic cases fails to maintain its speed, the supervisor of the group assembling the components could decide to continue production and add to inventories, even though there is no plan to do so. Decisions or actions in one group would then not have immediate implications for another.

Because of this possibility of loose coupling, a change in one part of the system need not immediately affect the other parts. Loosely coupled systems are characterised by the possibility of delays and changes in the sequences of events. And because of this we will find it difficult to predict what one group will do when another takes some action. The system becomes safer in the face of uncertainty, but the safety factor itself adds a level of complexity that makes it more difficult to determine how the system will behave or why it is behaving as it does.

Loose coupling means that the connections between decisions and actions in one part of the organisation and decisions and actions in other parts are often obscure. The connections between means and ends, and between problems and solutions, also become less clear. People, problems and choice opportunities are combined in confusing ways that make it difficult to predict agendas of matters to be attended to, and the outcomes of those matters.

When they deal with the ordinary day-to-day management of their existing businesses, successful organisations set up tightly coupled systems. Modern methods of operations management and inventory control, such as Just-in-Time delivery and Materials Resource Programming, are examples of this. But successful organisations always also have to face unpredictable changes to their activities. To deal with this they also evolve loosely coupled systems. Because they face both the predictable and the unpredictable, most organisations are systems that combine tight and loose coupling. The element of loose coupling often makes it very difficult to identify the events in one part of the system that are causing changes in other parts.

Links with the environment

Weick also explains the organisation's links with the environment in terms of feedback loops. The nature of these loops is illustrated in *Figure 6.7*.

First consider what the terms used in *Figure 6.7* mean and then what the loop connections between them signify.

1 *Ecological change* means the changes occurring in the market and wider environments that an organisation operates in. Such changes are primarily the actions undertaken by actors in the environment. These external actions may lead people in an organisation to undertake actions too – hence the arrow and the + sign running from ecological change to enactment.

2 *Enactment* describes what the actors within the organisation itself do; it is the actions they undertake. The term enactment is used rather than the term action, to indicate that people within an organisation do not simply anticipate, react or adapt to what actors in the environment can be objectively observed to do. Instead, people within an organisation are prompted by their subjective perceptions of what actors in the environment are doing or might do. It is those perceptions that drive their actions.

Furthermore, their actions may lead environmental actors to do what they do. Those within an organisation then perceive this and undertake further action. So they all keep going around a positive feedback loop, represented by the plus signs in the loop shown in *Figure 6.7* between ecological change and enactment. By taking a particular action, people within an organisation may cause people outside it to do what they do – the former are therefore in a real sense creating, or enacting, their own environment. Because they are driven by subjective perceptions it is also quite possible for people within an organisation to invent an environment and then cause it to occur. The reality people within an organisation respond to is being socially constructed by themselves. The question now is this: what causes actors within the organisation to perceive and act in the way they do? The answer lies in what they remember about what they have done before.

3 *Retention* is the process of storing what has been perceived and learned from previous actions. It is the shared memory of the collection of people constituting the organisation, built up from what they have done together over the past, reflecting their perceptions of what has worked and what has not worked. If particular actions worked in particular circumstances before, this will prompt a similar enactment now. So the link running back from retention to enactment can be positive or negative; that is, the organisational memory could prompt an action or stop it. The terms retention and organisational memory as they are used here mean

Figure 6.7 Weick's model: links with the environment
Source: K. Weick (1979), *The Social Psychology of Organizing*, Reading, Ma: Addison-Wesley

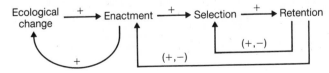

the same thing as the culture of the organisation, its recipe, the paradigm its managers subscribe to, their received wisdom. These terms all have to do with the shared mental models of organisational actors. The next question is this: how does retention come about? The answer lies in a process of selection.

4 *Selection* is the process through which organisational actors focus on some meanings of what they are doing and some perceptions of what others are doing, while ignoring yet others. What is selected for retention depends upon what has been done or enacted and what has been perceived (the positive arrow running from enactment to selection). And the selection itself is affected by what has been previously retained about how things should be perceived and done (the loop running back from retention to selection). What we select to focus on now depends on the mental models we have already built up. These may cause us to accept or reject a perception, hence the positive and negative signs in the retention–selection loop.

By looking at the interactions between an organisation and its environment in this way, Weick clarifies the concept of managers together creating the reality they respond to (see *Key Concept 6.2*).

■ **Key concept 6.2**
THE SOCIAL CONSTRUCTION OF REALITY

The environment which managers respond to is not a set of independently given, scientifically observable facts. It is a set of perceptions they have. These are determined by the mental models they have built up from previous education and experience and have come to share with each other. They continually amend these models through their ongoing experiences or enactments. In this sense they invent their own environment.

These perceptions are perceptions about the interactions between people inside one organisation and other people outside that organisation. People inside an organisation are taking part in these interactions and in this sense they are creating their environment. Ideas of creating and inventing, that is enacting, environments through interactions across the organisation's boundary, are going to be more useful guides to understanding what goes on in organisations than ideas of adapting to an environment.

Since managers are inventing and creating their own environments in conjunction with other actors in the environment in a positive feedback loop, they can easily generate vicious and virtuous circles, self-fulfilling prophecies, chain reactions and bandwagon effects. Because of all this, managers cannot know in advance what they are creating. They have to do something and then understand what they have done before they do the next thing. Here, then, people are attaching meaning retrospectively to what they have done, not deciding in advance what the meaning is of what they will do. In a sense the purpose of actions is defined after the actions have been taken. An organisation does not know what it is about until it looks back and imposes structure and meaning on what it has done.

■ **Illustration 6.3**
TIN CANS: INVENTING THE ENVIRONMENT

In the mid-1980s the UK manufacturers of tin can emulsion paint containers perceived that the main cause of the decline in the demand for their product was its propensity to rust. Market research at the time indicated that the more important cause was the poor levels of service provided to paint producers. Managers in the tin can firms ignored this and came up with a technical solution to the rust problem. By this time plastic cans backed by design support and high service levels had made major inroads into the market. They have now virtually replaced tin cans in the emulsion packaging market. Managers in the tin can firms were quite clearly enacting an environment, inventing it in fact. Because it bore little relationship to reality, the invention destroyed them.

But note that inventing or creating an environment does not always lead to disaster. Sony created a demand for personal entertainment systems by inventing the Walkman. This turned out to be an invention connected to reality.

Self-designing systems

The feedback system view of how an organisation works led Weick (1977) to the concept of an organisation as a self-designing system. Rigid rule-bound organisations that spell out exactly how people should behave are incapable of generating new forms of behaviour to meet new situations. To be able to meet the unexpected new situation, organisations need to be loosely coupled, self-designing systems. That requires establishing the following patterns:

- valuing improvisation more than forecasts;
- dwelling on opportunities rather than constraints;
- inventing solutions rather than borrowing them;
- cultivating impermanence instead of permanence;
- valuing argument more highly than serenity;
- relying on diverse measures of performance rather than on accounting systems alone;
- encouraging doubt rather than removing it;
- continuously experimenting rather than searching for final solutions;
- seeking contradictions rather than discouraging them.

Such patterns of behaviour will make organisations less efficient but more adaptable.

In the models summarised above, Weick has made a number of key points which have remained largely outside mainstream strategic management, despite the fact that they capture much of what we can directly observe to be happening. These key points are summarised in *Figure 6.8*.

We now turn to another important strand in management literature which has also received very little attention from those concerned with strategic management – system dynamics.

Figure 6.8   Weick's model: key points on organisational dynamics

- Organisations are complex feedback systems, starting right at the fundamental level of interaction between two or more people within the organisation.
- The systematic feedback structure of the organisation itself determines the pattern of behaviour over time. The standard assumption of today's dominant management theory is that the dynamics, the patterns of change, are due mainly to environmental forces outside the organisation. The proposition being made in the Weick models is that patterns of change are determined by the inherent nature of the system structure itself.
- A group of people does not necessarily have to have a shared, common purpose in order to be a group. People form groups before they have a common purpose because they have interdependent needs that require the resources of others. We group because we need each others' support, because of the means not the ends. Purpose comes later. So an organisation is not necessarily driven by goal-seeking behaviour, that is achieving a given goal. It may well be driven by searching for a goal in the first place. This is a very different perspective from today's dominant views on management.
- Meaning for an organisation is retrospective not prospective. We can only understand what we are doing by interpreting what we have done. We impose meaning on what we have done. So a vision would not be a picture of a future state but an interpretation of where we have now got to. Meaning, purpose, vision and mission emerge from what we have done and are doing – they are not

prior organisation-wide intentions.
- Organisations create and invent their own environment in the sense that the environment is their perception of what is happening and in the sense that their actions impact on the environment which then impacts back on the organisation. This is different to the simple adaptive view that is common in the dominant received wisdom.
- Predicting what complex feedback systems will do is very difficult. It is difficult to guess what people's preferences will be in the future and it is these preferences that will drive what they do.
- But despite the unpredictability and the complexity, people can operate as part of a system that is too complex for any one person alone to understand. Each plays a part in the complex unfolding of events, understanding only a part, and relies on others to play their parts.
- Loose coupling is important in the ability of such complex systems to remain flexible, but that loose coupling adds to system complexity and makes it even harder to understand and predict its behaviour.
- Such systems are essentially self-designing.
- Positive feedback, self-reinforcing processes play a very important part in what happens. Instability is an essential part of what goes on and we cannot simply ignore it or write it off as something to be banished by negative feedback controls. There is too much evidence that this focus on negative feedback alone leads to unintended positive loops and unintended consequences. People prize improvisation.

6.5 Jay Forrester's system dynamics models: cause and effect are distant

The most important development of complex systems models for application to organisational and social policy issues has been by Jay Forrester. His background is that of a servomechanisms engineer, digital computer pioneer and manager of a large R&D effort. He developed an approach to understanding human systems that is based on concepts of positive and negative feedback, nonlinearity and the use of computers to simulate the behaviour patterns of such complex systems. Feedback is the basic characteristic of his view of the world:

> Systems of information feedback control are fundamental to all life and human endeavour, from the slow pace of biological evolution to the launching of the latest satellite. A feedback control system exists whenever the environment causes a decision which in turn affects the original environment (Forrester, 1958, p. 4).

Here human decision-making is firmly linked to the feedback concept.

Production and distribution chains

Forrester has illustrated his approach by modelling the behaviour of production–distribution chains. A factory supplies a product, say beer, to a number of distributors who then ship it to an even larger number of retailers. Orders for the product flow back upstream from retailers to distributors and from them to the factory. The factory, the distributors and the retailers form a system and the links between them are flows of orders in one direction and flows of product in the other. Each part of the system tries to do the best it can to maintain inventories at minimum levels without running out of product to sell. Each attempts to ship product as fast as possible. They all do these things because that is the way to maximise their individual profits.

But because of its very structure – the feedback and lags in information flows – this system shows a marked tendency to amplify minor ordering disturbances at the retail level. An initial 10 per cent increase in orders at the retail level can eventually cause production at the factory to peak 40 per cent above the initial level before collapsing.

Peter Senge (1990) reports how he has used this example as a game with thousands of groups of managers in many countries. Even when people know about the likely consequences of this system, he has always found that the consequences of a small increase at the retail level is, first of all, growing demand that cannot be met. Inventories are depleted and backlogs grow. Then beer arrives in great quantities while incoming orders suddenly decline as backlogs are reduced. Eventually almost all players end up with large inventories they cannot unload. It is exactly this kind of cyclical behaviour we observe in real-life businesses.

Only by being aware of how the system as a whole functions, rather than simply concentrating on one's own part of it, can the extreme instabilities of the cycles be avoided. It seems, however, that these cycles can never be removed altogether.

The lessons of systems thinking

The lessons of the game are that:

- The structure of the system influences behaviour. The cycles in ordering, inventory levels and production in the game are really the consequence of the structure of the system. But, when people play the game in a classroom, or in real life, they blame others in the system for what is going on. For example, the retailers blame the distributors for running out of stock and not delivering fast enough.
- Structure in human systems is subtle. Structure is the set of interrelationships between people and, because of negative and positive feedback loops, that structure can generate unintended results.
- Coping effectively often comes from a new way of thinking. If one simply focuses on one's own part in the system, thinks for example always as a retailer, then one's behaviour of over- and under-ordering will simple contribute to the system's instability. If, instead, players think in terms of the whole system, they will behave differently. For example, they will realise that widespread over-ordering is likely to occur. They will realise that doing so themselves in this situation will not help them much in the short run, but will eventually lead to stock levels that are too high. They will avoid doing what everyone else is doing, even if this reduces profitability in the short run.

Principles of complex systems

By running computer simulations of a great many different human systems, researchers in the systems dynamics tradition have identified a number of principles about complex human systems. These are set out below.

1 Complex systems often produce unexpected and counter-intuitive results. In the beer game, retailers increase orders above their real need expecting this to lead to bigger deliveries, but because all retailers are doing this, and because of lags in information flows, the unexpected result is lower deliveries. Simulation of other situations suggests that increased low-cost housing in an inner city will exacerbate rather than arrest the decline of inner cities, because it creates ghettoes where social mobility is impossible. Policies of demolishing slum housing and discouraging the construction of cheap housing make the centre more desirable for the better off, but also create a more balanced social system in which there is the opportunity for upward mobility.

2 In complex systems – nonlinear relationships with positive and negative feedback – the links between cause and effect are distant in time and space. In the beer game, the causes of increased demand appeared at the retail end, distant in space from the factory and distant in time because of the lags in order flows. Such distance between cause and effect makes it very difficult to say what is causing what. Those playing the beer game always think that the fluctuations in deliveries are being caused by fluctuations in retail demand when in fact they are due to the manner in which the system operates. The problem is made worse by many coincident symptoms that look like causes but are merely relational. This means that it is extremely difficult to make specific predictions of what will happen in a

specific place over a specific time period. Instead, quantitative simulations on computers can be used to identify general qualitative patterns of behaviour that will be similar to those we are likely to experience, although never the same. Simulation here is being used not to capture the future specific outcome within a range of likely outcomes, but to establish broad qualitative features in patterns of behaviour. Senge (1990, p. 73) puts it like this:

> The art of systems thinking lies in being able to recognise increasingly (dynamically) complex and subtle structures, . . . amid the wealth of details, pressures and cross-currents that attend all real management settings. In fact, the essence of mastering systems thinking as a management discipline lies in seeing patterns where others see only events and forces to react to.

3 Complex systems are highly sensitive to some changes but remarkably insensitive to many others. Complex systems contain some influential pressure, or leverage, points. If we can influence those points we can have a major impact on the behaviour of the system. The trouble is that these are difficult to identify. Note how this concern with leverage points relates to the ideas introduced at the beginning of this chapter on chain reactions, bandwagon effects and virtuous circles of behaviour. In the beer game, the leverage points lie in the ordering practices of retailers and distributors. Unfortunately these pressure points, from which favourable chain reactions can be initiated, are extremely difficult to find. More usually, it seems, complex systems are insensitive to changes and indeed counteract and compensate for externally applied correctives. So when retailers find that deliveries from the distributors are curtailed, they respond by ordering even more and so make the situation worse. When aid programmes provide more dams and water pumps to halt the expansion of the Sahara, tribesmen simply enlarge their herd sizes, leading to overgrazing and the even more rapid encroachment of the desert.

Because of this natural tendency to counteract and compensate, that is to move to stability, it is necessary to change the system itself rather than simply apply externally generated remedies. By their very nature, complex systems often react to policy changes in ways that are the opposite to those which policy makers intend; and complex systems tend to a condition of poor performance because they resist change.

The above points lead inevitably to the conclusion that, because an organisation is a complex system, attempts to plan its long-term future and plan changes in its culture and behaviour patterns are all likely to prompt counter-forces and lead to little change at all or to unexpected and unintended changes. The very structure of a complex system makes it impossible to plan its specific long-term future. We have to operate within the system, in an ongoing way, guided by the general patterns that complex systems display.

Experience supports this conclusion. Individual organisations develop, as we all know, in unforeseen ways. On the national level we have seen the failure of grand design planning systems for whole economies: first in some Western countries such as the UK in the 1960s and 1970s and more recently in the countries of Eastern Europe. However, despite this experience and despite the research done by systems dynamicists, systems thinking attracts very little attention from either researchers into or practitioners of strategic management.

Archetypes of feedback processes

Once the strong possibility that complex systems will counteract correctives and produce unintended consequences is recognised, it becomes essential to analyse and understand the feedback connections in the system, to understand the system as a whole. It becomes vital for effective intervention in the behaviour of the system to understand the dynamics of the system.

Through their simulations, systems dynamicists have built up a set of templates, or archetype feedback processes, that are very commonly found in organisations of all kinds. The purpose of these archetypes is not to make specific predictions of what will happen, but to recondition perceptions so that people are able to perceive the structures at play, to see the dynamic patterns of behaviour, and to see the potential leverage in those structures. The templates are meant to be used in a flexible way to help understand patterns in events. You have to use the template as an analogy with which to build your own explanations of each specific situation you are confronted with. Some examples of these templates are as follows.

1 Limits to growth (*Figure 6.9*)

Limits to growth occur when a reinforcing positive feedback process is installed to produce a desired result (a positive growth loop) but it inadvertently creates secondary effects (a negative limiting loop) that puts a stop to the growth. We saw this in the discussion on positive and negative feedback in relation to population growth in an earlier section of this chapter, that on nonlinearity, negative and positive feedback. The 'limits to growth' structure is found wherever growth bumps up against limits.

The most immediate response to this structure is that of pushing harder on the factors that cause growth. In fact this is counterproductive because it causes the system to bump even more firmly against the limits. The solution is to work on the negative loop, on relaxing the limits.

For example, a company may grow through introducing new products flowing from its R&D efforts. As it grows it increases the size of the R&D department which becomes harder to manage. Senior engineers then become managers and the flow of new product ideas slows. Pressing for more new product ideas will simply lead to a

Figure 6.9   Limits to growth
Source: P. Senge (1990), *The Fifth Discipline*, New York: Doubleday

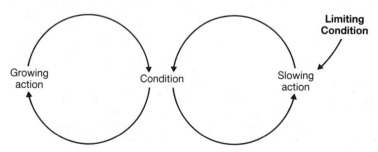

bigger R&D department and that will exacerbate the management problems, so reducing the flow of new ideas. We need instead to rethink the whole process of developing new products and running R&D activities. The leverage point is the way in which the actual R&D effort is organised and to see how this should be done we need to understand the whole system of which R&D is a part.

2 Shifting the burden (*Figure 6.10*)

Shifting the burden happens where some underlying problem generates a number of symptoms. Because the underlying problem is difficult to identify, people focus on the symptoms. They look for the quick, easy fix. While these temporarily relieve the symptoms, the underlying problem gets worse. People do not notice at first how the underlying problems are getting worse and as they avoid dealing with these problems the system loses its ability to solve them.

An example is bringing an expert into an organisation to solve a problem. This may leave a manager's ability unaltered and when related problems arise again the manager will be unable to cope without the expert.

3 Eroding goals (*Figure 6.11*)

Another template is that of eroding goals, where a short-term solution is effected by allowing fundamental goals to decline. This happens when managers accept a decline in performance standards as a temporary measure to deal with a crisis.

Figure 6.10   Shifting the burden
Source: P. Senge (1990), *The Fifth Discipline*, New York: Doubleday

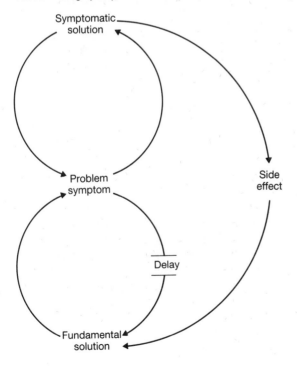

Figure 6.11   Eroding goals
Source: P. Senge (1990), *The Fifth Discipline*, New York: Doubleday

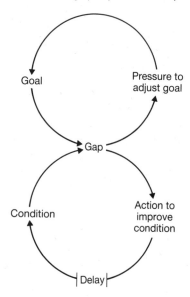

So for example, a company producing a good product attracting high levels of demand increases its delivery time to accommodate a backlog crisis. It then does little to increase production capacity. The next time it goes around the circle, it experiences even bigger backlogs and so it extends delivery time even further. This goes on until customer dissatisfaction suddenly reaches a critical point and demand falls away rapidly.

Simulations show that when firms allow their goals for quality and delivery time gradually to slip it has dramatic effects on their profitability, as shown in *Illustration 6.4*. The message is to beware the symptomatic solution and seek to understand how the system is working.

■ **Illustration 6.4**
PEOPLES EXPRESS

Peoples Express provided an innovative low-cost airline service between the US and Europe and within the USA. It was a no-frills service, but it was reliable. However, Peoples Express found that it could not build its service capacity to keep pace with the exploding demand. Instead of slowing its growth (by increasing prices) and focusing on training to increase service capacity, it continued to grow as fast as it could. Service levels declined more and more rapidly, staff morale collapsed, and competition became more fierce. Eventually customers no longer found Peoples Express attractive.

Source: Senge, (1990)

Figure 6.12 Growth and underinvestment
Source: P. Senge (1990), *The Fifth Discipline*, New York: Doubleday

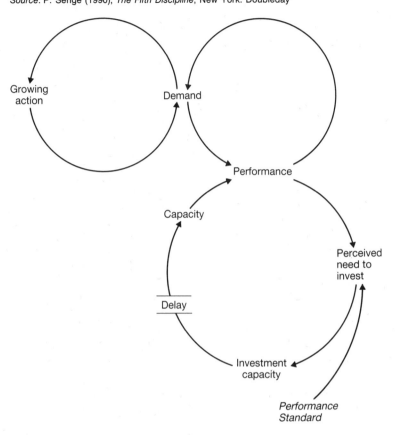

4 Growth and underinvestment (*Figure 6.12*)

This occurs when new investments in capacity are not made early enough or on a large enough scale to accommodate continuing growth. As growth approaches limits set by existing capacity, the attempts made to meet demand result in lower quality and service levels. The consequence is customer dissatisfaction and declining demand.

The systems dynamics approach to understanding how organisations work makes a number of important key points that are summarised in *Figure 6.13*.

6.6 Argyris and Schon's model: simple and complex forms of organisational learning

In the second section of this chapter, we discussed the nature of feedback systems, underlining the crucial role of human cognition – how we make sense of the world – in the operation of the feedback loops driving how we discover, choose and act in

Figure 6.13   System dynamics: main points on organisational dynamics

- Nonlinearity and feedback loops are fundamental properties of organisational life, properties we are unused to recognising.
- The feedback structure of the system itself generates patterns of behaviour and we find this confusing because we are accustomed to looking for causes in some discrete event. We believe that something or someone must be to blame when it is really the structure of the system that is leading to what happens.
- In complex systems of the type we are talking about, cause-and-effect links are distant and very difficult to identify.
- Behaviour patterns can emerge without being intended; in fact they often emerge contrary to intention.
- The result is unexpected and counter-intuitive outcomes.
- Forecasting specific sequences of events therefore becomes very difficult and seeing qualitative patterns becomes very important.

- Understanding the structure of the system could lead to the identification of pressure, or leverage, points where efforts to change behaviour have the most effect.
- These pressure points are difficult to find and most changes we try to make to a system simply provoke compensating and offsetting behaviour.
- Consequently, systems have a strong tendency to stabilise and so deteriorate in the face of change. This idea has much in common with that of the forces of differentiation and integration pulling organisations to extremes where they fail. The reader should refer back to Chapter 4, where the ideas of Miller on trajectories to failure are discussed.
- Successful organisations can approach stability and regularity if they understand the system as a whole and if they can identify the leverage points.

organisations. The environment managers respond to is the one that they together create through their shared perceptions – reality is a social construction. It is important therefore to be aware of how we make sense of the world and how we learn. Research on human cognitive ability shows that we are capable of retaining only up to seven bits of information in the short-term memory at any one time. A bit is a digit, or a letter of the alphabet, or some chunk of them such as a word. The information processing capacity of the human brain is thus very limited. The capacity of the long-term memory is apparently infinite, but it take seconds to store new information in that long-term memory. Our ability to absorb and process new information is therefore painfully slow.

Humans are therefore compelled by their limited brain capacity to simplify everything they observe; we are unable to know reality itself; all we can do is construct simplifications, that is mental models of reality. What we discover and therefore what we choose and how we act, all depend upon the mental model we bring to the task. When we look at a particular situation, we see it through the lens provided by the mental models we have built up through past experience and education. We approach each situation every day with a mindset, a recipe we have acquired from the past, that we use to understand the present in order to design our actions to cope with it. When we find that we are taking actions that fail to have the desired result, we often find that the reason lies in the way we perceived the problem in the first place. The remedy is to amend the mental model, the perspective, the mindset with which we are approaching the task.

The methods we use to store mental models and how we use what we have stored for subsequent discovery and choice have important implications. Research on cognitive ability shows that we do not normally store what we have previously observed and processed in any detailed form. We only store items and recall them in exact detail in exceptional circumstances, for example when we learn the lines of a play or prepare for certain kinds of examination. Normally we store and recall only some important category features of items we have observed. It is as if we label items according to the category they belong to, according to the strength of association they have with other similar items. We store schemas, frames or scenes and we particularly note exceptions. In other words, we store and recall according to degrees of similarity and irregularity, not according to the principles of sameness or regularity. The category features we use are rather vague and fuzzy. Mental models are sketchy, incomplete constructs used in a feedback way to affect what we discover next (Baddely, 1990). When we confront some situation we do not observe its complete detail. We select certain items and fill in others using our previously stored frames or scenes. Experiments have shown that we can be quite convinced that we have witnessed an event, even though it has not occurred, simply because that event normally occurred in a particular situation the experimenter now presents us with (Baddely, 1990).

These points about how we build partial, loose, flexible mental models based on similarities and irregularities in the patterns of events we observe, and then use them later partially to reconstruct what we then observe, are of great importance to our understanding of management. These points mean that managers will not simply observe a given environment and a given organisational capability – the facts. They, like all other humans, will sometimes inevitably invent what they observe. The whole process of simplifying and selecting means that the environment is in a real sense the invention and the creation of the managers observing it. It will then only be possible for managers to make sense of what they are doing after they have done it (Weick, 1969/79.) In highly complex and uncertain situations, then, explanations of strategic management need to take account of the possibility that environments may be invented or created in managers' minds and that they can often only make sense of what they are doing with hindsight.

Mental models

So far, a number of ways in which humans compensate for their limited brain processing capacity have been referred to. We simplify complex reality by constructing mental models of that reality in which data are classified in loose, fuzzy categories. We store those models and use them later to understand the next situation and indeed to fill in some of the detail of the next situation. We do not always use algorithmic step-by-step reasoning, but sometimes make intuitive jumps. In this way we can handle far greater levels of complexity and uncertainty, as well as far faster rates of change, than a straightforward use of our processing capacity would allow. But the consequence of this way of operating is that we may invent the reality around us. In some circumstances this may be a cost, while in others it may be the benefit of creativity.

In addition to all this there are two further means of great importance that we use to compensate for limited brain processing capacity in a complex world. First, we automate our mental models so speeding up the process of recall and application to a new situation. Second, we share those automated models with each other to cut down on the need to communicate before we act together.

Experts and unconscious mental models

A person would function very slowly if for every action that person had consciously to retrieve and examine large numbers of previously acquired mental models and then choose an appropriate one. Experts therefore push previously acquired models below the level of awareness into the unconscious mind. One aspect of learning is through repetition of an action in order to make the design of later similar actions an automatic process. The expert seems to use some form of recognisable pattern in a new situation automatically to trigger the use of past models developed in relation to analogous previous situations. Experts do not examine the whole body of their expertise when they confront a new situation. Instead they detect recognisable similarity in the qualitative patterns of what they observe and automatically produce models which they modify to meet the new circumstances.

For example, an expert chess player differs from a novice in terms of the richness of his or her mental store of patterns and relationships between the pieces on a chess board. On being confronted with some new juxtaposition of pieces, the expert perceives patterns missed by the novice. It is from these perceptions that the expert derives superiority. This conclusion is supported by the fact that the expert is no better than the novice in deciding what to do when the pieces have been set out randomly. It is not therefore that the expert has a better short-term memory or can process information faster. The expert's superiority arises because models of the moves appropriate to different patterns are stored in the expert's memory and drawn on as required through some form of analogous reasoning.

Analogy has been found to pervade thought. We use analogies to make the novel seem familiar by relating it to prior knowledge. We use analogies to make the familiar seem strange by viewing it from a new perspective. These are fundamental aspects of human intelligence used to construct new scientific theories, design experiments, and solve new problems in terms of old ones (Gick & Holyoak, 1983). Furthermore, paradox plays a crucial role in developing new insight.

One form of learning, then, is that which uses some form of repetition to push mental models into the unconscious where they can be recalled and used very rapidly. The richer the store of unconscious models the more expert the person. We can call this simple or single-loop learning. Each time we act we learn from the consequences of the action to improve the next action, without having consciously to retrieve and examine the unconscious models we are using to design the action.

But expert behaviour based on single-loop learning and unconscious mental models brings not only benefits; it carries with it significant dangers. The fact that the mental models being used to design actions are unconscious means that we are not questioning them. The more expert we are, the more rapidly we use unconscious models, and therefore the more easily we take for granted the assumptions and simplifications upon which they are inevitably built. This is highly efficient in stable circumstances but when those circumstances change rapidly it becomes highly dangerous. Mental models used without question can rapidly become inappropriate in rapidly changing conditions. The possibility arises of skilled incompetence (Argyris, 1990). The more expert we are, the more skilled we are in designing certain actions, the greater the risk we run that we will not question what we are doing, the more we are likely to become skilled incompetents. This gives rise to the need for double-loop or complex learning. Here we learn not only in the sense of adjusting our actions in the light of their consequences, but in the sense also of questioning and adjusting the unconscious mental models we are using to design those actions in the first place.

Teams and shared models

Managers do not choose and act as isolated individuals. They interact with each other, choosing and acting in teams or groups. Simply by being part of a group, individuals learn to share the mental models they use to discover, choose and act. In this way they cut down on the communication and information flows that are required before they can act together. In particular, the more they share those implicit, expert models that have been pushed into the unconscious, the less they need to communicate in order to secure cohesive action. This sharing of implicit models is what we mean by the culture of the group or the organisation. Groups and organisations develop cultures, company and industry recipes or retained memories,

---

■ **Key concept 6.3**
MENTAL MODELS, FEEDBACK AND SKILLED INCOMPETENCE

Mental models are the simplifications that humans construct and store in their brains of the world they encounter. These models are the lenses through which we perceive the world we have to operate in, the constructions we make to explain how it and we are behaving, the structures we use to design our actions. These models are based on loose flexible categories of information, where categories appear to be defined in fuzzy terms of similarity and irregularity. In totally new situations, we use processes of analogous reasoning to construct new mental models using those already stored. Coping with the world can be seen as a continuing feedback from one set of models to another.

We automate our mental models by pushing them into the unconscious – this is the process of becoming an expert. Some models, the expert ones, are therefore implicit and hardly ever questioned while others are explicit and are more likely to be questioned. The latter are the explanations of what we are doing that we articulate. We share the expert unconscious models when we work together in a group. Automation and sharing lead to the strong possibility of expert incompetence and groupthink when conditions are changing rapidly.

as they perform together, in order to speed up their actions. This is exactly what Kuhn was referring to as the paradigm that governs the conduct of ordinary science (see the section on how paradigms govern what we see and do in Chapter 3).

Individuals who are part of any group are put under strong pressure by group processes to conform, that is to share the mental models of the other members. While this may have great benefits in terms of efficient action in stable conditions, it becomes a serious liability when conditions are changing rapidly. It then becomes necessary to question the implicit, unconscious group models that are being used to design actions. As conditions change the unquestioned models may well become inappropriate. The powerful pressures that grow up within groups of experts to accept rather than question very fundamental values opens up the strong possibility of skilled incompetence in group behaviour, of groupthink.

Espoused models and models in use

We overcome our very limited physical brain working capacity to produce unlimited mental capacity by simplifying and selecting, building models, automating those models by pushing them below the level of awareness, and learning to share them with others in our group. We use qualitative similarities and dissimilarities between one situation and another when we develop more appropriate models in new situations. Managers design their expert actions in this way, just as physicians and physicists do. The more expert an individual or a group the more actions are designed in ways determined by unconscious, implicit models. Because the assumptions underlying those models are not surfaced and questioned it is quite possible that experts will articulate one model while designing their actions according to another. There may well be a difference between espoused models and models in use (Argyris and Schon, 1978). Experts are quite likely to say one thing and do another. The more expert people become in working together as a group the more prone they are to do this too. Ask managers what they do and most will say that they organise and plan. Observe what managers actually do and we see them dashing from one task to another in a manner which is not all that planned or organised.

When we recognise that there are frequent differences between what expert managers say they are doing and what they are actually doing, differences which they themselves are not usually aware of, we can see how easy it is for managers to play games and build organisational defences (Argyris, 1990). For example, most managers espouse a rational model of action and believe that they should uncover the facts and consider a sensible range of options before they take action. Most espouse free and open discussions because that is a rational position to take. But at the same time there is a widespread norm in our organisations requiring subordinates to withhold the truth from their superiors, especially if they believe that the superior will find the truth unwelcome and accuse them of being negative. Games of deception and cover-up are therefore played. All know they are being played but none openly discuss what is happening, despite espousal of rational behaviour. We say one thing, do the direct opposite, and rarely find this strange. Add to this the existence of skilled incompetence and you can see how very difficult it will be to change these games and break down these defences. Attempts to explain how strategic management is actually carried out and attempts to prescribe how to do it better will be misleading and perhaps dangerous unless they explicitly recognise the existence of skilled incompetence, the difference between espoused models and models in use, and the behavioural dynamics these lead to.

■ **Key concept 6.4**
ESPOUSED MODELS AND MODELS IN USE

Espoused mental models are those that we articulate and put forward to explain how we are behaving. Models in use are those mental models that actually drive our behaviour. The espoused models are simple to identify – they are what people say they are. The models in use are difficult to identify – they have to be reconstructed from what people are actually doing. Since models in use are often going to be those that are being unconsciously used, the actor using them will also have difficulty in identifying them. Experts have considerable difficulty in articulating their models in use.

The difference in espoused models and models in use means that we may well say one thing and do another. This is not necessarily intentional hypocrisy, since we may well be unaware of our models in use which we will normally hardly ever question.

Simple and complex learning

The simple form of learning can be illustrated by the activity of reviewing a budget and taking corrective action. There is a monitoring, or discovery, step in which an actual profit outcome is compared with the desired outcome set in the budget. If actual is below budget, the reason is discovered, a choice of corrective action is made, and action is taken. That action affects profit in the next period as do external changes, leading to the need for the next round of discovery, choice and action. Managers involved in this single loop are controlling and they are also learning. They are discovering the consequences of their actions and amending their behaviour according to what they discover. This kind of learning is simple or single loop because managers are not questioning what they are doing in any fundamental sense. The budget for example is not questioned. Taking another example, General Motors thought that high fuel costs and therefore smaller cars were the key issues and Japanese competence in offering small cars the key reason for their success in the 1970s. General Motors' managers focused on this explanation, never questioning their assumptions. This kind of single-loop learning is depicted in *Figure 6.14*.

Now consider what these managers would do if they were to learn in a complex or double-loop way. When they analyse why profit is coming in below budget, that is when they discover, they do so using their expertise, that is the implicit unconscious mental models they have built up through past experience and have come to share through working together. They have a recipe on how their organisation and its industry or environment works. The reasons they produce to account for poor profit performance will be determined by these unconscious shared mental models. Consequently their choice and their action will also depend on these

Figure 6.14   Simple single-loop learning

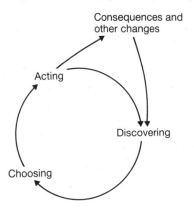

mental models. In the single-loop case they did not surface what the model was or question it; they simply used it. In double-loop complex learning they would, as part of the discovery stage, surface and question that model. They would be discovering not only what is changing outside and what the consequences of their actions are, but also what this all means for the unconscious models they are using, for their recipes and received wisdom. This simultaneous journey around two loops is depicted in *Figure 6.15*.

Complex learning, then, involves changing a mental model, a recipe, a mindset, a frame of reference, or a paradigm. It is a very difficult process to perform simply because we are trying to examine assumptions we are not normally even aware we are making. We will therefore keep slipping into single-loop learning because that is easier. But it is important to encourage double-loop learning since it is this that produces innovation. Kuhn has explained how most science is conducted within a given paradigm that scientists rarely question – a form of single-loop learning. Every now and then however, increasing discrepancies between what a science is explaining and what is happening lead to paradigm shifts in which the world comes

Figure 6.15   Complex double-loop learning

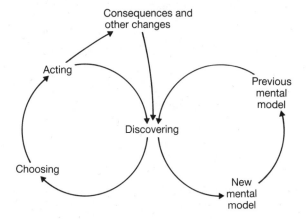

Figure 6.16 Organisational learning: main points on organisational dynamics

- Simple forms of organisational learning take the form of single negative feedback loops in which groups of people review and learn from the actions they have just undertaken.
- Simple forms of learning are conducted within a given paradigm and sustain the group learning in a state of stability, moving toward the realisation of a vision or the achievement of a goal.

- Complex learning is a double-loop phenomenon, partly the negative feedback learning about the consequences of actions, but also partly an amplifying, positive feedback loop of questioning the underlying assumptions.
- Complex learning is therefore essentially destabilising and revolutionary, but it is vitally necessary for innovation and creativity.

to be perceived in a different way – double-loop learning. Such shifts are associated with major new discoveries. One such shift is associated with the work of Newton and some believe that today is witnessing another such shift as the implications of complex system dynamics come to be understood. Managers who would innovate need constantly to be shifting, breaking and creating paradigms – they must engage in double-loop learning.

■ **Key concept 6.5**
SIMPLE AND COMPLEX LEARNING

Simple or single-loop learning is where we learn from the consequences of previous actions to amend the next action. It is a feedback process from action to consequence to subsequent action, without questioning the mental model driving the action.

Complex learning involves another feedback loop. It occurs when the consequences of actions lead to a questioning of the mental model, the underlying assumptions, that have been driving the actions. That questioning may lead to the amendment of the mental model, the reframing of the problem or opportunity, before action is amended. There is a double loop in which not only are actions amended, but the model driving the actions is too. Complex learning requires destruction – old ways of viewing the world have to be destroyed. Complex learning also involves creation – new ways of viewing the world have to be developed. Complex learning is the shifting, breaking and creating of paradigms.

6.7 Argyris's model: organisational defence routines and covert politics

In Chapter 5 we surveyed the general principles and the main techniques of Organisation Development (OD). You will recall that OD is the planned change of whole belief systems in an organisation such as to support and enable the implementation of its strategies. OD is the intentional change of a culture to be brought about through a systematic, organisation-wide, centrally planned programme of re-education. And this re-education programme has certain specific features: it is education based upon the consent and commitment of the people involved.

OD is based on the assumption that organisations will cope more effectively with change, will implement their strategies more effectively, if the creative potential of their people is unleashed. This is said to require:

- flat organisational structures;
- loose, overlapping job definitions;
- widespread participation in decision making; and thus
- the dispersion of power as authority to make decisions.

OD is about achieving planned changes in behaviour through empowering people in a particular kind of political system that we may call a democratic, collegial/consensus system (Greiner and Schein, 1988). The political system is collegial because it is based on dispersed power and widespread participation. It is a consensus system because it is all held together by strongly shared beliefs and decisions that are taken in a collaborative way. The aim is to move an organisation from a control model to a commitment one.

Despite the end point of dispersed power and consensus decision making, the OD programme is in fact about reaching that point in a planned manner. Someone has to decide in advance what the change in belief systems is to be; someone is in control of the process. OD is not about changes that emerge or evolve from a pattern of interactions: it is a comprehensive pre-designed programme. And herein lies its danger, for it can all too easily become a propaganda exercise. Herein lies what may be an insuperable obstacle – it is using a control model to install a commitment one. Note the concept of leadership in the OD project: the leader decides in advance what the organisation should do and then facilitates the acceptance of these decisions by others in the organisation. Contrast this with an alternative where leadership takes the form of facilitating a learning experience in which members of the organisation, including the leader, discover what decision to make. That would be a control model being used to lead to a commitment one.

Because of its emphasis on planning, OD is based on the unquestioned assumption that an organisation is a feedback system in which negative feedback is the dominant form. It is through the negative feedback of consensus planning and monitoring that the successful organisation is kept at, or returned to, stable states of consensus around a given culture or belief system, one that can be installed.

How well does this approach work? One study has described a long list of failed efforts at total culture change because of the neglect or lack of support from top management (Mirvis & Beerg, 1977). Another study of a number of companies (Beer, Eisenstat & Spector, 1990) leads to these conclusions:

- Corporate programmes to change the whole culture of a company in a top-down planned manner do not work.
- The most effective change programmes are those that start in a number of small peripheral operations and gradually spread throughout the organisation.

● Changes to formal structures, systems and policies come at the end of successful periods of change, not the beginning. Effective culture change focuses on the tasks people have to do in business units and it spreads not because the top is in control of the spread but because the top creates the right climate for change to spread.

There is therefore some persuasive evidence indicating that OD programmes simply do not work. A number of explanations have been put forward as to why they do not work. What these explanations all have in common is the introduction of self-reinforcing, amplifying feedback loops into the modelling of organisational life. Because the OD approach, with its emphasis on comprehensive plans, cannot assume the operation of amplifying feedback it produces inadequate prescriptions.

Consider some of the positive feedback loops commonly found in organisations.

Organisational defence routines

One of the main reasons for the failure of OD programmes is that they may well provoke and reinforce powerful organisational defence routines that are very difficult to identify and even more difficult to deal with effectively (Argyris, 1990). The activation of such defence routines is a specific example of the general point we discussed in the last section on systems dynamics: namely that complex systems tend to counteract planned changes to the system. OD programmes introduce negative feedback loops into an organisation, but they also unintentionally provoke positive feedback loops called organisational defence routines. Let me explain.

OD programmes are attempts to persuade managers to abandon a control model of managing and replace it with a commitment model. Consider first what is meant by a control model of managing. It is one in which:

● the manager's power is derived from position in the hierarchy;
● people are motivated by the task; and
● people respond most to short-term rewards in relation to task achievement.

These beliefs about the source of power and the way to motivate people are closely associated with the suppression of negative feelings and judgements about people's performance. Such judgements are usually not publicly exposed and tested in case they upset and demotivate others, so reducing levels of task performance. Instead evaluations are made privately and covered up in public. All understand that this is what is happening but they accept it as a necessary defence against hurting people's feelings and against the consequent organisational inefficiency.

When a manager is fired, this is frequently presented as a resignation due to health reasons or some other factor. Memoranda are distributed thanking the fired person for years of valued contributions. All know that this is a tissue of lies but none publicly say so. This is an example of a defence routine, a game people play to protect each other from having to face unpleasant organisational truths in public. As a result, the real reason for firing the person, a judgement that the person is incompetent, is never properly examined; it could well have been unjustified and turn out to be harmful to the performance of the organisation.

These kinds of beliefs about control lead to win/lose dynamics in which people adopt tactics of persuasion and selling, only superficially listening to others. People driven by win/lose behaviour also tend to use face-saving devices for themselves and each other. They save face by avoiding the public testing of the assumptions they are making about each others' motives or statements. This behaviour produces what has been called skilled incompetence: skilled in that the behaviour is automatic; incompetent in that it produces obstacles to work, real learning, effective decision-making. These obstacles take the form of organisational defence routines that become embedded in behaviour and are extremely difficult to change (see *Key Concept 6.6*).

■ **Key concept 6.6**
ORGANISATIONAL DEFENCE ROUTINES

Organisational defence routines are patterns of behaviour that people in an organisation deploy to protect themselves and others from embarrassment and anxiety.

The prime defence routine is to make matters undiscussable and to make the fact that they are undiscussable itself undiscussable. So subordinates refrain from telling their superiors the truth if those superiors are thought likely to dislike it. Subordinates do not publicly admit that they are doing this and of course superiors know that this is going on because they do it themselves. The result is an undiscussed game of pretence in which all indulge and all know they are doing it. The pretence enables all involved to avoid confronting embarrassing or potentially explosive behaviour.

Defence routines take the form of bypasses, cover-ups and games. For example, a manager may ask a colleague, with whom there is disagreement, for comprehensive proof of a proposal outcome when it is quite clear to all that such proof is impossible to provide.

A well-known game is to prevent a decision one dislikes by repeatedly calling for more reports and research on the grounds that a rational decision can only be made on the basis of the facts. For example, one company played the following game for over a year. One faction in the top management team thought that the company should diversify the range of its activities. Another faction led by the chairman thought that it should not. However the chairman did not openly quash the idea. He called for a paper setting out general diversification principles. After discussion at the formal executive meeting, specific proposals were called for – the principles paper was held to be too general. When the specific proposals were discussed, the chairman called for a discussion of the general principles. So it went on and needless to say, no diversification occurred. All involved knew it was a game and while they admitted this to each other in groups of twos or threes, no one ever raised it at the full meetings.

Long-term plans, mission statements and visions could well be games of a similar kind. They are usually abstract statements without operational content, simply to convey an impression of rational decision-making and to keep people quiet or feeling more secure.

Perhaps the most popular cover up, mostly unconscious, is to espouse a different style of management while actually continuing to use the control model. A manager ostensibly looking for team decision-making and open to different views can become visibly annoyed when such views are put forward. That manager makes it clear, by behaving in a particular manner, that team decision-making is not actually to occur despite any statements made to the contrary.

Defence routines become so entrenched in organisations that they come to be viewed as inevitable parts of human nature. Managers make self-fulfilling prophecies about what will happen at meetings, because they claim it is human nature; they indulge in the game playing, so confirming their belief in human nature. The defence routines, game playing and cover-ups can become so disruptive that managers actually avoid discussing contentious open-ended issues altogether. Even if this extreme is not reached, the dysfunctional learning behaviour blocks the detection of gradually accumulating small changes, the surfacing of different perspectives, the thorough testing of proposals through dialogue. When they use the control management model with the organisational defence routines it provokes, managers struggle to deal with strategic issues. They end up preparing long lists of strengths and weaknesses, opportunities and threats that simply get them nowhere. They produce mission statements that are so bland as to be meaningless, visions not connected to reality, and long-term plans that are simply filed. Or they may decide on an action and then not implement it.

Managers collude in this behaviour and refrain from discussing it. They then distance themselves from what is going on and blame others, the chief executive, or the organisational structure, when things go wrong. They look for solutions in general models, techniques, visions and plans. All the while the real causes of poor strategic management – the learning process itself, the political interaction and the group dynamic – remain stubbornly undiscussable.

People within an organisation collude in keeping matters undiscussable because they fear the consequences if they do not. Consultants too find themselves sucked into defence routines because they are nervous of the consequences of exposing them – they may be fired. The result of the defence routines we have been talking about is passive employees and managers, highly dependent upon authority, who are not well equipped to handle rapid change. In these conditions, managers produce vague, impractical prescriptions as a defence against having to do anything in difficult situations, such as 'we need more training' or 'we need a vision'. The organisation loses out on the creativity of people because of the management model it uses.

■ **Illustration 6.5**

THE CHALLENGER DISASTER

In 1986 a Presidential Commission enquired into the disaster that had occurred when the Challenger shuttle had crashed soon after launching. It concluded that NASA had sound structures, policies and rules to secure safety. What had gone wrong was that those most intimately involved with the launch had focused so heavily on the launch itself that they neglected safety matters. The conclusion was that there was nothing wrong with the organisation: the disaster was due to human failures. These were to be addressed in the future by making it compulsory for all launch constraints, and waivers of launch constraints, to be considered by all levels of management. In other words there was to be more referral up the management hierarchy.

Argyris (1990) analyses this episode to show how the disaster was actually due to organisational defence routines, which both NASA and the Presidential Commission were unwittingly covering up. The recommendation of more referral to higher management levels would do nothing to remove those organisational defence routines. It would therefore most probably be ineffective in preventing another accident.

Using the testimony presented to the Commission, Argyris shows the following. Before the launch, engineers had indicated that the launch should be delayed because of problems with O-rings, problems that ultimately caused the disaster. At a meeting with the engineers, one manager understood them to be advising a delay, but his superior concluded that they were simply raising some questions. The two managers did not explore their different understandings with each other; they did not test them publicly. The superior manager decided, without discussing it with anyone, not to report on the meeting with the engineers to higher levels of management. The engineers sounded a number of warnings and then stopped when they realised that no-one would listen. Engineers never questioned management as to why they would not listen; that would have been regarded as an affront to management capability.

At each level, the engineers and manages are covering themselves. The engineers raised the problem, but the next level did not heed them. Engineers were defending themselves by drawing attention to a problem and then giving up when it became clear that the next level would not listen. Engineers would not themselves take the matter further up the hierarchy because they knew that this would antagonise their immediate superiors. So they adopted the routine of raising the matter, knowing it would be ignored, and then dropping it, all in order to defend themselves – if anything went wrong, they would not be to blame. The first manager heard the message but bowed to his superior. He was covered because he was doing what the superior wanted. The superior was covered because he interpreted the points made by the engineers as simply raising questions and no-one contradicted him. He probably made this interpretation because he knew that those above him did not want bad news that they would have to convey to the President. In the end the disaster was due to all of these organisational defence routines and cover-ups. All knew that what was being covered up was important. They do not need rules to tell them this. Introducing rules is therefore unlikely to prevent this kind of thing from happening again. No rule can stop some manager from interpreting a warning as a question. If it is a warning it has to be conveyed up the hierarchy. If it is a question it does not. The only way around this is to require everything to be conveyed up the hierarchy and that is impossible. The real solution is to uncover the defences and discuss them, despite the anxiety and difficulty this involves. Argyris (1990, p. 43) concludes:

> Organizational defence routines make it highly likely that individuals, groups, intergroups, and organizations will not detect and correct the errors that are embarrassing and threatening because the fundamental rules are to (1) bypass the errors and act as if that were not being done, (2) make the bypass undiscussable, and (3) make its undiscussability undiscussable.
>
> These conditions, in turn, make it difficult to engage the organizational defence routines in order to interrupt them and reduce them. Indeed, the very attempt to engage them will lead to the defensive routines being activated and strengthened. This, in turn, reinforces and proliferates the defensive routines.

The way out of this impasse is to switch to a commitment model of managing. The commitment model seeks to take advantage of the inherent creativity of people by emphasising that:

- power flows from expertise and contribution, not simply position in the hierarchy;

- people are motivated primarily by their own internal commitment; and
- people respond to long-term rewards.

These beliefs about power and motivation tend to encourage the public exposure and testing of relevant feelings and judgements, even if they are negative, in order to ensure that decisions are being taken on valid data. Behaviour according to the commitment model should lead to cooperative dynamics and mutual control, allowing people to put their own creativity to use for the organisation.

The problem is that the attempt to move to the commitment model is itself likely to provoke the positive amplifying feedback loops of organisational defences. When people behave according to the control model, they set off amplifying loops of organisational defences. When they move toward behaving according to the commitment model, they are likely to set off amplifying loops arising from:

- the management fear of losing control;
- the clash of vested interests;
- the effects of power vacuums;
- the effects of unconscious processes.

These loops could quite easily completely immobilise learning, decision making and action. Here we consider the first of these loops and in later sections of this chapter we will consider the others.

The fear of losing control

The OD project is a programme of re-educating people from the control to the commitment model. That re-education programme is essentially about getting people to expose and question the values of the control model. They therefore have to expose their negative feelings, the basis of the judgments they make on the performance of others, the cover-ups and games they are playing.

The OD re-education programme is therefore bound to upset people and to arouse management fears of losing control. Such fears will reduce commitment to the programme, and consistent with the control model they are still using, even though they are trying to get away from it, people will also tend to conceal the diminishing commitment. The effect is to reduce the effectiveness of the re-education programme and the possibility of switching to the commitment model. The harder the re-education programme is pushed, the more it provokes the fears that impede it.

What we have then is a negative feedback loop running from the control model to the re-education programme which weakens the control model and builds up the commitment model. But movement around this loop itself touches off movement around another loop too. This is a positive, amplifying loop that undermines the re-education programme and therefore strengthens the control model. This is depicted in *Figure 6.17.*

When those running the OD programme find this happening, they may come to rely on using the control model themselves, the very model they are trying to remove. They may threaten to use, or even actually use, the power of the senior management supporting them to enforce cooperation in the programme. They may persuade the dissidents to suspend their disbelief in the programme and rely on the OD

Figure 6.17   Fear of losing control

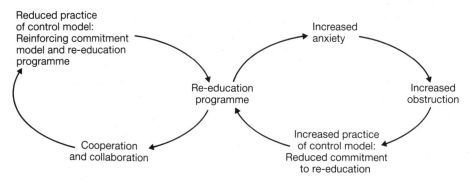

consultants. This establishes dependence on the consultants when the aim of the programme is to reduce dependence based on hierarchy. In this way another positive feedback loop is set up that will undermine the OD programme. Middle managers may cooperate with the programme only when it is supporting the short-term goals they are trying to achieve and withdraw support covertly when it is not. In this way the OD programme comes to bolster the control model instead of undermining it. OD consultants may then become unwittingly involved in bolstering authoritarian systems.

The result is the well-known phenomenon of the OD programme functioning while the consultants are there and then falling away within months of the consultants leaving.

Professionals who run OD programmes also make use of techniques that do not take realistic account of how managers actually behave (Argyris, 1990). For example, they may use organisational surveys in the form of questionnaires to find out what managers and employees think and how they are acting. But as we have seen, there is frequently a difference between what people say they do and what they actually do in organisations (Argyris & Schon, 1978). Surveys and questionnaires will uncover what people say they do, but are unlikely to reveal much about what they actually do and why they do it. In these circumstances, surveys and questionnaires will produce information that is highly partial and selective and therefore very misleading when it comes to designing ways of improving what the organisation does (Argyris, 1990). The point to note is that OD consultants may well be acting on incorrect information because of the information-gathering techniques they are using.

All the problems we have been talking about in this section are primarily due to the fact that people will continue to use the control model as they attempt to move from it to the commitment model. OD consultants tend to see this movement as one of empowering people throughout the organisation: they equate empowerment with democracy, dispersed power and widespread participation.

Simply dispersing power, inviting widespread participation, is no guarantee whatsoever that the organisation will function more effectively or make better decisions. First, widespread participation means that, although more people are being invited to take part in decision making, they are all still using the control model. We simply have more people behaving incompetently. There is no guarantee that lower managers or employees behave better than top executives. While the larger

Figure 6.18   Defence routines and covert politics: main points on organisational dynamics

- The behaviour of people in organisations is dominated by what Argyris has called the control model of management. This is usually operated within a pluralistic political system, in which a number of groupings have countervailing power.
- Use of the control model, the existence of different power groups, leads to win/lose behavioural dynamics. Here people employ a number of organisational defence mechanisms to protect themselves and others from the consequences of the win/lose pressures. They play games and make matters undiscussable. Consequently, decisions are often not made on valid data, implementation of decisions is often obstructed, small changes go undetected for lengthy periods. In short the ability of the organisation to develop strategically is severely impaired.

- But movement from the control model/pluralistic political system is fraught with difficulty. The most widespread idea of what to move to is a commitment model of control operating within a collegiate political system. This is the OD programme (and also the prescriptions of writers such as Peters, discussed in Chapter 2). Movement away from the control model, and particularly movement to the collegial model, touches off many positive amplifying feedback loops which undermine that movement.
- These positive feedback loops are activated because any attempt to change an organisation in a fundamental way upsets the balance and nature of power and raises the levels of uncertainty and ambiguity. All of these changes increase anxieties of one kind or another. And it is the anxiety that provokes positive feedback loops.

number involved in decision making continue to use the control model they will simply spread the win/lose dynamics more widely. The positive amplifying loops of organisational defences will be reinforced. Widespread participation is no guarantee of better decision making at all. People first have to learn how to operate on the basis of the commitment model and that is very difficult to achieve. Simply inviting people to do so will not have the required result. Widespread participation is no guarantee of better learning.

Furthermore, dispersing power more equally will tend to touch off two other amplifying loops: the first will have to do with vested interests and the second with the power vacuum that dispersed power may create. We now proceed to discuss each of these possibilities.

6.8   Greiner and Schein: vested interests and political interaction

The aim of the OD programme, as we have already seen, is to remove an authoritarian, rational/administrative political system and install in its place a collegiate/consensus political system. In the latter, power is more widely dispersed and based upon contribution rather than rules and hierarchical position. Highly authoritarian political systems based on mechanistic rules, however, are actually rather rare in practice. The point from which an OD programme starts is far more likely to be a complex pluralistic political system in which power is already spread around the organisation in groups with vested interests (Greiner and Schein, 1988). Thus, the typical modern corporation does not have a political system in which one or two powerful executives at the top control what goes on throughout the company. Instead we find powerful subsidiary companies and powerful departments in many different parts of the organisation and those at the top have to sustain enough support to govern. Any change of any significance is going to affect the balance of power, making one department, subsidiary company or management grouping weaker or stronger than it was before. Any sign of change will touch off fears that such power shifts might occur even before it is clear what they might be. People and groups will therefore start taking protective action as soon as they get wind of any possible change.

The OD re-education programme is just such a change, one that is directly concerned with changing power positions. It is therefore highly likely to touch off amplifying feedback loops of a political nature that will undermine and perhaps eventually destroy it. The more people are persuaded to move to a consensus collegiate way of making choices, the more powerful groups with vested interests are threatened and the more likely they are to put a stop to the programme. The more OD professionals try to head off this threat, the more they have to play by the rules of the political system they are trying to replace. If they do this they simply reinforce what they are trying to remove.

Once again, OD initiatives will fail if they do not recognise and deal with the amplifying feedback loops that are always present in organisations. And how to deal with these loops is far from clear.

Power vacuums and organised anarchies

If the OD programme does succeed in installing a collegiate political system and the commitment management model, yet other amplifying feedback loops may be activated by the shift in the distribution of power.

Figure 6.19 Threats to vested interests

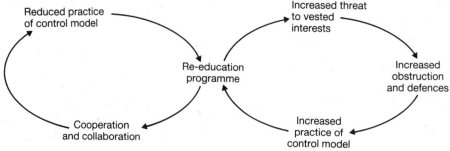

As authority and other forms of power are dispersed, as organisational structures are flattened, as job descriptions become looser, and as the establishment of widespread consensus comes to be required before decisions are possible, so the likelihood of a power vacuum at the centre increases. It becomes more and more difficult for anyone to exercise much authority; more and more people have to be able to handle their own independence. In situations in which most people seek the comfort of dependency this could create serious difficulties. We will explore what group relations theory has to say about this in a later section. Another way of understanding the consequences of changes in power distribution is provided by Greiner and Schein (1988).

Greiner and Schein use the device given in *Figure 6.20* to relate changes in willingness to assert and to accept power to the consequent group dynamic. When both leaders and followers consent freely to the exercise of power, there is a high probability of active consensus. When the leader exerts power but the followers do not consent, then we get the behaviour of covert resistance. You will see from *Figure 6.20* that as the leader becomes less able or willing to exert power, while followers still look for a lead, then we get the behaviour of passive loyalty. If, in the same circumstances, the followers too become less willing to accept the exercise of power, the group's behaviour is characterised by peer rivalry.

What we see, then, is that the dispersal of power and the spread of participation could set off amplifying feedback loops in which declining central power leads to greater rivalry throughout the organisation, or to passive loyalty, both of which will block the creativity that the OD programme is supposed to unleash. Indeed the amplifying loops could be much more complex than this if at the same time we raise levels of uncertainty and ambiguity by loosely defining people's jobs. We will explore the consequences of raising levels of uncertainty and ambiguity in the section later on to do with group relations theory.

Figure 6.20 Power and group dynamics

Source: L. E. Greiner & V. E. Schein (1988), Power and Organization Development: Mobilizing Power to Implement Change, Reading, MA: Addison-Wesley

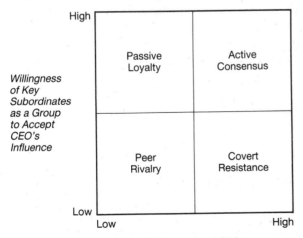

Figure 6.21 Vested interests and political interaction: main points on organisational dynamics

- Positive feedback loops are activated by any attempt to change an organisation in a fundamental way. This is because change upsets the balance and nature of power and raises the levels of uncertainty and ambiguity. Consequent anxiety provokes positive feedback loops.
- One positive feedback loop has to do with the fears of existing power groups that they will lose control. As change programmes are pushed, so these fears are increased leading usually to covert undermining of the programme. Organisational defence routines are then strengthened rather than weakened.
- Dispersing power and weakening central authority can set off positive loops leading to peer rivalry or passive loyalty. Both undermine creativity and decision-making ability.

Others have studied the decision-making processes in organisations such as universities, hospitals, as well as other public sector and professional bodies, that are characterised by the collegiate-type political system. They have described these organisations as organised anarchies and their decision-making processes as 'garbage can' decision making (Cohen, March & Ohlsen, 1972).

We will be discussing what these writers have to say in some detail in Chapter 8 in the section on models of decision making in conditions far from certainty. The point to be made here is this. When decision-making procedures are highly unstructured, as they tend to be when power is dispersed and widespread participation invited, then the particular decision taken on a particular occasion will depend almost entirely on the detailed context at the time. Here context means details such as: who attended the meeting at which the decision was taken; how important those attending were; what other matters they had on their minds. In this sense the particular decision made comes to depend upon chance. And in these circumstances there is a high level of probability that decisions will be postponed and, even if made, not implemented. Once again we can see that amplifying loops of behaviour may be set off by the political system that OD programmes try to install.

Changes in the nature of authority and power have important consequences, not adequately taken into account by mainstream OD literature or OD practitioners. Power vacuums and organised anarchies tend to raise levels of anxiety against which people defend themselves by regressing to infantile defence mechanisms. This gives rise to unconscious group behaviours – amplifying feedback loops we now go on to discuss.

6.9 Bion's models: unconscious group processes

The nature of interaction between people depends upon the extent to which those people are aware of the nature of their own and each others' behaviour. This point is made in *Figure 6.22*, a diagram known as JOHARI's window.

Figure 6.22 JOHARI window
Source: P. B. Smith (1969), *Improving Skills in Working with People*: The T Group, London: HMSO

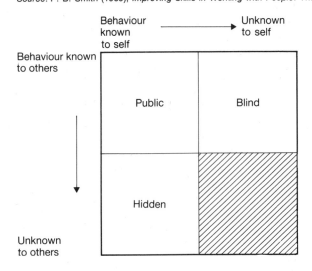

When people are aware of their own behaviour and those with whom they are interacting are also aware of that behaviour, then interaction between them takes on a Public form – we all know what we are doing together and why. But one group of people may be doing something that they are completely aware of to others who are unaware of what is going on. Such behaviour is labelled Hidden in *Figure 6.22*; some of us are manipulating others. Again, one group may be performing in a particular way, for reasons that they are unaware of, but their behaviour is transparent to others. Such behaviour may be called Blind: we may pretend we are doing one thing while we do another, but other people can see through this. The figure also shows a quadrant that is cross-hatched, depicting behaviour where those behaving and those responding are unaware of the true nature of their interaction. This is unconscious behaviour.

When individuals behave in such a way that they are not explicitly aware of the nature, or the quality, or the causes of that behaviour, then we can say that they are behaving unconsciously. For example, when we react in a hostile manner to a total stranger we have never heard about or met before, then we are behaving unconsciously – there is no obvious reason, no clear connection with external reality, to explain our reaction. The reason for our reaction probably lies in the unconscious mind; the particular person has activated a response from some other experience in the past that has been pushed into the unconscious. Whenever we react to some stimulus in a manner which others, and later we ourselves, perceive to be out of all proportion to the stimulus, then in all probability the cause of that behaviour lies in our unconscious.

When you lose your temper at a typist for making a small spelling error, the true source of the anger is most probably not the typist at all; you are simply projecting anger felt for someone else, who might well be yourself, onto the unfortunate typist. This kind of projection is an unconscious process in which all humans regularly indulge.

Since all of us as individuals behave in ways that are directed by unconscious as well as conscious processes, it is inevitable that, when we come together as a group, at least part of what we discover and choose to do in that group will be determined by those unconscious processes. In other words, unconscious group process will inevitably be an inextricable part of most decision-making processes in an organisation.

This is an obvious proposition, but one not recognised in most explanations of managing, organising and decision making. The role of unconscious processes is also firmly denied any explicit attention by the great majority of management practitioners. Such considerations tend to be dismissed as peripheral concerns for mature managers who are supposed to make decisions in largely technically rational ways. When unconscious processes are discussed they are normally seen as peripheral influences on a decision, usually adverse influences, which must and can be removed.

More careful reflection, however, makes it clear that unconscious processes are so deeply embedded in human behaviour that it is only some completely inhuman, and therefore non-existent, decision-making process that can occur in the absence of unconscious processes, or with those processes occupying a position of only peripheral importance. Unconscious processes are at the heart of the decision-making processes managers actually employ. It is therefore a matter of great importance for the effectiveness of strategic management to explore what impact these processes have and how they come about. First consider one way of becoming aware of what the processes we are talking about actually are.

Group relations conferences

A very powerful way of experiencing what unconscious group processes actually feel like is provided by what is known as Group Relations Conferences, or Tavistock Conferences (Miller, 1989). This approach to training in group awareness was popular in the 1960s but fell from favour largely because it did not produce predictable, long-lasting changes in people's skills in building cohesive teams. Since we are here questioning whether that is a valid aim, the criticism need not deter us from learning what we can from this approach and I would therefore like to describe some of the kinds of behaviour that always emerge in such events and then outline the explanations that have been put forward to account for it.

What I am going to describe is based on three separate conferences, each lasting two days over a weekend. The participants on each occasion were about thirty part-time MBA students, average age around thirty-five. Some points on the composition of these groups are as follows: about 15 per cent were female; perhaps 10 per cent of the total were from minority groups; about 70 per cent of the total were from the commercial and industrial sector and the remainder from public sector and charitable bodies; over 90 per cent had degrees or professional qualifications. All of these intelligent people held responsible managerial positions in their organisations.

Participants arrived at the residential weekend with some feelings of apprehension because they had heard rumours from others about the strange happenings likely to occur. At the start of the weekend, all of the participants met in a plenary session with the staff who were to act as consultants to groups of participants. The staff consisted of three visiting consultants with considerable experience in running such conferences and two teachers from my own institution who played a relatively minor consulting role. The task of the weekend was briefly outlined: it was to study group processes, particularly unconscious processes, so enabling each individual to examine the part he or she plays in those processes, including the exercise of authority.

Participants were then divided into Study Groups of 10–12 members each and the task of the Study Group was stated to be that of studying intra-group processes in the here and now, when they happen and as they happen. It was clearly explained to the participants that each Study Group would be attended by a consultant, who would not be there to teach, but to provide working hypotheses about the processes occurring in groups. It was quite clearly stated that participants must take responsibility for their own learning.

The Study Groups were therefore set up in such a way that there was nothing that the managers involved recognised as the kind of objective and task they were used to. Managers do not normally simply examine their own behaviour in a group – the behaviour normally lies in the background of dealing with an objective and a task. Here the behaviour itself is brought out of the background to actually provide the, rather unfamiliar, objective and task. The role that the consultants steadfastly occupy is also not one that the participants are used to. The consultant clearly occupies some position of authority as far as the participants are concerned, but that consultant abandons the participants in the sense that the consultant refuses to occupy the expected role of teacher, expert or leader. Then, however, having abandoned them in this sense, the consultant nevertheless keeps intruding in the role of consultant to offer interpretations of what the participants are doing (Gustafson & Cooper, 1978).

These two changes, the removal of what is normally regarded as a task and the removal of what is normally regarded as a teacher or leader, always provokes high levels of anxiety in the participants, anxieties which they are reluctant to recognise. Those anxieties find expression in all manner of strange behaviours. Group discussions may take on a manic form with asinine comments and hysterical laughter. In a remarkably short space of time the participants attack the visiting consultant for not playing a more usual and active role and openly question whether they are earning their consulting fees. Participants become incredibly rude to the consultants, behaviour they would not normally display to a visitor, no matter how poor the visitor's performance might be. Significantly, however, participants never attack my colleague and myself, perhaps because we represent the ongoing authority figures for the MBA course.

Members of Study Groups might try to find a leader to replace the non-functioning consultant but they rarely seem to be successful in this endeavour for very long. They begin to pick on an individual, usually some highly individualistic or minority member of the group, and then treat this person as some kind of scapegoat. They all become very concerned with remaining part of the group, greatly fearing exclusion. They show strong tendencies to conform to rapidly established group norms and suppress their individual differences, perhaps because they are afraid of becoming the scapegoat.

The Study Group events are followed by the Inter-Group Event. Here the participants are invited to organise themselves into groups and then study inter-group behaviour in the here and now as it happens. The sight of these mature people organising themselves into groups is quite astonishing. They do so without any forethought, all seemingly in a panic at the thought of being left out of a group. Within seconds the room is cleared of people who have all rushed off, away from the consultants, in one group or another. Then they begin to interact and within minutes the win/lose dynamic takes powerful hold. Even though there is no specific objective, other than studying behaviour, even though the groups have formed without any common purpose whatsoever, some groups at least start to talk about dominating the others. They then proceed to try to do so, brushing aside any quiet, puzzled voice that might ask why they are doing this. In their pursuit of domination, group members lie to each other, spy on each other, and play one deceitful game after another.

The one thing they hardly do at all is examine the behaviour they are indulging in, the task they have actually been given. Individuals and whole groups become scapegoats, set up by others and collaborating in that set-up. Very real emotions of anger and fear are evoked by what goes on, despite the fact that all know that this is 'only a training weekend'. Rumours spread about what other groups are doing, fantasies that participants afterwards realise are completely false. But at the time little effort is made to check on the data: all is wild assertions, building up fantasies of attacking and being attacked, rejecting and being rejected. People talk all the time about the group as some real thing separate from themselves as individuals. They place enormous store on being part of the group and on the group being cohesive. They talk about belonging to the strongest, most cohesive group, the best group, in a fantasy-like neurotic manner.

I personally find it most surprising that undoubtedly competent, mature people in responsible managerial positions react so strongly to two rather small changes from the normal. After all, there is a task: it is to study group processes as they happen and there is certainly much happening. There is assistance in performing the task in the form of comments and guidance from the experienced consultants, even though they refuse the role of teacher. But it seems that the original stimulus of two rather unusual changes sets off some kind of amplifying feedback loop in the behaviour of the groups of participants from which they seem incapable of escaping during the whole weekend. They, and even I as a rather peripheral consultant, become totally caught up in very strong and difficult-to-understand amplifying processes. The fact that the magnitude of the response is out of all proportion to the stimulus is a sign that we are dealing with unconscious processes. Throughout the experience it becomes apparent to many participants that processes of this kind occur every day within their own real life organisation, although usually at a much lower level of intensity.

How are we to explain the nature and cause of these unconscious processes that make it virtually impossible for a group of intelligent and competent managers to work on a task for a whole weekend? The most useful explanation seems to be that, when humans are confronted by high levels of anxiety provoked by unfamiliar tasks and lack of leadership, they revert very easily to infantile mechanisms. They begin to behave according to patterns they learned as infants. So first let us look briefly at what seems to be the most useful explanation of how infants cope with their world (Klein, 1975).

Infantile mechanisms

According to Melanie Klein's explanation (1975), infants are born with two powerful drives: the libido, or life force, which is the drive to love; and the morbido, or death wish, which is the fear of death and destruction, the feeling of persecution. The inner life of the infant is very simple – it is dominated by these two extremes of love on the one hand and persecutory fear on the other.

The infant's perception of its external world is also very simple, consisting of two part objects: a good part of the mother that feeds and comforts it and a bad part that denies it food and comfort.

The infant copes with this simple and also powerfully distressing world by splitting its inner life into a loving part that is projected onto the good part of the mother. The infant then identifies itself with that good part and introjects it back into itself. The same thing is done with the persecutory feelings and the aggression and hatred they arouse. These are all projected onto the bad part of the mother, and the infant identifies its own violent impulses with that bad part – it introjects that bad part of the mother back into itself.

This process of splitting, followed by projective identification and introjection, amounts to setting up feedback loops. The infant projects its feelings and then perceives those feelings as coming from the outside object. It therefore reacts to the object in a manner provoked by the feelings which originally come from itself. So it projects its own fears of persecution and then reacts to the object projected upon as if that object is actually persecuting it. This leads to a reaction of hate and aggression, strengthening the feeling of persecution. If the projection affects the behaviour of the object, then the whole feedback process becomes even stronger. It is through this feedback that the character of the infant is formed. If it experiences loving responses to its loving projections then the loving side of its character is strengthened. If the persecutory projections are reinforced by lack of love and actual persecution then this side of the character is reinforced. Right at the earliest stages of behaviour, then, positive and negative feedback loops play major parts in the development of each of us.

This first stage of infantile development is known as the paranoid–schizoid position. It is schizoid because the infant splits the external world and it splits its own internal world too. It is paranoid because of the persecutory fears of the infant. The infant deals with these fears by using the mechanisms of splitting and projective identification, putting what is inside its own mind out into some external object or person and then identifying with and reacting to what it has projected. It copes with harsh reality by creating an external fantasy world of separate objects, some of which are persecuting it. It is idealising the good parts and denying its own bad parts by projecting them, so building the external bad into a demon.

The infant who develops normally works through this position and comes to realise that the bad and good objects in its external world are really one and the same whole person. But having learned how to defend ourselves against the earliest anxieties, we lay those lessons down in the unconscious. In later life when we confront anxiety again, we are highly likely to regress to the infantile mechanisms of splitting the world and ourselves into extreme and artificial categories of the good and the bad, projecting the parts of ourselves we do not like onto others, so creating fantasies that have little to do with reality.

Once the infant realises that it loves and hates the same person it is filled with anxiety because of the feelings of anger and hatred previously projected into the mother. This causes the depressive position. The normal infant works its way through this position too, developing strong feelings of love and dependence on the mother, while seeking to make amends for previous bad feelings. It experiences hope from the maturer relationship with the mother.

Groups and infantile mechanisms

When mature, competent managers come together as a group, each brings along the infantile mechanisms of dependence, idealisation, denial, splitting, projection and fantasising which have been learned as an infant and laid down in the unconscious. Anything that raises uncertainty levels and thus anxiety levels could provoke regression to those infantile mechanisms.

Bion has provided the most insightful explanation of how these mechanisms are manifested in group behaviour, leading to the kinds of behaviour at the group relations conferences described above (Bion, 1961).

Bion distinguishes between two important aspects of any group of people. The first aspect is the sophisticated work group. This is the primary task that the group has come together to perform. So a team of top executives has the primary tasks of controlling the day-to-day running of the business of the organisation and also the strategic development of that organisation.

All groups are also at the same time what Bion called 'basic assumption groups'. A basic assumption group is one that behaves as if it is making a particular assumption about required behaviour. The assumption becomes most apparent when uncertainty and anxiety levels rise. What Bion is talking about here is the emotional atmosphere, the psychological culture, of the group. All groups of people have these two aspects: some task they are trying to perform together, accompanied by some emotional atmosphere within which they are trying to perform their task. That atmosphere can be described in terms of a basic assumption they are all making.

So, at any one time, a group of people may constitute a sophisticated work group characterised by a basic assumption on behaviour that occupies a kind of low-level background position, influencing the conduct of the primary task but not dominating or blocking it. Then when uncertainty and anxiety levels rise markedly the group can become suffused with and dominated by the basic assumption; a strong emotional atmosphere, or group culture, that blocks the group's ability to function as a sophisticated work group. The primary task will not be carried out, or it will be carried out in an ineffective manner.

Bion distinguished between three basic assumptions:

1 **Dependence**. Here the group behaves as if it has come together to depend on some leader. The members of the group seek a leader on whom they can depend. They abandon their individuality and critical faculties in favour of some kind of adoration of a charismatic leader. They actively seek a charismatic person who will tell them

what to do. Charisma lies not in the person of the leader but in the interrelationship between the followers and the leader.

In this state, members of a group will idealise the leader, expecting completely unrealistic performance from the leader. Groups working on this assumption are destined to be disappointed and will quickly abandon the leader. This dependence is an infantile mechanism because the members of the group are projecting their requirements for something to depend upon onto someone else. This projection will in effect select the leader. Note how this raises a possibility we do not normally think of. When a group is behaving in this mode it is creating its own leader through projecting demands on to a person – it is not the leader who is creating the group. If the person selected for this projection does not cooperate or disappoints, then members of the group project their frustration and fear onto that person and begin to attack. This brings us to the second basic assumption.

2 Fight/flight. Here it is as if the group has come together for the purpose of fighting some enemy or for the purpose of fleeing from some enemy. Members project their desire for fight or flight onto someone to lead them in fight or flight. Once again they may rapidly become disappointed with and attack the leader. Groups in this state invent fantasy enemies in some other department or some other organisation. The energy goes into competition and win/lose dynamics.

3 Pairing. Pairing is another mode a group might operate in. Here it is as if the group has come together to witness the intercourse between two of their number which will produce the solution to their anxieties. The atmosphere here is one of unrealistic hope that some experts will produce all the answers.

Turquet (1974) has added a fourth basic assumption.

4 Oneness. Here it is as if the group has come together to join in a powerful union with some omnipotent force which will enable members to surrender themselves in some kind of safe passivity. Members seem lost in an oceanic feeling of unity.

The dynamics

The explanation presented so far is summarised in *Figure 6.23*.

Once a group of people come to be dominated by one of the basic assumptions, they enter into volatile dynamics in which they switch, for apparently no reason, from one basic assumption to another. While people in a group are behaving like this they are incapable of performing the primary task or acting as a work group. They cannot remember what they have just discussed; they go around and around in incompetent circles; they suck unsuitable people into leadership positions; they create scapegoats; they act on untested myths and rumours; they build fantasies and lose touch with reality. Individuals sink their individuality in group uniformity and become deskilled. The organisational defence routines and game playing discussed in the last section provide examples of this in real-life organisations.

What provokes the switch from a work group with some background basic assumption, being used in a sophisticated way to support their task, to a group dominated by a basic assumption? The provocation seems to have a great deal to do with levels of ambiguity and uncertainty on the one hand, and with certain styles of

Figure 6.23 Unconscious group processes
Source: R. de Board (1978), *The Psychoanalysis of Organizations*, London: Tavistock Publications

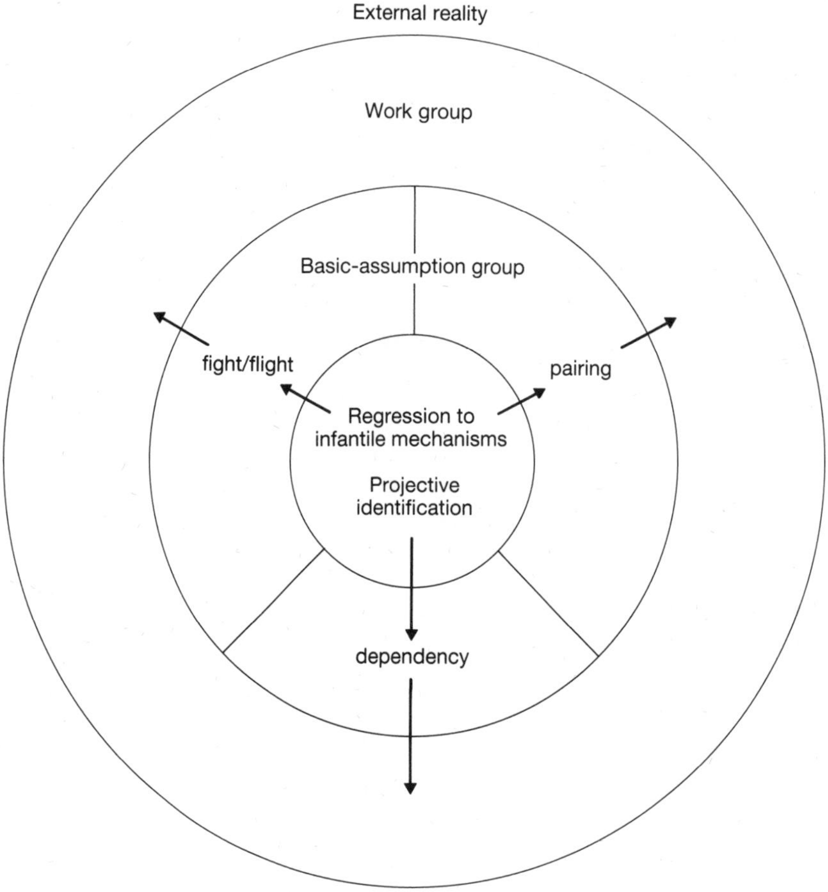

exercising power on the other. If leaders abandon groups in times of great uncertainty and ambiguity then they will develop into basic assumption groups and become incapable of handling the uncertainty and ambiguity.

But note that we are not talking about clear-cut causality between a specific action, say the withdrawal of power, and specific outcomes in behavioural terms. All we can say is that, when the nature of power in a group is changed so that people's requirement for dependency is frustrated, we will be able to observe general patterns of behaviour, archetypes, that we can label as fight/flight or some other label. We will not be able to say what form such fighting or such flight may take, or when it will occur.

Another point to make now, the relevance of which will become clearer in the next chapter, is this. When the nature of power and authority, the boundary conditions of the group, are changed, the group spontaneously displays a form of self-organisation. It spontaneously operates in fight/flight patterns for example. More supportive, more containing boundary conditions could result in a spontaneous switch to a serious work group. Forms of self-organisation may then be prompted by unconscious processes.

Implications for strategic management

Some important points follow from this analysis. Normally the role of power in the strategic management of organisations is discussed as one of the factors influencing the implementation of a strategy. There is also a quite separate literature, one taking a psychoanalytic view of organisations, where the possibilities and consequences of leaders becoming neurotic are discussed (Kets de Vries, 1984). But mainstream views on strategic management do not relate to this at all. Leaders are assumed to be perfectly healthy, balanced people, who set the direction of the organisation for others to follow. However, as soon as we recognise that basic-assumption groups can very quickly emerge from work groups we have to recognise that leaders can also be the creations of the group. It is quite possible that leaders are vainly trying to act out the fantasies that those in the management team are projecting. Reality is once again a feedback loop. Leaders affect what groups do, but groups also affect what leaders do through processes of unconscious projection.

The group relations approach also opens up these insights:

- Charismatic leaders and the strong cultures of dependence they provoke in followers may well be extremely unhealthy for organisations. Researchers (for example, Peters and Waterman, 1982) may therefore note the presence of charismatic leaders and superficially conclude that this is the reason for success, when it might well be a neurotic phenomenon that is about to undermine the company.
- A cohesive team of managers may not be a healthy phenomenon at all. It may be an unhealthy and unproductive reflection of the fantasy of basic-assumption groups acting out dependence or oneness assumptions. Again researchers not considering an organisation from a psychoanalytic point of view may well conclude that such neurotic cohesion is a reason for success.
- The idea of the group or the management team may itself be a defence mechanism. So, faced by high levels of strategic uncertainty and ambiguity, managers may retreat into the 'mother figure' of the team for comfort and in so doing fail to deal with the strategic issues.
- Groups clearly do not have to have a purpose or even a task to function very tightly as a group, even if it is a misguided one. Again, signs of close teams should provoke suspicion, not praise.
- Groups or teams are a two-edged sword. We need them to establish our identity. We need them to operate effectively. But they can also deskill us.
- The desire for cohesion may well be a neurotic phenomenon.
- Plans and rigid structures and rules may all be defences against anxiety instead of the rational way of proceeding we usually think they are. The way we cling to the dominant paradigm of strategic management, despite all the evidence to the contrary, is a sign of this.
- One aspect of culture is the emotional atmosphere, the basic assumption, that a group of people create as they interact.

Relationship to OD and strategic management

We can now return to the effect that unconscious group processes may be expected to have on OD programmes. A comprehensive OD programme will, by definition, raise anxiety levels because it is about major organisation-wide change. Such programmes, if effective, cannot but alter people's power positions and their jobs. And they all know this. Higher uncertainty levels and higher anxiety levels throughout the organisation are thus inevitable. Perhaps even the behaviour of the consultants could well create the conditions in which the work groups set up by their programme could be swamped by basic-assumption behaviour. For example, the consultants could encourage client dependence. If this happens then of course we will get a positive amplifying feedback loop that will offset the negative damping loop of the OD programme itself. This possibility is depicted in *Figure 6.24.*

The most important strategic issues, the response to which could alter the direction of the organisation, are by definition ambiguous with highly uncertain consequences. Such issues threaten the stability of how people work and their power positions. When teams of managers deal with strategic issues it is therefore inevitable that the basic-assumption aspect of any work group should come to occupy a more prominent role and even threaten to swamp the work group. This means that we have to see unconscious group process as an integral part of the process of making strategic choices, a part which is deeply embedded in human nature and cannot be removed. Inevitably, the handling of strategic issues activates positive feedback loops of unconscious behaviour.

The conclusion is that the basic OD model and mainstream models of strategic management with their emphasis on negative feedback do not take adequate account of the complex dynamics of organisations and will therefore not work. The consequence is that large-scale culture change programmes are highly unlikely to go according to plan as *Illustration 6.6* shows.

Figure 6.24 Unconscious group processes and organisation development

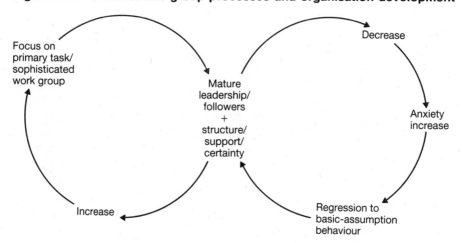

Figure 6.25   Unconscious group processes: main points on organisational dynamics

- Positive feedback loops are activated by any attempt to change an organisation in a fundamental way. This is because change upsets the balance and nature of power and raises the levels of uncertainty and ambiguity. Consequent anxiety provokes positive feedback loops.

- Increased anxiety unleashes unconscious processes of regression to infantile behaviour. Work groups become swamped with basic-assumption behaviour in which they are incapable of undertaking strategic developments.

- A group of managers facing strategic issues is, by definition, tuning up the levels of uncertainty and ambiguity since these are characteristics of strategic issues. Such issues, by definition, threaten power positions. It is therefore inevitable that strategic issues themselves will touch off the positive amplifying loops of basic-assumption behaviour. Such behaviour is an inevitable part of the process of making strategic decisions.

- In these circumstances it is quite likely that long-term plans, mission statements, visions and the like are simply being used as defence mechanisms. Perhaps we cling to today's dominant paradigm despite all the evidence to the contrary because it is our main defence mechanism against anxiety.

- The dynamics of any real life organisation are inevitably unstable, unless they are completely dominated by rules, fears or force, in which case they will atrophy and die. Strategic management proceeds as part of this unstable dynamic.

- Success has to do with the management of the context or boundary conditions around a group. The main factors that establish the context are the nature and use of power, the level of mutual trust, and the time pressures on people in the group. The purpose of managing the context, or the boundaries, is to create an emotional atmosphere in which it is possible to overcome defences and to test reality rather than indulge in fantasy. In other words, the context must be managed to create an atmosphere that enables complex learning.

■ **Illustration 6.6**
THE CULTURE CHANGE PROGRAMME

In early 1988, the senior managers at Apex Engineering were driven by increased international competition to find significant and permanent cost reductions. The management team examined the problem and decided to reorganise from a functional structure to one of profit-responsible business units. They employed consultants to identify international cost standards and set benchmarks relating to the level of inventories, product completion times, sales per employee, added value per square metre of space occupied, and people employed per project. They also employed consultants to develop a strategy to achieve the cost standards by 1994.

In early 1989, the management team in conjunction with the consultants, set out its mission. That mission was to become the prime world-class manufacturer of its main product and the strategy to achieve this consisted of installing just-in-time inventory control systems and cellular manufacturing; that is, small multidiscipline teams responsible for clearly specified parts of the total product. In addition, a leaner, flatter organisation was to be created by removing a rung of middle management.

The senior managers recognised that the strategy represented a major change in the way people worked and therefore it set up a culture-change programme. A change champion was appointed and management groups set up to deal with initiatives, problems and issues. The intention was to promote collective problem-solving and decision-making. But the role of the change champion was specified as that of ensuring that key people did in fact attend the groups. No-one seemed to think it odd that managers were to be compelled to cooperate. Right at the beginning a control model was to be used to install a commitment model.

The result was a network of people who were committed to the change but they tended to be located in the former department of the change champion – the personnel and purchasing functions. Little real support existed in the manufacturing function because so many managers stood to lose power from a switch to cellular manufacturing.

Senior management in discussion with each other stated that, without careful communication and selling to the workforce as a whole, the strategy would be viewed with scepticism, mistrust and outright rejection. So the managing director gave propaganda talks to people, a three-dimensional model of the new site configuration was built for all to see and questions were invited. This whole exercise might be viewed as a defence routine: senior managers are making presentations calling for group problem solving, but they are presenting a solution that has not been arrived at in this way. Those listening to the presentation know this but do not point it out.

The next step was to negotiate changes in work practice with the trades unions. When the unions asked what the mission and cost standards set for 1994 meant for work practices, the senior managers said that they could not readily be translated into specific work practices. They also said that the vision did not allow specific savings to be identified and so they could not identify any rewards for introducing new work practices. Managers are promoting a commitment model, but they are not being open with the unions. Or they are telling the truth and their missions and plans are so general and vague as to be meaningless.

In view of this the unions would not support the change programme and a small pilot programme was mounted instead. This was supposed to emphasise management commitment (but in fact the managing director showed little interest in it) and to test the cellular method of manufacturing. The pilot team was set up and received awareness training, diagnostic skills training and teamwork skills training. The pilot project was said by many to be a success, but no hard evidence to support this was produced and it did not run for its full time period – it has halted by a strike. Nine months later the unions agreed to cellular manufacturing but by this time, late 1990, the economy was in recession and the whole project was petering out.

6.10 Summary

At this point it will be useful to summarise the key points that have emerged so far from the survey of the models that focus exclusively on negative feedback (discussed in the last chapter) and those that also take account of positive feedback (discussed in this chapter).

There is one strand of thinking that derives from the engineer's concept of control as developed in communication theory and modern information technology. This is the idea of an organisation as a system of information flows consisting of a number of subsystems and embedded in a bigger environmental suprasystem. The behaviour of this system is thought to be driven by the need to achieve a predetermined goal that requires being adapted to a given environment. Such an organisation is kept on course to goal achievement by the operation of negative feedback in its control systems: it plans, monitors, reviews and takes corrective action. This concept of a system is also applied to behavioural interactions between the people in an organisation, to the values and beliefs these people hold, to the culture they share. Since all these factors affect goal achievement, they must match and be consistent with the goals and the plans. Appropriate behavioural systems must therefore be planned and installed (the discipline of OD). While these models do not usually make their assumptions about organisational dynamics explicit, we can now see that the this model of management leads to a state of stable equilibrium and those proposing this model are assuming that it is then that an organisation succeeds.

Stable equilibrium generates patterns of behaviour and performance that are consistent with each other – harmonious, regular over time, orderly and disciplined. Any irregularity is caused by unforeseeable changes in the environment – it is the environment that causes the organisation to be what it is. Or irregularity is caused by incompetence – proper stable systems have not been installed. Nonlinearity and positive feedback are largely ignored – they are harmful features to be removed.

This stable equilibrium view underlies the prescriptions for organisational success which today command the most attention of practitioners and researchers alike. Quite clearly these views underlie the whole budgeting, annual planning, product scheduling, managing information and control system, and short-interval control of organisations. The stable equilibrium mental model also underlies OD, the planning of cultural change. And it underlies the dominant views on strategic management. The key to it all is prior, organisation-wide intention – the goals and the application of negative feedback.

The second strand of systems thinking, some of which is also derived from engineering concepts of control (servomechanisms), makes it clear how narrow the focus of the negative feedback school of thought is. When account is taken of the inevitable existence of positive amplifying feedback loops together with negative feedback, a number of key points follow.

1 Organisations are characterised by fundamental contradictions: stability and instability; the need to differentiate and the need to integrate; the need for rule-based negative feedback control systems, and the need for flexible amplifying systems to deal with unforeseeable change which are impeded by the negative

feedback systems. One view is that successful organisations balance these contradictory forces in a planned equilibrium way dictated by contingency factors. Another view is that successful organisations sustain the contradiction in a non-equilibrium state. This latter view recognises strong forces pulling organisations to states of differentiation, integration, adaptation and isolation, all of which are seen as failure.

2 All organisations are characterised by nonlinearity and by positive and negative feedback processes. These processes are ubiquitous and of great importance but not taken much account of in the received wisdom.

3 Cause-and-effect links are problematic as is predictability. We commonly get unexpected and counter-intuitive behaviour.

4 Because of the problems with cause and effect and thus predictability, it becomes very important to be able to perceive patterns in behaviour and the structures that generate those patterns. Another way of putting this is to say that, since little can be said about the future of complex systems, it becomes very important to make sense of what has just been done. It is this kind of sense-making, identifying meaning retrospectively, that is essential for designing the next action.

5 Shared purpose established before any action is taken is not always necessary for a group of people to perform effectively. In complex, highly uncertain situations, purpose and patterns in action emerge from the interactions between the components of a system. In other words, people can perform quite effectively in complex systems even when they do not have a well-understood plan for the future. Then, the goals and the strategies to achieve them will emerge.

6 People operating in complex systems quite easily develop trained incapacity and skilled incompetence. If they are to combat this they need continually to question existing mental models and develop new ones to cope with the unfolding future of the organisational system they operate in. They need to think in system terms.

7 Complex systems spontaneously compensate when attempts are made to change them. Positive loops of behaviour are touched off when uncertainty and ambiguity levels rise and when the nature of power is changed. The result is organisational defence routines and unconscious defence mechanisms against anxiety. These are integral parts of the process of handling of strategic issues.

8 It is unlikely therefore that a comprehensive programme of specific changes can be planned for any organisation. Change is more likely to be brought about by attending to favourable boundary conditions, that is primarily favourable patterns in the exercise of power. Within the boundaries, creative development depends on some form of spontaneous self-organisation.

At this stage we can see quite clearly why there is persistent concern about the implementation of strategies that have been determined in a prior way. The system that managers have to cope with is too complex to allow them fully to intend the future strategic direction of their organisation. In other words, the complexity of the system is such that new strategic direction can only emerge.

We now turn to a new perspective that provides a framework within which we might be able to make sense of all these points.

Further reading

Richardson (1991) provides an excellent account of the use of feedback thinking in human systems and Senge's (1990) book is an excellent summary of systems thinking. de Board (1978) should be read as an introduction to a psychoanalytic approach to organisations. Argyris (1990) should be referred to for further information on organisational defences. Schein (1988), and also Greiner & Schein (1988), provide further detail on the criticism that can be levelled at OD.

7

What complex feedback systems lead to

Unpredictability and emergent strategy

7.1 Introduction

To clarify the purpose of this chapter it will be helpful to review the principal steps in the argument that has been developed in previous chapters.

Step one of the argument is the proposition that everything managers do depends at the most fundamental level on the mental models through which those managers understand their world, particularly the mental models they have come to share with each other. Those shared mental models determine how managers together construct their perceptions of reality and therefore what they agree to attend to. The strategic management processes managers use, the patterns in actions they develop, the positions and postures they establish and therefore the performance levels they achieve, all flow from their mental models. What managers believe about the causes of success, the explicit and tacit theories they hold to, determines what they do.

Step two of the argument states that we can quite easily detect the dominant body of theories of successful practice that the vast majority of managers today subscribe to. That is, we can identify the widely shared mental models that managers say drive their actions by asking them, by examining the management books that reach the bestseller lists, and by examining the content of textbooks. It is this that constitutes the conventional wisdom.

Step three establishes what this dominant set of beliefs about success is – although there are many different explanations and prescriptions that go to make up the conventional wisdom, they are all based on one dominant way of understanding organisational life. At the centre of the conventional wisdom is the belief that successful organisations are those that conform to one of a limited number of configurations; that is, typical arrangements of key organisational attributes such as: purpose or mission; strategies; hierarchical reporting structures; managerial roles and leadership styles; cultures, or belief systems; control systems; rewards systems; and so on. In the conventional wisdom, an appropriate configuration of these attributes is held to be determined by the size of the organisation and the nature of its environment; configurations that are close adaptations to the environment are believed to lead to success. It is thought possible to identify a configuration appropriate to particular circumstances by analysing the facts in a particular situation. It is also held to be possible to install the appropriate configuration into an organisation, taking the form either of the planning systems of the technically rational approach or of the visions and ideology of the more entrepreneurial approaches. Appropriate configuration then makes it possible for an organisation to determine the direction it should take to a fixed point in the long-term future and to maintain a controlled movement along the selected path to that point.

Step four of the argument demonstrates how this particular set of beliefs about the causes of success is based on unquestioned assumptions about the dynamics of successful organisations. The conventional prescriptions can work only in a world in which the dynamics are those of regularity, stability, harmony and consensus, all leading to predictable behaviour. When we make such assumptions, they amount to the belief that successful organisations are feedback systems dominated by negative feedback loops and that positive feedback loops are destabilising and hence to be removed or at least dampened down. Cybernetics, general systems theory, Organisation Development and the more visible theories of overt political behaviour provide well-developed explanations of such negative feedback functioning and these models underlie today's dominant views on strategic and change management. All of these unquestioned beliefs about the dynamic constitute a frame of reference we have called the stable equilibrium organisation paradigm. The whole validity of mainstream strategic management depends upon the usefulness of this paradigm.

Step five in the argument produces the empirical studies of Miller and Pascale and the conclusions those studies lead to. Miller demonstrates how companies that build on their strengths eventually move along trajectories that take them either to states of explosive instability or to states of stable equilibrium. In both states they ultimately fail: that is, they do not innovate and transform and therefore they become out of tune with a changing world. Pascale shows how companies that succeed are ones that sustain contradictions: contradictions generate tension; tension creates energy; with such energy, organisations innovate and transform themselves, so holding onto the prospect of continued life. Pascale explains success as operation in a state of non-equilibrium where companies follow circular, dialectical processes of rearranging paradoxical forces. These two studies therefore produce conclusions, supported by evidence, that directly question the validity of today's dominant explanations of success. And that questioning penetrates to a very basic level where the usefulness of the stable equilibrium paradigm itself is exposed to doubt. This is because Miller and Pascale are saying that failure flows from stability and success flows from some form of instability. These studies, however, do not produce compelling theoretical reasons for maintaining that successful organisations must generate instability; that is, why order leads to disorder.

Step six of the argument therefore explores what the literature has to say about the dynamics of instability in organisations. The models of Weick, Forrester, Argyris and Bion have in common the incorporation of positive feedback loops into their explanations of how organisations develop; it is these loops that are associated with the unstable dynamics of organisations.

Steps five and six of the argument produce the following important conclusions about the nature of organisations:

- **All human organisations are systems open to and interconnected with their environment**. They import labour and raw materials, they export value-added goods and services across the boundary between themselves and their environments, and how they do so is determined by the feedback loops that connect them to their environments. Organisations are webs of feedback loops of both the positive and the negative kind, not simply the latter. The positive loops are deeply embedded in human behaviour and can never be removed.

- **Patterns of behaviour in organisations flow from the autonomous flipping from dominant positive to dominant negative feedback loops and this happens because the loops have nonlinear structures**. The consequence is instability and irregularity in patterns of behaviour and that instability comes from the nature of the system itself, not simply fluctuations in its environment.

- **The organisation as a system is such that small changes are escalated into large consequences**. This leads to the phenomena of the vicious circle, the chain reaction, the bandwagon effect and the self-fulfilling prophesy.

- **The feedback connection of an organisation to other organisations and people in its environments means that it does not simply adapt to its environment, but that its managers take part in creating that environment.**

- **The system is such that connections between cause and effect are distant in time and space, making it very difficult to predict specific future situations.**

- **The complex systemic nature of the organisation results in the emergence of patterns of behaviour that are often unintended and unexpected**. Meaning can often be attached to these patterns only after the event; that is, missions and visions may be interpretations of current and past situations, not forecasts of future ones.

- **Managers in these circumstances have to use templates, or archetypes, to reason by drawing analogies between a specific present situation and others they have encountered before**. They cannot apply simple step-by-step reasoning to realistic assumptions about the future in these circumstances. Thus, although it is very difficult to forecast the specific behaviour of complex organisational systems, the archetypes, templates, or qualitative categories of behaviour provide guidance to thinking about whole systems. Systems thinkers see general patterns where others see specific events and look for specific causal connections.

- **Contradiction and paradox are fundamental to organisational life**, being expressed in the simultaneous presence of stability and instability, centralisation and decentralisation, division and integration, adaptation and isolation. All human organisations are simultaneously pulled towards diametrically opposed states of integration and differentiation, of maintenance control and adaptive control. However, contradiction and paradox provoke people into developing new insights.

- **In uncertain, ambiguous and paradoxical situations, organisations have to rely on self-designing forms of organisation and control.**

- **In these circumstances managers may not be able to direct the detail of what happens but may have to settle for managing the boundaries around instability.**
- **Consequently, strategic decisions may have to be made through political processes, through people trying things out and learning from them.** Political and learning processes are inevitably intertwined with unconscious group behaviours.

All of the above conclusions flow from models of managing and organising, mostly developed decades ago, that have been backed up by empirical studies, but for some reason they have never been absorbed into the conventional wisdom. What all these conclusions have in common is recognition of the significant and irremovable instability of organisational life if there is to be any innovation, transformation and new strategic direction. The models that we have so far surveyed, however, do not explain how the instability generated by amplifying feedback leads to success. In other words, there is no satisfactory explanation of how unstable behaviour produces creativity and innovation; that is, how disorder leads to new order.

Step seven in the argument, the focus of this chapter, will therefore be an explanation of the link between success and unstable dynamics; that is, with the question of why order leads to disorder and how order emerges from disorder. This chapter will be concerned with a framework or theory that can encompass the models of Weick, Forrester, Argyris, Bion, Miller and Pascale and explain the conclusions they reach. This framework represents a move away from the stable equilibrium organisation paradigm to a new paradigm, that of the far-from-equilibrium organisation. This move, as we shall see, has very important implications for strategic management action.

In this chapter, then, we are going to consider modern scientific theories of chaos and self-organisation and the insights they give to our understanding of organisational life. Before we do that, one word of qualification is required. I have been defining success as the ability of an organisation to survive by innovating and transforming itself. That is the criteria that most organisations today have to satisfy – but there are exceptions. For example, we probably do not want the nuclear industry to be highly innovative; it might be better for us all if it proceeds in a stable, bureaucratic way, having primary regard for safety. It is probably also unfortunate if the army or the police force becomes highly innovative. There will, therefore, be some organisations where the conventional wisdom is highly applicable. The point is, however, that in today's world they are the exceptions.

7.2 Feedback systems operating far-from-equilibrium – chaos and self-organisation

Our understanding of the behaviour of nonlinear feedback systems has been greatly enhanced by discoveries made by mathematicians and natural scientists during the last twenty years. They have discovered that dynamic systems have two fundamental properties of great importance: these properties have been called chaos and self-organisation. Some scientists regard these discoveries as among the most important of the twentieth century and believe that they constitute a scientific revolution, a whole new way of seeing the world (Gleick, 1988).

Since at least the time of Newton, scientists have understood the natural world in terms of machine-like regularity in which given inputs are translated through absolutely fixed laws into given outputs. For example, if you apply a force of ten pounds per square inch to a ball weighing fifteen pounds, the laws of motion will determine exactly how far the ball will move on a horizontal plane in a vacuum. Cause and effect are related in a straightforward linear way (see *Key Concept 3.3* in Chapter 3). On this view, once we have discovered the fixed laws and gathered data on the inputs to those laws, we will be able to predict the behaviour of nature's systems. Once we know how the system would have behaved without our intervention, we can then intervene by altering the inputs to the laws and so get nature to do something different, something we want it to do. According to this Newtonian view of the world we will ultimately be able to dominate nature.

This whole way of reasoning and understanding was imported into economics, where it is particularly conspicuous, and also into the other social sciences and the behavioural school of psychology, where it is somewhat less conspicuous. This importation is the source of the stable equilibrium paradigm that still today dominates thinking on managing and organising. That thinking is based on the belief that managers can in principle control the long-term future of a human system. Such a belief is realistic only if cause-and-effect links are of the Newtonian type described above, for only then can the future of a system be predicted, and only if its future can be predicted can it be controlled by someone.

The new way to make sense of the world is to take a dynamic feedback system perspective. From this point of view, nature is still understood to be driven by laws. The laws, however, are not ones of straightforward unidirectional causality; rather, they take the form of nonlinear feedback loops where causality is circular (see *Key Concept 3.3*).

What the theory of chaos tells us is this: any given nonlinear feedback system (loop, mechanism) can operate in a negative feedback manner to produce stable equilibrium behaviour; or it can be driven by positive feedback to generate explosively unstable equilibrium behaviour; or finally, it can operate in a mode in which feedback autonomously flips between positive and negative feedback to produce behaviour that is both stable and unstable. We have already seen that all human organisations are nonlinear feedback systems capable of generating all three of these states and we can see all of them in practice.

More specifically, the theory of chaos says that, when a nonlinear feedback system is driven away from the peaceful state of stable equilibrium toward the hectic equilibrium of explosive instability, it passes through a phase of *bounded instability* in which it displays highly complex behaviour, in effect the result of the system flipping randomly between positive and negative feedback. We might think of this phase as a border area between stable equilibrium and unstable equilibrium; that is, a state of paradox in which two contradictory forces, stability and instability, are operating simultaneously, pulling the system in opposing directions. While the system is in this border area neither of these contradictory forces can ever be removed; instead, the forces are endlessly rearranged in different yet similar patterns. When the system is in the border area it never behaves in a regular way that leads to equilibrium. Instead, it generates patterns of behaviour that are not only irregular but also absolutely unpredictable. Nonetheless, such behaviour has an overall, 'hidden,' qualitative pattern.

All these more specific conclusions are fundamental properties of nonlinear feedback systems no matter where they may be found; they are consequences of the nonlinear structure of the system itself, not due simply to any environment the system may operate in. Since, as we have already seen, innovative organisations are nonlinear feedback systems that operate between stability and instability, all these specific properties must also apply to innovative human organisations. Because of this, it is necessary to understand what these properties are and it is for this reason that we are now going to explore the theory of chaos.

Bounded instability far-from-equilibrium

The key discovery that scientists have recently made about the operation of nonlinear feedback loops is, therefore, that stable equilibrium and explosively unstable equilibrium are not the only *attractors*, or endpoints, of behaviour open to such systems. Nonlinear systems have a third choice: a state of bounded or limited instability far from equilibrium in which behaviour has a pattern, but it is irregular. This kind of instability is produced because the system's structure is such that, when the system is far enough away from equilibrium, it continually flips between negative and positive feedback. This means that the choice of far-from-equilibrium behaviour is a both/and one because the system is driven alternately by both positive and negative feedback and the outcome is both stable and unstable. And it is so driven, not because some agent within or outside it applies first one kind of feedback and then the other, but because the nonlinear structure of the loop causes this to happen autonomously in an apparently random way. Nonlinearity is in a sense its own constraint and stable instability is one of its fundamental properties. The choice of equilibrium behaviour, on the other hand, is an either/or one. Either the system is driven by negative feedback and then it tends to stable equilibrium, or the system is driven by positive feedback and then it tends to unstable equilibrium. If that instability is to be removed, then some agent or condition outside the system would have to 'step in and put a stop to it'. In other words, when systems are held far from equilibrium, they automatically apply internal constraints to keep instability within boundaries. This is so because of the nonlinear structure of the system. Once such a system moves into an unstable equilibrium position, however, any constraint has to come from outside the system.

When it operates in the border between stability and instability, the behaviour of the system unfolds in so complex a manner, so dependent upon the detail of what happens, that the links between cause and effect are lost. We can no longer count on a certain given input leading to a certain given output. The laws themselves operate to escalate small chance disturbances along the way, breaking the link between an input and a subsequent output. We have come across all these points before of course, but the conclusion we now reach is stronger, clearer and more definite: *dynamic nonlinear feedback systems generate completely unpredictable behaviour at a specific level over the long term.* The long-term future is not simply difficult to see: it is inherently unknowable. And it is so because of the feedback structure of the system itself, not simply because of changes going on outside it and impacting upon it. Nothing can remove that unknowability and it follows that, if an organisation is operating in the border area between stability and instability, as it must if it is to innovate, then any decision-making process that involves forecasting, envisioning future states, or even making any assumptions about future states will be ineffective. Those applying such processes in conditions of bounded instability will be engaging in fantasy activities. We can apply the conventional wisdom on strategic management only if we do not want an organisation to innovate, or if we accept that it will die. For example, we may not want organisations concerned with safety and security to innovate with these matters. However, when it comes to commercial enterprises operating in competitive markets, we quite clearly want them to be continually innovative for only then will they survive. The conventional wisdom on strategic management is not applicable to such organisations.

Although nonlinear feedback systems may generate unpredictable specific behaviour, that behaviour nevertheless has an overall qualitative pattern to it. Perhaps the easiest way to think of this is as follows. Dynamic feedback systems generate sequences of specific behaviours or events that fall into categories recognisable by 'family resemblance' type features which the behaviour or events share with each other. But within those very general, rather vague and irregular categories, each piece of behaviour or event is different. What we have is endless individual variety within broad categories – the templates or archetypes developed in the Forrester-type models for example (see Chapter 6). If we find ourselves operating in the border between stability and instability therefore, we will have to abandon all decision-making techniques that involve step-by-step reasoning from assumptions about the future. We will have to rely instead on using qualitative patterns to *reason by analogy and intuition* (we have come across this idea before in Chapter 6). Those who succeed in the borders between stability and instability will be those who see patterns where others search for specific links between causes and events.

The discovery then is the very surprising one that perfectly deterministic laws can yield behaviour that is in a sense random and that is why this behaviour has been called chaos. Note that chaos in its scientific sense is not utter confusion but a combination of qualitative patterns and specific randomness; a combination of fuzzy categories within which there is endless variety. The shape of a snowflake, for example, is generated by the feedback loop between it and its environment as it floats to the ground; it quite clearly belongs to the category 'snowflakes', but it is different from all other snowflakes and it is different because positive feedback loops have amplified tiny chance differences in the environment it experienced as it floated to earth, making it a product of its precise history.

So far we have been discussing how order (fixed laws) leads to disorder (random patterns of behaviour and completely unpredictable long-term futures). Now consider how disorder leads to unexpected new forms of order. Nonlinear feedback systems have also been discovered to possess another surprising and important property. Such systems are capable of spontaneously producing unpredictable, more complex forms of behaviour. They do this when they are pushed far from equilibrium into chaos; and they do it through a process of self-organisation. This means that, in nonlinear feedback systems, continuously creative and innovative behaviour emerges. Such innovation is not the result of any prior intention or purpose on the part of the system and it cannot be planned in advance. Experimenters seeking to provoke such unpredictable behaviour have to operate on the boundary conditions. They cannot determine what the system will do in specific terms but they can bring about some general patterns of behaviour if the right surrounding conditions are created. In these circumstances the system may be creative (see *Key Concept 7.1*).

■ **Key concept 7.1**
SYSTEMS AND CREATIVITY

At the border between stability and instability nonlinear feedback systems generate a whole world of forms that are neither stable nor unstable but a paradoxical combination of both. Their variety and beauty are such that we can describe such mathematical systems as ones that are continuously creative. If a system is not conscious and yet produces an endless stream of new and beautiful forms, it might be argued that it is just as creative as a conscious system doing the same thing. In the old mechanistic mind-set of the scientist, nature's systems were thought to behave in absolutely predictable, predetermined ways. From this perspective it would be absurd to talk about a natural system choosing to behave in a particular way or creating something new. Choice and creativity are, from this perspective, confined to consciousness and any order would be there by prior design. The new understanding is that nature's systems are driven by nonlinear feedback and the understanding of how these systems function changes the whole mind-set. We can now see that inanimate systems can choose and be creative; order can emerge unpredictably from chaos without prior design. In this way, nature produces the beautiful and the surprising.

These discoveries have extremely important implications for the way in which we think about creativity and about control. If systems are developing along inherently unpredictable specific paths, and if they spontaneously produce innovative forms through a process of self-organisation, then no one can be in control of such a system. It is totally impossible for humans to be in control of, or to dominate, systems such as this. The discoveries also mean that creativity arises out of instability. Looking at the world in this new way helps us to see why instability and unpredictability are essential to innovation and creativity.

The properties of chaos and self-organisation have been found to apply to nonlinear feedback systems in meteorology, physics, chemistry and biology (Gleick, 1988). Economists and other social scientists are now exploring whether these discoveries are relevant to their disciplines (Baumol & Benhabib, 1989; Kelsey, 1988; Anderson, Arrow & Pines, 1988). There are strong indications that chaos explanations apply to foreign exchange markets, stock markets and oil markets (Peters, 1991). Some have also applied these ideas to theories of managing and organising (Nonaka, 1988; Stacey, 1991; Zimmerman, 1991). It is this last application we now explore in the rest of this chapter. We will first explore in a little more detail what chaos and self-organisation mean and then we will look at the implications for managing and organising. It is worth doing this because the implications for decision making and control are so important.

7.3 Chaos

In the discussions on organisational dynamics in previous chapters, we have seen how:

- organisations are sets of nonlinear feedback loops;
- organisations are capable of generating stable equilibrium behaviour and also explosively unstable equilibrium behaviour;
- nonlinear systems containing both positive and negative loops can, simply because of their structure, flip from stability to instability and back again;
- successful organisations seem to be in a state that has characteristics of stability and instability, a state away from equilibrium that seems to be in the borders between stability and instability.

The theory of chaos explains the nature of this border area between stability and instability: it is a state in which a system combines both stability and instability to generate patterns of behaviour that are irregular and inherently unpredictable, but yet have a structure.

Mapping chaos

To illustrate this state of chaos, consider the following famous feedback loop. It is the equation that generates what is called the Mandelbrot set, named after its discoverer, Benoit Mandelbrot (Mandelbrot, 1982; Gleick, 1988; Stewart, 1989):

$$Z_t = Z_{t-1}^2 + c$$

This is a feedback loop because event Z now at time t is determined by event Z last time at time $t-1$ and it will determine event Z next time at time $t+1$. Starting with any Z event, this feedback relationship will generate a whole sequence of subsequent Z events over time; each Z event is simply fed back into the loop to generate the next Z event. Precisely what that sequence will look like will depend upon the parameter c. If we start with a Z and some value for c, we get one sequence of events. Change the Z keeping the same c and we get another sequence. If we start with the same Z but another c we will get yet another sequence of events.

Some of the sequences will be stable and orderly, settling down into predictable patterns over time. The patterns may be ones of constancy or of perfectly regular cycles. This is the equilibrium of stability. Yet other Z events will generate sequences that grow explosively to infinity in a perfectly predictable way – the equilibrium of explosive instability.

If we take many thousands of Z events and c parameters, examining them to see if they generate stable or unstable sequences, we will be able to draw a map of all the starting conditions leading to stability and all the starting conditions leading to instability. This will be a map of the two final states to which this particular nonlinear feedback system is attracted. It will be a map of the two attractors for the system.

A computer program (Peitgen, 1986) can be written to calculate sequences of Zs from the above equation (Z is a complex number, but it does not matter for our purpose what a complex number is) and that program plots a black point for all Zs that produce stable sequences and a white point for all Zs that generate unstable sequences. The result of doing this is shown in *Figure 7.1* and there is nothing at all surprising about it: there is a black blob in the middle representing all combinations of starting events that yield stable outcomes (attraction to stable equilibrium) and outside this blob there is a large white area for all events that lead to instability (attraction to explosively unstable equilibrium).

According to this map, this particular feedback system has a choice between being attracted to stability or instability. If this is the only choice we are aware of, we will quite naturally conclude that successful systems must be stable systems.

The surprise comes, however, when we start to look closely at the border between stability and instability, for we discover that the border is not the clean-cut clear line dividing stability from instability that we might have expected. Instead we discover that this border area is a completely different form of behaviour that scientists knew nothing about until the last twenty years or so. The discovery means that nonlinear feedback systems are not confronted by a simple choice between stability and instability – they could choose to operate in the third state, one of bounded instability. This is qualitatively different behaviour from either stability or instability.

We can see what this third attractor looks like on our computer map by taking smaller and smaller intervals between the Z events and the c parameters at the border line and plotting their resulting stability or instability. When we do this we find, as shown in *Figure 7.2*, that the borders are complex, highly irregular, wispy lines.

Now examine one of these wispy lines in more detail and your computer will draw a complex pattern of the kind shown in *Figure 7.3*. These patterns in the figure are in black and white, but you could instruct the computer to use different colours

Figure 7.1   A map of stability and instability
Source: R. Penrose (1989), *The Emperor's New Mind: Concerning Computers, Minds and the Laws of Physics*, Oxford: Oxford University Press

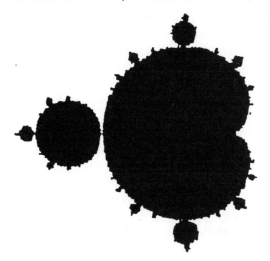

Figure 7.2 Mapping the borders between stability and instability
Source: R. Penrose (1989), *The Emperor's New Mind: Concerning Computers, Minds and the Laws of Physics*, Oxford: Oxford University Press

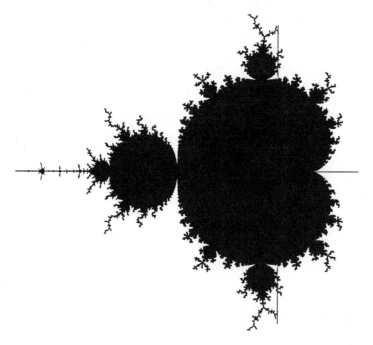

according to how long it takes to identify whether an initial point will end up as an unstable sequence. With these instructions, the computer will draw a contour map of the strength of the pull to infinity or instability and the result is patterns of great beauty (see for example, Peitgen (1986) or Gleick (1988)). Part of the pattern in *Figure 7.3* can now be blown up and you will see other patterns embedded in it. What you see depends each time on how closely you look and it is always different. But it is also always similar – recognisable irregular patterns always appear. Tiny differences in your perspective, tiny differences in the range of events or numbers you are concerned with, lead to very different, yet recognisably similar patterns, with the original shape, islands of stability, popping up over and over again. These patterns are constant only in the degree of their irregularity. Tucked between stability and instability, at the frontier, nonlinear feedback systems generate a whole world of creative, exciting, beautiful forms of behaviour that are neither stable nor unstable but continuously new and creative.

What this discovery, made only some twenty years ago, amounts to is this. There is no clear-cut border between stability and instability for a nonlinear feedback system. Instead there is an infinitely intricate border that is neither stable nor unstable, but a state of bounded instability, an intertwining of order and disorder. Perhaps one can think of it as a state of inherent contradiction between stability and instability in which order and disorder cannot be separated.

In this border area we cannot make clear-cut distinctions between stability and instability because the starting conditions that lead to one are so close to the starting

Figure 7.3 A closer look at the border
Source: R. Penrose (1989), *The Emperor's New Mind: Concerning Computers, Minds and the Laws of Physics*, Oxford: Oxford University Press

conditions that lead to the other. They are so close, in fact, that we could never measure or act upon the differences between them; we could never determine in advance which end condition was going to occur because we are incapable of infinite precision. For all practical purposes, then, instability and stability, irregularity and regularity, are hopelessly intertwined with each other here and, because of this, the specific future of the system is inherently unpredictable.

Ideas of this kind are certainly not new concepts. Many ancient mythologies incorporate them and artists and philosophers have spoken in these terms for a very long time. Jungian analytical psychology is built on the notion of contradictory opposites generating the tension that creates psychic energy from which the endless variety of human behaviour patterns emerges. What is astonishing, however, is that very simple, absolutely fixed mathematical equations can generate the kind of behaviour we have just discussed. What is equally astonishing is that such equations describe how a great many of nature's systems behave. These ideas are no longer confined to the realms of mythology, art, philosophy and psychology, but have moved to the centre of all sciences. If managers wish to adopt a scientific approach to understanding organisations, they must now take account of these properties of nonlinear feedback systems. *Illustration 7.1* provides some examples of chaos in nature's systems.

■ **Illustration 7.1**
CHAOS IN NATURE'S SYSTEMS

Chaos exists outside abstract mathematical equations in the earth's weather system. The weather is patterns in interdependent forces such as pressure, temperature, humidity and wind speed which feed into each other and thence back into themselves. The weather is generated by a nonlinear feedback system.

To model its behaviour, the forces have to be measured at a particular point in time, at regular vertical intervals through the atmosphere from each of a grid of points on the earth's surface. Rules are then necessary to explain how each of the sets of interrelated measurements, at each measurement point in the atmosphere, change over time. This requires massive numbers of computations. When these computations are carried out they reveal that the weather always follows what is called a *strange attractor*, another name for a chaotic pattern. The shape of that attractor is shown in *Figure 7.4*.

What this shape means is that the weather follows recognisably similar patterns, but those patterns are never ever exactly the same as those at any previous point in time. The system is highly sensitive to some small changes and blows them up into major alterations in weather patterns. Chaotic dynamics mean that we will never be able to

Figure 7.4 The strange attractor for the weather system
Source: R. Stacey (1991), *The Chaos Frontier: Creative Strategic Control for Business*, Oxford: Butterworth-Heinemann

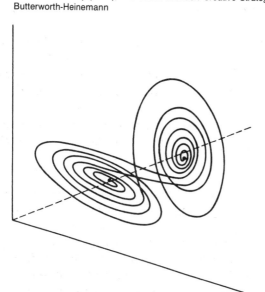

forecast the weather for more than a few days ahead. The theoretical maximum for accurate forecasts is two weeks, one meteorologists are nowhere near reaching.

Throughout the 1970s and the 1980s the principles of chaos have been explored in one field after another and found to explain turbulence in gases and liquids, certain pathological conditions of the heart, the eye movements of schizophrenics, the spread of some diseases, and the impact of some inoculation programmes against some diseases. The body's system of arteries and veins follows patterns determined by feedback rules with chaotic properties. The growth of insect populations has chaotic characteristics. The leaves of trees grow through a process of iterating deterministic rules contained in their spores; they are fractal and self-similar enough to allow us to distinguish one kind from another but no two of a kind are ever exactly the same. You can reproduce similar individuals, clearly belonging to one category, on a computer using the rules and iteration. Human cells divide in the same way following rules encoded in the DNA. The reason for no two snowflakes ever being the same can be explained using chaotic dynamics. The orbit of the moon Hyperion around Saturn follows a path which can be explained using the principles of chaos as can the Great Red Spot of Jupiter. Water dripping from a tap has been shown to follow a chaotic time pattern, as does smoke spiralling from a cigarette.

At this stage, note from our map in *Figure 7.2* that the particular system we are talking about there will find it most easy to be attracted to explosive instability – most Z events and c parameters produce this result. The next easiest option will be stability because large numbers of Z events and c parameters lead to this eventual outcome. The most difficult option to follow will be that of bounded instability because the range of Z events and c parameters leading to it is so much smaller. Indeed the area over which chaotic behaviour applies is so small that for centuries scientists did not notice its existence.

It is useful to reflect upon how the relative ease of reaching stability, explosive instability and chaos relate to the findings of Miller and Pascale discussed in Chapter 4. They too found that organisations seem to be attracted most easily to states of stability and explosive instability. What organisations seem to find most difficult is sustaining a state of contradiction, a state between the extremes of differentiation and integration, the extremes of instability and stability. The lesson seems to be that staying in the border area is a difficult task that requires continuing energy and attention.

Illustration 7.2 gives another way of looking at this important border area between stability and instability.

■ Illustration 7.2
CHAOS AND THE LOGISTIC EQUATION

Suppose that the profit level P of a particular company in a time period t depends exactly upon its advertising outlay in that period. Suppose further that there is a simple nonlinear relationship between profit and advertising. This means that increased advertising has a diminishing impact on consumers until eventually some increase in advertising brings in a profit which is smaller than the outlay, so that the total profit falls. Therefore, sometimes profit follows an amplifying feedback loop and sometimes it follows a damping feedback loop. To represent this behaviour in mathematical terms we can use the logistic difference equation already encountered in Chapter 6:

$$P_t = cP_{t-1}(1 - P_{t-1})$$

This nonlinear feedback loop will generate a sequence of profits over time for any value of c. The question is what patterns will profit follow as you raise the value of the parameter c (bigger impact of advertising on profit and/or bigger proportion of profit devoted to advertising).

At low levels of c, profit will settle into stable equilibrium paths of straight lines over time (values for c between 0 and 3), or of regular, repetitive cycles (values for c between 3 and 3.5). At high values for c (above 4), profits will show an unstable but uniform pattern of explosive growth to infinity. As with the Mandelbrot equation, therefore, we have states of stable equilibrium at first and later on states of unstable equilibrium, and we want to know what happens at the borders between them (values for c between 3.5 and 4).

To see this we have to perform thousands of calculations on a computer, gradually increasing the value of c. For example, at $c = 3.2$, we find that profits fluctuate along a regular two-period cycle with one peak and one trough. At a value for c of 3.5, a period four cycle appears – two peaks and two troughs. If you tune the parameter up to 3.56 the period doubles again and you get a period eight cycle. By 3.567 the cycles are to period 16. Thereafter there are rapid period doublings until you reach a value for the parameter c of 3.58 (Stewart, 1989).

This pattern is shown in *Figure 7.5*. Here the final values reached by profit are plotted (on the vertical axis) against the value of the parameter c (on the horizontal axis). So for each value of c between 0 and 3 we have a single stable point, a higher point for each value of the parameter shown by the rising curve from 0 to 3. At 3 we have two final values for profit: the peak and the trough of the cycle. The line splits into two, or

Figure 7.5   Mapping the logistic equation
Source: R. Stacey (1991), *The Chaos Frontier: Creative Strategic Control for Business*, Oxford: Butterworth-Heinemann

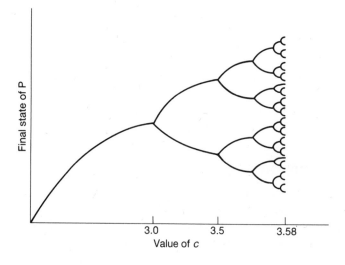

bifurcates. And the peaks and troughs diverge as we go from 3 to 3.5. At 3.5 we get a further bifurcation to show two peaks and two troughs. They in turn bifurcate and soon at 3.58 there are infinitely many bifurcations. This diagram has been called a fig-tree diagram, showing how, at successive values of the parameter, the trunk of final values splits into boughs, the boughs into branches, the branches into twigs, the twigs into twiglets and so on. The behaviour of the system is far more complicated than we could have imagined.

What happens as we continue to tune up the parameter *c*? At the parameter value of 3.58 the behaviour of the system becomes random (instability), within fixed boundaries (stability). There are no regular cycles; the values from each iteration shoot all over the place (within boundaries) and never return to any value they previously had. No matter how many thousands of iterations you try this remains true. There are cycles that you can recognise as cycles, but they are always irregular. This is chaos, also known as a strange attractor. There is no way you could ever forecast what will happen to profit if the parameter value is 3.58 – and that has nothing to do with environmental changes or random shocks. Nothing changes outside the equation, you follow the same constant rules as before and the parameter value sticks at 3.58, but the consequence is totally unpredictable disorder in the path of profit over time.

Figure 7.6 shows a representation of many thousands of iterations for parameter values between around 3.3 and 4. The black areas are chaos and the white stripes within chaos are windows of order.

You can now examine the first white stripe in the top part of *Figure 7.6* by iterating for very small intervals of the parameter value which yields that white stripe. In effect, you 'blow up' the picture within the window of order, and you find that this magnified portion resembles the whole diagram. This is shown in *Figure 7.7*. If you repeat the blow-up procedure for the first white stripe in *Figure 7.7* you will once again find a picture that resembles the whole diagram as shown in *Figure 7.6*. The structure is infinitely deep; there are pictures within pictures forever and they are always similar. What we have, then, is a very simple nonlinear feedback relationship, or decision-

Figure 7.6 Further map of the logistic equation
Source: R. Stacey (1991), *The Chaos Frontier: Creative Strategic Control for Business*, Oxford: Butterworth-Heinemann

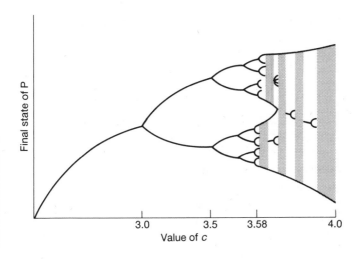

Figure 7.7   Yet another map of the logistic equation
Source: R. Stacey (1991), *The Chaos Frontier: Creative Strategic Control for Business*, Oxford: Butterworth-Heinemann

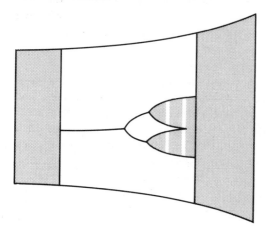

making rule, that produces a highly complex pattern of results over time. Between stability and instability there is a complex border that combines both stability and instability.

The properties of chaos

The discovery of the state of bounded instability is of such great importance because of what it means for the nature of cause and effect. Since, as we have seen, there are strong reasons for maintaining that innovative organisations must be operating in states of chaos, these important conclusions about cause and effect apply to organisations that are capable of innovating and transforming themselves.

Cause and effect

In bounded instability, or chaos, the system operates to amplify tiny changes in starting conditions into major alterations of consequent behaviour. This is called *sensitive dependence on initial conditions*. That sensitivity is so great that differences in the value of a variable or parameter to the thousandth or even the millionth decimal point can eventually alter the complete behaviour of the system. Tiny changes that we could not possibly hope to detect, measure or record could lead the system to completely different, qualitatively different, states of behaviour. This means that the links between cause and effect are lost in the detail of what happens. For all practical purposes the links have disappeared and we will therefore not be able to identify the specific consequences of a specific action nor will we be able to identify the specific cause of a specific event. Any claim that we have so done will simply be our own fantasy. To be connected to reality we will have to think instead in terms of general qualitative patterns related to the system as a whole.

The system dynamics we surveyed in the last chapter recognised that the links between cause and effect become distant in complex systems and are hard to detect. We can now see that it could be more extreme than that – the links can disappear altogether if the system operates in the area of bounded instability.

Chaos, cybernetics and statistical relationships

You will recall that those who developed cybernetics (see Chapter 5) were also concerned with what feedback meant for cause-and-effect links. They sidestepped the problem by saying that a feedback system is so complex that we cannot establish what the causal links are. But the way cybernetic models operate is based on the assumption that the links are still there, even though we cannot identify them. Those links are assumed to generate clear connections between inputs to the system and outputs from it. It is only because of this assumption that cybernetic control can be based on statistical relationships. We can now see that this connection is broken when the system operates in bounded instability and that must make cybernetic control absolutely impossible. When the cause-and-effect links are broken we may detect a strong statistical association in data from the past, but that association will not continue into the future.

Going back in time

Consider what this breakdown of cause-and-effect links means. Suppose a system has moved from a particular state A many periods ago and now occupies another state B. Could we take control of this system and take it back to state A? We could, if it were possible to identify the links between the causes and effects of its behaviour and we had a record of those causes over the past periods. We could then simply make the system retrace its steps and go back into its own history. If we did not have perfectly accurate records of past causes, and if we had not specified the causal links absolutely precisely, we could still hope to get the system back to a position approximating A, provided that the system does not escalate tiny differences in an unpredictable way. So we could only take a system back to some previous state if it is operating in equilibrium, either stable or explosively unstable. Only then are there the required clear-cut connections between cause and effect and only then do tiny differences not escalate in an unpredictable way.

If, however, the system operates in bounded instability it will be completely impossible to make it retrace its steps. For, on its journey through time from state A to state B, it will have lost some information (the law of entropy). It will have been impossible to keep infinitely accurate records of everything that happened to it, to measure with infinite accuracy to the millionth decimal place. This inability to retain every single scrap of information as the system moves from A to B is of great importance when the system operates in bounded instability. For, as we try to take the system backwards, we inevitably make a tiny mistake in reproducing what happened to it. Before long that tiny mistake takes over and we completely miss the state A that we are trying to take the system back to. Time is irreversible (because of the law of entropy and the nature of feedback) and we can never give an entirely accurate explanation of why the system now is where it now is (Prigogine, 1984). (As an aside, in a world of nonlinear feedback systems operating in bounded instability, the law of entropy makes it impossible for time machines to take us back into history. If this is how our world operates, and many scientists think it is, then time machines will always remain fiction.)

Going forward in time

The same points apply if we want to control the movement of a system to a fixed point in the future. There is no fundamental problem of principle in doing this if the system is an equilibrium one. But, to control movement to a future point when the system is boundedly unstable, we would have to specify with infinite accuracy each event, each action, required to reach that future state. If we make some tiny error in our specification the system could well amplify this and end up somewhere completely different. We cannot then decide on some future state for the system, say C, and identify the events required to take it there. We cannot measure or record in the infinitely accurate detail required to allow this to happen. The tiniest error could escalate and swamp the behaviour of the system. Nor could we fix on some future point and then get there by trial-and-error action because our errors would not cancel out.

We could imagine this desirable state C and stipulate that that is where we wish to go, but there is an infinitely small chance that we will actually reach it. Stipulating the future state is then an illusion, a waste of time, when the system is operating in bounded instability. Making some assumptions about what that future state might be is also rather pointless because we will have to keep changing those assumptions. If we make an assumption about the specific future of a chaotic system, then the only useful thing we can say about that assumption is that it will not happen. It then becomes difficult to see how the assumption helps one to make a decision. The real drivers of behaviour become what has just happened, not some hypothetical and unrealisable assumption about what might (see *Illustration 7.3*). There is no option but to create where the system is going through action and discovering where it is going as it is going there. This is a process of learning in real time, provoked by paradox and conducted through reasoning by analogy.

It follows that we cannot be 'in control' of a system that is far from equilibrium in the way we normally think about control. We cannot be in control because we cannot forecast the specific future of a system operating in bounded instability – it moves randomly at a specific level. We cannot envision it either, unless we believe in clairvoyance or prophecy. We cannot establish how the system would move before we make a policy change or then how it would move after the policy change. We have no option but to take a chance, make the change and see what happens. The future of a chaotic system is open-ended and inherently unknowable: it moves in a random way over the long term affected by small chance disturbances. Note that the future of the system is inherently unpredictable. It is unknowable. It is not just that it is difficult to forecast accurately. It is utterly impossible to do so. Such systems are an unravellable record of their own histories. This means that we have seriously to question any prescriptions based on assumptions that long-term futures can be forecast to any extent at all.

■ **Illustration 7.3**
MAKING ASSUMPTIONS ABOUT THE FUTURE

Take a very abstract case. Suppose we have to decide now whether we are going to invest in a particular project or not. The project will make a lot of money if certain conditions prevail in five years time but lose a great deal if certain other conditions prevail then. We decide that we cannot forecast what the situation is likely to be in five years time because of the level of uncertainty, but we believe that we must at least make some assumptions before we can take the decision and that we should make the decision on the basis of these assumptions.

Suppose that after much research and discussion we decide that the most reasonable assumptions are that conditions ABCD will prevail. On this basis we decide that the project will make money and we go ahead, even though we know that ABCD will not be what actually materialises. We believe we can live with that if we keep updating our assumptions as time passes. So we make the investment.

Nearly a year later, some way through to completion of the project, we review the situation and find that we need to change the basic assumptions – ABCZ is now a much more reasonable scenario we think. But three months later the project runs into a hitch and we review the situation again. Now we think that conditions XBCW make a more reasonable scenario. Even if these conditions indicate that we are unlikely to make much money, the project is now almost complete so we continue. Some three months later the project is complete and further reviews reveal that YPCW is now the likely scenario. This looks better so we set the project running. A month later we review the first month of full-scale operation and find that the situation likely to prevail at the end of our original five-year period is now assumed to be ZPNX.

Two years ago we decided to go ahead on the basis of assumptions ABCD, knowing that they would not actually prevail. Now, looking three years ahead, we are saying that the conditions will be ZPNX, completely different as we suspected all along. And no doubt we will continue to change the assumptions during the next three years. When we look back we have to admit that we decided to do something for reasons that were completely invalid and furthermore, we knew we were doing this at the time.

In what possible sense can we say that it was sensible or reasonable to make the decision on the basis of ABCD in the first place? The answer must be none. If we know that a set of conditions will not prevail it makes no sense at all to make a decision on the basis of such a fantasy. Yet this is exactly what boards of directors do when they use discounted cash flow calculations to make investments.

The properties of a system operating in chaos mean that we have to abandon hope of being in control of its long-term future. We will not be able to plan its long-term future nor envision it; but in the short term, because it takes time for small changes to build up, it is possible to forecast how the system will behave. It is therefore perfectly possible to be in control, to plan the short-term development of the organisation.

When it comes to the longer term, chaotic systems do have a property in addition to inherent unpredictability, one that enables us to cope. Systems operating in bounded instability always follow recognisably similar patterns, similar but always different too. The patterns are recognisable in terms of their similarity and their irregularity. *Illustration 7.4* provides an example of what is meant by this in a system in nature.

■ Key concept 7.2
CHAOS

Chaos is, in one sense, an inherently random pattern of behaviour generated by fixed inputs into deterministic (that is fixed) rules (relationships), taking the form of nonlinear feedback loops. Although the specific path followed by the behaviour so generated is random and hence unpredictable in the long term, it always has an underlying pattern to it, a 'hidden' pattern, a global pattern or rhythm. That pattern is self-similarity, that is a constant degree of variation, consistent variability, regular irregularity, or more precisely, a constant fractal dimension. Chaos is therefore order (a pattern) within disorder (random behaviour).

To see what the property of self-similarity, or recognisably similar patterns, means for an organisation, recall the templates or archetypes described in Chapter 6 in the section on Forrester's models: for example, patterns of shifting the burden, patterns of pushing the growth factors instead of relaxing the limiting factors. We can detect similar patterns of this type in one organisation after another, but they are never exactly the same. In Chapter 1 we talked about categories of patterns in actions – we called them strategies. One category is differentiation. We can observe many companies carrying this strategy out, but it is never the same from one company to the next. Chapter 1 also described categories of positions in markets; market leaders constitute a category but individuals within the category are always different. We also discussed categories of postures adopted by organisations. Chapter 2 discussed configurations and Chapter 4 reviewed the ultimate states typical trajectories led to from these configurations. In these cases too we were talking about rather loose categories, ones with similarities and differences, ones we would be able to recognise when they occurred although we could not necessarily predict their specific nature. Chaos is endless individual variety within recognisably similar, irregular categories.

We humans do not find it all that difficult to cope with chaos in the scientific meaning applied to it above. We saw in the section on Argyris and Schon's models in Chapter 6 how humans store their perceptions of the world in terms of family resemblance type categories rather than precise details. Humans cope with the unfamiliar through reasoning by analogy with other situations that bear some similarity to new ones, just as coping with chaos requires.

■ **Illustration 7.4**

THE WEATHER SYSTEM

Although the specific path of behaviour in chaos is random, that behaviour does have a 'hidden' pattern, a qualitative shape. *Figure 7.4* in *Illustration 7.2* above gave a simplified picture of that shape, the strange attractor which the weather follows.

That figure shows how the weather, described in terms of air pressure, humidity and temperature and so on, varies over time, moving around one of the lobes of the shape and then suddenly switching to the other. The weather system moves endlessly around this shape, never once returning to any point it previously occupied; the lines never intersect. (They appear to do so in *Figure 7.4* only because this is a two-dimensional representation of a three-dimensional figure.)

So the specific path of the weather is totally unpredictable in the long term, but it always follows the same global shape. There are boundaries outside which the weather system hardly ever moves and, if it does so, it is soon attracted back to the shape prescribed by the attractor. Some weather conditions are not allowed – snow storms in the Sahara desert or heat waves in the Arctic. There is an overall shape to weather behaviour because it is constrained by the structure of the feedback mechanisms generating it.

Because of this 'hidden' order, the system displays typical patterns, or recognisable categories of behaviour. Even before we knew anything about the shape of the weather's strange attractor, we always recognised patterns of storms and sunshine, hurricanes and calm, and seasonal patterns. These recognisable patterns are repeated in an approximate way over and over again. They are never exactly the same, but there is always some similarity. They are similar to what went before and similar to what is occurring elsewhere in the system.

The category winter follows the category autumn and within a particular winter we find typical patterns of temperature, rainfall and wind speed. As we enter a particular winter, we do not know whether the temperature will be very low or very high for that time of the year, the rainfall heavy or light, the wind speed moderate or at gale force.

This means that we cannot identify specific causes that yield specific outcomes, but we know the boundaries within which the system moves and the qualitative nature of the patterns it displays. We know that the very irregularity of the weather will itself be regular because it is constrained in some way – it cannot do just anything. We can use the resulting self-similar patterns of winter weather to prepare appropriate behaviour. We can buy an umbrella or move the sheep off the high ground. We can cope with the uncertainty and the lack of causal connection because we are aware of self-similar patterns and use them in a qualitative way to guide specific choices.

7.4 What chaos means for organisations

As we have seen at the beginning of this chapter, there are persuasive reasons for concluding that organisations must continually strive to operate in states of chaos if they are to be innovative.

Recall the model of Lawrence and Lorsch (in the section on general systems in

Chapter 5) and the study by Pascale (Chapter 4). A key point in both of those studies of large companies was the simultaneous presence of strong forces that pull them to states of differentiation or split on the one hand, and the equally strong forces that pull them to integration or fit on the other. Recall the Miller study (Chapter 4). This showed that some organisations give in to the forces of integration and move along trajectories until they become so ossified that they fail. Other companies pursue differentiation with such persistence that they follow trajectories to disintegration, where they also fail. Miller also talks about trajectories where organisations become either overadapted to, or isolated from, their environments and so fail.

According to these studies, organisations are powerfully attracted either to disintegration or ossification in terms of internal structure and control systems. They are also attracted either to adaptation or isolation in terms of their relationship to the environment. These are all equilibrium states of either the stable or explosively unstable kind and they are all states of failure. Success lies in the borders between these stable and unstable equilibrium states. Since organisations are nonlinear feedback systems, that borderline state must be what we can now understand as bounded instability or chaos (Stacey, 1991).

■ **Key concept 7.3**
CHAOS IN HUMAN SYSTEMS

In organisations, chaos takes the form of contradiction: the simultaneous presence of opposing ways of behaving. It is evidenced, for example, by managers who operate budgetary forms of control to keep the organisation stable, while at the same time they engage in amplifying forms of political activity in which they try to undermine the status quo. Chaos in its scientific sense takes the form of conflict, as when an organisation experiences the clash of countercultures, the tensions of political activity, the contention and dialogue through which managers handle ambiguous strategic issues. There is chaos when managers work in groups to learn and develop new strategies; the tensions they generate through the way they interact and exercise their power produce patterns of behaviour that fall into recognisable categories, but are always different in specific terms. Chaotic dynamics are evidenced by escalating small changes and self-reinforcing circles in the manner in which managers deal with events and actions that have long-term consequences. Chaotic dynamics result from the use of both amplifying and damping feedback and produce behavioural archetypes of the kind described in the section on dynamic systems in Chapter 6.

It is not therefore all that easy to observe chaos in organisations in the scientific sense meant here. In a company with chaotic dynamics, we would see visible order, tight short-term controls, consistent delivery of quality products, meeting of time and cost targets. These would all be secured through damping forms of control, through negative feedback applied to affect the short-term consequence of events and actions. In other words, the visible behaviour of a chaotic company would appear about the same as that of a company in stable equilibrium. We would not describe the dynamics as chaotic if we simply observe that there is no order at all; that is, managers run from one short-term crisis to another and fail to deliver products on time at the right quality and the right cost. Chaos in its scientific sense is not utter confusion or complete disorder.

The conclusion we reach is that the dynamics of success are such that organisations have to strive to avoid attraction to equilibrium states of stability and instability. They have instead to strive to stay in a state of bounded instability or chaos. This is a very difficult state to sustain. It requires continual inputs of energy, attention and information to keep an organisation far from the equilibrium of stability or explosive instability. This is so in nature's systems too and scientists use the term *dissipative structure* to describe a system held far-from-equilibrium because such systems dissipate energy into their environments – they require constant inputs of energy to replace this dissipated energy. A successful organisation is a dissipative structure in essentially the same sense.

■ **Key concept 7.4**
DISSIPATIVE STRUCTURES

This is a complex state of orderly behaviour which requires continuous inputs of energy if it is to be sustained. It is therefore unstable and difficult to maintain.

In the business setting, a dissipative structure refers to consensus on and commitment to the implementation of an innovation, that is a new strategic direction or significant change in some aspect of the business. It requires continual inputs of attention, time and resource to sustain this state of consensus, and commitment and cooperation. Such states are consequently short-lived, periodic rather than continuous.

These conclusions about the nature of the dynamics of successful organisations have a number of implications for some important concepts already presented in previous chapters.

1 Analysis loses its primacy

If you accept the proposition that a successful organisation is a dissipative structure operating in a state of chaos, then the long-term future of all successful organisations is unknowable. It is only the long-term future of failing organisations that is knowable. This is so quite irrespective of change in the environment – it is a fundamental property of the feedback system that is an organisation. And it means that we cannot use approaches or techniques for choosing courses of action that depend in any way on the predictability of specific outcomes. It is not logically valid to recognise that the long-term future is unknowable and then behave as if it is approximately knowable. We do this when we admit that we cannot make forecasts of the future but claim that we can make assumptions about that future to guide our present choices. This makes absolutely no sense when the future is inherently unknowable.

However, chaos also means recognisable patterns in the development of a system. It is this property we have to use to make sense of what is going on and hence to make sensible choices. We cannot know anything about a specific future, but as the future unfolds we will be able to recognise patterns in what is happening, if we are perceptive enough. We will then be able to use our powers of intuition and reasoning by analogy to make creative choices in relation to those patterns. These recognisable patterns are exactly what we were talking about in the section in Chapter 6 on system dynamics. You will recall the templates or archetypes presented by researchers in this field. It may be worth returning to section 6.5 at this point to fix your ideas on what is meant by the self-similar, recognisable patterns being talked about here and how they may be used.

2 Contingency loses its meaning

Once we accept that successful organisations operate in states of bounded instability where they escalate tiny changes into major outcomes, we have to reconsider the usefulness of the concept of contingency (see Chapter 2). Contingency postulates a linear connection between a cause (size of the organisation, degree of uncertainty in the environment for example) and a consequent effect (mechanistic or organic organisational structures for example). Such straightforward connections disappear when it is possible for a tiny change to be escalated into a major consequence. This is so because two organisations may be of exactly the same size, operating in the same environment, but some tiny accident in their histories could have taken them off along very different paths. The case of Litton Industries and Texas Instruments (*Illustration 3.2*) is an example of this.

Systems that are interacting closely with their environments, creating them in the manner that Weick envisages (see Chapter 6), will be operating in bounded instability. They will not be adapting to the environment in any simple way: they will be partially creating it through their interactions. Contingency then comes to lose its meaning. We would expect very different organisations to grow up in the same industry because small differences can have large outcomes. We would not look for simple either/or connections. For example, we would no longer link mechanistic-type organisations to stable environments and organic organisations to unstable environments. We would say all successful organisations have to be both mechanistic and organic at the same time (see *Illustration 7.5*). It is not an either/or choice but an and/both one. All successful organisations have to be a contradiction between the mechanistic and the organic, between the stable and the unstable. They have to be because they all have to handle predictable short-term futures and unknowable long-term ones if they are to survive.

■ Illustration 7.5
SUCCESSFUL COMPANIES IN JAPAN AND THE US ARE NOT ALL THAT DIFFERENT

An impressive study of the differences between Japanese and US companies (Kagono et al., 1975) produces an interesting conclusion. This is that the best of companies in both the US and Japan have much more in common than is usually supposed.

The study is an in-depth review of 19 Japanese companies (including NEC, Hitachi, Toyota, Sumitomo, Suntory and Matsushita) and a similar number of US companies (including General Motors, Sears, 3M, Texas Instruments and IBM). These in-depth studies were then followed by questionnaires completed by 227 US and 291 Japanese companies, all in the late 1970s. The samples were representative in terms of company size and industrial distribution.

The study identified significant differences between Japanese and US companies in terms of organisational form and strategic orientation. The former more frequently adopt the organic model of organisation with flexible structures based on group dynamics and they tend to pursue operations-led strategies. The latter more frequently adopt the mechanistic form of organisation, based on what the authors call bureaucratic dynamics, and product-led strategies. The authors ascribed this difference to the different environments in which the US and Japanese companies operated.

More interestingly, however, they then compared groups of high performers in the US with high performers in Japan and they also compared groups of low performers in both countries with each other. They found that the best performers in both countries operated in variable environments and combined some elements of mechanistic structures and operations-oriented strategies with organic structures and product-oriented strategies.

So, while the 'typical' approach in Japan differs from that in the US, the most successful companies in both countries adopt similar styles that combine the contradictory mechanistic and organic approaches.

3 Long-term planning becomes impossible

If successful organisations operate in states of bounded instability then they have completely unknowable futures in specific terms. The links between cause and effect disappear in the detail of what happens. Since analytical reasoning based on cause-and-effect links cannot be applied, and since predicting specific future states in any form becomes impossible, successful organisations cannot possibly plan their long-term futures.

This clearly means that corporate and strategic planning exercises will not achieve what they are intended to. They may serve other purposes, such as providing feelings of certainty, security and comfort, but, if the dynamics are those of bounded instability, then such planning approaches will not be able to secure the movement of an organisation through time in a direction intended by those at the centre. The same point applies to OD and culture-change programmes. In systems operating far from equilibrium, missions, cultures and purpose cannot be planned. They emerge from the operation of the system. The same point applies to new strategic direction – it too can only emerge from the complex interaction between subsystems and between one system and another.

It is possible to predict the short-term time path of systems operating far from equilibrium. Such systems are propelled forward by the momentum of their recent past. It takes time for small changes to be escalated into major consequences. For these reasons such systems follow roughly predictable short-term futures.

This then makes it clear that today's dominant paradigm and the models of managing and organising flowing from it are limited special cases applicable to the short-term development and control of organisations. This point applies to the fact-gathering, analysing and planning approaches as well as the visionary/ideological ones. When it comes to the longer term it is necessary to add something completely different to these models. A new far-from-equilibrium paradigm does not therefore lead to the rejection of all existing models. It puts them into context as models valid for short-term, day-to-day, or ordinary management. Strategic choice and action, extraordinary frame-breaking management, needs to be driven by different models. And since all organisations have to handle both ordinary and extraordinary management, they have to deploy both the old models and the new ones; the former for the day-to-day and the latter for cutting-edge strategic management.

If managers are operating in systems that need to be far-from-equilibrium to be successful and they approach their task with the planning mentality, they will inevitably find themselves repeating what they have already done successfully or imitating what others have successfully done. Their actions will reinforce a move to stability; the planning and strong ideology mentalities will be significant forces sucking an organisation to the stable equilibrium positions that ultimately lead to failure. Strategy can only be organisationally intended if it is a continuation of existing strategy and that is eventually a recipe for failure. In that far-from-equilibrium state required for success, new strategic directions cannot be intended; they can only emerge from an interactive, spontaneously self-organising process of complex learning in real time. This does not mean sitting back and waiting for things to happen – it is the taxing process of making creative things happen.

4 Visions become illusions

Since it is widely recognised that forecasting the future state of an organisation is extremely difficult, many recommend instead that leaders should develop visions. These are meant to be qualitative, general pictures of a realistically realisable future state; assumptions about a particular time period in the future against which to test here-and-now decisions; criteria anchored to a future reality for evaluating the actions we should consider and take now. The vision will turn out to have been useful if the future state occurs and useless if it does not – this is the ultimate test of the vision.

Many, however, use the word vision, or assumption about the future, in a different way. For example, the manager of an R&D department may declare a vision to build a team of researchers who challenge each other; a group of people, each with distinctive challenging contributions to make, who interact with and provoke each other to new discoveries. This is an obviously appropriate intention now and it would have been so ten years ago and will be so in ten years time. It is not time-specific, but timeless. If your purpose in life is to change things and develop the new, as it should be if you run an R&D department, then the aspiration of building a challenging team of people will always be right. It is not necessary to know anything at all specific about the future to make this statement. It does not depend upon particular events occurring. It is a statement in preparation for just about anything. In short, this is not a statement or assumption about the future at all: it is the statement of an already-existing ideal; it is a statement of a current challenge or aspiration not anchored to a specific future. Such a statement may be an important driver of behaviour, but setting it out as if it says something about the future is likely to add an element of the mysterious to the decision-making process.

Focusing on 'the vision' is dangerous in that it narrows the range of matters attended to, when an uncertain and ambiguous world requires the opposite. Any particular current challenge or aspiration that is dressed up as 'the vision' is likely to be one amongst many, rather than the single driving force that a vision is supposed to be. At some points the R&D manager will focus on the need to build a challenging team, but at other points focus will shift to other issues on the agenda. What we have then is not some vision or overarching assumption about a specific future, but a shifting set of stretching challenges, issues, problems, opportunities and aspirations all vying for organisational attention.

Others apply the words 'vision' or 'mission' very loosely to articulations of where they have come from and where they now are. For example, the chief executive of one of the UK's largest banks articulated his vision as 'a premier bank with a strong regional distribution network and a major international presence'. This has been true of that particular bank for at least fifty years now. In what sense then is it a vision of the future? The word vision is also frequently used in a retrospective sense to describe a particular successful venture and make it sound as if that success was intended right from the beginning. As part of creating this myth there is a strong tendency to ignore visions that failed.

When organisations operate far-from-equilibrium their long-term futures are unknowable. Strategic management then becomes not the control of future direction through plans or ideologies, but the management of a live, ever-changing agenda of issues and stretching challenges. The choices and actions cannot be driven by pictures of the future, but they can be driven by beliefs in the intrinsic merits of the task, by pride in skills and doing things that last.

5 Consensus and strong cultures become dangerous

If successful organisations operate in bounded instability, then their long-term futures cannot be planned or envisioned. For such organisations small changes will escalate into new strategic directions. New strategic directions and innovative forms of behaviour will emerge from the political interactions and learning activities of people in an organisation. In these conditions it is clearly stultifying if all adhere to a single view of the future and if all strongly share the same culture, the same values and belief systems. Such consensus will block the perception of small changes, it will block the development of different perspectives. Without the continual provoking of new perspectives, an organisation will be incapable of creating its future; it will simply repeat its past instead. Strongly shared cultures push an organisation back to stability, while countercultures are required to sustain the dissipative structure far from equilibrium.

This opens up the interesting thought that today's dominant prescriptions stressing management orientation to the future could actually lead organisations to repeat the past. On the other hand, Weick's ideas of strategy as making sense of the here and now through understanding the past, could lead organisations to create different futures.

6 Contradiction, conflict, dialectics and learning become essential

The five points made above all lead to the conclusion that successful organisations develop over the long term through a process of learning. Such organisations discover and create their environments and their futures. They do not simply take anticipatory and reactive action to adapt to given environments. It is more useful to think of successful organisations as creating and interacting rather than anticipating, proacting, reacting and adapting. Contradiction provokes the conflict that leads to the new perspectives and learning an organisation requires if it is to create its future. The process is a dialectical one as discussed in the section on the models of Miller and of Pascale in Chapter 4.

As soon as we think of a successful organisation in terms of bounded instability, we move away from today's dominant views on management towards those expressed by writers such as Forrester and Weick summarised in Chapter 6, and those of Pascale, Miller and Mintzberg summarised in Chapter 4. And all of these views have so far attracted very little attention from practising managers, nor do they constitute the current dominant research paradigm.

7 Statistical relationships become doubtful

In Chapter 3 we saw that the practical application of the strategy selection criteria of acceptability, feasibility and fit all relied on the ability to construct long-term financial and market models to forecast future developments. To construct all of these models we have to extract meaning from data collected on the performance of a business and the movement of the markets. That data has to be interpreted and used to establish the relationships that go to build up financial and environmental models.

For example, we have to establish the relationships between customer preferences and prices and volumes, between profits and volumes, between prices and volumes, between volumes and material and labour requirements, between volumes and quality. If we are able to identify long-term relationships in this way we can ask 'what if' questions and so determine the consequences of what we propose to do, before we do it.

To identify relationships for a general quantitative model, it is necessary to employ statistical techniques. The simplest and most widely used techniques are averages, the normal distribution, regression analysis and probability. We cannot deal with a whole time series of price data but we can collapse it into an average over the period and deal with that. And we can use the assumption that the deviations of actual prices from this average are normally distributed to measure the bands within which prices are likely to move around the average. Even more sophisticated, we can use regression analysis, based on assumptions of normal distribution, to identify the relationship between prices and volumes demanded by customers.

The problem is that, when the dynamic of the system we are dealing with is chaotic, all these approaches are flawed in their application to the long term.

When we average the data generated by a chaotic system, problems arise from the lack of uniform distribution which is a characteristic of chaos. The average you get will depend upon the particular time period you happen to select. If you did not understand the dynamics you could draw very misleading conclusions from an average which reflected more about the time period your data happened to cover than anything else of real significance. If data is in fact being generated by chaotic systems then the standard statistical techniques applied in economics and in business modelling become questionable. Fundamental concepts such as averages, normal distribution and regression are then of doubtful value in trying to derive relationships and build models. It would be necessary to fit exactly the right relationship to the data – some other linear or nonlinear approximation would not do (Stewart, 1989).

The statistical techniques that are commonly used in modelling the performance of organisations are based on the concept of the normal distribution; variances, standard deviations and correlation coefficients used to test the validity of the relationships identified all depend on this assumption. However, the behaviour of chaotic systems is not normally distributed or regular. Behaviour is fractal, that is irregular and jagged. When the distribution is fractal, variances become infinite or undefined. There is evidence that stock market prices, bond prices, foreign exchange rates, indices of production for the economy, and other economic measures are all fractal (Peters, 1991). This must raise major question marks over the methods being used to forecast and model organisational performance and relationships with environments.

Organisational decisions based upon financial models which are almost always linear approximations to the feedback mechanisms of an organisation can therefore only have any validity for very-short-term periods into the future. The very dynamics of the business organisation render general quantitative models useless for real strategic control.

8 Probability only helps in the short term

Faced with a number of possible outcomes, it is common practice in business to use some measure of which of them is more likely, in order to make a rational choice. An investment may be particularly sensitive to the level of the oil price. At $3 per barrel the investment will not yield a profit, at $5 it might, but at $6 it will. If the probability of each outcome can be measured this will greatly assist in making the best choice.

The concept of probability provides a practically useful approach when events are repeatable over time or where we are dealing with large numbers of the same kind of event. It provides the measures of risk, without which there would be no insurance industry, but in any practical sense it does depend on repeatability. We can only say that some event A at some point in the future is more likely than some other event B, if we can use past experience to show that events similar to A have occurred more frequently than events similar to B. We also need to believe that the underlying structures which generate A and B will continue to operate in the same manner into the future.

If you get the opportunity to repeat events A and B a great many times, the measure of probability provides you with a useful decision-making tool. However if you do not get the opportunity to repeat the rule, there is no practical value in any theoretical probability measurement. If your fortune depends on the occurrence of event A and ruin on the occurrence of event B, you may never get the opportunity to try again. In situations of true uncertainty (one unique occasion without close parallels in past experience) as opposed to risk (repeatable occasions or those where there is some precedent), probability provides no practical assistance because you only get one chance.

When the dynamics are chaotic, specific events will follow an unpredictable path over the long term. There will be an infinite number of possible long-term outcomes.

The probability of any single event occurring is then infinitely small and provides no assistance in making a decision. Because tiny changes can escalate into major consequences, it will in practice be impossible to generate the same sequence of events twice. In practice it is therefore impossible to measure probability.

Many quantitative decision-making techniques in business today are based on probability. Such techniques may have short-term validity but, if the dynamics of successful businesses are chaotic, then those techniques can provide no assistance when it comes to strategic control. Instead we have to deploy reasoning by analogy, making use of the qualitative similarities in the behaviour generated by chaotic systems (Stacey, 1991).

9 Long-term forecasts and simulations are impossible

The presence of chaos is the death knell to any form of quantitative forecasting or simulation in anything other than the short term. If a minute change can escalate into behaviour of a qualitatively different kind, then even the most sophisticated extrapolation of past trends will be of no use. It also does not help much to set out a whole range of forecasts, what we called simulations or scenarios in Chapter 2. Tiny imprecisions made in calculating the implications of each scenario rapidly take over, making it highly unlikely that any simulation we calculate will approximate to what will actually happen. The range of scenarios we generate will almost certainly not contain the outcome that eventually occurs. Simulation is pointless for a chaotic system because we only get the same amount of information out as we put in. More and more computing power is required to tell us less and less. In other words we are not predicting anything, merely describing the system to a certain limited level of accuracy as it evolves in real time. We cannot determine a chaotic path unless we are first given that path.

What we can do in the presence of chaos is to use simulations as a learning exercise. We can use them to practise moves we might make if events similar to those in the simulation occur. We are then not using the simulation as a basis for making a real decision. Simulating is simply playing practice games to build dexterity and skill, rather like a fighter pilot in a flight simulator.

Although we cannot predict the future of a chaotic system, we can predict the qualitative nature of the patterns it follows and the quantitative limits within which it will move. And it is quite possible that simple methods, which appear now to have very little scientific validity, may turn out to make more sense than much more respectable approaches. Experience-based intuition will be a more reliable approach to the overall shape of the dynamic in an organisational system than any analytical methods presently available to us.

As we saw in Chapter 3, the prescriptions for selecting strategies in advance of action are based firmly on the view that forecasting is possible and that the use of different scenarios provides some assistance. When organisations operate in bounded instability these things are not possible. It is therefore impossible to identify innovative new strategic directions in advance of action. If we try, all we will succeed in identifying is some repetition of our own past actions or some imitation of others and this will ultimately lead to failure.

10 Requisite variety loses its usefulness

You will recall from the section in Chapter 5 on cybernetic control principles that those principles are built on the concept of requisite variety. The idea is that a business which undertakes large numbers of trial actions in response to unpredictable changes occurring in the environment will find that mismatches between those unpredictable changes and the actions taken in response to them will cancel out. If we undertake a large enough number of experiments then the errors will largely cancel out. According to the laws of probability, we will be left with only a small percentage of mismatches or errors. Irregular performance should then be a very minor component of the total unless managers are incompetent, or they do not undertake a sufficient volume of trials. This notion is central to the prescriptions of writers such as Peters (1982, 1988) (see Chapter 2).

This cancelling out process can only work, however, if the unpredictable changes and the consequent actions occur in large numbers and they are largely repetitive. Furthermore, they must not be small changes which escalate into large outcomes. If they are, we cannot rely on errors cancelling out. It will be important to get the right response for that small change which might escalate, otherwise the consequence could be disaster. Where the dynamic is chaotic all these conditions for the cancelling out of mismatches between trial actions and unpredictable changes fail to be met. Chaotic dynamics generate long-term situations that are open-ended. Here the changes are unique, not repetitive; and small changes do escalate with large consequences. Stability can then be maintained only if we act in a manner that matches each specific change. We will always have to detect the change and get the timing right. That is, we will have to be able to forecast specific long-term outcomes. This is impossible in chaos. It follows that no matter how competent managers are, performance and behaviour will always display irregularity combined with regularity. We will not be able to fix on a future point and then reach that point by trial-and-error action.

The first property of nonlinear feedback systems, that of chaos, therefore has very important implications for how it is possible to control and develop a successful organisation over the long term. We turn now to the second property mentioned earlier, that of spontaneous self-organisation, which also provides significant insights into the nature of managing and organising.

7.5 Self-organisation

The chemist Illya Prigogine has shown how nonlinear feedback systems develop unpredictable new forms of behaviour when they are pushed far from equilibrium. There is a fundamental relationship between states of bounded instability or chaos on the one hand and innovation or creativity on the other: systems can only be creative through experiencing instability.

The state of chaos performs the important task of amplifying small changes in the environment, causing the instability necessary to shatter existing behaviour patterns and make way for the new. Creative systems pass through states of instability or crisis and reach critical points where they may spontaneously self-organise to produce some new structure or behaviour. The choice made at such critical points is unpredictable. The new more complex structure is dissipative because it takes energy to sustain the system in that new mode.

For example, as energy is pumped into a particular gas the molecules are put into a more and more excited state. They all move randomly in different directions – a state of instability or chaos. This instability is performing the function of amplifying or spreading the energy or information around the molecules in the gas. The instability is also shattering any relationship the molecules bore to each other before the energy was pumped in. In this state the gas emits a dull glow. As further energy is pumped into this system, it reaches a critical point. At this point the molecules appear to communicate with each other and suddenly they spontaneously organise themselves to all point in the same direction. The result is a laser beam casting its light for miles. The sudden choice of molecules all to point in the same direction is not predictable from the laws of physics. There is no central intention or law prescribing this behaviour; it emerges out of instability through a self-organising creative process.

■ **Key concept 7.5**
SELF-ORGANISATION

Self-organisation is a process in which the components of a system in effect spontaneously communicate with each other and abruptly cooperate in coordinated and concerted common behaviour.

Applying these ideas to an organisation we get a picture of the creative organisation as one that continually confronts instability and crisis, out of which it creates new order in spontaneous emergent ways. The studies of Miller and Pascale presented in Chapter 4 describe just such a development pattern for organisations.

Pascale (1990) was involved in and has sought to explain how Ford was transformed from a loss-making company that focused primarily on low costs in the late 1970s into a profitable quality-conscious concern by the late 1980s. He shows how this process was not the consequence of some master plan established early on in the period of transformation. Instead the changes came about as a large number of independently-started change initiatives built into a major movement. The at-first unconnected initiatives included schemes for employee participation, the use of multi-discipline teams to design the new Taurus, setting up various informally operating committees to examine how to break down barriers to change and extensive bureaucracy, the establishment of many task forces, and the use of training and development programmes. All of this did not happen as the result of some central intention, corporate plan or culture change programme. Pascale (1990, p. 122) concludes:

> The remarkable occurrence at Ford was that, somewhat mysteriously, a set of independent initiatives flowed together and became mutually reinforcing.

This is what is meant by self-organisation in human systems. The existence of such processes in successful organisations is also supported, as we have seen in Chapter 5, by studies of the political process in organisations. These studies depict stages close to the instability, crises, amplification and self-organisation described above.

Successful organisations seem to show the same temporal patterns of creative change as do systems in nature and the reason they do is that they too are nonlinear feedback systems.

7.6 What self-organisation means for organisations

Self-organisation theory provides an explanation of the stages a system passes through as it develops new, more complex forms of order. In organisational terms it establishes patterns in the change process through which new strategic directions or innovations emerge. This way of understanding human organisations makes it clear that new strategic direction can only emerge; it cannot be planned. And it makes it clear that the processes through which emergence occurs are ones of political interaction and group learning.

First, in what sense does self-organisation mean political interaction?

The way for spontaneous self-organisation is opened up by the manner in which nonlinear feedback systems amplify small changes in their environments. In human systems this happens when individuals detect some issue and then build support for it. The building of coalitions around issues, persuading and negotiating with others to support an idea, is clearly a political process. It requires the deployment and use of power. Innovations in organisations always begin with individuals and they can go no further than the individual unless the awareness of the issue is spread and commitment to it developed through the organisation. It is this political process that gets the issue onto the organisational agenda in the first place.

The importance of political interaction also clearly continues throughout the life of an issue. Politics is the process through which managers make and enact strategic choices. Whether an issue continues to sustain attention, what kind of attention it receives, whether it is ever tried out in the form of some experiment, and whether it is finally invested in or not, all depend on how its supporters use their power and sustain the support.

It is accurate to call the political processes we have been talking about self-organising. This is so because no-one centrally organises the support groups around particular lines. Nor can anyone because no one knows what the issues are until some coalition is formed around them. Whether an issue is ever noticed or not is self-organising in the sense of spontaneously gathering support or failing to.

Second, in what sense is spontaneous self-organisation in an organisation a learning process?

Nonlinear systems amplify changes and in so doing they shatter old patterns, making way for the new through a process of correlation or communication between components or agents of the system. In human systems this process of shattering the old and developing the new applies in the first instance to perceptions; only later on does it apply to structures, roles and so on. When we question and throw out old perceptions and then replace them with new ones we are learning. In organisations this kind of learning is done in groups. Group learning is thus the essence of strategic discovery and choice. The effectiveness with which groups in an organisation learn is the major determinant of whether that organisation takes effective strategic actions or not. But groups are affected by unconscious process as well as the primary learning tasks they have come together to perform. No-one can make a group learn. Whether or not it does depends upon its own spontaneous behaviour. That behaviour is all the more spontaneous because it is affected by unconscious processes, as we saw in Chapter 6. These unconscious processes make its behaviour patterns and what will emerge from its learning activities unpredictable.

We can interpret self-organisation in an organisation as the process of political interaction and group learning from which innovation and new strategic directions for the organisation may emerge. These processes are themselves nonlinear feedback ones. They too are only effective when they are held far-from-equilibrium in states of contention, contradiction and paradox. The outcome therefore emerges without central intention and is unpredictable.

Note that self-organisation is not the same thing as self-managing teams nor is it the same thing as democracy. A self-managing team or a democratic group is one that makes choices by some kind of majority vote, without being instructed what to do by its leaders or from outside its ranks. Self-organisation can and will occur even in a dictatorship: revolution may be a form of self-organisation and that is how dictatorships are overthrown. Self-organisation may well occur in bureaucratic organisations if managers from different hierarchical levels or different parts of the bureaucracy come to find themselves supporting and working together on some common issue. Self-organisation does not mean that job definitions are loose and overlapping. It can occur even when jobs are rigidly defined. Self-organisation is an irregular pattern of collaborative interaction: it can take many forms.

It is not a predictably mechanistic process as automatic control is in cybernetics. Weick's views on self-designing systems are a form of self-organisation, but so is a revolution or a coup.

■ **Key concept 7.6**
SELF-ORGANISATION IN HUMAN SYSTEMS

In organisations, self-organisation is the spontaneous formation of interest groups and coalitions around specific issues, communication about those issues, cooperation and the formation of consensus on and commitment to a response to those issues. The term spontaneous communication arenas, *that is meetings and document exchanges, may be used to describe the occasions on and the means through which this occurs.*

Self-organisation occurs when people form a group that produces patterns of behaviour, despite the absence of formal hierarchy within that group or authority imposed from outside it. Such groups could behave in what we would describe as a completely uncontrolled way, for example a mob, but such groups may also behave in a way that we would have to describe as self-controlled.

As soon as a collection of people begin to interact with each other, say at a party, we find that particular attitudes, ideas, enthusiasms, propositions and issues emerge spontaneously within a very short time. People form themselves into groupings around, say, some issue. One group may be for the issue and another against it. Soon the conversation will switch spontaneously to another issue and the groupings will spontaneously reform. No-one directs this process, nor does it move to a plan: it is a self-organising process. That process of spontaneous self-organisation can be seen quite clearly at a party, but it is also evident in all other human systems, including business organisations. It happens because of the intrinsic property of human systems to self-organise.

Informal groups and networks of managers within an organisation clearly form and conduct themselves through self-organising processes: no central authority organises the network of informal contacts and coalitions that develop in an organisation and yet that network can behave in a controlled way and become a vital part of the organisation's control system. Most managers are not used to the idea that a system, that is a set of interactions, can control itself. For them, control requires some individual to take charge.

Self-organisation differs from self-managing teams (to be discussed in Chapter 10) in the following important ways:

- Self-organisation is a fluid network process in which informal, temporary teams form spontaneously around issues, while self-managing teams are permanent or temporary but always formally established parts of a reporting structure.
- While top managers cannot control self-organising processes – they can only intervene to influence the boundary conditions around them – they can install a structure of self-managing teams and control them through the rules that govern how they are to operate.
- Participants decide on who takes part in self-organisation and what the boundaries around their activities are, while top managers make these decisions with regard to self-managing teams.
- Self-organising networks operate in conflict with and are constrained by the hierarchy, while self-managing teams replace the hierarchy.
- Unequal power energises networks through conflict but also operates as a constraint, while dispersed power is supposed to lead to self-managing teams and consensus.
- In self-organising processes, people empower themselves while, in self-managing teams, the top empowers people.
- The self-organising process is both provoked and constrained by cultural difference, while the self-managing process is based on strongly shared culture.

In Chapter 11, we will discuss the behaviour of self-organising small groups of people within organisations.

7.7 How the theories of chaos and self-organisation link success and dynamics

At the beginning of this chapter its purpose was stated as that of explaining the link between success and unstable dynamics. The Miller/Pascale studies show that successful companies are those that avoid stable equilibrium and operate in a state of contradiction and creative tension. This is essentially about the order of new strategic direction emerging from the disorder of contradiction and contention. The fundamental reasons why this should be so are however not made clear, nor is there a framework to understand why orderly organisational systems following rather simple decision rules should generate instability. There is no explanation of how disorder flows from order.

Approaching the matter from another angle, others have constructed complex feedback system models. They have shown that the connections between cause and effect are distant in these systems and that leads to unintended and unexpected consequences of actions. Successful action then has to depend on an understanding of the system as a whole, seeing qualitative patterns and using archetypes and templates to reason by analogy. The models explain the instability of the dynamics in terms of the complexity of the system, but they do not explain how such instability is essential to success. They explain how disorderly behaviour flows from orderly organisational systems, but they do not explain how new order flows from that disorder.

The theories of chaos and self-organisation provide the links. The first section of this chapter summarises the key points made by the complex system models surveyed in the last chapter. If you return to that summary (p. 209) you will see that all of these key points are consistent with the chaotic behaviour of nonlinear feedback systems. Disorderly dynamics are fundamental properties of nonlinear feedback systems wherever they are found. Such systems generate patterns of behaviour over time that are jagged or fractal. They display cycles of irregular periods and trends with sudden discontinuities. They move within irregular but recognisably similar categories, providing the archetypes and templates we observe. Orderly nonlinear feedback systems are structured so as to be capable of generating disorderly changes. Such systems use the disorder to destroy old behaviour patterns allowing the new to emerge through spontaneous self-organisation. This is why unstable dynamics are essential to success and how such dynamics may produce such success. This is the link back from disorder to order.

In addition to providing a coherent framework within which all the models of managing and organising discussed in Chapters 5 and 6 can be incorporated, the theories of chaos and self-organisation focus attention more clearly on certain important features of the dynamics. When you think within the framework provided by modern nonlinear dynamics you cannot escape the essential unknowability of the long-term future of any organisation. Once you accept this essential unknowability you have to reject a great deal of the received wisdom on strategic management and control. You have to accept the importance, instead, of forms of spontaneous self-organisation.

■ **Key concept 7.7**
A CHAOS THEORY OF ORGANISATION

A chaos theory of organising is built on the following propositions:

- *All organisations are webs of nonlinear feedback loops connected to other people and organisations (its environments) by webs of nonlinear feedback loops.*
- *Such nonlinear feedback systems are capable of operating in states of stable and unstable equilibrium, or in the borders between these states, that is far-from-equilibrium, in chaos or bounded instability.*
- *All organisations are paradoxes. They are powerfully pulled towards stability by the forces of integration, maintenance controls, human desires for security and certainty, and adaptation to the environment on the one hand. They are also powerfully pulled to the opposite extreme of unstable equilibrium by the forces of division and decentralisation, human desires for excitement and innovation, and isolation from the environment.*
- *If the organisation gives in to the pull to stability it fails because it becomes ossified and cannot change easily. If it gives in to the pull to instability it disintegrates. Success lies in sustaining an organisation in the borders between stability and instability. This is a state of chaos, a difficult-to-maintain dissipative structure.*
- *The dynamics of the successful organisation are therefore those of irregular cycles and discontinuous trends, falling within qualitative patterns, fuzzy but recognisable categories taking the form of archetypes and templates.*
- *Because of its own internal dynamic, a successful organisation faces completely unknowable specific futures.*
- *Agents within the system cannot be in control of its long-term future, nor can they install specific frameworks to make it successful, nor can they apply step-by-step analytical reasoning or planning or ideological controls to long-term development. Agents within the system can only do these things in relation to the short term.*
- *Long-term development is a spontaneously self-organising process from which new strategic directions may emerge. Spontaneous self-organisation is political interaction and learning in groups. Managers have to use reasoning by analogy.*
- *In this way managers create and discover their environments and the long-term futures of their organisations.*

7.8 Summary

This chapter has been concerned with the basic forces driving organisations over time – the dynamics of organising. The reason for this concern is that what managers implicitly believe about these matters will determine how they make sense of what is going on and therefore what they do.

The dynamics of organising can most usefully be understood by looking at the properties of feedback systems. Feedback in an organisational system can be negative or positive, or it can flip from one to the other to create complex patterns of behaviour. An organisation is a system that operates in some conditions in a manner that is well explained by the idea of stable equilibrium. Here it utilises negative feedback to limit its behaviour to predetermined patterns. It is also capable of operating in an explosively unstable manner where vicious and virtuous circles are generated by positive feedback. Where they are used exclusively, both of these modes of equilibrium behaviour lead ultimately to failure.

Successful organisations operate in states of bounded instability, using positive and negative feedback to create complex new patterns of behaviour – innovations and new strategic directions. Because they operate in this state they face reasonably predictable short-term futures but totally unknowable long-term ones. This requires us to review carefully what we mean by decision-making and control, and how we practise both, a task to be pursued in the next two chapters.

This chapter is a pivotal one in that it is concerned with scientific explanations of how and why nonlinear feedback loops, of which human organisations are composed, operate when they are creative and innovative. The conclusion we arrive at is that organisations must operate in states of chaos if they are to transform themselves and that the process of transformation is a spontaneously self-organising one. These properties lead us to see that the conventional wisdom on strategic management is a limited special case applicable only to the short-term control of an organisation or to the strategic development of organisations required simply to repeat their past. In all other cases the conventional wisdom cannot apply and thinking in those terms is a harmful fantasy escape from reality. Instead we need to think of an organisation as a learning community out of which new strategic directions may emerge.

Further reading

For those who wish to understand more fully how the concept of feedback systems is used in the social sciences, Richardson (1991) is an excellent source. Senge (1990) provides a very useful summary of the dynamic systems approach and the learning modes required to cope with it. On chaos there is the classic account of how chaos was discovered and what it means by Gleick (1988). A more mathematical but accessible treatment is Stewart (1989). On self-organisation it is useful to read Prigogine (1984) or Davies (1987). How chaos and self-organisation may apply to organisations can be explored further in Nonaka (1988) and Stacey (1991).

8

What unpredictability and emergent strategy mean for managers

Open-ended change and political decision-making

8.1 Introduction

It is the aim of this chapter to show how the feedback structure, and therefore the dynamics, of a successful organisation determine what decision-making processes it is possible for managers in that organisation to employ. By the dynamics, you will recall, we mean the fundamental nature of the patterns of change over time that a system's behaviour displays. The first step in this chapter will therefore be to translate the dynamics discussed in Chapter 7 into the types of change that an organisation faces. Then we will consider how people react to the different kinds of change that we will have identified. The nature of change and the human reactions it provokes will determine what kinds of decision-making processes it is possible to employ. We will therefore be looking at different modes of decision-making in relation to different change situations.

   Throughout the previous chapters we have been concerned with what the concept of equilibrium means for our understanding of organisational dynamics. In the next two sections we will draw together the implications of equilibrium and non-equilibrium dynamics for the nature of change: we will explore a theory of change.

8.2 Change situations confronting equilibrium systems

When a particular system is in equilibrium within an environmental suprasystem that is also in equilibrium, then the dynamics are simple: they are perfectly regular paths over time, straight lines or cycles, that are always repeated exactly. I will call such a situation of equilibrium and the regular patterns of change flowing from it, a closed change situation (see *Key Concept 8.1*).

■ **Key concept 8.1**
CLOSED CHANGE

Closed change describes a situation where the future behaviour of a system is perfectly predictable. Once the laws governing its behaviour have been identified, and once the determinants of its behaviour at any moment of time have been fed into the laws, its behaviour is known. Not only is there 'in principle' predictability, it is also possible to forecast with precision. It is helpful and legitimate to think in terms of clear-cut linear connections between a cause and an effect.

For example, for all practical purposes, the earth is an equilibrium system within an equilibrium suprasystem called the solar system. The earth follows deterministic laws that produce determined outcomes which we can forecast with great precision. There is no distinction between the long and the short term (at least in time spans that mean anything to most of us) – time is not important because the system always does the same thing.

Equilibrium systems do not generate change internally. They repeat their past until some external change requires them to adapt. Such systems then are not internally innovative.

Near to equilibrium

The next possibility to consider is that a particular system may be near to equilibrium in an environmental suprasystem that is also near to equilibrium. This will be the case when some disturbance has jolted the systems away from equilibrium so that they are in states of disequilibrium. Disequilibrium means that the systems are near to equilibrium; they are being powerfully pulled to some different state of equilibrium by the laws governing their behaviour. Non-equilibrium or far-from-equilibrium states differ from disequilibrium ones in that systems in the former state are not being pulled to equilibrium, but are being sustained away from equilibrium.

The usual analysis of market behaviour is an example of systems near to equilibrium. The market for houses may be near to equilibrium in the sense that it is responding to a sudden surge in the population of home buyers that has just materialised. Here the environmental suprasystem has experienced a change, a population increase, that has moved the housing market away from equilibrium. However, that market is now responding by building more houses and is moving back toward equilibrium where supply and demand are balanced. The disturbance in the environment has affected the housing market, but the system and its suprasystem are still following deterministic laws that produce determined outcomes; they are shifting from one equilibrium to another.

When we use the word disequilibrium, we are talking about a temporary disturbance to equilibrium only, one in which time is of some importance because adjustment takes time. However, over time there are still the clear-cut links between specific causes and specific effects: a disturbance in the environment causes a system to be dislodged from equilibrium, but the laws of its behaviour are returning it to that state. There is still 'in principle' perfect predictability. It is now much more difficult to forecast, however, because you have to be able to say what disturbances will occur in the future and when they will occur, if you are to forecast. Because agents in the system cannot forecast accurately and therefore control precisely, the system's behaviour over time displays irregularity. The irregularity is due to the disturbances coming from the environment, to the failure to forecast them, and to the imperfections in the system's ability to adjust. Irregularity here is basically due to ignorance of changes occurring in the environment, or the incompetence of the system in adjusting, or both.

I will call such a state of approach to equilibrium and the disturbance to basically regular patterns that it produces, a contained change situation.

■ Key concept 8.2
CONTAINED CHANGE

Contained change describes a situation where the state of a system is such that it means we can use the laws of probability to make forecasts of the system's behaviour. This is because when a system is close to equilibrium it makes large numbers of repeated moves back to equilibrium and the laws of probability apply only to situations where there are large numbers of repetitive events. Over time, however, the ability to forecast the behaviour of the system we are interested in diminishes, primarily because of the difficulty of forecasting the environment.

Note how we explain the source of uncertainty and the consequent irregularity in the time paths of behaviour, when we think in terms of systems being near to equilibrium. We seek to decompose the observed erratic patterns of performance into underlying patterns of uniformity – trends or cycles of one kind or another – on the one hand, and into the remaining irregular components on the other. The uniform part is then held to be generated by the underlying laws governing the behaviour of that system. That is, we look for the causes of the trends and cycles that we have extracted from the observed data. Since we usually cannot specify the underlying laws of cause and effect in an exact manner, we cannot explain the trends and cycles exactly; reality will deviate from our explanations and we call this deviation 'noise' or 'experimental error'. But if the causal model is good enough, this noise will be relatively unimportant and we can ignore it. The minor part of any irregularity we observe is therefore assumed to be noise. Now consider the major part of the irregularity we observe.

A system operates in an environment that may be changing. Much of this change is explainable by models of environmental behaviour and, to the extent this is so, we can determine the environmental impact on the behaviour of the system we are concerned with; we feed predicted environmental changes into our causal model and so generate predictions of the system's behaviour. The system can then take environmental change into account in its plans and so preserve behaviour close to regularity. If we cannot explain and predict the environmental changes, then we think of them as random shocks that impact on the system, moving it from the nearly regular path it would otherwise follow. The major part of the erratic, irregular behaviour we observe is then due to those random shocks coming from the environment.

It follows therefore that when systems are near to equilibrium we can explain the dynamics in two parts: the underlying laws governing the system generate regularity (disturbed in a minor way by noise) and random shocks from outside the system account for any significant deviations from this regularity. Uncertainty is then primarily the result of unpredictable random shocks hitting an organisation from outside it in its environment. A high level of uncertainty would then be due to our inability to explain and forecast all the changes in government policy, consumer fashions, technologies and so on. We see unpredictability as a consequence of our being ignorant of the full range of causes and effects, as well as the way in which they are related. Because of this uncertainty arising in the environment, the performance of an organisation or economy will display erratic movements around an otherwise regular path. Success then flows from adhering to the underlying laws, from creating a system that operates in an orderly and harmonious manner. To the extent that an organisation is affected by chance, that is due to random shocks coming from the environment and it must adapt to these as rapidly as possible.

Such an explanation leads to the conclusion that we should deal with uncertainty by overcoming our ignorance as much as possible by gathering more information and doing more research. The recognition of uncertainty in these terms strengthens the need for technically rational decision-making and leads to the conclusion that the qualitatively similar patterns we observe can be identified in more specific terms. We do not see these general similar patterns in more precise terms because we do not know enough. And this ignorance relates to what is happening in the environment, so our information gathering, research and analysis problems are mainly those to do with the environment. This kind of approach also leads us to think of irregularity as the consequence of incompetence: we have not designed the negative feedback loops regulating the organisation competently enough and that is why the system is behaving irregularly.

Furthermore, when we think of systems in this way, it is a nonsense to talk about systems being creative or behaviour being due to the nature of the system. Systems following deterministic laws that produce determined outcomes are in effect doing as they are told. Human systems of this kind perform according to the intentions of the people, or some of the people that constitute them. Any order that we observe is put there by the designing mind.

This is the explanation of uncertainty that underlies today's dominant models of managing and organising. As we will see, we reach very different conclusions about the nature of uncertainty and how it is possible to cope with it if we see the world of organisations from a far-from-equilibrium perspective.

8.3 Change situations confronting far-from-equilibrium systems

What we discovered in the last chapter is that there is a third state open to nonlinear feedback systems, one additional to stability and instability, that we now need to take into account. Our organisation could be far-from-equilibrium, operating within an environmental suprasystem that is also far-from-equilibrium.

Here the links between cause and effect are lost in the complexity of interactions within and between systems. The patterns of behaviour emerge from the detail of interaction within and between systems and those emergent patterns are essentially irregular. They are irregular not simply because of environmental change, but because of the very structure of the system itself. We cannot distinguish between underlying regular behaviour and irregular noise and random shocks. We have to deal with behaviour that is an inseparable mixture of regularity and irregularity; the feedback laws governing the system generate both inseparably.

In effect, systems in this state have a life of their own; a system itself can be creative and behaviour can be due to the nature of the system (see *Key Concept 7.1* in Chapter 7). All of these properties makes the specific long-term future of the system unpredictable, but that long-term future will display recognisable qualitative patterns, and in the short term specific behaviour will be predictable because of the momentum of the system. Chaos also means that the system will be irregular not because of ignorance or incompetence but because of its very structure. The problem of irregularity and unpredictability cannot then be overcome by gathering more information or doing more research. The problem is inherent and cannot be removed in any way. We will need to think far more fundamentally about how we actually deal with chaotic systems.

The change situation of far-from-equilibrium systems is therefore a complex one. It is a combination of approximations to the closed and contained change situations already discussed and another situation which I will call open-ended change (Stacey, 1990, 1991).

■ **Key concept 8.3**
OPEN-ENDED CHANGE

It is not possible to forecast the long term at all in open-ended change situations because it is not possible to predict; and it is not possible to predict long-term consequences because the connections between cause and effect are lost in the detail of the interactions that occur over time. Open-ended change situations are ones of unique uncertainty and ambiguity where the outcomes of actions are unknowable.

When a system is far from equilibrium, time is of the essence in that a system's current state is a record of everything that has happened to it, everything that the actors or components within it have done in the past. Its history is important and that history will continue to affect what happens to it in the future. That is why board and top executive meetings are so often dominated by accounts of what has happened. Managers concern themselves with the history of their organisation, with explaining how they have come to the current situation they find themselves in, because they cannot effectively decide what to do next until they understand what has happened.

We turn now to an explanation of the more complex change situations that faces far-from-equilibrium systems (Stacey, 1991).

Closed change

When we look back at the history of an organisation operating in conditions of bounded instability far from equilibrium, there are some sequences of events that we can clearly recount in a manner commanding widespread agreement of the managers involved. We are able to say what happened, why it happened, and what the consequences were. We are also able to explain in a widely accepted way how such a sequence of events and actions will continue to affect the future course of the business. This is close to what I have called a closed change situation.

The principal features of closed change are that the consequences of events are clearly understandable in their past form and accurately predictable in their future form. These principal features apply because the events and actions generating the consequences have already occurred and over short periods of time it is a reasonable approximation to think of causality as clear cut – there will not be time for small changes to escalate dramatically.

Such closed change would normally apply to the continuing operation of the existing business. For example, consider a business that supplies pop records and tapes to the teenage market. Managers in that business are able to say with some precision how the number of customers in that market has changed over the past and furthermore how it will change for the next fifteen years or so. Those customers already exist. The managers can establish fairly clear-cut relationships between the number of customers and the number of records and tapes they have bought and will buy.

Closed change is depicted in *Figure 8.1* as the darkly shaded area under curve A. This curve shows how the sequence of actions and events began at some point in the past, time t_{-1} on the horizontal axis, and then how the consequences developed to the present t_0, and will proceed into the future.

Contained change

Other sequences of events and actions flowing from the past are less clear-cut. Here we find that we are able to say only what probably happened, why it probably happened, and what its probable consequences were. The impact of such a sequence of events upon the future course of the business has similarly to be qualified by probability statements.

For example, the supplier of records and tapes will find it harder to explain why

Figure 8.1   The consequences of past change
Source: R. Stacey (1992), *Managing Chaos*, London: Kogan Page

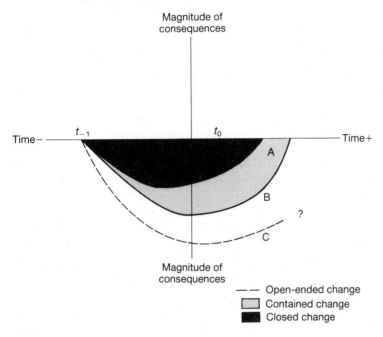

particular kinds of records and tapes sold better than others. That supplier will find it somewhat difficult to forecast what kinds of tapes and records will sell better in the future; but market research, life style studies and statistical projections will enable reasonably helpful forecasts for at least the short term.

It is reasonable to think of causality here as approximate or statistical, that is taking the form of probability statements. This approximates to what I have called contained change. It is represented in *Figure 8.1* as the lightly shaded area under curve B.

Open-ended change

There are yet other sequences of events and actions arising from the past and continuing to impact on the future where explanations do not command anything like widespread acceptance by those involved.

The company supplying records and tapes may have decided in the past to diversify into video film distribution, by acquiring another company already in that business. That acquisition may then become unprofitable and the managers involved could well subscribe to conflicting explanations of why this is so. Some may claim that the market for video films is too competitive. Others that the diversification was a wrong move because it meant operating in a different market with which they were not familiar. Others may say that it is due to a temporary decline in demand and that the market will pick up in the future. Yet others may ascribe it to poor management of the acquisition, or to a failure to integrate it properly into the business, or to a clash of cultures between the two businesses. What that team of managers does next to deal with low profitability obviously depends upon the explanation of past failure they subscribe to.

This kind of change situation is clearly what I have already called open-ended. Here we do not know with any clarity what caused the change, why the change occurred, or what its consequences were and will be. It is depicted in *Figure 8.1* as the blank area under the dotted curve C. That curve ends with a question mark because managers do not know what the consequences of the particular sequence of events and actions will be in the future.

The present and the future

As they stand in the here and now, at time t_0 in *Figure 8.1*, managers face three different kinds of change situation arising from sequences of events and actions that have already occurred.

There are, however, also sequences of events and actions that are starting up now, in the present. Some of these will approximate to closed change – an existing customer places a much larger order for an existing product line. Some sequences of events and actions will approximate to contained change – a new customer places orders for a modified range of products. And others will be open-ended change – setting up a new activity in Poland.

Yet other sequences of events and actions will be initiated at future points. Each of these sequences will also have closed, contained and open-ended components. *Figure 8.1* is completed in *Figure 8.2* by the addition of curves representing these present and future consequences. (The vertical axis measures the magnitude of the consequences without distinguishing between negative and positive. The diagram is drawn this

Figure 8.2   Change situations
Source: R. Stacey (1992), *Managing Chaos*, London: Kogan Page

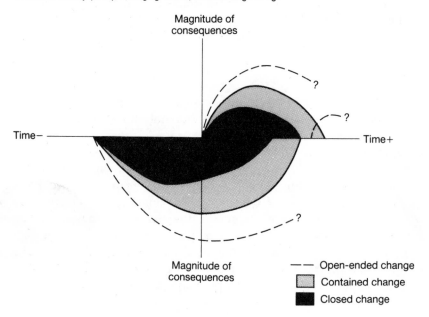

way simply for visual clarity.) The point the diagram makes is this. As they stand in the here and now, managers in any organisation face a spectrum of change situations in every time frame, from the past through the present to the future. At each point, that spectrum stretches from predictable closed change, through statistically predictable contained change, into unknowable open-ended change. The past and the short-term future are dominated by closed and contained change, but the long-term future is predominantly open-ended. The pattern of change situations alters as we look through time.

This pattern of change situations is a consequence of the dynamics of an organisational system. When the dynamics are chaotic, small changes escalate and self-reinforcing circles develop, making it totally impossible to predict the long-term future consequences of sequences of events and actions. In this sense the long-term future of the system is inherently unknowable. However, because it takes time for escalation to occur, it is possible to forecast the short-term future of the system.

Closed and contained change relate to developments that have short-term consequences. They are repetitions of what has happened before. They are large numbers of the same kind of event and it is therefore practically useful to apply probability concepts and statistical techniques to specify their consequences. Open-ended change is unique and has never happened in that specific form before. Measures of probability therefore have no practical use in decision-making. Simulating the future of the business, or building scenarios of its possible futures, will not provide forecasts of the likely range of outcomes. Simulation may be useful but only as a learning or practice exercise to get a feel for the kinds of future patterns that may develop.

The important point about these change situations is that managers cannot choose to focus on one kind of change or another. If they wish their organisation to survive, they will have simultaneously to deal with all forms of change. However, open-ended change is qualitatively different from closed and contained change, and because of that it must be dealt with in a completely different way. To see why this must be so, consider how managers' behaviour alters as they switch from dealing with issues arising in closed change situations to those arising in open-ended situations.

8.4   Behaviour and change situations

Closed/contained change situations

Over short time periods, the development of a chaotic system will usually approximate to that of a system near to or at equilibrium. It is then a useful device to think of the short-term development of the system as if it were an equilibrium system. Over the short term then we can think in terms of reasonably clear-cut links between causes and effects, of issues and actions whose consequences can be forecast to a reasonably useful degree of accuracy, of closed or contained change.

This means that the problems and opportunities facing managers are reasonably clear. Any difficulties lie in finding the answers, not in identifying the questions to ask in the first place. This is ordinary management that solves puzzles within an accepted paradigm that all share without question – akin to Kuhn's notion of normal science (see Chapter 3). The situation is not characterised by ambiguity and competent managers do not therefore behave in an equivocal manner. If they conflict, there is a substantial possibility of settling the conflict by rational argument, or through exerting hierarchical authority, or bargains of one sort or another. People by and large know what they are doing in closed and contained situations and they will often have decided what to do before the change occurs. The behaviour of groups of people and the models they use in common to design their actions are all understandable and reasonably predictable in these situations.

Open-ended change situations

However, when managers confront open-ended change the situation is completely different in every respect. They are faced with actions and events past, present and future that have unknowable long-term consequences. Links between cause and effect are lost in the detail of those events because small changes escalate and self-reinforcing circles develop. The key difficulty then, is that of identifying what the problems and opportunities are. The prime difficulty is not that of finding answers, but identifying *what questions to ask*. The situation is ambiguous and the responses of managers are equivocal. In these uniquely new situations, old shared mental models on how to design actions do not work and new mental models have to be developed and shared before anything can happen. We are talking about frame-breaking, extraordinary management, akin to Kuhn's notion of extraordinary science.

In open-ended change and the extraordinary management required to cope with it, conflict around how to interpret what is going on and how to design actions to deal with it becomes commonplace and inevitable. Such conflict is actually a vital part of developing the new mental models required to cope with the new situation. Predetermined rules and authority structures become useless as effective means of settling the conflicts, because they presuppose that someone has made a decision and knows what to do. This must be so, because it is these very rules and authority structures that are under question.

The unpredictability of specific events within fuzzy categories, which is the hallmark of open-ended change, leads to ambiguity and confusion. Although individual human minds are well equipped to deal with such situations, there are difficulties because new mental models need to be developed through analogous reasoning. That difficulty is magnified many times when a reasonably common mental model has to be shared by a number of people in the management team before they can take joint action. The manner in which they interact with each other then becomes a vital part of the decision-making process they employ. We cannot understand what they decide to do without understanding the impact of their personalities and the group dynamic on their decision-making processes. In open-ended change situations, people typically feel insecure and become anxious and the dynamic of their interaction becomes much more complex and can quite often be bizarre. There is a strong tendency to apply inappropriate mental models of the learning process.

The key point is this. When a system is chaotic, the long-term consequences of actions past, present and future are open-ended, where that means that they are unknowable, not simply currently unknown. This distinction between the unknown and the unknowable is an important one because if the future is simply unknown then there is the possibility that we will be able to identify it, if we gather enough information, conduct enough research, and perform enough analysis. If, however, the future is unknowable, then these things are a waste of time and we need to focus on different ways of doing things. *Illustration 8.1* indicates what these different change situations mean in practice.

■ Illustration 8.1
MÖVENPICK UNTERNEHMUNGEN

Mövenpick was set up by Ueli Präger in 1948 in Zurich, Switzerland. By 1977 it consisted of 56 restaurants, 7 hotels and 11 production and trading units dealing in food. In the mid-1970s Mövenpick set up an operation in Egypt. This is how Ueli Präger describes that decision:

> There are certain strategic decisions which are based on thorough analysis and planning. But there are also events which happen to you. Our international expansion falls into the latter category. . . . Our project in Egypt happened in this way. There is a publishing house in Zurich, they print souvenir books with photos of Egyptian treasures. They approached us with the proposal that it might be a good idea if the tourists in Egypt, tired from their visits to the museums, could rest in a Mövenpick restaurant. We were willing to entertain the idea, the Egyptians sent some plane tickets, and we went over to discuss the possibility of a restaurant in a museum. While we were there, I made a courtesy call to the Egyptian organization of tourism. The official in charge and I liked each other instantaneously, the way it sometimes happens when you meet somebody new. After a few minutes he posed the question: 'Do you want to build a hotel near the Pyramids?' I was not prepared for this question, but it was the beginning of a very successful cooperation.
>
> I had never planned to have a hotel near the Pyramids, but that's the way it goes, you open yourself gradually to such ideas and then comes the opportunity. Japan was similar. I had never had a long-range plan to expand in Japan; but then one day some Japanese businessman walked into our office with the idea of opening a chain of restaurants in Japan.

Source: Wiechmann & Gillespie, 1978

We now consider what these different change situations mean for the mode of decision-making it is possible for managers to apply to their business. We will see that managers have no option but to change the way they make decisions as the level of uncertainty, ambiguity and anxiety is tuned up.

8.5 The relationship between change situations and decision-making modes

Thompson and Tuden (1959) relate the mode of decision-making to the type and level of uncertainty in the following way. They identify different types of uncertainty in terms of:

- the lack of clarity in causal relationships;
- the lack of agreement over objectives.

Where there is very little clarity over causal relationships, and where there is little agreement on objectives, we have the change situation I have called open-ended. The opposite gives us closed change and the other possibilities fit what I have called contained change. In *Figure 8.3*, Thompson and Tuden show how managers shift from one mode of making decisions to others as they move from handling issues in closed change situations to handling issues in open-ended situations.

Where causal connections are clear and objectives shared, the conditions exist for managers to take decisions in a technically rational way. As they move away from these conditions it becomes impossible to apply technical rationality and so they have to use some other approach.

Thus, when causal connections are clear but managers conflict then the decision has to be made in a political manner – those with the greatest power will prevail. The decision-making process here will be one in which managers build coalitions (Cyert & March, 1963; Child, 1972 & 1984; Pfeffer, 1981) as we discussed in Chapters 2 and 5.

When managers are agreed on what they should be trying to achieve but the causal connections make it unclear how to do so, then they will have to use judgmental, or intuitive, modes of making a decision. They will have to reason by analogy; they will have to think laterally and use trial-and-error decision-making processes. We also discussed this approach in Chapter 2.

The most difficult situation is where causality is unclear and objectives conflict – the truly open-ended situation. Here managers will have to decide in a way that combines intuitive individual judgements with political interactions in a group.

Figure 8.3 Models of decision-making: types of uncertainty
Source: R. Turton (1991), *Behaviour in a Business Context*, London: Chapman & Hall

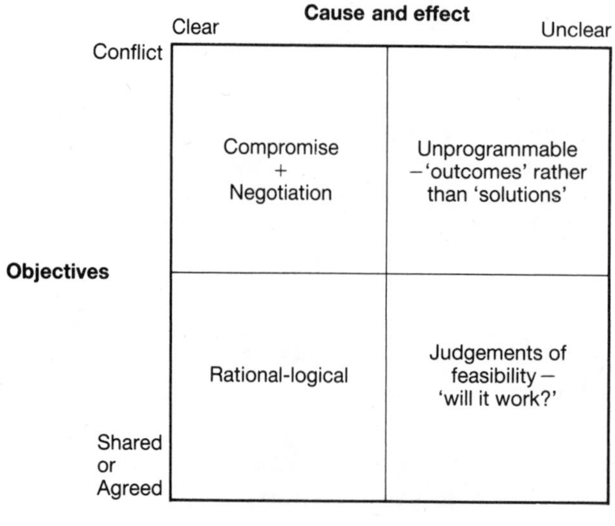

Figure 8.4 Dimensions of the environment
Source: R. Turton (1991), *Behaviour in a Business Context*, London: Chapman & Hall

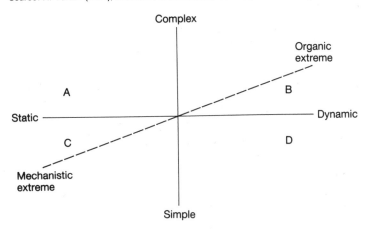

Duncan's approach

Other writers have also highlighted the connection between levels of uncertainty and modes of making decisions. Duncan (1972) for example relates modes of decision-making to degrees of environmental complexity and stability.

He distinguishes environments that are static from those that are dynamic, where dynamic means that the frequency, rate and extent of change are all high. He also categorises environments into those that are simple and those that are complex. In simple environments there are only a small number of variables that may change, while in complex environments there are many interconnected variables that may change. These two measures create four archetypal environments. The simplest archetype is the static and simple environment where the appropriate organisational system is the mechanistic one with its technically rational modes of decision-making. In the most demanding of these environmental archetypes, the complex dynamic one, it is only organic organisational systems that will survive, those with flexible, political, intuitive modes of making decisions. In between, some pragmatic combination of the mechanistic and the organic is required.

Perrow's model

Then, Perrow (1972) provides a model of the technology appropriate to different conditions, which makes much the same point. This is shown in *Figure 8.5*. The vertical axis depicts a spectrum of problem-solving procedures. At one end of the spectrum we have problem-solving procedures available that are analysable: they can be broken down into prearranged steps or rules of a logical kind. At the other end the only procedures available in a particular situation are unanalysable or unprogrammable. This means that the problem is such that we have to use some unique method of solving it, unique to that particular problem. Then on the horizontal axis we have the problem-solving situation classified in terms of the number of exceptions. Few exceptions means that there is little variability in the situation in which decisions have to be made. Actions and responses required are

Figure 8.5 The Perrow model of technology

Source: R. Turton (1991), *Behaviour in a Business Context*, London: Chapman & Hall

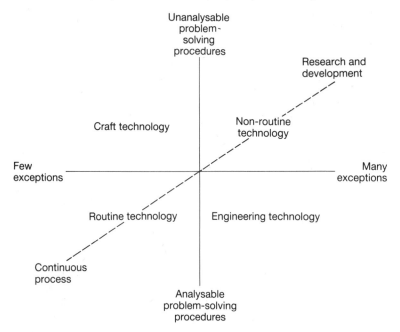

familiar and repetitive. At the other end of the spectrum there are many exceptions calling for different, unique responses.

In situations where there are few exceptions and analysable problem-solving techniques are available, then routine technology is appropriate. The decision-making mode here is clearly the technically rational one. As the situation and the problem-solving techniques become more complex the required technology has a higher skill content – engineering and craft skills are required. The corresponding decision-making mode calls for more judgement, but can still be reduced to step-by-step rules and procedures even though they may become very complex. But when the situation becomes complex and the techniques for solving problems become non-routine and unique, then the required technology is that of research and development. Here the decision-making mode involves unique methods of identifying new problems and finding unique solutions. Technically rational modes of decision-making become inadequate.

What emerges from all these analyses of decision situation and appropriate decision-making mode is this. Making a decision in a technically rational manner is only a possibility in the most restrictive of conditions. It will not be possible in conditions of disagreement, ambiguity and uncertainty. That is to say, it will not be possible when the change being faced is open-ended. But strategic issues are essentially those arising in open-ended change. The decision-making mode required in new strategic situations cannot therefore be that of technical rationality. Yet this is exactly what the dominant received wisdom focuses on: most strategic management prescriptions tend to be biased towards technical rationality, despite the availability of compelling reasons to the contrary for at least 30 years.

It is quite clear, then, that in conditions far from certainty managers have no choice but to apply significantly different decision-making modes to those required in conditions close to certainty (see *Illustration 8.1*). In the next two sections we will examine in more detail what these different modes of decision-making are.

8.6 Models of decision-making in conditions close to certainty

There are three very well known models of decision-making that can quite clearly be employed only in conditions close to certainty, that is in closed or contained change situations. These are technical rationality; bounded rationality, bureaucracies and dominant coalitions; and trial-and-error or logical incrementalism. This section examines each of these modes.

Technical rationality

When managers know what their objectives are and agree upon them in a closed change situation, then the effective mode of making a decision is that of technical rationality. Managers then discover how their environment and the capability of their organisation is changing by gathering the facts through a continuing process of scanning, research and monitoring. They analyse the facts using the step-by-step rules of logical reasoning to generate all the options open to achieve their objectives. They calculate the effects of carrying out each option on their objectives, choose that option which maximises their objectives, and then act to implement that option. What managers are doing or should be doing is explained in terms of pure rationality, the foundation of scientific management originating in the writings of Frederick Taylor back in the 1940s (Taylor, 1947).

We have seen that this is possible only when the dynamics are stable. Even then, however, the limits on human cognition make it impossible for the following reasons.

Given clear agreed objectives in relation to clear-cut problems, pure rationality requires the decision-maker to perceive the relevant objective facts in a direct manner. Perceiving directly means that we are not seeing the facts through some kind of lens or other means that could open up the possibility of distortion. Having perceived the facts directly, the purely rational person would then have to store them in an exact form so that they could be processed later on without distortion. This would mean storing facts in categories that are precisely defined – we put a fact into a category, if and only if it satisfies all the characteristics of that category. Having memorised the facts in this fashion and having memorised in much the same way the processing techniques required to manipulate them, the rational person would then process the facts in a step-by-step fashion according to the rules of logic and select the action option that maximises the objective. The choice is predetermined by the facts and the problem is simply one of calculation.

However, we saw in Chapter 6 in the section on the models of Argyris and Schon that humans do not perceive in this manner and they cannot therefore decide using this mode. As we saw, humans use selective models of reality, models they socially construct among themselves and share with each other. The models are constructed around categories of phenomenon that have fuzzy, irregular patterns in common. We do all this to overcome limited brain processing capacity.

Bounded rationality, bureaucracy and dominant coalitions

Recognising the restrictive circumstance in which pure rationality could be applied, Herbert Simon developed the concept of bounded rationality (Simon, 1960). He argued that managers could be rational only within boundaries imposed by resource availability, experience and knowledge of the range of options available for action. The collection, analysis and exchange of information uses resources, imposes costs, and is time consuming. It will therefore never be possible, or even sensible, to gather all the information and examine all the options.

Limited economic resources and limited individual brain processing capacity together impose constraints on communication and flows of information through an organisation. All of this makes it impossible for managers to use the exhaustive process of pure rationality. Instead of screening all the facts and generating all the action options before making a choice, managers in common with all humans take short cuts. They conduct trial-and-error search procedures to identify the most important bits of information in particular circumstances; they identify a limited range of the most important options revealed by the search; and then they act knowing only some of the potential outcomes of their actions. This means that they cannot take the action which maximises their objective. Instead they satisfice: they achieve the first satisfactory outcome they can in the circumstances. What they do then depends upon the sequence in which they discover changes, make choices, and take actions.

Limited resources and limited brain processing capacity are also compensated for by the use of bureaucratic procedures (March & Simon, 1958; Cyert & March, 1963; Simon, 1960). As managers act together they develop rules of action and standard operating procedures in order to cut down on the need to make decisions afresh each time. Precedents are established and subsequent decisions are taken without having to repeat the search process anew. Decisions and actions come to be outputs of standard patterns of behaviour. For example, next year's budget is often determined largely by uprating this year's spend. New alternatives tend to be sought only when a problem is detected, that is some discrepancy between what is expected and what happens. Once such a discrepancy is detected, a trial-and-error search for a new solution is undertaken. Since all possible outcomes are not known, the tendency will be to make incremental decisions, that is decisions with consequences as small and containable as possible. By relying on bureaucratic rules, and incremental decision-making, managers are able to reduce the levels of uncertainty they have to face. What the organisation learns will be embodied in its rules and procedures and these are used not to optimise outcomes, but to reduce uncertainty.

The lack of realism of the pure rationality model was recognised in other ways as well (Cyert & March, 1963). Although decisions and actions may flow from bureaucratic rules and precedent for most of the time, there are numerous occasions on which objectives and interests conflict. Which objectives are pursued will then depend on what the most powerful coalition of managers want. Organisational intention becomes the intention of the dominant coalition.

The above paragraphs indicate how and why bounded-rationality/bureaucratic explanations of how managers discover, choose and act differ from technical rationality. But there are also similarities. Bounded rationality also does not see problem-framing as the major difficulty. It is still about solving problems, even though they may not be as clearly framed. The processes described are still step-by-step or algorithmic procedures, differing from those of pure rationality only in that they are heuristic, that is involving rules of thumb to proceed by trial and error. These explanations are also within the tradition of organisational intention; the organisation is seen as searching for satisfactory attainment of known objectives according to known criteria for success and failure. The organisation is seen as succeeding when it adapts to a given environment. It learns from its experience and embodies this in its rules, unlike the purely rational organisation that learns in advance of experience through analysis, but the learning is still of the simple single-loop kind.

What these explanations do is recognise economic constraints and take a more complicated view of human cognition; they recognise the limitations of human brain processing capacity. They do not see the process of discovery or choice as problematic in any sense other than that of limited processing capacity. And these explanations make much the same assumptions about the nature of the environment and the relationship of the organisation to that environment: there are facts and there are clear-cut connections between cause and effect. Both bounded and pure rationality are, in the end, based on the same assumptions about the dynamics of the systems to which they are to be applied – stable equilibrium. They are therefore appropriate in conditions close to certainty and indeed these are the modes we can observe managers using when they handle closed and contained change in the day-to-day management of their business.

Trial and error – logical incrementalism

Quinn's research into the decision-making process of a number of companies revealed that most strategic decisions are made outside the formal planning system. He found that managers purposely blend behavioural, political and formal analytical processes together to improve the quality of decisions and implementation. Effective managers accept the high level of uncertainty and ambiguity they have to face and do not plan everything. They preserve the flexibility of the organisation to deal with the unforeseen as it happens. The key points that Quinn made about the strategic decision-making mode are as follows:

1 Effective managers do not manage strategically in a piecemeal manner. They have a clear view on what they are trying to achieve, where they are trying to take the business. The destination is thus intended.
2 But the route to that destination, the strategy itself, is not intended from the start in any comprehensive way. Effective managers know that the environment they have to operate in is uncertain and ambiguous. They therefore sustain flexibility by holding the method of reaching the goal open.
3 The strategy itself then emerges from the interaction between different groupings

of people in the organisation, different groupings with different amounts of power, different requirements for and access to information, different time spans and parochial interest. These different pressures are orchestrated by senior managers. The top is always reassessing, integrating and organising.

4 The strategy emerges or evolves in small incremental, opportunistic steps. But such evolution is not piecemeal or haphazard because of the agreed purpose and the role of top management in reassessing what is happening. It is this that provides the logic in the incremental action.

5 The result is an organisation that is feeling its way to a known goal, opportunistically learning as it goes.

In Quinn's model of the strategy process, the organisation is driven by central intention with respect to the goal, but there is no prior central intention as to how that goal is to be achieved; the route to the goal is discovered through a logical process of taking one small step at a time. In logical incrementalism, overall strategy emerges from step-by-step trial-and-error actions occurring in a number of different places in the organisation; for example, some may be making an acquisition while others are restructuring the reporting structure. These separate initiatives are pushed by champions, each attacking a class of strategic issue. The top executives manage the process, orchestrating it and sustaining some logic in it. It is this that makes it a purposeful, proactive technique. Urgent, interim, piecemeal decisions shape the organisation's future, but they do so in an orderly logical way. No-one fully understands all the implications of what they are all doing together, but they are consciously preparing to move opportunistically (see *Illustration 8.2*).

■ **Illustration 8.2**
EXXON EUROPE

Quinn (1978) illustrates his concept of strategies being developed through a process of logical incrementalism as follows:

> When Exxon began its regional decentralization on a worldwide basis, the Executive Committee placed a senior officer and board member with a very responsive management style in a vaguely defined 'coordinative role' vis-a-vis its powerful and successful European units. Over a period of two years this man sensed problems and experimented with voluntary coordinative possibilities on a pan-European basis. Only later, with greater understanding by both corporate and divisional officers, did Exxon move to a more formal 'line' relationship for what became Exxon Europe. Even then the move had to be coordinated in other areas of the world. All of these changes together led to an entirely new power balance toward regional and non-US concerns and to a more responsive worldwide posture for Exxon.

Source: Quinn, 1978, p. 102

Since in this model it is assumed to be possible to decide in advance where the organisation is going, it too can apply only in conditions of contained change. The degree of order and logic it describes is not possible in truly open-ended situations.

8.7 Models of decision-making in conditions far from certainty

In open-ended change situations, managers are by definition ignorant even of the outcomes that might possibly flow from a decision they make and an action they take. They do not know how their actions may be related in a cause-and-effect sense to the outcomes of those actions. In genuinely new situations it is not possible to assign probabilities to outcomes. In this section we are going to review models of decision-making that do not assume knowledge either of the final destination or outcome aimed for, or of the route to that destination or outcome. These, therefore, are the modes that can be applied in open-ended situations.

The search for error

Collingridge (1980) argues that effective decision-making in this situation is a search for error and a willingness to respond to its discovery. Instead of searching for the right decision as you would when using a technically rational mode close to certainty, you need to choose an option that can most easily be found to be in error, error that can most easily be corrected. In this way fewer options are closed off; you get more opportunities to adjust what you have done when the circumstances change.

For example, if you can forecast future electricity demand reliably, the right solution to increased demand may be to build one large power station now. If, however, the future demand for electricity is highly uncertain it would be better to build a number of small power stations, spread over a few years. That way you will find it easier to check for error in your forecast of future demand and easier to correct for mistakes. You may only have to close a small power station instead of running a large one at quarter capacity.

This kind of approach requires a considerable psychological adjustment. Most of us are used to being judged on whether we made the right choice. If it turns out to be wrong we devote much energy to concealing this fact, or in justifying our original decision. Applying technical rationality in conditions of great uncertainty leads us intentionally to avoid the search for error and to delay its recognition. If we abandon technical rationality in these circumstances and search for error instead, we would have to admit mistakes as soon as possible and avoid trying to justify them. Here we are talking about a mature recognition that being wrong is a valuable learning exercise.

The Mintzberg decision process model

Mintzberg, Theoret & Rainsinghani (1976) analysed twenty-five decision-making processes and formulated a descriptive model as follows. The decision-making situations they analysed were characterised by novelty, complexity and open-endedness. The research showed that a final choice was made in such situations only after lengthy periods that involved many difficult discontinuous and recursive steps.

They divided the decision process into three basic stages:

- identification
- development
- selection.

Within each of the stages a number of routines have been identified. We will now examine each stage and the routines it involves.

The identification stage

It is a feature of open-ended change situations that the issues which have to be attended to, the problems and opportunities requiring a decision, are not at all obvious or clear. The need to make a decision therefore has to be identified or prompted by signals from the environment or from the working of the organisation. The stimulus for a decision may be the voluntary recognition of a problem or an opportunity, or the result of some pressure or mild crisis, or the consequence of a major crisis that forces a decision. Many small stimuli may need to build up to some threshold before a decision need is identified and a decision triggered. In this regard the paradigm of the manager is important (Johnson, 1987). If the stimuli for a decision fall outside the currently shared wisdom on what the business is about and how it should be conducted, then managers will ignore the stimuli. It will probably require a crisis to force a decision. Where managers identify a problem to which there is no clear solution there will be a tendency to ignore it. Problems for which there are matching solutions will tend to be dealt with.

Note how the routine for recognising a problem depends upon the behaviour of individuals, is culturally conditioned, and involves political interaction.

Once managers have recognised a problem, the diagnosis routine is activated. Old information channels are tapped and new ones opened. The diagnosis may be formal or it may be very informal. It may be skipped altogether. What managers are doing here is trying to shape or structure the problems so that they may decide how to deal with them.

The development stage

The development stage takes up most of the time and resources in the decision-making process. It involves search routines and design routines.

The search routine is an attempt to discover a ready-made solution. These routines include simply waiting for an alternative to materialise, searching the memory of the organisation, that is the solutions to problems that have worked before, scanning alternatives, hiring consultants and so on. Search is a step-by-step or incremental process beginning with the easiest search routine.

The design routine consists of the steps taken to design a solution to the problem. Mintzberg et al. found that organisations avoid custom-made routines for making a decision because they are expensive and require many steps. In other words they tend not to consider large numbers of alternatives but to select one promising alternative, one that they have tried before. There is then a natural tendency to avoid innovative approaches to strategic decision-making.

Selection

Selection is often intertwined with the development stage and involves the routines of screening, evaluative choice and authorisation. The screen routine is used to screen out options that are clearly not viable. It is a superficial routine. The evaluation choice routine was not found to be one that involved the use of analytical techniques in the study that Mintzberg et al. conducted. The evaluation criteria were normally based on judgement and intuition. Managers dealt with information overload by using precedent, imitation or tradition. They made judgements on a proposal according to the reliability of the proposer rather than the project, on the track record of the manager.

The final routine is that of authorisation and legitimation of the choices that individuals and groups have made.

The decision-making process identified here is a number of routines that have behavioural, political and learning aspects. The routines are affected by interruptions caused by environmental factors, by scheduling and timing delays as well as speed-ups generated by those involved in the process, by feedback delays as people wait for information and authorisation, and by cycling back to earlier stages in the process.

A simplified version of this model is depicted in *Figure 8.6.*

Dialectical enquiry

Schwenck and Thomas (1983) also address the process of decision-making in open-ended situations. They identify three procedures for formulating problems and selecting outcomes:

- *Brainstorming*. Here a small group of people work together to produce as many ideas as they can on what problems they should be addressing and how they should deal with them. The ideas generated can then be ranked and subjected to further study and consideration.
- *The devil's advocate*. Here one or more persons play the role of trying to tear a proposal apart. They are performing the important function of identifying and questioning the tacit assumptions that are being made.
- *Dialectical enquiry*. This is similar to the devil's advocate approach but involves groups of people. Two opposing groups enter into a debate on a proposed solution to a problem. Again this focuses attention on tacit assumptions being made. From the two conflicting options being debated, a third, a synthesis of the two, may emerge.

These forms of stimulating the creative identification and handling of problems are illustrated in *Figure 8.7.*

Muddling through, organised anarchy, and garbage-can decision-making

Lindblom (1989) also describes the process of strategic decision-making as incremental but to him it is a form of 'muddling through'. His observations are derived from decision-making in state sector organisations, but they have

Figure 8.6 The Mintzberg et al. model of the strategic management process

Source: H. Mintzberg, A. Theoret & Rainsinghani (1976), 'The structure of the unstructured decision making process', *Administrative Science Quarterly*, vol. 21, pp. 246–75

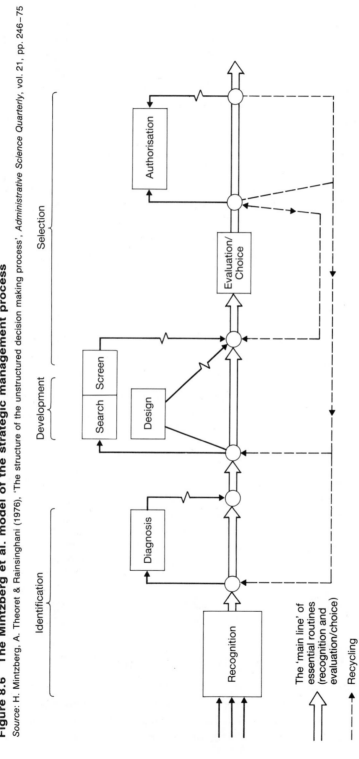

Figure 8.7 Techniques for identifying, formulating and resolving problems
Source: C. Schwenk & H. Thomas (1983), 'Formulating the mess: the role of decision and problem formulation',
Omega: The International Journal of Management Science, vol. 11, no. 3, pp. 239–52

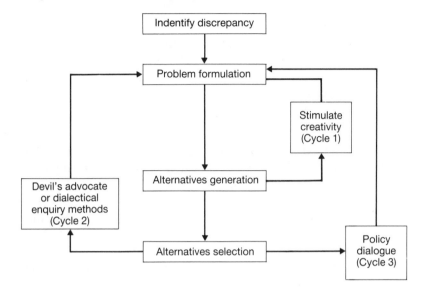

implications for private sector organisations too. Because in complex situations it is not possible to identify all the objectives of different groups of people affected by an issue, policies are chosen directly. Instead of working from a statement of desired ends to the means required to achieve it, managers choose the ends and the means simultaneously. In other words two different managers may choose the same policy or solution for different reasons.

This means that we cannot judge a policy according to how well it achieves a given end. Instead we judge a policy according to whether it is itself desirable or not. A good policy is thus simply one that gets widespread support. It is then carried out in incremental stages, preserving flexibility to change it as conditions change. The policy is pursued in stages of successive limited comparisons. In this approach, dramatically new policies are not considered. New policies have to be close to existing ones and limited comparisons are made. This makes it unnecessary to undertake fundamental enquiries. The procedure also involves ignoring important possible consequences of policies, a necessary evil perhaps if anything is to be done. But serious lasting mistakes can be avoided because the changes are being made in small steps.

Cohen, March & Ohlsen (1972) have carried this kind of analysis of state sector organisations further. They describe many of these organisations as organised anarchies and their decision-making process as garbage-can decision-making.

In their research, they found that universities and some state bodies are characterised by widely distributed power and complex, unclear hierarchical structures. The hierarchical structure is such that just about any issue can be taken to just about any forum, by just about anyone. These institutions are noted for widespread participation in decision-making, for ambiguous and intersecting job definitions, and a lack of shared cultural values across the whole organisation. What is found in the conditions prevailing at universities and some state bodies is the following:

- Individuals and sub-units do not have clear goals.
- No individual has much power and the distribution of power is not stably determined by sanctions, interdependence and contribution. It fluctuates with the context within which decisions are being made and consequently:
- the distribution of power over time is not constant and neither is:
- the distribution of power over issue. And furthermore:
- choices are often avoided, deferred, made by oversight, or never implemented.

Such organisations face open-ended change not only, or even primarily, because their environments are changing but because of the uncertainty of their technology. It is far from certain what good teaching is for example, or what good medical care is. Such organisations therefore have to be collections of relatively free professionals. This leads to a form that the authors call organised anarchy. Here decisions and their outcomes occur largely by chance. The flow of choices over time is erratic and haphazard. There is a continuing flow of problems, opportunities, solutions and choices coming together in a largely haphazard manner. This happens because there is no simple and clear hierarchy and because the distribution of power is close to equality.

Where power is widely dispersed so that there are no powerful actors who can enforce their wills; where power is therefore unstable over time and issue; where there is little sharing of values; where there are heavy workloads on individuals and meetings; where participation in decision-making is open and fluid; where access to choice situations and participation structures are open and unclear; then choice will be determined largely by chance. The choice will depend entirely upon the context in which it is attended to. It will depend upon the level of attention paid to it in the light of all the other issues; upon who was present and participated; upon how they participated and how others interpreted that participation. Looking back it will not be possible to say that the choice occurred because some individual or group intended it. In this sense intention or purpose is lacking in the choice process. There is no overall rhythm to the process and the specific sequence of choices is random and without any pattern. The sequence of specific choices can shoot just anywhere because important constraints provided by unequal power, clear hierarchies and job descriptions have been removed. Action is then the result of habit, custom or the unpredictable influence of others. It is impossible to predict the choice without knowing all the small details of the context. Intention is lost in the flow of events and goals are the product of sense-making activities after the event.

These studies have shown that where participation is widespread and power equally distributed; where job assignments are unclear and hierarchies complex; where values are not strongly shared; then we get sequences of choices that depend largely on chance.

Politics and agenda building

Chapters 5 and 6 reviewed the operation of political feedback loops in organisations and the impact these have on organisational dynamics. Political processes, the use of persuasion and negotiation to obtain desired outcomes where there is disagreement, is also clearly a decision-making mode. Since open-ended change is characterised by disagreement, the political mode will be of great importance.

Huff (1988) identifies the role of politics in strategic choice in the following terms:

- Organisation politics provides an arena for identifying and assessing new strategic alternatives which draw upon the varied experience of organisation members.
- Politics challenges organisation leaders to clarify and modify their thinking about strategic issues. In general, politics is more effective at this task than formal planning systems.
- Organisation politics identifies the individual and group commitments necessary for designing and implementing new strategy.
- Political diversity facilitates the succession of individual leaders, and promotes adaptations in the practices and beliefs which contribute to organisational culture.
- While organisation politics can be disruptive, routined decision cycles can channel potentially disrupting differences of opinion into manageable cycles of debate.

Dutton (1988) presents a model of decision-making in conditions of uncertainty and ambiguity which he calls an issue-building process. This is depicted in *Figure 8.8*. In this model, issues attract attention if they conform to the strategy and culture of the organisation – the idea of managers' paradigms governing what they see. If the issue is important and simple enough it will attract attention, otherwise the tendency will be to postpone it. This is much the same point as that made in the garbage-can model. To sustain attention an issue must be sponsored and this brings in the political process. Coalitions have to be built around the issue. Whether the issue gets onto the agenda or not will depend upon context, the other matters pressing for attention for example.

Figure 8.8 Issue agenda building
Source: L. Pondy, R. Boland & H. Thomas (Eds) (1988), *Managing Ambiguity and Change*, New York: John Wiley & Sons

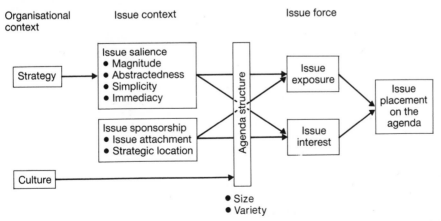

8.8   Summary

This chapter has identified the main kinds of change generated by the complex dynamics we find in those human systems we call organisations. It has shown how the characteristics of open-ended change make it impossible to apply rational, orderly decision-making techniques that rely on some ability to foresee the consequences of present actions. We must expect something messier and more opportunistic, involving political interaction and learning in groups. Open-ended change and political forms of decision-making have implications for what we mean by control and we turn to that in the next chapter.

Further reading

Turton (1991) contains excellent summaries of decision-making modes. For even further detail on particular decision-making modes turn to Quinn (1978), Mintzberg, Theoret & Raisinghani (1976) and Cohen, March & Ohlsen (1972).

9

What open-ended change and political decision-making mean for control

Simultaneous practice of ordinary and extraordinary management

9.1 Introduction

In the last chapter we saw how the system feedback structure of an organisation determines its dynamics; that is, the patterns of change over time that its managers must deal with.

Stable equilibrium systems generate patterns of behaviour that are regular and thus predictable; or to put it another way, they generate closed and contained patterns of change and it is with this kind of change that managers must deal when their organisation is close to equilibrium.

Far from equilibrium, however, nonlinear feedback systems generate much more complex patterns of behaviour over time: their short-term patterns approximate those of regularity and predictability, while their long-term patterns consist of that unpredictable specific variety within fuzzy, irregular categories called chaos. We can recognise the categories when we encounter them but we cannot predict their specific variety. In other words, far-from-equilibrium systems generate a spectrum of changes stretching from the closed and predictable, largely but not entirely in short time frames, to the open-ended and unknowable, largely but not entirely in long-term time frames.

Managers in innovative organisations have no choice but to deal with this complete spectrum of change, simply because organisations are nonlinear feedback systems that must operate far from equilibrium if they are to be innovative and creative. In certain circumstances, the stakeholders of an organisation may not require that it be innovative, but rather that it provide continuity and security. For example, members of a religious institution do not want its managers to innovate, but rather to preserve beliefs, traditions and practices unchanged for lengthy periods. To take another example, the community may well prefer its electricity industry, especially the nuclear component of that industry, to focus on continuity and safety rather than experimental change. In these cases, organisations likely to be judged successful will be those that operate close to stable equilibrium; that is, their managers will create systems of the negative feedback kind to preserve stability.

The primary task of commercial enterprises is, however, substantially different because key stakeholders want an enterprise to innovate – only then can it win competitive battles. In this case, managers must actually set out to create open-ended change and they must be able to cope with the unstable, uncertain and ambiguous consequences of such change. This inescapable need to cope with ambiguity and uncertainty has certain very important consequences for the mode of decision-making that it is possible for managers to employ:

- Managers can employ some approximation to a technically rational mode of decision-making only when they deal with issues arising in closed and contained change situations. It is only then that the dynamics at least approximate those of a stable equilibrium system, making the consequences of change predictable, and predictability is an absolute requirement for rationality. This means that in an innovative organisation approximations to technical rationality are possible for management only over the short term. This conclusion follows from the fact that the dynamics of an innovative nonlinear feedback system approximate those of stable equilibrium only over the short term. Over the short term, then, outcomes can be organisationally intended (see *Key Concept 2.2* in Chapter 2) for all organisations and in stable equilibrium systems they can be organisationally intended in all time frames.
- When they deal with open-ended issues, however, managers can make decisions only through complex procedures involving political interaction, group behavioural dynamics and double-loop learning. These processes provide the only realistic decision-making mode in open-ended change situations simply because the outcomes of actions in an innovative nonlinear feedback system are inherently unpredictable over the open-ended long term. Then, outcomes cannot be organisationally intended, but can only emerge from the detail of political and learning interaction between people.

In innovative organisations, managers have no choice but to employ both of these decision-making modes.

However, when the managers of an organisation find that they have, in certain circumstances, to employ decision-making modes from which outcomes emerge without organisation-wide intention, then it follows that no-one can be in control of those outcomes. A study of the dynamics of successful organisations, and the decision-making modes required to deal with the dynamics, requires us to think again about what we mean by 'the control of an organisation' and that reconsideration is the purpose of this chapter. We will be considering how the application of political/learning modes of decision-making in open-ended situations does not mean that there is no control, but that control takes a different form.

This chapter will argue that control must take a form in open-ended situations that is diametrically opposed to that which it takes in closed and contained situations. In the latter we find negative feedback forms of control in which the leaders are in control; in the former we find complex self-organising forms of control in which behaviour is controlled although no-one is in control. Furthermore, managers in innovative organisations have no choice but to employ both of these contradictory forms of control at the same time. This insight will lead us to draw a distinction between ordinary and extraordinary management.

9.2   The planning and monitoring form of control

In Chapter 5 we reviewed the theory of cybernetics and discovered that this theory underlies the notion of control to be found in today's conventional wisdom on successful management practice. Cybernetics is an approach in which control is thought of entirely in terms of negative feedback processes, the purpose of which is to sustain an organisation close to an organisationally intended position of stable equilibrium.

You will recall the review of the conventional notion of control in Chapter 2 in the section on implementing strategic plans, depicted in *Figure 2.2* as a negative feedback loop. The concern there was with installing hierarchical reporting structures, bureaucratic rules and procedures, standards in regulatory systems, and shared ideologies that, it was claimed, would enable managers to monitor and review performance as the basis for corrective action to restore that performance to target levels in both the short and the long terms. Through installing and operating these systems, it was claimed that those at the top could be in control of their organisation in both the short and the long terms.

You will also recall the discussions in Chapter 5 on general systems theory and planned culture change. The ideas reviewed there were also based on the conventional notion of control, with its emphasis on negative feedback processes through which it is supposed to be possible to change a culture intentionally from one state to another. The conventional concept confines control to notions of directing and converting leadership that ensures proper behaviour and allocates resources to meet known requirements.

Criteria for controlled behaviour

The process just described constitutes 'control' (see *Key Concept 9.1*) because the first general criterion for controlled behaviour is satisfied – there is a connected feedback loop between discovery, choice and action. In this particular case those elements of discovery, choice and action are defined in a particular, very precise way and the loop operates in a negative manner. It is these definitions and the characteristic of negative feedback that make this the planning/monitoring form of control; any other definitions would give us other forms of control.

The second general criterion for controlled behaviour is also satisfied by the control scheme shown in *Figure 2.2* of Chapter 2: there is control because the operation of the feedback loop is constrained. In this particular case it is constrained by organisational intention; that is, the standards those in the organisation agree or are compelled to operate to, the future states they agree to strive for, the actions they agree to undertake to achieve those future states. If the feedback loop is constrained in some other way then we will get another form of control.

The result of this particular form of control is a regular predictable pattern in the behaviour of people in the organisation and in its relationship to the systems that are its environment. Other forms of control could generate different patterns of behaviour, but provided that they still constitute recognisable patterns they would still qualify as control.

■ Key concept 9.1
CONTROL

Controlled behaviour consists of sequences of words and deeds over time that have some kind of pattern; that is, words and deeds that are not haphazard. The patterns in controlled behaviour do not have to be regular; they may be irregular but, nevertheless, recognisable as patterns and so still constitute controlled behaviour. Patterns will be generated when sequences of words and deeds are connected over time through some form of feedback and when those sequences of words and deeds are constrained in some way. The feedback connections and the constraints may take different forms; hence, control may take different forms. Negative feedback and constraint by intention give the planning/monitoring form of control. Feedback that flips from negative to positive, constrained by the need to persuade others and sustain support, results in self-organising political and learning forms of control.

The key to the planning and monitoring form of control is constraint by organisational intention. It will be possible to practise this form of control over a particular time period, therefore, only if it is possible to form organisational intention over that time period. If it is possible to form an organisational intention relating to a one-year period, for example, then managers will be able to control their organisation in the manner shown in *Figure 2.2* over that one-year period. The majority seem to agree that in most organisations it is possible to form shared intention covering short time periods ahead, sometimes a few weeks, sometimes for a year or so, and much more rarely for periods longer than that. But is it possible to do so over the longer term, say a five-year period? If it is not, then any attempt to use planning/monitoring as a form of strategic control will simply fail. It is therefore a matter of some importance to be clear on just what criteria must be satisfied for there to be organisational intention relating to long time periods into the future.

Criteria for long-term organisational intention

If control is to take the form of directing an organisation along an intended path (see *Key Concept 2.2* in Chapter 2) over a long time period, and this is what strategic control through long-term planning and monitoring means, then it must be possible for managers to set goals as follows.

Set goals that remain stable over time. Looking back, we will be able to say that managers have controlled their organisation according to an organisational intention if we can show that at the start of some long-term time period, say five years ago, those managers established what the future state (defined as a particular posture, position, performance – see Chapter 1) of their organisation was to be and then kept to that intention in a relatively constant form throughout the period. If the key managers kept changing their intended future state as they proceeded through the time period we are talking about, then they were in effect discovering their long-term intention as they acted. The intention emerged; it was not predetermined.

Set goals that are specific and clear. Looking back, the future state that managers intended to achieve must have been set out in a reasonably specific, unambiguous form so that it is possible to say at a later date whether the managers achieved it or not. If the intended future state was very general and ambiguous, it would usually be possible to provide some rationalisation with hindsight to conclude that an achievement had been intended. If the future state was one of a large number of different possibilities, we would probably be able to select one of them and conclude that managers intentionally achieved the state that actually materialised. Only if one selected future state was spelled out in a reasonably clear form and then realised can we unequivocally say that managers strategically intended what they achieved.

Set goals that are anchored to a future reality. Managers must have related their intended future state to some picture of the environment in which it was to be achieved. The end state must have been anchored in some way to a future reality. This requires a picture of a future market state containing enough information to enable the linking of organisational posture and position to performance. Intended financial objectives may well be stable over time, shared, specific and unambiguous, but on their own they fail the test of being anchored to a future reality unless those financial performance objectives are related to some future posture and position. Only then would it be possible to say whether they had been achieved by chance or not. We have to exclude the possibility of plucking some performance indicators out of thin air and then achieving them by chance, if we want to demonstrate that there was organisational intention.

Set goals that are overarching. Managers must have established a future state that covers the business as a whole. That state must have been overarching and central to the business. If this condition is not satisfied then the future state would relate to a small number of issues among many, rather than the intended direction for the business as a whole. If we find many different, unconnected aims then managers have intended many different specific responses to many different changes, but they will not have intended the future state of the organisation as a whole within a consistent framework, as organisational intention requires.

Share the same goals. If, instead of a shared overarching future state, we have a number of individual or sub-unit intentions then the future state realised will have emerged from the interaction between those individuals and sub-units. That state will not have resulted from organisational intention.

Set unique goals to differentiate themselves from the competition. Managers intend success and, in most markets today, firms survive and succeed when they deliver products that are different in some sense to those of competitors. The intended future state must therefore be a unique one, differentiating the organisation from its competitors. When a future state is defined simply in terms of a required return on capital or a required growth rate in profits or sales, this simply amounts to a restatement of one of the rules of the competition game, namely that a company must make an adequate return on its capital and generate the profit growth required by shareholders. Much the same point applies to long-term performance objectives taking the form of 'beating a prominent competitor' or 'delivering high quality and service levels'. These are simply rules of the competition game that apply to everyone and require no knowledge of a future state. Such aims do not define a state unique enough to provide competitive advantage and it will be left to some unspecified and therefore unintended factors to do this. We can only say that a future state was organisationally intended when the competitive advantage factors have been specified in advance.

Connect their goals deliberately to the action required to achieve them. Managers must have deliberately used the intended future state to govern their actions so that connections can be demonstrated between what they did and the state achieved. If this condition is not satisfied, their achievement may have emerged from a number of individual intentions, or even chance events. To meet the criterion of deliberateness, intended posture and position must be linked back to the pattern of actions necessary to produce them. The intended future state must be a guide to the selection and design of a sequence of actions. The aim must be specific enough for managers to screen out some actions and select others. Without this they cannot design actions in advance of the change and so intentionally secure a future state.

Have foresight. It must be possible to decide in advance what pattern of actions will yield the intended future state. This requires an ability to identify cause-and-effect links between the actions of managers in an organisation, the reactions of actors in their environment, and the consequences for the posture and position of the organisation. It must therefore be possible to forecast specific changes in the environment through time to a reasonable degree of accuracy. To establish a useful future goal it is necessary only to be able to forecast a picture at one future point in time. If the actions to reach the goal are to be intended, that is if there is to be a plan, then the developments leading up to that aimed-for future state must also be reasonably predictable. If we cannot foresee the pattern in actions, then we cannot intend it. It will emerge from the detail of what we do and any pattern will be evident only with hindsight.

It is only when the above eight conditions are satisfied that it will be possible for managers to control their organisation completely according to a shared organisational intention. Those eight conditions can be satisfied only when an organisation as a system is close to stable equilibrium, so that there are reasonably clear links between cause and effect and hence the 'in principle' possibility of prediction. It follows that the planning and monitoring form of control is possible only in conditions of closed and contained change and for an innovative organisation that confines it to the short term. Of course, where an environment supports a stable equilibrium organisation, then planning/monitoring control can be applied over much longer time periods simply because success here means continuity, repeating the past. It is also possible to apply planning and monitoring control over long time periods in a more limited sense, namely when executing a clearly specified project, such as building a new factory. Each step in the construction can, of course, be controlled according to plan, but the commercial outcome cannot be.

Despite the slim possibility of being able to satisfy the eight criteria for organisational intention in real-life management in demanding competitive environments over the long term, some managers still continue to believe that they are in control of the strategic direction of their organisation. They believe that it is approximately possible to control their organisation over long time periods in an organisationally intended way, using planning and monitoring forms of control. This will be possible, on purely logical grounds, only if that organisation is simply building on old strengths and repeating and refining what it has already done. In all other circumstances the belief in intentional long-term control must be a fantasy defence to protect managers against the anxiety that uncertainty and ambiguity generate (see *Illustration 9.1*).

The planning and monitoring form of control is, therefore, a restricted, special case view of control that can apply only in limited circumstances. Hofstede (1981) has developed a framework for categorising forms of control that makes this point clear.

■ Illustration 9.1
STRATEGY AT A CHEMICAL COMPANY

In 1985, the corporate level of an international chemicals company set growth rate objectives for the particular division with which this illustration will be concerned. It required the division to achieve annual growth rates of 10 per cent in sales and 15 per cent in pretax profits for the next five years. The division carefully examined its product portfolio and concluded that two of its major product lines – call them A and B – would be coming off patent towards the end of the five-year period, opening up the way for inevitable competition and loss of market share. The remaining product lines, C and D, were old ones unlikely to grow at all.

The divisional managers then examined the new product development portfolio and concluded that there was no way in which new products coming on stream, E and F, could compensate for the lack of growth in revenues and profits from the existing product portfolio. It was possible to quantify the negative gap between the corporately set objective for the division and the outcome likely to be generated by existing and new product portfolios by the end of the five-year period in 1990.

Divisional management concluded that in order to plug the gap they would have to adopt a strategy of acquiring products and/or companies. A divisional long-term plan was approved, setting out the objectives, the financial projections, and a general statement that the strategy was to be one of acquisition. The strategy did not specify anything about possible acquisition targets.

What happened between early 1985 and early 1989? At least one reasonably significant new product acquisition was identified and, after careful analysis, a proposal was put forward to the divisional board in mid-1987. But no decision was taken on this and no other significant acquisition was made in the period. Instead, in mid-1987, a merger was announced between the company and another major corporation. That merger was completed by mid-1988.

The two merging companies overlapped in some market segments, but the main effect of the merger was to increase the number of market segments operated in. The merged company was rationalised in a manner that involved some enlargement of the division this illustration is concerned with, but that enlargement by no means resolved the growth gap problem identified back in 1985.

Then in early 1989 the new corporate level set growth objectives for the division covering the five-year period to 1994. The objectives were once again annual growth rates of 10 per cent in sales and 15 per cent in profits. The situation was still one of projected decline in the market shares of the same two major product lines, the lack of compensating new product development, and a similar consequent 'gap'.

Whatever the merger may have done for the corporation as a whole, it had not substantially changed the overall prospects of the division. The divisional plan once again set out the objectives, the projections and the strategy of plugging the gap with acquisitions. A small group of managers was set up to identify suitable acquisitions.

Divisional managers interpreted what they had been doing, and what they were now proposing to do, as the activity of 'planning the long-term future of the division'. They claimed that this was an appropriate interpretation because they all shared clear, long-term, division-wide objectives and they shared a common view on the route to those objectives. They saw the division's future direction as intentional movement towards an identified future state.

When it was pointed out that the objectives, the performance gap and the route to the objectives were all exactly the same as those established nearly five years ago, they replied that the previous five-year plan had not been implemented because of the merger distraction. (Note, however, that this distraction occurred in the second half of the plan period. Even without the distraction, nothing had happened in the first half of the period.) The managers believed that it would be different this time around.

Is this interpretation of what they were doing – that of their organisation moving intentionally towards a predetermined future point – a reasonably realistic one?

The answer is no, because what these managers were doing does not even approximately pass the tests of intentionality. When they set their sales and profit growth targets, they are simply stating one of the rules of the competition game in a quantified form. Note how the rule is exactly the same in 1989 as it was in 1985. There is nothing unique about this at all – all their competitors must be doing much the same thing. They do not need to know anything about a future state to set these targets.

They have not related these aimed-for performance levels to a future posture or shape of the business. They have simply said that today's product portfolio (products A, B, C and D) will generate smaller volumes, new products added to the portfolio (E and F) will not compensate for this, and therefore achievement of performance targets depends upon some yet-to-be-identified acquisition. Nothing is said about that acquisition and the future posture of the business is thus undetermined.

They have also said nothing about the position of the future business in relation to customers and competitors, nor have they said anything about likely future market conditions. The link back from performance to posture and position is absent. The conclusion they have reached from identifying a performance gap is that they will have to do something different in the future to that which they have done over the past four years, but they have said nothing specific about what that something might be.

What they have done is simply stated yet another rule of the competition game. All their competitors are saying much the same thing – they will all probably compete over the same acquisition targets. But, in the end, which of them actually succeeds will depend on which of them does something different to the others.

The future state these managers have identified is therefore not anchored to any reality; nor is there overarching intention since there are many other issues to be dealt with, having little to do with acquisition. For example, there are issues around the effectiveness of the product development process, the productivity of the sales force, new manufacturing technologies and so on. There is also no deliberate connection between a future state and the actions required to achieve it, or any evidence of foresight in relation to those actions.

In this case we cannot point to organisational intention in relation to either the future state or the actions to realise it. It is far more realistic to say that both will emerge from what these managers do from now on. What these managers have done is to identify a key issue – the need for acquisition. That issue is one among many on the agenda. As they move into the future, new issues will be added and some existing ones will be dropped. What they will now do is use a task force to explore and learn about the acquisition issue, so discovering what they might do. Whether anything happens or not will depend upon the extent of political support built up around a particular acquisition proposal. It will depend upon the distractions provided by other issues. Recall why they did not acquire anything over the past few years – they were distracted by the merger issue.

There is intention, but it is intention to explore an issue. Any strategy will emerge from the diverse intentions and actions of key groups of managers, not a single overarching organisational intention. Proposals adopted and actions implemented will have more to do with behavioural interactions between the managers, with other pressures on them, than it will with analyses of potential acquisition targets.

Does it matter whether managers in the division of this chemical company interpret what they are doing as intentional or emergent? It matters very much from a highly practical viewpoint. If those managers interpret what they are doing as intentional planning, their strategic actions will focus on analysis, forecasting, trying to set targets, and allocating responsibilities. But they have been doing this for the past four years, at least, and there has been no acquisition. If instead they understand the emergent nature of what they are doing, they will focus on the effectiveness of their learning and political activities. They will seek to understand why the acquisition issue has received little effective attention. They will ask why they are not developing new products more rapidly because it is this that leads them every few years to the conclusion that they must acquire other companies.

9.3 Appropriateness of different forms of control

In Hofstede's approach to control, the situation in which control is to be exerted is defined in terms of:

- the degree of ambiguity in the objectives to be achieved;
- the measurability of the performance to be controlled;

- the extent to which the outcomes of actions are known;
- the extent to which the activity being controlled is repetitive.

Different combinations of these four factors require alternative forms of control and Hofstede distinguishes six of these, shown in *Figure 9.1*, which also indicates the control situation to which each is appropriate.

Figure 9.1 Hofstede's approach to control
Source: G. Hofstede (1981), 'Management control of public and not-for-profit activities', *Accounting, Organisations and Society*, vol. 6, no. 3, pp. 193–211

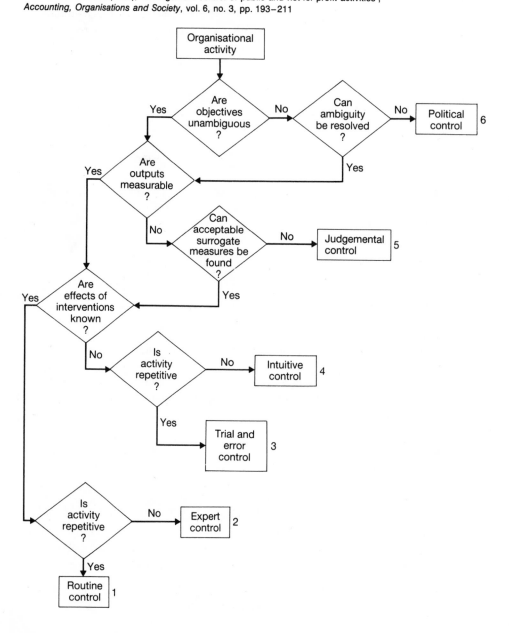

The six main forms of control Hofstede identifies are as follows.

1 Routine control. This is, of course, the pure cybernetic form of control that we discussed in Chapter 5 and it clearly applies only when there is no ambiguity in objectives, the consequences of performance are accurately measurable, the causal links are clear cut so that the outcomes of actions are known, and the activity being controlled is repetitive.

2 Expert control. If we relax the last requirement to do with repetitive activities then we can no longer practise routine, that is fully automatic control. But we can come pretty close to it, if we create the possibility of expert intervention at certain points. This is the planning/monitoring form of control discussed earlier in this chapter.

3 Trial-and-error control. Suppose now that the only condition we set for routine control that is not met is that the outcomes of actions are not known. Then, because we cannot predict, we cannot practise routine or expert control; instead we will have to discover the effects of our interventions through a process of trial and error which is possible because actions are repetitive. This is control through trial-and-error learning about the consequences of our actions. In Chapter 6 we referred to this as single-loop learning.

4 Intuitive control. What if the situation in which control is to be exerted becomes even more difficult in that, although objectives are unambiguous and performance is measurable, actions are not repetitive and their outcomes are not known? Then trial and error will not help much because in effect you will get only one chance to take a particular action – it is unique. In these circumstances Hofstede talks about control as intuitive, as an art rather than a science, where there are few rules to guide managers.

5 Judgemental control. If the control situation becomes even more difficult so that activity is not repetitive, its outcomes are unknown and now also not measurable, but objectives are still clear, then control has to take a subjective, judgemental form.

6 Political control. Finally, suppose that managers face unique situations in which the objectives to be achieved are unclear and the outcomes of actions are neither measurable nor known. Then the only form of control that it is possible to apply is political control. This relies on the use of power, negotiation, persuasion and manipulation, often expressed in rituals and symbols.

Hofstede's analysis can quite easily be recast into the terminology we have been using in this and previous chapters. When all of his six factors defining the control situation are present, then we have what the last chapter called closed change (clear objectives, repetitive actions, measurable and known outcomes). Contained change occurs when there are clear objectives, repetitive actions, imperfectly measurable and largely unknown outcomes. Open-ended change means that there are ambiguous and conflicting objectives, unique actions, non-measurable and unknowable outcomes. These change situations determine what form of control it is possible to apply:

- In conditions near to closed change, control can take forms close to the routine and expert; that is, the planning and monitoring form of control.

- In conditions close to contained change, control can take the form of shared cultures, political processes and trial-and-error action as advocated in the visionary/ideological approaches to management.
- In conditions that are open-ended, however, control will be possible only in its intuitive, judgemental and political forms.

We have already reviewed the nature of the planning and monitoring form of control and we now turn to a fuller examination of the other forms identified in the above paragraph.

9.4   The ideological form of control

We can understand Hofstede's other forms of control within the same framework as the planning/monitoring form by expanding the scope of the simple feedback control system depicted in *Figure 2.2*. We can do this by adding some of the feedback loops we identified in Chapters 5 and 6.

For example, in Chapter 5 (and also in Chapter 8) we reviewed the overt political feedback loop that is to be found in all organisations. Taking account of this, *Figure 9.2* makes the point that, when managers make a choice, that choice will frequently affect the vested interests of some individual or group of people in their organisation, or in other organisations that constitute the environment. This is particularly the case when managers make strategic choices – those affected tend to form special interest groups or coalitions to block some choices and foster others. As they attempt to apply rational decision-making and planning/monitoring control, therefore, managers inevitably activate overt political feedback loops. And that political activity in turn affects both the decision-making process and the nature of control. Not only does this loop allow us to incorporate political control into the system, but it also allows for trial-and-error control. It is through the process of champions forming around issues, building coalitions and trying out some responses that an organisation undertakes large numbers of trial actions to explore how to achieve its objectives.

We can similarly take account of Hofstede's intuitive and judgemental forms of control by incorporating yet another feedback loop to be found in all organisations. This time it is the loop labelled Culture and Cognition in *Figure 9.2*. This represents the feedback processes examined in the section on the models of Argyris and Schon in Chapter 6. There we considered how managers understand their world through mental models that they come to share with others as they work together. What managers consider to be irrelevant, what they pay attention to, and therefore what they do at any one time, are all determined by those shared mental models – the company and industry recipes (Johnson, 1987). In that section of Chapter 6, we also saw how shared mental models determine how managers learn. Mostly managers learn in a simple single-loop way about the consequences of their actions; they then adjust their behaviour according to the outcome of previous behaviour, without questioning their shared mental models. We also saw that, with less frequency, some managers may reflect upon their mental model itself and change that. When they do this they are engaging in complex double-loop learning.

Figure 9.2. The visionary/ideological form of control

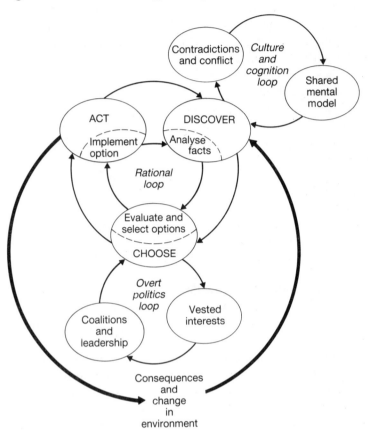

The culture and cognition loop in *Figure 9.2* shows that, as managers go about their tasks, they uncover anomalies, contradictions and conflicts that may provoke them to examine and question the mental models that drive their behaviour – double-loop learning. Or they may simply continue to use the same mental models – single-loop learning. Control by intuition and judgement clearly has to do with how managers are employing their mental models, how they are learning.

In *Figure 9.2*, therefore, we have a control system, a set of feedback loops, that is capable of including all the forms of control that Hofstede has identified and we can use it as a framework for reviewing what a number of writers have had to say about organisational control.

In Chapter 8 we examined a number of models developed by those who recognise the impossibility of utilising anything approaching technically rational decision-making and planning/monitoring forms of control in conditions of great uncertainty. Those models offer an interpretation of how the control system depicted in *Figure 9.2* might work.

One such group of models had to do with searching for error, logical incrementalism, and recognition/diagnostic/selection routines. We also discussed models of this kind when we reviewed the 'excellence' approach in Chapter 2.

You will recall that in these models top managers are 'in control' because they articulate a belief system; that is, a vision for the future and an ideology. Members of the organisation are inspired and persuaded to believe in the vision and ideology that then constitutes a strongly shared culture. Contained by this belief system, people in an organisation then conduct many experimental actions to discover how to reach the vision. Order is sustained by common culture and common intention.

Central to this visionary/ideological explanation of how successful organisations are controlled and developed is the leader as a charismatic political figure who builds and sustains a coalition of supporters. Political activity in this model takes the form of individual product or issue champions who detect, select and build support for particular issues and projects. They use temporary, informal, multi-discipline teams to develop innovative ideas and try them out in experimental form. To keep this overt political activity stable, vested interests must not be threatened. We saw in Chapter 6 how this loop can easily become an amplifying and thus destabilising loop. In the visionary/ideological model of control and development this does not happen because of the strongly shared belief system.

So, in the visionary/ideological scheme, the overt political feedback loop is kept stable through the way in which the culture and cognition loop is managed. In the visionary/ideological system, strongly shared mental models are promoted and this greatly cuts down on contradiction and conflict. It gives stability to the political system. People are controlled by belief rather than rules and regulations or authority.

This group of models retains organisational intention to do with the long run state managers are trying to achieve but introduces emergent, experimental ways of finding out how to achieve the intended state – Hofstede's trial-and-error control. Those emergent experimental ways are conditioned by managers' mental models or paradigms and how they share these, that is the culture of their organisation. These emergent experimental ways place particular emphasis on political interaction and upon learning about the outcome of actions.

What we have, then, is an interpretation of *Figure 9.2*, one that provides a fuller and more realistic model of the control system of an organisation. It includes the rational loop which is employed to deal with some issues and problems, but it now also takes account of other feedback loops that affect discovery, choice and action. There is control because there are regular predictable patterns in behaviour, and this occurs because there is feedback connection of the negative damping kind, as there was for planning and monitoring forms of control. The second general criterion for control is also present – constraint. Just as with planning/monitoring control that constraint is provided by organisational intention; the goal, the vision, is known. In the ideological form of control, behaviour is constrained by the ideology itself and by the criteria for trial-and-error action, namely that trial actions should constitute a logically incremental move from the existing core business. But now the route to the desired state is discovered through trial-and-error action.

Assumptions underlying the visionary/ideological form of control

This form of control and development is fundamental to the popular approach to success prescribed by writers such as Tom Peters (1982, 1988). He presses managers to form a vision, a picture of a future state, and then reach that vision by undertaking hectic trial-and-error actions that satisfy criteria set by shared values and logical connection to the existing business. But what conditions need to prevail if a process of trial-and-error action according to given criteria is dependably to lead to a vision decided in advance of the action? In other words, what is it necessary to assume about the nature of an organisation and its environment in order to make it sensible to prescribe this form of control and development?

The answer to this question is provided by Ashby's Law of Requisite Variety (see *Key Concept 5.2*). You will recall that this law states that a system will remain stable if its control system, or regulator, displays the same level of variety as the environment in which the control is to be exerted. The variety of the environment is simply the number of changes, or random shocks, it generates and the variety of the regulator in a system is simply the number of responses it can make to those changes or shocks. This is a rather elaborate way of saying that the faster the environment changes the faster the system has to respond to stay stable. What is not so obvious, however, is the mechanism that is proposed for responding. Ashby's law says that it is enough to have the same number of responses as environmental shocks, not that each response to each shock has to be the right one. In other words, the mechanism is trial and error and all that is necessary is to get the level or speed of the trial and error right. What is the justification for this?

The justification is the law of large numbers, or probability. If large numbers of random shocks, or unforeseeable changes, keep hitting a system and if that system undertakes large numbers of basically random small trial actions in response, then obviously only some random actions will match some of the random shocks in the sense of being appropriate responses. Most will not but, because of the large numbers involved, the inappropriate responses will tend to cancel each other out – the laws of large numbers. Provided that a system acts fast enough it will maintain stability and move toward its goal but only if shocks and responses are closely similar, or repetitive events of the kind we get, for example, when we toss a coin, where the result always is either heads or tails. It is only with large numbers of repetitive events that we can rely on the cancelling-out of mismatches between random shocks and random actions because it is only then that the law of large numbers works.

When a dynamic system operates in conditions of bounded instability, however, as an innovative organisation does in the long term, no specific event is ever repeated in exactly the same way. The probability of any specific event occurring is therefore infinitely small. Each specific event is unique, falling only into general qualitative categories in which items bear a family resemblance to each other. An organisation does not typically get a large number of chances to repeat events that bear a family resemblance close enough to apply probability in even an approximate way.

Under these circumstances there is no guarantee that trial-and-error mismatches with random environmental shocks will cancel out. Large numbers of random actions, even within boundaries set by logical connection with the existing business and core values, cannot be relied upon as a search technique that will take the business to its intended vision. The ideological form of control requires a causal connection between the vision and the actions required to realise it. It can therefore be applied only in situations of closed and contained change and attempts to apply it in other situations are based on unquestioned assumptions that clearly do not apply.

The ideological approach puts forward a very different mechanism for control, when compared to the long-term planning approach – it adds the loop of overt politics and the loop of cognition and culture to the specification of the control system. But both approaches seek to do the same thing. They are both concerned with the intentional adaptation of the business to its environment. Both see success as flowing from the maintenance of order and stability. The one secures order through hierarchy, formal rules, procedures and analytical techniques. The other secures order through ideology and belief. Both proclaim that a system of some sort, bureaucratic or ideological, can be installed to secure success. For both, prior, central intention and uniformity in behaviour provide the constraints that allow top executives to be in control of the outcome of strategic activity. Both propose a negative feedback form of control in which an organisation is kept to a predetermined path of some sort. The dynamic for both is the drive to equilibrium adaptation in which there are clear connections between cause and effect, even though we may not always be aware of what those connections are. Both are concerned with producing regular patterns in behaviour. Both can apply only to closed and contained change situations.

Since neither the planning/monitoring nor the ideological forms of control are practical propositions when managers wish to cope successfully with open-ended change, what is the form of control they will have to rely on? To answer this question we have to develop our model of the organisational control system further.

9.5   Self-organising forms of control

The essence of open-ended change is confusion and ambiguity leading to equivocal responses on the part of managers and provoking anxiety and conflict. The real problems of long-term control and development relate to identifying what the intentions and the objectives should be, what the problems and opportunities are. Since an innovative organisation always faces open-ended change, its managers have continually to cope with these conditions and these conditions always provoke certain kinds of behaviour that are not taken into account in the model depicted in *Figure 9.2* above.

The complex control system

To move closer to a useful model of the feedback structure of an organisation's control system, therefore, we need to add two additional loops to the model and these are shown in *Figure 9.3*.

The first additional feedback loop takes account of covert politics: as the level of uncertainty rises and as the applied power of leaders diminishes, fears of failure are aroused and people then develop organisational defences against this. This loop incorporates the ideas of Argyris on learning and organisational defences discussed in Chapter 6. In that discussion the importance of differences between espoused theories (what managers say they do) and theories in use (what they actually do) was emphasised. You will recall the organisational defence routines this distinction leads to and how ambiguous and uncertain situations are the ones where managers are

Figure 9.3 The self-organising form of control

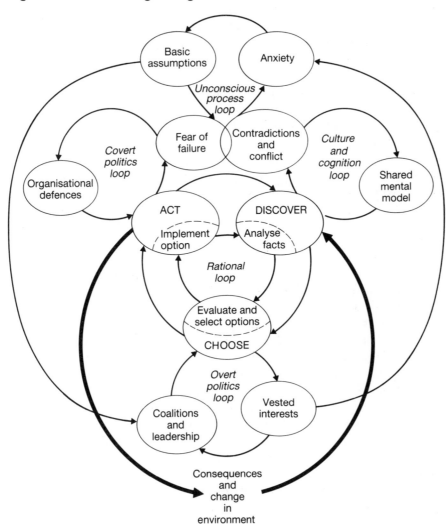

most likely covertly to abandon their espoused theories. It is extremely unlikely that there is any organisation in which these loops are absent. It is rather unlikely that any organisation could succeed in permanently removing them as opposed to diminishing their adverse impact. We must therefore add loops of this kind to our models of organisation control systems if we are to build a reliable picture of reality.

The second additional feedback loop takes account of unconscious group processes. You will recall from the section on those models in Chapter 6 that, when the level of uncertainty and ambiguity rises and as the pattern of power use changes, anxiety levels in groups are certain to rise. Such anxiety inevitably provokes unconscious defences such as dependence, fight/flight and pairing – the basic assumptions of Bion's group relations theory. It is extremely unlikely that we will find groups of people that do not exhibit behaviour of this kind and it is highly unlikely that any organisation will be able to remove such behaviour. A realistic model of an organisational control system must therefore include them.

These loops are added, in *Figure 9.3*, to give a fuller model of an organisation's control system. The figure also makes yet another connection. You will recall that basic-assumption behaviour affects the nature of leadership. It opens up the possibility of the leader becoming the creation of the group. *Figure 9.3* therefore shows a loop running from basic assumptions to leadership and coalitions. It thereby has an immediate impact on the nature of overt political activity in an organisation, threatening vested interests and directly raising levels of anxiety.

What this diagram depicts is a complex web of feedback loops. They could be joined to each other at any point – the arrangement in the figure is simply one possibility. All the loops are connected through some loop to all others. When people in an organisation deal with closed and contained change, that is when leaders can be relied on to exert authority and people carry out repetitive tasks to achieve known objectives, then decision-making and control can quite adequately be described by the rational loop in the middle of the diagram. It is as if the other loops all fade into the background and become of little consequence. Or in such closed and contained conditions we may find political activity kept stable by shared cultures. The control system model above has planning and ideological forms as special cases applicable to closed and contained change.

However, as soon as open-ended issues present themselves to people in an organisation, the level of ambiguity and uncertainty rise dramatically and leaders can no longer deal with the situation by applying their authority. We can think in terms of the level of ambiguity being tuned up while the level of applied power is tuned down. These inevitable consequences of the open-ended issues that are so characteristic of strategic management mean that the political, cognitive and unconscious loops that we previously ignored as background now become very important; they are activated to become major parts of the process of decision-making and control. The loops are not activated in any set order – each new situation provokes a new specific way of moving around the loops. In this system of feedback loops, some will inevitably operate in amplifying ways, opening up the possibility that the system will become explosively unstable, that is uncontrolled. The key question then is under what conditions we can expect such a complex system to generate controlled behaviour. The first general condition for controlled behaviour is still present: there is a feedback loop connecting discovery, choice and action as there was before; it is simply that the elements are defined in far more complex ways. The problem is that we can no longer rely on organisational intention to provide constraint. If the system is to be controlled we have to look for some other form of constraint.

Before examining this question of control however, we need to explore how we might use the model depicted in *Figure 9.3* to explain how managers deal with open-ended issues. *Illustration 9.2* relates this model to a case study. In the section on models of decision-making in conditions far from certainty in Chapter 8, we examined explanations of management as a process of muddling through, organisational anarchy, garbage-can decision-making, and political agenda building. All of these explanations incorporate the unstable overt and covert political activity that is part of the process of handling open-ended issues. These and other models of the political process (see Chapter 5) can be brought together in the following description of what managers do as they handle open-ended issues (Stacey, 1991, 1992). Once we have described this process and identified some of its key features we will be able to see the sense in which it can be identified as controlled behaviour.

■ **Illustration 9.2**
IMPERIAL INDUSTRIES

One of the largest divisions of a company I will call Imperial Industries consists of two main UK subsidiaries, as well as subsidiaries in the US and Sweden. Subsidiary A in the UK designs and installs information technology systems. It manufactures a few of the components required for these systems, but mostly buys them from other companies and assembles them. One of A's suppliers is its sister subsidiary in the UK, company B, which manufactures components which it sells to A and to A's competitors for integrated systems contracts.

The division therefore has a direct route to the end-user market and an indirect route through Own Equipment Manufacturers (OEM). Operating these two routes is a source of conflict between A and B in the marketplace because A demands preferential treatment from B, but B resists this pointing to the damage it does to its business with A's competitors. The difficulties are magnified when account is taken of export business since both A and B are trying to sell components to overseas OEMs.

The Swedish company also gets involved in the conflict because it operates in the same way and supplies components to A and to A's competitors. The company in the US combines both routes to market in one company, but conflict occurs where the UK and US companies appear in the same export market. The strategic issue then is which route to market is to be chosen: one or both? Is there to be an emphasis on one rather than the other? If both routes are to be retained and no particular emphasis laid on either, then what policies are to govern relationships between the companies? What organisational structure is likely to reduce conflict to manageable levels? This has all the hallmarks of the strategic issue: it is ambiguous; the outcomes of different solutions are uncertain; it is difficult to structure the problem; any change affects some power position; different people have different perspectives; it is characterised by paradox or dilemma; levels of anxiety are raised.

To deal with these issues, the Chief Executive arranged a one-day workshop with his executive team, the managing directors of the subsidiaries. Each of the four MDs was a powerful and ambitious figure intent on winning out in the battle. They all had considerable talent and the CEO did not wish to see any of them leave. For most of the day the workshop focused on general market conditions and how they were likely to develop in the future. They talked a lot about future market position. Then they turned to putting together a mission statement or a vision. After much amicable discussion they agreed that it was impossible to make a choice at this stage between one route to market and the other – the future of the IT industry was too uncertain. They agreed on a vision 'to be a leading player in the worldwide IT market'.

Then towards the end of the day they turned to the question of how the division might be organised to reduce levels of conflict in the marketplace. The meeting immediately broke into acrimonious bickering as each MD fought in a highly personalised way to preserve his power.

What emerges quite clearly from this is the following. Those managers were using a friendly discussion about the future marketplace and about a vague general vision to flee from dealing with the real issue of how to organise themselves in a sensible way. In this sense a focus on the future and on vision was simply a defence mechanism to keep conflict and anxiety at bay. When they did confront the real issue, the group became dominated by the fight basic assumption. What this workshop on strategic management clearly shows is that the covert and overt political loops as well as the unconscious group process loop explain what is going on. The rational loop in the middle of *Figure 9.3* plays the part simply of a smokescreen.

The CEO then invited a distinguished consultant to yet another workshop which was to address the issue. That consultant identified the key problem to do with relationships between the subsidiaries and their MDs and the need for policies and structures. But he said the first step was to form a dream or vision. This then let everyone off the hook again. They discussed the potential vision and decided that the one they had come up with before was the best they could do. Was this hiring of a consultant another example of flight behaviour? Did the consultant collude in this by providing another opportunity for flight in his insistence on a vision?

Yet another consultant was then employed. This time an attempt was made to unblock the political obstacle at the top by bringing together a working group of middle managers and asking them to propose policies and structures. They after all were at the forefront of the conflict. The idea was that pressure from their subordinates would move at least some of the MDs.

The proposals of the middle managers were presented to the MDs at a board meeting. Apparent peace prevailed while there was a discussion of the general principles of the restructuring proposed, but when it got close to anything specific a number of things tended to happen. The CEO chairing the meeting would get up and leave the room to attend to something urgent. The discussion would then peter out as soon as he left. On other occasions one of the MDs in particular would keep making personal remarks that he was quite aware would antagonise his colleagues. In this way he could sidetrack the meeting away from the real issue.

Once again, the point is that this process of making a strategic decision is characterised far more by covert political behaviour and unconscious group processes of flight and fight, than it is by analytical reasoning.

A few months later, the CEO built up enough support to implement a number of the proposals the middle management group had put forward and one of the MDs left. Had that MD been fired early in the process, a number of managers may well have left with him and, even if they did not, there would probably have been continuing covert opposition to the reorganisation. It happened, however, that no-one else left and there was considerable support for the new structure.

Clearly the outcome of this strategic issue emerged; it was not the consequence of organisational intention. It emerged from a complex process of moving around a number of interconnected feedback loops that had to do with overt and covert political behaviour and with unconscious group processes. It would be naive to believe that it is possible to remove these processes from an organisation. The behaviour of those involved was controlled in a self-organising manner, although no one was in control. Although the MDs conflicted, they did so within the boundaries set by each others' power.

How managers use the complex feedback control system in open-ended situations

The model of an organisational control system depicted in *Figure 9.3* is a web of nonlinear feedback loops that will operate in both damping and amplifying modes. When faced with clear, familiar tasks, leaders are likely to exert their authority and followers are likely to comply. In these conditions, the organisational feedback system will be close to stable equilibrium and operate in a negative feedback mode. The system will, in effect, be dominated by the rational loop at the centre of *Figure 9.3* and the other loops will fade into the background.

There are other conditions in which the organisational feedback system depicted in *Figure 9.3* will operate in an amplifying way leading to explosively unstable equilibrium. For example, confronted by the need to perform tasks that are ambiguous with outcomes that are uncertain, leaders may exert their power in the form of force and followers may rebel. The result is a highly unstable revolution. Again, leaders may not know what to do and in the ensuing power vacuum intense rivalry amongst followers might break out. The result is likely to be highly unstable conflict.

There are, however, other conditions that we will discuss later on and return to in Chapter 11, in which the feedback control system depicted in *Figure 9.3* will operate in an alternately damping and amplifying manner to produce chaos. Chaos is controlled behaviour because it is coherent and has a pattern that we can recognise when we encounter it even if it is irregular and we cannot predict its specific form. Control in this state of bounded instability takes on a self-organising form just as it does in the nonlinear feedback systems to be found in nature.

You will recall from Chapter 7 how nonlinear feedback systems amplify small changes to break the symmetry of existing patterns of behaviour and then self-organise to form new patterns. This process of symmetry-breaking and spontaneous self-organisation can be observed in organisations too. It takes the form of a rhythm to, a number of phases in, the behaviour of managers as they handle open-ended issues. These phases are depicted in *Figure 9.4* and briefly summarised below (Stacey, 1991 & 1992).

Detecting and selecting open-ended issues. Open-ended change is typically the accumulating result of many small events and actions. Since what is going on is unclear, ambiguous and confusing, with consequences that are unknowable, the key difficulty is that of identifying what the real issues, problems and opportunities are. The challenge is to find an appropriate and creative aspiration or objective. In these circumstances an organisation has no alternative but to rely on the initiative of individuals to notice and pursue some issue, aspiration or challenge. In order to do this, those individuals have to rely on their experience-based intuition and ability to detect analogies between one set of ambiguous circumstances and another. This activity on the part of an individual is spontaneous and self-organising in the sense that no central authority can direct anyone to detect and select an open-ended issue for attention, simply because no-one knows what it is until someone has detected it.

Gaining attention and building issue agendas. After some individual, at some level in the hierarchy, has detected some potential issue, that individual begins to push for

Figure 9.4 Political and learning processes: self-organising control

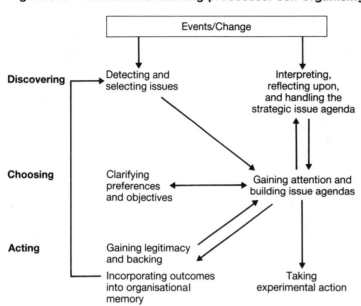

organisational attention to be paid to that issue. A complex process of building special interest groups or coalitions around an issue is required before that issue can be said to have gained organisational attention. This political activity of building support for attention to some detected issue is also clearly self-organising and spontaneous in the sense that it is informal and not part of the normal rules and procedures. No-one is centrally organising the factions and coalitions that form around detected issues. Once an issue has gained sufficient support, in the sense that it is being discussed by those with sufficient power to do something about it, then that issue becomes part of the organisation's strategic issue agenda. The agenda is a list of issues, aspirations and challenges that key groups of managers are attending to and it is always changing in a manner that reflects what is being detected, how the pattern of political interplay is developing, and what managers are learning. Once issues arrive on the agenda, some are attended to while others drop off the list without ever being acted upon, yet others are successfully enacted, and still others lead to actions that fail. There is no overall framework or grand design to which managers can refer before they decide how to tackle any issue on this agenda because they are unique and cannot be foreseen. Instead, managers discover what objectives they should pursue and what actions might work through discussion with each other and with customers, suppliers and even rivals. In this sense they are learning what to do as they progress the issue. They are in effect altering old mental models, existing company and industry recipes, to come up with a new way of doing things. Thus, when managers deal with the issues on their strategic agenda they are performing a real-time learning activity. The communication that this involves is spontaneous in the sense that it is not directed by some central authority, but depends upon the personalities of the individuals involved, on the context provided by the dynamic of their interaction with each other, and by the time they have available given all the other issues requiring their attention.

Interpreting, reflecting upon, and handling the strategic issue agenda. When managers deal with the strategic issue agenda of their organisation, they are performing a vitally important destabilising function. Open-ended strategic issues, by definition, threaten existing work patterns, organisational structures and power positions. Strategic issues are about new and different ways of doing things and different things to do. One issue has to compete with other issues for attention and scarce resources. Progressing open-ended issues through discussion, conflict and dialogue changes perceptions and is an activity that activates the covert political and unconscious process loops shown in *Figure 9.3*. This instability and confusion, or chaos, performs the function of shattering the existing order to make the new possible. In handling issues on the agenda, building support is an activity that amplifies this instability through the system. Instability breaks the existing order, making way for the new.

Clarifying preferences and objectives. Some issues on the agenda may be dealt with very quickly. Others may attract attention, continuous or periodic, for a very long time. How quickly an issue is dealt with depends upon the time required to reach enough consensus and commitment to proceed to action. It depends upon the course which the political and learning interaction takes. At some critical point, some external pressure, or some internal pressure arising from power, personality or group interaction, in effect forces a choice. The outcome on whether and how to proceed to action over the issue is unpredictable because it depends upon the context of power, personality and group dynamic. The result may or may not be some action. The point about this consensus required to proceed to action is that it is temporary, fragile and related to a specific issue. When the group of managers turns to the next issue, consensus has to be established anew. In a dynamic organisation, one dealing with an active, ever-changing issue agenda, consensus will be the exception, not the norm. It requires continuing inputs of energy and attention to sustain consensus – what scientists call a dissipative structure.

Taking experimental action and feedback. Action will usually be experimental at first, so providing a vehicle for further learning.

Gaining legitimation and backing. Building and handling strategic issue agendas proceeds largely outside the formal structures and procedures of the organisation. At various points in this largely spontaneous and self-organising process, however, the formal bodies and procedures of an organisation are required to legitimise the choices being made and to allocate resources to the exploration of, and experimentation with, issues. Although the support and interest of the formal bodies in the organisation is vital to the effective building and progressing of strategic issues, such bodies are essentially peripheral. They provide the boundaries within which the self-organising process of dealing with strategic issues occurs. As unclear open-ended issues proceed through learning and experimentation to emerge as potentially successful new strategies, the formal bodies of the organisation play a more prominent role. New strategies will emerge only if those bodies back potential success with sufficient resource to allow the new strategy to emerge.

Incorporating outcomes in organisational memory. Managers in a business come to share memories of what has worked and what has not worked in the past. In this way they build up a business philosophy for their company; they establish a company recipe and in common with other rivals they build industry recipes too. All of this is the same as developing a culture or a retained organisational memory. An organisation's memory has a powerful effect on what issues will subsequently be detected and attended to. It constitutes the frame of reference within which managers interpret what to do next – we have completed the circle and are back to individuals detecting issues. The retained memory provides a boundary around the instability of the political and learning processes through which strategic issues are handled. It is, however, a boundary that can easily become inappropriate to new circumstances. An essential part of the complex learning process required to handle strategic issues is the continual questioning of the organisation's retained memory.

An example of the process we have just considered is given in *Illustration 9.3*.

■ Illustration 9.3
AMSTRAD

In the 1970s Alan Sugar noticed that it would be much cheaper to make plastic covers for record players by injection moulding rather than vacuum forming and this led to his first successful product. Later, he became aware that, while people liked the fashionable appearance of a hi-fi set, they did not want to assemble a number of different units. This led him to market the highly successful tower system consisting of one unit that looked like a number of different ones. After that, he perceived the needs of potential customers for personal computers. Those potential customers knew too little about computers to be able to assemble a number of different units and load software onto them. Alan Sugar turned that perception into a low-cost product that could be taken from the store, plugged in and used immediately.

So one new product idea succeeded the other over the years, but at any one time managers at Amstrad were having to deal with a great many issues. For example, in the mid-1980s there were issues to do with different computer products, sourcing components in the Far East, manufacturing and assembly, setting up distribution channels in Europe, organisational structures and control systems, and many more. Which of those issues was attended to at any one time depended heavily on the political process in the organisation – in this case on the power of Alan Sugar himself.

Action on these issues took an experimental form: for example, Amstrad first set up agents in France, Spain and Germany. These operations all developed in different ways from which Amstrad learned, finally selecting the more successful French model to redesign operations in Spain and Germany. Only after it had learned from this experience did it set up subsidiary companies in those countries.

But Amstrad did not simply settle into a fixed mould. In the 1980s Alan Sugar abandoned crucial ingredients of the ultra-entrepreneurial, small business ethos and set in train the installation of structures more appropriate for the day-to-day management of a large company.

Source: Thomas, 1990

Spontaneous self-organisation produces controlled behaviour

In the paragraphs above we have described people spontaneously interacting to form a self-organising system that often amplifies their behaviour, leading to overt and covert political actions, unconscious processes, organisational defences and the questioning of shared mental models. That is, we have described the operation of a destabilising system that shatters existing structures and perspectives. It is nevertheless a system in which people sometimes spontaneously follow the phases described above to produce coherent patterns in behaviour that lead to new forms of order, given a favourable context. So, faced with open-ended situations, people in an organisation amplify small changes to form different patterns of behaviour that are irregular and unpredictable, but they are nonetheless coherent because we can recognise them when we encounter them even if we cannot predict their specific form.

The kind of self-organising behaviour described above is therefore controlled behaviour because it has a pattern and it satisfies the same general criteria for control as the planning/monitoring and ideological forms did, but in a different way:

- The first general criterion of controlled behaviour is satisfied because there is feedback connection between discovery, choice and action. It is simply that the feedback connection is a good deal more complex than it is when planning/monitoring or ideology is the form of control. The elements in the feedback loop are simply defined in a different, far more complex way – discovery involves questioning existing mental models and bringing unconscious processes to the surface; choice involves overt and covert politics; and action involves exploration.
- The second general criterion for control is constraint. In the system we have just been considering, however, constraint cannot take the form of organisational intention or strongly shared ideology because intention has to be discovered and ideology questioned if issues are to be surfaced and dealt with. Instead, constraint is provided by the boundaries around the amplifying manner in which the system operates.

Control through context

The most obvious boundaries around the instability created by the political amplification of issues are the legitimate formal bodies of the organisation needed to legitimise what is going on and to allocate resources on the one hand, and the retained memory, culture or ideology that must be questioned on the other. But less-obvious boundaries are even more important.

The first of these less-obvious boundaries arises from the very nature of a group of people who actually pursue a learning task. In such a group, individuals discover small changes, anomalies and ambiguities. They reflect upon these and push others to attend to them, so giving rise to conflict, contradiction, contention, dialogue and exploratory action – all essentially destabilising activities. However, behaviour is constrained partly by individual differences in culture and perceptions, by disagreements preventing a single view from dominating. Behaviour is also partly constrained by the shared views that groups working together come to acquire, but constantly have to question if they are to learn. Constraint then is a consequence of the tension between the simultaneous presence of both sharing and difference. The extremes of either sharing or difference both remove the constraints and lead to uncontrolled behaviour.

The second of these less-obvious boundaries, context factors or constraints arises from the very nature of political activity. People interacting politically form factions and build support through persuasion and negotiation. Their behaviour is constrained by the unequal distribution of power, by the existence of hierarchy, by the need to sustain sufficient support for the progress and enaction of issues. It is the tension inherent in an unequal distribution of power that acts as a boundary on what people can do in a political system. If power is not distributed at all but concentrated in the hand of one or two, the boundary is removed; those few can do whatever they wish and we get potentially explosive instability. If power is equally distributed, the constraint is also removed; there is no power grouping capable of restraining any individual from doing whatever that individual chooses to do and the result is once again potentially explosive behaviour. A context in which power is either concentrated or equally shared provides little control, but one in which power is both concentrated and shared – that is, unequally distributed – does provide the constraints necessary for controlled behaviour.

Note how it is uniformity that provides the constraint necessary for control in the planning/monitoring and ideological forms of control: uniform intention, uniform ideology. In the self-organising form, however, it is the tension created by difference that provides the constraint.

Top management and self-organising control

Top management exerts an influence on the learning and political form of coherent behaviour that is just as important as the influence it exerts through plans and ideologies – the area of influence is simply different. Instead of influencing through fixing intentions and establishing predetermined rules to yield an outcome, top management exerts its influence in open-ended change by operating on the boundary conditions surrounding the learning process in the organisation. In open-ended change there can be no central control over the choices made or their outcomes, but through operating on the boundary conditions, top managers determine whether learning occurs at all, how widespread that learning is, and what quality it displays. They operate on the boundary conditions (context) through the manner in which they use their power; in this way they provoke group dynamics that either help or hinder. Top managers allocate resources and so determine the time pressures learning groups face: if the pressures are too tight learning will not occur.

Note that central, shared intention is not an essential requirement for there to be controlled behaviour. We can intend explosive instability and that is not controlled. Behaviour may be chaotic, without central shared intention, and yet it is controlled. Predictability and stability are also not essential requirements for control. Explosive instability follows a perfectly predictable course and yet it is not controlled. Chaotic behaviour is unpredictable and unstable, but still controlled, simply because it is constrained and does display patterns even though they are irregular.

9.6 The paradox of control: ordinary and extraordinary management

Every organisation must retain the support of its environment if it is to survive; that is, it must perform the primary tasks that customers, owners, the community at large, and any relevant powerful others look to it to perform, and it must do so better than other organisations, otherwise those customers and others will simply withdraw their support. To put this notion in another way, every organisation must sustain a competitive advantage if it is to survive and for most organisations today that means continually innovating.

Chapters 7, 8 and 9 have demonstrated that a continually innovative organisation must simultaneously accommodate the impact of changes that range from the closed to the open-ended and that such profoundly different change situations require completely different, indeed contradictory, modes of decision-making and forms of control; approximations to technically rational modes of decision-making and planning/monitoring and shared ideology control forms are what work for day-to-day operational and repetitive strategic management (that is, handling closed and contained change); intuitive, political and group learning modes of decision-making and spontaneous self-organising forms of control are all that is possible in the open-ended situations out of which innovation and new strategic directions emerge.

Since it is necessary to make decisions and control in both closed/contained and open-ended situations simultaneously, organisations must combine fixed, directing forms of decision-making and control, operated largely through the hierarchy and the bureaucracy, with a flexible, opportunistic, political system that permits creative learning and operates largely through spontaneously formed personal networks. We see this happening in practice when managers function effectively in the morning as members of a formal hierarchy participating in institutionalised meetings and then function just as effectively in informal networks of colleagues, from different hierarchical levels, over lunch. In the morning they obey the rules of the hierarchy and over lunch they ignore or even plot to undermine them. The same managers alternate between one decision-making mode/control form and another, and different managers simultaneously apply different decision-making modes/forms of control in different parts of an organisation (Weick, 1969/79).

These different modes of decision-making and forms of control place demands on people and systems that are in direct contradiction to each other, making effective control a paradox that creates tension. For example, people must obey the rules without question when they operate according to one mode/form and then question and change those rules as they operate in the other mode/form. Such tension can never be removed or resolved permanently because the paradox, the requirement for stability and change/instability, can never be removed or resolved. All that can be done is the continual rearrangement of the paradoxical features of decision-making and control.

This distinction between two fundamentally different modes of decision-making and forms of control, and the need to apply them simultaneously, can be further illuminated by making use of Kuhn's distinction between normal and revolutionary science (we discussed this in Chapter 3). You will recall that normal science is practised when a community of scientists strongly share a common paradigm. But as they practise that normal science within the shared paradigm, anomalies build up and lead to the destruction of the paradigm and its replacement by another – a scientific revolution occurs. Very much the same distinction seems to apply to the manner in which organisations develop strategically – organisations require both what we might call ordinary and extraordinary management.

The normal day-to-day conduct of the existing activities of an organisation, together with the implementation of strategies that build on its existing strengths, is always carried out according to some paradigm that most within the organisation share. The circle at the centre of *Figure 9.5* depicts the organisational paradigm governing the shared perceptions that managers have of their task at any one time. That paradigm sets the agenda for the normal conduct of the organisation's activities and it is embodied in the:

- hierarchical reporting structure of the organisation;
- roles people take up within that structure;
- modes of decision-making they employ;
- forms of control they practise and the systems they use to control;
- culture, as well as the leadership and management styles they adhere to;
- kinds of ideology and forms of persuasion they use;
- way 'missions' and 'visions' are stated;
- rules of the competitive game they attach the most importance to.

The paradigm and its principal embodiments taken together lead almost inevitably to particular objectives, to particular conceptions of competitive advantage, and therefore to particular strategies. The ordinary management task is to solve the puzzle of how to implement the strategies and reach the objectives defined by the paradigm. Ordinary management (see *Key Concept 9.2*) is simply going around the

Figure 9.5 Ordinary and extraordinary management

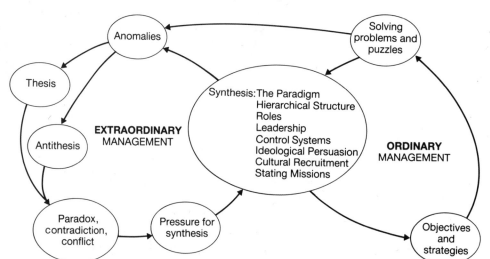

negative, damping feedback loop to the right of the circle representing the paradigm in *Figure 9.5*.

■ **Key concept 9.2**
ORDINARY MANAGEMENT

Ordinary management is practised when most of the managers in an organisation share the same mental models or paradigm. Cognitive feedback loops then operate in a negative feedback manner so that shared mental models are not questioned. Choices are made according to some approximation to technically rational criteria and this is possible because there is agreement on what the business is all about and what kind of environment it is having to cope with. Also, control is practised in its planning/monitoring and ideological forms through the instrument of hierarchy and bureaucracy. Ordinary management is about rational processes to secure harmony, fit, or convergence to a configuration, and it proceeds in an incremental manner. Ordinary management can only be practised in closed or contained change situations and indeed it must be practised in such situations if the organisation is to be able to deliver competitive advantage.

The paradigm, however, is a particular arrangement at a particular point in time of many paradoxes: division versus integration; preserving the status quo versus destroying it and creating the new; low cost versus high quality; and many more (Hampden-Turner, 1990; Quinn & Campbell, 1988; Kets de Vries, 1980). The paradigm is an arrangement of contradictory states that most managers in an organisation agree, perhaps only unconsciously, to be useful at a particular point in time. However, the effective practice of ordinary management inevitably uncovers anomalies, challenges to the current paradigm, that open up the paradox once more. This is inevitable because any given arrangement of paradoxes, of contradictory forces, must by definition be unstable. Once the nature of the paradox is reopened, the obvious contradiction leads to conflict and to pressure for a new synthesis, for a new arrangement of the contradictory forces, for a new paradigm. This paradigm-breaking is the extraordinary management depicted in *Figure 9.5* as the loop to the left of the paradigm circle; the connection with Kuhn's ideas discussed in Chapter 3 is clear.

■ **Key concept 9.3**
EXTRAORDINARY MANAGEMENT

Extraordinary management involves questioning and shattering paradigms, and then creating new ones. It is a process which depends critically upon contradiction and tension. Because it is outside the rules of an existing paradigm, because no-one can know what new paradigms will be shared, because no-one knows what the outcomes will be, rational analysis and argument cannot play much part in the developing of a new paradigm. Instead, frame-breaking extraordinary management is a process of persuasion and conversion, requiring the contributions of champions. It is not about consistency or harmony, rather it is destabilising and irregular. Paradigms cannot be changed incrementally. Instead, after long periods of grappling with anomaly, we seem to reach new paradigms in a sudden flash. The changing of paradigms is a revolutionary rather than an evolutionary process. Furthermore, paradigm changes cannot be organisationally intended. Those holding an existing paradigm do not decide in advance to find a new one. Indeed they resist the new one when it is first mooted. Consequently new paradigms have to emerge from the confusion created by anomalies and the contradiction of the existing paradigm. Ordinary incremental management with competitive trial-and-error experiments is bound to uncover anomalies and so lead to crisis and revolution. That revolution need not, however, be on a grand scale. Any small change in an organisation that requires groups of people to change their mental models qualifies as a revolution in the sense the word is being used here. Such revolutions are probably more prevalent than we might at first imagine.

Extraordinary management, then, is the use of intuitive, political, group learning modes of decision-making and self-organising forms of control in open-ended change situations. It is the form of management that managers must use if they are to change strategic direction and innovate.

The important point is that this extraordinary management is not some separate form of management: it is provoked by and in turn governs ordinary management. In *Figure 9.5* an arrow connects the solving of current puzzles with the raising of anomalies. The very activity of the day-to-day running of the existing business throws up anomalies that undermine the paradigm. The more effectively managers run their existing business, the more they uncover what is not working as well as it might. This uncovering of possibilities for improvement undermines the existing received wisdom. The cutting edge of strategic management is this frame-breaking extraordinary management and it flows from and determines the ordinary day-to-day repetitive management of the existing business, the continuing strategy of building on existing strengths. *Illustration 9.4* provides an example of this intertwining of ordinary and extraordinary management. Furthermore, ordinary and extraordinary management require completely different decision-making modes and control forms, matters we have already discussed, and also completely different institutional and behavioural frameworks through which those decision-making modes and control forms must be applied, matters we go on to discuss in the next two chapters. Finally, it must be stressed that we cannot choose to practise either ordinary or extraordinary management – we have to practise both at the same time.

■ **Illustration 9.4**
FOSTER BROTHERS

Johnson (1987) carried out a study of decision-making at the men's clothing retail chain, Foster Brothers, over a number of years in the 1980s. This company operated at the bottom end of the men's clothing market and its managers shared a number of unquestioned beliefs about the nature of their business: they assumed that competitive advantage flowed from high volumes of sales and low costs to be secured by sourcing in the Far East. Shops were seen as places to dispose of merchandise as quickly as possible and there was little in the way of marketing concepts. Then during the 1980s the company ran into difficulties and experienced declining profits. Some managers pushed for a move up market, a move that would require the company to focus on 'fashion'. Johnson describes how new people were brought in to create the necessary changes, but they never lasted long. Market research reports were re-interpreted so that they supported the shared beliefs that managers were having great difficulty in changing. When more managers did recognise the need to move up into the more fashionable segments, they tried to do so in a way clearly determined by their paradigm. They copied fashion items and had them made cheaply in the Far East, and then distributed them through low-cost channels, shops that paid little attention to ambience. Managers could not abandon ways of thinking that were driven by merchandise concepts and buying-driven responses, instead of design and customer satisfaction considerations. Johnson describes how the structure of the organisation, its culture and the decision-making processes managers used, their avoidance of challenging each other, all helped to perpetuate the paradigm. Eventually the company was acquired by a bigger stores group.

9.7 Summary

In general, controlled behaviour is the opposite of haphazard, meaningless behaviour on the one hand, and explosively unstable behaviour on the other. Controlled behaviour has some overall coherence, that is pattern, and for this to occur:

- There must be a feedback loop connecting discovery choice and action. It is possible, however, to define discovery choice and action in very different ways and still have control, provided that there is a feedback connection between them. For example, two people may not share the same ideology and they may not plan and monitor their behaviour when they argue fiercely with each other. Their behaviour, however, will still be controlled if each consciously or unconsciously discovers the reaction of the other to a statement and then makes the next statement in the light of that discovery. Where one simply makes a series of statements, not hearing or understanding the other, we get an uncontrolled argument that is either haphazard and meaningless or explodes into a quarrel. And this happens because the feedback connections are broken. The monitoring form of control defines connection in terms of comparing action outcome against standard. The ideological form of control defines connection in terms of shared belief and learning about the outcome of actions. The self-organising form of control defines connection in terms of reflection upon and learning about both action and belief systems.
- There must be some form of constraint on the feedback loop preventing behaviour from becoming explosively unstable. One way in which this requirement can be met is to ensure that the feedback loop operates in a negative manner. Constraint is then provided by the standard that is set or the belief that is shared, that is some

form of organisational intention (see *Key Concept 2.2* in Chapter 2). Organisational intention may be an end point all are striving for; it may be a path they all agree to follow; it may be a set of rules they all agree (or are compelled) to obey. Here constraint is provided by uniformity. This form of constraint requires central direction and mechanisms for securing agreement or acceptance. But we do not have to define constraint in this way and indeed, as we have seen above, in open-ended change we cannot. Instead, constraint is provided by the nature of the informal aspects of an organisational system itself, that is by differences in power and points of view. Those differences make it necessary to sustain support and this provides a constraint on what any individual or group may do. Constraint here is the direct opposite of the constraint required for control in closed and contained situations – difference, not uniformity. The result is a self-organising form of control, where the feedback loops operate in both positive and negative modes, but they do so within boundaries. In self-organising forms of control we do not restrict the feedback loops to negative operation; instead we control through intervening in the boundaries around the unstable operation of the feedback loops.

Control through planning/monitoring and through ideology is possible only in closed and contained situations. Only if the long term for an organisation is a repetition of its past can it control using strategic plans and milestones. In open-ended situations, self-organising forms of control are the only possibility and they are, in all important respects, the direct opposite of those forms of control that must be applied in closed and contained situations. It is hardly surprising, then, that these different forms of control produce different kinds of pattern in actions, different kinds of coherence. Competently operated negative feedback produces the regular, repetitive patterns of equilibrium. Controlled behaviour, however, could also take the form of irregular patterns and it will do so when self-organising forms of control are applied in open-ended situations. For example, the weather system produces controlled behaviour, but weather patterns are irregular.

The central conclusion reached in this chapter is this. Today's mainstream approach to strategy makes a number of rather specific assumptions, that are rarely questioned, about the system dynamics of an organisation. Those assumptions are not always applicable, making it useful to draw a distinction between ordinary problem-solving management on the one hand and extraordinary frame-breaking management on the other. In the former case, the body of knowledge on conventional strategic management can be applied in a relatively simple manner to derive prescriptions on how to manage, because the unquestioned assumptions on which it is based are valid. The body of strategy content knowledge constitutes the exemplars that encapsulate the current paradigm and this is what we need to see the world with in normal conditions. But in the latter case, extraordinary management, that existing body of knowledge is of far more limited use for reasons that have to do with the dynamics of organisational development. That use is confined to provoking anomaly and contradiction and to providing material for the development of analogous reasoning.

The distinction we have made in this and the last chapter between different modes of decision-making and different forms of control has led us to the notions of ordinary and extraordinary management. In the next two chapters we look at how managers practise these two different forms of management at the same time; that is, at the institutional and behavioural frameworks required to practise the different decision-making modes and forms of control that we have identified.

Further reading

Hofstede (1981) provides further detail on the classification of control forms. Goold & Quinn (1990) provide the case for strategic planning and milestone forms of control and Peters & Waterman (1982) provide a classic account of ideological forms of control. Stacey (1991) provides further discussion on self-organising forms of control.

10

What managers do when they practise ordinary management

Taking up roles in the formal hierarchy

10.1 Introduction

Throughout, this book has been at pains to demonstrate the limitations of today's received wisdom on strategic management. It has argued that when we focus on the dynamics, that is the patterns of behaviour generated by the nonlinear feedback loops that go to make up an organisation, we are constantly compelled to think in terms of very different types of change patterns, some regular with predictable outcomes, others irregular with unknowable outcomes. And when we do that we can see quite clearly that the received wisdom is relevant to situations of regularity and predictability only. The really interesting and exciting tasks of management, however, are those that involve creating and coping with the irregular, the exceptional, the ambiguous, the contradictory, the conflicting and the uncertain. Those tasks can be accomplished only through self-organising political and learning activities, an understanding of which falls largely outside the received wisdom.

Note, however, that today's received wisdom has nowhere been rejected as totally useless: rather, the concern has been with identifying when it is applicable and when it is not. In the last chapter, we reached the conclusion that it is applicable to a special case, namely the task of ordinary management. While this ordinary management may be less interesting and exciting than the creative and innovative process of extraordinary management, it is no less important. To reiterate, no organisation can carry out its day-to-day tasks effectively, no organisation can continue to build on and take advantage of its existing strengths, unless it practises ordinary management with a high degree of skill. Having taken up so much space in previous chapters identifying the failings and imperfections of the received wisdom, it is now time to redress the balance and that is the purpose of this chapter.

In Chapter 8 we have already identified the decision-making processes that are required for ordinary management. There they appeared under the heading: models of decision making that apply only in conditions close to certainty. You will recall that approximations to technical rationality, bounded rationality, trial-and-error experimentation to achieve a known goal, logical incrementalism, bureaucracy and dominant coalitions were all discussed as modes appropriate in conditions close to certainty. Then in Chapter 9 we discussed the forms of control that must be practised in ordinary management: planning and monitoring, and ideological conformity. But so far little has been said about the institutional and behavioural frameworks through which the processes of decision-making and control are applied; that is, the reporting structures, the formal groups, the information and communication systems, and the belief systems of an organisation. This chapter is concerned with such matters – with the instrument managers use to apply the decision-making and control processes of ordinary management, so vital to the orderly conduct of the existing business.

The basis of ordinary management is always some given paradigm that sets the agenda for the ordinary conduct of the organisation's activities. And the current paradigm of an organisation is embodied in its bureaucracy – the bureaucracy reflects and exists to enact and sustain that current paradigm.

■ Key concept 10.1
BUREAUCRACY

A bureaucracy consists of a set of offices or functions arranged in a hierarchy, that is ascending levels of office-holders where authority increases with upward movement. The office-holders are bound by strict rules that establish the extent of their authority and responsibility. People in a bureaucracy do not owe allegiance to other people, but only to the impersonal duties of the office they occupy. In a bureaucracy, people take up roles under a contract; they are appointed and their functions are carefully specified. Promotion is based on qualifications and there is an established career structure. The term 'bureaucracy' is usually used nowadays in a pejorative sense to mean an overburdensome administrative machine. The term is not used in that sense in this book, but in the sense of a clear reporting structure, accompanied by clear rules, procedures and plans.

When managers act in the ordinary mode they administer the bureaucracy and they bolster it by developing and reinforcing supportive ideologies. In more specific terms:

- They take up roles in formal hierarchies, designed and installed by top managers, that determine status, authority and responsibility for task performance.
- They process information, and they measure and monitor task performance, using the Management Information and Control Systems (MICS) and related reward systems of the organisation. The thought processes required are step-by-step analytical ones.
- They articulate the paradigm. Sometimes managers use mission statements and visions to make explicit some elements of the organisational philosophy that

guides the existing business. At other times they express the paradigm in symbols, myths, stories and rituals.

- They use top-down persuasion, exhortation and propaganda to reinforce the paradigm, directing attention to the rules of the competitive game, the timeless values governing behaviour, and other elements of the paradigm judged to be particularly important at any one time. As part of this process they tell stories and develop myths, manifestations of the culture that protect the paradigm, and recruit newcomers as adherents.

In the sections that follow we will consider each of these principal tasks of ordinary management. The first aspect to be discussed is that of the roles managers take up when they work in ordinary management, hierarchical task groups. Before we come to the ordinary management role itself, however, it may be helpful to some readers to go through a brief summary of the main types of hierarchical reporting structure and the dialectical way in which they evolve. Other readers, however, may wish to proceed directly to Section 10.3 on ordinary management roles.

10.2 The dialectic of hierarchical structure

At any one time, the hierarchical reporting structure of an organisation reflects or embodies its paradigm. The hierarchy represents a particular configuration of the most fundamental of the paradoxes of organising: the paradox created by the force of division on the one hand and that of integration on the other. Structure is a particular way of coping with the tension created by the forces of decentralisation and centralisation.

As an organisation grows in size and complexity, the tension between centralisation and decentralisation increases to a point where any existing structural arrangement can no longer contain that tension. The structure then has to be altered in some way and other mechanisms, for example temporary project teams, have to be added to deal with the complexity. But they, in their turn, bring further tensions. Every structural change or additional mechanism employed to deal with the problems created by the basic paradox, also reflects that paradox. Such changes and mechanisms can therefore only ever provide temporary relief to the tension; soon some other arrangement will be required. This dialectical process is depicted in *Figure 10.1*.

Organisational structure is, therefore, a dynamic evolving phenomenon, unfolding through a dialectical process. For short time periods, however, it provides a stable framework for control.

It is usual to distinguish three different structural arrangements of the paradox of division and integration, three different reflections of typical paradigms:

- simple structure
- functional structure
- divisional structure.

Figure 10.1 The dialectic of centralisation and decentralisation

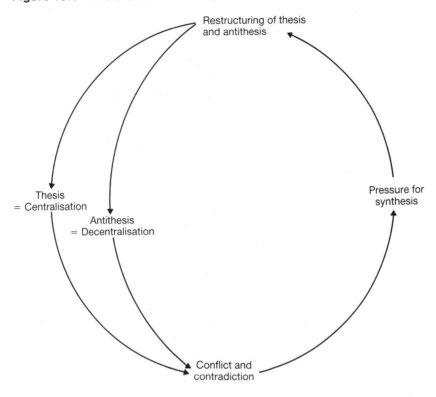

Simple structure

The simple structure resolves the paradox of division and integration by placing the emphasis on centralisation. In this structure, staff and workers report directly to a small number of managers – in most cases one person is very much 'in control'. As you can see from *Figure 10.2*, there is relatively little division of management responsibility and little formal hierarchy.

Because it relies heavily on informal personal contact, the simple structure has the flexibility required to deal with rapid change and high levels of uncertainty. As the size of the organisation expands, however, the vague, overlapping definitions of jobs,

Figure 10.2 The simple matrix

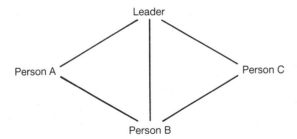

the loose reporting relationships, and the typical absence of formal controls increasingly create anomalies: for example, the flexibility makes the system good at acquiring new customers, but the absence of a bureaucracy means that it cannot retain existing ones. Growth demands the installation of more complex structural forms and more formal systems if control is to be effective; that is, more sophisticated bureaucracies are required.

Failure to recognise the size limitation of this structural form and the need it imposes for an efficient bureaucracy is perhaps the most frequent stumbling block encountered by the entrepreneurial founders of promising businesses.

Functional structure

The simple structure is typically followed by the development of a functional form. This form represents a significant shift from centralisation to decentralisation. Management is divided by primary and support tasks:

- getting the work (sales and marketing);
- carrying the work out (production, delivery);
- getting the raw materials (purchasing, stock control);
- getting, retaining and developing the labour (personnel);
- developing the products and processes (research and development, design, engineering);
- recording the transactions and arranging the finance (accounting and finance).

The integrating function is performed by a superior manager: the managing director, chief executive, or chairman, who acts as the leader of a formally appointed team of managers as shown in *Figure 10.3*.

The functional form is firmly based on specialisation and standardisation. It allows for:

- a greater injection of expertise and professionalism into the performance of each category of task in the organisation;
- more effective control in complex situations because it decomposes and localises the handling of disturbances to the business.

The functional form reaps the efficiency benefits of task division, but there are prices to be paid for these benefits and they become more evident as an organisation

Figure 10.3   The functional structure

continues to increase in size and diversity. The problems encountered in the functional form centre on:

- role duality
- functional barriers
- overlap
- interdependence
- size and diversity

These are the typical anomalies that the functional form creates and they eventually lead to contradiction and conflict, forcing a further rearrangement of the paradox of division and integration. Consider how these anomalies are typically dealt with.

Role duality, barriers, interdependence and overlap

As soon as people are divided into separately managed functional units, they are in effect being invited to take up two roles: one in relation to the function they belong to and the other in relation to the organisation as a whole. It is then inevitable that they will develop loyalties to their own particular part of the organisation, apart from, and usually stronger than, their loyalties to the organisation as a whole, so erecting barriers between one function and another. The consequence is usually conflict between functions and a tendency for their members to pursue their own functional goals. The separate functions, however, are all part of the same organisation: they are interdependent, their tasks are interconnected and quite often overlapping. If the organisation as a whole is to be effective, then coordinating devices to soften the impact of the barriers, recognise interdependence and manage overlaps are required.

Coordinating devices

There is a spectrum of coordinating devices:

- At one extreme, coordination is permanent and formally built into the functional structure itself. One example of this is the matrix structure where role duality and interdependence is explicitly and formally recognised by two lines of authority and responsibility which build overlap into the structure (see *Illustration 10.1*). While this structure does deal with overlap, it can lead to confused responsibility, high degrees of conflict, and long decision-making times. It is often accompanied by complex formal committee structures to try to iron out conflicts and monitor performance, the responsibility for which is dispersed among a number of managers.
- At the other extreme, coordination takes a flexible process form. For example, special task forces or specific project teams, which are not a permanent part of the formal hierarchy, may be set up to promote communication and cooperation across functional divides in relation to a specific project.
- In between these extremes we find forms of coordination that contain both structural and process aspects (see *Illustration 10.2*).

■ **Illustration 10.1**
THE MATRIX STRUCTURE

In the basic functional form, lines of authority and responsibility flow from and to one manager. But the team controlled by that one manager may also be central to the tasks that have been assigned to another manager and that other manager may in turn also require the services of the team under the control of a third manager. One way of dealing with these overlapping requirements is to establish a structural form with dual authority over and responsibility for those teams. This form occurs most frequently in relation to professional or scientific expertise.

For example, the research and development establishment of a major construction company may be organised into permanent sections, each with a manager, according to scientific expertise:

● aggregates section
● concrete section
● plant section
● chemicals testing.

At any one time there will also be a number of development projects, each with its own project manager. Staff will be assigned to the projects teams from their sections and they are then accountable to the project manager in respect of their duties on the project team, but accountable to their section manager in respect of professional competence. The section manager would carry out all managerial functions not directly related to the project.

Figure 10.4   The matrix structure

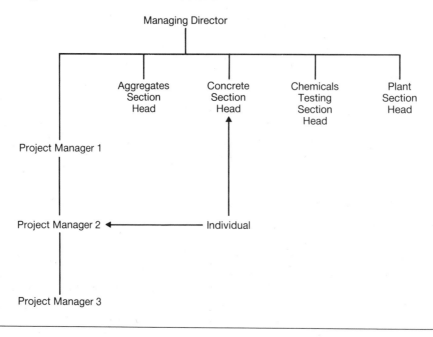

■ **Illustration 10.2**
BRAND MANAGEMENT

Brand management is a way of dealing with the considerable production facility and market outlet interdependence of different but closely related products. For example, the producer of five different brands of chocolate may use this approach. One manager is given responsibility for the development and marketing of a particular brand but has to secure production from the production function and sales of the product through a sales force that also sells the other brands. Here the brand manager is a permanent part of the formal structure; but there is no dual reporting. Effectiveness depends on the processes the manager applies to persuading and negotiating with others.

The problem of size and diversity

As the functionally structured organisation continues to grow in size without diversifying the range of its activities, the response to growing complexity may be to develop formal structures where there is even greater functional specialisation.

An essentially one-product and one-process business may therefore develop specialist engineering functions that deal with new construction and new plant, while another deals with repair and maintenance. A purchasing empire may well develop, with separate functions for different types of purchases. Separate design or development functions may develop that focus on different processes or stages of production. For example, there may be a research and development function that deals with chemical processes, while another deals with the mechanical processes relevant to the product. All of these departments may also have overlapping responsibilities for quality control and safety.

The possibilities of duplication and overlap between functions may increase dramatically as such an organisation tries to cope with the tensions of division and integration flowing from increased size and complexity. If, in addition to all this, the organisation diversifies its range of activities and the range of markets it operates in, the functional structure will be unable to stand the strain – some other structural form will have to be developed to deal with it.

Divisional structure

In the divisional structure, separate business units are established to:

● serve different market segments;
● provide different products;
● focus on different geographic areas;
● utilise different production processes.

We saw that the move from a simple to a functional organisation represented a move towards the decentralised extreme of the structure spectrum. The move from a functional to a divisionalised form represents a further movement towards that decentralised end of the spectrum. The organisation becomes a collection of separate, decentralised units each of which may then be functionally organised.

Figure 10.5 The divisional structure

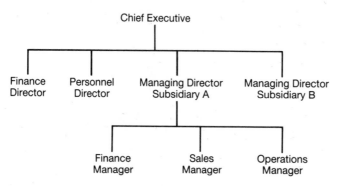

The further division of the management task in this way immediately raises the need for other integrative mechanisms. The first of these is provided by the establishment of a corporate head office with its own management structure headed by a chief executive.

It does not take long, however, before the anomalies of this divisional structure become apparent. As the number of business units increases, the span of control of the corporate chief executive becomes too great. The response is usually to group business units in some way under a divisional director. These divisions may develop their own management structures with their own divisional functions. In this way, the number of levels in the hierarchy proliferates, creating other centres of power and increasing coordination problems. Tensions grow between the top corporate level, the divisional barons, and the business unit managers. Conflicts on how to define roles, measure performance, allocate costs and capital all increase.

The tensions create three problems:

● Duplication of functional specialisms: corporate, division, and business unit levels tend to develop their own separate functions.
● Role duality, business unit barriers, interdependence and overlap: business units are profit-responsible but they should meet the requirements other units have of them in the interests of the whole corporation.
● Communication and flows of knowledge: knowledge held in one part of the organisation may be required for effective decisions in another part.

Duplication

Each unit in a divisionalised structure might have all of its own functional specialisms or some of them could be located at the corporate or divisional levels and shared by a number of units.

One solution: centralised corporate services

The most common centralised services are the finance and accounting functions, personnel, marketing, purchasing, research and development. The benefits of such centralisation are reduced costs, greater buying power, more marketing strength, better communication, and greater synergy between units. Furthermore, control problems may be eased by these shared services and by the usually large corporate staff.

However, there are also important disadvantages arising from this emphasis on centralisation:

- The autonomy of the business units is restricted and this could lead to inappropriate decisions.
- There is a powerful tendency for the corporate level staff to grow in size, soon offsetting any cost benefits from shared services.
- The number of management layers in the hierarchy tends to expand, increasingly divorcing those at the sharp end of the business from those at the top.
- Centralised staff functions seek to reinforce their own power by establishing vast numbers of rules and procedures. More layers of managers with closely defined and specialised responsibilities, imposing rules and procedures on those at the sharp end of the organisation's activities, slow down responses. The consequence is much slower reaction times and much reduced ability to innovate and to anticipate change.
- Motivation of those at the sharp end is also a casualty of highly centralised structures.

The opposite solution: self-contained business units

The opposite way of dealing with the problem of duplication is to ignore it: that is, to adopt a highly decentralised structure where each business unit is as self-contained as possible with all its own specialist functions.

The benefits of self-contained business units are:

- faster reaction times;
- more innovation;
- greater degree of anticipation of change;
- higher motivation of those at the sharp end of the organisation.

But there are also costs:

- in money terms, arising from the duplication of services in many business units;
- in the loss of synergy between different business units;
- in the increasing difficulties of communication and control of the day-to-day activities;
- in the increased need for formal systems of communication and control.

The holding company

The extreme form of an organisation consisting of independent business units is the holding company. This operates very much as a shareholder and banker. The head office is very small and considerable autonomy is granted to the business units: they are required only to make an adequate return on the capital invested and to seek authority for all capital expenditure. But these 'only' requirements place heavy constraints upon the business units, greatly reducing their scope for strategic manoeuvre. Control is exerted by regularly monitoring financial performance and in the event of poor performance the holding company will close or sell the unit. Holding companies generally grow by acquisition and are not noted for their organic growth. See *Illustration 10.3*.

Most companies tend to follow cycles of shifting first towards the centralised end of the spectrum and then back again towards the decentralised end. The tension between the requirements of division and integration in the organisation leads to continual change.

■ **Illustration 10.3**
HANSON TRUST PLC

Hanson Trust PLC is an acquisitive conglomerate that concentrates on acquiring businesses in basic industries with a clearly defined future. As it is acquired, each business is retained as a separate organisation. The managers of each business are set clear financial objectives and their performance is regularly monitored against these objectives. If they exceed target they are handsomely rewarded and, if they do not, they seek employment elsewhere. Capital investment is tightly controlled, with any unbudgeted item above a few hundred pounds requiring the approval of the Chairman. The corporate head office is very small, consisting of an accounts department to monitor performance against budget and a small acquisitions staff. Each business unit conducts its own affairs and is free to compete with other sister subsidiaries – there is no attempt to manage overlaps between businesses. This kind of company therefore operates very much like a group of separate businesses with only their shareholders in common.

10.3 Taking up a role in the hierarchy

The hierarchy in effect establishes formal interconnections between managers and in so doing sets up formal groupings in which they will be required to work. The key point about these formal groups is that they have clear tasks defined by the policies and rules of the bureaucracy to do with the day-to-day activities of an organisation and with reinforcing its existing strategic direction. When managers practise ordinary management they take up roles in these formal groups. In the next chapter we will contrast these formal roles with the informal roles that managers take up. But in this section we will consider two key questions relating to ordinary management roles:

● What is the nature of leadership in ordinary management task groups?
● What is the relevance of the group, as opposed to the individual manager, in ordinary management?

The nature of leadership in formal management groups

In an ordinary management context, the primary focus is on the leader as one who:

- translates the directives of those higher up in the hierarchy into the goals and tasks of the group;
- monitors the performance of the task in terms of goal achievement;
- ensures that a cohesive team is built and motivated to perform the task;
- supplies any skills or efforts that are missing in the team;
- articulates purpose and culture, so reducing the uncertainty that team members face.

When leadership is defined in these terms, the concern is with the qualities leaders must possess and the styles they must employ in order to fulfil these functions effectively and efficiently. Those who have put forward explanations on the nature of leadership have differed from each other over whether the effective leader is one who focuses on the task, or one who focuses on relationships with and between people. A related area of concern is whether the effective leader is one who is autocratic, or one who delegates, consults, and invites full participation. The question is which style of leadership motivates people more and thus gets the task done better. Consider three prominent theories.

Fiedler's (1967) Leader-Match Theory

Here managers are placed on a spectrum running from an orientation to the task at one end to an orientation to relationships at the other. Which of these orientations is more effective is said to depend upon the nature of the task, the attitudes of the subordinates, and the power of the leader. Where the task is clearly structured, and the leader has clear hierarchical authority and subordinates are supportive and willing to accept authority, then the task orientation works best. When none of these conditions is present, the task orientation still works best. The reason for this, perhaps surprising, result is that leaders with a relationship orientation would refrain from pressurising people in very unclear situations and thus not get the task done. However, where there is an in-between situation, then relationship-oriented leaders come into their own. The prescription for potential leaders is to discover their orientation and find a situation that fits.

Vroom and Yetton's (1973) Contingency Theory

This theory presents a spectrum of leadership styles from the highly autocratic at one end to the participative at the other. It is claimed that analysis of the problem situation determines which point on this spectrum provides the most effective leadership style for that situation. So, if there is likely to be a best rational solution, if there is sufficient information to reach the solution, if the problem is structured, if acceptance by subordinates is not all that crucial, and anyway they will accept it, then an autocratic style will yield the best results. But if there is unlikely to be a best rational solution, there is insufficient information, the problem is not structured, subordinate acceptance is crucial, goals are shared, but conflict is still likely, then the best style is a highly participative one. In between, various degrees of autocracy and participation would be called for.

Hersey and Blanchard's Situation Theory (1988)

Here, too, style and leader behaviour are to be adapted to the situation and to follower needs if they are to be effective. Task focus and relationship focus are related, however, and instead of being presented as alternatives, four leadership styles are distinguished. Leaders may adopt a 'selling' style, in which they focus heavily on both the task and relationships; or they may use a 'delegation' style, where they put a low emphasis on both task and relationships; or they may emphasise the task heavily and underplay relationships, in which case their style is 'telling'. Finally, they may focus heavily on relationships and underplay the task, in which case their style is 'participating'. The appropriate style depends upon how mature the group is. If maturity is low, then telling is the right style. As the group matures, the leader should move to selling and then to participating and finally to delegating.

Again you can see the paradoxical nature of leadership: on the one hand the leader needs to focus on the task, while on the other the need is to focus on the people, and these needs must both be met even though they can quite easily be contradictory.

■ **Key concept 10.2**
ROLES AND LEADERSHIP IN FORMAL GROUPS

Ordinary management is practised in formal groups that require the leader to arrive at the group with particular skills developed beforehand. The required personality, skills and styles (or, as they are sometimes called, competences) can be identified in advance since they depend upon the situation and this is specified by the bureaucracy. Leadership is about motivating people and the concern is with the appropriate role of the leader in securing efficient performance of known tasks.

As we shall see in Chapter 11, the role of the leader in extraordinary management situations is completely different.

The relevance of the group to ordinary management

Ordinary management is practised through a formal hierarchy, a formal set of legitimate representative bodies, and a formal administrative bureaucracy. These are all structures that formalise the division and allocation of tasks to individuals and groups of people on the one hand, and the legitimation, integration and control of those tasks through leaders and representative groups on the other. Individuals have roles as leaders and followers, they have roles in groups. But what, if any, distinctive part does the group have to play in how managers exercise their ordinary management role? We will now examine some answers to this question and in

Chapter 11 we will see how very different the role of the group is in extraordinary management.

Groups

A group is any number of people who interact with each other, are psychologically aware of each other, and perceive themselves to be a group. The groups of immediate relevance to ordinary management are the formal groups in an organisation. These may be permanent, for example the sales department; or they may be temporary as is the case when special task forces or multidisciplinary teams are appointed to deal with a particular task. Whether they are temporary or permanent, formal groups have clear goals and tasks; it is the purpose of formal groups to find solutions to structured problems. They usually have appointed leaders – leaders and managers have power given to them. However, they may also be autonomous, self-managing or democratic work groups that elect their own leader and design their own approach to a given structured task. Note that procedures are laid down in advance on how leaders are to be appointed and roles determined. This has sometimes been done to improve motivation and thus efficiency (Lindblom & Norstedt, 1975). However, even self-managing groups still have clear structures, tasks, objectives and procedures and so are formal groups.

Within, alongside and across the formal groups, there is a strong tendency for informal groups to develop. These may be horizontal cliques amongst colleagues on the same hierarchical level, vertical cliques that include people from different hierarchical levels, or random cliques. Informal groups develop primarily because of proximity (Festinger, Schachter & Back, 1950): through the contacts people make with each other given their physical location in relation to each other, the nature of their work and the time pressures they are under. From an ordinary management perspective, the immediate concern about these informal groups is whether they will support or counter the operation of formal groups. The concern is with motivating people to cohere into functional teams that will focus on clearly defined tasks, not dissipate energies in destructive informal groups.

From an ordinary management perspective, we are primarily concerned with the authority, responsibility and performance of individual managers in carrying out their pre-assigned tasks. From this perspective, our interest in groups relates to the circumstances in which groups may be more effective than individuals. Groups can:

- accomplish complex interdependent tasks beyond the ability of individuals working alone;
- solve complex problems that require many inputs;
- provide a means of coordinating activities;
- facilitate implementation through generating participation and commitment;
- generate new ideas and creative solutions within the paradigm;
- provide the opportunity of social interaction that improves morale and motivation.

Groups, both formal and informal, meet human needs for affiliation and self-esteem. They provide individuals with a sense of security, they reduce anxiety and the sense of powerlessness, and they provide opportunities for individuals to test reality through discussion with others. But they also create a vehicle for individuals to pursue their own self-interested tasks and problem-solving activities and so can be the enemies of effective ordinary management.

From an ordinary management perspective, the central concern in relation to groups is the same as that found in mainstream textbooks on organisational behaviour – motivating people to perform known tasks efficiently. This requires that people should behave in a cohesive manner and develop not counter-productive but supportive informal groups. Mainstream textbooks identify a number of factors that determine how groups will behave, how effective and efficient they will be. In the approach being adopted in this book, mainstream models are useful in understanding the ordinary management task, but restrictive when it comes to understanding the extraordinary management task to be explored in the next chapter. The factors that determine how groups behave in the ordinary management context where they have reasonably clear tasks and well-defined power structures are:

- *Environmental factors.* The nature of the work, the physical location of people and the time pressures they are under determine whether and what kinds of informal groups develop to support the formal groups. Key to the operation of the formal and their informal shadows is the managerial climate. This determines whether the logically designed formal groups can satisfy emotional needs or whether there will be strong pressures to develop alternatives. The conclusion generally reached is that groups designed on purely rational task-centred factors will lead to the emergence of anti-management informal groups. When, however, groups are designed according to social criteria, the result is cohesive teams. But social groups may not be all that logically related to the task, so it is generally thought best if groups are designed on self-actualising criteria. In this way individual motivational factors can be integrated with social factors to lead to cohesive functional teams that are motivated to deal with the task. Thus informal groups in themselves are not seen as relevant to ordinary management; they need to be pre-empted from emerging by the design of formal groups in such a way that those formal groups meet social and psychological needs.
- *Membership factors.* How a group performs will depend upon the personalities of its members, their personal background, status, who they represent and so on. Cohesion is brought about by putting together people with common experience or by creating opportunities for them to develop that common experience.
- *Dynamic factors.* The extent to which members of the group are socialised and sensitive to the group process and the extent to which they have been trained in these.

Mainstream textbooks are concerned with how it is appropriate to use and not to use groups. When it comes to problem solving, groups will generally be better at it than individuals when the problem has multiple parts requiring varied skills and knowledge. The principal reason usually given for using groups to solve problems, however, is that it makes it more likely that they will then implement the solution. Drawbacks are that groups tend to take riskier decisions than individuals (Stoner, 1968; Davis, Laughlin, & Komorita, 1976) because responsibility is diluted or because a group may amplify the positive cultural value of taking risks. Another drawback is 'group think' (Schachter, 1958). Members with deviant views are pressurised to conform if they are to retain membership. Informal groups have positive aspects too:

they relieve the frustration provoked by working in a bureaucracy and they augment the functioning of the bureaucracy when the rules are not appropriate.

As we shall see in Chapter 11, the extraordinary management perspective on groups is very different to this.

Having talked about the role that managers take up when they practise ordinary management, we now turn to what managers do within an ordinary role. In essence, they process information to do with problems that have already been framed and opportunities that have already been identified. In short, they manage by objectives and operate the Management Information and Control System. The next section sets out briefly what is meant by Management Information and Control System. Those familiar with the concept will want to proceed directly to the section after that.

10.4 Processing information and controlling through management information and control systems (MICS)

An efficient MICS (see *Key Concept 10.3*) is built on a painstaking analysis of the precise detail of each step required to perform every task at all levels in the organisation. Standards of performance are established for each task at every level and the information required for the performance of each task and the monitoring of that performance are identified. In addition, the chain of authority and responsibility for carrying out every task and for dealing with variations in performance are clearly set out.

■ **Key concept 10.3**
MANAGEMENT INFORMATION AND CONTROL SYSTEMS (MICS)

The MICS is a set of rules and regulations, procedures and codified traditions that have been built up through past experience and legitimised by those in the relevant hierarchical positions. The primary purpose of the MICS is the setting of objectives and standards for role-holders in the hierarchy and the processing of information on performance compared to standards and objectives, so that responsibility for corrective action can be identified and action taken.

To see what this means in practical terms, consider the formal procedures typically used to control the purchasing of supplies and equipment. This is shown in *Figure 10.6*.

The starting point in that figure is the originator of a purchase: someone in the organisation requires some raw material or some piece of equipment. The originator has to follow a formal procedure to obtain the required item. In the case of raw materials, the originator fills out a requisition form and sends it to Stores. A stock sheet is used to record the raw material supplied and the remaining inventory. If inventories of that item fall below a prearranged level, a preprogrammed response is triggered and a requisition is sent to the Buyer. The procedure the Buyer is to follow is clearly laid out. There is a separate procedure, specifying levels of authorisation, for the procurement of equipment. The processes used here are those of analysis,

Figure 10.6   A purchasing control system

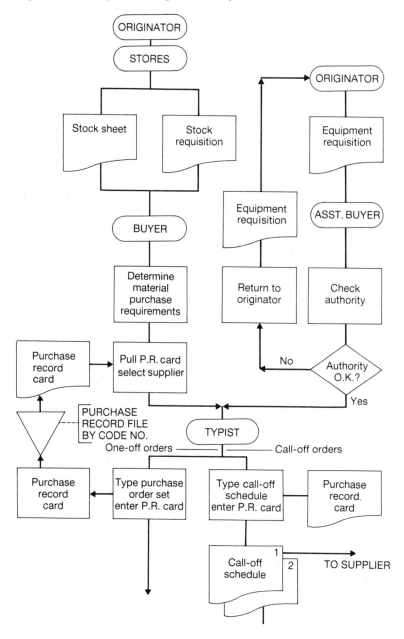

quantification, formal rules, procedures and communication. The intervention required of the higher levels in the hierarchy is minimal.

The intention is to get an organisation working like a machine. But the system will never work as smoothly as planned, because some open-ended change is present in all time frames, including the very short term. More intuitive intervention will occasionally be required to satisfy an unforeseen and urgent demand for some item. Informal rules will replace the formal, and originators will persuade and negotiate directly with the Buyer to secure what they need. In other words, political activity will be deployed to handle change even in the short term – but this is the exception.

This description of a requisition procedure is, of course, an illustration of only one small part of the formal procedures employed by well-run organisations of any size. *Figure 10.7* takes a step higher up the hierarchy and looks at the activities which precede a requisition. Quarterly, weekly and daily despatch schedules for the output of some part of the organisation are prepared. These form the basis for production schedules and thus requisitions for materials and equipment. Formal procedures lay down the reports to be prepared on the actual outcomes of despatch and production and the Daily Review Meetings to be held to compare outcomes against plan. Formal

Figure 10.7 The daily review meeting

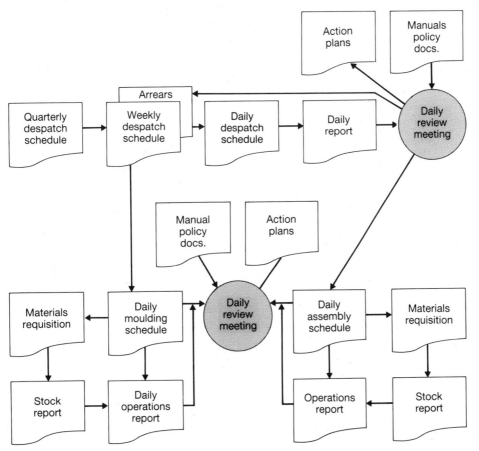

rules in policy manuals set out predetermined responses to variances. Formal action plans are prepared and implemented.

The dominant processes at review meetings are likely to be the instructing ones; effective action is usually the outcome of one-to-one contact between superiors in the hierarchy and those reporting to them, or to whom they report. But intuitive and informal negotiating processes are all used when unforeseen events occur.

A further step up the hierarchy reveals what happens to the Daily Reviews: there is a formal pattern according to which Daily Review Meetings lead to Weekly Reports, considered at Weekly Review Meetings by the next level up in the management

Figure 10.8 Weekly and monthly review meetings

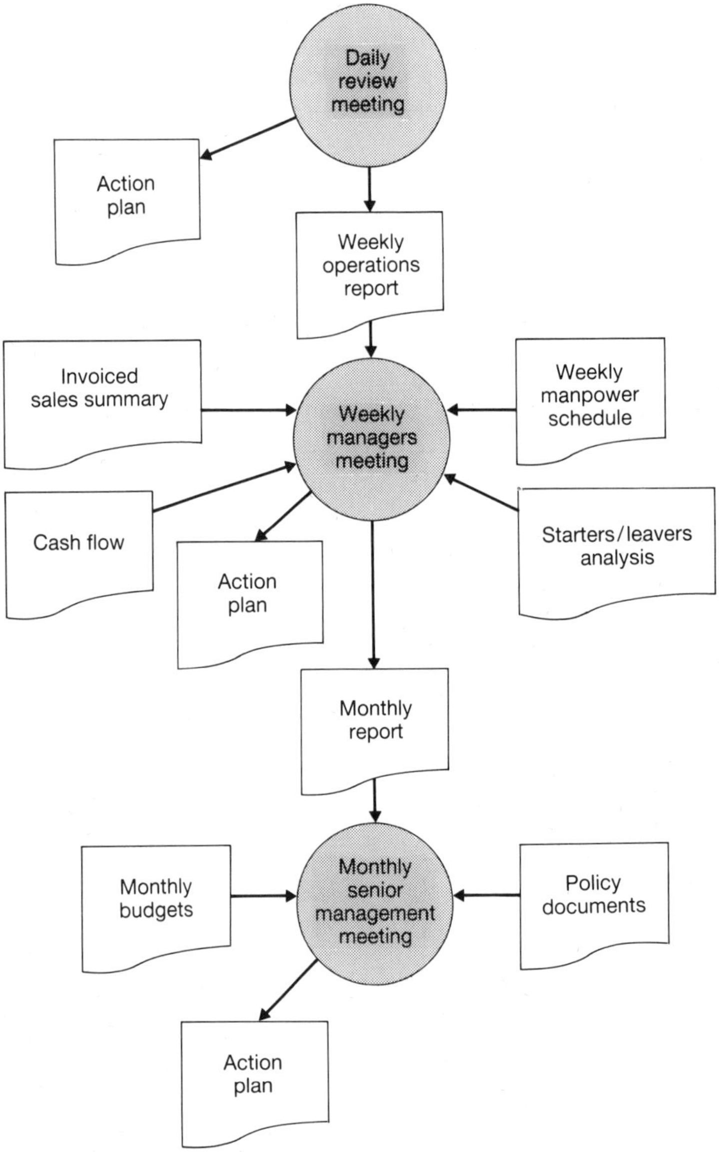

hierarchy. This in turn is fed into Monthly Review Meetings at higher management levels. Planning, monitoring and corrective action is initiated or legitimised at these meetings. (See *Figure 10.8.*)

Yet a further step up the hierarchy reveals how the formal procedures require each subsidiary to report its activities and actions by means of quarterly reports and budgets to the corporate level. Once again there are formal meetings, quantified budgets, and reports and formal policy documents which to some extent try to set predetermined responses to foreseeable changes. The process culminates in the annual meetings where budgets are set and then formally fed back down through the organisation. This is depicted in *Figure 10.9.*

Figure 10.9 Annual planning

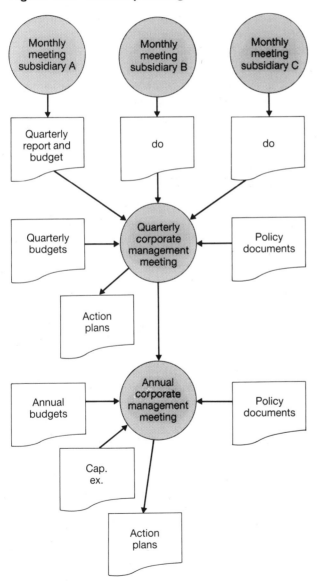

Note how an efficient bureaucracy is built upon simple hierarchies of managers in which roles are clearly defined. The planning and monitoring functions of the efficient bureaucracy involve the setting of hierarchies of objectives in relation to controlling and developing the existing business and the allocation of authority and responsibility for achieving them. Power in a bureaucracy is clearly derived from the rules, regulations and procedures of the organisation. The focus is therefore on administrative rather than political activity. Communication is institutionalised, rather than informal and spontaneous. Learning is of a simple, single-loop kind, concerned with discovering the outcomes of actions.

Note how MICSs focus on the formal, analytical processes. Leadership takes an instructing, directing form. Power takes the form of authority and the group dynamic is one of compliance and dependence. Discovering, choosing and acting are precisely defined as monitoring, planning and corrective action. Modern information technology is applied. MICSs are about adapting the organisation to its environment to achieve something approaching short-term equilibrium. If we focus simply on ordinary management it is a reasonable simplification to think in terms of stable equilibrium.

The MICS is one of the main forces for stability in an organisation. In one sense it makes it more possible for people in an organisation to handle uncertainty because it provides a secure boundary. At the same time it blocks change because it reinforces the repetition of existing behaviour patterns.

Note how the MICS separates out changes that have a high degree of regularity. It focuses on the repetitive and seeks to automate responses to that regularity.

Note also that the communication arenas, all the meetings and documents shown in *Figures 10.9* to *10.10*, are predetermined. They have already been set up in advance of the change; they are serially arranged with information flowing along prearranged channels from one arena to another. Those who are to participate in the arenas (meeting memberships, document circulation lists) are well defined and stable in the sense that the same group of people always participate.

The functions that each arena is to perform are quite clear. There are restricted membership meetings right at the top of the hierarchy that perform mainly symbolic functions (for example, approving budgets and plans, thus giving them legitimacy). Other meetings may perform administrative functions. Many one-to-one meetings perform choice or decision functions from which action flows. Many of the meetings and documents perform rationalisation functions of explaining what has already happened (for example, reviewing performance against budget). The point to note here is the importance of symbolic, legitimising, administrative, explanation of the past functions in these arenas. Making decisions is certainly not the only and may not even be the most important function of the meetings required for the MICS to operate.

At this point it may be interesting to reflect upon what would happen if we tried to build flexibility into the kinds of system just described: for example, if we were to follow the advice to avoid clear job descriptions and tear up the rule books (Peters, 1988). Clearly, the bureaucracy could not function and we might find that we have to sacrifice the benefits of orderly day-to-day conduct of the business that it brings. This matter will be discussed in Chapter 11 in Section 11.10.

10.5 Articulating the paradigm: stating the mission

For effective ordinary management people need to be motivated to fill roles in a stable hierarchy, protect the culture, and operate the systems to achieve the objectives set by the paradigm. This means that it is necessary to focus upon the motivators that drive people to take part in group life, to conform and share the same paradigm.

Management theories of motivation

There are a number of different theories of motivation that have been put forward in the management literature on how to secure consensus, cooperation and commitment:

Hertzberg's (1966) extrinsic and intrinsic motivators

Hertzberg pointed out that people are motivated to work in cooperation with others by both extrinsic motivators such as monetary rewards and intrinsic motivators such as recognition for achievement, achievement itself, responsibility, growth and advancement. Intrinsic motivation is the more powerful of the motivators and is increased when jobs are enriched, that is when jobs are brought up to the skill levels of those performing them.

Maslow's hierarchy of needs (1954)

Maslow distinguished between: basic physiological needs, such as food and shelter; intermediate social needs, such as safety and esteem; and higher self-actualisation needs, such as self-fulfilment. Maslow held that when the conditions are created in which people can satisfy their self-actualisation needs, those people are then powerfully motivated to strive for the good of the organisation.

Schein (1988) and Etzioni's (1961) framework for categorising motivation

These writers distinguished three categories of relationship between the individual and the organisation. The relationship may be coercive, in which case the individual will do only the bare minimum required to escape punishment. The relationship may be a utilitarian one where the individual does only enough to earn the required level of reward. Thirdly, the relationship may take a normative form where individuals value what they are doing for its own sake, because they believe in it and identify with it. In other words, the individual's ideology coincides with the organisation's ideology. This provides the strongest motivator of all for the individual to work for the good of the organisation.

Peters & Waterman (1982): the power of shared ideology as a driver of behaviour

They particularly emphasised the emotional content of motivation. They described successful organisations as ones in which people are driven by a sense of excitement and where they have strong feelings of belonging to the organisation.

Pascale & Athos (1981): the importance of organisational culture as a motivator

Their stress on organisational culture resulted from a study into Japanese management. They recognised that people yearn for meaning in their lives and transcendence over mundane things. Cultures that provide this meaning create powerfully motivated employees and managers.

What all these studies point to is this. An organisation succeeds when its people are emotionally engaged in some way, when they believe in what their group and their organisation is doing, when the contribution they make to this organisational activity brings psychological satisfaction of some kind, something more than simple basic rewards. People believe and are emotionally engaged when their organisation has a mission or set of values and when their own personal values match those of the organisation. Organisational missions develop because people search for meaning and purpose and this search includes their work lives (Campbell & Tawady, 1990). To win commitment and loyalty and to secure consensus around performing the tasks of ordinary management it becomes necessary to promote a sense of mission. And this is the same thing as the articulation, preaching and propagation of the organisational paradigm itself.

10.6 Reinforcing the paradigm: propagating the culture

The development of a sense of mission is a central leadership task in the ordinary management of an organisation. It is a vitally important way of gaining commitment to, loyalty for, and consensus around, the nature and purpose of the existing business. An organisation with a sense of mission captures the emotional support of its people, even if only temporarily. In the rest of this section we will first review what a sense of mission means, how it comes about, and how it might be managed.

A sense of mission

A sense of mission is more than a definition of the business, that is the area that an organisation is to operate in. A sense of mission is also to be distinguished from the ideas behind the word 'vision' or 'strategic intent'. The word 'vision' is usually taken to mean a picture of a future state for an organisation, a mental image of a possible and desirable future that is realistic, credible and attractive. The sense in which we are going to use the term mission here differs in that it refers not to the future but to the present. A mission is a way of behaving. Mission is concerned with the way an organisation is managed today, with its purpose or reason for being. Strategic intent is a desired leadership position. It too, therefore, is a desired future state, a goal to do with winning. Mission is to do with here-and-now purpose, the culture, the business philosophy, the paradigm itself.

■ **Key concept 10.4**
A SENSE OF MISSION

Campbell & Tawady provide a useful definition of a sense of mission (1990). A sense of mission is an emotional response to questions to do with what people are doing, why they are doing them, what they are proud of, what they are enthusiastic about, what they believe in.

The Ashridge mission model sees a mission as consisting of four components, shown in *Figure 10.10*.

1 An inspirational definition of what the organisation is there for. For some companies the purpose is to make money for shareholders. For example, this is quite clearly the prime purpose of Hanson PLC, a purpose frequently enunciated by Lord Hanson and one which quite clearly drives the behaviour of Hanson executives. Other companies have the purpose of satisfying all their stakeholders: shareholders, employees, customers, suppliers and the community. Other companies seek to fulfil a purpose bigger than satisfying stakeholders. For example Steve Job's purpose for

Figure 10.10   The Ashridge mission model
Source: A. Campbell & K. Tawady (1990), *Mission and Business Philosophy: Winning Employee Commitment*, Oxford: Heinemann

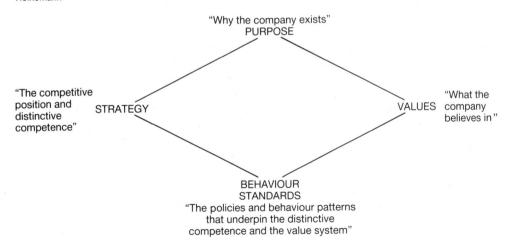

Apple was to bring computing power to the masses. The purpose of Marks and Spencer has been expressed as that of raising standards for the working man. At the Body Shop the purpose is to sell products that do not hurt animals.

2 The organisation's strategy. This is the commercial logic of the business. It defines the area in which the organisation is to operate, the rationale for its operation, the source of competitive advantage it is going to tap, the distinctive competence it is going to provide, the special position it is going to occupy. So one part of the Marks and Spencer business is food retailing in the UK where it seeks to secure a position as the best provider of high-quality food. Competitive advantage comes from dedication to quality.

3 The policies and behavioural standards, defining how managers and employees should behave. These are part of the organisation's way of doing business. For example, one of Marks and Spencer's standards is visible management – managers must be seen in the stores. Another example is given by Campbell, Devine & Young (1990, p. 30):

> British Airways provides a good example of how the company's purpose and strategy have been successfully converted into tangible standards and actions. It promotes itself as the 'world's favourite airline' and its mission statement declares as its aim 'To be the best and most successful company in the airline industry.' The strategy to achieve this is based on providing good value for money and service that overall is superior to its competitors and having friendly, professional managers who are in tune with its staff. These strategic objectives have been translated into policies such as the need for in-flight service to be at least as good as that of competing airlines on the same route, and the requirements that managers should be helpful and friendly at all times.
>
> By translating purpose and strategy into actionable policies and standards, senior managers at British Airways have dramatically changed the performance of the airline. Central to this effort was the training and behaviour change connected with the slogan 'Putting People First'.

4 The beliefs that constitute the organisation's culture and underpin its management style. People do things in organisations because there is a strategic logic and because there are moral or value based reasons for doing so.

A strong sense of mission comes about when personal and organisational values match and when the four elements are closely knitted together: when they support and reinforce each other.

> Take the clothing retailing activities of Marks and Spencer. The strategy is to produce better-quality classic products through close relationships with manufacturers. By selling these products at normal prices, Marks and Spencer create such a volume of sales that fixed overhead costs are much lower than for competitors and more than compensate for lower retail margins. Linked to this strategy are values based in quality, value for money, service and people care. Behaviour standards such as the company's human relations policies or visible management style tie the strategy and the values together. To sell goods in high volumes, service is critical. By looking after people well and being visibly interested in the operating issues of the business, managers create an atmosphere in which staff want to look after customers and help the business succeed. Finally, these elements of strategy, values and behaviour standards are linked together in an inspiring way by Marks and Spencer's purpose of raising the standards of the working man and woman.
> (Campbell, Devine & Young, 1990, p. 5.)

The sense of mission is important because it generates trust and belief in the activities in the organisation. It gives meaning to work, motivates people, and brings about consensus and loyalty. It provides the basis for making quick judgemental decisions without having to review things from basics or exchange a great deal of information. For example, a company faced with cash difficulties might dismiss an option of selling off subsidiaries on the grounds that it is there to build businesses, not trade in them. A strong mission provides the criteria for selecting and training people who will fit. It provides self-selecting criteria for conformity. People will leave if they come to realise that they do not fit. In organisations with a strong sense of mission there is conformity, cooperation, trust and consensus.

The research that Campbell carried out on missions in business led to the following conclusions:

- Creating a sense of mission is a long-term project that takes years rather than months. Missions emerge from the way people work together and those that are imposed from the top rarely take root. Top managers who wish to create a sense of mission therefore need to proceed slowly and there is little point in simply writing down intellectual statements of a mission.
- A true consensus at the top of the organisation needs to be developed before a sense of mission can be spread around the organisation.
- A sense of mission is spread through the actions of people at the top, not through their words.
- Top team visibility is essential if its views on mission are to be propagated.
- There must be continuity in the top team if a sense of mission is to be spread through the organisation.
- Any statements of mission need to be inspirational and reflect the personalities of those propounding them.
- Strategies and values should be created together.
- Managers should focus on the link between values and behaviour. Managers create meaning when they assist employees to see the link between tasks and values.

Campbell et al. maintain that a sense of mission can be managed. They draw a distinction between three approaches to managing mission:

- The first is the intellectual approach where managers go away for a weekend and write a mission statement, or they get some consulting expert to do so. The result, according to the research, is almost always a waste of time. No one believes the end product.
- The second approach is where some powerful founder of the organisation develops a business philosophy over a long period of time which takes hold in the organisation, becoming a set of timeless values that are deeply embedded in people's behaviour.
- The third approach is to focus on particular issues. These are usually rules of the organisational game as it were, values to do with service or quality or cost. People may have lost sight of the importance of these rules or values and the benefit of developing a mission lies in refocusing on them.

Campbell et al. offer this advice for developing and managing a sense of mission:

- Pick the most relevant theme in the particular circumstances, for example quality.
- Place the emphasis on action not words, for example a company-wide training programme, not a mission statement plastered on the walls.
- Focus on behaviour and stress one or two elements of behaviour such as putting people first.
- Expect it to take time.
- Build trust.

To see what this means in practice read *Illustration 10.4.*

■ Illustration 10.4
BRITISH AIRWAYS

In November 1983 British Airways introduced a training programme called 'Putting People First'. The aim was to put 12 000 customer-contact people through a two-day course to improve their customer service skills. The programme consisted of a mixture of presentations, exercises and group discussions in which staff reviewed their personal experience as customers of other service organisations. They also examined the implications for British Airways and were pressed to identify what they would do about these implications. The response to the training programme was mixed – some were sceptical, some saw it as a brainwashing exercise, some dropped out, and others were enthusiastic. But top management continued to support the programme, demonstrating their commitment to customer service. Then non-front-line staff began asking to be included and gradually the level of cynicism faded away. Staff began identifying the obstacles, confronting their managers with the fact that resources were insufficient to deliver the levels of customer care called for. The management responded to these issues and so encouraged staff to identify others.

Then in 1984, a programme for managers called 'Managing People First' was launched to change management styles. At the time, management style was perceived to be dominated by roles and procedures and the aim of the training programme was to replace this with something more open and dynamic.

Other changes were made to reinforce the training programmes. For example, quality assurance and performance-related reward systems were introduced. The services being offered by the airline were also improved, demonstrating to staff that they would get the resources required to deliver better service.

It was only once the changes in behaviour were starting to show up as better service and greater customer satisfaction that mission statements were formulated in 1986.

Source: Campbell, Devine & Young, 1990.

The Campbell & Tawady research also sounds warnings about developing a sense of mission:

- The strategies and values embodied in the mission could become inappropriate as the world changes and continued reinforcement of them would then lead to failure. Over decades the British motorcycle industry stuck to its traditional values and behaviours. This blinded them to the dangers of the competition from the Japanese and eventually led to the total destruction of the whole industry.

● Strong belief in a mission leads people in an organisation to resist change and to keep outsiders from occupying positions of any importance.

The authors advise that organisations should not try to develop a strong sense of mission in conditions of rapid change and great uncertainty, where the top team is divided or when the strategy is in a state of flux.

> There are therefore two ways to avoid the risks: avoid creating clear values and discourage employees from becoming emotionally committed to them; or formulate a well-founded mission with values that are timeless and a strategy that can be sustained for decades. The first way of avoiding the risks is appropriate when an organisation faces extreme and temporary uncertainty. In these circumstances it may be better to wait and see how events unfold before developing a mission ... in 12 months time everything is likely to become clearer, making it possible, even advisable, to develop a strategy and build a new organisation, a new mission, around it.
>
> For all other organisations, the pitfalls are best avoided by developing a timeless mission with values that need not change in fundamental ways.
>
> (Campbell & Tawady, 1990, p. 13)

In support of this conclusion the authors point to Marks and Spencer. Here the principles of good human relations and visible management have not changed, but the policy of buying British has – Marks and Spencer now has a large office in Hong Kong to help source product from the Far East.

The paradox of mission

People in an organisation find themselves pulled in two contradictory directions because of their basic psychological makeup: one force pulls each of them to conformity and consensus and the other pulls them to retain their individuality and difference. The first force leads people to develop a common set of beliefs, a paradigm or mission for their organisation. The second force leads them to pay lip service only to that common mission, or to try to undermine it, or to change it. The organisation's paradigm or mission is itself a temporary arrangement of conflicting motivational drives. The tension this leads to is the source of the dynamics of organisational behaviour, the prompt to the dialectic of continually rearranging the beliefs that constitute the paradigm, and one of the principal sources of both change and of anxiety in organisations.

Argyris (1957) stressed the conflict between the individual and the group. Argyris maintained that there is a conflict between the needs of healthy individuals and the demands of formal organisation. Chains of command and task specialisation require people to be passive and dependent, but psychologically mature individuals seek to be individual and different. The conflict leads to frustration, hostility and rivalry and a focus on a part of the organisation rather than the whole, as well as focus on short-term objectives. To adapt, individuals develop defence routines which then feed back into the organisation and reinforce the adverse effects.

One of the most common defences against anxiety is denial and repression, the result of which is a difference between what we espouse as the reasons for our behaviour and the reasons that actually govern our behaviour. There will then often be a difference between the 'espoused' mission of a group of people and the mission 'in use' (Argyris & Schön, 1978). The espoused mission will be very general so that it has more chance of commanding widespread support and not conflicting with individual desires. It will be general enough to encompass a great many of the more specific missions that will actually be driving behaviour. The more effective we are in creating a sense of mission, the more likely we are to arouse the individual motivator to be different, to explore for the new. Missions that are specific enough to drive behaviour are therefore inherently precarious. The more we articulate the timeless, the vague and the general, the more it is likely to last. But then the more it is likely to be the 'espoused' rather than the 'in use'. And the more we succeed in perpetuating a given mission in use, the more difficult we make it for the organisation to change.

Clearly, what is effective for ordinary management is the enemy of extraordinary management. In this chapter we have been concerned with the motivating forces that drive to conformity because that is what ordinary management requires. In Chapter 11, we will be concerned with the conflict that is the driving force in extraordinary management.

The conclusion we reach is that there is no quick-and-easy way to change the culture, to foster a sense of mission; it is something that emerges slowly from the way people work together. This is so because attempts to change what people believe provoke the amplifying behaviour that we discussed in Chapter 6. Top managers may, therefore, be able to encourage specific thrusts around some clearly focused issues such as those to do with customer care, but this a two-edged sword: what is helpful to ordinary management is harmful to extraordinary management.

10.7 Summary

Ordinary management enables an organisation to build on its strength, deliver competitive advantage, sustain continuity, and carry out the day-to-day activities of an organisation in an orderly and effective manner. It is essentially concerned with repetition and without it an organisation cannot succeed. The paradox, however, is that focusing predominantly on this form of management leads to success only if the organisation is supported by a stable environment or people want it to stay the same. If, however, a competitive environment requires an organisation to innovate and change, then focusing predominantly on ordinary management leads to failure. The conventional wisdom on strategic management is almost exclusively concerned with ordinary management and we can now see that it is a limited special case.

Ordinary management is therefore essentially temporary in nature, except for those institutions for which society sets a primary task of staying the same, preserving the traditional, or providing stability, security and safety. If an organisation is to innovate, then while its managers are acting within the paradigm, they must also be seeking to destroy it. In this sense it is instability that is the essence of success. The real cutting edge of strategic management is extraordinary management to which we now turn.

Further reading

Further information on organisational structures can be found in Mintzberg (1975b). For more detail on management information and control systems turn to Rowe, Mason, Dickel & Snyder (1989). Stewart (1983) provides a useful discussion on management roles and Campbell & Tawady (1990) should be referred to for a greater understanding of the mission concept.

11

What managers do when they practise extraordinary management

Taking up roles in an informal network of small groups

11.1 Introduction

In the last chapter we saw how managers practise ordinary management: they take up roles in work groups established by the hierarchical reporting structures and the rules and regulations of the bureaucracy. For the purposes of ordinary management, power is given to managers by hierarchical and bureaucratic arrangements and this applies even to self-managing teams because the roles and mode of operation of such teams are established in a formal and hierarchically legitimate way. The role of informal groups in the process of ordinary management is to relieve the frustration that bureaucratic processes provoke in people and to mould rules and regulations to everyday reality by dealing with the exceptional and the unforeseen outside the rules. The main task of ordinary management is to process information about the existing activities of an organisation, make rational decisions on that information, and take action to implement those decisions.

Ordinary management focuses on the consistent taking of concerted action in order to achieve known objectives. The objectives of ordinary management, its tasks and actions, its structures and processes, are all defined and shaped by a shared paradigm that managers articulate, preach and reinforce as part of their ordinary management task. It is the shared paradigm that enables them continually to take concerted action. Formal groups within the organisation enact the paradigm and the ordinary management task of informal groups is to cope with anomalies without undermining the paradigm.

The paradigm poses reasonably clear puzzles or problems and it is the task of ordinary management to solve them. But the very activity of solving these puzzles draws attention to anomalies and underlying paradoxes and as soon as managers respond to such anomalies and paradoxes they begin to undermine the existing paradigm, the whole orderly foundation of ordinary management. This undermining and changing of the current paradigm is the central task of extraordinary management and, if managers fail in that task, their organisation will not change.

This chapter is concerned with how managers go about the tasks of extraordinary management. It is concerned with how managers smash the existing paradigm and create a new one; that is, how they create the chaos required to destroy old patterns of perception and behaviour and how they self-organise to create new patterns of perception and behaviour. Finally, this chapter considers how managers establish an atmosphere that both contains the disorder provoked by questioning the paradigm and encourages the spontaneous self-organisation from which new order may emerge.

We have already explored, in Chapter 8, the decision-making processes appropriate for extraordinary management – the muddling through, 'garbage can', searching for error processes required in conditions far from certainty. We have also examined, in Chapter 9, the form of control employed in the course of extraordinary management – the self-organising control provided by differences in opinion when people learn, and the differences in power when they interact politically. What we will seek to do in this chapter is to understand the institutional and behavioural frameworks in which these decision-making and control processes are exercised.

Managers carry out the tasks of extraordinary management through a shadowy informal organisation simply because the formal organisation embodies and exists to protect the paradigm, the status quo, not smash and change it. For that revolutionary task managers have to operate in informal groups in which they spontaneously self-organise. Here the organisation does not empower managers as it does for the tasks of ordinary management. Instead, managers empower themselves as they self-organise into political factions and communities of practice that learn together. The role of informal groups is no longer simply that of oiling the wheels of the formal organisation, but that of creating and coping with uncertainty and ambiguity, the tools needed to undermine the paradigm. To carry out their extraordinary tasks, managers use informal networks to work alongside, to support and to undermine the formal organisation. This chapter will explore how managers:

- Take up roles in the informal organisation. We will be concerned with the parts that managers play in loose networks of informal contacts established in a self-organising manner, where membership is based on the contribution each person is perceived to be capable of making. These essentially political networks circumvent and undermine the centrally designed hierarchy and bureaucracy.
- Create new knowledge by interacting in the informal organisation in communities of practice. In this way managers tap each others' tacit knowledge of what is going on in the organisation and its environment. People in such groups think by analogy and are provoked by paradox, anomaly and conflict to new perspectives. In other words, managers create new knowledge when they learn together in informal groups.

- Present stretching challenges and fundamental aspirations that are ambiguous. This amounts to provoking equivocality and conflict. By creating such chaos managers destroy the existing paradigm, so changing the business philosophy. They promote counter cultures to question and destroy the existing paradigm.
- Manage the boundaries around the instability they create by promoting difference. Boundaries are set up when managers develop different perspectives and different amounts of power, because then no-one can do anything without persuading others and building and sustaining political support.
- Make periodic and partial interventions to improve learning skills, create the atmosphere conducive to spontaneous self-organisation, and manage the boundaries around instability.

Refer back to the first two paragraphs of this introduction and note how the tasks of extraordinary management require attitudes and actions that are directly opposed to those required for ordinary management: the nature of roles is different, the task is different, and yet managers have to practise both, switching all the time from one to the other. In this chapter we will explore the reasons for the development of an informal organisation; what that informal organisation is and how it operates; the functions it performs; the counter-responses it leads to; and what it achieves.

11.2 The need for an informal organisation

It has been recognised for a long time that bureaucratic control is neither rational nor efficient outside certain limited conditions and that it produces a number of negative behavioural consequences that undermine its effectiveness. The need for an informal organisation arises, then, simply because the formal bureaucracy often cannot work. There are two major reasons why a bureaucracy fails so frequently to produce what it is supposed to.

1 Adverse human reactions to bureaucracy

There is a considerable literature that identifies the adverse impact and consequent reaction of people to working in bureaucracies:

- Bureaucracies have an alienating impact on people. By definition, in a bureaucracy, people are allocated to narrowly defined roles and repetitive tasks and are thus treated as the means to some end (for example, profit). People are consequently separated from their own creativity and from social contact with their fellow human beings. This leads to feelings of powerlessness, isolation, frustration, dissatisfaction and aggression (Blauner, 1966).
- Bureaucracies tend to make people subordinate, passive, dependent, and lacking in self-awareness. Rule-regulated work limits people's behavioural repertoire, and confines them to interests that are superficial and cover short time spans. These are all the exact opposite of the characteristics of maturity and will therefore reduce motivation and efficiency (Argyris, 1957).
- Bureaucracies may lead to work that has lost its moral character and cultural

significance. People then perform according to rules they do not believe in. Without shared values to govern their work, their behaviour and the sharing of rewards, people feel that their work life has no meaning – a state of anomie. In this normless state, some will behave in ways that others regard as unacceptable. For example, the salaries that some company top executives pay themselves leads to envy and public outcries that escalate into strikes and other forms of disruption.

- Bureaucracies can deskill people, leading to trained incapacity (Merton, 1957). Merton's study, already referred to in Chapter 6, shows how exclusive reliance on bureaucratic systems develops trained incapacity so that people cannot make decisions to cope with the unforeseen.
- The operation of bureaucracies can contravene or provoke certain kinds of social behaviour and so touch off vicious circles. For example, in Chapter 6 we saw how an attempt to impose bureaucratic control can lead to unintended consequences in which people stick legalistically to the rules and are therefore less efficient; or they resist and so undermine the bureaucratic controls (Gouldner, 1964).

2 The bureaucracy's inability to handle ambiguity and uncertainty

Even if the operation of a bureaucracy does not itself provoke adverse human reactions that limit its operation, there are situations where the bureaucratic form of control cannot hope to work at all.

- Bureaucracies cannot cope with complex, unstable, unpredictable environmental and working conditions because they are inevitably too inflexible and slow to respond to change (Burns & Stalker, 1961). Rules and regulations cannot be established in advance to deal with the unforeseen. Chapters 8 and 9 were particularly concerned with this point and with the reasons why technically rational decision-making and control processes, an essential part of bureaucracy, cannot work in open-ended situations.
- Bureaucracies are filled with other functions and by their nature avoid the ambiguous. To see this consider what the functions of a bureaucracy are and on what basis people are supposed to perform those functions. The function of a bureaucracy is to divide up tasks in a predetermined way and ensure that those tasks are performed to a prearranged standard. To do this, task performance has to be regularly reported up the hierarchy and compared against standards at prescribed levels in the hierarchy. Instruction for action, or legitimation of decisions taken, has to be passed down the hierarchy. These flows of information, decisions, and instructions require a set of communication arenas (meetings, telephone calls, document circulations) to review what has just happened in the performance of current tasks, make decisions on how to respond, legitimise any deviation from the rules, policies and plans and perform symbolic functions to generate loyalty and security (for example, appearing to be in control even when events are occurring unpredictably). Who is to take part in each arena is determined by position in the hierarchy.

  The people taking part in any one arena have many tasks and so the capacity of any one arena will be limited. It will tend to fill with its obvious and primary functions of reviewing the past, legitimising decisions, and discussing symbolic actions. The higher up the hierarchy, the more this is likely to happen. Ambiguous issues with consequences that will probably not be felt for some time, that is the real strategic issues, will inevitably therefore be delayed, if they are ever accorded any attention in the first place. This will be most true of the board of directors and other formal top executive meetings. Some other type of communication arena will therefore have to deal with open-ended issues if they are to be dealt with at all and those other arenas will be the informal ones (Stacey, 1991).

People deal with these shortcomings of the bureaucratic system by colluding to operate a 'mock' bureaucracy (Gouldner, 1964) and acting instead within an informal organisation that they set up themselves (Blauner, 1964). The 'mock' bureaucracy is one in which all pay lip service to the rules but tacitly agree not to enforce them. The appearance of rationality and order is thus maintained, and any conflict that might have been generated by the application of inappropriate rules is avoided.

Since they are not actually using the bureaucracy to control and develop their organisation in these particular conditions, people have to turn to something else and that something else is the informal organisation that they spontaneously develop amongst themselves (see *Key Concept 11.1*). When they operate through the informal organisation, people are practising extraordinary management – they are undertaking activities that threaten, potentially at least, the operation of the bureaucracy and the paradigm it reflects.

■ **Key concept 11.1**
THE INFORMAL OR NETWORK ORGANISATION

Those who share similar experiences and expectations, who are affected by and take an interest in similar matters, who resent and try to offset the alienating, anomic and deskilling consequences of bureaucracy, form social groupings. People develop networks of contacts and relationships within their own department, across other departments, and even across other organisations that they then use in both social and work senses.

The groups are essentially political in nature; that is people handle conflicting interests through:

- *persuasion and negotiation;*
- *implicit bargaining of one person's contribution or interest for another's;*
- *the application of power that takes the form of influence rather than authority; that influence is derived from personal capability and the breadth of other network contacts.*

There are a number of important points to notice about this network organisation. The first is that it is self-organising in a rather obvious way (see Key Concept 7.6 *in Chapter 7). It is not established by some central, prior intention or design. Instead, it emerges from the interaction of people as they come into contact with each other and work together. It is self-organising too in the sense that the groups that result are governed by norms that emerge from the way people in those groups interact. What they do and how they do it is determined jointly by the people within the group, not by some hierarchical authority either within or outside the group. Networks, then, are not self-managing teams, but self-organising small groups of people.*

Second, those self-organising groups are not formal or legitimate in the sense that they have received any kind of seal of approval from the formal organisation.

Third, the groups that form may be fairly long-lasting social groups or they may be very-short-lived groups that come together to pursue a particular issue. The informal network organisation has a fluid, shifting aspect.

Fourth, the informal organisation, or network of political contacts, is the mechanism which people in an organisation use to deal with the highly complex, the ambiguous, the unpredictable, the inconsistent, the conflicting, the frustrating, and the alienating. They use it to satisfy social and motivational needs, as the means of operating organisational defences, as a means of dealing with conflicting demands placed on the organisation, and as the tool to promote innovation and change.

Fifth, it follows that the informal organisation is essentially destabilising. It exists, sometimes in place of the formal organisation and sometimes in competition with it, but always because the formal is defective in some way.

Sixth, the informal network organisation is the way in which the formal organisation is changed and it is so changed in the most fundamental way by altering the existing paradigm.

Another way of conceptualising the informal organisation is to think of it as a 'community of practice'; that is, a spontaneous grouping of people who carry out the same task and use their social network to learn informally from each other.

We are now going to look at the informal organisation and what it does from a number of different angles. The purpose will be to understand more fully what the informal organisation is, before we turn to the functions it performs. We are therefore going to consider the informal organisation as:

- a communication and social network
- an irrational decision-making process
- a learning community of practice
- a shifting set of self-organising small groups
- a political system.

11.3 The informal organisation: a communication and social network

When people work together they establish social relationships and customary ways of doing things – they form a social group (Stewart, 1983). Such groups will tend to develop their own aims and these may or may not coincide with those of the formal organisation. The informal group can often exert sanctions – the fear of rejection – that are stronger than those of the formal organisation. The great advantage of such groups is that they are self-disciplining and self-checking and therefore do not require superior management supervision for work to be carried out satisfactorily; indeed, their nature is such that they cannot be supervised. On the other hand, such groups could undermine and impede what superior managers want to do and they may protect the inefficient and ineffective.

The importance of social groups has been recognised for a long time; for example, in the 1930s, Chester Barnard (1938) stated that their function was the communication of intangible facts, opinions, suggestions, and suspicions that could not pass through the formal channels without giving rise to public conflict. He said that social groups made it possible for individuals to exercise influence far greater than the position they held in the hierarchy might indicate. The web of social groups was described as a hidden communication and operating structure. Thus, although four managers may all report directly to the managing director, one may be more important than the others because of close personal ties with the managing director. Another may have very little importance because the managing director in fact does not delegate any authority to that manager. What the managing director learns about the organisation will therefore come primarily from the personally closest manager. All those formally passing information will be sifting it and passing on only what they think the managing director should hear. It may well be the informal rather than the formal organisation, then, that determines actual communication flows.

The social system in multinationals

Interest in the functioning of the informal organisation has continued. For example, a study of multinational companies in the early 1980s found that they develop internal groups that allow the organisation to sense, analyse and respond to a far wider range of environmental factors than the formal organisation could (Bartlett, 1983). The web of informal groups across these companies allowed multiple perspectives to develop and it allowed greater flexibility in making decisions. The advice of the author of this study was that multinational companies should step off the endless merry-go-round of reorganisation in reporting structures and place greater reliance on the informal organisation. He did not, however, see the informal organisation as an uncontrollable by-product of the formal organisation. Instead, he maintained that top managers could influence the development of informal communication channels by overcoming barriers between operating units and building bridges between them. He recommended the greater use of temporary task forces and workshops. He stressed that these more informal mechanisms were to supplement not replace the formal organisation.

Social networks

More recently the informal organisation is frequently referred to as the network organisation. The network is an internal web of floating teams that work across functions and manoeuvre through the bureaucracy (Charan, 1991). It is also defined as the web of contacts managers in one firm have with managers in other organisations; or as a set of external relationships, alliances and joint ventures between one firm and other organisations. (Note that a computer network is one of the tools of the bureaucracy and is therefore fundamentally different to the way in which the word is being used here.) Networks have been described as the fundamental social architecture of the organisation, the mechanism through which key managers communicate, exert power, build trust, and make the trade-offs that shape the formal organisation (Charan, 1991).

Networks and networking cohabit with hierarchy and bureaucracy and should be identified and encouraged because this is how to make organisations more flexible and faster-acting (Mueller, 1986). Networks are like wild flowers – they cannot be cultivated, only permitted to grow – you cannot install them but you can create a favourable environment for them. For example, organisations that set up social occasions create the possibility of networks developing.

> Networks are informal systems where dissonance is encouraged and consensus a common goal. The nature of networks is that they are short-lived, self-camouflaging and adisciplinary. They are invisible, uncountable, unpollable, and may be active or inactive. In practical terms, networks nurture spontaneous feedback via telephone, mail, meetings, computers or a shout across the room.
> (Mueller, 1986, p. 155)

Mueller goes on to describe networks as independent, self-reliant groups of interdependent participants, where the border between one group and another is fuzzy and indistinct. Network groups tend to have many leaders. He claims that networking is vital to the introduction of novel products and processes and to the acceptance of other changes in an organisation.

There are, as we noted above, other ways of conceptualising the informal organisation.

■ **Illustration 11.1**
THE FRENCH BREAD INDUSTRY

There are 50 000 bread bakeries employing 80 000 people in France, one bakery per thousand people. Typically these bakeries are run by a baker, his wife and sometimes an apprentice or two. The organisational unit is in fact a married couple with the husband taking the role of artisan and his wife the role of shopkeeper – little has changed for a century. This is in marked contrast to other developed countries such as Germany, the United Kingdom and the United States where bread production is dominated by a small number of very large baking companies, in turn part of large food conglomerates. Why is it that France, operating in much the same environment as its industrial neighbours has never developed a modern bread industry?

It turns out that the answer is more complicated than simply one of cultural differences in eating habits. The answer has to do with the nature of the self-perpetuating social system to be found in the French bread industry. In the late nineteenth century, peasants stopped baking their own bread as large numbers of rural bakeries developed, drawing on the surplus labour of the French peasantry. The culture of the baking industry was, like that of the peasantry, based on fierce individualism and hard work. The large rural community in France still continues to supply apprentices to the bakeries. Typically a young man becomes apprenticed between the ages of 15 and 17 to learn the arduous trade. Then, at an early age, he seeks to set up independently as a baker, buying a business from a retiring couple. Since it is unlikely that the young purchaser will be able to raise the money to buy the bakery, the retiring couple lend it to him, using the repayments as a pension. To ensure the reliability of their pension, they first interview the purchaser's wife, since she is seen as the key to a successful bakery.

Large companies have made attempts to break up this system that brings in its recruits at one end and provides them with a pension at the other. In 1966, for example, the largest flour-milling group in France was rumoured to be preparing to build a large bakery on the outskirts of Paris. The flour company then changed its terms of trade with the small bakers so that only full truck loads of flour would be delivered. This threatened the bakers with serious storage problems and so they identified some smaller flour millers that were about to close down in response to the growing monopoly position of the large flour miller. News of flour suppliers available in the required quantities soon spread around the bakery network, demand was switched to smaller flour millers and the large company had to abandon its plans for a modern baking factory.

(Source: Clegg, 1990)

11.4 The informal organisation: an irrational decision-making process

Ultimately, the purpose of every organisation is to enable its members to take some joint action together – to take organisational, or concerted, action. People will act in a concerted way only if they have expectations in common, and they are motivated and committed to action (Brunsson, 1982). To act in concert, people must:

- expect that their individual action will be accompanied by the actions of others aimed at the same end result: these expectations are the individual cognitive requirements for concerted action;
- be motivated by having made a judgement as to whether the action and its intended end result are good or bad: such judgements are the basis of enthusiasm for action or the lack of it. This motivation is an individual emotional requirement for concerted action;
- be committed to the action in the sense that they can rely on others: this commitment is a social requirement for concerted action.

These three factors are interdependent and mutually reinforcing. Thus when a number of people in a group can rely on each others' commitment, this will reinforce individual expectations that it is worth performing the action, and this in turn will increase individual motivation. It is a strongly shared paradigm or ideology that provides the most important condition for self-reinforcing expectations, motivation, and commitment, and therefore for concerted action. This condition is met by ordinary management through the formal organisation, and such management therefore consistently produces organisational action.

However, when anomalies and uncertainties lead managers to question the current paradigm, they have to express their doubts through the social network and begin their manoeuvres in the political system – the formal organisation does not allow the questioning of the very basis upon which it is built. Furthermore, the discussions that occur in the informal organisation cannot be governed by the paradigm, since that is what is under question. The very framework that determines clear objectives and fixes the logical rules of discussion, reasoning, option generation, and evaluation are therefore suspended.

In other words, the basis for technical rationality is destroyed and it follows that, when they operate in the informal organisation, people have to use some 'irrational' way of conducting their discussions, making decisions, and eventually undertaking some concerted action to change the existing paradigm and the bureaucracy upon which it is built.

The extraordinary management task of changing the paradigm is, in the first place, one of destruction and, in the second place, it is one of one group persuading others to believe in a replacement paradigm. In other words, the task is first one of generating a variety of perspectives and beliefs, and in the second place the task is to reduce that variety enough to allow a new direction in organisational action to be taken. The rational decision-making process cannot help in the destruction phase because rationality is built on that which is being destroyed. Rationality also cannot help in the second phase, the reducing of variety to the point where action is possible, because of the effect it has on expectations, motivation and commitment (Brunnson, 1987). Consider why this is so.

An essential part of the technically rational decision-making process is that of generating as many different options for action as possible for rational evaluation. When this is done in conditions where people are not sharing the same ideology, the variety of options simply increases subjective feelings of uncertainty and confusion. That leads to conflict. Confused, uncertain, conflicting people are not motivated to act because:

- they quite rightly do not expect that others are likely to join them in action;
- since they are conflicting they, by definition, do not feel jointly committed to action;
- individual motivation to act is consequently greatly lowered.

The more technically rational people try to be in these circumstances, the less likely they are to take action. A divide therefore opens up between decision rationality and action rationality.

What kind of decision process is likely to promote concerted action in these circumstances? It will be one in which a particular group, the dominating group, has already made a choice by some means – probably intuitive and political – and then takes steps to reduce uncertainty and conflict in the wider group as part of persuading that wider group to adopt its choice.

The irrational decision process

This can be done, first, by avoiding the formulation of clear objectives in advance since people will simply disagree with whatever objectives are formulated. Indeed, given the uncertain conditions, the dominating group may not be sure what the objectives should be; it may simply have judged that some attributes of the action it is proposing are, in some sense, good. Objectives can be formulated later when it is clearer what they should be. Instead of trying to motivate by setting objectives, the dominant group focuses on bargaining and compromise about proposed actions – one group commits to action now in return for a favour later (Lindblom, 1959). The choice made by the dominant group is not a statement of preference but a commitment to action.

Second, the dominant group will be more persuasive if it reduces the number of options presented for consideration. The technique is not to generate as many options as possible for rational evaluation because this simply sows confusion, but to present the favoured action option together with one alternative. Only the advantages of the favoured option will be mentioned, with perhaps a few disadvantages that are obviously most unlikely to occur. The alternative option will be one that is quite clearly inferior or impossible to carry out and its presentation is weighed down with disadvantages.

Third, action is more likely to follow, when the paradigm is under attack, if managers suppress disturbing information, create illusions of unanimity, and take big risks. If action is the required outcome, these steps are not stupid, as they may seem to be from a technically rational decision point of view, but realistic ways of securing organisational action.

What has been described above is a decision process that is only apparently concerned with making a choice but is really about persuading others to accept a new paradigm embodied in the action being preached – the decision process follows the choice and is being used as propaganda. The irrational decision process maintains the pretence of being rational; it goes through the same steps of setting out objectives and options, but these are 'cooked' or 'fixed', and because of this it gives surface legitimacy to what is going on. It allows all the participants to pretend that they have not abandoned rationality. *Illustration 11.2* gives an example of the irrational decision process and the positive role it plays in generating concerted action.

According to the above analysis, attempts to make rational decisions when the paradigm is under question will simply destroy the organisation's ability to take concerted action. Here decision rationality would lead to action irrationality. Furthermore, when managers use the rational decision-making process in conditions of uncertainty, they try to reduce the risks to their organisation and to themselves by a number of means:

- refraining from action altogether;
- looking for less-risky actions;
- breaking the action down into smaller steps;
- trying to forecast the outcome and then later arguing that none could have foreseen what happened;
- trying to reduce their stake in the action by diluting personal responsibility in a group decision or by involving other groups and organisations in the action.

All these responses reduce the likelihood of concerted action. Higher commitment to action flows from irrational decision processes.

It is only once the process of conversion to a new paradigm has been accomplished that technical rational decision-making which produces concerted action will once again be possible.

Note the role that technical rationality plays in the informal organisation: it is a front used to reduce embarrassment by covering up what is really going on; it is a defence against anxiety because it preserves fantasies of control and rationality that cover up the extent of the uncertainty faced.

Defective learning

There is an alternative to this analysis and its conclusion that irrationality is required to generate concerted action. According to that alternative analysis, discussed in Chapter 6, the irrational processes just described are the consequences of an inappropriate learning model (Argyris & Schön, 1978). The argument here is that because the participants in the process are employing the win/lose unilateral control learning model in conditions of uncertainty, they end up playing games and using organisational defence routines. Thus the whole pretence of using a rational decision process, while actually employing an irrational one and then never discussing this, is a typical defence routine. The result will be an inferior choice because it is never exposed to wide-ranging questioning. The prescription then is not to accept decision irrationality for the sake of action rationality, but to educate people into using a more appropriate learning model in which they first question the choices and then commit to action. Those who propose the improved learning route admit, however, that this is a difficult task and that people keep slipping back into the old learning model (Argyris, 1990). Whatever we prescribe, we quite clearly have to base it on an explanation that is built on irrational, defective learning behaviour.

■ **Illustration 11.2**
THE SWEDISH STEEL CORPORATION

In 1975 there were three steel corporations in Sweden. One was the State-owned NJA situated at Luleå, the others were privately owned, one situated at Oxelösund and the other at Borlänge. At that time, the steel industry was in deep recession, profits had fallen for all, and NJA and Oxelösund were making losses. A government commission was set up to investigate whether the steel industry could be restructured and if so how. Its report was published in 1977 and its proposals were based on an analysis of the ways in which profitability could be achieved, irrespective of the employment consequences, in an industry that had a production capacity double what the market could bear. The principal proposal was to concentrate crude steel production at Luleå and Oxelösund, and close down crude steel capacity at Borlänge. The commission compared this solution with the alternative of maintaining crude production at all three plants. Calculations were not presented for other alternatives.

As a result of the report, merger discussions were initiated. At this stage the unions requested and were granted representation at the negotiations and consideration of the employment effects. They hired consultants to work on other alternatives, this time to minimise unemployment. The unions at Borlänge claimed that correct calculations would show that the best alternative was to keep crude production at all plants. But in the meantime, in order to proceed with the mergers, the negotiators had to agree on the size of the future government investment and that would depend on which plants were kept open. For the purpose of this calculation, all agreed to use an option that was much the same as the commission's report, but it was stressed that this was simply a 'forecast', without practical implications, that would allow negotiations to proceed.

The result was the creation of the Swedish Steel Corporation, partly State and partly privately owned, to be run on a commercial basis. It was agreed that the structure of the company was to be decided by negotiations between management and unions.

In January 1978 unions and management met, together with an army of experts, in negotiations that were to last for five months. The first task was to estimate the future volume of sales and then the size and distribution of production. The primary alternative was the 'forecast' used as an illustration case in the merger negotiations. The unions put forward an alternative that retained all sites – the 'reference' alternative. Seven variants of the forecast were proposed but eventually dropped. Most of the discussion concentrated on ways of calculating costs and prices. The two main alternatives were subjected to discounted cash flow calculations (see section on financial acceptability in Chapter 2) and at first there was no significant difference between them. Later calculations showed the 'forecast' alternative to be slightly better. The advocates of the 'forecast' now shifted ground and pointed out that Borlänge was an old plant not near the coast, a location essential to cut imported iron ore transport costs. This had been known all along and required no calculation. Calculations proceeded, while management and government supported the 'forecast' and unions the 'reference' alternative. Then the unions met for two days and agreed to the 'forecast' alternative provided that the employment situation was not allowed to deteriorate (but remember that the 'forecast' is based on the closure of Borlänge). Consultants were studying the effects of the proposals on employment but their findings were ignored.

After the decision had been made it was clear that the decision-makers did not agree on its interpretation. Unions at Borlange mounted a strike and a new commission was appointed, but eventually the original 'forecast' alternative was implemented.

Thus, the proposal made in 1977 was eventually implemented. The decision-making process was presented throughout as the means of making the choice. The choice, however, had already been made, informally out of the gaze of the formal organisation. The 'decision' process was really a way of gradually persuading people to accept the decision, while allowing action to proceed. The process was decision irrational but action rational.

Source: Brunnson (1985)

11.5 The informal organisation: a learning community of practice

Another way of conceptualising the informal organisation is as a community of practice that performs learning functions (Brown, 1991). A community of practice is a group of people who carry out similar tasks. So, physicists studying turbulence, the geography teachers at a school, the nurses on a ward, the managers on the executive team of a company, or the service technicians who repair the machines their company has sold (see *Illustration 11.3*) are all communities of practice. People performing closely similar tasks always form informal social groups in which they discuss what they are doing and the environment they are doing it in. They gossip, repeat anecdotes, and tell war stories. They recount the difficulties they have experienced in carrying out particular tasks and others compare these with similar experiences they have had. What is going on when this happens is, however, far more important than pleasant social exchange. What is going on is in fact a vitally important form of learning.

There have always been communities of practice and they have always played a major part in learning. The men of a primitive clan constitute a community of practice and it is by joining this that the boys learn to hunt. Apprentices join the communities of practice of craftsmen and that is how they learn. It is no different for managers. The method of learning such communities employ is embodied in their story telling. It is through telling stories that the knowledge required to deal with difficult situations is passed on. The stories are a rich source of analogies that people can subsequently draw upon to design new responses in unique situations. Furthermore, it is not just managers who learn in this way, but people at all other levels too, as *Illustration 11.3* shows.

Organisations can deal with the predictable using systems, procedures, rules and regulations, but when it comes to the unique, ambiguous, uncertain situation never before encountered, whether organisations cope well or badly depends upon how effective their communities of practice are. For predictable situations, people can be prepared by formal training and development courses, but for the unpredictable they have to learn by being members of a community of practice. Complex double-loop learning takes place informally in organisations through political and social interaction within a community of practice, often in conflict with the formal organisational procedures. Organisations are simply communities of such communities of practice and they develop in innovative new directions when the collection of communities of practice that constitute them are actively learning. Informal collaboration and social construction are essential aspects of this learning process. Furthermore, complex learning takes place at all hierarchical levels. It is not the hierarchical level that determines whether or not complex learning is required, but the level of uncertainty and ambiguity in the situations people are confronted with. Anything that obstructs complex learning at any level cuts down on the amount of uncertainty and ambiguity an organisation as a whole can cope with.

■ Illustration 11.3
NON-ROUTINE REPAIRS

In a large company in the United States, service technicians (reps) answer customer calls for the service and repair of the sophisticated machinery supplied by their company. The procedures for servicing and repairing the machinery are set out in great detail in manuals and rep training programmes are provided so that reps can learn to follow the directive procedures set out in the manuals. Those training programmes stress that any departure from the recognised procedures is to be regarded as deviant, unacceptable behaviour.

When they actually carry out repairs, however, the reps find that the mechanistic procedures and training programmes often obstruct rather than help. For example, the prescriptive documentation does not cover all the faults that arise in practice. When a problem arises that is not covered by the manuals, the reps improvise and then conceal what they were doing; they make it look as though they are employing the legitimate procedures because this is what they have been instructed to do.

For example, on one service call a rep dealt with a defective machine that produced the error codes upon which standard repair procedures were based. But the error codes did not match the nature of the machine fault and the repair manuals therefore provided no assistance. The correct procedure according to the manual would have been to replace the machine. The rep was reluctant to do this because he and his company would lose face and the disruption to the customer's work would damage relationships, endanger the rep's bonus, and make life more difficult in the future. He ignored the procedures, and since he had not encountered this particular problem before, he sent for a technical specialist who acted as a supervisor. The supervisor too had not encountered this problem before and was also reluctant to assign the machine to the scrap heap.

The rep and his supervisor then began to question the users and to swop stories about similar malfunctions each had encountered before or heard about from colleagues – they approached the task of diagnosis through a story-telling procedure that had nothing to do with formal manuals. Eventually the stories and anecdotes of similar experiences, conducted while the rep and his supervisor tried one experiment after another on the faulty machine, led to a correct diagnosis and repair.

Subsequently when they met with other colleagues they recounted the story of the repair and that story then became a part of the folklore of the rep community, folklore that would later be used to provide analogies that would assist in diagnosing unpredictable machine failures on future occasions. The reps were dealing with unpredictable problems using a process of narration through which they explored analogies and so jointly discovered an explanation of what had gone wrong. They constituted a community of practice and what they were doing was learning. What they learned was then embodied not in a rigid manual but in a loose story that would be remembered by others.

Source: Brown & Duguid (1991)

11.6 The informal organisation: a shifting set of self-organising small groups

So far, we have seen that the informal organisation present in every human society is a fluid network of contacts, nodes, links and interactions between people both within that society and across its boundaries with other societies. That network has many facets that can be explained and described in terms of:

- a social system that meets people's needs for mutual support and meaning in their work; and
- a communication system that enables rapid and sensitive flows of information; and

- a political system that deals with conflicting interests through persuasion, negotiation, bargaining, compromise, and the application of power; and
- a vehicle for hypocrisy and irrationality: in other words, a decision-making process that allows people to say one thing while doing another in the interests of mobilising concerted action; and
- a set of interactions through which people may learn.

Whatever facet of the informal organisation one focuses on, however, there is one property common to them all – they are all aspects of the behaviour of a shifting set of small groups of people that are self-organising (see *Key Concept 7.6* in Chapter 7). How the informal organisation actually works, whether its consequences help or hinder the organisation, all depend upon the behaviour of people in small groups. Ultimately, whether an organisation is able to change, innovate and develop new strategic directions, and what changes, innovations and new strategic directions it develops, therefore all depend upon how the network of informal small groups of people in the organisation behaves.

We have already discussed formal groups in Chapter 10 and the important distinction between the work and basic assumption aspects of any small group in Chapter 6 in the section on Bion's models. We may think of small groups in terms of a paradoxical constellation of behaviour that constitutes work on the one hand, and basic-assumption behaviour that makes work impossible on the other. The dynamic development of a group is a dialectical process in which these contradictory forces are continually rearranged. We now turn to a more detailed exploration of how small groups develop.

Patterns in small group development

Gibbard, Hartman & Mann (1974) distinguish between three models of group development: linear progressive, life-cycle, and pendular models. They describe each of these types of models in the following terms.

Linear progressive models

In this kind of model the explanations of group behaviour run in terms of progressive stages that the members of a group pass through and the resolutions they achieve in each stage before they can work effectively together. One of the best known descriptions of group development (Tuckman, 1965) identifies the four sequential steps that all groups are claimed to follow during the course of their development:

- *Forming.* When people first come together to form a group, they go through a hesitant testing stage in which they begin to identify their task, form relationships, and develop roles. It is a stage in which people are typically dependent and look for guidance.
- *Storming.* Having acquired some sense of security, the members of a group then conflict over what it is they should be doing, how they should do it, and what roles each should occupy. This is a stage of emotional expression.
- *Norming.* The next stage is that of working through the conflict and developing

shared values or norms to govern how they are to operate together. The outcome is conformity and cohesion.

● *Performing*. This is the stage in which the group produces what it has gathered together to produce; it performs its primary task.

You will recall from Chapter 5 that Lewin described the stages of change in an organisation and a group in terms of a period of 'unfreezing' (similar to forming and storming), followed by a period of 'reformulation' (similar to norming), followed in turn by 'refreezing' (similar to performing). Another model identifies two phases in group development, each of which consists of a number of subphases (Bennis & Sheppard, 1956):

● *The authority phase.* When people first come together to form a group they are preoccupied with the question of authority; that is, who is to be in charge, who is to be looked to for guidance, who is to be depended upon in performing the primary task. This phase is typically divided into subphases. First, people in the group behave in a submissive way, looking for and being willing to take guidance on what to do and how to do it. The hope is that some leader will provide the solutions that will allow the group to work. This is followed by the next subphase in which people rebel against those they have at first depended upon, hoping that conflict will provide a solution to the problems of group life. The third subphase is one in which members find a compromise solution and partial resolution of the dependency-authority/submission-rebellion issue, one that accepts their simultaneous presence.

● *The interpersonal phase.* Once the group has at least partially worked through the questions of authority and dependence, submission and rebellion, the concern then becomes that of interdependence between the members of the group. The first subphase here is one in which members of the group identify with each other, the subphase of 'enchantment'. The psychological force here is a desire on the part of individuals to find the security that comes from fusing themselves into the group. This is a primitive defence in which members seek the route to performing their primary task through group cohesion. This gives way to the second subphase in which members of the group experience 'disenchantment' with their interdependence and seek to establish their own individuality and independence of the group. The third subphase here is one in which there is some resolution of the fusion–individuation tension, one in which fusion and individuation are both present.

It is easy to see how these models are part of the stable equilibrium organisation paradigm – they seek ways of solving the paradox. These models appear to assume that a group reaches a peak of efficient work and then ends or continues at that level.

Life-cycle models

These models are an elaboration of the linear progressive models, the principal addition being the emphasis on the terminal phase for small groups. Thus Mills (1964) adds a stage of 'separation' in which the group begins to face and cope with its own death and members assess the success or failure of their efforts.

Pendular or recurring-cycle models

These models describe group development in terms of recurring cycles of issues or pendular oscillations between them. You will recall the description of Bion's theory of groups (Chapter 6) in which he describes groups moving between the primary task and various basic assumptions. Here there is no predetermined progression from one stage to another until the group functions properly. Groups may perform their primary task quite adequately for a time and then some event may provoke basic-assumption behaviour that interrupts efficient performance. Bion sees groups as perpetually trying to resolve their difficulties, endlessly rearranging their basic-assumption behaviour, but never succeeding in removing that behaviour completely for any length of time. Here the development of a group is seen in continuing efforts to deal with anxiety provoked by psychic non-equilibrium – tension between the pull to fuse with the group and the pull to develop as an individual (Jaques, 1955).

This view of group development is more realistic and fits well with the far-from-equilibrium organisation paradigm. Having discussed how small groups develop, we now turn to the roles people take up in those small groups.

Roles and leadership in small groups

In ordinary management, leaders are appointed to an office in a bureaucracy, or perhaps elected to a position in some representative body, where they take charge of a group of people who have also been appointed or elected in some formal way. People come to their roles in a formal fashion in groups that already have structures, procedures, norms, cultures, systems, goals and relatively clear primary tasks. In these circumstances the important question quite clearly is one of identifying how groups can most effectively and efficiently perform the task and reach the goal. When we observe that people have a natural tendency to develop informal social groupings as they work together in addition to the formal, the concern becomes one of harnessing that informal group to support and not obstruct the performance of the main task. The concern is with motivation and the prime role of the leader is to motivate, form the vision and clarify the cultural values. We then look to personality traits, styles and skills as the determinants of good leaders. We reach the conclusion that we can install techniques and programmes to develop good leaders and cohesive groups, ones that are aware of social and psychological self-realisation needs of individuals.

The extraordinary management perspective on roles and leadership is, as we have seen, a very different one. Here the point is to destroy the existing paradigm and the structures, cultures and styles that embody it, as the essential prelude to change. And the instrument organisations require to do this is the informal organisation. That informal organisation is the spontaneous emergence of small groups – the same groups we talked about as shadows to the formal in Chapter 10 – but now we see them not as purely social and psychological phenomena required to keep individuals healthy and motivated, but as instruments of change with vital tasks of their own. These groups are informal and unstructured, without a task or an objective – the task is to find and structure tasks and objectives.

People arrive at informal groups without roles and there are no leaders, the task is to develop these. Such groups do not relieve anxiety, they create it, and the group has to find out how to defend itself against that anxiety. When an organisation is able to produce such groups that do keep performing their obscure unstructured tasks then it is innovative and develops new strategic directions. If the organisation fails to produce such groups it is incapable of change.

The questions of interest are very different from this perspective to those that interested us from the ordinary management perspective. Now we want to know how such groups evolve, in other words how they develop differentiated roles and leaders, how they identify and structure their tasks. (See *Key Concept 11.2.*)

■ **Key concept 11.2**
ROLES AND LEADERSHIP IN INFORMAL GROUPS

Unconscious group processes produce informal roles in unstructured groups. The leader may well not create the group, but rather be the creature of the group. Leadership is the ability to interpret the processes of the group without being sucked into them, so as to help the group identify its task. From this perspective we can see how an organisation can quite easily become neurotic if its leaders produce or get sucked into neurotic processes.

Leadership

Bales (1970) identified the emergence of two kinds of leaders in small task-oriented groups: the task leader who gives suggestions, shows disagreement and presses the group to focus on task completion; and the social–emotional leader who asks for suggestions, shows solidarity, and soothes tempers by encouraging tension release. (The leadership theories discussed in Chapter 10 also focused on this dilemma of the task and the people.) These leadership roles are mutually supportive in that each helps the group solve different problems, provided that the role occupants can work together. Sometimes one person can combine both roles – the 'great man' leader (Borgatta, Couch & Bales, 1954). When specialist leaders of this kind do not emerge or cannot work together, then members begin to deal with their frustration in unconscious ways that lead to the emergence of scapegoat roles, enemy roles, messiah roles and so on. Bion (1961) distinguishes between different types of leader in the basic-assumption group: the fight leader, the flight leader, the dependency leader, and the leader who symbolises some unrealistic utopian, messianic, or oceanic hope. Bion points to the precarious position these leaders occupy. The important point here is that the leader is sucked into that position by the group and is controlled by the group, not the other way around as we usually believe.

An important distinction is that between the leader of a work group and a basic-assumption leader. An effective leader is one who maintains a clear focus on and definition of the primary task. That task determines the requirements of the leader, who must continually struggle to synthesise, participate, and observe. The effective leader operates on the boundary of the group, avoiding both emotional immersion and extreme detachment. Leaders are there to regulate transactions between their groups and other groups. Both immersion and distance make this impossible. When a group is dominated by basic-assumption behaviour it sucks into the leadership position one who is completely immersed in the emotional atmosphere, the basic-assumption behaviour of the group. This leader is subjected to conflicting and fundamentally impossible roles – to provide unlimited nurturance, to fight and subdue imaginary enemies, to rescue the group from death and dissolution, to fulfil utopian or messianic hopes.

> One of the most intriguing aspects of relatively unstructured and ego-involving small groups is the evolution of a constellation of informal roles that serve important social and psychological functions for the group. Most small-group research has addressed itself to groups that do not have formal statuses and ascribed social positions. The roles that emerge are usually described as 'behaviour patterns,' 'individual roles,' or 'interpersonal styles.' Under relatively unstructured conditions, psychological factors, conscious and unconscious, become increasingly important as determinants of role structure. ... Explicit and formal social prescriptions are replaced by fantasy conceptions of norms and sanctions. At the same time, it is assumed that such roles are not simply expressive of idiosyncratic needs but perform necessary and recurrent functions for the social system – such functions as impulse expression, group maintenance, tension release.
> (Gibbard, Hartman & Mann, 1974, p. 179)

The kinds of roles that have been distinguished are those of the aggressor, the seducer who tries to seduce people into exposing their feelings and positions, the scapegoat, the hero, the resistors, the anxious participators, the distressed females, the respected enactors, the sexual idols, the outsiders, the prophets (Dunphy, 1968). These informal roles develop in order to contain and deal with internal conflict, the tension of fusion and individuation. One of the key roles is that of leader.

Since strategic issues are ambiguous, ill-structured issues that usually start small and get bigger, it is the informal organisation that has to deal with them until they reach an advanced state of definition, at least. It follows that strategic choice and action will have more to do with these unconscious processes than any rational consideration. The example given in *Illustration 11.4*, based on actual events, demonstrates what is meant.

To summarise, we have discussed patterns of small group behaviour as the consequences of social interaction, the development of norms or a culture through the experience of being and working together – a behaviourist approach (see Chapter 10). We have also just been discussing patterns of small group behaviour as the consequences of unconscious processes – a psychodynamic approach that derives from Freud. Now we turn to another explanation that derives from Jung. While the Freudian approach tends to focus on drives and phases common to all of us, Jung stressed the differences between people that flow from the many instincts (archetypes) that drive us. He identified a number of common psychological types, preferred ways of behaving, or temperaments. From this perspective, patterns in the behaviour of small groups would be explainable from the manner in which different temperaments typically interact.

■ Illustration 11.4
CHOOSING A TRAINING PROGRAMME

David, the manager of a particular department, met with Judy, the personnel director, to talk about a possible training programme for his department. The idea had arisen casually before that in a conversation between David and Judy. David wanted to mount a team development weekend similar to one that he and his senior management colleagues had been on. During that weekend they had operated competitively in teams to win points in each of a series of events such as rock climbing, finding their way back to base over rough terrain and so on. He and his colleagues had enjoyed the event and felt that it had increased the team spirit among them.

Judy was supportive and so they involved David's secretary and the most senior supervisor in his department, Chris. As soon as he became involved, Chris suggested that they use a firm set up by his friends to run team training events on a yacht – crewing together develops team spirit. David opposed the idea on the grounds that many of the staff in the department were women who would not want to spend the weekend on a yacht. Privately he told Judy that Chris was an accomplished yachtsman and was pressing his idea simply so that he could win, something not all that good for the rest of the department.

In the end the yacht idea was dropped for what sounded like fairly rational reasons. However, frank discussions with David revealed completely different reasons. David was a sensitive, rather individualistic person who felt somewhat guilty about not being an enthusiastic member of the team who worked for him. Chris, on the other hand, was a boisterous, outgoing, macho man who was quite clearly a full member of the team. David felt threatened by Chris and his real reason for ensuring that the yacht weekend idea was quashed had to do with fears, probably about his own sexual prowess, in relation to Chris. In this way conscious and unconscious processes covered over with rational sounding reasons often determine what happens.

The impact of personality

Jung distinguished between preferences that go to make up different temperaments (Keirsey & Bates, 1978). First, people express preferred modes of behaviour somewhere between extroversion (E) and introversion (I). The E person derives energy from contact and interaction with others, while the I person is exhausted by such contact and seeks energy from internal, reflective sources.

Secondly, people have a preference along a spectrum that stretches from sensation (S) at one end to intuition (N) at the other. The S person prefers facts and knows through experience; such a person is firmly anchored to reality. The N person lives in anticipation and looks for change, skipping from one activity to another; such a person values hunches and prefers speculation.

The third pair of preferences are thinking (T) and feeling (F). The T person prefers the logical, impersonal basis for choice, while the F person prefers the personal, emotional basis.

Finally, there is the spectrum running from perceiving (P) to judging (J). The P person prefers to keep options open and fluid, seeing things from different points of view, while the J person prefers closure, that is narrowing choices down and reaching solutions.

The four pairs of preferences lead to sixteen possible temperament types and the possibility of having evenly balanced preferences adds a further 32 combinations to these. All these temperaments, however, can be sorted into four broad categories:

- The Dionysian or SP person. As a manager this type of person prefers not to be tied down by routine, but focuses on the present, seeks action, and tends to be impulsive.
- The Epimethean or ST person. As a manager this type of person is dutiful and desires to belong to the organisation. Such a manager is careful, thorough and accurate, a giver rather than a taker.
- The Promethean or NT person. As a manager this personality type is interested in power, control and predictability. They avoid the personal and emotional and want to be competent and in charge.
- The Apollonian or NF person. As a manager this type makes intuitive decisions, seeks to be unique, and finds it difficult to take negative criticism.

When people come together, their temperamental differences lead to misunderstandings and the widest gulf is that between the sensing and the intuitive types – the one insisting on logic and the facts, the other pushing proposals based on intuition and experience. People with the same personality type can also clearly have difficulties – a whole group of NT types all trying to control the group, for example, is a recipe for destructive conflict and inactivity. But differences bring contributions to relationships that would otherwise be lacking and some similarity provides the basis of understanding each other.

The behaviour patterns of groups of people would on this view be driven by the understanding and misunderstanding generated by the range of temperaments of the people constituting the group. The implication is that effective groups can be designed if we find out enough about the personality composition of sets of people, or group functioning can be improved by becoming more aware of the difficulties and contributions flowing from temperamental preferences.

Belbin's classification

Belbin has used teams of managers playing business games to identify the effects on group performance of different personality types (Belbin, 1981). He showed how some types work effectively together while others do not and that this has a greater impact on performance than the individual abilities of the people involved. Teams made up of people simply on the basis of their ability – how clever they are – do not make winning teams. Teams designed to include a balance of different personality types are much more likely to win even if they do not contain the most able individuals; it is actual contribution and interdependence that determines performance.

In Belbin's terms the basis of a good team is the Company Worker types – the conservative, dutiful and predictable, even if inflexible people (much the same as the Epimethean manager above). These Company Workers are the basis of a good team because of the stability they provide and the steady work contributions they make.

This is not enough for superior performance, however, In addition a team needs members paired into the 'Chairman' (Promethean) and the 'Shaper' (Apollonian) types. The 'Chairman' is calm, self-confident and controlled, arouses the contributions of many types, has a strong sense of objectives, but is average in creative ability. The 'Chairman' therefore needs to be balanced with a 'Shaper' who is highly strung and dynamic, challenges complacency and self-deception, and is impatient and irritable. The team is strengthened by the addition of the 'Plant' (Appolonian) and the 'Resource Investigator' (Dionysian). The 'Plant' is an unorthodox individualist who contributes new ideas but is apt to be 'up in the clouds'. The 'Resource Investigator' is an enthusiastic extrovert, eager for challenge but apt to lose interest quickly. These two types need to be balanced with sober and prudent 'Monitor Evaluators' and the orderly, conscientious 'Completer Finishers' (both Epimethean). Finally, superior teams contain 'Team Workers' who are socially oriented but tend to be indecisive in times of crisis (Apollonian, perhaps).

11.7 The informal organisation: a chaotic political system

The small group process is also a political process and we might think about the dynamics of this in the following terms (Stacey, 1991).

The dynamics in a political system are determined by the relationship between leaders and followers. Leaders derive power either from hierarchical position or from the contributions they are able to make to the group. Furthermore, leaders may or may not choose to exert that power. These sources of leaders' power and their willingness to exert it are set out on the horizontal plane in *Figure 11.1*.

Followers may consent to be led because they believe in the ideology propounded by their leaders, or because they accept the hierarchical authority of those leaders. Furthermore, followers too may withhold their consent to be led. These factors are set out in the vertical axis of *Figure 11.1*.

When these factors are combined in different ways, they lead to different forms of power and these in turn provoke different typical patterns of group dynamic, so creating a context within which a group works on its tasks. Five typical contexts are depicted in *Figure 11.1*:

1 **Authority and compliance**. Here both leaders and followers operate on the basis of their hierarchical position and shared ideology. The result is the exercise of authority and a group dynamic of compliance where followers suspend intellectual and moral judgements about the appropriateness of the superiors' choices and actions and willingly and unquestioningly do what the leaders want (Bacharach & Lawler, 1980).

2 **Influence and volatile group dynamics**. When both leader and followers work on the basis of their own personal skills and experience, then they influence each other by offering advice, entering into discussions, making suggestions, and persuading. A whole range of dynamics can emerge, from conflict to cooperation, from avoidance

Figure 11.1 Determinants of the form of power
Source: R. Stacey (1991), *The Chaos Frontier: Creative Strategic Control for Business*, Oxford: Butterworth-Heinemann

	Power not exerted	Exertion of power based on:	
		Contribution/ gain	Structure/ rules
Duty, obligation, strong belief	Vacuum	Authority	Authority
Contribution + gain	Vacuum	Influence	Force
Fear\n\nNo consent	Impotence	Impotence	Force

Consent to power based on: (vertical axis label)

to commitment, from compliance to dissatisfaction with the leader, from questioning and consensus seeking to game playing and making issues undiscussable.

3 Force, submission and rebellion. Where leaders apply force, the dynamic is either submission or rebellion. Force and its consequent dynamics are clearly not conducive to ordinary or extraordinary management, but may nevertheless be necessary in extreme circumstances.

4 Impotence. Where neither leader nor followers are willing to use or consent to power, there is a state of impotence. The typical group dynamic here is intense rivalry.

5 Power vacuum. Finally, where the leader is unwilling to apply power while followers are willing to consent, we get a power vacuum. Typical group dynamics here are passive loyalty, searching for a new leader, frustration.

Which of these five states prevails will depend upon the extent to which people share the culture and how power is distributed:

● When people in a group strongly share the same cultural norms and power is highly concentrated in clear hierarchies, then they will be willing both to exert and consent to the use of power. It follows that the context they will operate in will be that of authority and compliance. This is a psychologically secure state and it is highly appropriate for ordinary management. Consequently, all organisational political systems will be powerfully pulled to this state. As organisations try to take advantage of synergy and interconnection, as they drive towards commonly accepted goals and build shared cultures, they move to political systems where authority is the predominant form of power and compliance the predominant group dynamic.

- When people in a group do not share the same cultural norms and power is widely dispersed, there will be a low willingness to exert power and to consent to it. The result will be a state of political impotence in which the predominant group dynamic is one of intense rivalry. Since all organisations are powerfully pulled towards disintegration by the forces of division and differentiation, all political systems in business organisations will be pulled towards this state. As the organisation tries to deal with high levels of uncertainty and benefit from the division of tasks and the segmenting of markets, it develops many different units with different cultures. The power of the centre weakens and rivalry breaks out between the units.

- Organisations and their leaders may respond to weak sharing of values by imposing greater order and concentrating power at the top. Willingness to exert power is thus great but willingness to accept it is low. Power then takes the form of force and the predominant group dynamic is either submission, or resistance, or alternation between the two.

- Another response to the consequences of division and differentiation may be to offset the effects of widespread distribution of power by promoting the strong sharing of cultural norms over a wide range. Ability and willingness to exert power is then low and willingness to consent is high. This creates a power vacuum in which the typical dynamics are ones of passive loyalty, or frustration, or search for leadership.

Figure 11.2 depicts these four final states.

The political system of an organisation is therefore pulled in four different directions toward four different equilibrium states. It is very difficult to move an organisation away from any of these equilibrium states. It requires some political coup in which the leader is removed, or some major restructuring of the hierarchy, or alterations to systems and procedures. Furthermore, none of these equilibrium states can successfully deal with open-ended change because the group dynamics provoked by all of them simply obstruct questioning and complex learning.

Successful political systems are therefore those that are sustained far-from-equilibrium, by preventing:

- Strong sharing of cultural norms over a wide range and avoiding a state in which they are hardly shared at all. Organisational political systems are sustained far-from-equilibrium by weak sharing of cultural norms that occurs when people make different unconscious assumptions on what and how to learn. Differences in culture are essential to change.

- Widespread distribution of authority over strategic resource allocation and the confusion of hierarchical structures. The far-from-equilibrium state is one where authority is distributed, but not widely, and where hierarchies are clear, not confused. Difference in power distribution is also essential to change.

Successful political systems are those that enable people to cope with open-ended change and that can only happen when the political system allows and encourages

Figure 11.2 Equilibrium states for an organisation's political system

Source: R. Stacey (1991), *The Chaos Frontier: Creative Strategic Control for Business*, Oxford: Butterworth-Heinemann

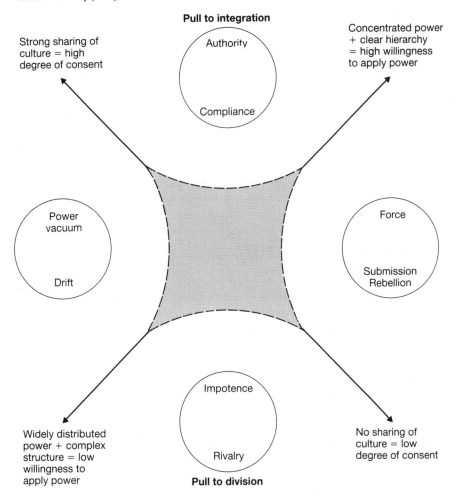

questioning and the exposure of new perspectives. Clearly, people are not open to persuasion and new perspectives when they strongly share a wide range of cultural norms and when they share none at all. They are also clearly not open to persuasion when power is so highly concentrated that those at the top do not need to listen, or when it is so widely distributed that there is not much they could do even if they did listen. Cultural difference and differences in power distribution therefore create the conditions in which people influence and are influenced. In other words, power is not continuously applied as authority or force, and continuous power vacuums and impotence are also avoided. It is in the border area between the equilibrium states of authority, force, power vacuum and impotence that we find power in its form of influence and that is what change requires.

11.8 The functions performed by the informal organisation

We have seen in this chapter so far that we can think of the informal organisation as a political system, a learning community of practice, a shifting set of small groups employing unconscious processes and fantasies, an irrational decision-making process, and a communication and social network. We have seen how people develop roles in the informal networks that are very different to the ones they play in the formal organisation and we have seen how the nature of leadership changes when it is exercised in the informal networks. The result is a many-faceted self-organising system that coexists with the formal organisation but that is far more flexible and therefore much more capable of dealing with the unexpected and the unknowable.

Beneficial functions

Our discussion so far indicates that an informal organisation performs some functions that are beneficial to both the organisation and its members:

- It enables more rapid responses to unforeseen changes than a formal organisation because it is inherently flexible.
- It generates change and new knowledge. It is the vehicle for political interaction and organisational learning out of which innovation and new strategic direction may emerge.
- It provides important psychological and social relief to individuals who have to operate in a bureaucratic system or have to confront great ambiguity and uncertainty. The consequence is that members are more motivated and psychologically able to operate effectively.

Harmful functions?

An informal organisation, however, also functions in ways that are quite clearly harmful to both members and the organisation as a whole; or are harmful to the organisation, in appearance at least, but are perhaps needed by the members of the organisation in some way; or that are quite difficult to draw immediate conclusions about. These judgements about the possible harmfulness of informal organisations are based on observing how people use informal groups to:

- achieve their own personal aims in conflict with the good of their organisation;
- practise hypocrisy in that they claim to be taking decisions in a rational manner in order to gain the support of, say, shareholders and bankers, when in fact they are taking decisions and acting on 'irrational' beliefs;
- operate organisational defence routines, to defend themselves and protect their colleagues in embarrassing and anxiety-laden situations (see Chapter 6);
- build symbols, practise rituals, develop ideologies, generate rumours, myths, dreams, visions, conscious and unconscious fantasies and other forms of irrational belief that then determines what they do; unstructured small groups with

unstructured tasks, the inevitable consequence of vague and ambiguous strategic issues, have been shown to be prolific generators of collective fantasy.

The dominant paradigm of the stable organisation predisposes us to reach the conclusion that all of the above factors are bad for an organisation and must be removed, or at least damped down if that organisation is to be successful. This is the dominant impression one is left with after reading most textbooks on strategic management, organisational behaviour and change management. A more careful review of the nature of the informal organisation, however, makes it clear that we cannot reach such easy judgements. To be sure, there are circumstances where most would agree that it is harmful to satisfy self-interests, practise hypocrisy, operate defence routines, and fabricate fantasies. But mostly it is not at all clear that this is the case.

We have seen, for example, that the practice of organisational hypocrisy may be required in the interests of concerted action. Such hypocrisy may also be required to deal with the inconsistent requirements of the environment. For example, when an organisation finds it impossible to predict events for more than about a year ahead, it clearly cannot prepare meaningful five-year plans. If its bankers nevertheless demand such plans to justify their financial support, then it is necessary to prepare fantasy plans to satisfy this demand. The decisions and actions, however, must be taken on some basis other than the rational to satisfy the requirements of unpredictable reality. Of course, the bankers will not believe the plans any more than the organisation's managers really do, but they will later be able to use them to demonstrate the rational basis of their lending decisions should anything go wrong. Those to whom they have to justify their decisions will also know that the plans are meaningless, but they will have some supposedly rational basis for judging what the bankers have done.

So, widespread hypocrisy of this kind can oil the wheels of action. We can no longer be so sure, therefore, that we need to banish it. Indeed as far as the managers of any single enterprise are concerned, they would be most unwise to try unilaterally to banish hypocrisy for reasons that are quite obvious.

Much the same point can be made about the pursuit of self-interest and the practice of organisational defence routines. A manager who really adopts a posture of altruism, avoids engaging in defence routines, and honestly exposes the routines others are engaged in will soon become an ineffective outcast. Changing patterns of behaviour is far more complex than simply recognising and confronting them.

Fantasy in organisations

Even the most 'hard-nosed' business people engage in fantasy activity: sometimes this is clearly an obstacle to effective management, but at other times it is a benefit. Mostly, however, fantasies have a paradoxical mixture of beneficial and harmful consequences. Consider some fantasy activities that have harmful aspects because they promote self-deception, but on the other hand may encourage and motivate people in situations that might otherwise be so depressing as to remove the incentive to act.

One frequent fantasy is the utopian one. When managers and their financial advisers prepare five-year projections of sales and profits, they generally make reasonable estimates for the next year or so, but almost always show massive improvements occurring after year three – the well-known 'hockey stick effect'. Also, it is not at all uncommon to hear managers describing their organisation's strengths and weaknesses, or the opportunities open to them, in terms that an uninvolved observer can see are grossly over-optimistic. Managers frequently have exaggerated ideas of the importance and standing of their organisation – they state that they are the best and the strongest without ever looking at any data to see if this is so.

Again, managers may blow out of all proportion some perceived threat presented by some other department and come to see that department as an enemy. On some occasions managers may develop messianic fantasies around some new chief executive appointed at a time of crisis. Chief executives can quite easily develop fantasies of deification with which their subordinates collude. Subordinates use terms such as the 'inner sanctum' to describe the executive suite consisting of a room for the secretary, leading to a room for the personal assistant, leading finally to a 'holy-of-holies' that contains the chief executive.

Fantasies come to be expressed in rituals such as the annual sales meeting in which people whip each other up to create a myth of invincibility in the marketplace. Or managers may go away for action-packed weekends to develop myths about their cohesiveness and fantasies about how good a team they are.

Why do we all engage in these activities and are they necessarily as dysfunctional as at first they sound? Fantasy activity in groups is thought to derive from:

- Individual intrapsychic and psychological sources: on this explanation, the social structure and fantasy activities of a group flow from what happens within individual psyches and how they are projected into group life.
- Group-based and sociological factors: here it is the social system that determines individual functioning and the social structure and fantasy activities of the group take the forms they do because they are acceptable to the group and fulfil some group need at the time.

Some writers adopt the psychoanalytic approach and others adopt the sociological approach. It would be more realistic, however, to see fantasy activity in a group as the consequence of a feedback loop that connects the intrapsychic with the social. We develop fantasies when we come together in a group for reasons that have to do with both individual psychological needs and social needs that operate in a circular self-reinforcing way. The consequence is that unpredictable variety in specific behaviour that nevertheless falls into recognisable categories – chaos.

From the psychoanalytic perspective, fantasy activity is usually seen as a defence against anxiety (see Chapter 6, the section on Bion's models). However, some psychologists have stressed the additional role of fantasy activity in integrating people into a group and in the ability of the group to cope with the world it operates in (Dunphy, 1968). It has been argued that fantasy activity is an alternative form of planning and imaginative thought that often plays an important part in problem solving just as dreams and daydreams are known to do (Singer, 1966). Others have described group fantasies as an intermediate area between inner and outer reality, an area of illusion on the way from hallucination and delusion to reality, that is vital for creativity (Gibbard, Hartman, & Mann, 1974). But myths and fantasies are irrational and may easily become highly unrealistic, thus serving as a hindrance to the tasks of a group.

The conclusion, then, is that the capability for creativity and flexibility provided by the informal organisation is inextricably wound up with its function as a vehicle for self-interest, hypocrisy, defence routine and fantasy. Trying to remove these manifestations would destroy the creativity and flexibility. Instead, it is necessary to create an emotional atmosphere in which self-interest, defence and fantasy activity might turn out to be primarily beneficial rather than harmful. Note that all we can hope for is that network activity might turn out to be primarily beneficial. In other words, there can be no prior guarantee that it will, nor is there any way of separating what we might regard as the harmful from the beneficial. The informal organisation is inherently unstable and this instability is the reason for its creative potential: it is the tension created by the paradoxical nature of informal networks of small groups that drives organisational creativity.

We turn now to the manner in which the informal organisation is creative and then to how it contains the instability that is so essential a part of that creativity.

Creating new knowledge

The practice of ordinary management through the instruments of hierarchy, bureaucracy and Management Information and Control Systems is all about the processing of information, primarily quantitative information. The practice of extraordinary management, on the other hand, is above all else concerned with the creation of new knowledge, largely of a qualitative kind – it is only through new knowledge that an organisation can innovate and develop new strategic directions. The informal organisation is the instrument managers have to use if they wish to create new knowledge. We can see why this must be so if we consider the nature of new knowledge, succinctly set out in an article by Ikujiro Nonaka (1991).

New knowledge is created when the tacit is made explicit and crystallised into an innovation, that is a recreation of some aspect of the world according to some new insight or ideal. New knowledge comes from tapping the tacit, subjective insights, intuitions and hunches of individuals and making them available for testing and use by the organisation as a whole.

■ **Key concept 11.3**
TACIT KNOWLEDGE

Tacit knowledge is personal and hard to formalise. It is rooted in action and shows itself as skill, or know-how. In addition to technical skills, tacit knowledge lies in the mental models, beliefs and perspectives ingrained in the way people understand their world and act in it (see Chapter 6). Tacit knowledge is below the level of awareness and is therefore very difficult to communicate. The nature of explicit knowledge, however, is easy to understand: it is the formal and systematic knowledge that we express and communicate clearly, for example product specifications or computer programs.

Tapping tacit knowledge

Nonaka gives an example of how tacit knowledge is tapped. In 1985, product developers at Matsushita could not perfect the kneading action of the home bread-baking machine they were developing. After much unhelpful analysis, including comparison of x-rays of dough kneaded by the machine and dough kneaded by professionals, one member of the team proposed a creative approach. She proposed using a top professional baker as a model, so she trained with a top baker to acquire his kneading technique and after a year of trial and error she was able to help her colleagues reproduce a mechanical kneading action that mimicked that of the professional. This example describes a movement between different kinds of knowledge, the tacit and the explicit:

- tacit to tacit as the product developer acquires the skill of the professional baker through observation, copying and practising, so internalising it and learning;
- tacit to explicit as the product developer articulates the foundations of her newly acquired tacit knowledge to her colleagues;
- explicit to tacit as the colleagues internalise the knowledge made explicit by the product developer and use it to alter their own tacit knowledge or mental models – in other words, they learn;
- explicit to explicit as the newly formulated product specifications are communicated to the production department and embodied in working models and final production processes.

Innovation then flows from a form of learning, that is new knowledge creation, that in turn flows from moving knowledge between one type and another.

New knowledge starts with an individual and its production cannot be centrally designed because no-one can know what will be produced until it is produced. Tacit knowledge has to travel from one person to another, also in a way that cannot be centrally intended because no-one knows what is to travel, or to whom, until it has travelled. New knowledge can therefore only be created when individuals self-organise into the unstructured small groups that make up the informal networks.

A key difficulty in the creation of new knowledge is that of bringing tacit knowledge to the surface of individual awareness, conveying tacit knowledge from one person to another, and finally making it explicit. This is so difficult because it requires expressing the inexpressible and this needs figurative rather than literal language.

Metaphors Metaphors have to be used to link contradictions to each other and express paradoxes. It is when we juxtapose seemingly illogical and contradictory things that we are stimulated to look for multiple meanings, to call upon our tacit knowledge, and so develop new insights. The ambiguity of metaphors provokes and challenges us to define them more clearly. Metaphors are formulated through intuition, a form of tacit reasoning that links images that may seem remote from each other. Nonaka describes how, in 1978, top management at Honda inaugurated the development of a new car concept with the slogan 'Let's gamble', indicating the need for a completely new approach. The development team expressed what they should do to deal with this metaphor in the form of another slogan: 'Theory of Automobile Evolution' (a contradictory idea of a car as both a machine and an organism). This posed the question: if a car was like an organism how would it evolve? The designers discussed what this might mean and produced another slogan: 'Man–maximum, Machine–minimum'. This conveyed the idea that the car should focus on comfort in an urban environment. The idea of evolution prompted the designers to think of the car as a sphere, a car that was 'short' and 'tall'. This gave birth to the idea of a 'Tall Boy' car, eventually called the Honda City.

Analogy Once metaphors have provoked new ideas, analogies between one thing and another can then be used to find some resolution (perhaps only temporary) of the contradictions that have provoked us into thinking new things. Analogy is a more structured process of reconciling opposites and making distinctions, clarifying how the opposing ideas are actually alike or not alike. To illustrate this, Nonaka recounts the story of Canon's development of the mini-copier. To ensure reliability, the developers proposed to make the copier drum disposable – the drum accounted for 90 per cent of maintenance problems. Team members were discussing, over a beer, the problem of how to make the drum easily and cheaply, when the team leader held up his beer can and asked how much it cost to make one. This led the team to examine the process of making cans to see if it could be applied to the manufacture of photocopier drums. The result was lightweight aluminium copier drums.

Models Finally, models are used actually to resolve the contradiction and crystallise the new knowledge: for example, a prototype kneading machine, or a prototype small photocopier.

As purported new knowledge is dispersed through a group and an organisation, it must be tested – that means that there must be discussion, dialogue and disagreement. The dispersion of purported new knowledge threatens people's existing perceptions and positions, raising anxiety levels and perhaps provoking strange groups dynamics. Insecurity, anxiety, conflict and confusion must be accepted as inevitable factors in the process of new knowledge creation; they can be removed only by stamping out the creation of new knowledge. It is the function of the informal organisation to use this chaos to generate new perspectives, learn, destroy existing paradigms and lead to the new. But it is also the role of the informal organisation to contain the instability, to keep it bounded, for without this we get utter confusion, not chaos – remember chaos is bounded instability.

11.9 Providing the boundaries around instability

To create new knowledge, top managers must intentionally encourage the development of an informal organisation and accept the consequent instability. Indeed, they must add to that instability by challenging and provoking people, so destroying belief systems. They must also intervene in order to affect the boundaries around the self-organising processes and consequent instability that produce unpredictable new strategic direction.

While no-one can control the network system, managers can affect the boundaries around that system, boundaries which affect the formation, activity levels and degree of stability of the networks (Stacey, 1992). It is possible for managers to intervene in such a way as to tighten the boundaries; they may become so tight that networks become relatively inactive and thus stable, or active in a covert way and thus unstable. Or it is possible to intervene so as to loosen the boundaries so much that networks become hyperactive and produce organisational anarchy. Yet other interventions can produce states of chaos in which instability is constrained and organisations can function creatively. What are these interventions and boundaries? The boundaries are provided on the one hand by hierarchical structure and the distribution of power, and on the other hand by organisational culture. Let us consider the sense in which each of these constitutes a boundary around self-organising processes and instability.

Hierarchy and power

The instability of the network organisation is constrained, first, because networks exist in contradiction and tension with the hierarchy and, second, because of the way networks operate. The manner in which network systems are constrained by the hierarchy is obvious: hierarchical authority confers important advantages to particular players in the network system and choices emerging from network operation have to be legitimised by those with hierarchical authority. However, the network system is a political one where power derives only partly from authority; influence derived from others' judgements of one's ability to contribute is just as important. Such a system produces sequences of behaviour and choice that are constrained by the need to convince, persuade and maintain political support.

The boundary is thus provided by the fact that different people have different levels of power, but none are too powerful. Wild swings in behaviour and choice are not produced unless the boundaries around this political activity, that is the need to obtain and sustain support, are either too tight or too loose. That tightness and looseness will be determined by the manner in which managers, especially those at the top, intervene to use their power. The choice for managers lies in when to use their authority derived from hierarchy, when to rely instead on their influence, and when to refrain from exerting their power at all. If managers always apply their authority no matter what the situation, they in effect intervene in the network system to establish very tight boundaries. They ensure a political system in which people are either dependent and submissive, or rebellious; that is, the self-organising networks are either largely dormant or operating in a covert manner. Perhaps surprisingly, the charismatic leader tends to have much the same effect. The followers of charismatic leaders are also dependent, willingly surrendering their critical faculties in the utopian hope that the leader will produce what is required. Such an emotional climate does not encourage the active operation of networks. Even more harmful, however, is that it greatly reduces the need to work at sustaining political support. The result is that it is much easier for top managers to pursue either haphazard sequences of decisions or to go off in one direction to disaster.

If, instead of a few at the top using their authority all the time, we have managers frequently using only their influence, or even making space for those lower down to take the initiative, then we have a different kind of boundary condition, a different context for the operation of the networks.

Culture and learning capability

Next, consider how conflicting cultures constitute a boundary around network operations and thus constrain instability. When managers explore open-ended issues in groups, they are in fact learning. Through this learning they discover how to frame issues and what to do about them. If they all share the same culture they will all reach much the same conclusions about how the issue should be framed and what should be done about it. If this consensus is wrong, as it often will be in a rapidly changing environment, then the whole group will pursue a given sequence of decisions for a long time before they realise their error. If, however, they all do not share the same culture, they will approach the issue from different perspectives and frame it in different ways. The conflict that this generates will prevent the group from pursuing one line of reasoning for lengthy periods. This constraint provides a boundary around learning and decision-making.

If on the other hand a group of people trying to learn together share almost nothing in cultural terms, they will do little but conflict. However, strong sharing and the failure to share culture at all both have the effect of creating boundaries that are too tight or too loose; that is, a context that is inappropriate to complex learning. Weakly shared, multiple cultures, on the other hand, both generate instability and provide a boundary around that instability. The boundary is provided by the need to convince and persuade others to follow a line of reasoning. There is a boundary when a group acts as a learning group and that happens when it is not swept along by a strongly shared emotional atmosphere, or shared culture, of fighting, fleeing from the issues, depending heavily on leaders, or indulging in unrealistic utopian fantasies. An effective learning group has its own inbuilt limits to instability and the more effective the people constituting the group are at complex learning the more they will be able to contain the instability their learning itself inevitably generates.

11.10 Prescriptions for the informal organisation

Mainstream prescriptions on organisational success largely ignore the informal organisation and many practitioners, as we have seen, cover up its use with a 'mock' bureaucracy. Those who have recognised the major part that the informal organisation plays in successful organisational development seem to have adopted one of two approaches:

- installing the flexible aspects of the informal organisation in place of the rigid aspects of the formal one;
- creating an atmosphere in which the informal organisation can function and then participating in that functioning.

Installing flexibility

The most frequent prescriptions flowing from a recognition of the importance of the informal organisation have been about building the flexibility of networks into the formal organisation. What is envisaged is:

- first, the removal of the demotivating, frustrating and ossifying aspects of hierarchy, bureaucracy and Management Information and Control Systems; and
- second, the installation of approaches that motivate and increase flexibility.

Thus, the earliest response to the deficiencies of scientific management and its bureaucracy was the 'human relations' movement (Mayo, 1945) that sought to empower people, enrich jobs, and create more democratic, autonomous work groups (referred to in Chapter 7 in section 7.6). Job enlargement schemes have sought to reduce the demotivating effects of extreme specialisation by rotating people between tasks and expanding the number of operations any one worker performs. These ideas were developed into those of job enrichment in which opportunities are designed into the work for achievement, recognition, responsibility and advancement. The idea is to design jobs that give people higher degrees of reponsibility for their own work. A natural extension of this idea is that of an autonomous team of workers that jointly take responsibility for the effective design of their own tasks. Here the group manages itself to achieve targets set for it.

These ideas were extended to an organisation-wide level by Burns & Stalker (1961) who distinguished between mechanistic (bureaucratic) organisations and organic (flexible network-type organisations) and prescribed the former for stable environments and the latter for volatile ones. Since dependence is a major cause of alienation, some (for example, Argyris, 1957) saw participation in decision-making, based on trust between superiors and subordinates, as one way of improving organisations. More recently, Ouichi has developed the idea of the 'theory Z organisation' which largely replaces control by rules with cohesion brought about through socialisation, that is sharing the same beliefs (Ouichi, 1981). This is the idea of an organisation as a clan rather than a bureaucracy. All of these ideas have found expression in the prescriptions of popular writers such as Tom Peters (1982, 1988) and Rosabeth Moss Kanter (1985, 1989).

Over the past decade there has been growing concern about the ability of rigid organisational hiererachies to cope with increasingly complex and turbulent business conditions. That concern has led to more and more top management interest in installing 'flexible organisational structures' and mounting 'culture change' programmes to empower people throughout an organisation. The aim of both the restructuring and the culture change is the same: to free employees and those below the top in the management hierarchy from instructions and controls, and allow them to take decisions themselves. It is believed that this approach will make organisations more responsive to the marketplace, encourage people to be more innovative, reduce administration costs by cutting out layers of management, and improve collaboration by making it easier for people to communicate horizontally from one business function or unit to another.

The mainline response to the drawbacks of the bureaucratic form of control has therefore been to try to replace it with some other kind of structure, that is replacing a structure of hierarchy with a structure of belief. More recently this idea of replicating some of the aspects of the network organisation into the formal one has been carried further to the point of a direct replication. Here it is proposed that Chief Executives set up teams of senior managers with the task of acting like a network (Charam, 1992).

Mueller (1986) too talks about designing the networks by deciding on the purpose to be achieved, preparing an inventory of networking skills, and so on. What is being sought then is a solution to, a resolution of, the paradox of freedom and control. The solutions are reflections of the dominant paradigm, in that they seek to establish cohesion and teamwork and so avoid conflict.

However, the attempt to install and institutionalise the informal runs the serious risk of damaging both the bureaucracy and the self-organising networks:

- Flexible structures and empowered people intentionally weaken the hierarchy and thereby destroy the short-term control system.
- The flexible organisation seeks to resolve the paradox of flexibility and control by choosing a balance that favours flexibility, but flexibility by design so as to reduce the tension. It is this very tension, however, that provides the creative drive of the informal organisation.

In the flexible organisation concept, therefore, managers face the choice of either tight short-term control or flexibility through what might be called 'self-managing teams' (dispersed power, widespread participation, wide spans of control, supportive supervision) and they make a choice that favours the latter (see Chapter 7, section 7.5). In the approach we have been following in this book, successful managers choose both strong hierarchies for short-term control and self-organising processes of political interaction and learning out of which new strategic direction may emerge.

A flexible organisation, then, consists of a particular constellation of self-managing teams that are a permanent part of a centrally installed structure. Self-managing teams have formal leaders, either appointed or elected, who have formally agreed, permanent roles defined as supportive rather than controlling. Self-managing teams also consist of permanent members formally appointed to the team with roles defined by loose job descriptions and rights to make suggestions and participate in what is probably meant to be democratic decision-making. What decisions they are to participate in, and how, is formally established when their team is set up. The climate the team is to operate in, is one that is set by the shared vision and values, and by the financial controls. That climate is intended to be one of stability with a state of consensus as the norm – the 'tight' property. It is also intended to be a climate of freedom – the 'loose' property.

Flexibility and short-term control

When one considers what is necessary for the operation of an effective planning/monitoring control system, however, it becomes clear that 'loose–tight' control is not a paradox, but a logical inconsistency. The essence of tight planning/monitoring control is the clear allocation of responsibility for carrying out predetermined tasks having reasonably predictable results to which rewards are tied. We cannot allocate clear responsibility for predetermined tasks unless those tasks are clearly defined. Loose role and job definitions accompanied by unclear hierarchies and organisational structures are completely incompatible with tight planning/ monitoring control. Such control is essentially management by rules and manuals. Tearing them up simply destroys the system. The essence of this form of control is frequent and regular formal review and reporting. The operation of an effective short-interval control system therefore requires managers to collect and present information, to attend review meetings, and promptly carry out corrective action. If stripping out layers of middle managers is carried too far, it will damage the ability to carry out tight short-interval control.

Widespread participation in decision-making and the dispersal of power to allocate resources are also incompatible with tight planning/monitoring control. The whole system is essentially a top-down one in which top management sets targets, after some negotiation with those lower down, and retains the power to allocate resources. It is through power to allocate resources that the top maintains short-term control and stability. Furthermore, the point of distributing power to allocate resources is to empower people to take action to deal with turbulent and complex environments; in other words, with events that have not been foreseen, whereas the essence of planning/monitoring control is to delegate power to use resources in predictable circumstances for predetermined purposes only. Allocating power to use resources in unforeseen circumstances would undermine the whole system.

Flexible structures and tight planning/monitoring control are thus completely incompatible and the choice is an either/or one. Either you have clear hierarchies with clear job definitions and power increasing markedly as you move up the hierarchy, or you have much diminished short-term financial control. The approach developed in this book advocates choosing quite clearly in favour of hierarchies and short-term control, thereby rejecting the idea of a comprehensive structure of loosely controlled self-managing teams.

Flexibility and strategic issues

On the face of it, widespread participation and more equally shared power should lead to more people detecting changes that occur in the environment and taking trial actions to deal with the uncertainty those changes provoke. However, as we have seen in Chapter 6, this does not guarantee that decision-making or organisational learning will improve. Dispersing power can lead to 'garbage can' decision-making and since almost everyone uses a mental model that blocks double-loop learning, opening up participation in the learning process to larger numbers of people simply means many more people performing learning tasks ineffectively. If managers wish to improve the ability of an organisation to learn, and thus to develop emergent new strategic direction, then the first step must be that of tackling ineffective learning models at the individual and small group levels. If participation is widened before this is done, the result is likely to be the spreading of organisational defence routines and game-playing and that will harm rather than help the business.

Flexible structures and dispersed power, then, tend to lead to decision-making processes in which the sequence of choices depends primarily on chance and to the spreading of organisational defence routines and game-playing rather than learning. They thus lead to potentially explosive instability (checked only by the extent to which people share a culture and a 'vision' rather than stability or bounded instability.

Elliot Jaques (1991) makes the point that it is a delusion to believe that a company's management can be improved simply by doing psychotherapeutic work on personalities and attitudes of managers. Insight into psychodynamics and small-group functioning on their own will fail to produce much change. This is because of the employment contract. Organisations do not employ groups, they employ individuals. It is individuals who have responsibility and authority. And large numbers of individuals have to be organised into hiererachies unless there is to be complete disorder. Attempts to replace hierarchy with groups will not work. Any use of informal groups has to proceed alongside clear hierarchies and effective bureaucracies and Management Information and Control Systems. Just as we cannot replace the bureaucracy with informal groups, so we cannot turn the self-organising network into a self-managing team where the hierarchy sets the goals. All we then do is set up an appendage to the hierarchy. The formal has to stay formal and the informal has to be really self-organising if they are to make their distinctive contributions to the organisation. So what, if anything, can managers do to improve the informal organisation?

Intervening rather than installing

The informal and self-organising nature of the network makes it impossible to formalise and install the fluid patterns of small groups that constitute the network and then control it and determine its outcome. As soon as we try to formalise, install and control it, we destroy it. It is possible, however, to say something about the contexts within which self-organising groups are: highly unlikely to form; likely to form and operate in a dysfunctional manner; and likely to form and operate in a helpful manner, although even then we will not be able to predict or control what they do. Our inability to predict and control the behaviour of the network, together with our ability to understand something about the impact of context on behaviour, allows us to make partial interventions only, so creating an atmosphere in which the networks might generate change.

A number of writers have set out measures that managers can take to create a context favourable to self-organisation. Nonaka (1991) sees senior managers managing the chaos generated by the informal organisation by articulating ideals, challenges, umbrella concepts and metaphors to guide the thinking and acting of people in the organisation. He sees it as vital for senior managers to present people with challenges that are open to many conflicting interpretations. For example, senior managers presented their people at NEC with the challenge of 'Computers and Communication' and Sharp presented people with the concept of 'Optoelectronics'. He advises senior managers to build redundancy into their organisations because the overlapping responsibilities and activities, the internal competition, encourage communication and provoke new perspectives, even if it all appears to be wasteful. He advises that people be rotated to create counter-cultures and he advises that access to information should be freed up.

Some of the key intervention steps that can be undertaken to create a context favourable to the functioning of networks as engines of enquiry and learning are listed below (Stacey, 1992).

1 Developing new perspectives on control

Many managers fear that piecemeal interventions in the context without much knowledge of the consequences amounts to an abdication of control. Either newly freed managers will enthusiastically undertake high volumes of inconsistent and duplicated actions that expose the business to unacceptable levels of risk; or managers exposed to the uncertainty accompanying the absence of clear organisational intention will focus excessively on the short term and avoid strategic thought and action altogether.

Establishing the conditions in which managers at different levels can create and discover emergent strategy does not necessarily amount to an invitation to people to do whatever they like, provided that there are boundary conditions. As we have seen earlier in this chapter, clear hierarchies of managers in which power is by definition unequally distributed provides an important boundary condition. Managers will then not do whatever they like because they know that they will need to build appropriate levels of support before they embark on any new direction. They will know that their proposals have to be legitimised, and resources allocated to carrying them out, according to the standard procedures in the organisation. In other words, the distribution of power and the operation of the political system of the organisation will perform control functions even where there is no prior intention or clear direction.

The first essential step toward creating a context for effective networking is the changing of the mental models of managers at the top. Without this, inappropriate forms of control will continue and they will block the emergence of effective networks.

2 Designing the use of power

The manner in which power is used has a direct impact on the dynamics of group interaction and group dynamics have a powerful effect on how managers in that group work together and what they learn. What they learn together determines the strategic choices they make and the actions they take.

If power is highly concentrated and always applied as force of authority, we get a very stable organisation in which very little complex learning occurs – the boundary conditions are too tight. The organisation can then only deal with whatever open-ended change the most powerful notice and are capable of dealing with. Strategy is the result of the intention of the top executive and, unless that executive is exceptionally talented, the organisation will fail to develop sufficiently creative new strategic directions to survive.

If power is widely distributed and hardly ever used as authority, we get conditions of organised anarchy in which there is also very little complex learning – the boundary conditions are too loose. The result is very little in the way of new strategic direction for the organisation as a whole. Instead we find fragmented individual strategies resulting from individual intentions which rarely converge because the group dynamics are those of continual conflict or avoidance.

If power is unequal, but distributed and applied in forms which alternate according to the circumstances, we find a flexible, fluctuating boundary around the political process that enables complex learning. But the important point is that establishing such a boundary does not ensure that such learning will occur or that it will produce some outcome that can be predetermined or guaranteed to be successful. The political and learning activity that may produce creative choices is spontaneous and self-organising. We cannot instruct anyone to have a creative idea in an open-ended situation. We cannot orchestrate factions and coalitions between people guaranteed to support the right idea, because when the situation is open-ended we cannot know what the right idea is. All we can do is control the boundaries within which behaviour favourable to the emergence of an innovative choice might occur. We have to leave the choice and the culture to the spontaneous self-organising ability of people in groups operating in favourable conditions.

3 Establishing self-organising groups

Top management can establish groups of key managers to operate in a spontaneous and self-organising manner. Workshops around issues or processes in general, or multi-discipline task forces set up to explore particular issues, are examples. For a team of managers to be self-organising, it has to:

- *have freedom to operate* as its members jointly choose, within the boundaries provided by their work together. This means that when they work together in this way, the normal hierarchy has to be suspended for most of the time. Members are there because of the contributions they have to make and the influence they can exert through those contributions and their own personalities. This suspension of the normal hierarchy can take place only if those on higher levels behave in a manner which indicates that they attach little importance to their position for the duration of the work of the group.
- *discover its own challenges, goals and objectives.* This means that top managers setting up such a team must avoid the temptation to write terms of reference, set objectives, or prod the group to reach some predetermined view. Top managers have to take the chance that the group will produce proposals of which they may not approve. Instead of a terms of reference, targets and agendas, top management establishing a self-organising team will present it with some ambiguous challenge. There is no point in setting up such a group unless those at the top are genuinely looking for a new perspective. The ambiguous challenge may be to find a better organisational structure; or it may simply be to identify strategic issues and choices the organisation should be attending to; or it may be to produce proposals for a new product or promotional campaign. The task is to work at contradictions and anomalies.
- *have a membership drawn from a number of different functions, business units and hierarchical levels.* The purpose is to generate new perspectives and this requires new groupings of people. Middle management is a much under-utilised resource in most companies when it comes to developing new strategic directions. These managers are closer to the action and more likely to be detecting contradictions, anomalies and changes from which new strategic direction is born. By drawing people from different levels and units, we widen perspectives and overcome the inherent inflexibility of existing structures and systems.

However, beware! It is quite possible for managers to use task forces and workshops as a defence mechanism. By setting up vast numbers of task forces and action teams, facilitated by armies of consultants, all of whom produce analyses and recommendations that are never acted upon, managers can create the illusion of action to cover up a determination, perhaps unconscious, to change nothing.

4 Developing multiple cultures

New perspectives are blocked when people strongly share the same culture. There are a number of ways in which management can develop counter-cultures. The first is to rotate people between functions and business units. The motive for doing this is usually one of developing wider experience in executives. It is usually seen as a method of management development, in which a cadre of managers with the same management philosophy is built up throughout the organisation. This tendency needs to be overcome by the design of development programmes that stress the importance of cultural diversity rather than uniformity.

A more effective way of promoting counter-cultures is that practised by Canon and Honda. Here managers are hired in significant numbers, mid-way through their careers in other organisations. The intention is the explicit establishment of sizeable pockets of different cultures that conflict with the predominant culture. It is important that this should be done at different levels in the hierarchy, not confined to one or two top executives.

A third possibility is to use outsiders on some of the self-organising teams in the organisation.

5 Presenting challenges and taking risks

Active strategic issue agendas evolve out of the clash between different cultures in self-organising teams. Top management can provide this activity by setting ambiguous challenges. Instead of trying to set clear objectives, top management should throw out half-formed issues for others to develop. Problems without objectives should be posed intentionally to provoke emotion and conflict, leading to active search for new ways of doing things.

This activity of presenting challenges should also be a two-way one. Top executives should hold themselves open to challenge from subordinates. General Electric has developed this into a regular process that it calls the 'work-out'. Here business leaders outline their views to a small group of employees drawn from all levels. The employees think about the ideas and about issues around their own jobs. They then reconvene to discuss the issues with the manager, who can accept or reject the ideas for improvement thrown up in the discussion, or can promise to think about them. If such a promise is made, the manager must report back to the group with a final decision within 30 days. This process is applied rigorously across the company, from top to bottom. It is structured so that managers cannot get away with doing nothing. Independent experts act as facilitators. They sit in on the sessions, make sure managers do not bully those who speak their minds, and check that they are sticking to their promises. The aim is to create an atmosphere where it is acceptable to speak out, where telling the truth is rewarded, and where bosses who yell at people for speaking out are not.

Provoking challenges and holding oneself open to challenge involves taking bigger personal risks; but taking chances and enabling creative strategies to emerge are closely intertwined. This applies not only at the personal level of the manager, but at the organisational level too. Some managers react to the idea that the future is unknowable and that the setting of prior organisational intention is impossible, by concluding that the organisation must avoid taking risks as much as possible. It should stick to the business it knows best and avoid uncertain long-term investments at all costs. The reaction amounts to saying, 'if you can't manage the outcome, don't do anything'.

6 Improving group learning skills

The role of top management in the strategic learning process is an enabling and provoking one. It is necessary to create the opportunities for, and the atmosphere of openness in which, many small changes and different perspectives may be surfaced. The role of top management is to create the context and provide challenges. Creating the context means identifying and overcoming the obstacles to complex learning. These obstacles take the form of unconscious and thus unquestioned assumptions about how groups should learn together. These assumptions generate organisational defences, game playing and cover-ups. It is these that have to be surfaced and worked on. Obstacles to learning also take the form of managers focusing their concerns on their own position without perceiving how they interact within the whole system of which they are a part. Obstacles take the form of managers distancing themselves from responsibility for the way they are interacting and so blaming others or the system.

In practical terms these obstacles can be overcome only by managers in groups actually working on them. This will require a programme of frequent workshops. Peter Senge (1990) recounts the story of the insurance company Hanover. Here a continuing, long-term programme was instituted for managers to work on their learning models and expose their defensive routines. That company has consistently outperformed the industry averages for profitability.

7 Creating resource slack

The creative work to deal with open-ended issues takes time and management resource, and investment in this resource has an unpredictable return. For lengthy periods it is quite possible that little will emerge from a great deal of discussion and experimentation. But without this investment in what appears to be management resource slack, new strategic directions will not emerge. A vital precondition for emergent strategy is thus investment in management resource to allow it to happen. This runs counter to the requirement for short-term profit and short-term efficiency, but it is a price which has to be paid if new strategic directions are to emerge. The current fashion for cutting out layers of middle management, for reducing numbers of senior executives and loading them up with day-to-day duties can easily be taken so far that it destroys the ability of a company to attend to open-ended issues. Executives who work 12 or 14 hour days are unlikely to have the mental resources to attend to such issues. A careful judgement therefore has to be made on the amount of management resource slack required to enable emergent strategy.

11.11 Summary

Every organisation is faced with the need to take concerted action in order to produce something that others – its environment – will want enough to support its continued existence. The need to be efficient in comparison with the competition pulls every organisation in two contradictory directions: the pull to divide tasks up to obtain the benefits of specialisation and the pull to integrate tasks and their outputs to produce a whole and obtain the benefits of synergy. People cope with this paradoxical situation by taking up roles in the hierarchy, the ancient instrument for enabling any group of people consistently to take concerted action. The set of formal hierarchical roles in an organisation embodies a particular shared belief (paradigm) on how the opposing forces of integration and division are best arranged at a particular time. The result is a formal organisation consisting of a bureaucracy, employing technically rational decision-making processes that are impersonal and can be seen to be fair, and produce concerted action. The formal organisation has clear-cut boundaries with its environment: it is easy to see who belongs to the organisation and who does not, because members have legal membership contracts with the formal organisation.

The bureaucracy, then, enables concerted action; it is the tool of ordinary management that solves problems posed by a given framework. The important point, however, is that any particular form of bureaucracy can be only temporary. It reflects a particular set of beliefs at a particular point in time, and because it is simply an arrangement of contradictory forces it will inevitably come under pressures that will generate new beliefs about division and integration and so change the hierarchy and the bureaucracy.

Every organisation is therefore faced with the need not only to take concerted action but to change and create the new, to provoke and confront the ambiguities and the conflicting forces that are its nature. There must be some mechanism that can cope with the unique and the unforeseen and if necessary arouse and focus the destructive new perspectives that will lead to the creation of new knowledge and action. That tool is the informal organisation and it is through this that managers are able to cope with the ambiguous and the uncertain through practising frame-breaking extraordinary management. This informal organisation is a fluid network of small groups, communities of practice, in which managers take up roles. Just as the hierarchy of ordinary management is subject to the contradictory pull of division and integration, so small groups are subject to the contradictory pulls to fusion and individuation experienced by their members. Just as the development over time of the formal organisation can be seen as a dialectical process of rearranging division and integration, so too can the development of small groups over time be seen in terms of the dialectical rearrangement of the forces of fusion and individuation. In both cases, the extremes of division and integration, of individuation and fusion, are dysfunctional if an organisation is to be innovative. The informal organisation functions effectively when its fundamental paradoxes are sustained, when it operates far from equilibrium between stability and instability in chaos.

At any particular point in time, the instruments of ordinary management, the hierarchy and the bureaucracy, look the same in an organisation close to equilibrium as they do in an organisation far from equilibrium. Where two such organisations differ is in the operation of their informal organisations. The difference, however, is not at all easy to see because of the very nature of informal organisations. Informal organisations are small group processes; that is, political and social interactions that often take place at an unconscious level and may well be irrational, but are normally concealed by mock bureaucracy, the appearance of rational process, organisational defences and hypocrisy.

Once identified, however, we find that organisations close to equilibrium have networks characterised by strongly held beliefs and stability – the fantasies people share have to do with togetherness, the power and goodness of their organisation. Here, the tension caused by the pull to fusion (a kind of stable equilibrium) on the one hand and the pull to individuation on the other (perhaps a kind of unstable equilibrium) has been resolved by moving close to the extreme of fusion. Such organisations do not change much – they simply keep repeating their past.

Innovative organisations, on the other hand, accept the paradox and use their informal organisation as the tool for destroying old paradigms and creating new ones that lead ultimately to concerted action, but of a kind different from the past. The informal organisation is decision irrational and, from time to time, action rational. The boundary with the environment is fuzzy because people in other organisations form part of the networks that change each other through mutual recognition and negotiation.

People operate within the formal organisation when they are faced with issues that are clear cut and have reasonably predictable consequences and when they feel motivated to do so. They do so in an automatic, skilled way, usually without being all that aware of it. When they are confronted with the unpredictable, the ambiguous, the embarrassing and the threatening, however, people turn to the network. They do so because they disagree, feel equivocal, alienated, or anxious. In organisations close to equilibrium, the network powerfully preserves the *status quo*. Every attempt to change it is sucked into repetitive behaviour patterns that transform the change into another version of what existed before. In organisations far from equilibrium, however, the network is the enemy of the formal and seeks to undermine and change it. We can tell in advance whether we are dealing with networks close to or far from equilibrium, but we cannot say in advance when people will switch to the network, whether the switch is appropriate, and what the specific outcomes will be. No-one tells people to do this and no one gives them permission. It is self-organising and it cannot be structured or arranged without destroying it. People probably switch from the formal to the informal many times a day.

The outputs of the informal organisation are:

- Talk: discussion and arguments that affect how people see things and begin to change the paradigm; talk is about generating new knowledge, often while fomenting dissatisfaction;
- Irrational decisions: in order to persuade people to adopt a new paradigm, people have to resort to presenting an obviously favourable option compared only with an obviously unfavourable alternative; or this may be dysfunctional and need to be overcome by improved double-loop learning;
- Learning and coping with the unique and the unknowable;
- Generating emergent strategy.

- Occasional concerted action, achieved through action rationality, or spontaneous consensus.

Because of its very nature, people deny that they are using the informal organisation for serious purposes; and they often make these denials to themselves as well. They have instead a presentation model or a theory in use that they claim to others and sometimes to themselves that they are using. The reasons for doing this are:

- partly to do with the fact that people behave according to a paradigm they are not all that aware of:
- partly to do with the demands that supervisory, regulatory and financial bodies place on organisations, requirements that conflict with what is possible in reality; the requirements have to do with rationality and control and make it necessary for managers to present the hyprocrisy that they are adhering to these things; they have to display structures and processes that are acceptable;
- partly as a defence against anxiety and embarrassment; if we admit that we are employing the defence routines found in the informal organisation rather than the formal one then we destroy the routine's efficacy; people may feel that they need the dream of rationality and the illusion of control in very hostile environments;
- partly because of moral feelings about protecting others from anxiety and perceptions of unfairness.

The need simultaneously to employ the informal organisation as the tool of extraordinary management and the formal as the tool of ordinary management, while covering this up leads to a situation where:

- there is a reluctance to discuss the informal organisation as a tool that managers must deploy;
- when it is recognised and discussed the first response is one of trying to formalise it, make it predictable, and bring it under top management control; to the extent that this succeeds it simply destroys the flexibility of the informal organisation;
- the dynamic of defence routines and organisational hypocrisy flourish, both internally and externally.

Further reading

Hirschhorn (1990) provides an important exposition of the role of the informal organisation as a defence against anxiety. Brunnson (1985, 1989) gives further development of the concepts of organisational irrationality and hypocrisy. Rush, White & Hurst (1989) explain how personality types affect decision-making, as does Belbin (1981). Kiersey & Bates (1978) give a questionnaire that you can use to identify your own personality type. Nonaka (1991) should be read to obtain a fuller understanding of how networks create knowledge and Mueller (1986) gives a good summary of the nature of networks. Finally, Turton (1991) provides a useful summary of many of the ideas mentioned in this chapter.

12

Strategic management in perspective

In Chapter 1 the field of study that we call strategic management was first described in terms of a number of elements. The first element is the feedback loop running from discovery, to choice, to action, and back to discovery again; that is, the process of strategic management which in turn generates the second element of the field of strategy study, namely patterns in organisational action that we may perceive either before or after the event. Those patterns in action continually alter the position of an organisation in relation to actors in its environment and its posture or internal shape. Position and posture determine the final element of the strategy field of study, namely performance. The task of students of management is to identify what kinds of circular feedback processes of strategic management generate patterns, positions, postures and levels of performance that are in some sense successful. In Chapter 1 it was stated that this would require consideration of nine important questions.

The first three of these questions had to do with the dynamics of organisational development: the stability or otherwise of the patterns associated with those dynamics; the kinds of feedback systems that generate those patterns; and the effect of uncertainty and ambiguity on the operation of those feedback systems. In relation to these questions we have discovered that:

- Organisations are systems that take the form of webs of nonlinear feedback loops connecting the individuals, groups, functions, tasks and processes within an organisation to each other, and connecting an organisation to those other systems that are its environment.
- As soon as we put forward prescriptions on how an organisation is to achieve long-term success, we make assumptions about the nature of those feedback loops, the state they operate in when successful, and the dynamics or patterns of change they generate over time.
- The prescriptions will succeed only if our assumptions about the dynamics are a useful simplification of the world we have to operate in.
- Those prescriptions that the great majority of practitioners find acceptable, espouse and believe in are all derived from the assumption that successful organisations are

dominated by negative feedback loops that keep them close to states of stable equilibrium where patterns of change in behaviour are regular and predictable. It is implicitly assumed that systems affected by positive feedback loops, apart from steady growth, will be explosively unstable and thus fail and that it is possible to remove or greatly reduce the impact of positive feedback loops in human systems.

- However, the closeness to reality of these assumptions and the usefulness of the prescriptions they lead to has been questioned for a long time. Systems dynamics, as well as models developed by social psychologists, have all pointed to the irremovable presence in real life human systems of amplifying, positive feedback loops leading to unexpected and unintended outcomes. More recently, studies have shown that companies moving to either stable or unstable equilibrium fail, that successful organisations operate in some state of non-equilibrium. That state is one of contradiction and continuing paradox which produces dynamics of irregular changes in behaviour that are difficult to predict.

- The modern science of complex dynamics, the theories of chaos and self-organisation, explains such states of non-equilibrium and the dynamics they generate. These scientific developments show that nonlinear feedback systems have a choice between operation in stable equilibrium, or unstable equilibrium, or the border between stability and instability. The border between stability and instability is a far-from-equilibrium state of chaos where specific long-term outcomes are unknowable, but they always display recognisable qualitative patterns that humans are capable of using to think by analogy.

- Since organisations are nonlinear feedback systems they must be capable of operating far from equilibrium, a paradoxical state that combines both stability and instability. For a long time now organisational theorists have pointed to the contradictory nature of organising. They have pointed to the diametrically opposed requirements to integrate and divide up tasks, to maintain the system and yet change it, and many others. It has been clear that a position in which one of these sets of forces dominates leads to failure. It is therefore clear that innovative organisations operate far from equilibrium.

- The very structure that causes long-term unpredictability also makes it possible for far-from-equilibrium systems to be continually creative. Such systems create variety, they innovate, through a process of self-organisation that also involves instability and destruction.

Returning to the questions identified in Chapter 1, we can now see that in the ensuing chapters we also developed some insight into those questions concerned with the roles of shared beliefs and intentions in driving organisational strategy, the impact of group behavioural dynamics, and the relationships between the formal and informal systems of an organisation. This insight has been achieved through comparing and contrasting two fundamentally different ways of conceptualising the process of strategic management.

On the one hand you can think of the successful organisation as the one that forms a clear intention of the future state it is to occupy and then intentionally follows a predetermined route to that state. Here the successful organisation is pulled by prior shared intention to an approximately known point in the long-term future. The strategic management task is then to identify the future state and take control of the path the organisation is to follow to reach it. This would be the task of managers at the top of the hierarchy and the more stable the organisation the more likely it would be to succeed in identifying and reaching the future point.

On the other hand, you can think of the successful organisation as one that is propelled from its current state to create and discover a long-term future that its managers cannot now foresee. Here the successful organisation is driven by contradiction and conflict in the here-and-now to develop new ways of understanding what it is doing, new ways of more usefully rearranging the paradoxical forces of organising. The strategic management task is then itself a paradoxical one. It is, firstly, to promote and protect order and stability in the day-to-day conduct of the existing business and in its existing strategic direction; in other words to practise ordinary management which is the operation of an efficient bureaucracy. But, if this is all that managers ever did, then their organisation would simply repeat its past or imitate what others had already done. So the strategic management task is also, secondly, to create an atmosphere of questioning and contention, disorder and chaos, that threatens the bureaucracy, and then manage the boundaries around the instability that has been generated. In other words, the second task, in direct opposition to the first, is to nurture an informal network of managers that in effect invites and encourages them to self-organise spontaneously to destroy the bureaucracy. This second task is what opens up the possibility of innovation.

Through such spontaneous self-organisation managers may identify small ambiguous strategic issues, build dynamic agendas of such issues, and continually experiment with responses to those issues. Such responses will inevitably undermine the bureaucracy. Successful organisations have vibrant issue agendas frequently leading to exploratory actions from which new strategic directions may or may not emerge. Here organisations do not know where they are heading and no-one can be in control of the journey, but the behaviour of the organisation may nevertheless be controlled and creative new strategic directions may emerge, although there can be no guarantee of that.

Let me underline the point this book has been making. One approach to strategy is based on the idea that successful organisations are pulled to an identified future point. The task of management would then be relatively simple: it would be to maintain order in all time frames across all issues. However, this book has argued that the dynamics of organising make this an impossible approach to apply in practise and succeed. Those that do apply it are ultimately led to failure. To succeed, managers must practise the other approach, the one based on the idea that successful organisations are driven from where they are now to a destination that they create and discover. And this process of creation and discovery is paradoxical management; that is to say, the simultaneous application of two contradictory forms of management – ordinary management and extraordinary, revolutionary management.

Ordinary management preserves, protects and enacts the existing paradigm. That existing paradigm is the same thing as the culture or the business philosophy; that is, the shared framework that managers use to make sense of their world. The paradigm is a shared repertoire of examples, images, understandings and ways of acting. The paradigm is used by managers in an automatic unquestioning way that binds them together. It enables them to explain their world to each other without having to justify each step in the argument. The paradigm enables managers to agree relatively rapidly on actions to deal with their environment. The objectives managers set, the actions they design, the outcomes they expect all flow from the paradigm. The paradigm is expressed, is made particular, in the hierarchical structure of the organisation, the shape that managerial roles display, the control systems managers employ, the management styles they adopt, the strategies they are pursuing, and the manner in which they manifest a common culture in their physical environment and through the stories they tell.

For example, the core of the paradigm may be the belief that success flows from providing mass-produced low-cost products to customers. This will probably be reflected in the primacy of the financial function that exerts its power through tight financial control systems, so managing the business by cost objectives. Or the core belief may be that success is reaped from high-quality products for selected niche markets. Here it may be the marketing and sales functions that exert the most power, so managing the business according to prescribed quality measures.

Ordinary management is the process of finding out how to achieve known objectives and expected outcomes; it is all about finding solutions to organisational puzzles within the existing paradigm. Ordinary management solves the puzzle of how to achieve the low-cost or the high-quality targets in the above example. Ordinary management is the enactment of the organisational intention set by the paradigm.

The more effectively managers carry out the ordinary management of their existing business, the more they will identify the excesses such beliefs take them to: the more, in other words, they will uncover anomalies to the existing paradigm. So, as managers in the first company pursue their low-cost targets, they will find that quality deteriorates and sales decline; or the other company focusing on quality will find that this leads them to higher and higher cost levels, also causing a loss of sales. This will make it harder for managers to continue sharing the paradigm in an unquestioning way. The paradigm, anyway, is hardly ever a clear-cut, monolithically shared set of beliefs. It is the sharing of a few key beliefs about what is important to the successful conduct of the organisation's business accompanied by conflicting interpretations of other matters: a mixture of stability and instability. Eventually these conflicting interpretations will spill over to undermine the core beliefs. The paradigm is essentially paradoxical: it is both stable and unstable.

That extraordinary or revolutionary management that questions and threatens the existing paradigm therefore flows quite naturally from the effective conduct of ordinary management, unless obstacles both structural and behavioural are put in the way. For example, the doubts raised about the low-cost paradigm in the above example could lead to its replacement by a paradigm of high quality and this will occur through the processes of extraordinary management, unless people's roles are so constrained and they are so demotivated that they cannot be bothered. Extraordinary management produces emergent new strategic direction.

At this point we can return to the key questions posed in Chapter 1 – question 8 had to do with the relationship between success and stability and we can now see how previous chapters have dealt with this.

There has been little attempt so far to define success – it has simply been argued that success requires an organisation to be innovative. For most organisations this is so obviously true today that there is little need to justify the assertion. It is, however, not universally so and we can see this if we consider how we might define success.

A sensible definition of success might be as follows: an organisation can be judged successful if it reasonably consistently sustains the support of its environment for lengthy periods of time. Organisations exist because people within them and outside them are willing to support them in financial, political and legal terms. Successful organisations are those that do reasonably enough what those inside and outside principally expect from those organisations or will accept from them. Success can then be judged only in terms of the nature of the primary task that the community sets for an organisation. Failure at that task leads to the withdrawal of support.

If an organisation is a commercial enterprise operating in a fiercely competitive international market, its primary task is quite clear and that is to innovate. If those who constitute such an organisation fail to innovate then they will fail simply because customers withdraw their support. This book has argued that such an organisation can succeed only if it sustains itself far from equilibrium with all that this means about instability, unpredictability and self-organising creativity.

At the other extreme, people in a community may want some organisations that operate in stable equilibrium. Those who support religious institutions, for example, set a primary task, not of innovating but of preserving age-old beliefs. That primary task will require the organisation to stay close to stable equilibrium. If those managing the institution begin to innovate with its beliefs, they will soon lose the support of their members and their environment. They will then either be removed or cause the existing organisation to fail by splitting into schismatic parts. Here any attempt to move toward the far-from-equilibrium state leads to failure in terms of the primary task.

Much the same point may apply to other organisations whose primary tasks have to do with security and safety. For example, the primary task of an army or a police force is that of protecting a community. The community will support such organisations when they function in a stable, predictable manner; they may be innovative in the weapons they use and the information systems they employ, but in fundamental terms they are not required to be innovative, for example regarding when, whom and to what extent they protect and punish. For such organisations, then, success will be a state close to stable equilibrium. Another example of success as a state of stable equilibrium may well be the nuclear industry. Perhaps one might argue that the primary task the community wants this industry to perform is that of protecting them from nuclear accident – safety may be the primary task and as such would be prized far above innovative flair. For such organisations, success may be a state close to stable equilibrium. When this is the case, the management task is primarily an ordinary one and today's received wisdom, by and large, provides the appropriate set of prescriptions.

However, for the vast majority of organisations today, some form of innovation seems to be connected to their primary tasks. When this is the case, extraordinary management becomes of major importance. For extraordinary management, a dialectical, paradoxical and chaotic conceptualisation of the strategic management process, in which strategy emerges, is far more useful than is the received wisdom, derived as it is from the stable equilibrium paradigm. This conclusion is supported by studies showing that those who try to practise according to the intentional conceptualisation eventually fail. Those who practise according to the emergent conceptualisation may succeed, although success is not guaranteed. The intentional approach leads to the certainty of eventual failure. The emergent approach leads to the possibility, but not the certainty, of success.

Finally, question 9 in Chapter 1 is all about paradox and how managers cope with it. The fundamental paradox is expressed in the need to sustain and manage the continuing tension created by simultaneously practising two diametrically opposed forms of management: one that sustains the paradigm and the other that destroys it and creates a new one.

We have seen in previous chapters how managers often deal with the anxiety such paradoxes and tensions bring by colluding among themselves, often unconsciously, to erect defences against their anxiety, that is all manner of games and cover-ups. One such defence may well be the insistent claim that the conventional wisdom on strategic management is applicable to innovative situations. It is so much easier to sustain the fantasy that we can plan the unknowable than it is to delve into the group processes that obstruct complex learning in organisations. The question nowadays, however, is whether we can afford such protection from anxiety. If we become convinced, however, that we cannot afford the price, care must be taken in removing organisational defences. If the primary task of an organisation is that of safety, it may be disastrous to strip away the apparently rational procedures people are using to defend themselves against their anxiety, at least without being satisfied that the boundaries around any consequent instability are manageable.

CASE STUDIES

Case study 1

THE SUTER PACKAGING DIVISION

In August 1985 Larkfield Management Consultancy Ltd wrote to Francis Packaging Ltd introducing its strategic management service. In late August Larkfield were invited to a meeting with the Francis Chief Executive and in preparation for this meeting one of the Larkfield consultants put together a recent history of Francis Packaging Ltd from published accounts, newspaper reports and discussions with a colleague who had run a production and cost improvement assignment at Francis back in 1982.

The business of Francis Packaging Ltd

Francis Packaging operate in the general line sector of the tinplate packaging market. This market can be divided into a number of sectors which are described in Appendix 1A. Briefly, these are:

- open top cans for beverages and processed food. This is a high volume business and in 1984 sales amounted to over £500m;
- aerosols for a wide variety of uses and total sales of around £80m;
- collapsible tubes for toothpaste and a variety of other uses with sales of about £20m;
- closures, that is the tops, for a wide variety of containers with sales of around £74m;
- general line containers. This category covers many shapes and sizes of container and usually

those produced in smaller volumes. Total sales here were about £190m in 1984 (round lever lid cans £60m; rectangular cans about £35m; tinplate drums £20m; others such as biscuit tins, tins for toiletries £75m).

Francis Packaging and its subsidiaries manufacture round cans mainly for the paint industry, rectangular cans for the lubricating and edible oil markets, tinplate drums for a variety of uses and a range of other tinplate containers for tobacco, milk powder, and shortbread. Francis Packaging itself operated from two factories: one at Greenwich, London, which produced paint cans, rectangular cans and drums; the other at Wrexham in Wales which had a similar product range. A subsidiary company, Shemtec Packaging Ltd produced paint cans only at its Leeds factory. Another subsidiary, Drummond Packaging Ltd located in Glasgow, Scotland, produced a variety of tinplate containers for powdered food, tobacco and shortbread as well as 10-litre paint pails.

As a back drop to considering the history of Francis over the 1980s certain key points on the packaging market should be noted:

- after growing more rapidly than the economy as a whole, expenditure on all packaging materials began to grow more slowly than the economy around the turn of the decade;
- the share of tinplate packaging in the total began to decline around the turn of the decade to the benefit of plastic and fibreboard;
- the result was a sharp decline in the volume of materials contained in tinplate.

Strategy over the early 1980s

Going back to 1980, Francis Packaging Ltd had a sales level of £14m on which it earned a profit before tax of £0.3m (see Appendix 1F). At that time, Francis Packaging Ltd was a subsidiary of Francis Industries Plc. The other subsidiaries were Clearplas Ltd and Clearplas France SA, manufacturers of plastic products that had nothing to do with packaging; Sagar Richards Ltd; and Lacrinoid Ltd, manufacturers of blow-moulded plastic products, including plastic containers. Francis Industries' sales were nearly £30m on which they earned a profit before tax of £1.8m (see Appendix 1B).

Since 1980 Francis Packaging had adopted a strategy of dealing with the decline in its markets by increasing market share, partly through organic growth and partly through acquisition. Thus in May of 1981 Francis Packaging had acquired Drummond Packaging Ltd from the receiver. The business of Drummond was that of a jobber (short runs, speciality products) rather than a volume producer. The receiver had been called in five months previously, so it took some time to recover customers and build turnover up to £1.8m in 1982. Since that time, however, turnover had shown little growth and profitability had fallen dramatically.

In 1982 Francis Packaging acquired some of the assets and customers of one of its competitors, DKS, who had been making losses in the very difficult market conditions of 1980/1981. The turnover of the businesses whose assets were bought was around £4m. Francis transferred most of the purchased equipment to its factory at Wrexham and a line for producing 10-litre paint pails was transferred to the Greenock factory of Drummond. Then, in 1984 Francis Packaging made a further acquisition, this time of a small family-owned and -run company called Shemtec. This company manufactured round cans mainly for the paint industry and its turnover in 1984 was £4m.

The management at Francis had become increasingly concerned over the years at the penetration of plastic in their markets. The lubricating oil producers switched to plastic for 1-litre containers in the early 1980s – plastic containers of this size were reusable whereas the 1-litre metal containers had a tear off strip which meant that all the contents had to be used at once. The oil producers had drawn this problem to the attention of the tinplate manufacturers but there

had been no effective response. Also, some of the paint companies expressed their discontent with rust in the tinplate containers for emulsion paint and in 1981 they drew this to the attention of the tinplate manufacturers. In view of the threat from plastic, the management of Francis gave some consideration to the development or acquisition of a plastics capability, but this never came to anything. In fact, Lacrinoid, the sister company, which did operate in this area, was far from successful and so in 1982 Francis Industries decided to sell it. Some thought was also given to the application of a more effective lacquer to the rim of paint cans, but it was to be some years before this was made available and by that time ICI had already started to pack its emulsion paint in plastic cans.

Mostly as a result of the acquisitions mentioned above, the turnover of the Francis tinplate packaging companies rose from £14m in 1980 to £18.5m in 1983, while the profit increased substantially to £1.5m. The importance of the tinplate companies in Francis Industries had therefore increased considerably (see Appendix 1F).

The Suter takeover

During 1983, Suter Plc (see Appendix 1C), an acquisitive conglomerate chaired by David Abell and owning a range of companies in the refrigeration, air conditioning and hairdressing equipment industries, had built up a significant holding of shares in Francis Industries. By January 1984, Suter owned just over 26 per cent of Francis shares and rumours of a takeover bid increased. In March of that year it was announced that preliminary discussions had taken place between Suter and Francis which could lead to an offer being made by Suter. Suter then made a £13.4m bid which was rejected by the Francis Board as inadequate. Francis announced its excellent 1983 results and the Francis Board said that it expected record results for 1984. Suter increased its offer to £14.4m and acquired further shares in Francis, taking its stake to 34 per cent. Through April and May the battle to gain control of Francis continued with the Francis Directors announcing in May that they expected profits to rise 40 per cent to over £2m. Mystery buyers acquired significant numbers of Francis shares and so the matter was referred to the takeover panel by Francis. But no breach of the takeover code was found to have been committed by Suter.

Through May and June, Suter continued to build up its shareholdings and by 5 July it held 42.5 per cent. On 25 July, D M Saunders, Chairman of Francis Industries, resigned from the Board. At the same time D Crosby, the Managing Director of Francis Packaging Ltd was appointed to the Board. Then in September the Francis Board announced first half results of £1.25m pre-tax profits, in line with the more than £2m which the directors had projected for 1984 as a whole. During October there were a number of false reports of agreement being reached on a new, revised bid. Finally, on 2 November the Francis directors halted dealings in the company's shares after a bid of £18.5m by Suter was agreed. The next day, Suter discovered that Francis would not reach its profit forecast of £2.35m (in fact less than half of this forecast was eventually achieved). By 4 December Suter held almost all of the Francis equity. After taking advice, Suter decided to sue the directors of Francis Industries as well as their merchant bank and accountants for the losses it had suffered as a result of the incorrect forecast. Writs were finally issued in early 1985.

The situation after the takeover

Through the first half of 1985, D Crosby continued as the Managing Director of Francis Packaging, reporting to the Chairman of the Francis Packaging Board, D Burnett, who also remained in office. The other members of the Board and an organisation chart are given in Appendix 1D. The Francis Packaging board remained responsible for Shemtec Packaging Ltd (Managing Director, C Crabtree) and Drummond Packaging Ltd (Managing Director, F Lysons).

By July 1985 D Burnett had left and at the end of July 1985 Suter installed a new Chief Executive, Paton Wallace. Paton Wallace was to take over the packaging companies of the former Francis Group, now to be known as the Suter Packaging Division – other Francis companies such as Clearplas were placed in other Suter Divisions. The Chairman of Suter had appointed Paton Wallace with the clear purpose of achieving an acceptable profit, that being at least 20 per cent on capital employed. The former Managing Director,

D Crosby continued as a consultant to the company and the Production Director left. When Paton Wallace arrived Francis Packaging was forecasting a profit before tax of less than £300,000 compared to the £1m that had been achieved in 1984. Mr Wallace was told that substantial business had been lost for a number of reasons. First, a major competitor, Nacanco, had taken advantage of the situation at Francis to mount a price war and had taken away large contracts with the oil companies. This had a major impact on the volume of sales from the Greenwich and Wrexham factories. Second, an important customer of Shemtec, the paint manufacturer Kalon, had not renewed its contract for reasons which were not clear. Finally, Drummond was suffering from the decline of major customers in the tobacco industry and of a major customer, DCL, who produced yeast.

In late August Larkfield consultants met the new Chief Executive. Mr Wallace outlined the recent history of Francis Packaging and then went on to discuss the problems that he was currently facing. Paton Wallace invited the Larkfield consultant to discuss the problems of the business with colleagues on the Board, a brief summary of which is given in the following paragraphs. He also commissioned the consultants to carry out market research and this is summarised in Appendices 1H to 1M.

A number of points emerged from the discussions that the consultants had with other members of the board. The view was widely held that tinplate would inevitably continue to lose market share to plastic. The conversations centred on the paint market and the dominating position that ICI held in that market. The consultants were told how ICI had taken a policy decision some years before to move to plastic containers for all their emulsion paints. Although solvent-based paints could not be contained in plastic because of the chemical reaction, it was thought that it was only a matter of time before water-based gloss paints would be developed to the point where they would be acceptable substitutes for solvent-based paints. Then ICI, it was felt, would use plastic containers for these paints too. The immediate threat, however, was to the emulsion paint business. ICI had encouraged Mardon Illingworth and Reed Packaging (a subsidiary of Reeds, who also owned Crown Paints) to develop straight-sided plastic cans with the same dimensions and specification as the metal cans. This had been done and ICI was transferring all of its emulsion paint to plastic containers as fast as the production capacity of the plastic can manufacturers would allow. The view at Francis was that, as soon as they could, the other paint producers would follow the ICI lead. In addition, solid emulsion was packaged in a plastic tray and this was also eroding the share of tinplate.

There seemed to be nothing that Francis could do to counter these trends – all the tinplate producers supplying the major paint companies provided a standard can (to Metal Packaging Manufacturer's Association standards) and in the oversupply conditions of the industry there was little scope for price increases.

After completing the discussions with Board members and the market research, the Larkfield consultants then worked on a strategic plan for the Division and its subsidiaries. This plan was prepared in close consultation with the Chief Executive of the Division. Mr Wallace was required to present his strategy to the main Suter Board in December 1985, only five months after taking up the position of Chief Executive. The time constraints were therefore such that it was impossible to involve the other members of the management of the Division.

Towards the end of November the outline of the strategy that Paton Wallace had developed with the consultants was presented to the Managing Directors of the three subsidiaries, the Board of Francis Packaging and two managers whom Paton Wallace had identified for promotion. Initially there was some disagreement on certain points in the market analysis and some reservations on the magnitude of the change which the new strategy represented, but at a second presentation there was a general agreement that it represented the way forward.

Appendix 1A
BACKGROUND NOTE ON THE PACKAGING INDUSTRY

Expenditure on packaging materials grew more rapidly than total expenditure in the economy over the second half of the 1970s. Metal packaging was holding its share. Around the turn of the decade there was a sharp change in trend with packaging growing more slowly than the economy and metal packaging losing share within the industry as a whole. These remarks on total value apply even more forcibly to volumes – the packaging industry as a whole and metal packaging in particular had not recovered to 1979 volume levels. Plastic packaging and to a lesser degree fibreboard have been gaining market share from metal and paper and to some extent, glass. Paper prices have risen much faster than inflation generally, as have prices of fibreboard. Metal packaging prices have increased much in line with inflation, but glass and plastic prices have tended to increase more slowly.

Metal packaging accounts for just under one quarter of the total packaging industry and has a total sales level of around £900–1000m. It employs about 21 000 people. The metal packaging industry can be subdivided into segments discussed in the following paragraphs.

Open top cans

These are either three-piece or two-piece. Three-piece is where the body is bent and the tops and bottoms are applied; two-piece is where the body is drawn up from the bottom and a top applied. The two-piece can was introduced in 1973 and currently nearly all beverage cans are of this variety. Here the printing is added to the cylindrical shape while in the case of the three-piece cans the printing is added before the metal is bent. Imports and exports are relatively small, although imports have been tending to rise.

Most open top cans are made of tinplate. Almost all open top cans for food are of tinplate, although about 65 per cent of the ends are made from tin-free steel. About half the beer and soft drink cans are now made of aluminium. The principal technical trends have been towards lighter weight, the use of welded rather than soldered joints and the substitution of aluminium for tinplate. In the past, tinplate cans took market share from glass but future trends are likely to be ones of substitution of tinplate by plastic, composite materials (for example, foil and plastic) and combined forms of packaging such as the bag in the box.

This is a volume production sector – about 9m cans a year. Of these about two-thirds are used by the canned food industry. This demand has been in decline due to the concern for healthier food and the greater demand for frozen food. However, growth in the production of pet food has compensated. Most of the remaining third of open top cans are used in the beverage industry.

The largest producer of open top cans is still Metal Box, but this company has lost market share (now about 50 per cent) to Nacanco (US owned) and American Can (Canadian owned), who together have about 30 per cent of the market. Crown Cork and Continental Can together have about 17 per cent of the market, leaving about 3 per cent for a few small producers. Some food producers manufacture their own cans.

Closures

These are the tops for various kinds of tinplate container. There has been strong substitution in this area by plastic.

Aerosol cans

These containers constitute a sizeable market and are used in a wide variety of applications, particularly in the toiletries and household cleaner markets. The major producer is Metal Box and there are relatively few other producers.

Collapsible aluminium tubes

These are used for tooth paste and ointments. Plastic is increasingly penetrating this sector.

Metal drums

These are made from steel, tinplate and aluminium. About 80 per cent in volume and 25 per cent in value of metal drums are in the 25 litres and less size range and these are predominantly tinplate. Those above 25 litres are made from cold-reduced mild steel. The main end uses of metal drums are as follows:

60% chemicals and petrochemicals;
25% oil products/lubricants and grease;
5% food, drink and tobacco;
10% other (including paint).

This sector has also been affected by the advent of plastic. Steel and tinplate have a technical advantage in the transport of solvent-based paints, food and oil. Furthermore they are re-usable. But plastic drums are lighter and they have an advantage in the transport of some corrosive liquids and dyestuffs. Bowater has developed blow-moulded plastic drums up to 220 litres.

There are only a few producers of metal drums: Metal Box, Van Leer, Francis, Reads, and Rheem Blagden.

Francis Packaging: Composition of the metal packaging industry

1984		£m
Open-top cans		540
Closures		74
Aerosol cans		81
Collapsible aluminium tubes		21
Metal drums		
– 25 litres and smaller	30	
– Above 25 litres	94	124
Other general line		
– Paint cans	50	
– Automotive product cans	15	
– Powdered food	47	
– Tobacco	21	
– Toiletries	19	
– Household	18	170
Total		1011

Other general line containers

These are predominantly round cans (mainly used for paint), rectangular cans (main uses being lubricating oil and edible oil) and a wide variety of smaller containers used for toiletries, and gift-ware. Production is characterised by much smaller runs than in the case of open top cans and these production runs are particularly small for the wide variety used in toiletries.

Appendix 1B
FRANCIS INDUSTRIES PLC

Activities: manufacture of packaging and industrial products for petroleum, food, paint and automotive industries.

Subsidiaries: Clearplas Ltd; Clearplas France SA; Drummond Packaging Ltd; F Francis and Sons Ltd; Lacrinoid Products Ltd; Sagar Richards Ltd; Shemtec Packaging Ltd (acquired in 1984).

Extracts from published accounts:
Year ending 31 December (£m)

Year	Turnover	Net profit before tax
1979	32.8	1.9
1980	29.7	1.8
1981	29.9	1.7
1982	32.7	0.0
1983	35.1	0.7

Geographic analysis of turnover (£m):

	1982	1983
UK	28.6	29.8
Rest of Europe	3.5	4.0
America	0.6	1.2

Appendix 1C
SUTER PLC

Activities: Manufacture and wholesaling of commercial refrigeration, air conditioning and hairdressing salon equipment. As a result of the Francis Industries acquisition, Suter also manufactures round and rectangular tinplate containers, die castings, mechanical components and precision injection moulding.

Extracts from published accounts:
Year ending 31 December (£m)

Year	Turnover	Net profit before tax
1980	4.2	0.5
1981	45.0	0.6
1982	58.2	(1.3)
1983	44.9	2.2
1984	47.3	4.1

Composition of turnover by activity (£m):

	1983	1984
Hairdressing equipment	3.8	4.8
Refrigeration and air conditioning	27.6	36.2
Francis Industries		3.3*

* results for six months as a related company and one
month as a subsidiary.

Geographic analysis of turnover (£m):

	1983	1984
UK	29.0	37.3
France	3.6	4.7
West Germany	1.8	0.8
North America	3.9	0.1

Appendix 1D
FRANCIS PACKAGING LTD: ORGANISATION CHART (MAY 1985)

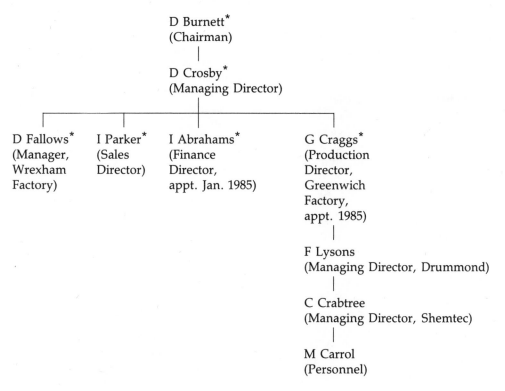

* Members of the Board of Francis Packaging

Appendix 1E
PRODUCTION FACILITIES

Francis Packaging itself operates from two factories, one at Greenwich in London and the other at Wrexham in Wales. The Greenwich and Wrexham factories each have the following production facilities.

- Tinplate printing facility. This is of major importance given the requirement for high print quality for final customer-appeal reasons. The sides of the containers are printed in sheets according to the design specifications of the purchasing company. Stocks of printed tinplate are held for the major customers. The printed sheets are then cut into individual pieces when required and passed onto the production lines.
- Lines producing paint cans (1-, 2.5- and 5-litre sizes). The printed container sides are bent into the required round shape by one machine and then automatically passed onto the welder where the ends are welded. The bottoms are next welded to the base and the ring components fixed to the top. Greenwich and Wrexham produce high quality cans to MPMA specifications. Order sizes are generally large (15 000 containers plus) although nowhere near as large as in the case of open top cans, which also differ in another respect – they are not usually printed.
- Lines producing rectangular containers (2.5- and 5-litre sizes). The production process is much the same as that described above and these too are the high volume products of the general line business.
- A line producing 20-litre and 25-litre tinplate drums. These are also standardised relatively high volume products.
- Areas for producing components, e.g. lids, bottoms, handles and rings for container tops.
- Quality control. Samples are regularly checked for strength, leakage and print quality.

Stocks of completed cans are not generally held for any length of time because the space occupied would be considerable. There had been some investment in the previous few years in the facilities at Greenwich, but the drum line at that factory was very old and conditions were very crowded in the factory.

The Shemtec subsidiary has a factory in Leeds which produces paint cans only (0.5-, 1-, 2.5- and 5-litre sizes). These cans do not conform to MPMA size dimensions and are therefore not usually purchased by the paint company majors. They are not regarded as of the same quality as the Greenwich and Wrexham cans. The Leeds factory has a print facility and a number of paint can production lines. The equipment is considerably older than that at Greenwich and Wrexham. There had been little investment for some years. Components produced here were not compatible with those at the other factories.

The Drummond subsidiary has a factory in Greenock, Scotland. The business of this factory is substantially different from that at the other factories discussed above. The operation here is at the jobbing end of the tinplate business. Order sizes are generally much smaller, less than 10 000 containers. Round cans used to pack powdered food are the only products with order sizes which approach those for rectangular and paint cans. The factory has a good print facility and lines to produce round cans (powdered food), rectangular cans (usually for cooked meats), rectangular tins for shortbread, tins for cigars and small round containers for tobacco. There is also a line for 10-litre paint pails. It should be pointed out that the round and rectangular tins produced at this factory are very different from those produced at the other factories for paint and oil. There had been no investment in this factory for some years; for example, an automatic welder required for top-quality cans for the powdered food industry was lacking.

Appendix 1F
SUMMARY OF THE PAST FINANCIAL PERFORMANCE OF THE COMPANIES IN THE SUTER PACKAGING DIVISION (£m)

	1980	1981*	1982	1983	1984†	1985‡
Sales						
Francis	14.0	13.4	14.7	16.9	20.8	20.1
Shemtec					4.0	3.4
Francis/Shemtec					24.8	23.5
Drummond		0.8	1.8	1.6	1.8	2.1
Total					26.6	25.6
PBT						
Francis	0.3	0.7	0.9	1.5	0.8	0.6
Shemtec					0.3	0.2
Francis/Shemtec					1.1	0.8
Drummond		0.0	0.1	0.0	(0.1)	0.0
Total					1.0	0.8
Capital employed						
Francis	3.8	3.8	3.8	3.1	6.1	5.8
Shemtec					1.2	1.1
Francis/Shemtec					7.3	6.9
Drummond		0.5	0.3	0.3	0.4	0.5
Total					7.7	7.4
Return on capital employed						
Francis	8	18	24	48	13	10
Shemtec					25	18
Francis/Shemtec					15	12
Drummond		0	33	0	(25)	0
Total					14	11

* Drummond acquired in 1981.
† Shemtec acquired in early 1984.
‡ Companies acquired by Suter in late 1984.

Appendix 1G
MARKET RESEARCH: COMPOSITION OF SUTER PACKAGING DIVISION'S BUSINESS

At the start of the market research (points from which are summarised in Appendices H–M) which Larkfield had undertaken to complete for the Suter Packaging Division, the consultants prepared an analysis of the current composition of the Suter Packaging business. They saw the Suter companies as two distinct businesses.

- Francis Packaging Ltd plus Shemtec Packaging Ltd, whose business is the volume production of standard general-line tinplate containers (round cans, rectangular containers and drums) for the following industries:
  - paint;
  - miscellaneous chemicals (bituminous products, structural and preservative products, paint removers and strippers, putties, fillers, sealers and adhesives, printing inks and insecticides);
  - lubricating oil (largely retail);
  - edible oil for the catering sector.
- Drummond Packaging Ltd, whose business is the short-run production of off-standard, speciality tinplate general-line containers for the cooked meat, powdered food, biscuit and confectionery, and tobacco industries.

The Francis/Shemtec business

The breakdown of Francis/Shemtec business was found to be as follows:

	Sales (£m) 1984	1985	Units (m) 1984	1985	Litres contained (m) 1984	1985
Rounds	12.7	11.4			81	83
5 litre			10.5	10.9		
2.5 litre			8.8	8.8		
1 litre			5.1	5.2		
0.5 litre			2.0	2.2		
Rectangulars	6.6	6.5			80	55
5 litre			11.9	8.5		
4 litre			4.2	2.5		
2.5 litre			1.0	1.1		
Drums	5.5	5.6	3.6	3.8	84	88
Total	24.8	23.5			245	226

Francis/Shemtec (F/S) shares of the total tinplate container market (by product) in 1985 were estimated to be as follows:

	Units (m) F/S	Total	Litres (m) F/S	Total	Percentage of F/S Share
Rounds					
5 litre	10.9	42	55	210	26
2.5 litre	8.8	40	22	100	22
1 litre	5.2	52	5	52	10
0.5 litre	2.2	22	1	11	10
Rectangulars					
5 litre	8.5	30	42	150	29
4 litre	2.5	6	10	24	42
2.5 litre	1.1	2	3	5	55
Drums					
20/25 litre	3.8	13	88	313	28
Total		226		864	26

Using the distribution of deliveries to types of customer for the first nine months of 1985, the consultants made the following analysis (in percentage terms) of the markets into which the products were going:

	Round cans units	litre	value	Rectangular cans units	litre	value	Drums units	litre	value
Paint	87	92	89	10	10	10	23	25	24
Chemical	11	6	9	25	25	25	11	11	11
Lubricating oil	–	–	–	54	54	54	25	28	27
Edible oil	–	–	–	7	7	7	39	34	36
Other	2	2	2	4	4	4	2	2	2
Total	100	100	100	100	100	100	100	100	100

The Drummond business

The composition of the Drummond business (percentage of turnover) over the past two years is summarised as follows:

	1984	1985
Tobacco Clipovac tins and cigar ovals	47	28
Oblongs and squares for meat, yeast and Fetta cheese	26	56
603 diameter round for powdered food and some chemicals	7	3
Flat rectangular for shortbread	6	5
10-litre pails for paint	4	2
Other	10	6

Appendix 1H
PACKAGING IN THE PAINT MARKET

An overview of the paint market in 1985 (millions of litres) is given in the following table. The paint market here is defined to exclude paint-related products: structural and preservative products; bituminous products; putties, fillers and sealers; paint removers and strippers; and printing inks.

Sector	Total	Metal			Plastic				Steel drums bulk containers
		Cans	Rect.	20/25 drum	Tray	Can	Pail	Other	
Decorative									
Trade (water)	92	78				10	4		
Trade (solvent)	70	70							
Retail (water)	82	35			17	30			
Retail (solvent)	46	46							
Total (water)	195	119		6	17	40	5	8	
Total (solvent)	136	125		11					
	331	244		17	17	40	5	8	
Industrial									
Refinishing	24	10	4	10					
Cars	21								21
Commercial vehicles	11								11
Can coatings	18								18
Coil coatings	46								46
Marine	16	7	3	6					
Other/General Industry	129	32	5	12					80
	265	49	12	28					176
Other paint									
Wood finishes	21	5	8				8		
Miscellaneous	8	2	3				1		2
Thinners, etc	7							7	
	36	7	11				9	7	2
Total	632	300	23	45	17	40	14	15	178

The building sectors in which paint is professionally applied (the trade segment) are:

Industro–commercial	17%
New housing – public	7%
New housing – private	25%
Repair and maintenance	51%
	100%

Past trends in the use of paint in the trade segment were:

Year	Litres (m)	Percentage per annum	R&M	New housing Pub.	Priv.	% per annum comm.
1980	147	−3	4	−19	−27	2
1981	139	−6	−9	−34	−9	7
1982	146	5	−1	−16	15	14
1983	160	9.5	7	6	20	2
1984	163	2	5	−9	−3	4
1985	162	−1	−4	−23	1	6

The largest manufacturer of paint for the trade sector is ICI. The next three in size are owned by major industrial groupings: Crown owned by Reed International; Berger by Hoecsht; McPhersons by the major Finnish chemical company, Kemira oy. Kalon is an independent company which has been pursuing an aggressive acquisition policy and by this means built up a significant market share. ICI exerts an influence on the market which is far greater than its market share alone would suggest. It is the price leader.

ICI	22%
Crown	16%
Berger	7%
McPherson	9%
Blundell	17%
Kalon	10%
Goodlass Wall	4%
	85%

Over half the paint used by professionals is distributed directly by the paint manufacturers.

	1964	1970	1979	1985
Direct sales	47	49	53	55
Wholesalers/merchants	48	47	43	42
Retail sales	5	4	4	3
	100%	100%	100%	100%

Paint in the trade segment is packaged in round containers up to five litres, with five litres as the predominant size. The decorative quality of the container does have an importance, but not nearly as marked as in the retail market. Concern over corrosion of tinplate containing water-based paint is not marked in this sector, partly because paint stocks move much more quickly. The professional user is generally reported to have a preference for tinplate containers, mainly for strength reasons. The builders merchant consulted in the market research expressed a preference for tinplate, mainly for stacking reasons.

Recent trends in retail paint demand are given below:

Year	Litres (m)	Percentage (pa)	Spending on DIY as percentage (pa)	Home decorating DIY (%)
1980	115	−2.5	−11	45
1981	115	0	−7	44
1982	115	0	−3	43
1983	116	1	−0.5	43
1984	123	6		
1985	128	4		

Market shares in the retail sector are shown below:

	%
ICI	33
Crown	20
Berger	7
McPherson	7
Kalon	10
Goodlass Wall	4
Johnstone	2
	83

Shares of distribution outlets in retail paint (percentage by volume) are shown below:

	1977	1983
Paint and wallpaper specialists	46	35
DIY stores	8	25
Supermarkets	8	15
Woolworths	10	8
Builders merchants	7	5
Other	15	10
	100	100

The market research revealed that paint manufacturers in the decorative sector had the following requirements of packaging.

(a) Service provided by the container manufacturer. This covers reliability in terms of delivery; flexibility in terms of responding at short notice to orders or changes in orders; and communication of any delivery problems which are likely to be encountered. The large paint makers were moving to the 'just-in-time' method of production control.

(b) Responsiveness by the container manufacturer to changes in the requirements of the paint industry in terms of service, quality and marketing.

(c) Package quality: standard dimensions appropriate to filling lines, strength appropriate to warehouse stacking arrangements, a low propensity to leak, dent or corrode.

(d) Appearance and decorative quality so as to enhance the paint product. This is of particular importance in the retail sector.

(e) Container price. The container represents 6 per cent of the final sales price of the paint and it has been increasing much more rapidly than the price of paint.

The requirements of distributors of paint focus primarily on appearance, that is, packaging is very much a marketing factor. As far as they are concerned denting, corrosion and leaking are appearance-related factors, as is the propensity of the package to attract dust.

The requirements of the final user of the package do not seem to attract much attention from either the paint manufacturers or the distributors.

The market research revealed a widespread dissatisfaction with the service provided by the manufacturers of tinplate. The industry was criticised for its lack of flexibility, its poor communication and its old-fashioned attitudes. The lack of response by tinplate manufacturers to the perceived requirements of the paint industry were frequently commented upon. Some of those paint makers currently using plastic regard the service provided by the plastic manufacturers as superior; none thought that it was worse. There was much less of a consensus on the quality of the tinplate

product. Some large paint makers did regard leakage as a problem, others thought that the incidence was so low that it was not significant. Denting was also mentioned, but it was not generally seen as a widespread or major problem. There was no unanimity on the view that tinplate is incompatible with water-based materials. Those DIY distributors interviewed did not see corrosion as a problem. There is no readily available information on whether the final user is concerned about corrosion. The price of tinplate containers was not generally regarded as a problem.

ICI had decided to package its emulsion paint in plastic because tinplate corrodes and, despite invitations to address this problem, the tinplate manufacturers had done nothing. ICI introduced the paint tray for solid emulsion and Crown and Berger followed. ICI encouraged Reed Packaging and Mardon Illingworth to develop plastic paint cans with the same dimensions as tinplate cans to avoid investment in filling lines. But some stacking and warehouse rearrangement was still required because of the lower strength characteristics of plastic. These plastic containers are currently sold at the same price as tinplate. The Metal Box, straight-sided plastic can did not meet ICI specifications (overhanging lid). But it is sold at a 10 per cent price discount and is used by some paint manufacturers. The tapered pail had not succeeded in taking market share because of the stacking problems.

Estimates of current plastic can manufacturing capacity are as follows.

	Units 2.5L	5L	End 1985 Litres (m)	End 1986 Litres (m)
Reed Packaging	3	3	22.5	22.5
Mardon Illingworth	3	3	22.5	22.5
Metal Box	2	2	15.0	30.0
Metal Box (new can)	–	–	–	22.5
Total			60.0	97.5

As at November 1985 the market research indicated the following intentions by paint makers (millions of litres).

| | 1985 | | | 1986 | | | 1987 | | |
	Emuls. Total	Plastic Tray	Plastic Can	Emuls. Total	Plastic Tray	Plastic Can	Emuls. Total	Plastic Tray	Plastic Can
ICI	54	9	25	55	10	44	57	10	47
Crown	35	5		36	5		37	6	
Berger	14	3		14	3	3	15	3	6
McPherson	16			16			17		
Blundell	16			16			17		
Kalon	19			19			20		
Goodlass	7		5	7		7	7		7
Johnston	4		3	4		4	4		4
Sigma	2		2	2		2	2		2
Others	28		5	30		10	29		15
Total	195	17	40	199	18	70	205	19	81

In the longer term there is the strong possibility that solvent-receptive plastic containers will be developed. This might occur through the development of special plastics or, more likely the coating of the interior of plastic containers with a solvent-resistant substance. The overwhelming consensus in the paint industry is that this will occur; developments are already underway. However it is generally regarded as unlikely that this will occur before the 1990s. Another development could be the introduction of water-based gloss paints. These already exist and are extensively used in the US. However, they do not display the high gloss characteristics required by the UK market. Further work is proceeding to remedy this and the general consensus is that they will appear on the market in the 1990s.

About two thirds of industrial paint is transported by bulk means. The main categories of industrial paint not transported in this way are:

(a) refinishing paint sold to garages and body shops. The main producers are ICI, followed by Ault and Wiborg. ICI does not exert the dominant role here which it does in the decorative market;
(b) marine paints;
(c) less than 40 per cent of the remaining general industrial paints.

Past trends in some parts of the industrial paint market are summarised below (millions of litres).

Year	Marine	Other industrial (not bulk transported)
1980	25	65
1981	22	64
1982	22	60
1983	18	68
1984	18	68
1985	16	73

Important developments now occurring in the industrial paint segment are the improvement in spraying techniques and the increasing application of powdered coatings, particularly coil coatings. The increasing import penetration of finished goods also has implications for the industrial paint market. In the longer term there is likely to be a trend towards the gradual reduction of the proportion of aggressive solvents in industrial paints. These paints are also likely to be affected by the development of water-based paints in the 1990s. The appearance of solvent-receptive plastic containers also looks likely.

Current forms of packaging for industrial paint (not bulk transported) are confined to tinplate because of the aggressive solvents used. Packaging is widely spread over the size range with around half in the larger round cans, about one-third in the 20/25-litre drums and the remainder in the larger rectangular containers.

Attitudes to the tinplate are very similar to those held by manufacturers in the decorative paint market.

Customers' opinions of the Suter Packaging companies are varied. None of those interviewed hold the view that either Francis or Shemtec are any worse than the other tinplate manufacturers. A number hold the view that there is nothing to distinguish either Francis or Shemtec from the other tinplate manufacturers. Generally, how-ever, the opinion is that both Francis and Shemtec provide a better service than other tinplate manufacturers in terms of reliability and flexibility. Only a few think that quality is poorer than the competition. But Francis/Shemtec are seen as the number three supplier, mainly on capacity grounds and on the belief that they do not have the resources or the support to function as top suppliers.

Appendix 1I
PACKAGING IN THE MISCELLANEOUS CHEMICALS MARKET

In 1985 some 18 million litres of bituminous product were produced and sold into the DIY and building markets (mainly industrial building) for waterproofing purposes. Both the DIY and building applications have been growing over the past few years. About 30–40 per cent of these products are water-based. In their packaging, the producers of these products are looking for: reliability; flexibility; modern and appealing design; adequate strength and protection. For the water-based products the manufacturers tend to use plastic because it is cheap (tapered pails), less easily damaged and the decorative qualities are acceptable. For the solvent-based products they use tinplate. The view is that tinplate manufacturers are unreliable and not innovative enough, and in these respects are inferior to the manufacturers of plastic containers. Francis is highly regarded in comparison to other tinplate manufacturers.

An estimated 20 million litres of preservative and structural paint products were produced in 1985. They include wood preservatives and concrete additives. Some of these products (e.g. wood preservatives) are sold into both the DIY and building markets, others (e.g. concrete additives, plasticisers, etc) are sold entirely to building and civil engineering contractors. Some of the products (e.g. wood preservatives) are solvent-based while others (e.g. agents for concrete) have a high proportion of water-based products. A wide range of container sizes is used and the penetration of plastic into the water-based products is heavy because the cheaper, tapered plastic pails are used. Packaging priorities are price and compatibility with the material. The same views as those described above were expressed on tinplate manufacturers.

Paint strippers, fillers, sealers and adhesives are in highly fragmented industries selling mainly into the DIY market, but with an industrial market for adhesives. The DIY products are now almost entirely packaged in plastic and, to a lesser extent, in collapsible aluminium tubes. The main use of tinplate seems to be in 25-litre drums for export.

Demand for printing inks has been growing rapidly over the past few years. Water-based products account for about 30 per cent and plastic-tapered pails are used for packaging because they are cheaper. Requirements of packaging are: strength and compatibility; sales appeal; and price. In future, containers will have to meet United Nations regulations on the carriage of dangerous materials. Sericol import 5-litre tapered tin pails from Holland because they cannot obtain a container of the required quality from UK producers. The views on tinplate versus plastic manufacturers are the familiar ones, as described above.

Insecticides represent a rapidly growing market.

Appendix 1J
PACKAGING IN THE LUBRICATING OIL MARKET

The volume (millions of litres) of lubricating oil supplied to the UK market in 1985 were as follows.

	Volume	*< 5L*[*]	*5L†*	*25L‡ + 205L + bulk*
		Form of packaging		
Transport				
Retail	105	15	90	
Vehicle servicing	65			65
Commercial	170		10	160
Marine/aircraft	70			70
Agriculture	40			40
Industrial	475			475
Total	925	15	100	810

[*] Predominantly plastic
† Approximately 70 per cent tinplate and 30 per cent plastic
‡ Predominantly tinplate

The commercial sector covers all deliveries to vehicle manufacturers, transport authorities, bus companies, nationalised industries and transport companies. While some of the oil is for new cars, the bulk of it is supplied to the operators of commercial transport fleets. The remainder of the transport sector consists of supplies to agricultural machinery, ships and aircraft. The industrial sector includes metal working oils, process oils, greases, fuel oil sold as lubricant and all other oils used in industrial processes.

The demand for lubricating oil for both retail and vehicle servicing is shown below (there are no statistics on the split between them). However, retail demand is probably about 65 per cent of the total and has probably remained a constant proportion of the total over the 1980s.

Year	Total sales litres (m)	Percentage (pa)
1980	195	
1981	182	−7
1982	178	−3
1983	172	−3
1984	170	−1
1985	170	0

The decline in lubricating oil demand (despite the slow growth in the vehicle population) in the retail segment has been caused by two factors.

(a) Vehicle engines have been improved leading to longer maintenance intervals and thus fewer oil changes. Sumps are also now significantly smaller.

(b) Lubricants themselves have been improved by the addition of additives, also leading to less frequent oil changes.

The retail market can be segmented both by purchasing motivation and by the type of product. By purchasing motivation the market can be divided into:

(a) emergency top up consumers – purchases tend to be in 0.5- and 1-litre packs;

(b) take away consumers, e.g. DIY car servicing – purchases are usually in 5-litre packs.

During the 1970s there was a large shift to DIY car servicing. The proportion of people both topping up and changing their own oil increased from 42 per cent to 60 per cent. During that period the fall in lubricating oil usage in the retail plus vehicle servicing sectors was therefore not reflected in the retail sector – it fell largely on the vehicle servicing sector. It appears that the trend to DIY ceased in about 1980 due to the large proportion of company cars in the UK. The continuing fall in lubricating oil demand in the 1980s has therefore come to be reflected in retail sales.

By product-type, the market can be segmented into the following.

(a) Multi-grade oils (about 85 per cent of the retail market). The multi-grades subdivide into premium multi-grades and the cheaper multi-grades. The former are the brand leaders and are, technically, superior blends of the latter. The latter tend to be own-brand products and are aimed at the economising motorist. The premium multi-grades tend to be in tinplate at the 5-1litre size, while the cheaper multi-grades are in plastic. For both premium and other multi-grades, the smaller packs are almost all now in plastic.

(b) Single-grade oils. These are the old-fashioned oils specific to particular vehicles and seasons. The usage of these oils in the car market is dying out, but they are still important in the high-mileage commercial vehicle sector where oil changes are more frequent. The share of single-grade oils in the retail sector has fallen from 30 per cent in 1970 to around 15 per cent at the present time.

(c) Speciality oils. These are a new generation of high-tech, hyper-grade oils, many of which are synthetic. They can be used in all types of vehicle and in all conditions, although currently they tend to be used only in expensive cars. Speciality oils are available in all retail sizes and are packed in plastic.

Over 70 per cent of retail oil falls into the 5-litre takeaway multi-grade segment.

Castrol and Duckhams have maintained brand leadership in the retail lubricating oil market for many years. The other companies with significant market shares are the major oil companies: Shell, Esso and BP.

	1981 (%)	1983 (%)
Castrol (Burmah)	30	30
Duckhams (BP)	16	15
Shell	10	11
BP	8	7
Esso	8	7
Mobil	4	3
Own label	14	16
Others	10	11

The market has become increasingly competitive with large short-term swings in market shares. Own brands have used price to gain share at the bottom end of the market. The big companies have tended to compete increasingly on promotions, involving free gifts or possible prizes. A major promotion this year, which is viewed as being very successful, was Castrol's offering of 10 per cent extra oil free.

The split between oil distributed by garages and retail outlets is shown below (percentage by volume).

	1971	1979	1981	1985
Garage forecourts	75	50	54	60
Retail shops	25	50	46	40

Within the garage forecourt sector, the relative importance of the major oil companies is shown (percentage shares in the number of garage outlets).

	%
Shell	15
Esso	14
BP/National	12
Texaco	7
Jet/Globe	5
Burmah	4
Mobil	4
Other (50)	39

The major oil companies largely restrict the sale of motor oil on their own forecourt to their own brands. The major brands are also generally not stocked in retail outlets. The exceptions are Castrol and Duckhams, both of which are available over a wide range of garage outlets and retail shops. In the 1970s there was a switch to purchasing oil from retail outlets. This switch has now to some extent been reversed.

The oil companies have all introduced tendering procedures for their supplies from packaging companies.

At present, the oil industry has expressed a preference for 5-litre tinplate rectangles, while at the same time expressing a belief that plastic will take over in the long term. At present, tinplate is seen as having the following advantages:

(a) an up-market connotation;
(b) superior printing qualities;
(c) easier handling and quicker filling times;
(d) greater strength and therefore higher stacking as well as simpler palletisation.

However the oil companies did point to:

(a) the rapid advances in plastic printing technology;
(b) methods of designing production and storage to reduce the costs of using plastic containers without substantial investment.

The oil companies do not have a high opinion of the tinplate manufacturers. They are seen as performing the commercial aspects adequately but they are regarded as highly complacent. There are variations in product quality, reliability and speed of delivery, flexibility and general service. But none of these aspects are considered critical, nor are there differences between suppliers such as to give any of them a major advantage. The oil companies see the tinplate manufacturers as lacking in innovation, product promotion, product differentiation and imagination. While they would like to keep stocks to a minimum, there is not sufficient trust in the suppliers to move to 'just-in-time' production scheduling.

The major distinguishing criterion in placing orders between the four major suppliers (Metal Box, Nacanco, Reads and Francis) is price. Except over very small price variations, differences between the four suppliers on other product/service parameters would need to be much greater if they were to form the basis of contract-placing decisions.

The plastics companies have a much higher reputation in a market which now places so much emphasis on promotions with the consequent requirement for off-standard sizes. Plastic has therefore been making in-roads despite the fact that its products are non-standard and therefore difficult to multi-source. By contrast, both Burmah and BP have been experiencing difficulty in securing the containers they need for their promotions from their tinplate suppliers.

The oil companies regard Francis as the 'best of a bad bunch'. Quality is considered to be about the same as Metal Box. On delivery and flexibility, Francis are considered to be the best in the industry. There is a considerable amount of goodwill towards Francis and they are considered to be the nicest company to deal with. But Francis does not escape the general criticisms of the tinplate industry.

Market shares (as a percentage of litres produced) for competitors in the retail lubricating oil market can be measured in two ways (see table below). The first column shows the share estimates for 1985 as a whole. The second looks at current contracts alone. The share which Francis had of the total retail market over 1985 as a whole is likely to be of the order of 30 per cent. However, if only current contracts are taken into account, then the Francis share of the rectangular 5-litre market falls to 10 per cent. This dramatic fall in share is the consequence of losing the contracts with Castrol, Shell and Esso in the price war instigated by Nacanco. Reads, and to a lesser extent Metal Box, have followed Nacanco in its price cutting.

	1985 (%)	Current contracts (%)
Nacanco	22	35
Metal Box	13	15
Reads	5	10
Francis	30	10
Plastic	30	30

In the garage servicing, commercial transport, agricultural, marine and aviation sectors the increasing efficiency of oils and engines has led to the demand for oil declining at a rate of 1.5 per cent a year. The decline in heavy manufacturing in the UK has resulted in lubricating-oil use in industry falling at a rate of around 2 per cent a year.

The major requirements (for 25-litre drums, used to a considerable extent in the segments given in the above paragraph) are utility and cost. Specification is made according to usage and, within the specification, price is the determinant. Plastic is considered inferior to tinplate because it is not strong enough for required stacking and is unstable for filling and handling. It cannot be multi-sourced because each company's product is different. Plastic has failed to establish a price advantage.

The customers in the other sectors of the lubricating oil market are the same as in the retail market. In these sectors, Nacanco is not a competitor but Van Leer and Tanks and Drums are. With the same customers and mostly the same competitors it is not surprising that customer perceptions of both the tinplate industry and of Francis are the same as they are in the retail sector. Generally, product reliability and flexibility are more important here, while image and other marketing factors are less so.

Appendix 1K
PACKAGING IN THE EDIBLE OIL MARKET

The volumes of refined edible oils consumed (000 tonnes) in the UK in 1983, and how they were contained, was as follows.

Manufacture of fats, margarine, etc.	988	Bulk tanker
Bottled oils	70	Glass/plastic
Canned oils	80	Tin/plastic

The product transported by bulk tanker is either transformed into margarine and solid fats or is used by food manufacturers. While imports of edible oils are about 15 per cent of consumption and exports only 3 per cent, in the UK most of the imports are in bulk form and are then packaged for consumption. The recent UK expansion of rape seed production is likely to reverse the adverse import/export balance and, to the small extent that packaged cooking oil is currently imported, growth in production is likely to exceed growth in demand.

The remaining raw edible oil is sold into the domestic and catering markets. Bottled oil roughly equates with the domestic or retail market. Oil here is packaged largely in pack sizes up to three litres and is mainly in plastic. Canned oils are used mainly in the catering sector and are packaged in tinplate in 5-litre and 20-litre sizes.

Retail demand for edible oil in recent years was as follows.

Year	Tonnes (000)	Litres (m)	Percentage (pa)
1981	52	60	3
1982	55	63	5
1983	59	68	8
1984	64	74	9
1985	70	81	9

The food market is a mature one and growth in most sectors tends to be minimal. But in the case of edible oil the marked shift away from high-cholesterol fats for health reasons has led to the growth trend evident in the statistics shown in the table above.

In the retail sector very little is sold in container sizes above three litres. Only a small proportion of the oil sold in 5-litre sizes in this sector is in tinplate. Plastic is much cheaper than tinplate. Tinplate has an unacceptable image in the retail market because it is not transparent and clean looking.

Recent growth trends in the demand for edible oil in the catering sector were as follows.

Year	Tonnes (000)	Litres (m)	Percentage (pa)
1981	66	76	3
1982	68	78	3
1983	71	82	5
1984	77	89	9
1985	85	95	7

There is no clear distinction between the packers and distributors of edible oil. The packing/distribution structure consists of:

(a) refiners who distribute in bulk to packers, but who also pack for final distribution to caterers, either direct or through wholesalers and specialist catering distributors;

(b) packers who purchase bulk supplies from the refiners and then pack for distribution to caterers either direct or through the wholesalers/distributors;

(c) wholesalers and specialist catering distributors who provide a cash-and-carry service.

Shares of the top refiners in 1985 were:

	%
Acatos and Hutchinson (Pura)	35
Van Den Burgh/Bibby	10
Top Three	50

The top three refiners account for a significantly smaller share of distribution. However Acatos and Hutchinson are aggressively trying to increase their share of both production and distribution. They are pursuing a modernisation and cost-cutting strategy in order to meet foreign competition in a highly price-conscious market. They have taken over a number of other companies recently, (e.g. Pura and Britannia) and are engaged in a rationalisation programme. They are talking about the introduction of a just-in-time system to reduce stock holding. They are exploring the possibility of producing their own 20-litre drums, both to cut costs and discourage the specialist packers, and so gain a higher share of distribution. Van Den Burgh regard the edible oil market as a commodity market with margins which are too low to justify an aggressive expansion strategy.

Packing and distribution are fragmented, with the refiners themselves having only a small share. The remainder of packing and distribution includes a large number of ethnic packers who fill by hand.

The largest distributor accounts for about 20 per cent of sales and the next largest for less than 10 per cent. The rest of the distribution network is highly fragmented.

Forms of packaging currently in use in the catering segment of the edible oil market are:

Size	Litre (m)	Material
5-litre	10	Tinplate/plastic
10-litre	–	Tinplate
20-litre	85	Tinplate

Packaging requirements vary to some extent in different parts of the catering market:

(a) at the bottom fragmented end, packers are looking for the cheapest form of packaging;
(b) the larger refiner/packers aim at minimising production and distribution costs. Their emphasis is on a standardised container for automatic filling with good strength characteristics for stacking, handling and transport. Minimising stock holding is of major importance.

Where price is the major factor, plastic has made in-roads and this applies particularly to the 5-litre size. At the 20-litre size the plastic product is not sufficiently technically developed, and is no cheaper than tinplate. At this size plastic is not rigid enough and there are leakage problems.

At the mass production end of the market the tinplate manufacturers are regarded as complacent, spending insufficient time identifying their customers needs or trying to satisfy them. It is felt that communication is poor.

In terms of quality, reliability and flexibility, Francis are regarded as the best of a bad bunch. But Francis were criticised for poor communication, lack of sales literature and lack of warning on price increases.

Francis has a competitive advantage in terms of location – most of the mass fillers are located in the South East. Francis has a market share of about 30 per cent of the more than four million 20-litre drums used in this market. The competitors are the same as those for 25-litre drums. Francis are in a similar position in the much smaller, 5-litre segment.

Appendix 1L
PACKAGING IN THE MARKETS FOR DRUMMOND'S PRODUCTS

Drummond sells its products to the fillers of cooked meats requiring non-standard containers, to segments of the powdered beverages markets, confectionery, biscuits, and tobacco.

The 1982 breakdown (£m) of canned meat consumption in the UK is given below. Imports probably account for a small proportion of the 'hot' sector, most of the imports being of 'cold' meats.

Bacon and ham	50
Corned beef	155
Sausages	10
Chopped ham and pork	25
Tongue	10
Poultry	8
Luncheon Meat, other	12
Total cold	**270**
Pies and puddings	20
Mince, stewed steak	25
Pie fillings	15
Casseroles	5
Others	25
Total hot	**90**
Total	**360**

Most of these meat products are contained in open-top cans. The sectors of most relevance to Drummond's products are bacon and ham (mostly filled abroad); and pies, puddings, pie fillings and casseroles (mostly filled in the UK).

The UK canned fish market is worth around £130m, but the bulk is of imported filled cans.

Fetta cheese is packaged in tinplate since no rectangular plastic cans exist at this time. In the export market the tinplate can be used as a cooking utensil in less developed countries.

Infant milk and instant milk powders constitute an important user of general line containers, but some 25 per cent of their requirement for such containers is manufactured by the users. The UK instant milk market has declined in line with birth rates, but the export market continues to play an important part with a substantial proportion of filled containers going abroad, mainly to third-world countries. In export markets the tinplate container has considerable advantages over its principal domestic competitors – the pouch and lined carton – because of its protective qualities against both climate and impact damage.

The gourmet tea market, characteristically packed in distinct, square, tinplate lever-lid containers and fancy boxes was formerly an important market for the tinplate container. However, rapidly rising tea prices have caused a marked decline. High quality teas are packaged mainly for the export market.

Ground coffee has now followed instant coffee

in switching from metal to other forms of packaging – in this case, flexible bags – although an important (but declining) metal container market remains for exports.

For confectionery, the tinplate container is used mainly for exports, specialities and promotions.

The large unit, decorated tinplate biscuit tin market has always been dependent on a few major customers with a quarter of total usage made in-plant. While there is an export element, the substantial seasonal home market is the dominating factor. The biscuit producers seek three suppliers of tins. A few years ago these were Wilkie Paul, Huntley Bourne & Stevens, and Metal Box. Wilkie Paul went bankrupt and Metal Box bought their machinery. Linpac then invested in the necessary machinery. It subsequently bought Huntley Bourne & Stevens. Drummond has just ordered the necessary machinery to become the third biscuit-tin supplier.

For a long time tinplate containers have taken only a small proportion of tobacco packaging and their share has been further eroded by both the decline in smoking and the switch to new packaging materials. The resurgence in demand caused by the cigar, pipe and cigarette hand-rolling markets have now been reversed by the use of polythene pouches and the general fall in demand for all tobacco products. Again, it is the gift and export markets for the premium products (cigars) that offer the most lasting prospect for tinplate sales. Drummond supplies oval cigar tins and Clipovac tins for tobacco. The main tobacco tin alternative is the screw-top tin produced by Metal Box. Gallaher has recently decided to purchase all Clipovac tins from Barnsley Canister, all its oval cigar-tin requirements from Drummond, and all screw-top tins from Metal Box.

Several attributes are important when assessing potential suppliers, varying according to the product being packed:

(a) quality – sizes outside tolerance ranges stop production lines; badly welded cans do not protect the product; the container has to ensure a long shelf-life for products;
(b) consistency of quality in seaming, internal lacquers, size and printing;
(c) sales appeal – the quality of printing is important;

(d) reliable delivery and flexibility – in some markets, producers have to respond rapidly to the demands of retailers or wholesalers for large quantities over short periods of time;

(e) price;

(f) commitment to the user's business;

(g) technical support;

(h) sales contact – regular communication from can makers on availability, problems on the horizon, pricing issues, quality control developments and new ideas.

Drummond's main tinplate competitors are as follows.

- Meat products: Metal Box; American Can; Carnaud; Haustrup; Thomasen & Drijver.
- Biscuits/shortbread: Metal Box; Huntley Bourne & Stevens: Robertson Canisters.
- Tobacco: Metal Box; Huntley Bourne & Stevens.
- Yeast: Cebal.

Customers dual source to give security of supply, ensure a competitive situation (on price, quality and delivery); and encourage more ideas on new developments in packaging. There is no single supplier who meets all of the evaluative assessment criteria discussed earlier, and who produces the full product range required.

Virtually all of Drummond's customers felt that it was falling short of the standards they expect. But customers recognised the efforts which Drummond staff made under difficult circumstances. Although some customers had taken business away from Drummond on quality grounds (seaming was quoted frequently), changing suppliers creates uncertainty and companies do not therefore switch suppliers often. Customers felt that Drummond showed flexibility and willingness to supply smaller volumes, and small company characteristics which enabled the buyer to talk directly to the appropriate person. A notable degree of goodwill was felt towards Drummond. Several customers felt that Drummond took an active interest in how their business is going.

Drummond was criticised in the following respects: quality (cans shorter than specification, wrong tinplate used, seam problems, panels concaving, contents leaking, top and bottom of can printed in different shades); poor quality control; old technology and machinery; little investment, perhaps due to changes in ownership; poor delivery times; few technical support facilities; slow to respond to customer's needs; and a poor response to new business enquiries.

Appendix 1M
THE VIEWS OF PACKAGING DESIGNERS

1 A number of packaging designers were consulted to obtain their views on tinplate as a packaging material, both from the functional and decorative points of view. Their views are set out below.

2 Tinplate is inherently compatible with solvent-based liquids and with foodstuffs where a high oxygen barrier is required or where the container is filled with hot substances. It is not inherently compatible with water-based liquids. Tinplate possesses inherent strength advantages which lead on to lower storage and transport costs. The decorative qualities of tinplate and the high quality of print which it achieves are a major strength which the manufacturers of tinplate have grossly undersold. Tinplate has a quality image and a retention value for uses other than containing the material sold in it. This advantage is not aggressively exploited.

3 The designers suggested going back to how the final user of the container actually uses the container. For example, the lid arrangement of the paint container could be re-designed so that lacquer protection is not damaged on opening. The

designers who were consulted felt that plastic would ultimately displace tinplate in many uses, leaving a role for tinplate as a specialist, low-volume material in applications where decoration and re-use are important. This view is based on the contention that the cost advantage ultimately lies with plastic. But the time period before the ultimate penetration of plastic is achieved can be greatly extended by the imaginative design of tinplate.

Case study 2

GREEN HOLDINGS LTD

In January 1988, Charles Green, Chairman and majority shareholder of Green Holdings Ltd, appointed consultants to advise him on how to deal with the problems facing his business. Green Holdings Ltd operates as an agricultural merchant, grain trader, seed and fertiliser producer predominantly in Worcestershire and Lincolnshire. The significant profits of the early 1980s had turned into a breakeven position in the financial year June 1986 to May 1987. Although prospects are believed to be improving, Charles does not feel confident that the improvement will be sufficient and therefore wishes to undertake a thorough review of the business. The major bright spot in the situation lies in the value of the company's property assets. Over the years a number of properties had been acquired, largely for the purpose of the business. The expansion of nearby towns, with the consequent increase in traffic, had rendered some of these properties unsuitable for the business of agricultural merchant or seed and fertiliser producer; but they are now ripe for residential development. These properties are probably worth over £4m and negotiations are already proceeding to acquire the necessary planning permissions and to sell them to property developers. The consultants commenced work at the beginning of February. Interviews were held with the members of the Board and with a number of senior managers. The notes made of these discussions follow. The Appendix gives the management accounts for 1986/7.

Notes of meeting with Charles Green

The business was founded by Charles's grand-father, a farmer, in the 1930s and then significantly expanded by his father and uncle. Charles had become the Managing Director in the 1970s and then, three years ago, had concentrated on the role of Chairman, appointing a Managing Director from within the company. This appointment had not proved successful and a new Managing Director, Tony Douglas, had been appointed, also from within the company.

At the present time the business consists of a number of activities. The Seed Division is run by Paul Green, the son of Charles's uncle. Paul has a small shareholding and a seat on the Board. He reports to the Group Managing Director, Tony Douglas, but this reporting relationship is made difficult by personality clashes between the two men. The Division contracts with farmers to grow seed to a certain specification and it then cleans and grades it. This business had been built up since the end of the War under the brand name 'Greenseed.' The branding of seed in this way had been an innovative idea and the brand had made the company's name. The seed is sold direct to farmers in Worcestershire by the Group Sales Force (sales about £1.3m), and in the rest of the country through agricultural merchants. Competitors had long since followed the 'branding' approach and the market is now highly competitive with major companies, like Dalgety, as the market leaders. Greenseed sales amount to around £3m per annum.

The Fertiliser Division is the responsibility of the Group Managing Director, also a member of the Board. Reporting to him are the Commercial Director, David Dunn; the Production Director, Seph Lonsdale; the Sales Director, Richard

Oldham, responsible for sales to merchants in the Eastern part of the country; and Nick Foley, responsible for sales to merchants in the Western part of the country. Sales in Worcestershire are made through the Group Sales Force direct to farmers. This business had been developed some years ago by Tony Douglas from the lime quarrying and spreading activity. (Lime quarrying and spreading is now being phased out because farmer requirements have changed and the activity has been losing money for some time – it is not a major part of the business.) The Fertiliser business had also been characterised by innovative ideas. The basic raw materials, phosphate and potassium are purchased from overseas producers and blended to the requirements of the farmers. Tony Douglas had identified an unsatisfied market niche for a specific crop at an early stage. Farming efficiency could be raised by blending a fertiliser (with the addition of sodium) suitable for that specific crop. A soil testing service was provided to determine the most suitable blend and a spreading service was then provided to apply the fertiliser to the land. The product is marketed by Green Fertiliser Ltd under the name 'Greengrow'. Competitors had soon followed and Green now has a market share in Worcestershire of 25 per cent. Greengrow accounts for approximately half the sales of about £4m, the other half being mainly blends for cereal farmers. About 60 per cent of sales go through the Group Sales Force and the rest through merchants in other parts of the country.

The major component of fertiliser is nitrates, a by-product of the activities of the major chemical companies. The market leaders are ICI, Norsk Hydro (a Swedish company who had bought Fisons) and UKF (a Dutch company). These have a market share of about 80 per cent. They sell through agricultural merchants, generally a limited range of products combining nitrates, phosphates and potassium. Over recent years ICI has been trying to undermine the competition provided by the smaller fertiliser blenders such as Green by waging a price war. Margins have therefore been seriously eroded.

Green also operates in the market for crop care and protection chemicals. Some years ago Green had acquired Horchem in Lincolnshire, a company specialising in the merchanting of chemicals primarily for horticultural farmers (about two thirds of their total sales of about £6m, the remainder being of chemicals to arable farmers). The Managing Director of Horchem, Rod New, reports to Tony Douglas. Horchem is profitable but has shown little real growth since its acquisition. Competition in the specialist horticulture market is not all that intense and good margins on sales of around 15 per cent are available. In Worcestershire, sales of chemicals are made through the Group Sales Force and are mainly to arable farmers (around £3m per annum). A small merchant specialising in horticultural chemicals was acquired in late 1987 to augment the limited sales of horticultural chemicals. This activity is the responsibility of Duncan Blacks who reports to Tony Douglas. A further acquisition of a small merchant specialising in arable chemicals was made in early 1988. The former owner of this business (Ike Owl) and his team of two salespeople are now employed to continue their selling activities for the Group. Ike Owl reports to Tony Douglas. Purchasing of the chemicals is, of course, a vitally important function. Tony Douglas conducts the major negotiations with the suppliers – major chemical companies. These negotiations determine likely total annual buy and the associated volume discounts. During the year the detailed negotiations and call off in Lincolnshire are the responsibility of Rod New, and in Worcestershire it is managed by Sammy Vincent, who reports to Tony Douglas. The large national merchants such as Dalgety are the major players in the arable chemicals market and competition is fierce.

In Worcestershire there are four sales centres or depots which are regarded as essential to the ability to sell chemicals. Farmers want to be able to call at the depot and collect chemicals during the spraying season. The sales centres are also important in managing the sales force. An opportunity has been identified in selling sundries (small equipment and clothing and materials required by farmers) from these sales centres and Adam Green, the 26 year-old son of Charles, has been put in charge of developing this.

The final activity of the business is conducted by the Grain Division, located at Warley. This consists of a storage activity (surplus EC grain is stored for the government) and a trading activity. The Group Sales Force identifies sellers of grain and the Grain Division then tests it, negotiates the purchase and sells the grain on to maltsters, bakers and shippers. The Division is run by Herbert Fowler who reports to Tony Douglas and is assisted by Berty Higham. About £1m is tied up in working capital and fixed assets are worth just under £0.5m.

At the Group level the key managers are as follows. Harry Hall, the Sales Director, reports to Tony Douglas and is responsible for the members of the sales force. Tim Davis, Finance Director and member of the Board reports to Tony Douglas. John Green, Charles's brother, is the Personnel Director and a member of the Board.

Looking at the overall competition, most competitors are now making losses. There are a few specialist companies which seem to be doing well. There is a specialist chemicals merchant in Worcestershire called Bakers, who make about £1.5m profit per annum. Sims, a major grain trader, makes about £2m and Nils, a fertiliser blender, with sales about 20 per cent above Green is also thought to be making good profits.

Against the above background Charles sees the need to rethink and reshape the business. The former innovation seems to have disappeared, the market conditions are very difficult and for years now the Green business has not shown any solid or sustainable growth. They seem to be lost between being producers and merchants. They have been acquiring smaller companies and they are now the largest private merchant company in Worcestershire. They are certainly the largest in terms of net assets. There is also the question of when to sell the properties and what to do with the proceeds.

Notes of meeting with Tony Douglas

A major problem facing the Group is the price war that has been going on in the fertiliser market for about three years now, as ICI seeks to regain market share. The price war looks unlikely to end in the foreseeable future. The arable chemicals market is also very competitive and over the last two years Tony has pursued a policy of focusing the sales force on the high margin chemicals. This has meant lower volumes sold, but the total contribution to profit has increased: margins in Worcestershire are up from about 8 per cent to over 15 per cent. Tony keeps very close to the

Fertiliser Division and to chemicals – in both of these areas buying is important and Tony has developed very good relationships with the suppliers. Another problem experienced by the Group over the past year was the very bad weather, which hit sales of fertiliser and chemicals.

There had been problems with the sales force but the situation is now improving. Tony is concerned at the diversion which the Grain Division creates for the sales force. Selling chemicals requires a high degree of expertise and it is unrealistic to expect salespeople to develop this expertise, as well as that in seed and fertiliser, and then also identify grain purchasing opportunities. His view is that the Grain Division must stand on its own. He is expecting the Grain Division to make a profit of £100 000 this year.

Another concern is the size of the sales force. Out of a total of 160 employees (16 employed at the fertiliser factory) there are just over 40 salespeople. Is this sufficient for a business of the Green type?

Notes on the meeting with Paul Green

About 550 000 tonnes of seed are produced annually in the country as a whole. The market is dominated by Dalgety with a 30 per cent market share; Green sells just over 7000 tonnes per annum. In Worcestershire they sell through the Group Sales Force (just over 3000 tonnes per annum) and in the rest of the country through other merchants (at a discount on retail price of about 13 per cent, out of which the merchant has to pay transport costs to the customer). A distinction must be drawn between new varieties of seed and speciality seed (this usually means seed treated with chemicals against disease, etc) on the one hand, and basic seed (called C2) on the other hand. The market for new varieties/speciality seed is smaller but higher prices can be charged and higher margins earned. The policy of Green is to focus on the high-margin, high-quality end of the market. The competition in the C2 segment is very fierce with suppliers now selling through merchants at prices that are below cost. The Green policy is to avoid competition on purely price terms. Representatives in the Group Sales Force are given fixed prices and they either sell at these prices or walk away from the sale. Over the past few years the volumes of seed sold through the sales force have been on the decline. Paul is very critical of the sales force. He feels it is not well managed or directed and that there is too much emphasis on training the reps to act as technical advisors to farmers on chemicals, rather than training them on how to close sales.

Notes on the meeting with Harry Hall

Harry Hall is the Group Sales Director. Basically Green is selling crop nutrition, crop care and protection. He outlined some of the history behind the sales force. A few years ago the Group was organised into separate companies. Green Fertiliser produced and sold fertiliser with its own sales force. Green Chem and Frank Green and Sons sold chemicals and seed with their own sales forces. Then about three years ago all the sales forces were amalgamated into one to sell all the Group products in Worcestershire. This had caused problems with the fertiliser salespeople who had to acquire highly technical chemicals product knowledge. To sell chemicals the rep had to be able to walk the farm with the farmer and identify pest and other problems and recommend the best solution. The change also meant that chemical specialists had to acquire fertiliser product knowledge. It is feasible for a rep to be highly expert in one product, very proficient in a second, but only knowledgeable in a third. The tendency therefore is for reps to specialise in either chemicals or fertiliser and relegate seed to third place. In addition, salespeople have to identify grain purchases for the Grain Division. This tends to come very much in fourth place. After the reorganisation of sales, many of the sales force had left and had been replaced with less expert, younger people. The sales force now tends to be somewhat unbalanced with a number approaching retirement and the remainder being mostly young and relatively inexperienced people. On average the sales per rep in Worcestershire are around £300 000 per annum.

The sales force situation is improving – a good deal of effort has been put into training, concentrating on chemicals product knowledge. However, the training programme is criticised by some of the reps as being too disjointed and 'bitty'. There is an incentive system under which the contribution earned on sales by each rep is compared to his or her salary and if it exceeds salary then incentive payments come into force. However for most, the contribution on sales never exceeds salary and the incentives therefore do not work. The contribution from sales is also used to allocate sales force costs to the producing activities. The formula is such that total costs are never fully allocated and nearly half is left as an unallocated group overhead.

Two years ago the decision had been taken to set up sales centres. These serve as depots for chemicals and also as centres for sales teams. At each centre there is a Team Leader who manages the reps. There is a sales centre at Knutsford run by Bill Sutter with a team of six reps. The location of this centre is very poor because of problems from industrial traffic. But the intention is to sell the land and buildings (the site is also used for the Head Office and the seed factory) and build a new Head Office, sales centre and seed factory on another site owned by the Group. Further north is the Fitter sales centre run by Cain Anderon. This is also the location for Ike Owl's chemicals' sales team. There is a sales centre at Mableham where the Team Leader is Steve Binder, who joined the company six months ago from Norsk Hydro. The fourth sales centre is in Raleigh and is run by Larry Fell. Duncan Blacks, the manager of the horticultural chemicals sales team is located there, but his team of five salespeople is spread around the depots.

Notes on the meeting with Rod New

Rod New is the Managing Director of Green Horchem in Lincolnshire. About two-thirds of his sales are in horticultural chemicals and the rest is in arable chemicals. The latter is a much more competitive market. Chemical reps have to be experts: there is some specialisation between horticultural and arable reps but they do sell to both types of farmers. There are nine reps with sales of about £6m per annum. There are three sales centres. They have a market share of about 60 per cent of horticultural chemicals in Lincolnshire.

Notes on the meeting with David Dunn

David Dunn is the Commercial Director of the Fertiliser Division. He buys, in the main on his own, phosphates and potash from overseas producers. He also buys nitrogen products but Green do not have a UK supplier. They simply sell the nitrogen on to farmers. There is not much margin in this but they do it to be able to provide a complete service to farmers.

He sees some prospect of change in the fertiliser market. The chemical majors may well decide to concentrate on selling nitrogen, their main product. These majors have to buy in phosphates and potash from the same sources as the small blenders such as Green. There is, therefore, nothing very attractive to them in this business. A threat to the market for nitrogen is the environmental pressure to reduce the quantities of nitrates in the water supply.

The Fertiliser Division sells 60 per cent of its product through the Group Sales Force and the remainder through merchants in the rest of the country. The volumes sold through the sales force have been on the decline but there has been an increase so far this year. Steve Binder is now trying to develop sales through other merchants in Worcestershire. They are finding that they have to give these merchants a discount of around 13 per cent on average, out of which the merchant has to pay transport costs to the customer, leaving the merchant with a margin of about 8 per cent. The fertiliser factory is not capacity constrained and could produce 50 per cent more. The obstacle is the state of the market where the demands for fertiliser is not growing. The EC policy of cutbacks on cereal production could lead to declines in the future.

Notes on the meeting with Tim Davis

Tim Davis is the Finance Director. He went through the management accounts and explained some of the items in those accounts which were not clear to the consultant. The item called credit in the group accounts represented charges which were made on the late payment of invoices. Tim did not have much confidence in the forecast profit of the Grain Division. He was doing some work which indicated that there could be a substantial loss.

Other points from meetings

The sales force lacks direction and control and the sales policy is not clear or consistent as far as the reps are concerned. The reps feel they are under attack from the production activities which impose rigid prices on them and then complain about declining volumes. Management style was felt to be dictatorial, with the team leaders of the reps complaining that they are given responsibility without the authority and flexibility to achieve results in a highly competitive marketplace. The reps feel that they are the best people to make detailed judgements on price since they are at the sharp end.

Appendix 2A
FINANCIAL INFORMATION ON GREEN HOLDINGS

Group Trading Summary for month of May 1987

	Year to date Actual	Budget		Year to date Actual	Budget
Fertiliser – Net trading	−73.9	365.3	Selling costs	−277.7	−105.1
Seed – Net trading	161.9	77.2	Credit	94.7	35.1
Grain – Net trading	−40.3	144.1	Net trading profit	17.4	630.2
Chemical – Net trading	152.7	113.6	Central costs	27.5	20.1

	Year to date	
	Actual	*Budget*
Management & retirement costs	429.1	360.8
Finance – bank	106.8	159.3
Finance – other	2.9	3.1
	566.3	543.1
Finance charges received	702.1	350.1
Net central cost result	264.2	193.1
Total trading profit	−246.9	436.9
Other income	33.0	35.0
Group profit – current year	−213.9	471.9
Group profit – previous year	206.1	

Department: Fertiliser

	Actual	*Budget*
Sales total – units	42425.0	53080.0
Sales total – value	4322.1	5984.5
Costed margin	923.2	1448.1
Hauliers	256.1	203.6
Adjustment		
Gross margin	666.1	1244.4
Wages	97.3	122.5
Fixed	319.3	346.6
Direct	89.3	469.1
Cars	18.0	18.8
Total costs	523.9	620.1
Added value	142.2	624.4
Group selling	114.1	180.7
Gross contribution	28.1	443.7
Finance costs	57.0	60.1
Net contribution	−28.9	383.7
Central services	42.1	42.1
Other income	−2.9	23.7
Net trading result	−73.9	365.3

Department: Seed

	Actual	*Budget*
Sales total – units	6930.0	7400.0
Sales total – value	2140.1	1896.1
Costed margin	547.6	460.1
Hauliers	63.4	53.4
Adjustment		
Gross margin	500.2	422.7
Wages	44.7	40.1
Fixed	81.1	90.3
Direct	94.3	76.1

	Year to date	
	Actual	*Budget*
Cars	6.7	7.2
Total costs	226.7	213.7
Added value	257.5	193.1
Group selling	78.6	72.9
Gross contribution	178.9	121.6
Finance costs	6.1	15.1
Net contribution	172.8	106.6
Central services	46.2	46.2
Other income	35.3	16.8
Net trading result	161.9	77.2

Department: Grain

	Actual	*Budget*
Sales total – units	122822.0	128000.0
Sales total – value	14599.1	15040.1
Costed margin	703.9	801.7
Hauliers	199.6	222.7
Adjustment		
Gross margin	504.3	579.1
Wages	15.4	26.2
Fixed	115.9	116.7
Direct	186.9	143.8
Cars	15.1	9.5
Total costs	333.2	296.2
Added value	−52.5	64.6
Group selling	41.1	43.4
Gross contribution	−93.6	21.2
Finance costs	53.1	53.1
Net contribution	−146.7	−31.9
Central services	30.8	42.8
Other income mainly storage	137.1	218.8
Net trading result	−40.4	144.1

Department: Worcestershire Chemicals

	Actual	*Budget*
Sales total – units		
Sales total – value	3194.6	4905.1
Costed margin	422.0	460.5
Hauliers	42.6	
Adjustment		
Gross margin	418.8	460.5
Wages	7.7	7.5
Fixed	25.7	28.6
Direct	113.1	84.7

	Year to date				*Year to date*	
	Actual	*Budget*			*Actual*	*Budget*
Cars	17.3	11.8	Hauliers		33.1	30.7
Depot costs	51.4		Adjustment			
Total costs	215.2	132.6	Gross margin		686.1	649.9
Added value	164.2	283.5	Wages		18.2	18.6
Group selling	54.3	179.1	Fixed			
Gross contribution	109.9	104.4	Direct		459.1	497.9
Finance costs	79.0	90.1	Cars		40.1	45.5
			Total costs		517.3	562.1
Net contribution	30.9	14.5	Added value		168.8	87.9
Central services	42.1	42.1	Group selling			
Other income			Gross contribution		168.8	87.9
Net trading result	−11.2	−27.6	Finance costs		107.1	140.1
Department: Horchem			Net contribution		61.7	−52.2
Sales total – units			Central services		28.1	28.1
Sales total – value	5449.1	5850.1	Other income		130.1	221.3
Costed margin	719.1	680.6	Net trading result		163.7	141.1

Capital employed

	May 1987			December 1987		
	Fixed	*Working*	*Total*	*Fixed*	*Working*	*Total*
Fertiliser	250	600	850	250	85	335
Seed	100	(53)	50	100	27	127
Worcs. Chems.	250	868	1118	250	692	942
Horchem	500	991	1491	500	1093	1593
Grain	200	200	400	200	852	1052
Central	–	–	–	–	–	–
Total Group	1318	2612	3930	1300	2749	4049

Case study 3

Z HOLDINGS LTD

Z Holdings is the wholly-owned subsidiary of a major multinational company called Alpha International. It is the vehicle that Alpha International uses to group together a number of companies which it had acquired some time ago and which represent a significant diversification away from its major core businesses. Alpha International controls Z Holdings by appointing a Chairman of the Board of Z Holdings, generally an executive with other responsibilities at the Alpha Head Office. It also appoints the Z Holdings Chief Executive, Finance and Personnel Directors from the ranks of management in its core businesses. The three top Head Office executives generally serve at Z Holdings for periods of three to four years and sometimes for shorter periods than this. Periods at Z Holdings are seen as part of the management development programme of some of Alpha's fast-track managers. Control is also exerted by Alpha in the form of setting return on capital and growth objectives, monitoring against budgets which have to be presented to top Alpha management once a year and also by calling for five-year-plan presentations once a year. In addition, Alpha also imposes stringent safety requirements on Z Holdings and requires it to adhere to other general policies, particularly personnel policies. Z Holdings is required not to undertake activities that might conflict with other Alpha businesses. Within these limits, however, the management of Z Holdings has considerable freedom and for some years now has enjoyed the generous financial support of Alpha for its expansion strategy.

Z Holdings has five major, wholly-owned subsidiaries.

- Company A operates in the building products market in the UK and it controls two fairly recently acquired subsidiaries in the same general markets.
- Company B manufactures road construction products and is organised by region, also with a recently acquired subsidiary in the same markets. Recently it has undertaken some small road construction projects.
- Company C covers the same market segments as Companies A and B, but in Canada.
- Company D operates mainly in the UK but it also has substantial export business. It manufactures and applies industrial paints.
- Company E covers the same market segments as D but in France and Germany.

The Managing Directors of each of the five major subsidiaries have not come from the ranks of Alpha management. They have all come from the industrial sectors in which their companies operate. They all sit on the Board of Z Holdings, as do the three Head Office Directors and the Chairman. This Board meets every quarter and the same group, without the Chairman, meets once a month as the Management Meeting.

For some time now Z Holdings has been pursuing an active strategy of growth, largely by acquisition. Most of the acquisitions have been put forward by the operating subsidiaries. The normal practice has been for a subsidiary Managing Director and his team to identify and put forward a potential acquisition. This is discussed with the Chief Executive and then reported on to the monthly Management Meeting. If the proposed acquisition is approved by the Chief Executive then Head Office staff prepare a capital requisition for submission to Alpha International. This requisition has to follow a format and meet criteria laid down by Alpha. The requisition is prepared by Z Holdings Head Office staff who also assist the subsidiary Managing Director with the financial and legal aspects of the acquisition. Once the acquisition is made it becomes the clear responsibility of the acquiring subsidiary.

Each of the five major subsidiaries holds a Board Meeting once a quarter, chaired by the Chief Executive of Z Holdings. A typical agenda for one of these meetings is given as Appendix 3A. A significant part of these meetings is taken up with item 2, Last Period Results. A 50-page document is distributed before the meeting. It consists of summary sheets and each item on these summary sheets is then broken down into considerable detail in the rest of the document. Subsidiary management meet on the day before the full Board Meeting to prepare for that meeting at which they report to Z Holdings' Chief Executive, Finance Director and Personnel Director. In between the Board Meetings the management of each subsidiary meets formally on their own each month. A consultant attended a number of the meetings and noted that:

- significant amounts of time were taken up with overlap problems with other subsidiaries and complaints about the policies of Alpha;
- a large loss on a small civil engineering contract was reported on and reasons for it given, but very little discussion took place on what was a relatively new activity for the company.

The monthly Management Meeting of the Head Office Directors and the subsidiary Managing Directors follows a standard agenda, an example of which is given in Appendix 3A. This meeting considers monthly results for the month completed two months before the meeting. A consolidated summary of profits plus total profit for each subsidiary is discussed. A consultant who attended this meeting made the following notes:

- matters arising took up the first hour, of which safety matters accounted for 15 minutes and incentive schemes for employees another 25 minutes;

- discussion on the May financial results took 50 minutes, including some discussion on problems in the building products market and some difficulties on attempts to diversify into small engineering works, and the effects of a government moratorium on local authority spending;
- reports on prospective acquisitions took 30 minutes;
- all afternoon was taken up with reporting on subsidiary company business, as well as highlights and complaints about restrictive Alpha policies.

The Chief Executive has to make a five-year plan presentation to the Chief Executive of Alpha. This occurs in early September and is followed by a more detailed budget presentation in late November. Z Holdings therefore requires submission by its subsidiaries of five-year plans and budgets which allow its timetable to be met. Appendix 3C gives the plan letter sent out and the timetable which subsidiaries are required to follow.

The reward system employed at Z Holdings includes an element which is performance-related and this can amount to 20 per cent of salary. For the subsidiary Managing Directors the bonus is tied to the achievement of target return on capital and profit growth. Subsidiary Managing Directors apply similar schemes to their senior managers.

In early 1988 the board of Z Holdings attended a one-day workshop at which they discussed with consultants the appropriateness of the control style they were employing. They expressed some concern that they had not foreseen in time the deterioration in profitability which had occurred in 1987. This had been due mainly to price cutting to build up volume in Company B. The Management Meeting had been informed that such a price-cutting policy was being employed but had not fully appreciated the consequences. The consultants directed attention to the work which Goold & Campbell (1988) had done on styles of management and the role of the Head Office. The participants of the workshop concluded that the 'strategic control' style of management was appropriate to their business, but that it should be supplemented by an emphasis on financial control. They hired the consultants to assist them to improve the approach of Z Holdings to control and to clarify the role of the top management level of the group as a whole.

At the beginning of the assignment the consultants interviewed all the top managers. The following is a summary of points made during those interviews.

The Management Meeting and the Board are not really consulted on capital expenditure or acquisitions, they are merely informed. They do not generally see the papers submitted to Alpha. Collective responsibility is not exercised. Authority for running the business must be left with the Managing Director of that business. Colleagues on the Board do not know enough to make much con-tribution to this. The attitudes and values of Alpha conflict with those of the subsidiaries. Is there any point in a Group Board? What are the expectations of Alpha? The Head Office Directors keep changing. Management Meetings and Boards do not provide a forum for input into the development of other Managing Directors' businesses. Should one Board member make comment on and take part in decisions on the business of another Board member? The Management Meetings are a useful forum for discussing overlaps between businesses. Board and Management Meetings are a waste of time. The Chief Executive meets Managing Directors once a month but they rarely talk about the budget.

Appendix 3A
COMPANY B LTD: BOARD MEETING AGENDA

1 Matters arising
2 Period results
3 Capital expenditure
4 Debtors
5 Health and safety
6 Properties
7 Acquisitions
8 Major projects
9 Interface with Alpha
10 Any other business

Appendix 3B
MANAGEMENT MEETING AGENDA

1 Matters arising

2 Finance
  (i)   Monthly results
  (ii) Acquisition/disposal report
  (iii) Pension

3 Personnel
  (i)   Group staff handbook

4 Safety
  (i)   Monthly performance
  (ii) Fatality
  (iii) Product safety manual

5 Business highlights/matters of general interest
  (i)   Company A
  (ii) Company B
  (iii) Company C
  (iv) Company D
  (v)   Company E

6 Central purchasing

7 Internal audit

8 Report on R&D meeting

9 Any other business

Appendix 3C
PLANNING PROCEDURES

MEMORANDUM TO: See attached list
FROM: David Douglas
SUBJECT: Business Plan and Budget
DATE: July 1988

There are some general assumptions specific to Z Holdings to which you will wish to refer. A copy of the Z strategy document is enclosed, and you will wish to note:

(a) As a group we must achieve at least 12.5 per cent operating profit improvement in 1989 on the Business Plan for 1988.

(b) We should finance organic growth out of current cash flow, and should expect, in addition, as individual businesses, to be able to pay a dividend out of cash flow of not less than 8 per cent of equity and interest free funding. Actual payment will depend upon financing considerations.

(c) Individual businesses should not include potential acquisitions in their 1989 budget. However, extra resources will be available for expansion through acquisitions.

(d) Health, safety, environment, quality, integrity and honesty will remain our absolute business philosophy.

A Business Plan is not merely a set of numbers. In relation to the business the Management team should discuss and agree:

(a) WHAT IT IS NOW;
(b) WHAT IT SHOULD BE;
(c) HOW WE WILL GET THERE.

The following is a guideline you will wish to use:

1 Outline present business position, including strengths and weaknesses. Compare with previous Business Plan.
2 Identify critical success factors and activities which will influence the successful achievement of your business plans.
3 Agree objectives and timing.
4 Specify assumptions and strategy, both in the long and short terms.

5 Evaluate monthly or quarterly financial plans for 1989 on basis of the agreed objectives. Quantify risk of assumptions being incorrect.
6 Review (5) above. Accept or modify as appropriate.

While we do not require a financial evaluation of the years 1990–94, we wish to fully discuss your five-year strategy. It is only in this context that we can properly consider your plan for the ensuing year. You should therefore, describe how you see your company in 1994 and how you intend to get there.

To meet the enclosed timetable requirements, it will be necessary for you to start the plan process now.

Please would you include a page in the planning package on the use of Information Technology in your business. You should cover:

(a) a statement of your objectives for using IT in your business and the competitive edge you expect this to give you; and
(b) strategies for meeting the objective.

Planning Timetable

---

1 Managing Directors Outlook Reports		29 August
2 Outline Five-Year Plan to Alpha		9 September
3 Forecasts for 2 years to Alpha		9 September
4 Plan Meetings All data to Head Office 1 week prior to meeting		
	Central Office	1 October
	Company A	7 October
	Company B	11 October
	Company C	13 October
	Company D	18 October
	Company E	21 October
5 First draft budget		31 October
6 Management team Discussion		8 November
7 Final Budget		14 November
8 Presentation to Z Board		21 November
9 Presentation to Alpha Board		24 November

Group Strategy Statement

The Strategy:

- Our group will be operated to the highest standards of safety, honesty and integrity.
- Our products and services will be of a consistently high quality.
- We recognise our responsibility to our customers, the community and our employees.

Our Objective:

- We aim to grow profitably and to maximise our shareholders' interests.

Our targets:

- 20 per cent return on capital at the operating level.
- Sales growth of 12.5 per cent per annum.
- Capital expenditure to be funded from cash flow.
- Recruitment and development of high calibre staff.

Our limits:

- We will concentrate in our existing areas of activity.

Case study 4

STRATEGIC PLANNING AT FEDMET INC.[1]

Federal Metals: history and context

Federal Metals (Fedmet) is owned by Federal Industries Limited (FIL), a Canadian conglomerate with four industry groups. Fedmet, with revenues of over one billion dollars in 1988, was the largest of FIL's groups. In 1988 Fedmet accounted for over 50 per cent of the revenue of Federal Industries.

The organisation chart of Fedmet is shown in *Exhibit 4.1*. With the exception of Manfred Wirth and Carol Besner, the members of the management team attended the formal strategic planning meetings during the 1989 planning cycle.

Federal Metals was primarily a carbon steel distributor which had two main types of steel: flat-rolled, which is used in consumer products; and general line, which has more industrial applications. The Canadian carbon steel industry was approximately ten million tons in 1988 of which 75 per cent was sold directly from the mills to the end-user and the remaining quarter was sold to service centres such as Russelsteel and Drummond McCall, which were divisions in Fedmet. The percentage sold through service centres had been increasing over the past few years primarily due to flat-rolled products. The mills were unwilling to cut the flat-rolled into small quantities that the consumer often needed. Fedmet had approximately 20 per cent of the carbon steel business in Canada which goes through service centres. They were the largest in the industry with the next three largest making up about 50 per cent of the industry volume. In addition to carbon steel, Fedmet also distributed non-ferrous products. Fedmet's international division was a trading operation where they imported and exported metals, primarily steel.

Fedmet focused on metals distribution. The executives said they were not fabricators and hence upward vertical diversification was not considered a viable option for the organisation. Their key product was service – the service of providing the metals to customers in quantities and with the frequency of deliveries that the customer needed. Pat Eckersley, President of Drummond McCall, argued that 'if you think of steel distribution as a stock market you will go bankrupt'. He said there was some friction in the pricing over a broad price band within which orders can be satisfied. He argued that they moved people up the price band by providing excellent service. When asked to define this both he and Al Shkut, President of Russelsteel, argued that customers were willing to pay for trust and comfort. They need to trust that the metals will arrive on time, will fit their engineering specifications and will be cut to fit exactly in their manufacturing process.

Their customer base was mixed. The majority of

[1] Case copyright 1991 by Brenda Jane Zimmerman. Full version of case appears in unpublished doctoral dissertation, *Strategy, Chaos and Equilibrium: A Case Study of Federal Metals, Inc.*, 1991, York University, Toronto, Canada.

Exhibit 4.1 Formal structure of Fedmet Inc.

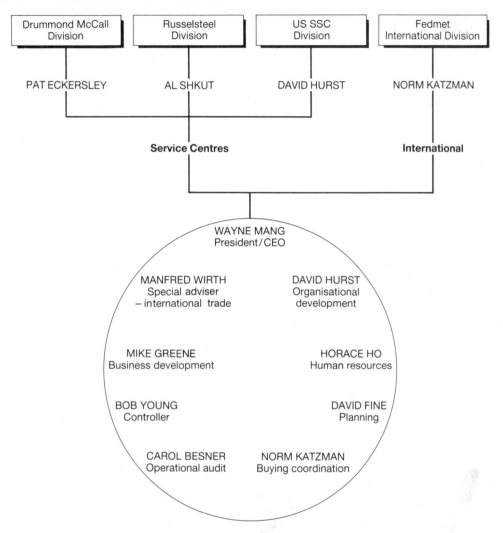

their business was 'broken bundles'. Mills have minimum quantities that they are willing to sell, and thus many of their customers needed quantities of metals that were too small to be serviced by the mills directly. Some broken bundle customers were large users of metals and normally bought from the mills and used Fedmet to fill in the gaps when they ran short of certain metals. Others needed special cutting or processing that the mills would not provide. This was primarily flat-rolled metals where they slit or cut to length. They also cut plate metal in shapes for manufacturing parts for heavy machinery. A third type of

business that Fedmet's service centres were involved in was 'direct mill sales'. In these sales, Fedmet acted as a broker for a fabricator or manufacturer who for some reason failed to meet all of the mills' criteria. This was not business they sought since it tended to be low margin. Shkut and Eckersley said they spend a great deal of time trying to strengthen their relationships with their customers. Shkut argued that what they wanted to achieve was to 'pull a customer into our rhythm – you know, so we just become part of their business'.

In addition to strengthening their relationships

with customers, Fedmet had spent a great deal of effort reaching out to their suppliers. Shkut argued that they approached the mills with a 'how can we help you?' attitude. The logic was that they were part of a 'community of metals' which will work better with cooperation, said Eckersley.

Federal Industries annually prepared a five-year strategic plan. Their plan was complete by mid-January. The four industrial groups, including Fedmet, were required to prepare a five-year plan by mid-April and their divisions' plans were due in the middle of July. The 1989 strategic planning process for Fedmet began with a meeting of nine executives on 23 January, 1989.

23 January, 1989: 'Warm bubbles and little arrows'

The planning documents from previous years and the memo for the upcoming strategic planning day in January stressed the need to look on planning as a learning process. The following three paragraphs are an excerpt from the 1988–93 strategic plan.

Successful companies that survive and prosper in the long run are ones that seem able to learn and adapt. Such companies have an ability to live in harmony with their business environment, to switch from a survival mode when times are turbulent to a self-development mode when the pace of change is slow. Many companies, however, do not learn to adapt or, at least, not very quickly; a full one-third of the Fortune 500 industrials listed in 1970 had vanished by 1983! Russelsteel only just survived.

In this context then what is planning's role in corporate learning? In a nutshell the role of planning is to act as facilitator, catalyst and to help accelerate the corporate learning process. The most relevant learning is done by the people who run the business – the operators. So the real purpose of effective planning is to facilitate the ongoing development of the emerging strategies and thinking that the decision makers carry in their heads.

Our ability to learn faster than other players in the industry may be our only long run competitive edge. The tremendous improvement in the results of recently acquired steel service centres is, to a large extent, a result of exposure to the thinking of people in the Metals Group and the resulting

'fast learning' experienced by the management teams in the newly acquired units.

In preparation for the 1989 planning cycle, David Fine, Vice-President of Planning, circulated a memorandum. The memo had a series of questions which were to be addressed in the meetings over the next three months. On the first page, Fine introduced the role of planning at Fedmet.

The planning process requires us to talk to each other on a scheduled basis – that's about all – and then take a snapshot of our conversations.

The all-day meeting took place in a picturesque country club several miles from Head Office. They sat around a series of tables organised in a U-shape. The agenda was very loose.

Fine: Our agenda today is 'Warm Bubbles and Little Arrows'. The morning session on 'Warm Bubbles' is soft. We will review the visions and values of the group and address four questions. The afternoon is a little more focused as we discuss the initiatives of 1988 and propose new initiatives for 1989 and the 1990s.

After a little more description of the stated visions and values of the group, he put an acetate slide on the projector with the following four questions preceded by Fedmet's vision statement 'EVERY PERSON A MANAGER':

(1) What configuration of the vision and value 'bubbles' do we envision for the Metals Group?
(2) Which ones do we feel good about?
(3) Which ones do we not feel good about?
(4) What revisions to group vision and values would we like to see?

'Let it happen' was a guiding principle of the Fedmet team. During the meeting almost every member used the phrase repeatedly in describing what was happening or could happen in their divisions or areas of responsibility. Although the Fedmet team believed in the philosophy of 'let it happen', they often struggled with its implementation, particularly in Drummond McCall. Drummond McCall and Russelsteel were major competitors for over one hundred years. In 1987, after Federal Industries purchased Drummond McCall, it immediately became a separate division of the Fedmet group. The cultures of the two competitors were different and had resulted in a very different orientation in many dimensions of the business. Pat Eckersley became president of Drummond McCall at the time of purchase, after being with the Russelsteel organisation for many years. Shkut argued that Eckersley was inculcated with the Russelsteel culture which made the transition very difficult at times. Eckersley argued passionately about the need for the line workers to be closer to the customer in order to improve the productivity of the operations. However, he was struggling with the process concept of 'letting it happen' and the content of this idea which he felt sure was valid.

Eckersley: I don't think we'll ever sell the concept of quality to our people in their hermetically sealed plants, who only see steel pass through the airlock and see it come back in with a label on it that says it wasn't any good. I don't think we'll ever really crack quality until our people who are producing or working with our product have a feel for what happens to that product outside. The only way they can do that is to talk to the guys in the customers' plants who use the product. I mean our hourly guy talking to the customer's hourly guy to understand the goddamn problems they have with the product which comes out of our plant. . . . I can order them to do this but that won't work, we have to let them come to the idea themselves and want to do it and see the value in it. I am looking for an easy acceptance of a worthwhile thought but the structure of Drummond McCall is so hard edged.

Middle management was the focus of much of the discussion. They argued that middle managers inhibit the process of 'let it happen'.

A key struggle the Fedmet team had during the day was the concept of the sequence of plans and actions. The team explicitly eschewed the idea that plans precede actions. They argued that a major purpose of the annual planning sessions was to reflect on the past actions and attach meaning to those events. They referred to this concept as retrospective sessions. They institutionalised

retrospective sessions for all levels of the organisation, arguing that there was a significant learning process in reflecting on the past.

The meeting concluded with Fine expressing the thought that translation of the visions and values into actions was the 'missing link' that Fedmet needed to understand. Fine agreed to work on a summary document which would take a 'snapshot' in words of the process and the outcomes of the meeting. They would then use the snapshot to continue in developing the concepts and material for the five-year strategic plan.

'Executive pornography'

The executive team of Fedmet occasionally referred to strategy as a four-letter word, an obscenity. As an example, they labelled an article in the business press which focused on Chief Executive Officers (CEOs) and their strategic decision-making role in an organisation's 'executive pornography'. The management group identified and commented on some of the pornographic words, phrases and images in this article. They appear in *Exhibit 4.2.*

At the meeting on 23 January, 1989, the team discussed the article. David Hurst, Executive Vice-President, argued that it presumed that the ideal manager is some sort of genius who can analyse reams of relevant data and use the analysis to make the key decisions which will then be implemented by the people in the organisation. There are a number of facets to this image which the Fedmet team found obscene. First, they objected to the implied controller–controlled duality. Second, they objected to viewing the 'people side' of the organisation as one that involves 'motivating people'. This insinuates that there is a need and a right to manipulate people to act in the manner the CEO requires in order to implement his, or her, plan. It also suggests some unique personal ownership of the strategy by the CEO.

One of their central concerns about a conception of strategic management hostage to such obscene images, is the time dimension implicit in strategic thinking. They argued that an understanding of where they are and where they are going can only be grasped in retrospect. They questioned the

Exhibit 4.2 Executive pornography

Pornographic words, phrases and images of the Chief Executive Officer:

- masterminding;
- manoeuvring;
- it's fun to move the company in the direction you want it to move;
- he [or she] is expected to be above the fray, reading, thinking and developing long-term strategy;
- he [or she] has got to figure out how to get the company to understand where he [or she] wants to go and to help him [or her] get there;
- the challenge of motivating people;
- strategic management is the absolute key element of success;
- engineered a turn-around;
- the CEO is in control.

(The 'obscenities' were underlined in Hurst's copy of the article 'The Boss Under Fire', Report on *Business Magazine*, February 1989.)

presumed sequence of (1) analysis, followed by (2) decisions and consummated by (3) action. In the terminology of management strategy, they were not convinced that implementation follows planning or decisions. They implicitly believed in experiential learning rather than learning by analysis. Their key phrase which reflects this was 'Let it Happen.'

The Fedmet team eschewed many traditional strategic management procedures. In particular its members objected to the emphasis placed on developing a strategic plan. The process of planning was considered useful but the 'black marks on white paper' or the plan itself was of significantly less value. They viewed all management as a process in which the best one can do at any point in time is to capture the process in a two dimensional way, as in a snapshot or photograph. Fedmet labelled their 1990–94 plan 'A Series of Snapshots of the Group Planning Process'. The metaphor of the snapshot permeated the entire document. Since a snapshot can only picture the external dimensions of a situation, visions and values, which were the critical management focus of the Fedmet team, could not be adequately captured in a snapshot.

Another dimension of the snapshot analogy is the connotation that strategy is enacted. Thus a photograph can only capture one point in time, which is over as soon as the photograph has been taken. In the 1990–94 strategic plan they stated that a snapshot cannot capture motion and therefore is limited to portraying dynamic interaction as a static arrangement. The Fedmet team focused on the process elements and suggested that the structures or plans were merely temporary manifestations of the process.

24 January – 15 March 1989: 'Living the vision'

During the next two weeks, Fine worked on the concept of translating the vision into reality. Fine and Wayne Mang, CEO, met frequently to discuss the issues. Hurst was often present at these meetings. They discussed what the 'linkage' process between the vision and the reality should be and the conversations often centred on the need for appropriate body language or actions rather than words. There was considerable jousting in the discussions but Mang's influence was evident. More often than not, the phrases or words he suggested were included in the final chart which can be seen in *Exhibit 4.3*.

The team reconvened on 8 February at the Fedmet offices to discuss Fine's approach. Although there was considerable discussion about the appropriateness of the approach – including concerns about the 'linearity of the process' – all agreed to work through the ideas as the next step to develop the plan. The task was broken down into five subgroups each charged with the responsibility to investigate further the linkage and the reality of the visions and values. The first three values listed in *Exhibit 4.3* below were combined since all dealt with the linkage process of 'living 60/60'. (The '60/60' concept indicates that each side in a relationship has to go more than half-way to make it work.) The other four groups each had one value to address. Fine prepared lists of questions to stimulate the discussions.

The subgroups consisted of three people, in addition to Fine who participated in all the subgroups. Each member of the executive team volunteered to work on two subgroups. The subgroups

Exhibit 4.3 Fedmet: 'Living the vision'

FEDMET: LIVING THE VISION

The Vision:	**Living 'Every Person a Manager':**	**The Reality:**
'Every Person a Manager'	*'Linkage' Processes*	*'Every Person a Manager'*
• Customer is king	• Living '60/60', person to person	• Front line people, fully mobilised, flatter organisation
• Small company feeling	• Living '60/60', team on team	• 'Big company' opportunities
• Excellent supplier relations	• Living '60/60', president to president	• Cooperative initiatives
• An environment for free thought	• A retrospective by unit	• Goals to 'get better'
• People-oriented	• Fedmet; creating and living the environment	• Magnetising group and division offices, e.g. a Fedmet Library
• Plans its future	• Living our plan for growth	• Growth in the 1990s
• Profit is a requirement	• Living 'a federal industries company'	• Embracing the FIL ESOP 'RONA never below 20' – a reality

were expected to meet once for approximately half a day and to report their findings at the next strategic planning meeting on 29 March, 1989.

After the five subgroups had met, David Fine prepared a draft strategic plan which was intended to reflect the subgroup discussions. In consultation with Mang and Hurst, he summarised the subgroup discussions into seven priorities. The document was circulated to the Fedmet executive team a week prior to the meeting. The draft plan used the photography analogy and presented the plan as a series of snapshots. The memo attached to the draft indicated the need to continue to challenge the document. One section of the draft dealt specifically with the subgroup discussions. The 'realities' were outlined along with the linkage process to move the value into reality. Under each of these seven items was a blank section entitled *Questions*. The questions, Fine told us later, were intended to be 'wicked' questions in that they would be challenging and equivocal, often with a paradox or an oxymoron embedded in it.

29 March, 1989: The 'wicked' questions

The group's priorities were the centre-piece of the day's discussion. The seven 'realities' or priorities for the next five years are shown in *Exhibit 4.4*.

Under each reality was the list of the translation processes to convert the priority into a 'living process'. These were essentially the summary of the subgroup meetings as Fine saw them.

After some heated debate about the document, and in particular the implications for the divisions' long-range plans, which were supposed to reflect Fedmet's plan at least to some extent, the discussion moved to the 'wicked' questions. The rest of the day was spent discussing the linking processes before the wicked questions were finalised. Mang sat back away from the table for most of the meeting, only occasionally raising a

Exhibit 4.4 The seven priorities

1 **Create and maintain an appropriate environment**
2 **Mobilise and empower front-line people**
3 **Capitalise on 'big company' opportunities**
4 **Promote cooperative buying initiatives**
5 **Goals to 'get better'**
6 **Focus on earnings per share**
7 **Growth in the 1990s**

question or reiterating someone's comment. Fine played a more active role at this meeting than at previous meetings. The deadline for completing the strategic plan was mid-April so there were certain pressures for closure.

There was some discussion about how much of the document was retrospective versus future-oriented.

Shkut: Wayne, I think your caution is don't make it a total retrospective document. So we need to look at items six and seven on the list because that is where we really go forward. Are we really comfortable with that?

Hurst: I don't agree that is where we go forward. I think all of them are forward looking. Creating and maintaining an environment can't affect yesterday's business but it sure as hell affects tomorrow. We will only get to point six by going through points one to five.

Shkut: OK. Yep, you're right.

Hurst: At this instant we have an historic RONA (return on net assets) of whatever it is and the only way to affect tomorrow's RONA is through the people. We can't work on the numbers directly. The numbers are a result of action, behaviour . . . . All we can work with is people in such a way that when the numbers are measured the results are favourable. So we have to think about what we can do now which may impact the results later.

Eckersley: But it is a bit of a circle because it is looking at the numbers which leads you to think about things which would impact the numbers so it goes round and round.

Greene: And surely in that process you have to get as many people as possible keying in on those numbers.

Exhibit 4.5   The wicked questions of the seven priorities

---

1   Create and maintain an appropriate environment
- Do our 'body language' and our everyday actions reflect what we write?
- Are we committed to practising this – if so what change does this require in my own behaviour?

2   Mobilise and empower front-line people
- Are we ready to put the responsibility for the work on the shoulders of the people who do it?

3   Capitalise on 'big company' opportunities
- How can we maintain the advantages of inter-divisional rivalry while also achieving all the benefits of close cooperation between divisions?

4   Promote cooperative buying initiatives
- How can we maintain the benefits of autonomy while taking full advantage of our size?

5   Goals to 'get better'
- Have we learned anything from our history?

6   Focus on earnings per share
- What needs to happen in order for us to state 'RONA never under 20' is a reality?

7   Growth in the 1990s
- Where will we find the people to achieve this growth?
- Will FIL be able to balance their portfolio with growth in other groups to permit our growth?

They agreed that the past and the future were reflected in the seven priorities and then spent the next three hours developing the wicked questions related to each priority. The questions are noted in *Exhibit 4.5*.

Fine noted that the questions were to be presented in the strategic plan, rather than the answers, with the expectation that the divisions would address these questions and raise these and other questions with their branches. They discussed at some length the need to keep the questions both ambiguous and challenging, to create some discomfort among people at all levels in the organisation. Fine argued that using questions indicated that the process is continuous.

The strategic plan was viewed as a snapshot of one point in time of the ongoing process.

After the meeting the 1990–94 strategic plan was written by Fine and distributed to the members of the Fedmet team, the divisions and FIL. The process of preparing the plan began with a very loose, broad agenda and focus, and gradually narrowed into some specificity of actions, only to broaden and loosen again at the end with the wicked questions. The ambiguity inherent at the beginning of the process was also inherent at the end. Hurst said they trusted the process to develop the content. He said that objectives of what to do should *not* be clear at the beginning, rather they become clear through the process.

Case study 5

POTAIN SA[1]

It was 8 January, 1985 and Pierre Perrin, Chief Executive Officer (CEO) of Potain SA, had just received a letter from MACHIMPEX (China International Machinery Import–Export Company) requesting a proposal for a five-year licensing contract on Potain's FO23B crane. The Chinese wanted total know-how and know-why for crane design and manufacturing. (See *Exhibit 5.1*.)

Perrin asked his secretary to send a copy of this letter to the Export Director and to the SEREX Manager (Service Assistance Technique Export) immediately. An urgent meeting had to be arranged to discuss the Chinese opportunity before putting together an offer, and to select Potain's delegation that would go to Peking to negotiate the licensing contract.

What did technology transfer mean to Potain and how should Potain handle it? Should Potain provide the Chinese with all its technology? What should the price be and what conditions should be made?

Market trends

In 1979, 16 000 tower cranes (including both top-slewing and bottom-slewing or self-erecting cranes) were sold worldwide. Since then, the world market had weakened and continued to

decline. In 1983, world sales were just slightly over 9000 units, and the first half of 1984 had led market followers to believe that the world market could fall below 7000 units for the 1984–85 fiscal year (1 March–28 February). The forecast for the 1985–86 fiscal year offered little hope for improvement.

Potain's situation

In one year, the number of employees at Potain SA had been reduced from 2900 to 1460. Heavily dependent on the crane market, Potain was near bankruptcy; a loss of FF 94 million on a turnover of FF 750 million had been estimated for the 1984–85 fiscal year (these figures included the expenses and necessary financial arrangements incurred by layoffs). There was even a question about whether Potain's 1984–85 forecasts for turnover would be achieved. In addition, the market decline was expected to continue for the next three years. (The financial information can be found in Appendix 5A.)

Factory workers were worried about the rumours of bankruptcy, and some were already looking for other jobs. Perrin needed to take immediate action to put the company back on its

[1] This case was based on teaching materials originally developed at the Lyon Graduate School of Business by Professors T. Atamer, Francis Bidault, Ham San Chap and Frank Zaeh. The English version of the case has been prepared by Research Associate Kimberly A. Bechler, under the supervision of Professor Francis Bidault, as a basis for class discussion rather than to illustrate either effective or ineffective handling of a business situation.

feet, limiting the impact of a short-term problem on Potain's long-term future.

Competition

Potain's major competitors were: Liebherr and Peiner of Germany, and Edilgru, Alfa, and Cibin of Italy. The Dutch company, Kroll, was also a top challenger (see Appendix 5B.) Even though Italian manufacturers had the largest volume worldwide, with 4430 cranes per year, these were mainly bottom-slewing cranes.

Most competitors were either already licensing or moving in that direction, and it was clear that if Potain did not go into China, another company would be sure to claim that market.

History

Potain was founded in 1928 in the same town of La Clayette in France's Sâone and Loire region by Faustin Potain, an iron craftsman. In the beginning, Potain manufactured building equipment such as cement mixers, scaffolding parts and small cranes. At present, the Potain Group essentially manufactured tower cranes for buildings and public works projects. Potain had tried to diversify but had remained heavily concentrated in tower crane manufacturing.

In 1985, with its corporate headquarters in Ecully, near Lyon, the Potain Group consisted of Potain SA (holding company), BPR (a former competitor purchased in 1977), Sologat (a crane rental subsidiary), Sambron (a lift-truck manufacturer purchased in 1983), Simma (an Italian crane manufacturer that had been 51 per cent controlled by Potain since 1972), Potain Iberica (a crane manufacturer and vendor in Spain) and sales subsidiaries in the US, West Germany and Switzerland.

Diversification efforts

In the mid-1960s, the directors realised that Potain had become too specialised and started thinking about diversification. Potain formed an alliance with Poclain in 1968, creating Potain, Poclain Material (PPM) and targeting the mobile crane market. Mobile cranes were self-propelled cranes with a single telescopic arm, which were often used to erect top-slewing tower cranes. However, this alliance had the effect of limiting Potain's activity rather than providing a vehicle for expansion; Potain could not sell mobile cranes with a load capacity of greater than 1600 lbs (8 tons).

Potain had also tried to develop new products: tower cranes providing fast assembly and transport, mobile cranes travelling over any surface and lift-trucks. However, none of these products had a commercial success. Potain remained dependent on its original business of manufacturing tower cranes.

In 1977, under the pressure of the French Ministry of Industry, Potain agreed to take over BPR, a company combining three of its competitors – Richier, Boilot and Pingon – this move marked an end to its diversification efforts for the time being. In spite of the costs of its aborted diversification efforts, Potain remained a strong company. At the end of the 1970s, Potain completely dominated the French market and shared the world leadership position with Germany's Liebherr, both companies enjoying a 30 per cent market share.

Finally, in 1980, after a long history of family control, Potain hired its first 'outsider' as CEO. Pierre Barrot believed that Potain's 'best diversification' was the tower crane and that further diversification should be limited in order to refocus the Group on its business and accelerate international growth. Due to a disagreement with the board on the best way to manage the crisis, Barrot left Potain in June 1984. He was succeeded by Perrin, a long-serving senior executive who had held various positions, mainly in technology, engineering and business development.

Crane developments

In the early 1920s, the technology for cranes with liftable jibs was invented by the German firm, Wolff. The trolley-jib was developed in the early 1930s. The jib (or arm) that had always been attached to the top of the mast was now laid horizontally across it. Underneath the jib was a trolley car running on tracks which served to distribute the load with more precision than the liftable jib alone. Trolley-jib cranes enabled the load to be moved at any height, distance or direction by using four movements: hoisting, slewing, trolleying, and travelling or ground movement.

In 1935, Potain developed its first small crane with a liftable jib; gradually this technology was adopted by different manufacturers. Then in 1953, Potain introduced its first trolley-jib crane. Each one of the crane movements could be controlled by the crane operator by remote control either from his cabin or from the ground. These 'firsts' were followed by: in 1956, the development of a telescoping system, enabling tower cranes to self-erect automatically; in 1961, the launch of electrical mechanisms with variable speeds, enabling better control of crane movements and at the same time better precision in the 'delivery' of loads; and in 1969, Potain received the world record for its '982' crane weighing 250 metric tons.

Cranes were defined according to six characteristics:

- *the height under the hook* (vertical distance between the hook and the ground), the counterweights being at the extreme opposite end of the jib and the jib in its fully upright position);
- *free-standing height* (maximum height under the hook at which the crane could operate faced with bad weather conditions, without requiring auxiliary means for ensuring its stability;
- *the reach* (horizontal distance between the crane's point of rotation and the hook;
- *serviceable load* (weight of the load that could be suspended on the hook, this weight varying with the reach;
- *maximum load* (maximum serviceable load that the crane could lift; and
- *the load at the tip* (serviceable load that the crane could lift at its maximum reach.

However, the features that were most commonly used to describe cranes were: free-standing height, maximum reach, maximum load and load at the tip. (See *Exhibits 5.2, 5.3 and 5.4*.)

In addition to cranes used in the construction industry, there were other types of cranes. Each type of crane exemplified a different technology as the usage determined the required features. For example, harbour cranes required less precision in lifting and rotating than building cranes as port 'loads' were not as fragile as prefabricated boards. However, harbour cranes required greater durability for heavier loads and uninterrupted handling. Other examples were: forest cranes requiring shorter jibs and counter-jibs, and off-shore cranes requiring special tempering and steel casings.

Potain manufactured and sold two types of cranes: construction cranes and travelling cranes (for industrial applications). In the construction crane segment (or tower cranes), Potain's product range spanned the two main categories: top-slewing and bottom-slewing (self-erecting tower cranes). Top-slewing tower cranes rotated at the *top*, had free-standing heights of 108–328 feet, reaches spanning 131–262 feet, and load capacities from 2200 lbs at 131 feet to 44 000 lbs at 262 feet. Site applications included small, low and high-rise buildings, power plants, dams, and bridges.

Potain's FO23B crane, for instance, was a top-slewing tower crane. Having a free-standing height of 202 feet, a reach of 164 feet, a maximum load of 20 000 lbs and load at the tip of 4600 lbs, the FO23B was priced at FF 1 400 000 (which included Potain's 20 per cent margin on completed cranes). Adding the costs of transportation, customs and commissions, importing an FO23B would cost the Chinese FF 2 100 000.

On the other hand, bottom-slewing or self-erecting tower cranes rotated at the *bottom*, had free-standing heights of 52–108 feet, reaches spanning 43–180 feet, and load capacities from 1000 lbs at 40 feet to 4400 lbs at 180 feet. Site applications included small- to medium-sized buildings (ten floors), individual houses, condominiums, small bridges and as auxiliary cranes on large projects such as dams or bridges.

Manufacturing

Cranes were not mass produced but, rather, parts were specially made to meet the various crane and usage requirements. The entire crane was manufactured by Potain except for the electric motor, which was purchased from another company, Leroy-Somer.

Potain's crane manufacturing took place in four factories: La Clayette, Montbrison, Charlieu and Moulins. These factories had diverse responsibilities. La Clayette was dedicated to the more technologically sophisticated components (such as electrical parts); Montbrison subcontracted mechanics and/or soldering to Charlieu and Moulins. Moulins and Charlieu were each responsible for a particular range of crane models. The distribution of work between these two factories was often problematic as the market growth for the two main product lines was very different.

Marketing

Over the past years, Potain had experienced sustained growth, which placed it in the uncontested leadership position in the French market with a market share of 85 per cent. On a worldwide basis, Potain's share of the crane market had increased to roughly 20 per cent of the bottom-slewing crane market, and to 40 per cent of the top-slewing crane market. Potain's market presence was expanded and enhanced through its subsidiaries and licensees. For example, Potain was present in Italy via its 51 per cent ownership interest in Simma (since 1972), which had a 35–40 per cent share of the Italian crane market.

Potain did not have much information about its customer base as it sold mainly to dealers and seldom to end-users. However, Potain's market share had continued to increase due to Potain's reputation for quality, service and industrial dominance. Potain placed a high priority on service, including training and technical assistance, and after-sales service.

The Potain Crane Institute was based at La Clayette and employed about a dozen people. Training covered areas such as crane assembly, maintenance and repair (especially electrical and electronic), and crane handling. Potain's after-sales service included preventive maintenance, crane renovation and repair. 25 per cent of its after-sales activity was dedicated to the assembly and disassembly of top-slewing cranes; an activity which was not really profitable for Potain as there were many smaller firms offering this type of service at lower prices (FF 90–95 vs Potain's FF 120 per hour).

Internationalization

Export sales and subsidiaries

Potain 'internationalised' its business by emphasising export sales; the development of sub-

sidiaries and cultivation of licensees. Potain's International Business Organisation was responsible for all of Potain's international operations: exports, subsidiaries and licences.

Export sales were divided into three zones: Asia, America, and Europe–Africa. Potain had exported cranes since 1958 – first to Britain and the Commonwealth, then to Germany and Italy. In fact, exports were such a major portion of Potain's business that, in 1971, Potain received the 'Grand Prix de l'Oscar de l'Exportation'. For the 1983–84 fiscal year, 70 per cent of Potain's crane sales had been made outside France.

Potain had five foreign subsidiaries, four of which were located in the largest tower crane markets: Germany, Switzerland, Italy and Spain. The fifth one was located in the USA which, although a minor market, was considered strategically important as all the major competitors (especially Germany) were there.

Licensing

Licensing policy Potain's licensing policy was developed during the 1970s in reaction to the slowdown in the major European markets. Licensing was seen as a means to reach remote or protected markets where it was almost impossible to import finished products. Typically, Potain looked for a licensee that would locally manufacture the heaviest and bulkiest parts of the crane. The most sophisticated parts would be imported by Potain and then assembled by the licensee.

To support this licensing policy, Potain developed a group of principles and tools composed of: a coherent international development strategy, capable technical support, a flexible business policy and precautions to manage the risk of creating potential competitors. Until the present time, the precautions taken by Potain to protect itself against a licensee turning into a competitor included:

- not selling its latest technology, while at the same time being careful not to sell the licence to products that were no longer part of its product line;
- requiring a minimum level of quality for products manufactured under licence in order not to compromise its brand image;

- establishing a minimum of five years for the contract – reserving the provision of components, especially of mechanical parts which would always be manufactured in France;
- not giving the licensee exclusivity in areas considered outside the licensee's national territory, and to establish Potain's own sales network in these areas; and
- in the event of a major long-term strategic position, considering a 'joint venture' which would enable Potain to control the licensee's activity by linking him as a partner.

Integration of technology The integration of Potain's technology for production was done in phases. For the proposed China deal, integration of the technology for manufacturing the FO23B crane would have five phases, with one phase integrated per year. During Phase I, the technology for the whole mast and jib would be integrated; Phase II included the technology for the counter-jib and cat head (or 'A' frame); Phase III comprised the technology for the crane chassis; Phase IV included telescoping accessories; and Phase V comprised the technology for the four mechanisms of hoisting, sewing, trolleying and travelling, plus the cabin with electrical switchboard, crane driver's post and control instruments. Phase V was usually not part of the 'technology transfer package'.

SEREX Potain was experienced in technology transfer, signing its first licensing contract in 1972 with South Africa. Recognising the need for the formalisation of its know-how and technology, Potain created its SEREX (Service Assistance Technique Exports) department also in 1972. Within the Potain organisation, SEREX reported to the Industrial Director, while functionally working with the Export Sales organisation.

Initially, SEREX only served to provide licensees with technical documentation adapted to each country. But, its general role had evolved to where SEREX was responsible for identifying potential licensing partners, and then for managing the transfer of technology and overseeing its local adaptation and implementation. Specifically, SEREX was: analysing potential licence candidates; defining the conditions for the integration of manufacturing by the licensee in coordination with the Export Sales organisation; preparing the

necessary documents and equipment for manufacturing; following up licensee orders for components, organising training and technical assistance; and monitoring overseas licensee quality production.

Licensing contracts Potain's licensing contract with South Africa was followed by agreements with: Yugoslavia (1974), Iran (1974), Poland (1975), Venezuela (1976), Argentina (1976), South Korea (1978), Turkey (1979), Egypt (1980), Singapore (1980), Mexico (1981), Morocco (1981), and India (1983). These 13 licensing contracts were in various stages of activity, ranging in status from active to inactive.

Potain's partner in South Korea, for instance, was Hyundai, a company which produced two models of top-slewing cranes and one bottom-slewing crane. Until 1985, Hyundai had produced a total of 97 top-slewing and 11 bottom-slewing cranes; this licensing contract was slowly dying due to the incompatibility of the partners' objectives. In Singapore, as the market for new cranes had almost disappeared, Potain's licensing agreement was totally inactive. Therefore, the partner was moving towards Australia. The licensee, which had been a former agent in this marketplace, produced three different models of top-slewing cranes. Until 1985, this partner had produced a total of 80 cranes.

In contrast, Potain's licensing partnership in India was an example of a durable relationship. The licensee, a construction company, produced three models of top-slewing cranes and two models of bottom-slewing cranes. Up until 1985, 47 top-slewing and 59 bottom-slewing cranes had been produced.

China

The marketplace

Potain had access to China through two channels: directly to China or indirectly via Hong Kong. Selling directly to China was Potain's weakest position; there were several sales agents with undefined territories and with little motivation to sell, and prices were not very competitive. However, Potain had a strong position in Hong Kong with almost 40 per cent of the market.

In 1983, China's crane imports were FF 32

million, while in Singapore they were FF 79 million and in Hong Kong FF 20.5 million. In 1984, China's crane imports were only FF 12 million, where Hong Kong's were FF 39 million. However, 50–70 per cent of Hong Kong's imports were then sold to China. Over the next three years, total direct imports of completed cranes were estimated at FF 50–100 million.

History of Potain in China

Since Deng Xiao Ping's arrival to power in 1978, the operational word in China was 'modernisation'. To achieve this objective, Chinese leaders expressed their desire to introduce equipment, advanced technology and management experience from developed countries. The construction industry was China's priority for modernisation.

With the agreement of the Chinese and French governments, a mission to China was organised by French construction companies in 1979. Pierre Perrin, then deputy operational director, accompanied by the director of international development, led this mission for Potain. They were received by the Vice-minister responsible for technology transfer. The mission turned into a symposium on materials, and equipment for building and public works projects. At the time of this trip, Perrin understood that China was not interested in importing products, merely product technology. Despite a letter expressing an intent to cooperate sent by Perrin to the Vice-minister, no activity or further communication had followed this visit.

Then, in 1982, after three years of silence, MACHIMPEX sent a letter to Potain's International Business Organisation requesting Potain to submit an offer for a licensing contract for the manufacture of construction cranes. MACHIMPEX invited Potain's technical experts to visit one of its factories in order to help them identify and define their technological needs. When two salespeople arrived and were unable to answer MACHIMPEX's questions, the Chinese concluded that Potain was not serious about the proposition. Later, when one of Potain's engineers went to a construction site in Peking, he was invited to visit Peking's crane factory. As this engineer *was* able to answer all their technical questions, the Chinese had added Potain to their list of programmed

visits for 1984 (which also included Liebherr and Peiner).

In January 1984, a Chinese delegation (composed of the Peking factory director and directors of research from the Institute of Technological Research for Mechanical and Electrical Construction) visited Potain; the delegation noted that Potain was well equipped to handle the transfer of its technology. However, the Chinese remained unsure about Potain's willingness to cooperate. Therefore, in March 1984, Perrin, Gendrault (Research Director), Liger (SEREX Manager) and a sales representative went to China. This visit lasted two weeks and ended with a 2-day cross-examination, during which the Chinese engineers asked over 150 pointed technical questions to establish Potain's level of expertise.

The letter that Perrin had just received was the first news since that visit.

The China deal

MACHIMPEX was demanding the whole technology – '100 per cent integration' – for Potain's FO23B top-slewing crane. This 'licensing opportunity' represented a new situation for Potain; the Chinese wanted to produce everything, including the mechanisms, and wanted the 'know-why' for crane design which was a determining competitive advantage in the industry. In the past, Potain had only agreed to license Phases I–IV. Perrin also considered the opportunity cost; Potain's margin per crane was FF 280 000, but if Potain did not sell the technology, the market would be closed to Potain.

Looking at it from MACHIMPEX's perspective, Perrin thought about the costs incurred by China as a potential licensee. According to a SEREX study on China's production costs, China would save significantly on transportation and labour costs (direct production costs). Shipping and transportation costs for an FO23B crane would be FF 350 000 before the transfer of technology process began. Over the proposed 5-year contract period, these costs would vary according to the number of completed products versus components imported by China.

SEREX produced a forecast of the full cost of an FO23B in China (see *Exhibits 5.5* and *5.6*). This forecast showed that the full cost of an FO23B would decrease from FF 2 100 000 before the transfer of technology to FF 383 000 when the licensee reached full integration. The final price to the end-user would then be determined by a mark-up set by the Chinese Ministry of Industry. In similar industries, according to other Western companies that had done technology transfer in China, the mark-up was usually around 40 per cent (i.e. margin of 28 per cent), leaving almost no profit to the factory. The price of the FO23B crane in China would thereby be fixed by the Ministry in terms of a 'cost +' basis (full cost + margin), keeping the retail price at a minimum in order to make the product affordable to local construction companies; profit in China did not seem to have the same meaning as it did in France.

In preparation for his meeting with his colleagues, Perrin consulted a memorandum he had received from Antoine Colas, Export Director (see *Exhibit 5.7*.) Faced with an 'all or nothing' deal, Perrin thought about the complexity of the decision faced by Potain and the possible resulting long-term consequences.

Market considerations in the region

The world crane market basically included three zones: Europe (80 per cent), the Far East and Asia 10–15 per cent), and the Middle East (5–10 per cent). The Far East and Asia, and the Middle East were the two markets expected to experience high growth in the future: the four 'dragons' – Japan, Korea, Singapore and Taiwan – were expected to exhaust their stock of cranes in 4–5 years; Indonesia, Malaysia and the Philippines were believed to be waiting to 'take off'; and Japan's construction companies were rapidly augmenting their technological expertise and developing a presence in foreign markets.

In addition, the Far East was potentially the second largest market after Europe for top-slewing cranes. With a potential market of 500 cranes, representing a turnover of roughly FF 200 million, China would possibly be the fifth largest market after West Germany, Italy, the former USSR, and France. China also had liberal technology transfer legislation (see Appendix 5B) as well as legislation providing cooperation and financial incentives for the development of 'Special Economic Zones'. (See *Exhibit 5.8*.)

However, it was uncertain how long Deng's policy of openness would last, and Potain did run the risk of the Chinese becoming competitors in the fast growing markets of the Far East.

The meeting

It was 11 January, three days after Perrin had received the letter from MACHIMPEX. Pierre Perrin (CEO), Antoine Colas (Export Director), Bernard Liger (SEREX Manager), Philippe Gauguin (Director of Sales, Far East), and Paul André (Director of Operations) were assembled to discuss MACHIMPEX's letter and the implications for Potain. Perrin asked Liger to kick off the meeting by talking about SEREX's findings. (The following discussion took place at the meeting.)

Liger: The FO23B top-slewing crane is the crane model that we believe would best meet the Chinese's needs. The integration of Potain's technology for manufacturing this model would be done in five phases, or one phase per year. During this 5-year period, the percentage of production costs per unit remaining with Potain would be:

Yr 1	Yr 2	Yr 3	Yr 4	Yr 5
66	55	41	34	0

This would leave Potain with a significant amount of exports to China. In addition, the weighted average margin (%) on sales to the licensee for each phase would be:

Yr 1	Yr 2	Yr 3	Yr 4	Yr 5
25	28	30	35	0

This illustrates that mark-up margins on components increase as the components become more sophisticated.

Perrin: What if the Chinese decided to develop their own crane technology?

André: If we look at R&D costs in China, the estimated development cost for a crane like the FO23B would be roughly FF 2.6 million, including two elements, the crane structure at FF 1 635 000 and the mechanisms and control units at FF 1 050 000. But, this would take several years, four to five years at least.

Liger: Actually, R&D costs are not relevant since the Chinese have decided to buy technology from the 'outside' – either from Potain, Liebherr or Kroll (already producing in Hong Kong). The Chinese are in a hurry and they want the technology today! The idea would be to share the profits that would otherwise go into our competitors' pockets with our Chinese partners; that's the licence's appeal. Especially as China has decided to manufacture cranes, China will do it with others if not with us. China is a country where we sold one crane in 1983 and six in 1984.

Gauguin: Yes, but China has only been importing cranes for the past two or three years. In 1984, we sold six of the 20 cranes imported. In fact, 50 per cent of the cranes imported by Hong Kong are then sent to China, where we represent 42.5 per cent of the market.

André: We also need to consider what will happen three to five years from now. Where will we be? Potain will not be selling them anything and they will take the Asian markets away from us.

Perrin: It's true that we must consider the risks in the long term. The transfer of technology to China cannot be contemplated without considering our own strategy in the Asian zone. However, let's also review the facts of China's current situation. China's objective is to produce 1000 cranes per year. There already exist seven factories in China producing tower cranes with jibs of less than 98 feet in length. They have manufactured a few jibs longer than that, but these are not appropriate; this is why they seek to acquire Western technology. For the moment, they want to manufacture jibs 131–196 feet long with reliable materials. For these models, they have defined a need for 500 cranes per year, and they have estimated production at 500 cranes per year by the end of the third year of licensing. Looking at the construction activity in hotel and apartment complexes, it is my opinion that their needs will grow. In this type of situation, I believe, however, that the Chinese estimations will be cut in half; it would not be unrealistic to think that they will manufacture 25 cranes the first

year, followed by 100 in the second, 150 in the third and then 250 in both the fourth and fifth years.

In relation to our strategy in Asia and according to what I saw in China during our visit to their factories, I think it will be a long time before they will be able to export cranes. Their needs are great, and it would be difficult to imagine them producing at a level above their needs. Given their technological level, I would agree with André's evaluation that it would take them four to five years to integrate the production of mechanical parts. Furthermore, I believe that they will have to increase their imports of cranes having jibs longer than 196 feet to complement the local production of the FO23B which has a jib of only 164 feet. By the way, Mr Liger, what would be your best estimation of the transfer cost for the production of FO23B in the Chinese factory?

Liger: SEREX would need a budget of FF 2.5 million (with 1.5 million being spent in the first six months) to cover the transfer costs including: training of Chinese staff in France, provision of technical assistance, preparation of the technical documentation, provision of the specifications for equipment and plant layout, preparation and negotiation of the contract, hiring of consultants (lawyer and interpreter), supervision of the transfer, and monitoring of the licence.

Perrin: And Mr Colas, do you have any news about our competitor's bidding price?

Colas: In spite of Potain's intelligence effort, the export department has not been able to determine the price that the other crane manufacturers will be asking for a licence. But, let me say that, looking at the developing market in South-East Asia, I think we should also seriously consider proposing a joint venture with the Chinese, in addition to a licensing contract. A joint venture would enable us to sell on the Asian market with competitive prices; we could economise on transportation and labour costs at least for the mast and jib. At the same time, we would establish a strong market position for the larger crane models.

Perrin: Yes, we should consider the possibility of a joint venture carefully. The 'Special Economic Zones' defined in South-East Asia have advantages which should not be overlooked. However, China's definition of these zones is a recent development. We should look at the operations already executed in formulating a conclusion. We will be better able to understand the movement of the South-East Asian markets after seeing the transparencies that Mr Gauguin has prepared. [See *Exhibit 5.9.*]

Gauguin: Planned construction in South-East Asia includes two nuclear generating stations, and several other energy stations and hotel complexes. It would therefore not be surprising if China imports 50–100 more powerful cranes than those manufactured under licence. Of course we must wait and see if China will have the money to finance these imports and whether its openness policy will continue.

I believe that we should see China as another opportunity for additional finished products sales. China has an immediate need for 25 model FO23B cranes, and I think that Potain would certainly be chosen as the supplier if it would show its 'good citizenship' by agreeing to transfer technology. In addition, this is an opportunity for the Chinese to become familiar with Potain's products, and we could expect Potain to be in a good position to provide specialised cranes (high-rise tower cranes and special cranes for complex construction sites) which would generate further revenue in the future. For me, the licence with China could enhance Potain's market position in the short term. In the long term, if the Chinese do their own manufacturing, it is difficult to say what our position will be. However, a joint venture in a 'Special Economic Zone' could consolidate our position in the long term.

The group's consensus remained unclear: should Potain submit an offer for a licensing contract with MACHIMPEX? If yes, Perrin was still undecided about: the length of the contract, the use of Potain's brand name, export rights, what to include in the transfer of technology 'package' (old versus new technology), the price of the 'package', and the degree and form of Potain's involvement.

Exhibit 5.1 Letter from MACHIMPEX

Request For Submission of Offer

MACHIMPEX

POTAIN SA
18, rue Charbonnières
69130 ECULLY
FRANCE

Peking, December 28, 1984

SUBJECT: Request submission of an offer for the provision of know-how and know-why for the production of a top slewing crane by the Peking construction machine factory.

Gentlemen,

Following our visit to your factories and your 1984 visit to Peking, we would like to request that you submit an offer for the provision of know-how and know-why for a top slewing crane with a 20,000 lbs maximum load and 164-foot jib, which could be manufactured at our Peking factory.

The offer should include a description of the know-how and know-why concerning: crane design and calculation, specifications of raw materials, manufacturing, quality control, testing, as well as crane installation, maintenance and utilization. The price for the know-how and know-why, and a proposed payment schedule should be sent with the offer no later than February 1, 1985.

We would also like to invite you to come to Peking in April for final negotiations, after which, MACHIMPEX and the PRC Ministry of Urban Construction and Environmental Protection will choose the technology transfer partner; our goal is to start production as quickly as possible and according to the most advanced techniques.

Thank you in advance for your timely handling of this matter.

Exhibit 5.2 Topkit 50/23B

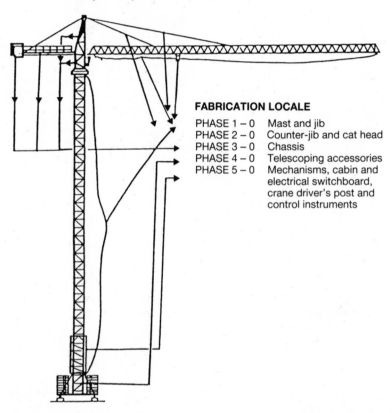

FABRICATION LOCALE

PHASE 1 – 0 Mast and jib
PHASE 2 – 0 Counter-jib and cat head
PHASE 3 – 0 Chassis
PHASE 4 – 0 Telescoping accessories
PHASE 5 – 0 Mechanisms, cabin and
electrical switchboard,
crane driver's post and
control instruments

Source: Potain Company Materials

Exhibit 5.3 Tower cranes (top-slewing)

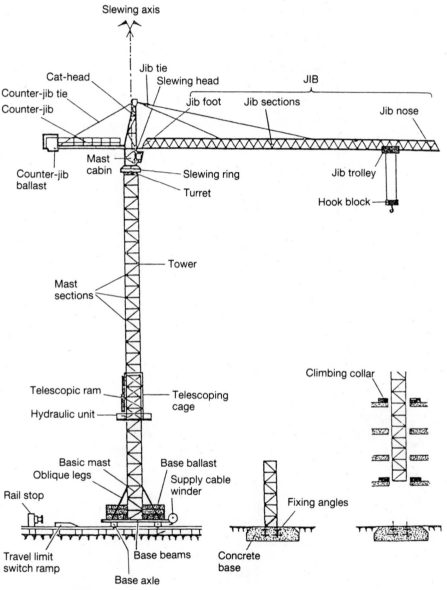

Source: Potain Company Materials

Exhibit 5.4 Tower cranes (bottom-slewing; self-erecting)

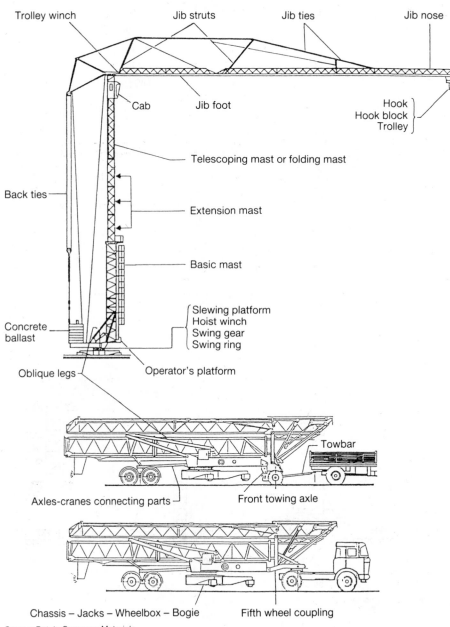

Source: Potain Company Materials

Exhibit 5.5 Structure of Potain's production costs for FO23B

Raw materials (steel)	18%
Components (electrical devices, etc.)	12%
Factory cost (labour and amortisation = factory hourly rate)	35%
General and administrative	15%
Selling costs	20%
Full cost	100%
Margin = 20 percent	25%
(Mark-up = 25 per cent)	
Total	125%
Ex-factory price of FO23B (before tax)	1 400 000
Shipping and Forwarding	25%
Customs duties	25%

Exhibit 5.6 Breakdown of the full cost of FO23B in China (in 1000 FFr)

	Year 1	Year 2	Year 3	Year 4	Year 5	Before TT
1. Integration Phase (operational)	Phase I	Phases I–II	Phases I–III	Phases I–IV	Phases I–V	
2. Cost of components and parts shipped by Potain to China	739.2	616.0	459.2	380.8	0.0	1120
3. Margin	246.4	239.5	196.8	205.0	0.0	280
4. Price including margin (ex-factory before tax) = 2 + 3	985.6	855.5	656.0	585.8	0.0	1400.0
Shipping and forwarding per unit						
5. ● Percent	51%	38%	21%	15%	0%	100%
6. ● (1000 FFr)	178.5	133	73.5	52.5	0	350
7. Cost of imports per unit (before customs duties) = 4 + 6	1164.1	988.5	729.5	638.3	0	1750
Local costs of licensee (according to integration level)						
8. ● Percent	34%	45%	59%	66%	0%	0%
9. ● (1000 FFr)	130.2	172.3	225.9	252.8	383	0
10. China costs before customs duties	1294.3	1160.8	955.4	891.1	383	1750
11. Customs duties rate	15%	15%	15%	15%	0	25%
12. Customs duties (1000 FFr)	147.8	128.3	98.4	87.9	0.0	350.0
13. Full cost per unit in China (before tax) = 10 + 12	1442.1	1289.1	1053.8	979.0	383.0	2100.0
14. Price per unit in China (fixed by Ministry of Industry)						

Source: SEREX (disguised data)

Exhibit 5.7 Memorandum from Pierre Perrin to Antoine Colas

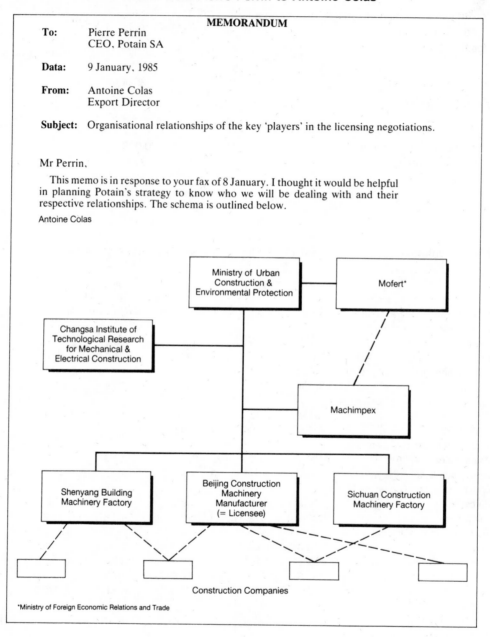

MEMORANDUM

To: Pierre Perrin
CEO, Potain SA

Data: 9 January, 1985

From: Antoine Colas
Export Director

Subject: Organisational relationships of the key 'players' in the licensing negotiations.

Mr Perrin,

This memo is in response to your fax of 8 January. I thought it would be helpful in planning Potain's strategy to know who we will be dealing with and their respective relationships. The schema is outlined below.

Antoine Colas

Ministry of Urban Construction & Environmental Protection

Mofert*

Changsa Institute of Technological Research for Mechanical & Electrical Construction

Machimpex

Shenyang Building Machinery Factory

Beijing Construction Machinery Manufacturer (= Licensee)

Sichuan Construction Machinery Factory

Construction Companies

*Ministry of Foreign Economic Relations and Trade

Exhibit 5.8 Note on tax issues

China places great importance on the introduction of new technology and foreign investment in China. Foreign companies not residing in China and receiving Chinese revenues (including interest, dividends, licensing fees and royalties) will be taxed at the source at a rate of 20 per cent.

However, the French–Chinese Convention provides for 'tax sparing' so that a French company having done technology transfer in China can attribute a tax credit on its French revenues equal to 20 per cent of the gross income earned.

Source: Droit Chinois des Affairs, Meyer, Verva and Dupont, September–October 1987.

Exhibit 5.9 Far-East: Market trends & Potain Group's market position

	POTAIN SALES**				Market		Market Trends	
Country	1983 Units	1983 in 1000 Ffr	1984 Units	1984 in 1000 Ffr	1984 Units	1984 in 1000 Ffr	Short-term 1986	Long-term 1989
Singapore	20	10912	30	16705	43	22670	−	=
South Korea	46	47380	21	8844	35	29444	−	=
Thailand	6	6200	5	3429	18	11424	−	=
Indonesia	0		2	2451	8	7561	−	+
Malaysia	7	10550	7	6277	16	10001	−	+
Philippines	0		0	0	0	0	−	−
China*	3	6500	6	2630	20*	11834	+	=
Taiwan			2	2099	5	11983	=	=
Hong Kong	10	11864	17	21883	40	38843	=	+
Australia			0	0	1	261	−	−
New Zealand			0	0	1	1299	=	=
Japan	0		0	0	0	0	=	+
Total Far East	92	93406	90	64318	187	145320	=	+
World Market	1845	935851	1316	659739	6178	1906543	=	=
FE/WM	5.0%	10.0%	6.8%	9.7%	3.0%	7.6%		

* Imports only.
** Includes sales from Potain, its subsidiaries and licensees.

Appendix 5A
POTAIN SA: FINANCIAL INFORMATION

**SITUATION FINANCIERE PREVISIONNELLE
1984–86**
(Fiscal year: 1 March–28 February)
**POTAIN: COMPTE DE RESULTAT PREVISIONNEL
POUR L'EXERCICE 84–86**
(en 1000FF)

CA	761 088
Autres produits d'exploitations	2 622
Consommation	500 150
Valeur ajoutee	263 560
Impots, taxes, assimiles	− 20 149
Charges de personnel	− 347 455
Subvention d'exploitation reçue	106
EBE	− 103 938
Dotations d'exploitation	− 21 755
Autres charges	− 7 168
Autres produits	64 989
RE	− 67 872
Resultat financier	− 65 239
Resultat courant avant impot	− 133 111
Resultat exceptionnel	38 698
Resultat net	− 94 413

**BILAN PREVISIONNEL SIMPLIFIE POUR
L'EXERCICE 1984–85**
(en 1000 F)

Immobilisations (1)	187 000	C. Propres (2)	42 000
Stocks	241 000	Provisions	46 000
Creances Clients	211 000	Pour P. et C.	
		Dettes (3)	604 000
Autres creances	46 000		
Disponibilites	7 000		
Total	692 000	Total	692 000

(1) dont:	Immobilisations corporelles		130 000
	Immobilisations financières		55 500
(2) dont:	Ecart de réévaluation		21 400
	Réserves		63 100
	Report à nouveau		− 105 270
	Résultat d'exercice		− 94 410
	Provisions réglementées		51 500
(3) dont:	DMLT		168 300
	Fournisseurs		151 000

Comptes de pertes et profits compares (en 1000 FFr) de Potain SA

	Au 2.29.1984	*Au* 2.28.1983	*Au* 2.28.1982	*Au* 2.28.1981
Perte d'exploitation	56509			
Participation salariés		2029		
Pertes sur exercises antérieurs	23450	8600	5868	1237
Pertes exceptionnelles	3995	9192	4761	9923
Dotations aux comptes de provisions hors exploitations ou exceptionnelles	68455	15939	17544	36203
Provisions pour impôts sur les Sociétés			16670	6033
Bénéfice net		4256	19043	6621
Total	152409	40016	63886	60017
Bénéfice d'Exploitation		2121	28662	14375
Profits sur exercises antérieurs	17366	3910	3248	1778
Profits exceptionnels	7491	7242	8373	2983
Reprise sur provisions hors exploitation ou exceptionnelles	22279	26743	23603	40881
Perte nette	105272			
Total	152409	40016	63886	60017

Comptes d'exploitation comparés (en 1000 FFr) de Potain SA

DEBIT	*Au* 2.29.1984	*Au* 2.28.1983	*Au* 2.28.1982	*Au* 2.28.1981
Stocks au début de l'exercice	230356	221062	230140	217138
Dépréciation	33589	29827	29090	22474
	196767	191235	201050	194664
Achats	490699	449243	415529	447714
Frais de personnel	311295	268620	239995	223006
Impôts et taxes	17429	15064	13171	10959
Travaux, fournitures et services	134839	141622	135449	117087
Transport et déplacements	44416	47503	43261	34488
Frais divers de gestion	21942	24576	18728	16743
Frais financiers	43522	39318	37432	35160
Dotations aux comptes amortissements	23481	17665	15811	17573
Dotations aux comptes de provisions	17671	13486	16314	11279
Quote-part stés en particip	2			
Bénéfice d'exploitation		2121	28663	14375
Total	1302062	1210453	1165403	1123048

(*continued*)

CREDIT	Au 2.29.1984	Au 2.28.1983	Au 2.28.1982	Au 2.28.1981
Stocks à la fin de l'exercice	316000	230356	221062	230140
Depreciation	42395	33589	29827	29090
	273606	196767	191235	201050
Ventes et produits	925008	951687	927391	876544
Subventions d'exploitation	283	27	56	47
Ristournes fournisseurs	964	3678	1858	2452
Produits accessoires	12819	12494	10565	17961
Produits financiers	17261	21446	17169	13010
Travaux faits par l'entreprise pour elle-même	5407	11035	6769	8151
Quote part résult. participation		40		
Perte d'exploitation	56509			
Travaux et charges non imputables à l'exploitation de l'exercice	10205	13279	10360	3833
Total	1302062	1210453	1165403	1123048

Bilans comparés (en 1000 FFr) de Potain SA

ACTIF	Au 2.29.1984	Au 2.28.1983	Au 2.28.1982	Au 2.28.1981
Valeurs Immobilisées				
Frais d'établissement	69	94	184	137
Immobilisations	118191	123158	107358	113288
Autres valeurs immobilisées	115854	97382	100207	105328
Valeurs d'exploitation	273606	196767	191235	201050
Valeurs realisables à court terme ou disponibles	262686	277444	253907	211397
Resultats (Perte de l'exercice)	105272			
Total Actif	875678	694845	652891	631500

PASSIF	Au 2.29.1984	Au 2.28.1983	Au 2.28.1982	Au 2.28.1981
Capitaux Propres et Reserves	214632	214570	200414	189806
Subvention d'equipement	12	19	25	31
Provision pour pertes et charges	70457	24254	30631	37190
Dettes à long et moyen terme	127769	113212	77551	94302
Dettes à court terme	462808	338534	325227	303550
Resultats (Benefice de l'exercice)		4256	19043	6621
Total	875678	694845	652891	631500

Appendix 5B
POTAIN'S COMPETITORS

Crane Market 1984 (in units)

	POTAIN		BPR		SIMMA		LIEBHERR		PEINER		EDILGRU	ALFA		CIBIN	KROLL	
	Bottom*	Top*	Bottom	Top	Bottom	Top	Bottom	Top	Bottom	Top	Bottom	Bottom	Top	Bottom	Bottom	Top
Total Europe	467	148	95	49	76	115	718	125	94	40	192	100	42	500	69	10
EC Countries	358	102	87	18	76	115	567	87	77	33	150	100	42	500	36	4
COMECON		5														
Other Europe	109	41	8	31			151	38	17	7	42				33	6
Total Africa	91	31	35	9			25	19							1	15
Maghreb	80	10	26	3			12									15
Other Africa	11	21	9	6			13	19					3		1	
Middle East	23	11		4	1		5	18	1	5			2			
Far East	6	47		15			1	14	1	5			15		2	2
Total Asia	29	58		19	1		6	32	2				17		2	2
Oceania								1		40						
Total Americas	5	3	2	7				3		40					15	
North America	1	1		2				3							15	
Latin America	4	2	2	5												
World Total	592	240	132	84	77	115	749	180	96	120	192	100	62	500	87	27

* Bottom or top refers to whether the crane turns at the bottom (bottom-slewing) or top (top-slewing).

Appendix 5C
LEGISLATION CHINOISE SUR TECHNOLOGY TRANSFER

Regulations of the People's Republic of China on the Administration of Technology Acquisition Contracts

Promulgated by the State Council on 24 May 1985

Article 1

These Regulations are formulated with a view to further expanding foreign economic and technical cooperation, upgrading the scientific and technical level of the country and promoting national economic growth.

Article 2

Importation of technology referred to in these Regulations means acquisition of technology through trade or economic and technical cooperation by any corporation, enterprise, organisation or individual within the territory of the People's Republic of China (hereinafter referred to as "the recipient") from any corporation, enterprise, organisation, or individual outside the territory of the People's Republic of China (hereinafter referred to as "the supplier"), including:
1 Assignment or licensing of patent or other industrial property rights;
2 Know-how provided in the form of drawings, technical data, technical specifications, etc. such as production processes, formulae, product designs, quality control and management skills.
3 Technical services.

Article 3

The technology to be imported must be advanced and appropriate and shall conform to at least one of the following requirements:
1 Capable of developing and producing new products;
2 Capable of improving quality and performance of products, reducing production cost and lowering consumption of energy or raw materials;
3 Favourable to the maximum utilisation of local resources;
4 Capable of expanding product export and increasing earnings of foreign currencies;
5 Favourable to environmental protection;
6 Favourable to production safety;
7 Favourable to the improvement of management;
8 Contributing to the advancement of scientific and technical levels.

Article 4

The recipient and the supplier shall conclude in written form a technology import contract (hereinafter referred to as "the contract"). An application for approval of the contract shall be submitted by the recipient, within thirty days from the date of conclusion, to the Ministry of Foreign Economic Relations and Trade of the People's Republic of China or any other agency authorised by the Ministry (hereinafter referred to as "the approving authority"). The approving authority shall approve or reject the contract within sixty days from the date of receipt. Contracts approved shall come into effect on the date of approval. Contracts on which the approving authority does not make a decision within the specified period of time shall be regarded as approved and shall come into effect automatically.

Article 5

The conclusion of technology import contracts must conform to the relevant provisions of the "Foreign Economic Contract Law" and other laws of the People's Republic of China. Both parties must specify in the contract the following items:
1 Contents, scope and essential description of the technology provided, and a list of patents and trade marks if they are involved;
2 Technical targets to be reached and time limit and measures for accomplishing the targets;
3 Remuneration, composition of remuneration and form of payment.

Article 6

The supplier shall ensure that it is the rightful owner of the technology provided and that the technology provided is complete, correct, effective and capable of accomplishing the technical targets specified in the contract.

Article 7

The recipient shall undertake the obligation to

keep confidential, in accordance with the scope and duration agreed upon by both parties, the technical secrets contained in the technology provided by the supplier, which have not been made public.

Article 8

The duration of the contract shall conform to the time needed by the recipient to assimilate the technology provided and, unless specially approved by the approving authority, shall not exceed ten years.

Article 9

The supplier shall not oblige the recipient to accept requirements which are unreasonably restrictive. Unless specially approved by the approving authority, a contract shall not include any of the following restrictive provisions:

1 Requiring the recipient to accept additional conditions which are not related to the technology to be imported, such as requiring the recipient to purchase unnecessary technology, technical services, raw materials, equipment and products;
2 Restricting the freedom of choice of the recipient to obtain raw materials, parts and components or equipment from other sources;
3 Restricting the development and improvement by the recipient of the imported technology;
4 Restricting the acquisition by the recipient of similar or competing technology from other sources;
5 Non-reciprocal terms of exchange by both parties of improvements to the imported technology;
6 Restricting the quantity, variety and sales price of products to be manufactured by the recipient with the imported technology;
7 Unreasonably restricting the sales channels and export markets of the recipient;
8 Forbidding use by the recipient of the imported technology after expiration of the contract;
9 Requiring the recipient to pay for or to undertake obligations for patents which are unused or no longer effective.

Article 10

In applying for approval of contracts, applicants shall submit the following documents:
1 Written application for approval of the contract;
2 Copy of the contract concluded by both parties and its Chinese translation;

3 Documents evidencing the legal status of the contracting parties.

Article 11

Application and approval of any revision and renewal of the contract shall be made in accordance with the provisions stipulated in Article 4 and Article 10 of these Regulations.

Article 12

The authority to interpret these Regulations and to formulate detailed rules for implementing these Regulations resides in the Ministry of Foreign Economic Relations and Trade of the People's Republic of China.

Article 13

These Regulations shall enter into force on the date of promulgation.

24.9 Procedures for examination and approval of technology import contracts

Approved by the State Council on 26 August 1985 and published by the Ministry of Foreign Economic Relations and Trade on 18 September 1985

Article 1

These procedures (hereinafter referred to as the "Procedures") are formulated in accordance with the provisions of the "Regulations of the People's Republic of China on the Administration of Technology Import Contracts".

Article 2

Technology import contracts hereunder listed must be submitted for governmental examination and approval in accordance with these Procedures regardless of country of origin, sources of funds and method of payment:

1 Contracts for transfer or licensing-in of industrial property rights and technical know-how;
2 Contracts for technical services, including that of feasibility studies or engineering designing entrusted to or in cooperation with foreign enterprises, that of provision of technical services through employing foreign geological exploration or engineering team(s), that of provision of technical services on technical renovation, technology or product design improvement, quality control and enterprise management, etc. but exclusive of

that for foreigners to be employed to work in Chinese enterprises;

3 Contracts for co-production which involves the transfer of industrial property rights and technical know-how or licensing, but exclusive of that for SKD or CKD operations, and processing with supplied materials or samples;

4 Contracts for the supply of complete sets of equipment such as plant, workshop or production lines, the aim of which is to transfer or licence-in industrial property rights and technical know-how as well as provision of technical services; and

5 Other contracts for the purchase of machinery, equipment or goods which involves the transfer of or licensing-in of industrial property rights and technical know-how as well as provision of technical services, but exclusive of those for the straightforward purchase or leasing of machinery and equipment, nor their after-sales provision of technical data, random operation manuals and maintenance instructions or maintenance service in general.

Article 3

For technical import contracts in which technology is acquired from foreign investors or other foreign parties in enterprises owned by foreign interests, and equity and contractual joint ventures that are established in the People's Republic of China, they must undergo the process of examination and approval according to these Procedures.

For contracts in which the industrial property rights or technical now-how concerned is entered as an equity share by foreign investors, they must undergo the process of examination and approval according to the provisions of the "Regulations for the Implementation of the Law of the People's Republic of China on Joint Ventures Using Chinese and Foreign Investment" and other relevant laws and/or administrative regulations.

Article 4

Technology import contracts are examined and approved respectively in the light of the following conditions:

1 Given existing norm stipulations, the contract for an above-norm project, the feasibility study report or equivalent document(s) of which are approved by the State Planning Commission is to be examined and approved by the Ministry of Foreign Economic Relations and Trade;

2 Given existing norm stipulations, the contract for a below-norm project, the feasibility study report or equivalent document(s) of which are approved by the responsible ministry or administration directly under the jurisdiction of the State Council is to be examined and approved by the Ministry of Foreign Economic Relations and Trade or the above-mentioned responsible ministry or administration entrusted by the Ministry of Foreign Economic Relations and Trade, which, however, is invested with the overall responsibility to issue the "Approval Certificate for the Technology Import Contract";

3 Given existing norm stipulations, the contract for a below-norm project for which the feasibility study report or the equivalent document(s) is approved by provincial, autonomous region or municipality government directly under the jurisdiction of the Central Government, special economic zones, coastal open cities and cities which come separately under national economic plans is to be examined and approved by the respective departments (commissions or bureaus) of the Ministry of Foreign Economic Relations and Trade. The contract or project for which the feasibility study report or equivalent document(s) is approved by city or county government is to be examined and approved by the respective departments (commissions or bureaus) of the Ministry of Foreign Economic Relations and Trade of provinces, autonomous regions and municipalities where the organs of the above-said cities or countries are located; and

4 Except those stipulated in item 2 of Article 3 of these Procedures, a technology import contract signed by a foreign-owned enterprise, equity joint venture or contractual joint venture of other foreign parties is to be examined and approved by the departments (commissions or bureaus) of provinces, autonomous regions, municipalities directly under the jurisdiction of the Central Government, special economic zones, coastal open cities and cities which come separately under the national economic plans where the above-said enterprises are registered.

Article 5

Application for examination and approval for a technology import contract mentioned in Article 4 must be submitted by the contract recipient to the

organs in charge within 30 days from the date of signature along with the documents as listed below:
1 Application;
2 Contract copy and its Chinese version; and
3 Certificate referring to the legal status of the contracting parties.

If the organs in charge consider it necessary, the applicant may be asked to submit other documents/data needed for the examination and approval of the contract.

Article 6

After receiving the application, the organs in charge must pay attention to the following points:
1 Whether the contents of the contract conform to that of the feasibility study report or the equivalent document(s) approved;
2 Whether the essential articles in the contract are as required;
3 Whether the property rights of the transferred technology and, where disputes arise over such property rights in the technology transfer, the obligations as well as the solutions thereof are explicitly and reasonably stipulated in the contract;
4 Whether there are reasonable stipulations in the contract for the technical level which should be achieved by the transferred technology, including the product quality guarantee, through the application of the said technology;
5 Whether the price and method of payment are reasonable;
6 Whether the stipulations in the contract for the contracting parties relating to their rights, responsibilities and obligations are definite, reciprocal and reasonable;
7 Whether any preferential taxation commitment is made in the contract without the consent of the Chinese Tax Authority;
8 Whether any provision is found in the contract violating the existing laws and regulations of China; and
9 Whether any provision is found in the contract that constitutes an encroachment of the sovereignty of China.

Article 7

The organ in charge must complete its contract examination and approval process within 60 days from the date of receipt of the application:
1 Once a contract is approved after examination, the organ in charge shall issue the "Approval Certificate for Technology Import Contract" printed and numbered by the Ministry of Foreign Economic Relations and Trade; and
2 If a contract is not approved after examination, the organ in charge shall put forth as soon as possible the reason thereof and request the recipient signatory party to hold renegotiations with the supplier of the technology and then grant the approval provided that the contract is amended accordingly.

To facilitate approval for the contract, the recipient negotiator may consult the organs in charge for the main contents or certain articles in the contract before or during the renegotiations or requests for pre-examination.

Article 8

After approval of the technology import contract by the government authorities concerned, all organs in charge shall submit a copy of the "Approval Certificate for Technology Import Contract" as well as the relevant data to the Ministry of Foreign Economic Relations and Trade for unified registration. The specific requirements for the data to be submitted shall be further notified by the Ministry of Foreign Economic Relations and Trade.

Article 9

The "Approval Certificate for Technology Import Contract" or a copy thereof must be presented when arranging for a bank guarantee, letter of credit, payment, settlement of exchange accounts, Customs clearance, payment of taxes or application for reduction or exemption of taxes or duties during the course of execution of the technology import contract; unless the said approval certificate is submitted, the bank, Customs and tax authorities are not entitled to process or handle the above request.

Article 10

Where substantive amendment or extension of the contract duration is made during the course of the execution of the technology import contract, re-application for examination and approval shall be made according to the relevant stipulations of these Procedures.

Article 11

The Ministry of Foreign Economic Relations and Trade shall be responsible for interpreting these Procedures.

Article 12

These Procedures shall enter into force from the date of promulgation.

Source: *The China Investment Guide*, 3rd Edition, Hong Kong 1985.

Case study 6

LOGITECH INTERNATIONAL SA (A)[1]

[handwritten: Culture — open ended change.]

'I don't know where I'm going, but I'm on my way,' stated a poster that used to hang in the offices of the people who created Logitech SA – one of Switzerland's most successful start-up companies of the 1980s. Founded in 1981, it had rapidly grown so that by 1990 it had a sales turnover of SF 205 million and employed 1450 people on three continents. While the academic community had been debating the characteristics and merits of global strategies throughout the decade, Logitech was already actually confronting them. In general, these strategies tended to be discussed in the context of large established multinational companies, seldom with start-ups. Logitech, however, had succeeded in assuming many of the essential features of such companies.

Although the poster had long since disappeared, the spring of 1991 made people remember that cheerful self-mocking message. It was time to take stock in preparation for the decade ahead; while some things had obviously been done well, others could have been handled differently. One issue was the company's international strategy. Was, for instance, the pattern of investment and trade that had evolved appropriate for the new challenges ahead? How global was Logitech? What changes were necessary to become a more effective competitor internationally? These questions assumed an even greater importance because the company's business scope had begun to change. Best known as a leading mouse company, it had started to position itself as a supplier of a broad range of desktop tools for personal computers. *[handwritten: — Product diversification]*

The beginning

Logitech had been incorporated in two locations almost from the start: as Logitech SA in Apples, Switzerland, in 1981 and as Logitech Inc., in Palo Alto, California, in 1982. This dual incorporation occurred because of the nature and domicile of the *[handwritten: history]* main founders – one Swiss (Daniel Borel) and two Italians (Pierluigi Zappacosta and Giacomo Marini).

Borel and Zappacosta had met while studying computer science at Stanford University in 1976. After graduation, Borel returned to Switzerland, but Zappacosta stayed behind in California. The two, however, shared a common interest in person computers and soon started to work together on developing a generalised word processing system for desktop publishing. Bobst Graphic, a Swiss typesetting company, supported their work over a three-year period. However, just as the system was up and running, Bobst Graphic

[1] This case was prepared by Professor Vijay K. Jolly and Research Associate Kimberly A. Bechler, as a basis for class discussion rather than to illustrate either effective or ineffective handling of a business situation.

The authors wish to acknowledge the generous cooperation and assistance given to them by a number of managers at Logitech International SA in the preparation of this case, especially the Chairman, Mr Daniel Borel.

was sold, leaving the two of them empty-handed with a staff of ten.

In order to continue what they had started, Borel and Zappacosta teamed up with Giacomo Marini, who had just opened his own software consulting company in Ivrea, Italy, after a career with IBM and Olivetti. The three became the principal shareholders in the new company, Logitech SA; a few others, like Jean-Luc Mazzone, a former collaborator at Bobst Graphic, also joined the company as shareholders.

On the organisational side, Borel looked after marketing and the office in Switzerland, while Zappacosta managed the US operation, where Marini joined him. By the end of 1982, there were six employees working in Switzerland and twelve in the company's Palo Alto office.

In line with the work Borel, Zappacosta and Marini had been doing, Logitech too started out as a software consulting company. Based on its expertise in word processing and desktop publishing systems, it won, among others, a $2 million development contract with Ricoh. Logitech was to analyse and design a graphics workstation into which the latter's peripheral products could be integrated. Most of the work on this contract was performed in Logitech's US office. Meanwhile, recognising the need for a good software environment for such applications, Logitech approached Professor Wirth of the ETH in Zurich. Known as the 'father of *Pascal'*, he had recently developed a new high level language called *Modula-2*, which was particularly suited to desktop publishing systems. With Professor Wirth's cooperation, Logitech gradually developed special capabilities in this new language. — Specialisin

From software to the mouse

It was the interest in *Modula-2* and the Ricoh contract that eventually led the founders of Logitech to think about the mouse.

Starting already in the 1950s, a range of pointing devices had been developed to facilitate interaction with computers. These included *light pens, keyboard cursor keys, cursor disks, touch screens, touch pads, trackballs, joy-sticks* and the *mouse*.

The world's first mouse was developed by Doug Engelbart at the Stanford Research Institute (SRI) in 1964 as part of a programme researching screen selection techniques. Engelbart had long been interested in how computers could augment the human intellect and ways to improve man–computer interactions. After trying out all the commercial pointing devices then available, he had decided to develop something himself.

The term 'mouse' originated with the device created by Engelbart; its shape, a round-edged wooden box with a cable, resembled a mouse. It consisted of two wheels placed perpendicular to one another; when rolled forward, one wheel rotated freely while the other dragged along without turning. When rolled at an angle, each wheel turned in direct proportion to the extent of horizontal or vertical motion. The wheels functioned as a potentiometer, similar to the volume dial on a home stereo, sending different voltage levels as they turned, which were then translated into digital signals for the computer. Although the wheels were big and noisy, and the resolution they provided inadequate for most purposes, the device worked and Engelbart was issued a patent on it in 1970.

The Engelbart mouse was picked up by Xerox PARC and further developed by one of its staff, Jack Hawley. Licensing the basic wheel system from SRI, Jack Hawley replaced the potentiometers with a digital encoding system in 1972. Then, in 1975, Xerox commissioned Hawley to improve a mouse developed by another Xerox employee, Williard Opocensky, which used ball-bearings instead of wheels. This mouse became the first commercial mouse, establishing the standard for mechanical mice.

Professor Wirth, whom the Logitech team knew through *Modula-2*, had seen this Hawley mouse when on sabbatical at Xerox PARC in 1976. It had been used with the famous Xerox *Alto*, the first screen-based graphics machine with WYSIWYG (What You See Is What You Get) capability. Returning to Switzerland, he persuaded an acquaintance, Professor Nicoud of the Ecole Polytechnique Fédérale de Lausanne (EPFL), to develop the device further for possible use on a workstation he was designing based on *Modula-2*.

The mouse that Professor Nicoud developed in Lausanne in 1978 was an opto-mechanical one, in which wheel motion was detected by opto-electronic components. He was also the first to use a floating ball concept in place of wheels. Not only was this mouse design technically superior, but it also became a familiar and popular feature when Apple introduced it with its *Lisa* computer in 1982.

In parallel with the development of opto-mechanical mice, some people had begun work on pure optical mice as well. These optical mice required specially designed pads to communicate movement to the cursor. Instead of balls they used LEDs (Light-Emitting Diodes) to reflect position.

Compared to other pointing devices, the mouse quickly became the preferred computer interface. Typically, early users tended to be engineers, using the mouse for computer-aided design and manufacturing. All three major technologies – mechanical, opto-mechanical and optical – had their own following in the beginning, with the opto-mechanical concept eventually dominating.

Logitech as a value-added distributor of mice

After Professor Nicoud had developed his opto-mechanical mouse, he contacted a small company, Depraz SA, near Lausanne, Switzerland, to arrange for a regular supply. These mice were sold mainly to universities and laboratories.

While working on the Ricoh job, Logitech observed these developments close up and became convinced that mice could easily become a popular tool in creating a user-friendly interface with computers. Indeed, Logitech saw the mouse as a new business opportunity rather than a mere development tool.

'We were a small group of people with a great dream', Borel said about this opportunity. 'From the beginning, we dreamt of the day when Logitech would grow beyond its role as a consultant for other companies and would be established in the world market with a recognized name, providing fun and innovative products.'

As more people began to inquire about the device, particularly through the ARPANET (Advanced Research Projects Agency Network), Logitech approached Depraz in August 1982, obtained worldwide distribution rights to Professor Nicoud's *Series 4* mouse and began selling it under the Logitech name.

The relationship with Depraz, however, left much to be desired. Being a small company, it was unable to meet the quality standards that Logitech

deemed essential for the product. Soon after the introduction of the *Series 4* mouse, Professor Nicoud, therefore, started work on its successor, the *Series 5* mouse, using the market feedback Logitech could provide. This new model, however, was turned over to a larger Swiss company, Câblerie de Cortaillod, for manufacture.

Unfortunately, the experience with Câblerie de Cortaillod was no better. After nine months, when the company was not making the large sales promised by Logitech, Cortaillod became reluctant to invest further in the product's manufacture. Costs were high, too.

Buying rights to the mouse

In October 1983, realising that it either had to control everything or get out of the mouse business, Logitech bought the rights to the *Series 5* opto-mechanical mouse from Cortaillod for about SF 1 million – a combination of cash and a commitment to buy a certain number of mice at a high fixed price.

When Logitech acquired these rights, it had had no prior experience in volume hardware manufacturing. The device was still used mainly by universities and laboratories, with a worldwide market of barely 15–20 000 units in 1983.

The early competition

Although the personal computer industry was starting to take off, it was not clear which pointing devices would benefit most and to what extent. Furthermore, Logitech was neither first nor alone in the market.

Among the companies already in the mouse business in 1982 were: Mouse Systems Corp. (MSC) with its optical mouse; and Mouse House, founded by Jack Hawley himself, which made a mechanical mouse. MSC was strong in the retail segment, while Mouse House mainly pursued the own equipment manufacturers (OEM) market. Both subcontracted out the manufacture of their mice to other companies. MSC, for example, first used a Silicon Valley company for its manufacturing and, then later, used a company in Singapore.

In 1983, Microsoft was the next one to enter the market. Using the mouse as a complement to its

Highly competitive – speed

application software business, the company soon built up a strong position in the retail segment. It, too, subcontracted the manufacture of its mouse – to Alps of Japan. Apple Computers had also developed its own mouse. In addition, two other companies were getting ready to enter, KYE, a Taiwanese company that made PC housings, and Mitsumi, a Japanese company. Both were adopting Logitech's opto-mechanical technology.

Growing the business internationally

The Swiss base

After taking over the manufacturing rights from Cortaillod, Logitech built a small 'factory' in Apples near Lausanne in 1983, concentrating both its hardware and software development there. Since the mouse design evolved rapidly in response to market feedback and developments in technology, manufacturing was kept light and flexible. The total capacity installed was around 25 000 units per year.

Close to customer

Logitech also immediately set about improving Professor Nicoud's mouse. Among the early achievements of its R&D were: the development of a cordless mouse; a patented, lightweight ball-cage system which, in addition to improving resolution, was easier to manufacture and handle; and the use of data signals to power a mouse, thus eliminating the need for a separate power cable.

Although the development and manufacture of the mouse was based in Switzerland, the main market was in the USA. Therefore, promoting the business was handled by the company's Palo Alto office.

Hewlett-Packard OEM contract

It was the early market development in the USA that led to Logitech's first major breakthrough. Hewlett-Packard, also based in Palo Alto, was looking for a mouse in 1983 and became interested in Logitech's product. But, H-P wanted a high quality, reasonably priced product made to its specifications. Therefore, from the summer of 1983 until May 1984, H-P helped Logitech not only redesign the mouse for its proprietary use, but also provided instruction and training on mechanics, manufacturing and quality. In order to supply the OEM contract placed by H-P in 1984, Logitech decided to set up its own manufacturing facility in California.

Joint venture / need

emergent

The US site

Until this time, there had been the inevitable debate inside Logitech about whether or not to become a manufacturing company. The H-P contract, in fact, resolved the debate. As Zappacosta recalled, 'We basically needed to manufacture in order to have a chance with the OEM market; if we had been selling to the retail market instead, we probably would never have said "Oh, how beautiful – manufacturing", because people who sell to retail always feel that a little bit of marketing wizardry can take you a long way.' Borel then went on to explain why the company had established manufacturing in the US, 'OEMs want you to be nearby, they want to be able to inspect.'

California gradually became Logitech's main production facility, although mice continued to be developed and built (in smaller quantities) in Switzerland. The 'H-P mouse', furthermore, was followed by other mice designed for AT&T and Olivetti. By the summer of 1985, Logitech had about 10 large OEM accounts. The manufacturing capacity installed to support them was about 300 000 pieces per year.

emergent strategy

From OEMs to retail

A couple of years after the OEM contract with H-P, which had turned Logitech into a manufacturing company, Logitech's founders decided to gamble on the retail market while pursuing other OEM customers. This effort was first launched in the US in early 1986 with the introduction of the *Logimouse C7*.

'However', Zappacosta recalled, 'although the C7 was an excellent product, probably the best available at that time, we had no retail presence. Also, using the traditional channels to access the retail market meant going through distributors, convincing them to take the product, and hoping they would do a good job in reaching dealers. It also meant that significant advertising support would have to come from Logitech, which we could hardly afford.'

Then, the experience of one of Logitech's

engineers, Fabio Righi, provided the company with an idea. He had been trying to sell the *Modula-2* software package for $495 and was getting nowhere. He had concluded that there was indeed a big demand for the product but that the price was too high. Promising to sell 'a ton of the stuff' if it were priced at $99, he was able to convince Logitech to lower the price and advertise it widely. It worked.

In order to bypass the traditional channel for accessing the retail market for mice, Logitech tried the same approach. Advertisements for a $99 mouse were placed in trade publications like *PC Magazine* and *Byte*, together with coupons that people could send in to buy directly from the company.

With Microsoft, whose leading brand was selling at $179, this $99 price not only attracted great interest but turned Logitech into a pioneer in buying such products by mail order. Given the fact that production volume was still small, it was also a viable method. Zappacosta recalled, 'Even with a price of $99 we made money, because our costs were around $40; if we had gone through a distributor, we would have had to give a 50 per cent discount and would have gotten nowhere. This way, we could also put money into advertising and that created brand recognition early on'.

The success of this direct selling effort later facilitated Logitech's entry into the retail market by the more traditional distributorship route. As more customers began to inquire about Logitech's products, dealers and then distributors were eager to carry them.

Taiwan – the second non-Swiss site

Parallel to pursuing the retail market in the US, Logitech continued to search for other OEM customers as a means to grow the business. Apple and IBM were the OEM accounts most sought after by the company. Both sourced from Alps, a large Japanese manufacturer of electronic components, which had also become the exclusive supplier to Microsoft.

The fact that it was much smaller and relatively inexperienced compared to Alps did not deter Logitech's managers. To acquire the Apple business, however, Logitech had to be able to produce at high volume and at a low cost, as well as offer a better-designed mouse.

Although still not sure about the Apple account, Logitech started to look for an additional manufacturing base and eventually selected Taiwan. With luck, and the help of a good lawyer, the company was accepted in the Science-based Industrial Park in Hsinchu for an affordable 'entrance fee' in 1986. 'It was rather like hang-gliding, you jump and you hope the wind will be there', Borel described the prematureness of this investment. Then, Apple demanded terms that were more challenging than Logitech had expected. 'We took the business at a price we could not meet, but sometimes you have to force yourself to reach certain goals', Zappacosta explained.

Cost had been influential in choosing Taiwan, but there were also other reasons for the choice: a well-developed supply base for parts, qualified people and a rapidly expanding local computer industry. In fact, direct labour accounted for only 7 per cent of the cost of Logitech's mouse.

Starting with a mere $200 000 investment, the Taiwanese factory soon surpassed Logitech's US facility as a manufacturing base. After the Apple contract, other OEM contracts also started being served from Taiwan, increasing the total capacity to 10 million pieces per year. Finally, in late 1988, the company also obtained an important contract with IBM, after offering a highly competitive price.

Europe and the Irish site

At the time the Taiwanese factory was being built, in mid-1986, 7.5 per cent of Logitech's sales came from the US, mainly from OEM customers.

The company's first major breakthrough in Europe happened early on. Soon after winning an OEM contract with AT&T in the US, Logitech succeeded in gaining a similar contract with Olivetti in Europe in 1985, which was supplied by the Swiss facility. One reason Logitech won this contract was that it was already qualified as a supplier for AT&T, which had a recently made alliance with Olivetti at that time.

The European retail market took more time to develop. The problem had to do with the nature of the market and the way Logitech positioned itself. The US was one big market which could be reached through a handful of publications. There was also a well-developed home-use market which, being price sensitive, was especially attracted by Logitech's low-price positioning.

'Europe', according to Borel, 'was completely different, and we learned through a number of mistakes. The main market in Europe was corporate, which tended to be brand rather than price sensitive. It instinctively preferred to buy IBM and Microsoft. Users, moreover, were engineers and production people. Each country's market profile, use pattern, and distribution channels were also different'.

Realising that the 'mail order' strategy was unsuitable in Europe, Logitech approached distributors. Compared to the US, where there was a trend towards no-fringe low-cost mass outlets, European distributors preferred high margins rather than market share. Logitech wanted them to price its mouse at SF 199 against Microsoft's SF 600, in order to repeat what it had done in the US. The distributors, however, insisted on a SF 300–350 price, which they felt was competitive enough. 'Unfortunately', Borel recalled with some bitterness, 'the Taiwanese did to us what we had done to Microsoft in the US. They got in at a DM 99 price, catching us in a higher price position than we intended. In a few years we lost a lot of the market to them and, when we reacted strongly in 1988, it was rather late. Now, we are trying to regain the position we could have had all along'.

With a strong commitment to developing both the retail and OEM segments, Logitech started to look for a manufacturing site in Europe and opened its fourth manufacturing plant in Cork, Ireland, in the autumn of 1988 – barely 18 months after starting up in Taiwan.

Locating in Ireland brought Logitech closer to its major European customers. Apple, for example, was located in Ireland as well, while Apollo, IBM and Compaq had their facilities nearby in Scotland. As Borel put it, 'We could not have developed OEMs like Apple Europe and IBM Europe, and we would have had a problem delivering to Olivetti; OEMs expected to receive delivery from inside Europe. Retail-wise, too, we wouldn't have been able to serve the market in French, Italian, German and Spanish without a European site'.

The choice of Ireland was influenced by a number of other factors. Apart from being an EC member, it offered investment subsidies, low tax rates (10 per cent), a skilled and motivated labour force at a reasonable cost and, compared to Switzerland, no problem with work permits. When the Irish plant came on stream with a capacity of 1–1.5 million pieces per year – comparable to the US level at that time – all manufacturing in Switzerland ceased.

The Japanese and East Asian market

The retail market in Japan and the Far East was even more difficult. For a long time, the Japanese market for PCs had been dominated by NEC, which supported its own input devices. There was no Japanese software running a mouse, and the PC market as a whole had taken longer to emerge. When Logitech entered the Japanese retail segment through a small distributor in 1988, it was soon in a stagnating situation.

In the Far East, the main market was for OEM products. The retail segment was small and, especially in Hong Kong and Singapore, re-exports occurred frequently. While developing whatever retail potential there was, Logitech was worried that such re-exports might mean losing some control over its worldwide marketing policy.

The net result was that Logitech's market coverage began to trail somewhat behind its manufacturing base. While it fairly quickly established a global manufacturing infrastructure, most of its revenues came from the US. *Exhibits 6.1 and 6.2* show the growth in Logitech's sales and its distribution by area and principal segment.

Managing its infrastructure

The international spread of Logitech's investments eventually raised the issue of assigning roles to the various sites and, within them, to each of the functions.

The trend until 1987

Until 1987, when Switzerland, the US and Taiwan were the main sites, the trend was towards functional specialisation. Switzerland, where Logitech's Chairman, Daniel Borel, resided, and from where most of the early financing was raised, naturally became the locus of the finance function.

Historical structure

After successfully adapting and improving Professor Nicoud's *Series 5* mouse, the Swiss site also became the centre for hardware development for mice. The fact that some manufacturing took place there as well facilitated design and prototyping in one location. Finally, given its location, the facilities in Apples, Switzerland, took on the responsibility for developing European sales.

California, where Logitech's software expertise had been located from the beginning, became the centre for software development. Since the US was Logitech's principal market and Zappacosta was based there, this facility also took the lead in worldwide marketing coordination.

Taiwan, in addition to becoming the main manufacturing site, first took on some manufacturing engineering roles, then some mechanics development and procurement of certain components. The last two roles had to do with the local supply base.

The evolving network

The picture started to become more complex when the Irish plant came on stream in 1988 and each of the three 'regions' began to grow in size. Practical considerations and the way Logitech had become an international company started to make these units more and more self-contained.

In manufacturing, both the US and Ireland started to develop capabilities in engineering alongside Taiwan. To some extent, this was aided by the new CAD/CAE (computer-aided design/computer-aided engineering) technologies that diminished the advantages of using Taiwan for prototyping and tooling.

It was natural that the marketing function should become the most regionalised, especially when the European market grew in importance. Rather than rely on product management and marketing support from the US, another group was created in Switzerland. Although not the initial intent, Taiwan too gradually started to assume some marketing responsibility for the Far East. It succeeded in introducing a Chinese version desktop publishing software package for its regional market and, more recently, had taken the lead in establishing a new venture in Shanghai to develop software for mainland China.

To support its marketing effort, the company decided to establish a number of regional and national sales companies over time, which were also grouped under the three regional centres.

R&D and Engineering (employing 170 people out of a workforce of 1450) also became dispersed. Roughly 80 per cent of the R&D and Engineering resources were devoted to new retail products, the rest being allocated to supporting OEM product development. Four principal areas of expertise were covered: optics, electronics, mechanical engineering and software.

Inevitably, each site developed its own support and administrative functions too. Switzerland continued to act as the locus of the finance function – even more so, in fact, as Logitech went public there in June 1988. However, the three units – Europe, USA and Taiwan – each had their own finance function, and managed their own investment and performance control systems. They were also responsible for their own human resource management. *Exhibit 6.3* shows the way the company's infrastructure evolved and *Exhibit 6.4* the growth in headcount by function and region.

Costs and benefits of the infrastructure

While a network of 3–4 full-function units – plus a number of sales companies – did carry a cost penalty, Logitech also saw the advantages this situation provided.

All production facilities shared a common manufacturing process (see *Exhibit 6.5*). A typical line included 25 stations, was 25–40 metres long, and had a throughput time of about 20 minutes. Each line had a capacity of about 1800 mice per day and could handle multiple models. Compared to the US and Ireland where three lines were installed, Taiwan had 16 identical lines.

Borel summed up his assessment of the manufacturing function:

> The trick is to deliver fast, but without tying up your inventory with anything specific before it is necessary. It is really a trade-off between ... 'What do I do if I get an order of 500 tomorrow morning that needs delivery within 24 hours?' and 'How fast should I be ready?' So the complexity is high in Ireland where one has to deliver in several languages. In the US, you have one mouse and one documentation language that is the same all

over the US. There, you can prepare yourself, you can build inventory ahead of time – that is, in the summertime for the Christmas season. In Europe, you cannot do that to the same extent.

Sourcing from plants was initially on an *ad hoc* basis. Gradually, the criterion when selecting sites for sourcing became total acquisition costs – not just the cost of the product but the cost of shipping, duties and flexibility, i.e. the ability to deal with changes in customer orders. If Ireland or the US could manufacture at Taiwan's cost plus roughly 10 per cent, then the company would prefer to manufacture for local markets.

Being present in three regions had a procurement advantage, too. Since the material content in the mouse represented around 70 per cent of the cost, procurement was always an important function at Logitech. With the bulk of the components being sourced in the Far East (see *Exhibit 6.6*), the Taiwanese factory had a key role in qualifying and dealing with suppliers for the entire group. Each facility was, however, free to do its own sourcing.

In marketing, too, there were certain benefits. For example, no one was exactly sure about Logitech's 'nationality'. In fact, a Taiwanese journalist once asked the General Manager of Logitech–Ireland why a Taiwanese company had chosen to locate in Ireland as a way to penetrate the European market!

It was this 'localness' that also helped the Taiwanese unit win an OEM contract with IBM Asia. Y S Fu, the Head of Logitech Taiwan, and Jim Ho, one of Fu's colleagues, found someone in IBM's Taipei International Procurement Office (IPO) they knew and, after doing some design work together, got the Taiwanese unit of Logitech approved as a worldwide supplier for IBM's PS/2 and PS/1 personal computer models – a very satisfying achievement for them.

The worldwide mouse market

From a slow start in 1982, the worldwide market for mice expanded rapidly to reach approximately $500 million by 1990.

The mouse itself was a fairly standard product. As Zappacosta described it, 'We believe strongly that most of the world has similar requirements. Certainly in our market – computers – it's hard to imagine why a European user should need a

mouse that is different. In fact, the reason we stopped using a power supply was that it was one element we had to adapt for Europe, Asia and the US. We wanted one product.'

Even so, there were a number of ways to segment the mouse market: by product, channels, buyer groups and even by geography.

Product

In terms of positioning, mice could be roughly placed in three categories: upper-end, middle and low-end products. In 1991, the manufacturers' list prices ranged from around $100 for upper-end products to $6–10 for the cheapest, with corresponding retail prices anywhere from 20–100 per cent higher. Microsoft was well established as the 'leading brand', commanding a premium price at the retail level, partly because of the parent company's reputation and the perception 'that the safest way to run Microsoft software is by using a Microsoft mouse'. MSC, which dominated the optical mouse business, had long been considered the 'Rolls-Royce' of the industry. It gained this reputation in part because of being the major supplier to workstation manufacturers such as SUN Microsystem and Silicon Graphics. Over time, however, MSC had become a marginal player in the industry overall and was bought by KYE in 1990.

Logitech, which entered in the middle, gradually covered the entire range. In 1988 it launched a low-end product under a new brand name called *Dexxa* whose retail price was in the $18–30 range. This competed against KYE's *Genius* brand and against several other Far East Asian manufacturer's products. Later, in order to compete directly with Microsoft and MSC, Logitech launched the *Series 9* in January 1989, followed by the *MouseMan* (corded and cordless) models. At this time, Logitech also introduced its *Logimouse Pilot* (known as *First Mouse* in the US) for first-time users, to strengthen its position in the low-to-middle end of the product spectrum. *Exhibit 6.7* summarises Logitech's product introductions; *Exhibit 6.8* illustrates positioning changes of various companies over time both in the US and Europe.

Channels and buyer groups

The two main channels for distributing mice were

barriers to entry – few

OEMs and retail. There were two main sub-segments within the OEM group: customised and non-customised. In the former the mouse was either jointly developed by a mouse manufacturer and an OEM, for example, the Logitech/Apple project for the latter's high-end product, or was fully specified by the OEM, with a mouse company acting mainly in a subcontracted manufacturing role. In the non-customised segment, the mouse was typically designed and built by a mouse company and supplied off-the-shelf to OEMs. Logitech was mainly active in high-end products for both customised and non-customised versions, especially the former (as shown as *Exhibit 6.9*).

Both in the USA and in Europe, there were four main sub-segments within the retail market: home, education, corporate and small business. *Exhibit 6.10* summarises the main characteristics of these four sub-segments in Europe. The US profile was comparable, with an additional 'government' sub-segment that had its own buying process and criteria. Logitech served all of these retail segments.

Geography

The behaviour of each of these segments in the retail market varied somewhat from country to country. There were, moreover, some distinct differences between the US and Europe. The US was a large market, with a few nationwide distributors (such as Softsell and Ingram), and retail chains (such as Egghead Software and Businessland) that had a close relationship to suppliers. Also, as Marc Chatel, Vice-President of Marketing and Sales in Europe, observed, 'High prices and discount channels seem to co-exist well in the US, while Europeans do not accept large price differences for the same product.' The European market also remained fragmented, although the UK was starting to approach the US in some regards. Elsewhere, the cost of distribution tended to be significantly higher than in the US. The relationship between manufacturers and distributors/retailers was also weaker; whereas, for instance, service tended to be the manufacturer's responsibility in the US, European retailers considered service to be a value-added feature which justified asking a higher price. The independent role played by

distributors in Europe also created a market that was wide open to low-cost mice from the Far East. Many distributors simply went directly to Taiwan to source their products, thus compensating for their higher costs.

The retail or 'street' price differences between the US and Europe reflected these market characteristics. While the street price was 20–60 per cent higher than the distributor's list price in the US, it was 50–100 per cent higher in Europe depending on the country and channel.

The differences in product acceptance were more subtle but existed nevertheless. As Ron McClure, Vice-President Strategic Marketing in the USA, put it, 'Europeans tend to like "high-tech" features with an Italian/German look, while Americans prefer something in beige, and Japanese want small products. Also, while products tend to be accepted more quickly in the US, the slow pace in Europe means that once accepted, you are safe for a while'.

Logitech and its competitors

In the OEM segment, Logitech's main worldwide competitor was Alps of Japan, a $3 billion company that was Microsoft's exclusive supplier. It had recently announced a collaboration with Lunar Design of Palo Alto, California, to design new 2- and 3-button mice to sell to OEMs, and was targeting Thailand and Malaysia as sites for new production facilities. In 1990, Logitech had 35 per cent of the OEM market compared to Alps' 43 per cent. Mitsumi, the other major player, had a share of approximately 10 per cent. An all-round electronic parts maker, Mitsumi was a leading manufacturer of OEM keyboards sold to makers of portable computers. It too was opening new plants in the Philippines, Thailand and in Mallow, Ireland. Two or three other companies accounted for the remainder of this segment, including KYE/MSC.

The leader in the retail segment was Microsoft, with a 39 per cent share; Logitech was next with a 27 per cent share, followed by KYE with 23 per cent (see *Exhibit 6.11*). In Europe, control of the retail segment varied from one country to another. Logitech was clearly the dominant player in Switzerland; in France, Microsoft was in the lead; in Germany, while Microsoft held the 'corporate' market, several Taiwanese companies had established a strong position in the 'home' market; in the UK, Amstrad sold its low-end microcomputers with its own mouse sourced on an OEM basis. Overall, however, KYE had the largest market share in terms of units (28 per cent) followed by Microsoft (23 per cent), Logitech (20 per cent) and IBM (9 per cent). The remainder was accounted for by some 20 other companies.

Except for KYE/MSC Logitech was the only company competing in both the OEM and retail segments. It made over 20 different mice models in a variety of configurations.

In addition to offering technically superior and customised products, Logitech also emphasised the service dimension in its business. Service was defined differently for the OEM and retail segments. For the OEM market, service meant designing to customer specifications, having one person from Logitech deal with a particular OEM account on a dedicated basis, and meeting delivery targets in a flexible manner.

In the retail market, service included a 30-day money back guarantee and access to a technical support group. Logitech tried to answer all user questions, even if they were not related to the mouse. Although this service orientation cost the company 1–2 per cent of turnover, management believed that, in reality, service was free because of the word-of-mouth benefits that would follow. One example was a thank you letter received by the company. At the end, the letter said, 'I only paid $99 for your mouse, but with the telephone calls and the time you people spent solving my problem, you must have really lost money'. This was true but, as Zappacosta said, 'The customer had bought the mouse for his granddaughter and so it was important that he be completely satisfied'.

In contrast, Microsoft was successful with just one shape and colour at the upper end. It also continued to source its products outside, mainly from Alps. The several Taiwanese and Far-East Asian companies did their own manufacturing but competed with standard products too at the low end. Although active in Europe they did not manufacture there. Most had one product, one manual with different languages and one box.

In response, Borel stated, 'we too could manufacture everything in Taiwan and sell in Europe. But then, Logitech would have the complexity of a bigger Taiwan, a longer lead time and a greater overhead. It is easier to manage two companies with 500 people each than one company with 1000'.

Challenges for the 1990s

The overall market for pointing devices, especially mice, was continuing to grow rapidly. Even so, just as with many other new 'high-tech' industries, fast growth and a rapid rate of new product introduction could not prevent the mouse from becoming a 'commodity'. (*Exhibit 6.12* summarises the distribution of value-added over the business system for mice and *Exhibit 6.13* Logitech's financial performance.)

Recognising the dangers of being a 'single product' company, Logitech had already begun to broaden its offerings. In addition to maintaining its software business and introducing new products based on *Modula-2* and desktop publishing applications it successfully introduced a hand-held optical scanner in 1988. The latter was first bought from Omron, a Japanese company, on an OEM basis. In order to differentiate and add value to this product, Logitech developed its own interface protocols. Later, as the product gained acceptance, it worked on improving and manufacturing it in-house. By 1990, the company was gaining 75 per cent of its total revenue from mice, 15 per cent from the scanner and 10 per cent from various software products.

The natural question was whether the approach taken until 1990 was sufficient to sustain profitable growth for the company in future. Apart from deciding on the nature of the business, the company needed to reassess its international infrastructure. On the latter, Borel remarked, 'Being international can sometimes be a liability. The goal is to turn it into an asset. But, the ones who will never make it an asset had better stop right away!'

Exhibit 6.1 Logitech International SA: sales and net profits 1986–1991

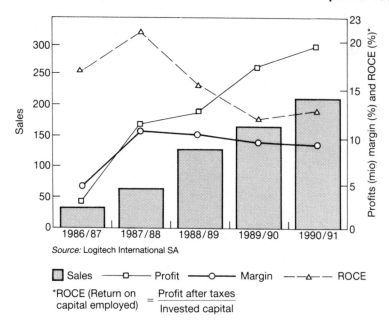

Source: Logitech International SA

*ROCE (Return on capital employed) = $\dfrac{\text{Profit after taxes}}{\text{Invested capital}}$

Exhibit 6.2 Logitech International SA: growth in sales and percentage accounted for by OEMs 1986–1991

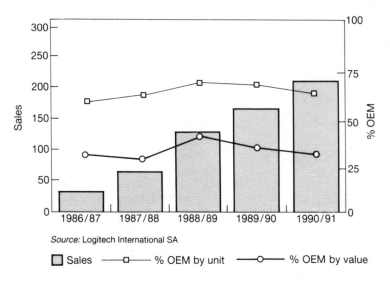

Source: Logitech International SA

Exhibit 6.3 The Logitech infrastructure: end 1987 & 1990

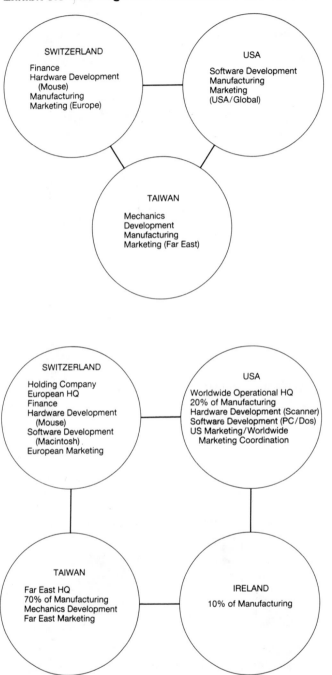

Exhibit 6.4 Logitech International SA personnel

A: Growth in headcount (permanent and temporary) by location (31 March of each year)

	1982	1984	1986	1988	1990	1991
Switzerland*	2	10	40	82	110 **	123
USA*	5	20	87	228	378	456
Ireland					75	153
Taiwan*				141	400	712
Sales Offices	3	3		12	17	26
Total	10	33	127	463	980	1470

* Includes country sales offices.
** Closed production in Switzerland, moved to Ireland.
Source: Logitech International SA.

B: Headcount (permanent only) by functional area (31 March 1991)

Functional Area	Far East	N America	Europe	Total
Administration	32	61	47	140
Sales	10	60	50	120
Marketing	4	47	29	80
R&D/Engineering	42	83	45	170
Manufacturing				
– Direct	487	126	80	693
– Indirect	58	30	23	111
– Staff	82	49	25	156
Total	715	456	299	1470

Source: Logitech International SA

C: Distribution of R&D and engineering personnel by location and discipline (31 March 1991)

Discipline	Europe	N America	Far East
1. Software	11	21	9
2. Electronics Engineering	13	17	11
3. Optics	1	1	0
4. Mechanical Engineering	2	14	7
5. Other (manufacturing, engineering, quality assurance, product management)	8	30	15
Totals	45	83	42 = 170

Source: Logitech International SA

Exhibit 6.5 Steps in the manufacturing process for mouse

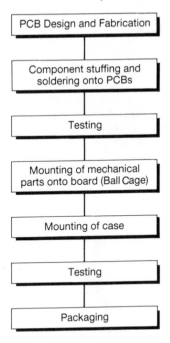

Exhibit 6.6 Material procurement for mouse products

Major Commodities[1]	Procured from			
	Taiwan	Japan	USA/SA	Europe
Plastic raw material	X	X	X	X
Plastic injection	X		X	X
Diecasting and machining	X		X	X
Stamping	X			
Cable/connectors	X			
PCB (under 6 layers)	X			
Passive components	X			
Semi-conductors	X	X	X	X
Distribution by area (%)[2]	69	13	11	7

[1] Representing 75 per cent of total material inputs for mice.
[2] By value. The 69 per cent procured in Taiwan represents 60 per cent from Taiwan itself and 9 per cent from the rest of the Far East excluding Japan.

Exhibit 6.7 History of product introductions

Products	*1982/83*	*1984*	*1985*	*1986*	*1987*	*1988*	*1989*	*1990*	*1991*
1. Mouse									
(a) Upper-end							*Series 9* *TrackMan* Trackball	*MouseMan*	*MouseMan* *Cordless* *TrackMan* Portable
(b) Middle	*Series 5*		*Series 7*		High resolution Mouse			*Logimouse* *Pilot*	
(c) Low-end						*Dexxa-I*		*Dexxa-II*	*Dexxa-III*
2. Software									
(a) Development tools	*Modula-2* Compiler	*Modula-2* Cross development system		: *Modula-2* Windowing : *Modula-2* Translator : *Logi Cadd*		*Modula-2* os/2			
(b) Applications				: *Logi Paint*	*Paintshow*		*Finesse*	*Catchword*	
3. Other Products for 'Computer Cockpit'						*ScanMan* Optical scanner		*ScanMan* 256	*ScanMan* 32

Exhibit 6.8 Competitive positioning in the retail mouse market

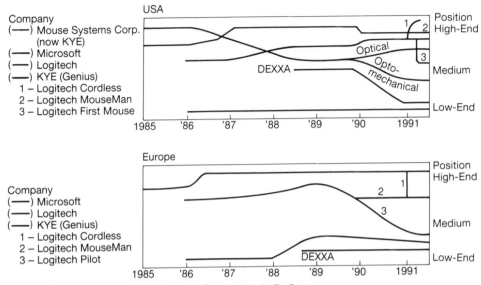

Note: There are over twenty other mouse manufacturers based in the Far East, all of whom compete in the low end of the market, especially by providing standard products to OEMs.

Exhibit 6.9 Market segments

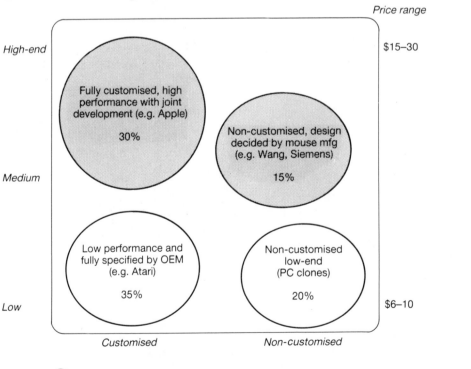

Percentages give the approximate relative size of each segment by unit

Exhibit 6.10 Profile of the major sub-segments in the European retail market

Profile	Home	Education	Corporate	Business
1. Personal Computers				
% of total market	23	10	33	33
By Type				
IBM PC Compatible	48	80	94	89
Apple		11	6	6
Non-Compatible	52	9		5
Distribution	• Consumer electronics • Computer stores • Dept stores • Specialised 'school' dealers	• Direct from manufacturer • Specialised dealers	• Specialised dealers • VARs	• Computer stores • VARs • Catalogue
2. Mice Who	• Adults (20–55) for education/business and entertainment • Children	• Teachers (25–55) • Educational purchasing units	Central purchasing unit (MIS)	Individual users (25–55)
Values	• prices (1) • ease use/install (2) • aesthetics (3) national versions (4) • SW bundle (5) • accessories (6) • quality (7)	• price (1) • quality (2) • national versions (3) • compatibility (4) • support (5)	• compatibility (1) • ease use/install (2) • quality (3) • HW performance (4) • ergonomics (5) • price (6)	• compatibility (1) • ease use/install (2) • quality (3) • price (4) • support (5) • aesthetics (6)
Channel	Retail: CE, Dept, computer stores	Specialised dealers	Specialised dealers	Store front, catalogues, VAR's, computer stores
Platform	52% non-compatibles	PC & Apple	IBM compatibles	IBM compatibles

Exhibit 6.11 Worldwide market shares in the mouse business (by units)

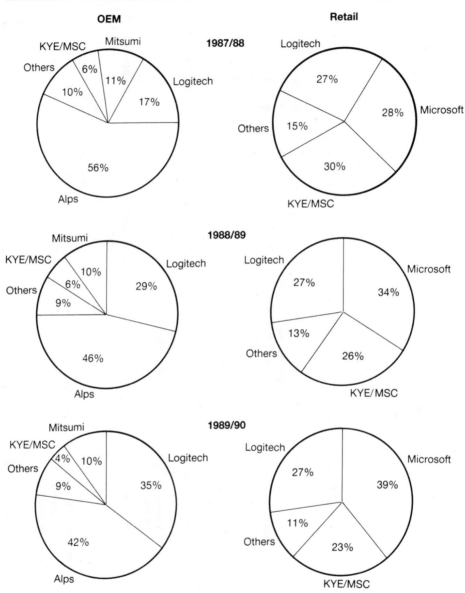

Source: Logitech International SA

Exhibit 6.12 Value-added distribution over the mouse business system (percentage of suggested retail price)

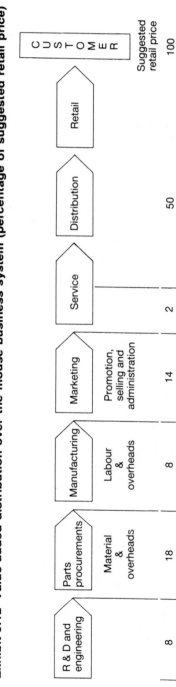

R & D and engineering	Parts procurements	Manufacturing	Marketing	Service	Distribution	Retail	CUSTOMER
	Material & overheads	Labour & overheads	Promotion, selling and administration				
8	18	8	14	2	50	100	Suggested retail price

Exhibit 6.13 Logitech International SA: Selected consolidated financial data

Logitech International SA selected consolidated financial data

(In '000 – except')	Swiss Francs	Swiss Francs	Swiss Francs	US Dollars
Full Year ending	31/3/89	31/3/90	31/3/91	31/3/91
Consolidated revenues	124 111	179 786	205 871	154 907
Net income after tax	11 207	14 161	16 872	12 695
% of revenues	9.03	7.88	8.20	8.20
Cash flow	14 290	17 450	23 287	17 095
% of revenues	11.51	9.71	11.31	11.04
Earnings per bearer share*	76	96	114	86.07
Dividend per bearer share*	12	16	20	13.71
Engineering, research & development expenses	8397	13 710	17 999	13 543
% of revenues	6.77	7.63	8.74	8.74
Number of personnel*	731	980	1470	1470
Current assets	75 527	107 859	128 782	88 343
Property, plant & equipment gross	22 422	30 571	51 287	35 182
Less accumulated depreciation	(5223)	(8511)	(14 926)	(10 239)
Property, plant & equipment net	17 199	22 060	36 361	24 943
Other non-current assets	1184	3926	5599	3841
Goodwill	13 094	11 193	9294	6376
Total assets	107 004	145 038	180 036	123 503
Current liabilities	36 776	32 212	54 217	37 192
Long-term debt & deferred taxes	10 541	43 489	46 109	31 631
Stockholders' equity	59 687	69 337	79 710	54 680
Total liabilities & stockholders' equity	107 004	145 038	180 036	123 503

Case study 7

LOGITECH INTERNATIONAL SA (B)[1]

'Structure is there to support the growth of the company; moreover, a company is not really something that you can put on a piece of paper; it is something which breathes, which lives', stated Daniel Borel, Chairman of Logitech International SA.

The people who founded Logitech in 1981 really had two aims: to participate in the fast-growing personal computer industry by providing software and hardware products; and to create an organisation that would span the world imbued with their own sense of excitement, aggressive opportunity-seeking, and flexibility. The word 'flexible', in fact, pervaded every aspect of the company. Words such as 'flat structure', 'open-door policy', 'team work', 'employee participation', 'networks of small groups' became the building blocks of the organisation.

However, when the business and international strategy of the company was being reviewed in preparation for the 1990s, the question had come up: Was Logitech's organisational structure still appropriate? This question was debated with characteristic informality, with the result that there was no consensus on whether or not any change was even needed.

Among the founders, Giacomo Marini was the only person who had previously worked for large international companies (IBM and Olivetti). Being the Chief Operating Officer, he felt the need for a more formal structure and had been instrumental in designing whatever structure the company did have in 1989/90. Neither Borel nor Zappacosta felt any urgency in this regard. 'Zappacosta is our visionary, our long-term thinker who wants to make sure the business is on the right track', Borel explained. In turn, one of his colleagues described Borel with a different compliment: 'Borel is for action yesterday, he is a doer'.

How the organisation evolved

The fact that Logitech virtually started as a multinational company influenced the way its organisation evolved.

In 1982 the company had two sites: Switzerland and the US. For personal reasons, Daniel Borel (Chairman) lived in Switzerland, while Zappacosta (Chief Executive) and Marini (Head of Operations) were located in the US. Mutual empathy, frequent travel and an electronic mail system linked the two sites.

When the mouse business started in 1983, the Swiss group became the principal development unit. Since the main, if not only, market for the device was California, all the marketing effort was

[1] This case was prepared by Professor Vijay K. Jolly and Research Associate Kimberly A. Bechler, as a basis for class discussion rather than to illustrate either effective or ineffective handling of a business situation.

The authors wish to acknowledge the generous cooperation and assistance given to them by a number of managers at Logitech International SA in the preparation of this case, especially the Chairman, Mr Daniel Borel.

concentrated there. Borel, who was engaged in all aspects of the business, often travelled to the US for extended periods of time between 1983 and 1987 and had a formal role in the USA as head of marketing and sales. *Exhibit 7.1* shows the organisation of the US company in September 1983.

Meanwhile, Jean-Luc Mazzone, one of the earliest collaborators, started assembling a European team in Switzerland. With Borel absent in the USA and later in Taiwan, Mazzone was actually the Chief Operating Officer for Europe. He looked after manufacturing and sales, as well as finance. The latter function, finance, was clearly important for the start-up company and, since most of the funds came from Switzerland, Mazzone's role was critical.

When Logitech set up a US factory to supply H-P in 1984, the US became the operational HQ, a logical development since the three founders were present there.

Despite its enhanced role, very little direction was actually given by the US unit. The European facility was really on its own, developing its own markets. It was, however, contributing to the global business by supplying R&D, manufacturing and sales support. Moreover, the linkages between the US and Switzerland were reciprocal. The Olivetti contract, for example, which was handled in Switzerland, was won partly because Olivetti had an alliance with AT&T, which had already prequalified Logitech in the US.

Since the two Logitech companies were separate legal entities and evaluated individually, the structure could best be described as 'confederal'. As Hank Morgan, who joined Logitech in 1989 from Wyse technology, put it, 'There was nobody clearly in charge. You had a number of different people who shared the power. And the roles evolved. The people running the US organisation did not feel they should tell Switzerland what to do, even though they were collectively the principal shareholders. The hierarchy was very, very fuzzy'.

This network of part-specialised, but autonomous, units simply got extended when the Taiwanese operation began. Initially, it was Borel who took responsibility for Taiwan and spent long periods of time there. He worked closely with a local Chinese, Y S Fu, whom he had hired as General Manager.

Between 1984 and 1988, Logitech's managers were far too busy working on many different projects; there was no time to think about a formal structure. Business was booming and, after the Taiwan facility was underway, there was the Irish factory to set up. Being practical, the three founders just assigned themselves different roles and got the job done. With his interest in sales and manufacturing, Borel assumed the role of Vice-President of Manufacturing for the entire Group in 1986. (See *Exhibit 7.2* for the organisation chart of the US company in 1986.) Marini, who became interested in R&D and materials, took charge of operations while Zappacosta concentrated on marketing. Together, they started to coordinate all the functions of the Group and shared responsibility for business development. The culture, organisational processes and policies they had established made a more formal structure at all levels seem unnecessary during that time period.

Logitech's organisational structure in 1990

In order to cope with the larger and more complex infrastructure that evolved, Logitech made some organisational changes in April 1990. The main purpose was to bring together the geographic units and the functions of the company on a more global basis than previously. On 26 April, 1990, an internal memorandum from *Daniel Borel* announcing these changes stated:

> The success, the growth and the maturity of the Logitech Group worldwide requires a new, more cohesive international management structure.
>
> We believe that the new organization structure will allow [us] to best compete in the worldwide market [by] making the most of being a truly internationally minded company. This structure will allow us to think globally and act locally. It will give us the flexibility to adapt to change and market evolution. It will support entrepreneurial spirit, creativity and technological innovation, which are key for our long-term success.

One feature of the new organisation was the creation of an 'Office of the President'. Although the three founders had performed this role informally, the new structure formalised its existence and clarified reporting relationships at the Group level. A small corporate staff team was also created to assist this 'Office' in planning, control and communication activities.

With Daniel Borel as Chairman, taking care of special projects and acting as Group coordinator, the Office of the President consisted of Zappacosta, President and Chief Executive Officer (CEO) of the Group, and Marini, Executive Vice-President and Chief Operating Officer. All geographical areas and worldwide functions would report to this 'Office', with direct reporting to Marini. Moreover, this 'Office', in addition to Group level management responsibility, had direct management responsibility for the US site and its corresponding geographic area. *Exhibit 7.3* provides an organisation chart of the new structure.

In terms of their respective roles, Zappacosta would 'concentrate on the activities of setting directions, making the synthesis of strategies, identifying and setting corporate goals'. Marini would 'concentrate on translating corporate directions and goals into operating plans, initiating and controlling their execution, and exercising the day-to-day management process with the operating managers'. To symbolise their joint role, Zappacosta and Marini moved their offices (in the US) next to each other, whereas previously they had been at opposite ends of the building.

To assist and complement the Chairman and the Office of the President in top-level management activities of the Group, the Executive Management Committee (formed in 1989) was expanded in April 1990 to include – apart from the three founders – Morgan (Chief Operating Officer, Europe), Fu (Senior Vice-President & General Manager, Far East), and Mazzone (Vice-President Strategic Marketing for the Group, but based in Europe).

The main organisational units, however, continued to be the areas. Logitech retained its traditional policy of giving local management at each site full profit and loss responsibility.

For cohesiveness at a global level, some executives were, however, given worldwide mandates for certain functions. The worldwide functional manager was not really expected to direct oper-

ations; rather, he would coordinate and provide team leadership for the particular function, working closely with site managers responsible for their function at the local level. The latter had a dotted line reporting to the worldwide functional manager and direct reporting to the site chief executive or general manager. In most cases, the worldwide functional manager resided in the US, but this was not a requirement.

Functional managers with worldwide responsibility and their locations were: Morgan (Finance and Administration, Switzerland); D'Ettore (Human Resources, US); Righi (Sales, US); Van Natta (Corporate Communications, US); Mills (Quality, US); Marini (Engineering, US); and Zappacosta (Marketing, US). Both Marini and Zappacosta were 'acting' heads of their functions, until someone else was appointed.[2] *Exhibit 7.4* shows the allocation of worldwide functional responsibility and *Exhibit 7.5* the structure of the US company.)

Logitech's values and culture

'We work in one place, the globe'. This simple phrase stated the business spirit and the cosmopolitan attitude at Logitech; the basis of its founders' beliefs from the beginning. The composition of the Executive Management Committee – Borel (Swiss), Fu (Chinese), Marini (Italian), Mazzone (Swiss), Morgan (American), and Zappacosta (Italian) – not only tangibly expressed the company's philosophy, but guaranteed that different geographic and cultural perspectives would inevitably be advocated within Logitech.

Coupled with its cosmopolitan make-up, Logitech's management reflected youthfulness, daring and a spirit of adventure, a combination frequently found in high-tech start-ups with excellent results. At Logitech in 1991, the emphasis was on small groups that met 'horizontally' for particular issues and projects; direct contact between senior management and employees was promoted; employees were urged to be more involved in running Logitech; and, the one thing to be abhorred was formal policies. As the head of

[2] Recently, a Vice-President for Engineering, Rick Money, was appointed, and Fabio Righi took on the marketing role as Vice-President, Sales and Marketing.

administration, Bavaud stated, 'We don't want a police state at Logitech'.

Logitech's basic values consisted of a belief in people, trust, caring for the feelings of others and the ability of everyone to do what is right. The metaphor often used to describe the organisation was 'a family that has bridged national differences'.

Although at the time this case was written, no formal mission statement existed, it was felt that if one were ever created, it should reflect the fun, the creativity and the responsibility experienced by each member of Logitech. Since Logitech's key descriptors and the usual format of a mission statement did not seem compatible, the question was raised: Should Logitech's statement be a written document? Or perhaps a cartoon or even a videotape!

The evolution of the Logitech logo also illustrated the company's self-image. Until 1988, Logitech's logo was a square surrounding a circle divided into four equal parts; the 'framing' square represented Logitech's engineering background, the circle indicated its flexibility, and the darkened square represented the letter 'L' in Logitech.

After the company went into the consumer market, the logo was redesigned (see *Exhibit 7.6*) to reflect the company's values and its vision of humanising the computer: the irregular green shape represented the company structure, present yet enabling Logitech to 'break away', to look towards the future and be innovative; the eye in the centre represented the human aspect of the company, both in terms of its attitude towards employees as well as humanising computer use; the red arrow pointing top right symbolises Logitech's moving forward, leading the change, while the three black lines represent the company's flexibility, coordination and equilibrium.

Organisational processes

Despite giving freedom to individuals and groups to pursue their tasks in a creative and responsible manner, no effort was spared to establish links throughout the company.

Communication was one of the important tools used. The electronic mail system, installed in 1982 the same day that Logitech had two locations, was continuously expanded. As Morgan put it, 'We send and receive messages or copies of messages from all over the world every day. So we tend to know very quickly what is going on'. *Logi News*, an internal newsletter, and formal meetings were other ways of keeping people involved.

Setting overall direction took place at two levels: the Executive Committee and the functions. The Executive Committee met every two months, with the discussions going on for a long time, sometimes over two days. A lot of things would be talked about. Decisions were not always made, but direction nevertheless evolved at these meetings. The decisions that were taken then were communicated and discussed throughout the organisation via monthly company meetings at each site.

At the operational level, functional heads from each site met approximately once a year in order to coordinate policies and practices worldwide. Depending on the function, there would be frequent telephone and electronic mail exchanges as well.

In addition to these functional meetings and exchanges, a number of cross-functional, inter-site teams were created. The main ones were *project teams* built around the introduction of new products, taking projects from initial development to mass production. *Exhibit 7.7* reproduces the membership of a recently constituted project led by the US organisation.) In 1991, there were some 20 *project teams* with about half led by the US organisation and the remainder by other sites. Marini had coordinated the work done by these teams in the past, but they became the responsibility of the head of engineering, Rick Money, with the organisational restructuring.

The other main area where multi-functional, multi-site teams were used was in *product management*. These teams worked to launch new products on the market which also included making competitor assessments, preparing translations and manuals, and designing and placing advertisements. In 1991 *product management* teams were being coordinated by Fabio Righi, Vice-President, Sales and Marketing.

Policies

In June 1988, Logitech went public in Switzerland. Previously, there had been occasional attempts to consolidate the operations worldwide, but they had resembled 'exercises' to ascertain what the total entity might look like. A worldwide budget was, in fact, put together for the first time in 1988, enabling Logitech finally to compare 'actual' with 'budgeted'.

It was still not entirely clear where Logitech's HQ was located, although the US unit gradually started to assume that role mainly because, according to Marini, the Silicon Valley played an important role as a lead market, as well as providing Logitech with credibility. In any case, management believed that 'headquarters' should provide a 'service' rather than a 'control' function and should not have the power that most companies normally would give to headquarters.

Each site also had its own policies with no formal 'central' coordination. One policy area shared by all the company's locations was human resource management. Although acknowledging local practices and legal requirements, Logitech tended to hire people who would fit into its culture. Potential employees were expected to be flexible, internationally minded and good team workers. Due to this careful selection process, Logitech had a very low turnover rate, a particularly remarkable achievement given its location in the Silicon Valley.

The company also encouraged transfers between sites. It hoped, thereby, to increase intercultural awareness within the company, decrease friction between sites and increase employee identification with Logitech International, rather than with a particular unit.

The strategy for the 1990s

The strategy for the 1990s was framed to build on Logitech's evolving competence as a first-rate manufacturer of small electronic devices sold to a wide cross-section of computer users. Fulfilling this strategy meant constantly introducing new products, all nevertheless aimed at facilitating access to personal computers. 'Our goal', explained Zappacosta, 'is to have one or more Logitech products on the desk of every personal computer user'. As for the mouse itself, he wanted to transform what had become a commodity product into a fashion statement. 'We want people

to look at the mouse sitting next to their computer and say, "I like it, it's cool!"'

Logitech's expanded business scope was evolving towards the *'senses of the computer'*. Whereas the mouse represented the hand and the scanner the eyes (by perceiving 256 shades of grey and eventually colour) it was expected that 3-D and sound too would provide new avenues for product extension. The company's long-term strategy and outlook was to heighten brand awareness in the mass market, be the volume and share leader in the retail market, fuel growth through continuous product-line extensions and innovations, and acquire or partner for competitive advantage.

As for geographical ambitions, Logitech wanted to strengthen its presence and reach into all world markets and be close to its customers. As Borel put it, 'Unless you go out on the street, see what your competition is doing, see what is changing every day, you are lost. And it can happen very quickly'. Also, compared to the present geographic distribution of sales – North America 65 per cent, Europe 28 per cent and Far East 7 per cent – Logitech expected the following distribution over the next few years: North America 40 per cent, Europe 45 per cent (including Eastern Europe) and Far East 14 per cent.

The debate on organisation structure

The starting point for the debate on organisation was at the time of the April 1990 structure. While some managers were satisfied, others wanted to see greater clarity in the reporting relationships. Who, for example, should functional heads really report to, especially when they carried global responsibilities for their function? They would also like to see more effective team *processes* without, however, creating a bureaucratic organisation. The engineering function had already set up a 7-man 'Engineering Services Group' to oversee quality assurance, alpha and beta testing, cost and reliability, and documentation control. Working in matrix, their role was to make sure the twenty or so project teams maintained adequate standards, especially since that was what OEMs wanted. Similarly, Marini had previously coordinated procurement and operations through intersite teams, but then in 1991 the company decided to create two new posts: Director for Strategic Procurement and Operations Planning Manager. *Exhibit 7.8* summarises their job descriptions.

Regarding the *project* and *product management* teams, there were two issues: how to make them smaller and less cumbersome; and how to maintain accountability and responsibility at the functional manager level for the tasks being accomplished.

Some people at Logitech felt undisguised nostalgia for the informal networking character of the company's earlier organisation. With all the information technology at Logitech's command, they asked: 'Why not simply continue as a modern distributed network structure, especially since so many management experts write about its virtues?' Even Borel admitted, 'Why can't we operate as fast as we did when we were twenty employees?'

A more general issue was how to preserve Logitech's ability to act as a global company. Although the three founders were the main locus for a global view, they also realised that the company had become too large and complex for them to play this role exclusively. If changing Logitech's organisation structure could be a way to meet this challenge, what sort of configuration would be most appropriate?

If Logitech stayed with its present *area* organisation – with separate structures for Europe, the Far East and the USA – it would still be able to focus on different segments (e.g. Taiwan could handle all OEM business), but would lose important synergies in product development and production planning. How, moreover, would business functions be governed and on what basis would competitors be identified?

Another option was to organise by *product technology*: mice and trackman (both sharing pointing device technology), scanning devices, application software, etc. Alternatively, it could organise along *product/market segments*, such as pointing devices and application software for scanning devices. The latter approach would, at least, maintain the link between hardware and software which groupings along '*products*' might lose.

Making a choice was not expected to be easy. As Y S Fu, the General Manager of Logitech Taiwan, explained, 'We try to be locally present, this is both our strategy and our strength; we deal with local customers as local people; when IBM's Taiwanese International Procurement Office (IPO) talk to us, they feel they are talking to an independent company; we can make all the decisions, provide all the support; we don't have limitations from Switzerland or the USA, which is different from other foreign companies'. A counter argument was found, however, in Borel's example of the way the company worked: 'When Logitech Europe launched its Pilot Mouse (for first-time users) in order to combat the Taiwanese, the US did not think an introduction was warranted in that region since there was already a strong presence at the low end. Eventually, the product was introduced at a later date'.

Attention also needed to be focused on some *functions*. One such area was procurement. Compared to the current practice of letting each site procure on its own behalf, the idea was to centralise purchasing in order to gain better overall terms for Logitech. By creating several International Procurement Offices (IPOs) – like at IBM, where staff would be paid a commission on what they could source locally, the hope was to diminish the present dependence on the Far East for components. This would also introduce some competition in the procurement function itself. What would be the effect of these IPOs be on Logitech's structure? 'You have an IPO in Taiwan, does he report to the local manufacturing site or does he report to a worldwide sourcing organisation?' Borel asked.

Finally, another question relating to organisational dimension was whether, and to what extent, the company should begin to set up divisions. Its initial software engineering business had been spun off into a new company, MULTISCOPE Inc., but so far, Logitech had gone no further toward creating *divisions*.

Exhibit 7.1 Logitech Inc. (US): organisation structure (September 1983)

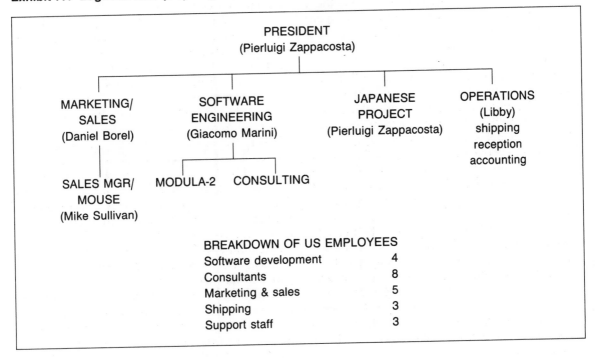

PRESIDENT
(Pierluigi Zappacosta)

MARKETING/
SALES
(Daniel Borel)

SOFTWARE
ENGINEERING
(Giacomo Marini)

JAPANESE
PROJECT
(Pierluigi Zappacosta)

OPERATIONS
(Libby)
shipping
reception
accounting

SALES MGR/
MOUSE
(Mike Sullivan)

MODULA-2   CONSULTING

BREAKDOWN OF US EMPLOYEES
Software development   4
Consultants   8
Marketing & sales   5
Shipping   3
Support staff   3

Exhibit 7.2 Logitech Inc. (US): organisation structure (Summer 1986)

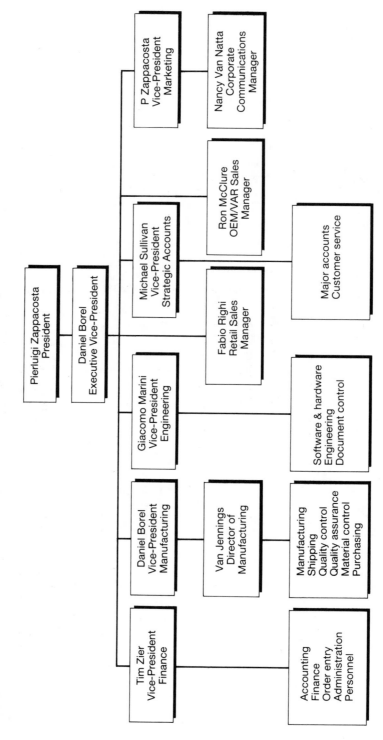

Exhibit 7.3 Logitech International: organisation structure (April 1990)

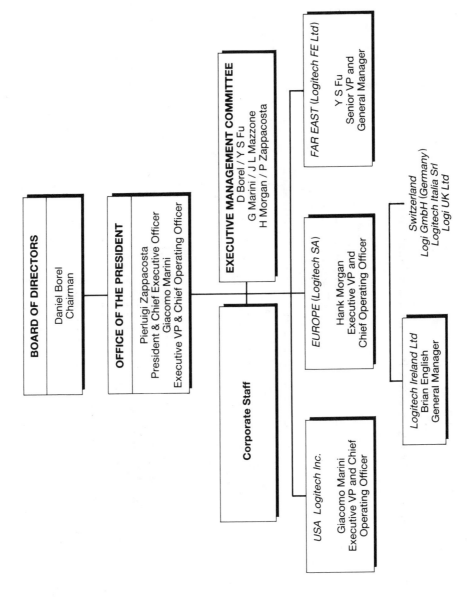

Exhibit 7.4 Logitech International: group level functions (April 1990)

Office of the President
Pierluigi Zappacosta
President & Chief Executive Officer
Giacomo Marini
Executive VP & Chief Operating Officer

Corporate Communications
Nancy Van Natta

Corporate Communications USA
Corporate Communications Europe
Raffaella Ettore

Human Resources
Fiorella D'Ettore

Quality
Kevin Mills

Quality USA
Quality TAIWAN
C.S. Chen
Quality IRELAND
Denis McCarty

Marketing
Pierluigi Zappacosta

Finance & Administration
Hank Morgan

Finance & Administration Europe
Finance Holding
Otto Kunkel
Finance & Administration USA
Tim Zier
Finance & Administration Taiwan
Eric Su

R & D/Engineering
Giacomo Marini

R & D/Engineer USA
R & D/Engineer Taiwan
Hank Wang
R & D/Engineer Switzerland
Alain Wegmann
R & D/Engineer Ireland
Rory Dooley

Sales
Fabio Righi

Sales USA
Marketing & Retail Sales Europe
Marc Chatel
OEM Sales Europe
Heinz Ettinger
Sales & Marketing Taiwan
M F Yen

Exhibit 7.5 Logitech Inc. (US): corporate headquarters' organisation structure (April 1990)

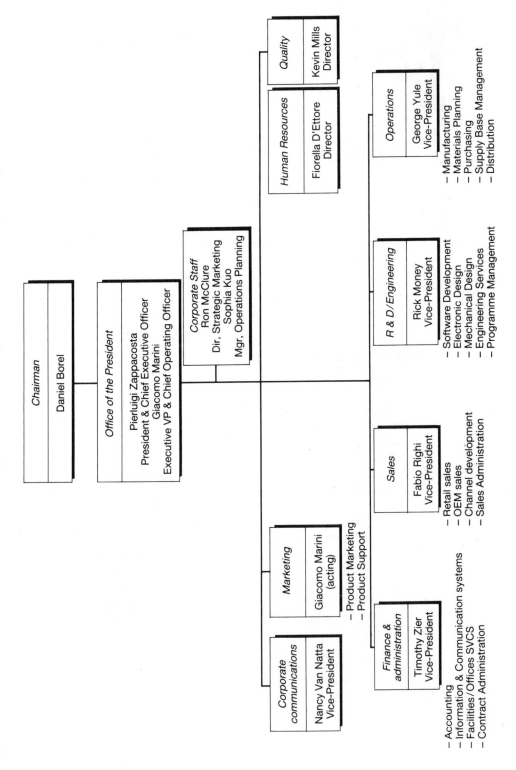

Exhibit 7.6 Logitech logo

Exhibit 7.7 Logitech International SA: composition of a recent project team for developing and manufacturing a new product

(Number of individuals from each function in parentheses if more than one)

1. **USA**
   Product Marketing (3)
   Mechanical Engineering (2)
   Cost & Reliability Engineering (3)

   Electrical Engineering
   Software Engineering
   Product Quality Assurance
   Technical Publications (3)

   Technical Support
   Supply Base Management
   Quality Assurance
   Materials Planning
   Production Engineer
   Test Engineer

2. **Logitech Switzerland**
   Product Marketing
   Product Management
   Project Planning

3. **Logitech Taiwan**
   Product Engineering
   Project Planning

4. **Logitech Ireland**
   Product Engineering
   Project Planning

Exhibit 7.8 Logitech Inc. appointments. Job descriptions for new appointments in operations

Director, Strategic Procurement

As Strategic Procurement Director, you will work closely with the Chief Operating Officer in the formulation and implementation of procurement strategies for LOGITECH manufacturing worldwide. Your major responsibilities will include; establishing, communicating and maintaining the international procurement policies, working with a global team to implement strategies, providing directives and recommendations to the worldwide procurement groups, identifying areas where multiple sources will be needed, defining strategic commodities and project needs, maintaining a database of strategic commodities, vendors and relevant data, and preparing reports and analyses.

Operations Planning Manager

Reporting directly to the C.O.O., you will be involved in the formulation and implementation of worldwide operations planning and strategy for new products, manufacturing and distribution. Your job responsibilities will include: developing global manufacturing strategies, allocating manufacturing tasks to worldwide facilities, establishing performance measurements and monitoring the results, analysing worldwide shipments and forecasts, reviewing operation reports, and preparing site reviews.

Case study 8

SOCIETE GENERALE DE BELGIQUE[1]

In June 1988, the dust was finally settling after the largest cross-border takeover in European history. The Belgian industrial and financial giant, Société Générale de Belgique (SGB), had been acquired by the French holding company, Compagnie Financière de Suez. In its initial step at securing control over its latest acquisition, Suez had appointed Mr Hervé de Carmoy, previously the director of international operations at the British Midland Bank PLC and a Frenchman, as SGB's first Chief Executive Officer.

The mandate given de Carmoy was, however, still clear: define and implement a strategy to revitalise SGB and its many holdings and make the SGB empire a competitive and profitable force in Europe. It would not be an easy task. As the new Chief Executive Officer (CEO), Mr de Carmoy assumed many of the managerial responsibilities of the former Governor of SGB, Mr René Lamy, who remained as Chairman of the SGB Board. By appointing a non-Suez executive to run SGB and initially keeping Mr Lamy, a Belgian, as Chairman, Suez had sought to allay the suspicion harboured by many Belgians that Suez was intent on dominating and perhaps absorbing SGB. SGB was closely tied to Belgium, and the government, unions and public would be watching the changes made under de Carmoy with interest. Publicly,

the Suez group professed interest in keeping SGB independent.

The company that de Carmoy found himself running in 1988 was a very large amalgamation of holdings in generally unrelated financial and industrial companies, concentrated in Belgium. Additionally, tradition was strong at SGB and the old order was deeply intrenched: many believed the nickname *la vieille dame* (the old lady) had been well earned. Founded in the early 1800s, the company had grown to become one of the pillars of the Belgian economy although it suffered from years of ineffective management and mediocre performance.

Historically, La Générale, as the company was more commonly known, had taken a passive approach to its subsidiaries, rarely interfering or showing much interest in their activities as long as dividends were paid. Complicating the problem, many of SGB's holdings were only minority stakes: SGB frequently relied on its ability to influence decision-making at the subsidiary level rather than taking formal control through majority ownership. However, changes in the commercial environment of Belgium, stemming from the increasing momentum behind the drive for a unified market in the European Community in 1992, were forcing all domestic businesses to adopt new

---

[1] This case was prepared by Research Associate David H. Hover, under the supervision of Professor John J. Pringle, as a basis for class discussion rather than to illustrate either effective or ineffective handling of a business situation.

ways of operating, and SGB was no exception. (The financial statements can be found in the Appendix at the end of the case. Unconsolidated financial statements exclude balance sheet items held by subsidiaries.)

Belgium and the European Community

Belgium is a small country of less than 10 million inhabitants sandwiched between France, Luxembourg, West Germany and The Netherlands. The population is divided into two primary cultural and linguistic groups: the French-speaking Walloons in the southern half of the country (Wallonia), and the Flemish-speaking (similar to Dutch) Flemings in the north (Flanders). The Flemish constituted approximately 56 per cent of the country's population. In the 1980s, about 11 per cent of the population lived in Brussels, the capital. Although French-speaking, the residents of Brussels were not considered Walloons.

Prior to World War II, economic growth had been concentrated in the south because of local deposits of coal and minerals (notably iron). After the war, however, the centre of economic activity shifted to Flanders as the coal and steel industries in Wallonia declined, exacerbating previously existing linguistic and cultural animosities between the two regions. Increased autonomy for Flanders and Wallonia had helped relieve some of the pressures, but a strong rivalry for political and economic gain remained.

Perhaps because of its history, cultural background and location, Belgium had been a founding member of the European Community and was an avid supporter of inter-European cooperation. One SGB executive described Belgium's relationship to Europe, 'What is good for Europe is good for Belgium. Belgium will only survive within Europe. Belgians shouldn't be worried about who controls what'.

La Vieille Dame

Société Générale de Belgique/Generale Maatschappij van België (the company's formal name in French and Flemish) was a part of Belgium. The company had been established in 1822 by the royal decree of the Dutch King, William I,[2] as a development bank to promote industrial development in the southern part of the kingdom. The new bank was financed through contributions from the large banking families in Brussels and the King's own coffers. A history published in honour of the company's 150th anniversary identified the company's mission: '[SGB] would have as its object, participation in any undertaking of a useful character . . . able to take part in any limited company . . . and supply development funds for industry by way of loans or [shareholdings]'.

After Belgium became independent in 1830, SGB continued its role as the region's development bank. During the early years of Belgium's independence, a large number of the company's shares which still belonged to the former King, William I, were repurchased by Belgian investors. Ironically, given the events in 1988, the nineteenth century repurchase was described in 1970 by a company historian as, 'a necessary action if foreign takeover was to be avoided'. Deepening the company's ties with Belgium, the Belgian royal family became closely associated with La Générale over the years although the nature of its influence remained obscure.

Through its banking and investment activities, SGB had accumulated substantial interest in companies throughout Belgium and its former colonies, particularly the Belgian Congo (Zaire).[3] At the end of 1986, SGB had direct or indirect

---

[2] The region that eventually became Belgium had been most recently occupied by France. At the end of the Napoleonic wars, the region was united with Holland to form the new Kingdom of the Netherlands ruled by King William I. The southern region of the new kingdom, where SGB operated, later seceded from the rest of The Netherlands to become Belgium.

[3] SGB's operations in the Congo played a minor role in World War II. At the beginning of the War, Union Minière, an SGB subsidiary, suspecting its potential value, shipped 1200 tonnes of high grade uranium ore from the company's Shikolobwe mine to New York to prevent it from falling into German hands. The existence of the ore, however, was not known to the directors of the Manhattan Project and the shipment spent over two years in storage on Staten Island. The oversight was eventually discovered and the ore was integrated into the refining operations while more was imported from the Congo. Superior to domestic ores, the uranium ore from the Congo helped speed the development of the atomic bomb.

holdings in 1261 companies worldwide ranging from a railroad in Angola to a film production company in Los Angeles. In 1988, one Belgian newspaper claimed SGB, through its subsidiaries and holdings, contributed a third of the total Belgian economic output.

SGB's long history as development bank and venture capital fund had created an unusual legacy. Some of the infant industries, including mining, railroads, and steel, in which SGB had acquired and maintained investments during the 1800s had become mature or declining industries in the late 1900s. While these industries had originally been very important to the economic development of Belgium and Europe, in 1988 they were considered by many to have little potential for future growth or profits.

Attempts at diversifying into new fields in the 1970s and 1980s had been generally unsuccessful. For example, one effort, ACEC, an electro-technical equipment and computer manufacturer succeeded in accumulating extensive debts without making any significant in-roads into its targeted markets. Diversification remained an interest, however, and SGB maintained holdings in a number of companies in expectation of future growth opportunities.

An additional problem for SGB was that many of its ownership positions were relatively small. In general, SGB policy had been to hold equity investments at 'a significant level, [but] seldom exceeding 50 per cent'. A 'significant' level for SGB meant 'sufficient to influence the activities of the company'. The diverse and fragmented shareholder base of many of the companies partially owned by SGB frequently allowed SGB to exert influence without having to purchase controlling interest. For example, because SGB was the largest stockholder in Generale Bank, it had been able to influence Bank policy, despite owning only about 20 per cent of the stock. Although it permitted SGB to conserve capital, company management increasingly found minority ownership was insufficient to effectively guide strategy and

implement the changes necessary to meet the challenges of the coming European internal market.

Europe 1992: 'Completing the Internal Market'

A free internal market in which goods, services, people and capital would move unimpeded across national borders had been the objective when the Treaty of Rome was signed in 1957, creating the European Economic Community.[4] Substantial progress in achieving a common market had been made since the EC was established, notably in the creation of a Community-wide customs union in 1968, but a truly integrated market remained elusive and significant barriers to free trade persisted. In the mid-1980s, however, the situation had begun to change.

When the EC established the customs union in 1968, it was anticipated that free flow of trade between the member countries would be substantially realised. Under the customs union, tariff levels were unified for trade within the EC. However, varying standards of taxation, safety, and product quality remained. Countries allowed only products meeting local standards to be imported. These non-tariff barriers continued to restrict the free movement of goods, services, people, and capital. Preoccupied with protecting domestic markets, member countries had resisted efforts to remove the remaining impediments to free trade. Few observers, especially during the late 1970s when poor economic conditions existed throughout Europe, thought the Community would ever achieve its goals.

During the early 1980s, however, EC member countries gradually began to realise that global competition was increasing and that Europe's divided markets were limiting the efficiency of European companies. The renewed interest led directly to the European Commission White Paper, *Completing the Internal Market*, published in 1985. In the Paper, the Commission set out a detailed agenda together with a timetable for

---

[4] Belgium, France, West Germany, Italy, Luxembourg, and The Netherlands were the original members of the European Economic Community (EEC). Denmark, Ireland and the United Kingdom became members in 1973. Greece became a member in 1981 and Portugal and Spain became members in 1986. The European Community (EC) was created by the merger of the European Coal and Steel Community, the EEC, and Euratom in 1967.

establishing a single internal market among the member nations. The main objective of the programme outlined in the White Paper was to remove the remaining non-tariff barriers to trade within the Community and create an 'area without frontiers' by the end of 1992.

Many of the Paper's key points, including its guiding principle to establish open frontiers, were embodied in the Single European Act, adopted in 1985 by the unanimous approval of the European Council of Ministers. In an important step toward speeding up the necessary legislative process to make the internal market a reality, the Act provided for majority (rather than unanimous) voting on many issues. By accepting majority voting, member states surrendered some of their sovereignty. Importantly, majority voting was not extended to fiscal policy regulations.

In total, the Commission had identified 286 regulatory issues that needed action before the internal market could be realised. By June 1988, approximately 60 of the necessary actions had been taken, and, although short of the final goal, the result had meaningfully changed the way businesses operated in the Community. Many knowledgeable observers believed that '1992' was best viewed as a process and not a date; even if the 1992 deadline were missed, the major goals would be achieved.

Corporate strategy at SGB in the 1980s

While Europe moved towards realisation of the dream of the internal market, SGB had also worked on preparing itself for the new economic environment although progress had not been smooth. One of the major stumbling blocks for SGB was the stagnant and myopic senior management and Board of Directors. Before the restructuring which followed the takeover, the SGB Board had been comprised exclusively of SGB executives. Although an exaggeration, one executive was not far from the general perception when he described the qualifications for Board membership as 'French-speaking and blue-blooded'.

Certainly, the vast majority of senior executives were French-speaking.

Board meetings had been sedate affairs; embarrassing questions were not asked by Directors, knowing similar questions about the results, strategy and difficulties at their own subsidiary would not be asked. Those SGB Directors also serving as the CEOs of subsidiaries, one observer later commented, saw their subsidiaries as personal fiefdoms; meddling in their internal affairs by the parent at 'rue Royale' was not appreciated.[5] Reports to the Board were frequently based only on annual reports with almost no supporting documentation. Auditors, working on behalf of SGB, were known to have been denied access to subsidiaries – 'pas de chiffres' (no numbers) was the effective response.

It was within this old traditional environment that René Lamy had become CEO in January 1981, determined to restore the glory and image of SGB. Beginning in 1979, the holding company had identified its role in coordinating and providing new ideas to the subsidiaries as an area needing further improvement. The effort to strengthen the centre of SGB and increase its control over the far-flung parts of the organisation took time to develop. As with many would-be Don Quixotes, Mr Lamy and the managers at 'rue Royale' were up against a deeply entrenched opponent steadfast in its opposition to change.

In the company's 1981 annual report, the formation of a strategic management group was announced. Its ambitious goals included establishing future policy guidelines, monitoring the parts to ensure maximisation of growth and prevent over-diversification, and, finally, to oversee group strategy. The objective was the coherent synthesis of individual corporate programmes while improving the group's ability to find and exploit promising new areas of activity.

The tools to carry out the new policy were concentrated in the financial and organisational areas. Included would be a corporation-wide information system. Later, a human resources committee with representatives from the SGB Board and management, as well as the subsidiaries, was organised. The implementation, however, was

---

[5] SGB's headquarters were located at 30 rue Royale which formed one side of a square, the other sides of which were occupied by the Belgian parliament building and the royal palace.

slow. The 1984 annual report noted that only then were results (in the form of a report) being seen from the strategic planning initiative launched in 1981.

The growing competitiveness in world business was also noticed by SGB management, and statements about the need to ensure the efficiency of the company as a unit were made repeatedly. In the 1985 Annual Report a new organisational concept, which identified 10 Business Sectors, was planned:

> The grouping of available resources around [the 10 major subsidiaries] is designed to meet the basic criterion of efficiency. In effect the object is to put together a number of entities which are sufficiently integrated so as to enable a [united] policy of technical marketing and financial rationalization [creating new entities] better adapted to face up to international competition.

The company stressed, however, that strengthening SGB with respect to the subsidiaries did not imply that the decentralisation concept was being abandoned.

Despite efforts to persuade the subsidiaries, resistance to the enhancement of SGB's power over the units was extensive and the implementation of Lamy's revitalisation plans was stymied. The poor rate of progress eventually attracted the attention of stockholders and, in turn, others interested in the potential returns available from reorganising or breaking up the company. In response to the many claims that SGB was directionless during this period, Jean Duronsoy, a Gechem executive, stated later, 'It isn't true that Lamy didn't have a strategy, and it also isn't true that Carlo De Benedetti did'.

The takeover

The battle of control for SGB, launched by Carlo De Benedetti in January and won by Suez in April 1988, ended with the largest cross-border takeover in Europe. Many of the biggest names in European finance had been involved in the struggle at one point in time or another. However, as Philippe Bodson, a member of the post-takeover SGB Board brought in as an ally to the Suez-led investor group, said afterwards, 'The details of what happened during the takeover will perhaps always remain a mystery'. Regardless, when Carlo De Benedetti, the CEO of Olivetti SpA, made his bid for control of SGB on 18 January 1988, he forever changed the course of the company's history.

The Belgians were seen by many as dedicated Europeanists. Prior to the Single European Act, cross-border takeovers, especially hostile ones, were unusual in Europe, although other foreign takeovers had been allowed in Belgium before. However, the SGB case was unique. It was the largest cross-border takeover ever conducted in Europe and, moreover, SGB was a significant economic and cultural force in Belgium. As one SGB executive noted, however, 'SGB's former managers saw themselves as more important than the Belgian government did. Evidently, they didn't read the cards right.'[6]

SGB's attractiveness as a takeover target had been clear to the Board. In September 1987, an anti-takeover plan was prepared to operate in conjunction with the company's previously established contingent of loyal shareholders. The stockholders considered loyal to SGB management were mostly large French and Belgian corporations, many of which were also partly owned by each other and SGB. The group included: Groupe AG (20 per cent held by SGB); Artois (a Belgian brewery); Assubel; Royale Belge (other large Belgian insurers); Compagnie Générale d'Electricité (a French telecommunications company); Cerus (an investment company); Suez; and others. Together these companies owned approximately 25 per cent of SGB's shares, enough, it was hoped, to thwart an attempted takeover.

The test came in January 1988. After bidding the price of SGB shares up to BEF 3250 (Belgian francs) from BEF 2230 ten days before, Carlo De

---

[6] The immediate political situation in Belgium may also have been a factor in the SGB takeover. In December 1987. following a parliamentary dispute over economic reforms, the governing Belgian coalition failed, the government dissolved, and new elections were held. The election results gave fewer seats to the leading party in the previous coalition, forcing it to form a new coalition. While the new coalition was being organised, the country was run by a largely ineffectual interim government. By the time the new coalition government assumed power in May 1988, the battle for SGB was over.

Benedetti made his intention to control SGB public.[7] Mr De Benedetti was well known as a sophisticated investor interested in establishing a pan-European empire capable of fully exploiting the opportunities promised by the proposed internal market. He had also successfully purchased and revived Olivetti SpA, an Italian office automation company. De Benedetti held a seat on the Board of Directors at Suez and owned a majority of Cerus, among his many other interests.

Most observers were not surprised by De Benedetti's move, only by its size. By targeting one of Belgium's largest corporations, however, many wondered if he had attempted too much. Turning around Olivetti had been a major success, but was on a much smaller scale than the reorganisation of a conglomerate like SGB. His action plan for SGB, if he won, was unknown. Many assumed that De Benedetti would sell some of the poorer performing parts and use the proceeds to strengthen the remaining holdings. De Benedetti, perhaps in an attempt to deflect nationalistic criticism, denied that his intent was to break up SGB. Rather, he claimed to be interested in building a new management team capable of revitalising the company.

The alliance which wrestled control away from De Benedetti's grasp was formed by Mr Maurice Lippens, the Chairman of Groupe AG, and consisted of a mix of Belgian and French shareholders, most of whom were members of SGB's original group of loyal shareholders. Suez, initially hesitant to enter the conflict, had been persuaded to act as the leading 'white knight' and dominated the group. At the end of February, the group claimed more than 50 per cent of the outstanding shares. Virtually all of SGB's shares were held by one of the two sides, and trading activity effectively ceased. Despite repeated attempts, the De Benedetti camp could only muster control of 47–8 per cent of the shares. The Suez faction called for an extraordinary shareholders' meeting in April to decide the outcome.

At the extraordinary shareholders' meeting on 14 April 1988, it was clear that Suez had won, although De Benedetti was still in a position of power due to his large minority interest.

Compagnie Financière de Suez

The company that won control of SGB was itself a major conglomerate closely associated with its national colonial history. The company was founded in 1858 to build and operate the Suez canal. The canal, however, was nationalised in 1956 by President Nasser of Egypt, leaving the company floundering. Through a determined effort, the company changed its focus and gradually grew into the second largest *banque d'affaires*, a cross between a holding company and investment bank peculiar to France. The company was nationalised by the French government in 1982 and then re-privatised in mid-October 1987.

Suez could be described as a French counterpart to SGB: a large holding company with a multitude of minority positions in generally unrelated (French) businesses. At the centre of the Suez empire was Banque Indosuez, an investment bank owned 100 per cent by Suez. When De Benedetti began his assault on SGB, Suez, partly held by De Benedetti's Cerus group and SGB, was a member of SGB's secure shareholders. Initially Suez stayed out of the contest but gradually came to oppose De Benedetti. Observers believed that Suez wanted to stop De Benedetti from acquiring SGB because, if he won, his next target would likely be Suez. The SGB purchase cost Suez almost $2 billion, financed primarily through new equity issues.

The Company, June 1988

SGB's many shareholdings had been organised into ten business sectors focused around the primary subsidiaries and related companies in the 1985 reorganisation (see *Exhibit 8.1*). Of the ten sectors, eight were considered 'strategic holdings', while the other two sectors held companies which SGB considered important but not core operations. The strategic groups were Financial Services, Energy (including engineering, industrial contracting, electronics, telecommunications and media), Non-ferrous Metals, Cement, Transport, Diamonds, Chemicals, and International Trading. *Exhibit 8.2* provides a breakdown of SGB's portfolio by relative value and

[7] On 7 March, the stock price hit a high of BEF 8530. The price in June 1988 ranged between BEF 4205 and BEF 5000.

dividends. *Exhibit 8.3* provides information on ownership.

In the prospectus for a stock offering in October 1987, companies were considered affiliated enterprises or subsidiaries if SGB could control either the composition of the Board or management policy. In a number of cases where it could not exercise control, SGB, still a significant stockholder, was able to exert influence over important decisions. Companies in the latter group included Generale Bank, Groupe AG, and Arbed, among others. After 1986, if SGB were able to influence decisions, the results of the subsidiary would be fully consolidated in SGB's annual report, even if less than 50 per cent were held. A final category existed in companies where SGB desired a 'lasting relationship'. Few holdings came under this heading, although SGB's interest in Royale Belge, Belgium's number two insurer, was listed.

Financial Services

The Financial Services sector was the largest of SGB's strategic groups in terms of both value and dividends. In 1987, the group accounted for 32.2 per cent of the SGB's portfolio value and 41.8 per cent of total dividend contributions. Growing out of the company's original mission as a development bank, the Financial Services group contained companies deeply rooted in SGB.

Tanks Consolidated Investments Tanks Consolidated Investments was a holding company centred around a large portion of SGB's 'strategic reserves' and investments in international financial services. One of the company's major holdings was a 50 per cent stake in the London-based subsidiary of Dillon, Read, the New York investment bank. Tanks also held 33.3 per cent of Sodecom, an investment company fully owned by the SGB Group, in which part of SGB's shareholding in Groupe AG was located. Through Tanks, SGB held interests in a number of other companies, including Tanks Investments (Zimbabwe) and Benguela Railway in Angola.

Generale Bank Generale Bank was perhaps the most important of any single one of SGB's holdings. The bank was the largest in Belgium with 1157 branches. Its overseas operations were significantly smaller, although international

growth was a major objective. In anticipation of 1992, the bank had concluded an alliance with the Dutch bank, Amro in early 1988. Under the agreement, the two banks exchanged shares equivalent to 10 per cent of outstanding equity and had the option to increase cross-ownership to 25 per cent in the future. Together the two banks would form one of the ten largest banking groups in Europe.

Generale Bank
Abbreviated consolidated figures (BEF m)

	1987	1986
Total assets	2 175 143	2 080 365
Shareholders' equity (Group share)	48 986	47 252
Turnover (sales)	NA	NA
Profit (group share)	6409	5896

Groupe AG The Financial Services group, additionally, held SGB's interests in Groupe AG and Royale Belge, the number one and two insurance companies in Belgium respectively. Groupe AG had been instrumental in the takeover as Suez's main Belgian ally. Groupe AG was also an important holder of Generale Bank stock. Groupe AG had acquired substantial holdings in Assubel, a Belgian insurance company, during January 1988.

Groupe AG
Abbreviated consolidated figures (BEF m)

	1987	1986
Total assets	206 957	186 772
Shareholders' equity (Group share)	15 286	8887
Turnover (sales)	NA	NA
Profit (group share)	4126	2728

Rounding out the Financial Services group were two venture capital companies, one each in Wallonia and Flanders, as well as specialised financial subsidiaries.

Energy, Engineering and Telecommunications

Energy; Engineering, Industrial Contracting and

Technical Services; Electronics, Telecommunications and Media, was the formal designation for SGB's second largest sector by value. The sector accounted for 19.3 per cent of the total portfolio value and 17.8 per cent of gross dividends. As the name implied, this sector comprised a wide range of different activities, most of which were organised as subsidiaries of the primary company in the sector, Tractebel, making it a major conglomerate in its own right. Besides Tractebel, other holdings in the sector included Electrafina, Belgatel (a shareholder in Alcatel, a telecommunications joint venture between ITT and Compagnie Générale d'Electricité of France), and Havas (a French media and advertising company). When Havas was privatised by the French government in 1986, Société Générale de Belgique had purchased 5 per cent on behalf of Tractebel. ACEC, an attempt at entering the electronic hardware business, was an unsuccessful subsidiary in this group and had accumulated extensive tax-deductible losses.

Tractebel SGB directly owned 15.6 per cent of Tractebel and was its largest single shareholder. Six SGB Directors also sat on Tractebel's 30-man Board, including Mr René Lamy who served as Chairman. Formed by the merger of two energy and related consulting companies at the bidding of SGB in 1986, Tractebel was one of the top five firms in market capitalisation on the Belgian stock exchange. The company had a complex holding structure, similar to SGB's, with interests ranging from nuclear power plants (66.3 per cent of Belgium's power came from nuclear energy) to a specialty food company. The company's primary holdings were in three electric utilities, which together produced 92.6 per cent of the power generated in Belgium. However, Tractebel's ownership of each was limited to about 25 per cent. The other major shareholder was Groupe Bruxelles Lambert (GBL), another Belgian conglomerate.[8] The engineering and financial services units had grown directly out of the needs of the utilities and remained largely dependent on them for business.

Tractebel had made a number of diversification efforts over the years, including construction and robotics, inherited from FN Industrial Systems.

Tractebel
Abbreviated consolidated figures (BEF m)

	1987	1986
Total assets	120 224	91 141
Shareholders' equity (Group share)	53 098	48 324
Turnover (sales)	28 641	25 818
Profit (group share)	6785	6024

Non-ferrous metals: Union Minière

The non-ferrous metals sector was operated through Union Minière, a wholly owned holding company, originally formed in 1906 to operate mines in the Belgian Congo. In 1987, the sector contributed 17.3 per cent of the value of the portfolio and 14 per cent of dividends. Its primary investments were in Metallurgie Hoboken-Overpelt (MHO), founded in 1919 to process the copper, gold, cobalt and other mineral ores coming from the Katanga mine in the Congo, and Vieille-Montagne, which began exploiting Belgian zinc reserves before 1850. UM also mined and processed germanium, a promising semi-conductor, and recycled precious metals, especially platinum, from catalytic converters.

In 1987, UM made another loss despite rising prices in copper and stable prices in most other products. The operations of Vieille-Montagne suffered sharp losses as the Belgian franc appreciated against the US dollar, the reference currency for zinc. Vieille-Montagne operated two zinc smelters, one with a 205 000 ton capacity (the largest in Europe) and the other with a capacity of 180 000 tons. The operations at MHO, on the other hand, were profitable. MHO operated a 120 000 ton zinc smelter, although this operation was secondary to the company's copper business. Total zinc smelter capacity in Europe, divided among fourteen companies, was approximately 1 730 000 tons per year (1988), 33 per cent of world production.

The copper and zinc industries had faced an extended period of low growth, chronic excess

---

[8] GBL was a major shareholder in the Belgian petrochemicals group Petrofina and was believed to be interested in controlling the company. SGB's 15.5 per cent minority position in Petrofina (4.4 per cent of which was held by Electrafina, a joint subsidiary of SGB and GBL) acted as a counterweight to GBL's influence in the utilities.

capacity and intense competition from non-European suppliers during much of the 1980s. Forecasts for the industries expected more of the same, with only temporary price increases stemming from short-term supply constraints. One executive noted that, given the cyclical nature of the minerals processed by UM, it was advantageous to have a secure shareholder like SGB willing to take a long-term perspective. Under René Lamy's SGB, however, the long-term perspective had been to gradually sell part of SGB's interest in UM once operating profits were generated, despite UM's dominant position in the industry and low-cost production facilities.

Union Minière
Abbreviated consolidated figures (BEF m)

	1987	1986
Total assets	80 388	80 648
Shareholders' equity (Group share)	18 924	20 106
Turnover (sales)	84 871	77 782
Profit (group share)	(831)	(734)

Cement: CBR

CBR was a manufacturer of ready-mix concrete and aggregates, 38 per cent directly owned by SGB. In 1987, 7.2 per cent of portfolio value and 3.6 per cent of gross dividends were contributed by CBR. CBR's operations were concentrated in Europe and North America, and were the fifth largest in the world. The cement industry was dependent on the general level of construction. CBR had made both revenue and productivity increases in recent years.

CBR
Abbreviated consolidated figures (BEF m)

	1987	1986
Total assets	32 787	35 350
Shareholders' equity (Group share)	13 455	11 665
Turnover (sales)	36 226	30 339
Profit (group share)	2338	1440

Transport: CMB

The CMB shipping line accounted for 3.1 per cent of portfolio value and 4.3 per cent of gross dividends. CMB had been able to maintain its profitability despite extensive excess supply in the maritime shipping industry. CMB's tramping operations (mostly iron ore and coal for the steel industry in Belgium and Luxembourg run through its Bocimar subsidiary) had increased market share as freight rates for bulk cargo improved. The important regular line operations had, however, suffered from the industry-wide 40 per cent oversupply in container ships. CMB owned approximately 36 ships at the end of 1987, and chartered others as needed. The company also had smaller operations in road transportation and port facilities.

CMB
Abbreviated consolidated figures (BEF m)

	1987	1986
Total assets	38 907	42 509
Shareholders' equity (Group share)	6590	6585
Turnover (sales)	30 376	31 214
Profit (group share)	533	520

Diamonds: Sibeka

Sibeka was involved in the mining and processing of natural and synthetic diamonds, and the manufacturing of diamond tools. Sibeka contributed 3.1 per cent of SGB's portfolio value and 6.6 per cent of gross dividends. SGB owned 54 per cent of Sibeka directly. The company's 48 per cent drop in

Sibeka
Abbreviated unconsolidated figures (BEF m)
(Consolidated figures were not available.)

	1987	1986
Total assets	5978	5608
Shareholders' equity	5380	5002
Turnover (sales)	NA	NA
Profit	218	420

profits between 1986 and 1987 was attributable to the persistence of poor market conditions in the diamond tools business. The important drill bit industry had been especially hard hit as the rate of oil exploration decreased. However, 1987 had been a good year for diamond jewellery. Sales of synthetic diamonds had also been strong over a number of years.

Chemicals: Gechem

SGB owned 52 per cent of Gechem, which accounted for 2 per cent of the portfolio value. Plagued with flat results from its diverse range of activities, Gechem did not contribute dividends to SGB in 1987. Although ranked only seventh among SGB holdings in value, Gechem was important to the parent company and, thus, was the first target of de Carmoy's reorganisation plan. The company had not only lost BEF 2236 million in 1987, but had, in fact, been a 'problem child' for at least ten years.

Gechem was created by merging SGB's chemicals-related holdings in 1985. The fertiliser operations, which had been a loss, were sold off soon after the merger, and the remaining parts were reorganised as Recticel (polyurethane foams), Sadacem (metallic oxides and salts), PRB (munitions), and Omnichem (fine chemicals). Recticel was a world leader in the manufacturing of foams used for car seats, beds, acoustical applications, and packaging. Metallic oxides and salts were also a promising area for Gechem because of their substantial market presence. The munitions group suffered from poor market conditions and relatively dated products. Omnichem was a significant player in the severely fragmented fine chemicals industry. SGB was well aware that

many parts of Gechem would be closed down if sold individually.

International Trading: Generale Trading Cy

International Trading, which accounted for 1.1 per cent of SGB's portfolio value and 2.5 per cent of gross dividends, actively traded in non-ferrous metals for UM as well as other commodities for outside accounts. SGB and its subsidiaries (primarily UM) owned 95 per cent of Generale Trading Cy.

Generale Trading Cy
Abbreviated consolidated figures (BEF m)

	1987	1986
Total assets	17 420	4258
Shareholders' equity (Group share)	4504	2649
Turnover (sales)	42 258	7792
Profit (group share)	(387)	357

Other shareholdings: financial and industrial or services

The financial holdings sector accounted for 7.7 per cent of SGB's portfolio value and 6.9 per cent of dividends. The leading company in this group was the holding company, Sofina, and its important holdings in Tractebel and in Petrofina, a large petroleum refiner and a major player in the Belgian economy. Additionally, the sector contained SGB's 1.5 per cent holding in Suez.

As with SGB's miscellaneous financial holdings, the industrial and services held in this sector were generally unrelated to the company's other holdings. Some of the holdings in this group were, however, important to SGB, especially Arbed and FN. Overall, the industrial and services holdings accounted for 7 per cent of SGB's portfolio value and 2.5 per cent of gross dividends.

Arbed In 1987, Arbed was one of the ten largest steel producers in Europe with an output of between 7 to 8 million tons per year. SGB held a minority position with 25 per cent of Arbed's outstanding voting stock. The Luxembourg

Gechem
Abbreviated consolidated figures (BEF m)

	1987	1986
Total assets	36 837	45 373
Shareholders' equity (Group share)	1463	3269
Turnover (sales)	39 125	54 976
Profit (group share)	(2236)	(3663)

government owned 30 per cent while the balance was held by others. Because of industry-wide difficulties, Arbed had posted a loss in 1987 after three years of good performance.

Arbed
Abbreviated unconsolidated figures (BEF m)
(Consolidated figures were unavailable.)

	1987	1986
Total assets	70 613	72 474
Shareholders' equity	24 124	26 627
Turnover (sales)	47 971	57 808
Profit	(2217)	890

Fabrique Nationale Herstal – FN Located in Wallonia, Fabrique Nationale Herstal SA (FN) was famous for manufacturing light arms and munitions for military forces and for sports use throughout the world. Its Browning brand name in the USA was well known. Plagued by labour and management problems as well as poor market

Fabrique Nationale
Abbreviated consolidated figures (BEF m)

	1987	1986
Total assets	34 404	33 836
Shareholders' equity (Group share)	1624	753
Turnover (sales)	23 762	28 092
Profit (group share)	(1510)	(2836)

conditions, FN had been unprofitable since 1985. FN operated a small and slightly profitable engine group which did contract work for the larger engine makers such as Pratt & Whitney of the USA. The company received financial assistance from the Walloon regional government in 1987, underscoring its importance to the region.

The future of SGB

De Carmoy was well aware of how much trouble and expense Suez had invested to secure control of SGB. His appointment had followed a much publicised battle for control, and the spotlight was now on him to perform. It was clear that Suez expected him to clean up the SGB house and improve its profitability quickly. Suez was intent on making SGB work and would ensure that the necessary means were available. Between the two companies (SGB and Suez) substantial financial resources were available; each company had the capacity to raise funds in many ways.

The central issue was how the company should be restructured. Georges Ugeux, the Finance Director appointed by de Carmoy, raised a key question, 'How does the holding company add value?' It was clear that the other shareholders in the Suez camp would be unwilling to see SGB completely broken up even if buyers could be found and approval granted. Mr de Carmoy saw a great challenge ahead as he pondered the appropriate strategy for SGB. He was convinced that there were some excellent parts to SGB and, with the right management input, the company could become an important contributor to Suez.

Exhibit 8.1 Société Générale de Belgique: group organisation chart at 31 December 1987

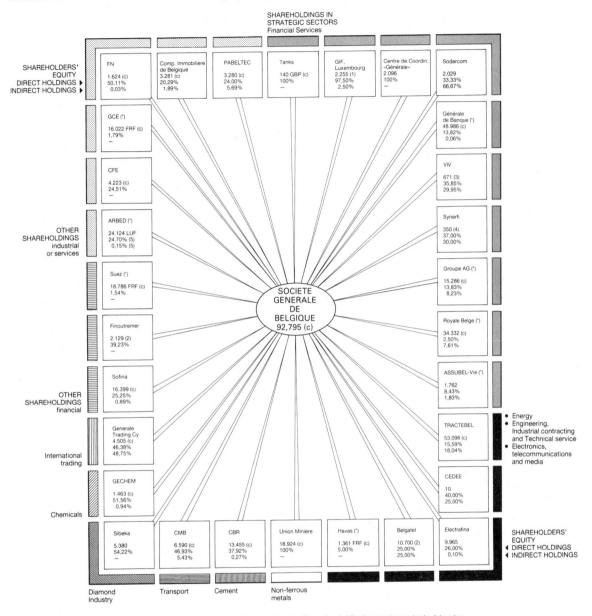

This chart includes the main companies in which Société Générale de Belgique holds a significant shareholding in percentage or in absolute value.
For each company, is mentioned in the following order:
● shareholders' equity (in millions) as at end of 1987 except if otherwise mentioned, consolidated (c) if the case;
● the percentages of direct and indirect shareholdings of the Société Générale de Belgique.
(*) Companies which are not linked.
(1) As at 31.3.1988. (2) As at 30.6.1987. (3) As at 30.9.1987. (4) Created 27.4.1987, capital of BEF 500 million, 70 per cent fully paid up. (5) Percentages of shares with voting rights attached.

Exhibit 8.2 Shareholdings in strategic sectors – 1987

Sector	Book value* BEF Millions	Percentage	Estimated value BEF Millions	Percentage	Gross dividends (percentage) 1987	1986	1985
Financial services	22 482	30.7	29 102	32.2	41.8	34.8	35.6
Energy etc.	13 212	18.1	17 429	19.3	17.8	16.7	14.5
Non-ferrous metals	15 668	21.4	15 668	17.3	14.0	15.5	16.7
Cement	4051	5.5	6510	7.2	3.6	2.9	2.7
Transport	1950	2.7	2795	3.1	4.3	4.3	4.0
Diamond industry	1517	2.1	2782	3.1	6.6	7.1	7.5
Chemicals	1650	2.3	1789	2.0	0.0	4.4	3.7
International trading	613	0.8	949	1.1	2.5	2.6	2.6
Other financial	4305	5.9	6954	7.7	6.9	7.3	7.5
Other industrial	7731	10.6	6338	7.0	2.5	4.4	5.2
Total	73 179	100.0	90 316	100.0	100.0	100.0	100.0

* Unconsolidated.

Exhibit 8.3 Important holdings by sector – 1987

	Important subsidiary holdings (direct and indirect (%))	SGB ownership Direct (%)	Indirect (%)
Financial			
Tanks		100.00	0.00
Dillon, Read Ltd.	50.00		
Benguela Railway Co.	90.00		
Sodecom		33.33	66.66
Groupe AG	7.83		
Generale Bank		13.82	0.06
Groupe AG		13.83	8.23
Generale Bank	8.71		
Royale Belge		2.50	7.61
Assubel		8.43	1.83
Energy, engineering and other			
Tractebel		15.59	18.04
Petrofina	8.64	0.42	15.07
Belgatel	20.00	25.00	25.00
Havas		5.00	0.00
Electrafina		26.00	0.10
Tractebel	9.72		
Petrofina	4.39		
Non-ferrous metals			
Union Minière		100.00	0.00
Metallurgie Hoboken-Overpelt	61.57		
Vieille-Montagne	50.15		
Cement: CBR		**37.92**	**0.27**
Transport: CMB		**46.93**	**5.43**
Diamond industry: Sibeka		**54.22**	**0.00**
Chemicals: Gechem		**51.56**	**0.94**
International trading: Generale Trading Cy		**46.38**	**48.75**
Other shareholdings:			
Sofina		25.25	0.89
Petrofina	1.59	0.42	15.07
Tractebel	8.16		
Belgatel	5.00		
Finoutremer		39.23	0.00
Petrofina	0.47		
CMB	1.99		
Belgamanche		50.00	0.00
Eurotunnel (s.a. and Plc.)	3.44		
Compagnie Financiere de Suez		1.54	0.00
Arbed (Voting shares only)		24.70	0.15
Compagnie Generale d'Electricite (CGE)		1.79	0.00
Fabrique Nationale Herstal (FN)		50.11	0.03
Browning (USA)	81.00		
Beretta	36.00		
FN Aeronautique	50.00		

(Indirect ownership is through subsidiaries.)

Appendix 8A
FINANCIAL INFORMATION OF SOCIÉTÉ GÉNÉRALE DE BELGIQUE

Balance sheet, 1984–87
Unconsolidated
(Thousands of Belgian francs)

	1987	1986	1985	1984
Assets				
Current assets				
Cash	834 256	60 330	119 155	30 430
Current investments	12 389 006	11 494 063	6 444 636	4 854 769
Accounts receivable	1 702 282	1 346 098	2 793 443	1 782 510
Notes receivable	443 337	45 662	85 148	540 148
Other	674 589	57 356	58 997	76 445
Fixed assets				
Financial Assets*				
Affiliated companies	54 309 979	47 973 624	41 804 979	36 872 576
Participating interests	13 749 798	8 784 703	8 525 384	6 974 449
Other financial assets	6 908 127	3 144 471	1 139 371	1 234 496
Tangible assets	697 576	729 290	760 911	795 971
Total	91 708 950	73 635 597	61 732 024	53 161 794
Liabilities				
Accounts payable				
Current notes payable	141 692	503 001	55 932	179 684
Financial debt	1 530 315	5 751 001	58 156	1 241 000
Trade debt	23 773	30 507	2682	12 736
Taxes & remuneration	131 358	169 625	102 110	103 570
Other	8 919 298	12 029 844	12 759 763	8 909 762
Notes payable				
Financial debt	8 898 037	1 072 075	1 596 378	1 684 503
Other	2 385 111	25 909	28 422	29 810
Other	1 105 206	207 733	269 168	91 199
Total	23 134 790	19 789 695	14 872 611	12 252 264
Provisions	1 017 911	1 035 650	1 330 450	1 067 954
Capital and reserves				
Capital	35 254 289	30 100 000	27 220 000	24 100 000
Reserves	14 911 807	14 848 773	13 392 872	13 380 872
Other	17 318 734	7 796 791	4 874 893	2 326 334
Accumulated profits	71 419	64 688	41 198	34 370
Total	67 556 249	52 810 252	45 528 963	39 841 576
TOTAL	91 708 950	73 635 597	61 732 024	53 161 794

* Primarily shares.

Income statement, 1984–87
Unconsolidated

(Thousands of Belgian francs)

	1987	1986	1985	1984
Charges				
A. Interest and debt charges	922 942	892 186	890 922	1 314 462
B. Other financial charges	1 169 556	533 123	94 689	221 342
C. Services and goods	194 652	149 686	106 691	107 377
D. Remuneration and pensions	354 279	356 828	335 057	289 618
E. Other	83 113	51 530	33 323	33 153
F. Depreciation	367 800	244 087	340 219	247 975
G. Amounts written off				
Financial assets	3 330 955	1 582 348	781 935	637 453
Current assets	285 266	20 208	4974	49 294
H. Provisions	0	508 115	328 502	316 358
I. Loss on disposal[*]	17 731	156 422	71 596	9812
J. Extraordinary charges	24 130	23 534	164 971	19 780
K. Income taxes	213	76 225	492	122
L. Profit	4 137 536	5 311 617	2 821 435	1 974 647
Total charges	10 888 173	9 905 909	5 974 806	5 221 393
Income				
A. Income from financial assets	4 314 080	3 974 250	3 571 159	3 176 566
B. Income from current assets	414 877	639 554	395 341	337 926
C. Other financial income	1 415 538	631 852	199 604	112 860
D. Income from services	79 137	78 164	73 977	70 923
E. Other current income	58 368	40 497	38 902	35 474
F. Write-backs	125 493	78 121	98 815	7213
G. Write-backs of provisions	7540	158 756	8536	11 364
H. Gains on disposal[*]	4 169 840	4 278 451	1 557 906	1 427 777
I. Extraordinary income	289 699	23 574	10 021	34 620
J. Income tax adjustments	13 601	2690	20 545	6670
Total income	10 888 173	9 905 909	5 974 806	5 221 393

[*] Primarily from fixed financial assets.

Consolidated balance sheet, 1986–87
(Millions of of Belgian francs)

	1987	1986
Assets		
Current assets:		
Cash	15 297	12 751
Current investments	60 434	58 040
Accounts receivable	101 748	110 939
Inventory	103 071	110 573
Notes receivable	7747	5382
Other	9574	7147
Fixed assets		
Financial assets (mostly shares)		
Affiliated companies	89 315	78 030
Participating interests	35 958	22 722
Other financial assets	18 602	13 942
Formation expenses	3944	1982
Intangible fixed assets	6310	4799
Consolidation goodwill	9056	2087
Tangible assets	101 315	94 636
Total	562 371	523 029
Liabilities		
Accounts payable		
Current notes payable	12 276	14 074
Financial debt	45 791	44 239
Trade debt	95 666	105 424
Taxes & remuneration	18 333	18 730
Other	44 443	36 451
Notes payable		
Financial debt	86 409	67 969
Other	10 250	9365
Other	18 249	17 169
Total	331 416	313 421
Provisions	27 367	22 217
Capital and reserves		
Capital	35 254	30 100
Reserves	38 240	37 133
Other	22 497	12 050
Exchange differences	(3196)	(1787)
Third-party interests	110 793	109 896
Total capital	203 588	187 392
TOTAL	562 371	523 029

Consolidated income statement, 1986–87
(Millions of Belgian francs)

	1987	1986
Operating income		
Turnover	336 804	341 012
Change in inventory	(75)	(1543)
Other income	11 278	11 349
Operating charges		
Raw materials & consumables	174 016	170 692
Services, other goods	63 646	67 788
Remunerations, pensions	80 924	84 931
Other charges	23 456	21 969
Operating profit	5965	5438
Financial income (from:)		
Fixed financial assets	4569	4476
Current financial assets	5716	6170
Other financial income (non-interest)	6534	6277
Interest	(10 490)	(10 325)
Other charges	(7736)	(6577)
Extraordinary income	13 237	20 539
Extraordinary charges	(11 303)	(19 722)
Profit before taxes	6492	6276
Income taxes	(2231)	(2056)
Profit after taxes	4261	4221
Results of companies consolidated (using equity method)	6509	5262
Profit	10 770	9482
Group share	3611	6334
Third-parties' share	7159	3148

* Prior to 1986 the equity method was used for affiliates 20–50 per cent held by SGB. All linked companies in which SGB had a direct holding were fully consolidated beginning in 1986. This was intended to provide a more accurate view of the group by representing SGB's effective control. As a result of the change, third-party interest in the 1986 group's equity went from 12 billion BEF (out of 90 billion BEF), to 110 billion BEF (out of 187 billion BEF) as stated above.

Case study 9

HOLLYWOOD IN THE ALPS[1]

The company

The Vocatron Corporation was set up about fifteen years ago by Stephan Muller, who believed that there was a niche in the market for private vocational training programmes, particularly for younger people. His hunch proved to be right, and over the years the company had steadily expanded. Muller had branched out from his home base in Denmark and set up sales subsidiaries in most European countries, the United States, Canada and Australia. Almost all of his fifty regional sales offices were run by women, who were usually in their twenties or early thirties. Most of the selling took place by telephone and through home visits. For tax reasons, Muller had very recently decided to move the Head Office from his home country to Lichtenstein.

Vocatron was facing some specific problems. After a period of sustained, steady growth, profits were beginning to decline. Stephan Muller had also begun to consider the question of his successor and was concerned whether his son, who had been working for the company for two years, would eventually be capable of taking over from him. For advice, Muller turned to Robert Houtman, a consultant specialising in entrepreneurship and family business.

The company visit

Robert Houtman's initial visit to Vocatron was engraved on his memory. Vocatron's Head Office commanded a spectacular view of snowcapped mountains. The small parking lot in front of the building was full of Porsches and Mercedes, which were completely upstaged by a splendid red Ferrari which stole the scene. Once past the heavy security at the entrance, Houtman discovered an opulent interior with white wall-to-wall carpeting and modern paintings and sculptures, including a Henry Moore. An attractive secretary pointed out a fitness centre, complete with sauna, whirl bath and swimming pool. The whole complex was less than a year old.

Houtman had to wait for ten minutes before being greeted by Stephan Muller. The president was very well, if conservatively, dressed, and seemed young for his age. His height, bushy eyebrows and penetrating stare left a lasting impression. His manner of speaking was obviously that of a man used to giving orders.

Muller explained that all was not well at Vocatron. After a period of rapid expansion, with sales doubling every three years, growth had levelled off and profits were falling. An explosive increase in the number of sales offices had come to a halt

[1] This case was prepared by Manfred F R Kets de Vries, Professor at INSEAD. It is intended to be used as a basis for class discussion rather than to illustrate either effective or ineffective handling of an administrative situation.

during the last year and a half. Muller attributed these new circumstances to the fact that his top management group had become seriously over-extended.

The president was clear about what he expected from Houtman: he wanted him to investigate how the company could continue to expand. Arrangements had already been made for Houtman to interview his top management team and some of the more experienced subsidiary directors. Muller also wanted Houtman to assess his son David. He mentioned as an aside that he had heard rumours which had sown doubts about his son's competence.

The interviews quickly revealed a number of problematic issues. The directors of the subsidiaries, who were specially flown in for the occasion, turned out to be a deeply disgruntled group. These young women were very unhappy about the way their careers were progressing. At first, working for Vocatron had seemed very glamorous. They had had early responsibility, excitement, adventure and travel. But as the years passed, the glamour had gradually worn off.

Houtman was astonished to discover that none of the female directors had ever been at the new Head Office before. Most communication took place by telephone, fax, letter or personal visits from senior management. Comparing the modest conditions under which she worked with the opulence of Head Office, one of the directors exclaimed, 'This place is unbelievable, it's like Hollywood in the Alps!' During her visit, this particular woman said she had made several attempts to see the President. She was prevented from doing so by his secretary, who consistently maintained that he had gone out for a business meeting. The President had, however, been seen in the office. Houtman learnt that Muller had made promises about this woman's future career which had come to nothing, although she had apparently been running the most profitable sales subsidiary for the last ten years. A previous attempt to pacify her by giving her a sports car as a bonus had obviously met with only partial success. While Houtman was present, in an angry attempt to get through the door to the President's office, this woman 'accidentally' spilled a cup of black coffee on the immaculate, deep-piled white carpet.

A complaint repeatedly made by the Sales Directors was that they all felt stuck in their present position. When they had joined the company in their early twenties, working for Vocatron had seemed very exciting. There were very few companies offering this kind of opportunity to people with their relatively limited education and lack of work experience. Setting up a sales office in a foreign country had been a great challenge. Over time, however, the long hours and only average salaries had killed the spirit of adventure. Since most of the selling took place in the evening, and there was a lot of pressure to perform, their social life had been seriously affected. Almost none was married or had a long-term stable relationship. Indeed, the only relationships most appeared to have were with some of the men from Head Office who made regular visits to monitor their performance. Quite a few of the women complained of stress symptoms. Some had repeatedly been put on medication and even been hospitalised. The major criticism was that career progress stopped with the position of Director of a sales subsidiary. No woman had ever been promoted to Head Office.

A close inner circle of all-male executives, many of them old school friends of Stephan Muller, ran the Head Office. Some of the Sales Directors compared this group to the KGB because of the control systems they used to monitor sales performance. When asked why they didn't leave, the Subsidiary Directors seemed lost, not only for a reply but literally, not knowing where they could go. Many of them had left their home countries long ago and had a sense of rootlessness – their only feeling of belonging anywhere was in the ambience created by Vocatron. Whatever might be wrong with company policy, they hung on to the belief that people at Head Office would look after them, whatever the circumstances.

During the interviews, some of these Subsidiary Directors talked about David Muller, the President's son. According to them he was incompetent, and, without his father's influence, would never have got on in business. They drew their conclusions from his behaviour during internships at three of the sales subsidiaries and cited some rather vague incidents illustrating what a disaster he had been.

This view of David rather surprised Houtman.

He was unconvinced by the Subsidiary Directors' comments. David Muller had come across as a rather thoughtful individual when Houtman had interviewed him. He appeared to be reasonably well-educated, having obtained a business degree. However, Houtman had discerned a certain amount of ambivalence toward his father who, according to David, 'gave him impossible assignments, never praised him for work well done, kept checking up on everything he did, and chastised him in front of everybody'.

David Muller told Houtman that he had not been a good student, more interested in cafés and parties than studying. He explained that it had not been easy to grow up in his father's shadow. Only after leaving home and doing his military service (when he received a commission and became aide to a general who had taken a liking to him), had he become more sure of himself.

During an interview with Stephan Muller, Houtman asked him why, given his own assessment of the need for more top management talent in his company, did he not do the obvious thing and select the most capable Subsidiary Directors for promotion to Head Office? Muller reacted with astonishing violence. He became very agitated and then stiffened up, saying, 'Impossible! Women have only limited capabilities and running a sales office is as far as they can go'. According to Muller, having women in senior positions at Head Office would seriously disrupt the general atmosphere. He then said, rather wistfully, 'Wouldn't it be nice if only I could get rid of all these older women in a pleasant way. They were alright when they were younger but they turned into such bitches later on!'

In contrast to the female Subsidiary Directors, the six male executives who made up Muller's inner circle at Head Office seemed to be quite happy working at Vocatron. They shared their boss's perception of women, believing that it would be very disruptive to have them at Head Office in anything other than secretarial positions. In their opinion these particular women needed continuous surveillance, otherwise they would begin to act irresponsibly. Then they jokingly said, with an obvious sexual innuendo, that they knew how to keep their subordinates in line.

This group of executives seemed to be quite satisfied with the existing reward structure. Further prompting revealed, however, that at Vocatron bonuses were given rather haphazardly. For example, one of the executives had once gone to Muller saying that he needed a yacht and, surprisingly enough, in due course he had received one.

Personal background

During a subsequent dinner with the President, Houtman learnt more about Stephan Muller's background. He was an only child. From his conversation, it was clear that he had not been happy growing up. A key event in his childhood had been his parents' divorce when he was only five years old. His father had moved to another country where he had started a new family. His son had not seen him since.

Muller had described his mother as a very irresponsible, unreliable individual who went through an endless series of short-lived love affairs. He felt that his father's departure had really changed her. She had become very moody, lashed out at her son and ordered him around. He cherished, however, a few early memories of family togetherness. His tactics for survival at home, while growing up, had been to minimise his stays there. He spent most of his time with a close circle of friends, some of whom now worked for him. The interest shown in him by an uncle who regularly took him on excursions had also helped him to overcome his feelings of desertion by his father. This uncle had provided some kind of stability and Muller felt close to him. Muller explained that his own marriage had not been successful. He and his wife had come to an arrangement, living together for the children's sake, but each of them leading a separate life. Although it had never been explicitly stated, his wife was aware that he had had a number of mistresses.

After some prompting about stress symptoms, the President said that at times he had stomach problems. He also complained about recurring nightmares. When asked to say something more about them, he described a dream in which he was cornered by a horrible looking witch who would jump on his back and almost choke him. He would begin to scream, and that would wake him up.

Houtman was somewhat taken aback by Muller's confessions. He had to puzzle out the meaning behind them, and behind the serious problems at Vocatron. He knew his task was now to sort out the different issues, offer Muller an analysis of the various problems, and present a set of recommendations.

Case study 10

ENIGMA CHEMICALS (A)

Enigma Chemicals is a large company producing a limited range of chemical products from three sites in the UK, mostly for the domestic market, although it does export about 20 per cent of its output. The chemicals that Enigma produces are important inputs into the production processes of a number of other major companies. Although the Enigma products are important to its customers' production processes, they do not constitute a major cost component in the final products of those customers. Furthermore, through control over a vital raw material and through various patent arrangements, Enigma occupies an almost monopoly position in the UK and has done so for many years.

Another fact about Enigma's products is also important; they are of a hazardous, environmentally threatening nature and this makes Enigma an ideal target for environmental pressure groups. The company is frequently attacked by the media, despite the fact that it has, on the whole, a rather good safety record – its policies and monitoring systems certainly place tremendous importance on these matters. However, over the past few years there have been two serious incidents of a rather dramatic nature: in one of these incidents pollutants were accidentally released into the atmosphere causing health problems for people living in the vicinity of the plant concerned; and in another serious incident pollutants leaked into a river, killing fish, birds and other wild life over an area of many miles. Periodically, there were fires in the manufacturing plants and some former employees were suing the company on the grounds that the

manufacturing process had damaged their health. These incidents had created a public image that Enigma was experiencing great difficulty in changing.

The patents that afforded Enigma a near monopoly position were due to expire in ten years' time, after which Enigma could expect fierce competition to cause a dramatic decline in its sales. Over the past few years, Enigma's managers and employees had experienced a foretaste of what this might be like: the long recession of the early 1990s had caused a significant decline in sales and for the first time in its 30-year history Enigma had been forced to reduce its work force. Although the reduction in the numbers of both managers and employees had been accomplished entirely through early retirement and voluntary redundancy, it had unsettled people at Enigma, the great majority of whom had come to believe that they had 'jobs for life'.

As part of the strategy for coping with the new commercial realities, the management reporting structure of Enigma had been reorganised. Before the reorganisation, there had been a monolithic functional structure: main Board Directors were responsible for personnel, R&D, health and safety, finance, engineering and production. The production function, by far the largest employer, was subdivided according to geographic sites, each of which was run by a General Manager to whom a number of works managers reported. These works managers were responsible for a number of plant managers, in turn responsible for supervisors, to whom foremen reported. After the reorganisation, Enigma consisted of five divisions, each responsible for its own profitability and having a wide range of its own functional activities such as personnel and engineering. The corporate level still had functional responsibilities, but in theory at least, much of the responsibility and the authority had been devolved to the divisions.

At the time of the reorganisation, the Board had also reviewed its strategic planning process and decided to devolve much of the responsibility for this to the divisions. Whereas the central planning function had in the past prepared five- and ten-year plans with little involvement of managers at the site level, it was now to act more as an adviser to divisional management which was charged with preparing the five- and ten-year plans for the approval of the main Board. In future, the Chief Executive would lay down a general framework to establish future direction and he would articulate some important strategic thrusts, but then it would be up to divisional managers to develop the strategy.

The Chief Executive, Harry Bream, had spent his entire career at Enigma and consequently knew it well. He could recall previous reorganisations and previous attempts to change strategic direction, none of which had actually done a great deal to change the way people at Enigma worked. He knew from experience, therefore, that simply reorganising and pushing strategic responsibility further down the hierarchy would not necessarily lead to the strategic actions that a more hostile world and the eventual running out of the patents would create. He therefore contracted with a team of consultants to advise how the inevitable obstacles to implementation might be removed. The consultants conducted a series of interviews with a sample of managers and staff at all levels in order to identify what the issues were and what sort of company Enigma was. The notes that follow on three of these interviews turned out to be rather typical of all of those conducted with top management and the views of supervisory and middle management are indicated in a summary of interview notes prepared by one of the consultants, which is given below after the interview notes. The consultants now faced the task of formulating an approach to assisting their client.

Notes on an interview with Adrian Sinclair, Director of Division X

Adrian Sinclair had been with Enigma since he left university with an engineering degree some twenty years ago. In his interview with the consultant he started by describing how the organisation had changed since he joined it. Twenty years ago it had been an extremely bureaucratic, status-conscious organisation. Thus, there had been a sharp divide between the shop-floor workers on the one hand, and the staff on the other. Staff in turn were divided into professional and scientific streams; people entered the company either as a technician or as an administrator and tended to remain in the stream they had joined, moving regularly up the strictly graded structure. Relationships between people at different levels were very formal – you always addressed a more senior person as 'Mr', and you always communicated in strict hierarchical order. No one ever went around their boss to a higher level.

The system had changed when the distinction between the professional and the scientific grades was abolished. All new entrants now came into a unified stream and then progressed up the grades according to experience. As they progressed, they encountered two important break-points in the pay grading structure. At the first of these points, those promoted were given significantly better terms and conditions. So, when entrants joined from university, they had terms and conditions set out in a staff handbook with a brown cover and at the first important break-point, the ranks of middle management, they acquired the terms and conditions set out in a green staff handbook. Then, when a person reached senior management status, the terms and conditions changed once more and this time they were set out in a blue staff handbook. Managers therefore came to be classified into clear-cut groups known as 'Greens' and 'Blues'. Everyone knew to which group a manager belonged and every year there were separate conferences for 'Greens' and 'Blues'.

One thing had not changed, however, and that was the open-interview procedure for promotions up the grade structure. Competent people could expect promotion as a matter of course. All openings were publicly advertised throughout the company and applications were invited from anyone with the right qualifications. Those selected had to attend a Promotions Committee consisting of three people, two of whom were outside the department in which the promotion was to be made. In this way, said Adrian, 'We can be seen to be fair and it prevents people from promoting their blue-eyed boys'. With this system, everyone got a fair chance and the company benefited when new talent was unearthed.

Adrian outlined how it was everyone's ambition to reach 'Blue' status and how he had thought of the 'Blues' as a kind of 'club' or 'secret society' until he had joined it. Once one reached the 'Blue' level, one was entitled to the BMW grade of car, a secretary, personally selected office furniture, private medical assurance and other benefits.

Adrian reiterated how the company had changed, how people had become much more flexible and less status-conscious than they were, but he did say that there were 'many images of old ways of behaving still lurking about', and it was these that he saw as the major obstacles to achieving the low-cost regimes and the entrepreneurial behaviour that were called for in the ten-year corporate plan.

According to Adrian, one of the principal images of the past, which were still 'lurking about', related to the manner in which managers at Enigma typically handled poor performance. There was a system in which people's performance was appraised each year. Although the system allowed people to be placed into one of five performance categories, ranging from the 'completely unsatisfactory' to the 'excellent', in fact managers tended to put almost everyone into the average performance category. Most people consequently got the average level of bonus and incentive pay. It was very difficult to fire nonperformers because of agreements with powerful unions and because of the complex procedures that had to be followed before anyone could be fired. But quite apart from this, managers did not like to apply sanctions to anyone anyway. There was therefore a widespread perception that managers avoided tough decisions and personal confrontation. 'We do not like to go home at night feeling that we have been unpleasant to people', is how Adrian put it. He also felt that if managers

lower down were suddenly given the right to appoint and fire staff without going through all the laborious procedures, they would simply not take up that responsibility.

Adrian did point out, however, that if he was determined to do something, then the bureaucratic systems simply did not stop him. He got around the bureaucracy through his informal contacts. He felt that those who complained that they could not manage because of bureaucratic systems imposed on them by the corporate centre, were simply using this as an excuse for not managing. When he had a staff member who did not perform he usually managed to find someone inexperienced enough to take that person, or he privately convinced the non-performer to go, or he just found the non-performers something else to do, usually a promotion that got them out of the way. He felt that managers at Enigma did not sack people because they had not got the stomach for it. They all felt that they had a job for life and if that was changed in one case, who knew where it might stop. Anyway, it was a bad idea to do anything that would provoke a strike because that would simply attract media attention and the old environmental scares would simply be revived.

Notes on an interview with Adam Frusquin, Director of Division Y

Adam had joined the company 25 years ago after completing his doctorate in chemistry. He described how for years people at Enigma had seen their company as a good employer operating in a stable industry, giving people jobs for life. He described the family atmosphere that prevailed and gave examples of the caring attitude the company adopted to its people. He also described Enigma as a not particularly demanding employer.

In his view this was a company in which, even nowadays, 'people tended to know their place' in a clearly structured hierarchy. It was also a company in which everything was done by negotiation rather than instruction. The result was a relatively comfortable, conflict-free and content organisation. However, Adam was convinced that these attitudes would have to change and he talked about the need 'to be seen to be more commercially aggressive. Instead of operating strictly according to hierarchical position and following well-established negotiating procedures, Adam believed that people at all levels would have to be empowered to take their own decisions. But he recognised that many managers would find this threatening and would not want the responsibility.

Notes of an interview with Anita Cummings, Director of Human Relations

Anita was a highly unusual manager at Enigma: first, she was the only woman in a senior position; and second, she had been at Enigma for only a year. Harry Bream had brought Anita on to the Board as his way of signalling that he wanted a change in behaviour throughout the organisation and that personnel practices and systems were going to change to bring this about. He 'was tired of having everything he tried to do disappearing into a fog'. Anita's arrival had caused quite a stir because she had previously been the Personnel Director of AMR, a ruthless conglomerate, and in that position she had acquired a reputation for being tough with non-performing managers.

In the interview with the consultant, Anita confessed that she was still surprised at the lack of focus on costs and financial performance generally. She found the style of management to be highly bureaucratic, proceduralised and very slow-moving. As far as she was concerned, people did not seem to recognise any pressures for change, but channelled much of their energies into what she called 'sibling rivalry'. She explained how people tended to form fairly cohesive teams in the department or immediate project group they worked in, but built up animosities against other groups and did their best not to cooperate with them. She spoke with some amusement about the classification of managers into the 'Greens' and the 'Blues'. As far as she was concerned these were secretive 'men's clubs' that were not open to her and were, anyway, irrelevant as far as the business was concerned. She said that people at Enigma 'react to newcomers with fear'. She said that managers felt that 'they had to be seen to be members of the "Blue" club'.

She still found it surprising that senior managers kept starting new initiatives that somehow always required a committee, a task force or a workshop and often the assistance of consultants. There was so much activity examining everything and suggesting changes in everything and yet so little change itself.

She described the culture of the organisation as a comfortable family atmosphere in which people saw their roles in terms of the pay grade they had reached.

Summary notes on interviews with middle managers

In almost all the interviews managers stated their support for the company which they viewed as a good employer that provided them with job security. However, they were also critical of more senior managers who, they said, avoided tough decisions. Senior managers tended to communicate with them using memos rather than walking around. Despite all the efforts to promote participation, most middle managers saw it as a sort of front – they believed that decisions were really taken in a rather autocratic way. Middle managers complained about communication with higher levels where they had to rely on the grapevine and they thought this was wrong. They called for more detailed and precise information on the company's objectives and strategies. When the consultant pointed out that they had been sent summary copies of the ten-year plan, some said they could not remember what it said, others said it was in a drawer somewhere, others said it was not detailed and precise enough. They claimed that top managers had no sense of direction and they, at the middle level, needed to be told what this direction was before they could function properly.

As far as the outside world was concerned, few middle managers talked about the prospects facing the company as its monopoly hold on its chief product weakened. But they all mentioned the unreasonable way in which pressure groups and the media pilloried them for what they felt were imaginary environmental dangers.

Case study 11

ENIGMA CHEMICALS (B)

Case Study 10, Enigma Chemicals (A), gives more information on the company but, for the purpose of this Case Study, it is enough to know that Enigma is a rather bureaucratically managed company that has recently moved from a highly centralised functional structure to a more decentralised, divisionalised structure in which the divisions are responsible for profit. This case is concerned specifically with the performance appraisal system that was used for judging people's performance, informing them of what that judgement was and then rewarding them accordingly. The system was also used to design people's training and development needs, as well as to plan their career progression. It was a tool that some found useful in planning management succession.

Before the reorganisation there was a large central personnel function that had unilaterally designed all the personnel systems, including the annual performance-appraisal procedure, and then negotiated their acceptance by the Unions. After the reorganisation many of the personnel staff had been transferred to the divisions and there was now a much smaller Central Personnel function. Managers of this new Central Personnel department believed that the appraisal procedure provided valid data of a detailed kind on managers and staff alike and that this information was particularly vital for top corporate managers to carry out their tasks of planning management succession. One of the personnel managers said, 'Regular updating of information of this kind enables the Chief Executive to plan management succession and move senior managers around for the good of the corporation as a whole. Any change in the system should therefore be small and gradually implemented after careful consultation and negotiation with the Unions'. Central Personnel feared that any major change to the procedure would lead to divisional empire building and to the hoarding of managerial talent at the expense of the corporation as a whole.

A group of divisional managing directors and their personnel managers, however, believed that the annual appraisal procedure took too long and the forms that had to be completed were too complex and laborious. They argued that the procedure generated a great amount of detailed information that no one wanted or used. They were therefore pressing for a much simpler form and a much less laborious procedure. More specifically, they argued that each division should be free to develop its own procedure subject only to providing certain clearly specified pieces of information that were needed by corporate management. They felt that Central Personnel was trying to hang on to as much of its former power as it could. They argued that substantial change was required and that the divisions needed to develop their own appraisal systems if they really were to manage their own businesses. Furthermore, they maintained that the appraisal system was a matter for managers and that there was no need at all to negotiate its form with the Unions.

This debate between the centre and the operating activities had been going on for years, even before the reorganisation into divisions had occurred. The centre had, from time to time, responded by altering the appraisal form, but there had been little real change. Now, with increased operating activity power through the divisionalised structures, the whole matter was opened up again. The Central Personnel activity also saw quite clearly that some changes would have to be made now that the divisions had increased responsibility.

Both sides to the dispute agreed that the appraisal system was an issue that had to be attended to. Therefore, a committee including representatives of Central Personnel and divisional management was formed to make recommendations to top management on the appraisal system. Before the first meeting, consultants interviewed the representatives from the centre and from the divisions.

In the interviews, the divisional representatives were fairly unanimous in maintaining that Central Personnel were:

- old fashioned bureaucrats unable to adapt to the changing world. They were incapable of understanding modern commercial pressures;
- well meaning people, but they were blind to their own faults and the foolishness of the policy they were trying to preserve. They were really trying to hang on to their own power; and
- seeing divisional managers as potential robber barons. One divisional manager said, 'They believe that if you let the divisional barons loose, those barons will destroy the synergy and corporate identity they [Central Personnel] have worked all their lives to uphold and those barons will destroy the relationship they [Central Personnel] have built up with the Unions over many years'.

The consultants also interviewed the Central Personnel representatives on the Committee. The central staff believed that:

- there was a need to review the procedures but it must be done gradually and in negotiation with the Unions;
- the divisions were overreacting to problems with the present procedure. 'If we are not careful we will undermine the relationship with the Unions and divisional warfare for the best

managers will break out. Also we will be undermining the standards of objectivity, rationality and fairness that the present system embodies. They [the divisional managers] will destroy the identity of the corporation'; and that

- the divisions were well-intentioned but they simply did not understand the power of the Unions and the importance of synergy. They were taking the position they take simply because they wanted to grab power. 'And the divisions see us as hopeless bureaucrats who do not understand commercial realities.'

At the first meeting of the Performance Appraisal Procedure Review Committee, divisional representatives proposed that the Committee would proceed faster if it established a working party consisting of lower-level experts to draft new performance appraisal forms. In their presentation to back up this proposal, they kept repeating that although any new appraisal form would certainly not solve all the problems, it would be a step forward. But this step would simply build in a modest way on what was already being done. They said that it would be experimental and it would not threaten anyone. It would certainly not affect the ability to move staff from one division to another. All were in favour of synergy and the use of all senior managers as a corporate resource, not simply a resource for a division, but they did point out how the information generated by the appraisal procedure was used to move staff away from a division to the detriment of that division. There had to be some balance, they said, between the power of the centre to move people about and the power of the division to retain key managers. They recommended that this topic undergo further study and a task force be set up to look at it.

The Central Personnel representatives repeatedly stated how much they supported the ideas of moving carefully and experimentally and trying to make better that which already existed. (The personnel representatives later told the consultant that they saw their approach of selectively agreeing with the divisions as a means of holding them down to gradual change only.) Central representatives also agreed that there was room for improvement but emphasised the importance of regarding senior managers as a group constituting the most important corporate resource. They emphasised the importance of the Unions. They said they would themselves already have made improvements in the procedures but they were overloaded with work due to the reorganisation.

From time to time a central representative made an impassioned plea that they avoid the dangers of disintegration of the corporation; or a divisional representative said that it would be quite impossible to achieve corporate goals unless the procedure was changed. Such pleas were received in embarrassed silence by the other members of the committee until someone introduced a new topic for discussion.

After a number of meetings that continued in much the same fashion, an outline of a new appraisal form was eventually agreed upon and presented to a joint meeting of top corporate managers and Union leaders with the recommendation that it be a guide to divisions but that it should not be imposed upon them. After some argument, the top managers and the Unions agreed that they would appoint a permanent Appraisal Committee with representatives of management and Unions to put 'flesh on the bones' of the form recommended to them and also to administer the new appraisal procedure, and in particular administer any departures from the norm that a specific division might propose. They also set guidelines for this new permanent committee. It had to be fair and objective and provide enough information to enable top managers to plan management succession, but the committee was to avoid costly changes. The meeting ended with a buffet lunch, wine and feelings of cooperation. There was a common feeling that progress had been made.

Case study 12

SMALL FIRMS IN A SWEDISH CONTEXT: Måleräs, Pilgrimstad and Söderhamn[1]

Sweden, the largest country in Scandinavia, has a population of about nine million distributed quite unevenly over an area of 450 000 square kilometres. Sweden's government promotes a viable private business sector through industrial and regional policies and maintains its position as a welfare state with social services organised mainly through the public sector. The result is that general living conditions in terms of basic infrastructure and social services are about the same all over Sweden. Access to qualified business services, however, varies considerably between metropolitan areas and peripheral regions.

The Swedish small business sector is of considerable importance to its economy; as many people are employed in firms with less than 20 employees as in corporations with 200 employees or more. Furthermore, in spite of the increasing internationalisation of the relatively small Swedish economy and the higher level of merger activity, the small business sector has increased in importance. Over the period 1983 to 1988 the increase in the number of jobs in firms with less than 20 employees was 16 per cent while the larger firms provided only an additional 6 per cent of jobs.

In 1978 a structure for implementing small business policy was set up, consisting of 24 regional development funds jointly financed by the state and the regional county councils. Each regional development fund included representatives from industry and the Unions and was run by a Board appointed by the county councils. Development Funds provided loans to supplement bank loans, services such as training to supplement private services, and technology-transfer assistance. In 1990 the government reduced the financing role of the regional development funds, transferring these functions to six new regional venture capital companies.

The Swedish government therefore recognises the importance of the small business sector in its sectoral, industrial and regional policies, but it sees general measures, such as providing an appropriate infrastructure, as its major contribution to the promotion of small businesses. Thus, out of total direct state financial support to industry in 1987/88, only 2 per cent was explicitly directed to small firms. Swedish municipalities are restricted in terms of the financial support they may provide to individual companies: basically, they are limited to the provision of liaison services and premises. The government also promotes specific initiatives from time to time: for example the targeting of women through special start-up groups, selective measures to improve design, assistance in dealing with environmental issues, etc.

The creation of science parks, i.e. industrial and commercial complexes focusing on high-technology activities and usually located close to a university, is a consequence of a national technology policy. But local economic development also occurs more or less spontaneously as 'industrial districts' evolve in the absence of any specific policy initiative. In the Swedish context, the success of any of these local development efforts is conditioned by the ability to cope with four important power centres. Very few local initiatives, either planned science parks or spontaneously developing industrial districts, can succeed without building alliances with one or several of the four cornerstones of Swedish society, namely, the large corporations which dominate the markets, the political system, the public administrative machine, and the powerful interest groups, such as the centralised labour movement, the large-scale Cooperative Societies, and the traditional Agricultural Associations.

Local economic development strategies are affected by the Swedish municipalities who are subject to strict legal limits but may use their financial resources to cope with the consequences of decreasing population and increasing unemployment. Also, task forces, usually including Union or Cooperative Society representatives, are often specially set up to cope with realised or expected unemployment. The need for modernisation of industry is especially prevalent in central Sweden, dominated as it is by one-company towns based on iron manufacturing. Unions and Cooperative Societies often play a major role in dealing with the decline in a town's main industry. Finally, there is the part played by the local inhabitants themselves and this obviously varies from case to case. Three specific examples are provided below that illustrate typical processes of local entrepreneurial development in Sweden.

Måleràs

At the end of the 1970s the small community of Måleràs had a population of 300 that had declined by two-thirds over a 30-year period. The dominant glassworks had come under external control and had shrunk to a fraction of its former size. How-

ever, a strong local identity had survived, due to geographic isolation and to kinship ties among the inhabitants reaching back several generations.

One of the 300 inhabitants, Mats Jonasson, was active in various local arenas such as the sports association, the local orchestra and the village committee. He recognised the potential of the social resources of Måleràs and perceived that they could be mobilised to create businesses and jobs. So, Mats founded a local organisation, Project Måleràs. People taking part in this project collectively approached banks, local authorities and various other organisations for venture capital, inexpensive premises and professional advice. Mats supplied ideas and designs for new products to the local leather industry, to a small iron foundry and to a trading company. The iron foundry and a local metal manufacturing company became sub-contractors to the glass works. Mats also formulated the idea of taking over the local glass works.

Once the project gained momentum, however, it became difficult to control and it proved impossible to provide facilities for all the new projects that were created in Måleràs or were attracted to the community.

Over a period of five years the number of companies and the number of locally employed workers more than doubled in Måleràs and the number of inhabitants increased slightly. The glass works became a local company owned by employees and the local people. But it was not all plain sailing: there were close-downs and bankruptcies; the second largest company in the community came under external control and its work force was reduced. The commercial success of the glass works provoked a hostile take-over bid from one of the major corporations in the glass industry and this led Mats Jonasson to acquire the majority of the stock. Local ownership was thus retained but Måleràs is again approaching the status of a one-company town.

Pilgrimstad

Pilgrimstad is located in the centre of Sweden and has a population of 3500. In 1986 it was economically completely dependent on an externally controlled fibreboard plant built in the early 1950s. At the beginning of 1986 the plant owners decided to concentrate production in another unit located on the Baltic Sea.

Pilgrimstad is located in the municipality of Bracke and one of the main political leaders in Bracke was Erik Magnusson: he was the Chairman of the Municipal Board for the district that included Pilgrimstad. In addition he was a Union representative on the Board of the company that owned the fibreboard plant. Professionally, he was in charge of the maintenance of the plant. In January 1986, when the company had announced that it would close the plant in six months' time, he had organised a project group to cope with the situation. That group's ambition was either to rescue the factory or to find alternative products for the plant. For this mission, Erik used his contacts in the Unions and also in the political sector and the public bureaucracy. Despite all his work, however, the plant was closed down.

When the 90 employees of the plant were laid off, about one-third were interested in participating in local efforts to create new jobs locally. Another third of the previous work force was granted early retirement and the youngest third preferred to move immediately to jobs in adjacent villages. For the first-mentioned third, a training programme was organised and it attracted 19 persons.

Erik Magnusson's strategy was, first, to make sure that his former workmates got jobs and social security, even if it meant commuting to a nearby town, Ostersund. Second, he recognised the need to guarantee the maintenance of private and public community services. Third, he wanted to initiate a self-supporting local business development programme. At first, therefore, he focused on finding large external companies that could fill the employment gap quickly. The local group even suggested appropriate ventures. However, it was impossible to find a suitable prospect for the available premises.

In 1987 the new management of the parent company of the fibreboard plant dismantled the machinery and virtually donated the premises to the community early in the following year. The premises were then managed by the municipality's technical department. These changes forced Erik Magnusson to re-define the economic development concept in line with an alternative plan he had mentally been preparing since 1986.

He thought of attracting small firms that could not pay high rents but wanted to operate close to the regional centre of Ostersund. Eric and two other colleagues set up a task force to prepare the premises provisionally and offer them to prospective tenants. They restructured the factory into what they called an 'industrial hotel'. They shaped the areas tenants wanted in consultation with them so as to meet their requirements. Erik had great difficulty persuading his political colleagues that this project was viable – many wanted to tear down the factory or at least employ a recognised consultancy agency to do the job professionally. Many referred to Erik as the 'village idiot'.

By the end of 1990, however, more than half of the potential premises had been put to use. About a dozen companies were active within the premises and all the original 90 jobs had been replaced.

Söderhamn

Söderhamn is located in north Sweden on the Baltic Sea. The municipal area has for centuries been dominated by large corporations exploiting the rich natural resources of the hinterland: iron ore, timber and hydropower. However, all of these companies have for a long time been externally controlled by national corporations within the private as well as the state sectors. Until 1975 huge production units, mainly within the forest and engineering industries, provided the town with increasing employment. But in the late 1970s several major plants were closed down due to changed business conditions and restructuring because of ownership changes. In less than one decade employment was reduced by more than 2500 and the population decreased from 32 000 to less than 30 000 between 1976 and 1984. In 1989 about 30 per cent of the remaining jobs were in the manufacturing industry (the national average is 21 per cent).

Towards the end of the 1970s Söderhamn's town authorities mobilised administrative resources to deal with the increasing problems. A development corporation was established and an industrial liaison officer engaged. The focus was then on various defensive operations such as lobbying for state money and revitalising companies in crisis. The most speculative move was the acquisition of a company that manufactured heavy chain cables, mainly for oil platforms. The company was at that time a subsidiary of a state-owned conglomerate within the steel industry. The local development corporations took over ownership under pressure from the employees and their Unions. When the oil extrusion industry stagnated after some successful years, the company went bankrupt. Municipal involvement in individual business is illegal in Sweden and indirect ownership through development companies is questionable. Therefore, Söderhamn and its politicians had to face media scrutiny when the company went bankrupt. The effect of this was to tarnish the image of Söderhamn nationally and spread a negative self-image among the local populace.

Under pressure from the Ministry of Industry, another local development company was set up, this time by the large, private cooperative and state corporations. But by 1989 this company had invested only 20 per cent of its original capital and contributed little to job generation.

In 1983 three businessmen organised a planning committee for a local trade show in order to counteract the emerging defeatism in the community. Later the same year, the local authorities, in their capacity as owners, planned to demolish the premises sold off by a major, shrinking engineering company. Sven-Mikael Mickelsson, who had worked for the factory for 16 years, organised a protest movement for the preservation of the abandoned premises. He argued that these should be used for a revitalisation of the indigenous local, small business sector.

Mickelsson and a partner had for several years run a company in another municipality 50 kilometres from Söderhamn. This firm, with fifteen employees, specialised in the development of new machinery for the major manufacturing corporations. Together, Mickelsson and his partner had more than one hundred patents. In 1984 Mickelsson started an inventors' workshop on the rescued premises. He also conducted other educational activities on how to start a business and set up an inventions competition for all ages.

Also in 1983, Ingvar Oremark, the Chief Executive Personnel Officer of the major regional forest industry, retired. In the 1970s he had organised the resistance to the closure of the local hospital and was very highly regarded by members of the community. In 1984, Oremark joined the task force that Mickelsson had set up. He organised special days when potential 'returnees' were persuaded to return to the community. On the 1985 and 1986 days Söderhamn was invaded by returning 'emigrants' and they were registered for future contacts by what had now become known as the 'Söderhamn Spirit Task Force'. The task force set about changing the negative image of Söderhamn by systematically informing the national media about developments in the local community.

Then the 'Söderhamn Spirit' was formally organised as an association with about 1000 members including local firms. Ingvar Oremark became the Chairman and the purpose was to mobilise the inventiveness of the community in both the technical and the business senses.

In 1983, Hans-Olof Olsson, in charge of the finance of the local public administration, was recruited to the Board of 'Söderhamn Spirit'. Then in 1986, Hans-Olof Olsson was appointed mayor in Söderhamn in charge of industrial issues and had to resign his position on the 'Söderhamn Spirit' Board. However, he moved his office from the town hall to the Development Centre as a symbol of support. He was also in a position to supply practical support through his department's budget. By 1990 the Development Centre included an inventors' workshop, an exhibition hall, a restaurant and training facilities. Sven-Mikael is consultant to the Centre and he organises courses on how to transform technical ideas into business ventures.

The decline of Söderhamn's population has slowed and the image of Söderhamn has improved.

Case study 13

APEX ENGINEERING PLC[1]

Apex Plc is an internationally diversified corporation with a portfolio of activities in the heavy engineering, control systems and information technology markets. The corporation has undergone many transformations during the past twenty years as a result of mergers and acquisitions as well as organic growth. One of the larger subsidiaries, the one in the heavy engineering industry, is called Apex Engineering Ltd and it operates from a number of factory sites in the UK.

In 1988 a new Chief Executive was appointed to run Apex Plc and one of his first steps was to announce a rationalisation strategy for Apex Engineering Ltd: this would involve closing three sites and reducing costs by 30 per cent within four years at the remaining three sites. Between 1988 and 1990 those three sites were indeed closed and, in accordance with the cost-cutting strategy, many thousands of people were made redundant at the others.

The recession of the early 1990s made life even more difficult and by mid-1992 it was clear that a further site would have to be closed. Sites at Warrington, Newcastle and Birmingham were therefore vying to secure a position as one of the survivors.

This case is concerned with events at the Warrington site, the principal activity of which was the manufacture of heavy equipment. In 1988 the production process was one of batch manufacture of components and flowline assembly. The site was run by a General Manager and reporting to

him there were a number of Directors of support functions (Finance, Engineering and Personnel) and also a Production Director. The General Manager and the Directors together formed an Operations Executive Committee (OEC). A number of Production Managers reported to the Production Director and to each of them, a number of works managers reported. Each works manager had a number of product managers reporting to them and they in turn had supervisors to whom foremen reported.

The Warrington strategy

In 1988, in response to the Apex Chief Executive's strategy on rationalisation, Warrington's OEC appointed consultants to assist in formulating a strategy for the survival of the Warrington site. About a year later, the strategy agreed upon was that of dividing the operations function at Warrington into smaller, more manageable units, flattening the reporting structure of the manufacturing activity by reducing the levels of management to three and empowering people at lower levels to make decisions and become accountable for their actions. The new organisational structure was therefore to be one in which a number of work shop managers were to report to the Production Director. Each work shop was to consist of a number of cells, each with its own cell supervisor, and each manufacturing cell was to be given responsibility for a section of the final product. Each cell would include staff from the support function and they would report to the cell supervisor, retaining only a functional link to the old support function departments, which would become advisory in nature. So, instead of some people manufacturing parts of a component while others assembled them all, components would in future be manufactured and put together into sub-assemblies before going on to a higher-level assembly operation. In addition, the manufacturing cells were to operate just-in-time (JIT) inventory policies, pulling their supplies from other units as they needed them. And the way accountants, controllers and personnel people would work would, of course, be significantly changed because they would now relate to cell teams.

The old performance reporting system

These changes in work practices in turn required changes in the way that performance was measured, controlled and rewarded. Under the batch production and flowline assembly system, performance measures were built up from data collected at the level of the individual operator to construct manhour and cost indicators for batches of components. Reporting for monitoring and control purposes was against batch cost standards and the performance measures were therefore cost accounting measures. It was, consequently, the function of the site's Finance Department to set the standards, collect the cost data and report on performance.

In 1988, the key performance measures were:

● batch delivery times to outside customers;
● manhour costs per batch;
● actual hours against standard;
● numbers of quality defects per batch.

Although these measures were generally considered adequate, it was known that the reporting system was not distributing costs into the right cost categories, but because the interest was only in cost at a higher level of aggregation, the system was not changed.

Throughout the history of the Warrington plant the accounting system measured shop floor workers' output against standard packages of work and the individual bonus schemes and payments by results systems were tied to this. Both shop floor operators and managers were thus interested in maintaining 'accurate' data. Although the data was perceived to be 'accurate', the operator's bonuses grew each year until in 1978 they had become unacceptably high. The bonus payment system had then been replaced with one based on components delivered to outside customers and applied to all people in the company. This meant that operators away from the final assembly activity could not relate their performance to the final product and so they had lost the incentive to work against target. They also lacked the motivation to collect accurate data since they could not see what purpose it served. The recorded manhours against the job increased and performance deteriorated.

The project to develop and apply new performance measures

Operating a strategy of cellular manufacturing and JIT would clearly require a different system for measuring performance and monitoring and controlling it. It would be essential to measure not the batch cost, but the cost of each item that a manufacturing cell produced. Without this information, cell team members would not be able to identify areas for improvement. In the new system information would not simply be reported up the hierarchy for attention by senior managers. Instead, cell team members would monitor their own performance and decide how to keep to target. For this new method of control to work faster information feedback to team members themselves would have to be ensured.

OEC members recognised the pivotal importance of performance measures for the new manufacturing strategy and so appointed a project leader to design a new set of performance measures. The project leader appointed consultants to design appropriate new performance measures and the consultants' proposals for a new set of six measures was accepted.

The pilot cell

The first step in implementing the new manufacturing strategy was to set up a pilot manufacturing cell. A joint Union/Management committee was set up to monitor the progress of this pilot over a three-month period, after which the committee was to review the conditions under which the trial would continue. The trial was to include a shift from an external department, measuring individual performance, to the cellular team, measuring themselves and then doing what was needed to improve performance. It was necessary, however, to ensure that links were maintained between the old method of measuring performance and the new one during the trial period. Therefore, an informal management review board, including representatives of all site functions, was set up to monitor the use of the new performance measurements. This board sent a project leader into the pilot cell to work with the cell team to design and implement new performance measures.

Before the three-month trial was up, however, the Unions withdrew their support, ostensibly because of a disagreement on overtime in another part of the site, and the informal board refused to approve the specific performance measures that cell members proposed. The operators in the trial cell then withdrew their cooperation with the engineers and controllers who had been allocated to the team from the site's support functions. The operators continued to produce the performance data in the form they had recommended to the informal board, but of course, the data was not used for anything.

Six months later, the objection to the pilot cell was withdrawn and the trial continued. A formal initiative called Performance Management and Reporting (PMR) was established to look at performance reports. A new project leader was appointed and he set up an informal working group, consisting of the support departments. A number of meetings were held but little progress was made because individuals had other priorities. One meeting resulted in a slanging match between Finance and Operations – both complained about each others' ability: Finance accused Operations of not managing its people, while Operations claimed that financial reporting was useless because it was so out of date and not at the level of detail required to understand the problems. The informal group was also criticised for not including operators and cell supervisors. In the end the frustrated project leader defined his own set of performance measures, but these too failed to secure senior management approval.

Shortly after this, senior Apex Engineering Ltd management arranged for a group of experts to present their ideas on performance to the management of all sites in the company. The presenters were highly critical of the Apex approach to performance measurement and those attending reacted with disbelief to the adverse comparisons made with their competitors. When the Apex Finance Director arrived to close the day's event, he presented a message that conflicted with the presenters' emphasis on long-term thinking – the Finance Director stressed the importance of short-term financial results.

By late 1990 the Operations function at Warrington had initiatives of one kind or another running into double figures. Senior managers became concerned at the number of changes that were being examined and the PMR board was called together to try to obtain an understanding of what all these initiatives were and what they were supposed to achieve. A small working group was asked to define a ten-point plan to prioritise the initiatives. When this plan was discussed it was decimated and no action was taken. Instead people said things like, 'This topic is already covered by another initiative', or 'That has already been completed', or 'This topic is something that needs to be looked at in the future'.

After these failed PMR meetings, Operations circulated a list of performance measures defined by an engineering support function leader. In response to this, a number of memos were issued by the Finance Department on cell accounting. Operations did not respond to these memos – they said the memos were not comprehensible – and so Finance let the matter drop.

Consultant intervention

Then in January 1991, the Managing Director of Apex Engineering Ltd suggested that consultants be appointed to define performance measures at the Warrington site. A joint Consultant-Operations team was set up and, after eight weeks' work, the following set of performance measures, to be taken at the manufacturing cell level, was agreed by the PMR board, with the exception of the cost statement that required the agreement of the Finance Department and this was not forthcoming:

- delivery time compared to plan;
- order-delivery response time;
- capacity utilisation against plan;
- stock levels;
- costs.

These were designed to be simple measures that operators and management could understand at a glance. The measures were to be displayed on charts on the wall for all to see. The data for the charts was to be collected by team members themselves. Problems were to be reported up the hierarchy only on an exceptions basis.

A senior Operations Manager then requested that an analysis be made of all current performance reports so that some could be dropped when the new measures came into force. The consultant did not want to be involved in a discussion of what were the best measures so the analysis was conducted by another group. This analysis showed that 90 people in Operations and Finance were generating data in 85 reports coming mostly from support departments that had no relevance to the

manufacturing cells. The reports were too complex to understand quickly and were the result of years of *ad hoc* accumulation. This confirmed what had been known for years – that there was too much irrelevant information.

Implementation

The next step was that of setting up a Performance Reporting Board to manage the implementation phase of the now agreed performance measures. The consultant left and a new project manager was appointed. Implementation was seen as the joint responsibility of Operations and Finance, but gradually Finance withdrew and eventually the Finance Director stopped attending meetings of the Performance Reporting Board. The fifth agreed performance measure, the cost statement, was therefore not developed further or applied.

In the meantime, as we have seen, Union resistance to cell manufacturing had been overcome and a number of Manufacturing Centres and their constituent cells had been set up. In the absence of site-wide agreed performance measures, each cell was using its own.

References

Aacker, D. (1988), *Strategic Management*, New York: John Wiley.

Anderson, P. W., Arrow K. J. & Pines, D. (1988), *The Economy as an Evolving Complex System*, Menlo Park, Ca.: Addison-Wesley.

Aldrich, H. E. (1979), *Organizations and Environments*, Englewood Cliffs, NJ: Prentice-Hall.

Alexander, L. D. (1985), Successfully implementing strategic decisions, *Long Range Planning*, vol. 18, no. 3, pp. 91–97.

Ansoff, I. (1990), *Implanting Corporate Strategy*, Hemel Hempstead: Prentice-Hall.

Argenti, J. (1980), *Practical Corporate Planning*, London: Allen & Unwin.

Argenti, J. (1984), Don't let planners meddle with your strategies, *Accountancy*, April, p. 152.

Argyris, C. (1957), *Personality and Organization*, New York: Harper & Row.

Argyris, C. & Schon, D. (1978), *Organizational Learning: A Theory of Action Perspective*, Reading, Ma.: Addison-Wesley.

Argyris, C. 1990, *Overcoming Organizational Defenses: Facilitating Organizational Learning*, Boston: Allyn & Bacon, Prentice-Hall.

Ashby, W. R. (1945), The effect of controls on stability, *Natura*, 155, pp. 242–43.

Ashby, W. R. (1952), *Design for a Brain*, New York: John Wiley.

Ashby, W. R. (1956), *Introduction to Cybernetics*, New York: John Wiley.

Bacharach, S. B. & Lawler, E. J. (1980), *Power and Politics in Organizations*, San Francisco: Jossey-Bass.

Baddeley, A, (1990), *Human Memory: Theory and Practice*, Hove, Sussex: Lawrence Earlbaum Associates.

Bales, R. F. (1970), *Personality and Interpersonal Behaviour*, New York: Holt.

Barnard, C. I. (1938), *The Functions of the Executive*, Cambridge, Ma.: Harvard University Press.

Bartlett, C. A. (1983), MNLs: get off the reorganization merry-go-round, *Harvard Business Review*, March-April.

Baumol, W. J. & Benhabib, J. (1989), Chaos: significance, mechanism and economic applications, *Journal of Economic Perspectives*, Winter, vol. 3, no. 1, pp. 77–105.

Beck, P. W. (1982), Corporate planning for an uncertain future, *Long Range Planning*, vol. 15, no. 4.

Beer, M., Eisenstat, R. A. & Spector, B. (1990), *The Critical Path to Corporate Renewal*, Boston, Ma.: Harvard Business School Press.

Beer, Stafford (1959/67), *Cybernetics and Management*, London: English Universities Press.

Beer, Stafford (1966), *Decision and Control: The Meaning of Operational Research and Management Cybernetics*, London: John Wiley.

Belbin, R. M. (1981), *Management Teams: Why They Succeed or Fail*, Oxford: Heinemann.

Bennis, W. G. & Shepard, H. A. (1956), A theory of group development, *Human Relations*, vol. 9, pp. 415–57. [Republished in Gibbard, G. S., Hartman, J. & Mann R. D. (Eds.) (1974), *The Analysis of Groups*, San Francisco: Jossey-Bass].

Bion, W. R. (1961), *Experiences in Groups and Other Papers*, London: Tavistock Publications.

Blauner, R. (1964), *Alienation and Freedom*, Chicago: University of Chicago.

Borgatta, E. F., Couch, A. S. & Bales R. F. (1954), Some findings relevant to the great man theory of leadership, *American Sociology Review*, vol. 19, pp. 755–59.

Bowman, C. & Asch, D. (1987), *Strategic Management*, London: Macmillan Education.

Brown, J. S. & Duguid, P. (1991), Organisational learning and communities of practice: toward a unified view of working, learning and innovation, *Organisational Science*, vol. 2, no. 1, Feb., pp. 40–57.

Brunson, N. (1985), *The Irrational Organisation*, Chichester: John Wiley.

Brunson, N. (1989), *The Organisation of Hypocricy*, Chichester: John Wiley.

Burns, T. & Stalker, G. M. (1961), *The Management of Innovation*, London: Tavistock Publications.

Buzzell, R. D. (1983), Ciba-Geigy Pharmaceuticals Division: multinational strategic planning, in Buzzell, R. D. & Quelch, J. A. (Eds.) (1988), *Multinational Marketing Management*, Reading, Ma.: Addison-Wesley.

Buzzell, R. D. (1984), Citibank: marketing to multinational customers, in Buzzell, R. D. & Quelch, J. A. (Eds.) (1988), *Multinational Marketing Management*, Reading, Ma.: Addison-Wesley.

Buzzell, R. D. & Gale, B. T. (1987), *The PIMS Principle: Linking Strategy to Performance*, New York: Macmillan.

Campbell, A. & Tawady, K. (1990), *Mission and Business Philosophy: Winning Employee Commitment*, Oxford: Heinemann.

Campbell, A., Devine, M. & Young, D. (1990), *A Sense of Mission*, London: Hutchinson.

Chandler, A. D. (1962), *Strategy and Structure*, Boston, Ma.: MIT Press.

Charan, R. (1991), How networks reshape organizations – for results, *Harvard Business Review*, Sept-Oct.

Child, J. (1984), *Organisation*, London: Harper & Row.

Child, J. (1972), Organisational structure, environment and

performance: the role of strategic choice, *Sociology*, vol. 6, no. 1, pp. 1–21.

Clegg S. R. (1990), *Modern Organizations: Organizational Studies in the Post-Modern World*, London: Sage Publications.

Collingridge, D. (1980), *The Social Control of Technology*, Open University Press.

Cohen, M. D., March, J. G. & Ohlsen, J. P. (1972), A garbage can model of organizational choice, *Administrative Science Quarterly*, vol. 17, pp. 1–25.

Cooke, S. & Slack, N. (1984), *Making Management Decisions*, Englewood Cliffs, NJ: Prentice-Hall.

Cyert, R. M. & March, J. G. (1963), *A Behavioural Theory of the Firm*, Englewood Cliffs: Prentice-Hall.

David, F. R. (1989), *Strategic Management*, Columbus, Ohio: Merrill Publishing Co.

Davies, P. (1987), *The Cosmic Blueprint*, London: William Heinemann.

Davis, J. H., Laughin, P. R. & Komarita, S. S. (1976), The social psychology of mixed groups: cooperative and mixed motive interaction, *Annual Review of Psychology*, vol. 27, pp. 501–41.

de Board, R. (1978), *The Psychoanalysis of Organizations*, London: Tavistock Publications.

De Geus, P. (1988) Planning as learning, *Harvard Business Review*, March-April, pp. 70–74.

Duncan, R. (1972), Characteristics of organisational environments and perceived uncertainty, *Administrative Science Quarterly*, vol. 17, pp. 313–27.

Dunphy, D. C. (1968), 'Phases, roles and myths in self analytic groups', *Journal of Applied Behavioural Science*, vol. 4, pp. 195–226.

Dutton, J. E. (1988), 'Understanding strategic agenda building and its implications for managing change', in Pondy, L. R., Boland, J. R. & Thomas, H. (Eds.) (1988), *Managing Ambiguity and Change*, New York: John Wiley.

Etzioni, A. (1961), *Complex Organizations*, New York: Holt, Reinhart & Winston.

Festinger, L., Schachter, S. & Back, K. (1950), *Social Pressures in Informal Groups: A Study of a Housing Project*, New York: Harper & Row.

Fiedler, F. E. (1967), *A Theory of Leadership Effectiveness*, New York: McGraw-Hill.

Forrester, J. (1958), Industrial dynamics: a major breakthrough for decision-making, *Harvard Business Review*, vol. 36, no. 4, pp. 37–66.

Forrester, J. (1961), *Industrial Dynamics*, Cambridge, Ma.: MIT Press.

Galbraith, J. R. & Kazanian, R. K. (1986), *Strategy Implementation: Structure, Systems and Process*, St. Paul, Minnesota: West Publishing.

Gemmell, G. & Smith, C. (1985), A dissipative structure model of organizational transformation, *Human Relations*, vol. 36, no. 8.

Gibbard, G. S., Hartman, J. J. & Mann, R. D. (Eds.) (1974), *Analysis of Groups*, San Francisco: Jossey-Bass.

Gick, M. L. & Holyoak, K. J. (1983), Schema introduction and analogical transfer, *Cognitive Psychology*, vol. 15, pp. 1–38.

Gleick, J. (1988), *Chaos: The Making of a New Science*, London: William Heinemann.

Goldsmith, W. & Clutterbuck, D. (1984), *The Winning Streak*, London: Weidenfeld & Nicolson.

Goold, M. & Campbell, A. (1987), *Strategies and Styles*, Oxford: Blackwell.

Goold, M. with Quinn, J. J. (1990), *Strategic Control: Milestones for Long Term Performance*, London: Hutchinson.

Gouldner, A. (1964), *Patterns of Industrial Bureaucracy*, New York: The Free Press.

Greenley, G. E. (1986), Does strategic planning improve performance?, *Long Range Planning*, vol. 19, no. 2, pp. 101–9.

Greenley, G. E. (1989), *Strategic Management*, Hemel Hempstead: Prentice-Hall.

Greiner, L. E. (1972), Evolution and revolution as organizations grow, *Harvard Business Review*, July-August.

Greiner, L. E. & Schein, V. E. (1988), *Power and Organization Development: Mobilizing Power to Implement Change*, Reading Ma.: Addison-Wesley.

Gustafson, J. P. & Cooper, L. (1978), Toward the study of society in microcosm: critical problems of group relations conferences, *Human Relations*, vol. 31, pp. 843–62.

Hamel, G. & Prahalad, C. K. (1989), Strategic intent, *Harvard Business Review*, May-June, pp. 63–76.

Hampden-Turner, C. (1990), *Charting the Corporate Mind*, New York: Free Press, Macmillan.

Handy, C. B. (1976), *The Gods of Management*, Sovereign.

Handy, C. B. (1981), *Understanding Organisations*, Harmondsworth: Penguin.

Handy, C. B. (1984), *The Future of Work*, Oxford: Blackwell.

Hannan, M. & Freeman, J. (1977), The population ecology of organizations, *American Journal of Sociology*, vol. 83, pp. 929–64.

Hartley, R. F. (1991), *Management Mistakes*, New York: John Wiley.

Hayes, R. & Abernathy, W. (1980), Managing our way to economic decline, *Harvard Business Review*, July-Aug, pp. 11–25.

Henderson, B. D. (1970), *The Product Portfolio*, Boston Consulting Group.

Hendry, J. (1990), The problem with Porter's generic strategies, *European Management Journal*, vol. 8, no. 4, pp. 443–50.

Hersey, P. & Blanchard, K. (1988), *Organizational Behavior*, Englewood Cliffs, NJ: Prentice-Hall.

Hertzberg, F. (1966), *Work and the Nature of Man*, Cleveland: World Publishing Co.

Hirschorn, L. (1990), *The Workplace Within: Psychodynamics of Organizational Life*, Cambridge, Ma.: MIT Press.

Hofer, C. W. & Schendel, D. (1978), *Strategy Evaluation: Analytical Concepts*, St. Paul, Minnesota: West Publishing.

Hofstede, G. (1981), Management control of public and not-for-profit activities, *Accounting, Organisations and Society*, vol. 6, no. 3, pp. 193–211.

Hsieh, D. (1989), Testing for nonlinear dependence in daily

foreign exchange returns, *Journal of Business*, vol. 62, no. 3.

Hurst, D. K. (1986), Why strategic management is bankrupt, *Organizational Dynamics*, Autumn, pp. 4–27.

Hurst, E. G. (1982), Controlling strategic plans, in Lorange, P. (Ed.) (1982), *Implementation of Strategic Planning*, Englewood Cliffs, NJ: Prentice-Hall.

Huff, A. S. (1988), Politics and argument as a means of coping with ambiguity and change, in Pondy, L. R., Borland, J. R. & Thomas, H. (Eds.) (1988), *Managing Ambiguity and Change*, New York: John Wiley.

Hussey, D. E. (1991), Implementing strategy through management education and training, in Hussey, D. E. (Ed.) (1991), *International Review of Strategic Management*, vol. 2, no. 1, Chichester: John Wiley.

Jacques, E. (1991), In praise of hierarchy, *Harvard Business Review*, Jan-Feb.

Jacques, E. (1955), Social systems as a defence against persecutory and defensive anxiety, in Klein, M., Heimann, P. & Money-Kyrle, P. (Eds.) (1955), *New Directions in Psychoanalysis*, London: Tavistock Publications. (Also published in Gibbard, G. S., Hartman, J. J. & Mann, R. D. (1974), *Analysis of Groups*, San Francisco: Jossey-Bass.)

Johnson, G. (1988), Rethinking incrementalism *Strategic Management Journal*, vol. 9, pp. 75–91.

Johnson, G. (1987), *Strategic Change and the Management Process*, Oxford: Blackwell.

Johnson, G. (1988), *Exploring Corporate Strategy*, Hemel Hempstead: Prentice-Hall.

Kagono, T., Nonaka, I., Sakakibara, K. & Okamura, A. (1985), *Strategic Versus Evolutionary Management: A US–Japan Comparison of Strategy and Organisation*, Amsterdam: North-Holland Publishing.

Kanter, R. M. (1985), *The Change Masters: Innovation and Entrepreneurship in the American Corporation*, Englewood Cliffs, NJ: Simon & Schuster.

Kanter, R. M. (1989), *When Giants Learn to Dance: Mastering the Challenge of Strategy Management and Careers in the 1990s*, Englewood Cliffs, NJ: Simon & Schuster.

Kast, P. & Rosenzweig, F. (1970), *Management and Organization*, New York: McGraw-Hill.

Katz, D. & Kahn, R. L. (1966), *The Social Psychology of Organizations*, New York: John Wiley.

Kelsey, D. (1988), The economics of chaos or the chaos of economics, *Oxford Economic Papers*, vol. 40, pp. 1–31.

Kets de Vries, M. F. R. (1980), *Organizational Paradoxes: Clinical Approaches to Management*, London: Tavistock Publications.

Kets de Vries, M. F. R. & Miller, D. (1987), *The Neurotic Organization*, San Francisco: Jossey-Bass.

Kiersey, D. & Bates, M. (1978), *Please Understand Me: Character and Temperament Types*, Del Mar, Ca.: Prometheus Nemesis Books.

Klein, M. (1975), *The Writings of Melanie Klein*, London: Hogarth Press.

Kuhn, T. S. (1970), *The Structure of Scientific Revolutions*, University of Chicago Press.

Lawrence, P. R. & Lorsch, J. W. (1967), *Organization and Environment*, Cambridge, Ma.: Harvard University Press.

Lewin, K. (1947), Feedback problems of social diagnosis and action, Part II-B of Frontiers in Group Dynamics, *Human Relations*, vol. 1, pp. 147–53.

Lewin, K. (1951), *Field Theory in Social Science*, New York: Harper & Brothers.

Lindblom, L. (1959), The science of muddling through, *Public Administration Review*, vol. 19, pp. 79–88.

Lindblom, L. & Norstedt, J. (1971), *The Volvo Report*, Stockholm: Swedish Employers Confederation.

Lorenz, C. (1986), Metamorphosis of a European laggard, London: *Financial Times*, 12 May.

Mandelbrot, B. (1982), *The Fractal Geometry of Nature*, New York: W. H. Freeman.

March, J. G. & Simon, H. A. (1958), *Organizations*, New York: John Wiley.

Marquand, J. (1990), *Autonomy and Change*, Hemel Hempstead: Harvester Wheatsheaf.

Maslow, A. (1954), *Motivation and Personality*, New York: Harper & Brothers.

Mayo, E. (1945), *The Social Problems of an Industrial Civilization*, Cambridge, Ma.: Harvard University Press.

Mayes, B. T. & Allen, W. R. (1977), Towards a definition of organizational politics, *Academy of Management Review*, vol. 2.

McKelvey, W. (1981), *Organizational Systematics*, Los Angeles, Ca.: University of California Press.

Merton, R. K. (1957), Bureaucratic structure and personality, in *Social Theory and Social Structure*, New York: The Free Press.

Miles, R. E. & Snow, C. C. (1978), *Organisational Strategy, Structure and Process*, New York: McGraw-Hill.

Miller, D. & Friesen, P. H. (1980), Momentum and revolution in organizational adaptation, *Academy of Management Journal*, vol. 23, pp. 591–614.

Miller, D. (1986), Configurations of strategy and structure: towards a synthesis, *Strategic Management Journal*, vol. 7, pp. 233–49a.

Miller, D. & de Vries, K. (1987), *The Neurotic Organization*, San Francisco: Jossey-Bass.

Miller, D. (1990), *The Icarus Paradox: How Excellent Organizations Can Bring About Their Own Downfall*, New York: Harper Business.

Miller, E. J. & Rice, A. K. (1967), *Systems of Organization: The Control of Task and Sentient Boundaries*, London: Tavistock Publications.

Miller, E. J. (1989), *The Leicester Conference, Occasional Papers*, London: Tavistock Publications.

Mills, T. M. (1964), *Group Transformation: An Analysis of a Learning Group*, Englewood Cliffs, NJ: Prentice-Hall.

Mintzberg, H. (1975a), The manager's job: fact and folklore, *Harvard Business Review*, July-Aug.

Mintzberg, H. (1975b), *The Structuring of Organizations*, Englewood Cliffs, NJ: Prentice-Hall.

Mintzberg, H., Theoret, A. & Rainsinghani (1976), The structure of the unstructured decision making process, *Administrative Science Quarterly*, vol. 21, pp. 246–75.